Financial Risk Management

Financial Risk Management

Editor: Brian Hurley

NY RESEARCH
PRESS
New York

Published by NY Research Press
118-35 Queens Blvd., Suite 400,
Forest Hills, NY 11375, USA
www.nyresearchpress.com

Financial Risk Management
Edited by Brian Hurley

International Standard Book Number: 978-1-64725-455-1 (Hardback)

Cataloging-in-Publication Data

Financial risk management / edited by Brian Hurley.
p. cm.
Includes bibliographical references and index.
ISBN 978-1-64725-455-1
1. Financial risk management. 2. Risk management. 3. Management. I. Hurley, Brian.
HD61 .F56 2023
658.155--dc21

Contents

Preface

This book has been an outcome of determined endeavour from a group of educationists in the field. The primary objective was to involve a broad spectrum of professionals from diverse cultural background involved in the field for developing new researches. The book not only targets students but also scholars pursuing higher research for further enhancement of the theoretical and practical applications of the subject.

Financial risk refers to the possibility of losing money in an investment or in a business venture. This risk can come in a variety of forms including operational risk, credit risk and liquidity risk. Both individuals and organizations can experience these kinds of risks. The practice of assessing and managing potential and current financial risks in order to reduce an organization's exposure to risk is known as financial risk management. It entails recognizing the risk, quantifying it, assessing all viable solutions, formulating a plan and then implementing the steps and financial tools required to mitigate its potential consequences. The primary strategies for financial risk management are risk reduction, risk retention, risk avoidance and risk transfer. This book explores all the important aspects of financial risk management in the present day scenario. It consists of contributions made by international experts. A number of latest researches have been included to keep the readers up-to-date with the global concepts in this area of study.

It was an honour to edit such a profound book and also a challenging task to compile and examine all the relevant data for accuracy and originality. I wish to acknowledge the efforts of the contributors for submitting such brilliant and diverse chapters in the field and for endlessly working for the completion of the book. Last, but not the least; I thank my family for being a constant source of support in all my research endeavours.

Editor

Risk Management in the System of Financial Stability of the Service Enterprise

Svetlana Drobyazko [1,*], Anna Barwinska-Malajowicz [2], Boguslaw Slusarczyk [2], Olga Chubukova [3] and Taliat Bielialov [4]

1 European Academy of Sciences, London 71-75, UK
2 Faculty of Economics, University of Rzeszow, 35-310 Rzeszów, Poland; anna.barwinska@yahoo.com (A.B.-M.); boguslaw.slusarczyk@yahoo.com (B.S.)
3 Faculty of Economics and Business, Kyiv National University of Technology and Design, 01011 Kyiv, Ukraine; chubukova@ukr.net
4 Department of Finance and Financial and Economic Security, Kyiv National University of Technology and Design, 01011 Kyiv, Ukraine; talyatb@ukr.net
* Correspondence: drobyazko.s.i@gmail.com

Abstract: The article is devoted to the theoretical substantiation and development of methodological approaches and practical recommendations for modeling the assessment of the financial stability of a service sector enterprise. To assess the financial condition of the hotel industry, a visual interpretation of the neural network, a model of self-organizing Kohonen map, was used. It is proven that by the method of Kohonen maps for each service provided by the hotel industry, in a certain period of activity, it is possible to establish certain objective limitations of structural characteristics that will prevent the transition to problem clusters or ensure the transition to better ones. The authors propose an economic and mathematical model of the process of assessing financial stability by calculating the integral indicator of financial stability of the service sector. The types of control maps for each of the coefficients that have a significant impact on the assessment of the financial stability of the enterprise in the service sector were identified. Control maps were constructed for each coefficient, which are part of the integrated indicator of financial stability, and their analysis was carried out for the presence of special reasons for the variability of the process of financial stability assessment. The concept of modeling a system for assessing the financial stability of service enterprises is developed in the article, which is based on the collection of financial data, a comprehensive analysis of factors influencing the financial condition, a study of the controllability of the process of assessing financial stability, building a model of an integral indicator of financial stability, and its program implementation.

Keywords: risk management; financial stability; coefficient of seasonality; control chart; expert system

1. Introduction

Every year, the share of services production is increasing in the structure of the economy of developed countries of the world. Studying the problem of the financial stability assessment of the respective service enterprises is an important aspect of the industry's development. The market conditions of the economy and the problems of financial support for the activity of the service sector enterprises (SSE) necessitate the change of the financial and economic policy and the qualified assessment of the financial state with a view to the functioning of SSEs in crisis situations and their further economic growth.

Over the past decades, the service sector (SS) has become a significant source of innovation and economic growth. In the member countries of the Organization for Economic Cooperation and Development (OECD), SS covers about 3/4 of total employment and gross output (National Accounts—Analysis of Main Aggregates 2019). Hence, that SS is the largest sector of the economy, there is a need, on one hand, to explain the mechanism of the transition to a post-industrial economy and, on the other hand, to study the factors that cause structural changes.

These stylized facts are well traced in the example of the US economy. In 1810, the share of people employed in the US agricultural sector was about 80%. Two hundred years later, this share was already 1.5%. The share of those employed in SS in 1810 was about 10%, and in 2010—about 80% of total employment (National Accounts—Analysis of Main Aggregates 2019).

Assessment of financial condition is an integral part of the economic analysis of the enterprise, without which it is impossible to rationally manage the economy of any entity.

Acharya et al. (2017), Liu and Arunkumar (2018), Wagner (2017) have made a major contribution to the development and solution of the problem of financial stability. However, it is not enough to have only retrospective information on the financial state of an enterprise to study the financial stability of the SSE. The basis of the assessment is estimated figures of the financial stability, which can be obtained primarily through its modeling.

The following studies are devoted to the implementation of models, methods, and information technologies for financial analysis of enterprises' activities: Adrian et al. (2018), Fazio et al. (2018), Nyman et al. (2018), who have developed methods of calculation and analysis of indicators of the enterprise's financial condition.

Despite its difficulty of creating, the financial stability calculation system on the basis of mathematical models using modern information technologies is a powerful tool for solving the above problems, which determines the objective need for further development of the basic theoretical approaches and practical ways of ensuring sustainable financial development of the SSE. However, the problems of managing the financial stability of SSEs, which have significant specificity of activity, have not been sufficiently addressed in the works of these scientists. Thus, the development of models for assessing the financial stability of the SSE is an urgent scientific task, defining the topic of the work, its goals, and objectives.

Coefficient analysis is one of the methodological approaches to assessing the financial condition of enterprises. The essence of the analysis of financial position by the coefficient method is the calculation of relative indicators as the ratio of absolute indicators of assets and liabilities of the balance (Leva et al. 2017).

The analysis of financial coefficients is to compare their values with the baseline values, as well as to study their dynamics over the reporting period and over several years. The values of indicators of the enterprise for the past year, industry average values of indicators, and values of indicators of the most promising enterprises can be used as the base values (Afonso et al. 2018). In addition, as bases of comparison can be theoretically substantiated or obtained as a result of expert assessments of the value characterizing optimal or critical (limit) values of indicators in terms of stability of financial conditions.

There is a large number of works (Singh et al. 2018; Almasi et al. 2017) on the coefficient analysis of the financial condition of enterprises. They propose the calculation of a certain number of financial coefficients for a given period of operation of the enterprise, followed by a comparison of the values of these coefficients with similar coefficients of other enterprises or with the critical values of these coefficients. However, analytical methods that have been tested and proved to be of practical value at the micro level may not always be feasible or appropriate for the analysis of generalized information (Agénor and da Silva 2017).

If it is sufficient for the researcher to know how the financial state of the enterprise changed by a train of a certain period or in comparison with its competitors, then the tasks for the analysis of the financial state of the enterprises at the regional level are much more complicated and wider in the state (Culpeper 2018; Kryshtal 2019).

For this purpose, it is necessary, first of all, to have a small complex number of indicators that reflect the main characteristics of the financial condition of the enterprise and allow performing timely identification of changes in the general development trends (Chang et al. 2018) and, second, to develop a methodology for determining the baseline values of these indicators, which can be used to compare certain sets of enterprises combined by certain criteria (the type of activity, region, ownership, etc.) (Nasreen et al. 2017).

The analysis of scientific literature (Lin et al. 2018) shows that there are different views on the construction of the system of financial coefficient, its structure, and typology. Depending on the purpose of the financial analysis, the authors use different approaches to grouping and classifying coefficients.

Financial stability is a reflection of a stable excess of income over expenses, provides free maneuvering of the organization's funds, and, through their effective use, contributes to the uninterrupted process of production and sales of products (Anton 2018).

Consequently, financial stability is the main element of the overall stability of enterprises and is considered as the stability of the financial condition, the ability to fulfill obligations to creditors, the budget and owners by balancing their own financial resources and loans. At the same time, there are four types of financial stability: internal, external, "inherited", and general.

Financial stability is the most important characteristic of the financial and economic activity of an enterprise in a market economy. If an enterprise is financially stable, then it has an advantage over other enterprises of the same profile and attraction of investments, in obtaining loans, in choosing suppliers, and in the selection of qualified personnel. Finally, it does not come into conflict with the state and society since it pays timely taxes to the budget, contributions to social funds, and wages—to workers and employees, dividends—to shareholders, and guarantees to banks the loss of loans and payment of interest on them.

The higher the stability of an enterprise, the bigger it is, regardless of an unexpected change in market conditions and the less the risk of being on the verge of bankruptcy.

The purpose of the work is to develop models for assessing the financial stability of a service enterprise to objectively analyze its financial status and make effective management decisions to ensure sustainable development.

The scientific novelty of the study lies in solving a new, important for the economy, the task of modeling the processes of assessing the financial stability of enterprises in the service sector, which provides for an increase in their overall efficiency.

The assessment of financial condition is an integral part of the economic analysis of the enterprise, without which it is impossible to rationally manage any business entity.

The main areas of crisis management at the level of the business entity are constant monitoring of the financial and economic condition of the enterprise, development of new management, financial and marketing strategies, reduction of fixed and variable costs, increasing productivity, attracting funds of founders, and strengthening staff motivation.

The study of the concept of financial stability has been conducted by many scientists, but there is no single view on the solution and study of this concept, The issue of the essence of financial stability of the enterprise, the factors that provide it, and the assessment of financial stability through mathematical modeling remains open.

2. Materials and Methods

In order to understand what methods are used in the article, we first consider the general methodology of the study.

The following research methods were used to solve the purpose of the work: conceptual and categorical analysis—for studying the concept of "financial stability of the service sector enterprise"; analytical method—for theoretical generalization of scientific concepts of financial analysis; expert assessments method; economic and mathematical methods—for constructing an integral indicator of the financial stability assessment of the service sector enterprise and determining the optimal form of change for the coefficients of the integral indicator; induction and deduction method—when studying the theoretical and methodological foundations, based on the principles of economic theory on one hand, and on the conceptual bases of economic and mathematical modeling on the other; comparison method—for studying the coefficients of influence on the financial condition of the enterprise and assessing their significance; economic and mathematical modeling method—for development of models of the financial stability assessment of the service sector enterprise; methods of random variables and fuzzy sets—for the numerical expression of the seasonality coefficient as a linguistic variable and the factors of influence on the regional location of the service sector enterprise.

The information base of the research consists of materials of scientific-practical conferences, scientific works of scientists, monographs, collections, periodicals of domestic and international organizations, resources of the Internet, financial statements of enterprises, as well as the author's own calculations.

To assess the level of financial stability, the indicators presented in Appendix A are used.

In our opinion, it is necessary to dwell in more detail on the modified Shewhart chart methodology.

To investigate the stability and controllability of the coefficients of influence on the financial stability of the enterprise, the use of the Shewhart control charts (SCC) is suggested. Control charts do not solve the issues that are usually posed before statistical procedures.

Instead of looking for a theoretical model for data obtained for some well-defined phenomenon, one can decide using the control chart whether it is possible to use a sequence of data to predict what will happen in the future. When predictions are possible and done appropriately, control charts become the basis of such predictions. When prophecy is impossible or unsuitable through unmanageable variations, control charts will warn of this instability.

Shewhart suggested dividing the set of data into subgroups. If several measurements are taken at some point in time, their results can be grouped and considered as a single set of data (Makedon et al. 2019; Nesterenko et al. 2019; Siddique et al. 2020).

The Shewhart chart requires sample process data obtained at approximately equal intervals. Intervals can be set either by time (for example, hourly) or by the amount of production (each batch). As a rule, each subgroup consists of the same type of products or services with the same controlled indicators, and all subgroups have the same volume. For each subgroup, one or more characteristics such as the arithmetic mean of subgroup X and the scope of the subgroup R, or the sample standard deviations.

The Shewhart chart is a graph of the values of the found characteristics of subgroups depending on their numbers. The chart has a centerline corresponding to the reference value of the characteristic. When evaluating whether a process is in a statistically controlled state, the arithmetic mean of the data considered is usually the reference. During the management, the long-term value of the characteristic set in the technical conditions, or its nominal value based on preliminary information about the process, or the intended target value of the characteristic of the product or service, serves as the reference process. The Shewhart chart has two control limits (which are defined statistically) relative to the centerline (CL), which are called the upper control limit (UCL) and the lower control limit (LCL).

3. Results

The successful functioning of enterprises in the conditions of unstable economic situation is possible only under the condition of overcoming of the crisis phenomena, which may arise at the appropriate stage of their development. This can be done through timely analysis of the financial stability of the enterprise. The detailing of the procedural side of the financial stability analysis methodology depends on the goal, tasks, and various factors of information, temporary, methodological, technical, and personnel support. However, it should be noted that the results of formalized analytical procedures performed should not be the only and unconditional criterion for making a decision.

Modeling the assessment of the financial stability of a service sector enterprise is a laborious process. To model the assessment of the financial stability of an enterprise, various factors of influence on it, which were described in the first chapter of the candidate's work, are taken into account.

Modeling the assessment of the financial stability of the SSE includes:

- determination of significant factors of influence on the financial condition;
- determination of internal and external factors of influence;
- establishment of normative values of internal indicators and the optimal form of changing these indicators;
- determination of the current values of internal indicators of a service sector enterprise;
- determination of the periods of seasonality and factors of the location of the service sector enterprise;
- estimation of the seasonality coefficient based on linguistic variables and estimation of the location coefficient based on stochastic variables
- defuzzification of the value of the coefficient of seasonality and determination of the coefficient of location, assessing the impact of external factors on the financial condition of a service enterprise;
- construction of a matrix of pairwise comparisons of external and internal coefficients of influence on the assessment of the financial stability of an enterprise in the service sector on its basis, to determine the priority of the coefficients;
- study of the controllability of the process of assessing the financial stability of a service sector enterprise by building Shewhart control charts for each coefficient;
- building a model of an integral indicator of the financial stability of the SSE;
- implementation of a model for assessing financial stability by using an expert system;
- obtaining research results.

As a result of the above-described process, an algorithm for modeling the system for assessing the financial stability of a service sector enterprise was developed (Figure 1).

In order to study the coefficients of the financial stability assessment of the service sector enterprise with the help of the Shewhart charts, their calculation on the financial statements of the enterprise is carried out.

For control charts using quantitative data, a normal (Gaussian) distribution of deviations within the samples is provided, and deviations from this assumption influence the performance of the charts. The coefficients for the calculation of the control limits are derived under the condition of a normal distribution. Since most control limits are used only as empirical criteria in decision making, it is advisable to neglect small deviations from normality. In any case, due to the central limit theorem, sample averages have a distribution that approaches normal with the increase in the sample amount even when individual observations do not obey the normal law. This justifies the assumption of normality for X-charts even with such small sample amounts as 4 or 5 units taken for control.

Quantitative data charts can describe sample process data because of scattering (variability from unit to unit) and because of the center position (process average). Therefore, control charts for quantitative data are almost always used and analyzed in pairs—one chart for the position of the center and one for the scatter. Pairs of X- and R-charts are most commonly used. Tables 1 and 2 and the formulas of the control limits and the coefficients for the corresponding charts are given.

Table 1. Formulas of control limits for Shewhart charts using quantitative data (author's study).

Statistics	Default Values Are Not Set		Default Values Are Set	
	CL	**UCL and LCL**	**CL**	**UCL i LCL**
$\overline{X}$	$\overline{\overline{X}}$	$\overline{\overline{X}} \pm A_2R$ *or* $\overline{\overline{X}} \pm A_3\overline{s}$	$\overline{\overline{X}}_0$ *or* μ	X_0 *or* $A\delta_0$
R	$\overline{R}$	$D_3\overline{R}, D_4\overline{R}$	R_0 *or* $d_2\delta_0$	$D_1, \delta_0, D_2\delta_0$
s	$\overline{s}$	$B_3\overline{s}, B_4\overline{s}$	S_0 *or* $c_4\delta_0$	$B_5, \delta_0, B_6\delta_0$

Note: X—values of the measured quality characteristic (individual values are written as: $X_1X_2, X_3, \ldots$;$\overline{X}$—mean for the subgroup; R—size of the subgroup: difference of the largest and smallest values in the subgroup; $\overline{R}$—mean of the R-value for all subgroups; s—selective standard (mean squared) deviation; $\overline{s}$—mean of standard samples (mean squared deviations of subgroups; δ—true group standard deviation; A, B, C, D—coefficients for the calculation of control limits; CL—centerline; UCL—upper control limit; LCL—lower control limit.

Table 2. Coefficients for the calculation of control chart lines (author's study).

№	Coefficients for Calculating Control Limits										Coefficients for Calculating Center Line			
	A	**A2**	**A3**	**B3**	**B4**	**B5**	**B6**	**D1**	**D2**	**D3**	**D4**	**C4**	**1/C4**	d_2	$1/d_2$
2	2.121	1.880	2.659	0.000	3.267	0.000	2.606	0.000	3.686	0.000	3.267	0.7979	1.2533	1.128	0.8865
3	1.732	1.023	1.954	0.000	2.568	0.000	2.276	0.000	4.358	0.000	2.574	0.8862	1.1284	1.693	0.5907
4	1.500	0.729	1.628	0.000	2.266	0.000	2.088	0.000	4.698	0.000	2.282	0.9213	1.0854	2.059	0.4857
5	1.342	0.577	1.427	0.000	2.089	0.000	1.964	0.000	4.918	0.000	2.114	0.9400	1.0638	2.326	0.4299
6	1.225	0.483	1.287	0.030	1.970	0.029	1.874	0.000	5.078	0.000	2.004	0.9515	1.0510	2.534	0.3946
7	1.134	0.419	1.182	0.118	1.882	0.113	1.806	0.204	5.204	0.076	1.924	0.9594	1.0423	2.704	0.3698
8	1.061	0.373	1.099	0.185	1.815	0.179	1.751	0.388	5.306	0.136	1.864	0.9650	1.0363	2.847	0.3512
9	1.000	0.337	1.032	0.239	1.761	0.232	1.707	0.547	5.393	0.184	1.816	0.9693	1.0317	2.970	0.3367
10	0.949	0.308	0.975	0.284	1.716	0.276	1.669	0.687	5.469	0.223	1.777	0.9727	1.0281	3.078	0.3249
11	0.905	0.285	0.927	0.321	1.679	0.313	1.637	0.811	5.535	0.256	1.744	0.9754	1.0252	3.173	0.3152
12	0.866	0.266	0.886	0.354	1.646	0.346	1.610	0.922	5.594	0.283	1.717	0.9776	1.0229	3.258	0.3069
13	0832	0.249	0.850	0.382	1.618	0.374	1.585	1.025	5.647	0.307	1.693	0.9794	1.0210	3.336	0.2998
14	0802	0.235	0.817	0.406	1.594	0.399	1.563	1.118	5.696	0.328	1.672	0.9810	1.0194	3.407	0.2935
15	0.775	0.223	0.789	0.428	1.572	0.421	1.544	1.203	5.741	0.347	1.653	0.9823	1.0180	3.472	0.2880
16	0.750	0.212	0.763	0.448	1.552	0.440	1.526	1.282	5.782	0.363	1.637	0.9835	1.0168	3.532	0.2831

Table 2 presents the coefficients for the calculation of the Shewhart chart control lines.

The purpose of the process management system is to obtain a statistical signal of the presence of special (non-random) causes of variations. The systematic elimination of special causes of excessive variability puts the process in a state of statistical controllability. If the process is in a statistically controlled state, the product quality can be predicted, and the process is fit to meet the requirements set out in the regulatory documents.

The process capabilities are determined by the total variability (process scatter) caused by common causes, that is, the minimum variability that remains after eliminating all non-random causes. The process capabilities are represented by process indicators in a statistically controlled state. The process is first brought to this state, and then its capabilities are determined. Thus, it is necessary to start determining the process capabilities after the control problems with X- and R-charts are solved, that is, specific causes are identified, analyzed, corrected, and their repetitions are diverted, and the current control charts demonstrate the persistence of the process in a statistically controlled state, at least for 25 subgroups. The process output data scatter is then compared with the specifications to confirm that these requirements can be confidently met. The criteria for the specific reasons for the Shewhart charts are presented in Figures 2–4. The calculation of Shewhart charts is performed in Microsoft Excel.

As can be seen from Figure 3, the impact of seasonal activity on the financial condition of the service sector enterprise is very large. In the "high season", the net profit increases, and therefore the financial position of the enterprise is in the stage of growth, which, to a certain extent, requires a possible increase in labor resources, additional raw materials, and also increases the investment attractiveness. The lowest income is in the December–February, the "low season", which indicates the deterioration of the financial situation. This period encourages management to reduce labor resources, search for product sales, hotel services, and find ways to increase investment attractiveness.

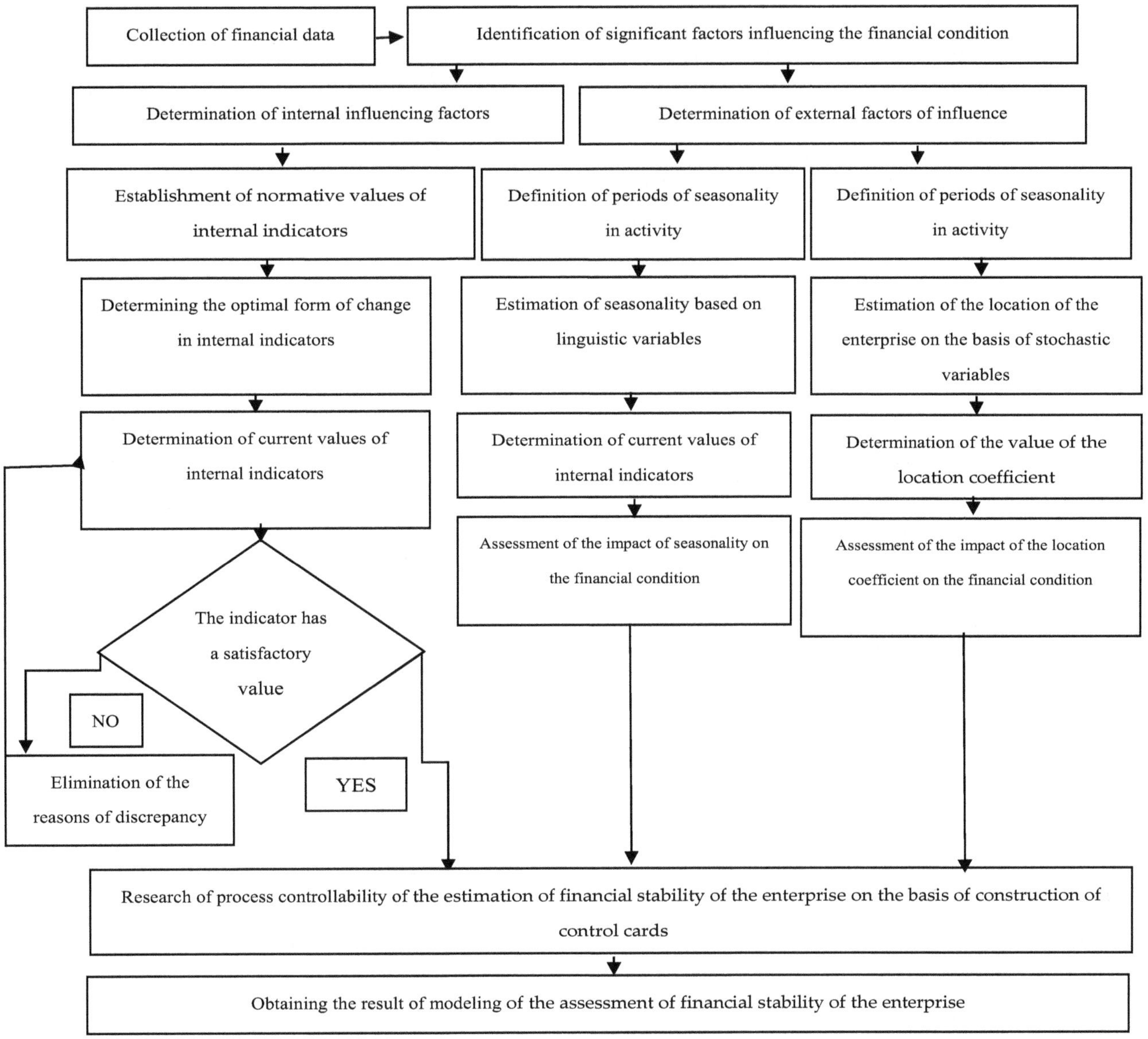

Figure 1. Algorithm for modeling the system for assessing the financial stability of the service sector enterprise (author's study).

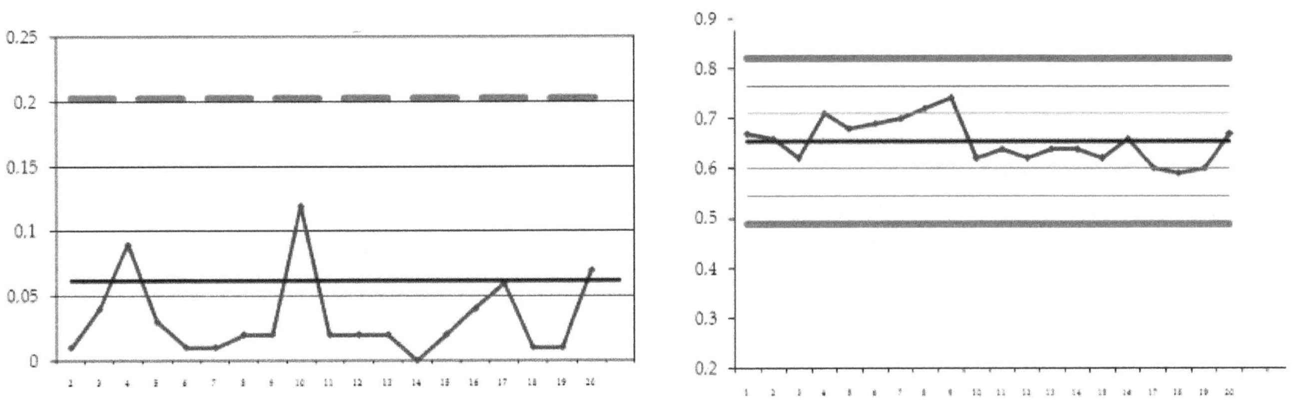

Figure 2. Shewhart's control charts for the fixed asset index (author's study).

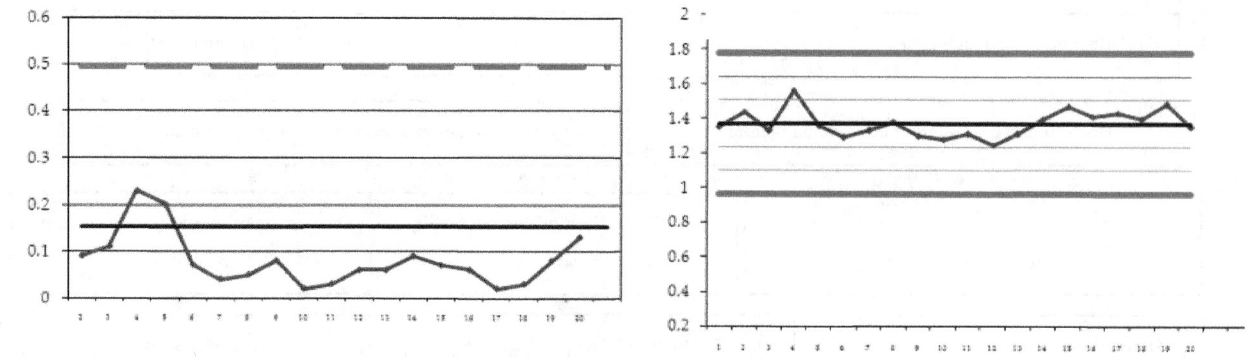

Figure 3. Shewhart's control charts for autonomy ratio (author's study).

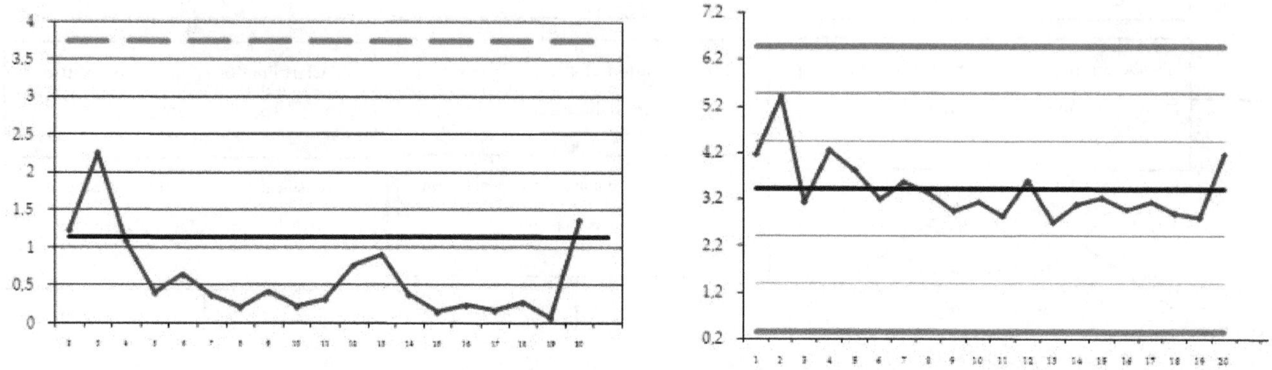

Figure 4. Shewhart's control charts for seasonal ratio (author's study).

One example of a solution to the problem of seasonality is the widespread system of contracts with companies that provide the hotel with business travelers.

Let us consider some measures that help reduce the seasonality index of a service sector enterprise:

- the provision of several types of services, the demand for which fluctuates in the antiphase (seasonal decline or rise). For example, targeting vacationers in high season and business travelers in low season;
- seasonal pricing policy—the use of progressive pricing depending on the expected consumer demand for a particular hotel service, as well as their ability to respond to such changes;
- the widespread use of the mass media to generate demand for services and attract customers by alerting them to the properties and quality of services provided;
- the use of progressive forms of customer service to shape the competitive advantage of the enterprise in the market;
- comprehensive improvement of the provision of the services for the establishment of the enterprise in the competitive market;
- formation of a base of regular customers and discount system for them;
- formation of special package deals in the low season, for example, three nights for the price of two ones;
- registration in the systems of reservation and use of contracts with corporate clients.

For example, we will analyze the company's services and segment the visitor base, build profiles of service users by identifying their similar behavior in terms of frequency, type of services ordered and evaluate the most and least profitable segments. To analyze and to build a map of Kohonen, we use data from the company "HOTEL AND RESTAURANT PREMIUM CLUB". The result is shown in Table 3.

Table 3. Information about the services of the hotel-restaurant "HOTEL AND RESTAURANT PREMIUM CLUB".

No.	Service	Description of the Service	Cost of the Service
1	Restaurant and bar	The hotel invites its guests to use the services of a restaurant and bar located on the territory. Modern interior, author's cuisine, cozy atmosphere, pleasant music, and professional service—all this will give guests the opportunity to get maximum comfort from their rest.	The price varies
2	Hotel	There are rooms in the hotel for every taste and at different prices. The hotel features: duplex apartments, family apartments, apartments, luxury, junior suite, standard with an extra bed, standard with balcony, economy class apartments.	From $1000 to $2400
3	Conference hall	The services of the hotel are regularly used by organizations for the purpose of holding various corporate events on its territory: seminars, training, negotiations, presentations, or small group meetings.	$300/h
4	Spa zone	The spa area includes an original design Roman bath, an indoor heated pool, and a relaxation room Maximum number of visitors—6 adults or 4 adults + 3 children	$800
5	Sports hall	An important part of the hotel's infrastructure—the gym is equipped with all the necessary equipment.	$50/h
6	Accommodation with pets	B Pets of small breeds up to 10 kg and up to 45 cm tall are allowed in the hotel.	$300

Hotel-restaurant visitors were segmented using an approach based on the Kohonen algorithm, objects were clustered according to the Kohonen algorithm, and an interpretation of the Kohonen map was built based on the company's financial revenues from services provided. The results are based on the company's activities for one month (Table 4).

Table 4. Financial revenues from the provision of services for August 2019, US dollars.

Day	Restaurant and Bar	Hotel	Conference Hall	Spa Zone	Sports Hall	Accommodation with Pets
1	4700	14,000	0	0	400	300
2	1000	12,000	0	800	450	300
3	3800	15,000	1200	800	300	300
4	2000	16,000	600	0	450	0
5	4500	12,000	0	0	300	0
6	3650	13,700	0	0	0	0
7	2766	13,700	0	0	0	0
8	6536	15,000	1500	800	350	600
9	3440	13,000	1200	800	450	600
10	5423	7000	900	0	200	600
11	3429	14,900	0	800	250	600
12	5443	15,000	1200	0	0	0
13	4121	15,400	1500	0	800	0
14	7537	15,400	900	0	600	300

Table 4. *Cont.*

Day	Restaurant and Bar	Hotel	Conference Hall	Spa Zone	Sports Hall	Accommodation with Pets
15	4569	12,350	600	0	0	300
16	3246	13,450	0	0	0	300
17	4537	14,400	1500	0	550	0
18	7648	12,350	1800	800	0	0
19	3452	13,700	1200	800	400	0
20	5259	14,900	900	800	300	0
21	4627	14,350	1200	0	450	0
22	3730	17,900	0	0	0	900
23	8551	17,900	1200	0	150	900
24	4653	15,350	900	0	100	900
25	5438	15,350	0	800	0	900
26	5334	15,350	1200	0	350	0
27	3076	12,400	900	0	200	0
28	3435	12,400	1500	0	150	0
29	5946	12,400	1800	0	0	0
30	4335	12,350	1200	800	0	0
31	5419	12,350	900	0	350	0

Figure 5 shows the obtained Kohonen maps based on Table 4, which shows the company's financial revenues from services provided. The results are based on the activities of the company "HOTEL AND RESTAURANT PREMIUM CLUB" for one month.

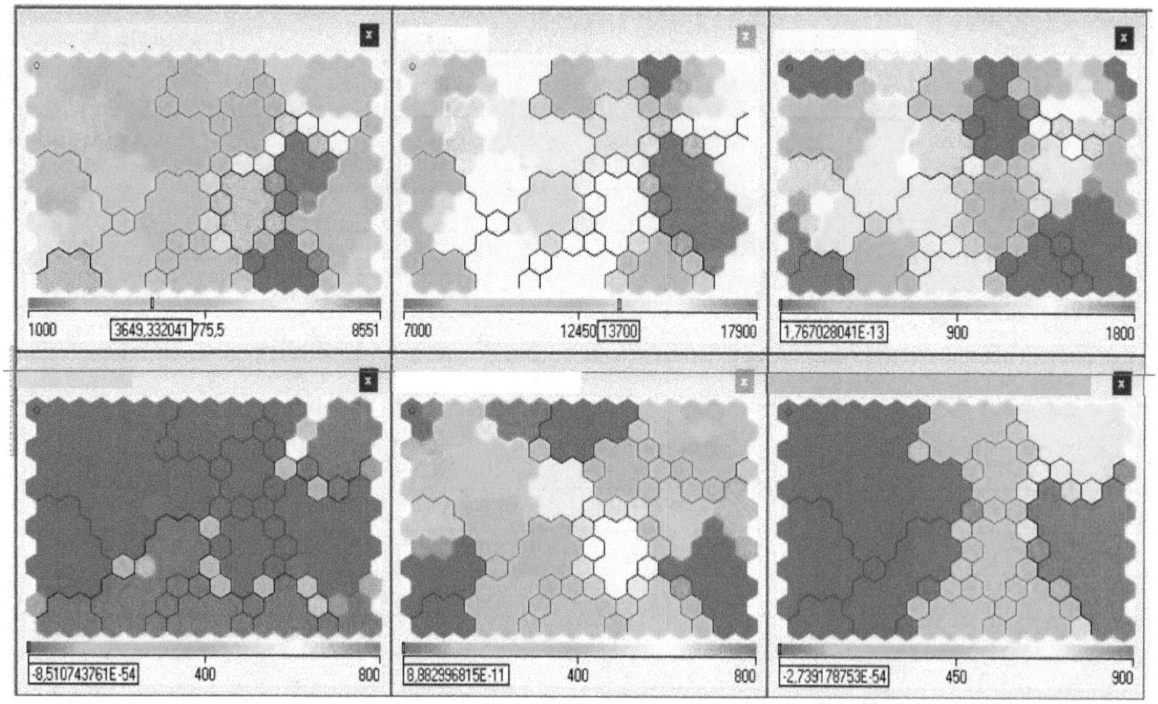

Figure 5. Characteristics of financial income in the form of two-dimensional Kohonen maps.

When assessing financial stability, an analytical approach is applied; that is, the actual financial stability indicators calculated are compared with extreme ones.

As can be seen from the above figures, the clear leader in terms of financial receipts of a service sector enterprise is the hotel service, receipts from this service were $431,350 in August 2019.

Restaurant and bar service, which brought $141,600 in a month, is in second place.

Conference hall service with an income of $25,800 is in third place.

Spa zone service with an income of $8000 is in fourth place.

"Accommodation with pets" service with an income of $7800 is in fifth place.

Sports hall service with an income of $7550 is in sixth place.

The survey results were conducted for August 2019, which may also affect the financial receipts from each service, as some of them are seasonal.

The formed structure of sources of funds, the turnover of current assets, the reputation of the enterprise, etc. Therefore, the acceptability of the values of the coefficients, the assessment of their dynamics and directions of change can be established only for a specific enterprise, taking into account the conditions of its activity.

The algorithm is based on a comprehensive analysis of financial stability indicators that will predict the future level of economic stability of the enterprise. The constructed algorithm gives an idea of the nature of the impact and the degree of correlation of the coefficients with each other, and the indicator of economic stability. This will give recommendations on the impact of a particular activity (personal, fixed assets, capital structure, etc.) of the enterprise on its economic stability.

4. Discussion

A study of the features of the financial activity of an enterprise in the service sector was carried out, and it was determined that a distinctive feature of this industry is a significant number of qualitative indicators of activity, which are difficult to express in a quantitative format.

To determine the system of optimal indicators for assessing the financial stability of an enterprise, a comparative characteristic of methods for assessing the financial condition by absolute indicators and an assessment of the financial condition using relative indicators, which use various data of the enterprise's activities that affect the assessment of financial stability, are carried out.

To analyze a significant number of factors influencing the financial stability of enterprises in the service sector, which leads to a variety of classifications of these factors, the research of factors influencing the assessment of financial stability has been deeply studied, and the classification of factors has been improved by introducing external factors of seasonality and regional location of the enterprise in the service sector.

To determine the significance of the influence of external factors on the financial stability of the hotel business, such factors as seasonality and regional location, which are complicated by problems of their uncertain nature and discretization, which is necessary for calculating and assessing the financial stability of the enterprise, were researched in the paper. To assess the financial condition of a hotel enterprise, a visual interpretation of a neural network was used—a model of a self-organizing Kohonen map. It was proved that using the Kohonen map method for each service provided by a hotel enterprise, in a certain period of activity, it is possible to establish certain objective limitations of structural characteristics that will prevent the transition to problem clusters or ensure the transition to better ones.

An important tool for ensuring the financial stability of the enterprise in the long term is a set of activities and procedures for managing risks that influence its level. The organization of risk management at the enterprise simultaneously allows deciding or creating favorable conditions for the solution of the main tasks of its activity, among which are: planning of expected profits and losses, reduction of unexpected expenses, optimization of tax payments, increase of credit and investment rating, strengthening of financial stability, and the like. The solution of these tasks will contribute to the achievement of strategic financial goals of the enterprise.

This approach is due to the dual response of strategic management to external change: long-term and operational one simultaneously. The long-term response is laid down in strategic plans, and the operational one is implemented in real time. Therefore, the enterprise risk management subsystem must provide for risk control and management both in strategic decisions and in tactical and operational decisions.

Measures aimed at optimizing the risks of financial stability of the enterprise should not reduce the stability of its financial environment. The risk management system for reducing financial stability can only be considered effective if the costs of optimizing it are less than the expected loss.

In today's economic environment, characterized by a high level of uncertainty, the achievement of strategic financial goals of enterprises and ensuring their long-term financial stability are impossible without creating an effective system of strategic financial management, an integral element of which is a mechanism for managing the risk of reducing financial stability.

Tax, investment, operational and liquidity risks are the main risks that hamper long-term development and cause a loss of financial stability for economic entities. Building an effective system of strategic financial stability management, which contains a risk management subsystem, will enhance the financial stability of the enterprise in the face of increased competition and uncertainty in the domestic and global markets.

Considering different approaches to calculations of the optimal capital structure of the company, it should be noted that the choice of methodology depends on the specific conditions of activity of the enterprise and the decisions of its management.

Depending on the goal—to minimize the risks or cost of capital or to maximize its profitability, the management of the company chooses the appropriate approach.

In the process of functioning, each enterprise must maintain not only the stability of its position but also balance the internal capabilities with the influence of the external environment to achieve a state of new quality, which will allow development.

The expert system was developed to assess the impact of external and internal factors on the financial stability of the enterprise. Of course, the company is not able to influence most external factors, but with information on the numerical assessment of financial stability, it can adapt to their impact and prepare effective strategies to address potential financial problems (Shim 2017).

The presence or availability of the enterprise with labor resources affects the volume and rhythm of production and sales of products in the case of the hotel industry for the implementation of services, the efficiency of using fixed assets, the cost of products, works, services, profit, profitability, and the financial condition of the enterprise. The analysis of the availability and provision of the enterprise with labor resources is carried out in the following sequence: research of the composition and structure of personnel; calculation and study of indicators of the movement of labor; assessment of the provision of the enterprise with labor resources; search and calculation of reserves for increasing the efficiency and completeness of the use of labor resources.

The provision of an enterprise with labor resources is a relative indicator calculated by dividing the actual number of employees by category and profession by the planned need.

The analysis of the provision of the enterprise with labor resources should be carried out in close connection with the study of the degree of implementation of the plan (program) of the social development of the enterprise—the provision of housing for employees, ensuring their social and cultural needs, and the like.

In the course of the analysis, the reserves for reducing the enterprise's need for labor resources as a result of these activities should be identified. Distribution and redistribution of workers is the distribution of personnel, positions, and jobs, which ensures the implementation of the necessary types and volumes of work. The use of workers involves the definition of such a structure of work that allows maximizing the opportunities and individual characteristics of workers.

Thus, the given expert system represents the calculation of the coefficients of influence on financial stability. The system indicates the input and output information (data that we have from the financial statements of the enterprise and, accordingly, the indicators that we obtain as a result of the analysis). The input indicators used in solving financial stability and initial information are described: the results of calculation of coefficients and their analysis, the system builds a matrix of pairwise ratios and transmits data for calculation of the integrated indicator of financial stability of SSE.

5. Conclusions

The comprehensive study of the problem of assessing financial stability was carried out in the paper, and new methodological approaches to solving the assessment of financial stability as leveling the risks of activities of enterprises in the service sector were implemented. To study the stability and controllability of the process of assessing financial stability, the types of control maps for each of the coefficients were determined. They have a significant impact on the assessment of the financial stability of a service sector enterprise. The control maps were built for each coefficient included in the integral indicator of financial stability, and their analysis for the presence of special reasons for the variability of the process of assessing financial stability was carried out. To assess financial stability, taking into account many criteria, a software implementation of a model for assessing the financial stability of an enterprise in the service sector was carried out in the form of an expert system, which provides for the calculation of coefficients of influence on financial stability, and the formation and analysis of an integral indicator of financial stability.

The method of constructing Kohonen maps was used for the segmentation of visitors. It can be argued that using the Kohonen map method for each service provided by a hotel company, at a certain period of activity, it is possible to establish some objective limitations of structural characteristics that will prevent the transition to problem clusters or ensure the transition to better ones. We are talking about the financial structure of indicators corresponding to the established level of financial stability of a service sector enterprise. Thus, the proposed apparatus of neural networks makes it possible not only to determine the most profitable activity of an enterprise but also to assess the financial condition of each of its research objects.

In the difficult financial and economic situation in the world, which is connected with external problems and complex internal situation, it is necessary for enterprises to take all possible measures to stabilize their own financial activities. To this end, it is advisable to recommend further research prospects:

to carry out constant monitoring and operative analysis of indicators of financial condition of the enterprise, taking into account features of the service sector;

to improve information support for analysis and forms of financial reporting, which will increase the analytical capabilities and the reality of assessment of the property of the hotel enterprise;

to study the implementation of neural network analysis to the analysis of the financial stability of the service sector enterprise.

Author Contributions: Conceptualization, S.D. and B.S.; methodology, A.B.-M.; software, T.B.; validation, S.D., A.B.-M. and O.C.; formal analysis, T.B.; investigation, B.S.; resources, O.C.; data curation, B.S.; writing—original draft preparation, T.B.; writing—review and editing, O.C.; visualization, T.B.; supervision, A.B.-M.; project administration, O.C.; funding acquisition, T.B., please turn to the CRediT taxonomy for the term explanation. Authorship must be limited to those who have contributed substantially to the present work reported. All authors have read and agreed to the published version of the manuscript.

Appendix A

Table A1. Indicators for assessing the financial stability of the enterprise.

Name of Indicator	Content of the Indicator
Autonomy ratio	The ratio of the amount of own funds to the balance sheet. The greater the value of the ratio, the less dependence on external sources
Loan capital concentration ratio	Characterizes the share of borrowed capital in total capital
Financial leverage	Shows how much borrowed funds are attracted per one hryvnia invested in the assets of own funds
Equity maneuverability ratio	Characterizes the degree of mobility of the use of own funds
Financial dependence ratio	The indicator is inverted to the autonomy ratio, shows the amount of the total value of the property per 1 dollar of own funds
Financial stability index	Characterizes the ratio of own and borrowed funds
Ratio of borrowed sources in non-current assets	Shows the part of non-current assets that is financed by long-term borrowed funds
Long-term borrowing ratio	Shows the share of long-term loans used to finance the company's assets along with its own funds
Long-term liabilities ratio	Determines part of long-term liabilities in the total amount of sources of formation
Current liabilities ratio	Determines the share of current liabilities in the total amount of sources of formation
Own funds ratio	Displays what part of current assets is financed by own current assets
Financial leverage ratio	Characterizes the dependence of the enterprise on long-term liabilities
Working capital stock ratio	Characterizes the level of coverage of current tangible assets
Business insurance ratio	Shows the amount of capital reserved by the company for each dollar of property
Share capital insurance ratio	Shows the amount of capital reserved by the company for each dollar of the authorized capital
Equity insurance ratio	Shows the amount of capital reserved by the company for each dollar of equity
Current assets working capital ratio	Characterizes the share of free current assets of the enterprise
Ratio of borrowed and own funds	Characterizes the structure of the financial resources of the enterprise. It is calculated as a share of the distribution of the amount of borrowed funds to the amount of equity. The maximum allowable value is 1

References

Acharya, Viral V., Imbierowicz Björn, Steffen Sascha, and Daniel Teichmann. 2017. Does the lack of financial stability impair the transmission of monetary policy? *SSRN*. [CrossRef]

Adrian, Tomas, Dell'Ariccia Giovanni, Haksar Vikram, and Tomammaso Mancini-Griffoli. 2018. Monetary Policy and Financial Stability. In *Advancing the Frontiers of Monetary Policy*. Washington, DC: International Monetary Fund.

Afonso, Antonio, Baxa Jaromir, and Michal Slavík. 2018. Fiscal developments and financial stress: A threshold VAR analysis. *Empirical Economics* 54: 395–423. [CrossRef]

Agénor, Pierre-Richard, and Luiz Pereira da Silva. 2017. Cyclically adjusted provisions and financial stability. *Journal of Financial Stability* 28: 143–62. [CrossRef]

Almasi, Moein, Hemmati Hadi, Fraser Gordon, Arcuri Andrea, and Janis Benefelds. 2017. An industrial evaluation of unit test generation: Finding real faults in a financial application. Paper presented at 39th International Conference on Software Engineering: Software Engineering in Practice Track, Buenos Aires, Argentina, May 20–28; pp. 263–72.

Anton, Sorin Gabriel. 2018. The Impact of Enterprise Risk Management on Firm Value: Empirical Evidence from Romanian Non-Financial Firms. *Inzinerine Ekonomika-Engineering Economics* 29: 151–57. [CrossRef]

Chang, Chia-Lin, McAleer Michael, and Wing Keung Wong. 2018. Management Information, Decision Sciences, and Financial Economics: A Connection (No. TI 2018-004/III). Tinbergen Institute Discussion Paper. Available online: https://www.econstor.eu/handle/10419/177694 (accessed on 1 September 2020).

Culpeper, Roy. 2018. Systemic reform at a standstill: A flock of "Gs" in search of global financial stability. In *Critical Issues in International Financial Reform*. London: Routledge, pp. 203–36.

Fazio, Dimas Mateus, Silva Thiago Christiano, Tabak Benjamin Miranda, and Daniel Oliveira Cajueiro. 2018. Inflation targeting and financial stability: Does the quality of institutions matter? *Economic Modelling* 71: 1–15. [CrossRef]

Kryshtal, Galyna. 2019. Conceptual approaches to forming the directions of the development of system synergy of the state regulator, economic sector and the banking system. *Economics and Finance* 3: 59–65.

Leva, Maria Chiara, Balfe Nora, McAleer Brian, and Michael Rocke. 2017. Risk registers: Structuring data collection to develop risk intelligence. *Safety Science* 100: 143–56. [CrossRef]

Lin, Edward M. H., Edward W. Sun, and Min-Teh Yu. 2018. Systemic risk, financial markets, and performance of financial institutions. *Annals of Operations Research* 262: 579–603. [CrossRef]

Liu, Chang, and Nior Arunkumar. 2018. Risk prediction and evaluation of transnational transmission of financial crisis based on complex network. *Cluster Computing* 22: 4307–13. [CrossRef]

Makedon, Vyacheslav, Drobyazko Svetlana, Shevtsova Hanna, Maslosh Olha, and Maryna Kasatkina. 2019. Providing security for the development of high-technology organizations. *Journal of Security and Sustainability Issues* 8: 757–72. [CrossRef]

Nasreen, Samia, Anwar Sofia, and Ilhan Ozturk. 2017. Financial stability, energy consumption and environmental quality: Evidence from South Asian economies. *Renewable and Sustainable Energy Reviews* 67: 1105–22. [CrossRef]

National Accounts—Analysis of Main Aggregates. 2019. Available online: https://unstats.un.org/unsd/snaama/ (accessed on 1 September 2020).

Nesterenko, Svetlana, Drobyazko Svetlana, Abramova Olha, and Natalya Siketina. 2019. Optimization of Factorial Portfolio of Trade Enterprises in the Conditions of the Non-Payment Crisis. *IBIMA Business Review* 2019: 278890. [CrossRef]

Nyman, Rickard, Kapadia Sujit, Tuckett David, Gregory David, Ormerod Paul, and Robert Smith. 2018. News and narratives in financial systems: Exploiting big data for systemic risk assessment. *SSRN*. [CrossRef]

Shim, Jeungbo. 2017. An investigation of market concentration and financial stability in property–liability insurance industry. *Journal of Risk and Insurance* 84: 567–97. [CrossRef]

Siddique, Asima, Masood Omar, Javaria Kiran, and Dinh Tran Ngoc Huy. 2020. A comparative study of performance of commercial banks in ASIAN developing and developed countries. *Insights into Regional Development* 2: 580–91. [CrossRef]

Singh, Sujit, Olugu Ezutah Udoncy, Musa Siti Nurmaya, and Abu Bakar Mahat. 2018. Fuzzy-based sustainability evaluation method for manufacturing SMEs using balanced scorecard framework. *Journal of Intelligent Manufacturing* 29: 1–18. [CrossRef]

Wagner, William P. 2017. Trends in expert system development: A longitudinal content analysis of over thirty years of expert system case studies. *Expert Systems with Applications* 76: 85–96. [CrossRef]

The Determinants of Credit Risk: An Evidence from ASEAN and GCC Islamic Banks

Faridah Najuna Misman [1] and M. Ishaq Bhatti [2,*]

1 Department of Finance, Faculty of Business and Management, Universiti Teknologi MARA, Segamat 85000, Johor, Malaysia; farid978@uitm.edu.my
2 Department of Economics, Finance & Marketing, La Trobe Business School, La Trobe University, Melbourne, VIC 3086, Australia
* Correspondence: i.bhatti@latrobe.edu.au

Abstract: In less than a decade, the Islamic Banking (IB) industry has become an essential part of the global financial system. During the last ten years, the IB industry has witnessed changes in economic conditions and proved to be resilient during the periods of financial crisis. This paper aims to examine the important issues related to credit risk in selected Islamic banks in nine countries from Association of South East Asian Nations (ASEAN) and Gulf Cooperation Council (GCC) regions. It employs the generalized least squares panel data regression, to estimate the ratio of non-performance financing to total financing as dependent variables and bank specific variables (BSV) to determine the credit risk. It uses 12 years of unbalanced panel data from 40 different Islamic banks. The overall findings show that financing quality has a significant positive effect on credit risk. It is observed that the larger IBs owned more assets with lower credit risk compared to smaller banks. The bank's age is also an important factor influencing the credit risk level. Moreover, regulatory capital significantly reduces the credit risk exposure adherence to the minimum regulatory capital requirements which help IBs to manage their credit risk exposures. It was also observed that IBs were not affected by the global financial crisis due to less credit risk compared to the conventional banks.

Keywords: credit risk; Islamic Bank; financial crisis

JEL Classification: C1; G01; G21; G29

1. Introduction

The recent growth and development of the Islamic banking (IB) industry has prompted attention and further investigation towards the management of IBs, specifically risk management. At present, the total assets of Islamic banks have amounted to more than USD 3.2 trillion[1], holding the largest share of total Islamic finance assets and owning approximately 76%. This highlights the importance of comprehensive risk management, as the IB business model significantly differs from conventional banks (CB). Islamic Banks must also adhere to regulatory requirements, such as, *Shari'ah* compliance (see Akkizidis and Khandelwal 2008; Cihák and Hesse 2008), thus resulting in an additional element of risk when compared to conventional banks. Amongst the various types of risk faced by banks, credit risk serves as the primary threat to financial stability in the banking industry (Basel 1999). For IBs, credit risk may be more essential to handle due to the nature of the financing model (modes) itself (Cihák and Hesse 2008; İncekara and Çetinkaya 2019). It offers financing with several different models;

1 https://www.arabianbusiness.com/islamic-finance-assets-forecast-be-worth-3-2trn-by-2020-641156.html.

for example, some financing modes are based on profit and loss sharing (PLS) while others are based on debt or trading financing modes (non-PLS). As a result, credit risk may arise in different circumstances according to various PLS vis-à-vis non-PLS financing modes. Credit risk is measured by referring to the size of non-performing loans (NPL). According to Reinhart and Rogoff (2011), the size of NPL is an important benchmark in evaluating a banking crisis. Therefore, the need to understand the determinants of credit risk is essential.

Compared to the extensive literature published on conventional banking (CB), there are limited studies regarding the credit risk in IBs[2]. The number of empirical studies on Islamic banks' credit risk are minimal and very few attempted to address the issues related to this specific kind of risk[3] (Al-Tamimi and Al-Mazrooei 2007; Hassan 2009). Researchers have addressed various risk management issues including credit risk without due regards being given to the study of credit risk in member countries of the Association of South East Asian Nations (ASEAN) and the Gulf Cooperation Council (GCC) which contribute more than 50% of IBs size.

This paper attempts to fill this gap in the literature. It investigates the key determinants of credit risk in IBs in the ASEAN and the GCC regions, as these two regions are at the forefront of global Islamic banking industry. IB in the GCC started its journey in 1975 with the establishment of the Islamic Development Bank (IDB). Since then, other gulf countries have gradually implemented Islamic banking in collaboration with the conventional system with a similar trend being seen in ASEAN countries. Acknowledging the difference in market structure and regulations among ASEAN and GCC countries, it is appreciated to examine the determinants of credit risk using seven (financing, financing quality, capital buffer, capital ratio, net interest margin, management efficiency and age) bank specific variables (BSV) in selected IBs. To this end, this paper seeks to answer the following four research questions (RQ) related to the credit risk associated with BSV in IBs.

RQ1. Are the BSVs used as exploratory variables, the key determinant of credit risk?
RQ2. Is there a significant different between IBs credit risk level of the two regions; ASEAN and GCC?
RQ3. Does the age of the banks also influence the credit risk?
RQ4. What are the effects of the global financial crisis (GFC) on credit risk across various countries?

This paper employs an unbalanced panel data regression model to examine the determinants of credit risk in Islamic banks across GCC and ASEAN regions. It estimates the fixed effects (FE) and random effects (RE) using generalized least square (GLS) estimation method. It computes the ratio of non-performance financing (NPF) to total financing as dependent variables and bank specific variables to determine the credit risk determinants.

This paper contributes to the Islamic banking and finance industry literature in three ways. Firstly, it examines the determinants of credit risk across different regions rather than focusing on a single country or region. Bank level data was used rather than an aggregate data, capturing different characteristics amongst banks (IBs) in both regions. It also addresses the research question of whether there are significant differences in credit risk between the two regions. This is important as it can be utilized by policy makers in the process of structuring a better credit risk management framework.

Secondly, it focuses on the impact of age on the credit risk level. There is a notable difference in years of establishment between ASEAN and GCC, and IB poses a question on the significance of this factor in influencing credit risk levels. With different levels of experience in the industry, we may or may not see a relative deviation in credit risk. Finally, this study examines whether the global financial crisis (GFC) had a significant impact on the credit risk level of Islamic banks in ASEAN and GCC regions. This will help to identify whether the two regions were impacted differently. The motivation to examine the GFC impact is to determine if the IB structure reacts differently to the crisis as compared

---

2 Most studies include the Islamic window which is embedded in conventional banking institutions.
3 An extensive recent literature review is done by Al Rahahleh et al. (2019) on the developments in risk management in Islamic Finance.

to the conventional system. This is an important and timely research question in the presence of COVID-19 financial crises (see McKibbin and Fernando 2020).

The rest of this paper is organized as follows. In the preceding sections, the research question is introduced and the brief literature review relevant to the study is given by incorporating important existing research in this area. Section 3 describes the selected data used, sample selection procedure of unbalanced data over time and countries and the research methodology adopted to conduct empirical research using complex unbalanced clustered panel data. Section 4 examines the results on credit risk in the IB industry along with the effect of GFC which enable to make analogue discussion about the COVID-19 effects on financial portfolios. The final section summarizes the main findings and elaborate on limitations of the study.

2. Literature Review

Understanding financial stability in the banking sector, particularly in managing credit risk, is increasingly important especially when industry faces extreme events; like GFC and/or COVID 19 types of uncertain events. Research on credit risk management have attracted the attention of many academician and financiers, from developed and developing countries. Moreover, Investigating the factors that drive the credit risk in the banking sector is vital to the bank's management, finance industry and their regulatory bodies. Most of the studies about the credit risk of commercial banks focus on developed countries, ignoring due research on banks from developing countries. For example, (Bonfim 2009; İncekara and Çetinkaya 2019; Louzis et al. 2012) are among others who worked on developed country's data. They investigated various issues of credit risk, such as the effect of macroeconomic and banks specific variables on credit risk, the relationship of credit risk and liquidity risk, and gave evidence from the latest financial crisis like AFC and GFC.

Some prior studies have measured credit risk by using the ratio of non-performing loans (NPL). Among these are the work of (Alandejani and Asutay 2017; Bonfim 2009; Misman et al. 2015; Rahman and Shahimi 2010). Moreover, recent literature reviews were completed by Bhatti et al. (2019) and Al Rahahleh et al. (2019). In banking studies, the loan is classified as NPL when the payment of interest and principal are overdue by 90 days or more. Higher NPL causes the banks to experience lower profit margins and if the problem increases, it can lead to a crisis. Potential influences on the NPL include the types of borrower, bank management and adverse changes in the economic situation. The importance of efficient credit risk management invites many parties especially researchers, regulators and banks' management to investigate the determinants of credit risk in banking. This will help them to understand and propose a comprehensive credit risk management framework. The level of credit risk is found to be a significant influence in the performance of banks (Ahmadyan 2018). Therefore, examining the key drivers of credit risk is important for the banks to manage its function in an efficient way.

This study links the two main areas of credit risk research. Firstly, it aims to discuss the significance of bank specific variables (BSV) or microeconomics and their impact on credit risk level for the selected data in our empirical study. Secondly, it intends to examine the effect of the changes in macroeconomic variables on credit risk. A dummy variable to represent GFC was used to examine the impact of financial crisis on credit risk management.

Bank-Specific Variables and Credit Risk

Current literature related to credit risk management suggests two important determinants of credit risk, namely systematic factors and unsystematic factors. Systematic risk refers to risk that cannot be eliminated and controlled by the bank itself. For example, (i) macroeconomic factors like inflation, changes in interest rate and unemployment rate; (ii) changes in economic cycle like a recession and financial crisis; (iii) political factors. All these factors will influence the capacity of the borrower to repay back the loans and a failure to do so will classify the loan as an NPL. Despite the importance of systematic risk in influencing the credit risk, the unsystematic risk should not be ignored. Louzis et al. (2012) claim in their study that a distinctive structure of banking industry across different countries and the individual bank management will vary the impact of unsystematic risk on credit risk level.

Moreover, the literature revealed that unsystematic risk or bank specific variables (BSV) are hypothesized to have either a positive or negative relationship with the level of NPL. The important BSV discussed in previous studies included financing variables, capital, cost of fund, management quality, and efficiency. Some of these studies examine the link between BSV and credit risk by focusing on the efficiency and problem loans matter. For example an early study by Berger and DeYoung (1997) focuses on bad management, skimming and moral hazard issues. These issues are related to the relationship between loan quality, cost efficiency, bank capital and credit risk. Evidence from the US banking sector (for example, Angbazo 1997; Berger and DeYoung 1997; Cebenoyan and Strahan 2004; Gallo et al. 1996) indicates that BSV have a significant effect on credit risk of commercial banks. Moreover, Cebenoyan and Strahan (2004) in their study on US commercial banks from 1987 to 1994 find that the type of loan has a positive and significant influence on credit risk. Another study using a dataset from developing countries conducted by Eng and Nabar (2007) also concludes that a few BSV did significantly influence bank risk using data from 1993 to 2000.

Furthermore, previous studies have also discussed the effect of lending or financing variables on various risks faced by commercial and/or Islamic banks. To empirically test this, the authors used two financing variables against credit risk, namely financing quality and financing expansion. Financing quality is measured using a ratio of loan loss provision[4] to total assets. Banks make a provision for losses in order to adjust loan loss reserves to reflect expected future losses. This provision does not involve direct cash outflows. It is instead decreased as reported net income, retained earnings and shareholders' equity. In the case of IBs, this provision is made in order to anticipate future losses for financing and investment accounts such as Mudharabah, Murabahah and Musharakah (see Zoubi and Al-Khazali 2007, for sukuk see Azmat et al. 2020; Khawaja et al. 2020). Previous studies found that financing quality has a positive-significant relationship with credit risk (Ahmed et al. 1999; Eng and Nabar 2007). When banks make a higher provision for loss, the loans or financing is argued to be of low quality or carry a higher risk of default, leading to an increase in credit risk exposure.

The second variable related to credit risk is the proportion of loans or financing to the total bank assets. Financing item is generally perceived to be a higher risk compared to other asset items. Holding a larger amount of financing (loan) relative to total assets, exposes banks to high default risk and less liquidity compared to other asset components, in addition to creating a credit and liquidity risk conflict (Hassan et al. 2018; Imbierowicz and Rauch 2014; Zarei et al. 2019). However, as loans or financing are major services provided by banks, this problem cannot be avoided. Therefore, a higher proportion of total financing to total assets will potentially increase NPL and create a credit risk for banks. Love and Turk Ariss (2014) claim that a rapid growth in financing will give an adverse impact on credit risk. A positive coefficient is commonly assumed between financing expansion and credit risk. However, a negative coefficient might also appear when the banks have better credit risk management strategies. Gallo et al. (1996) and Madura et al. (1994) document mixed results on composition relative to total assets. Madura et al. (1994) demonstrate a negative relationship between the proportion of loans to total assets and bank risk but when considering only on real estate loans, a positive significant relationship exists.

Recently, Louhichi and Boujelbene (2016) claimed that capital plays an important role in the banks' management of credit risk. Banks' capital consists of ordinary shares and retained earnings. Traditionally, banks hold larger amounts of capital to reduce the risk of insolvency and to buffer losses from unexpected circumstances. Cebenoyan and Strahan (2004) noted in their study that banks can reduce the possibility of failure by holding appropriate amounts of capital buffer, liquid assets and employing an active risk management system. Banks with active risk management strategies can retain less capital and invest in

---

4 IFRS-9 standard on expected credit losses (ECL) in three different stages, Stage 1, Stage 2, and Stage 3, which is different from the existing loan loss provisions and has been in the industry and IBs are yet to implement that standards and the implications will be different which are not captured in this study.

more risky assets and illiquid loans (see Froot et al. 1993). In bank management, the amount of capital required to be maintained by the banks is monitored by bank regulators. In practice, bank regulators require banks to hold minimum amounts of capital to promote safety and soundness. The Basel committee on banking supervision (BCBS) introduced in June 2006 represents a capital adequacy requirement under Basel II with the intention of controlling or reducing risk-taking by the banks.

The BCBS provides a guideline for all commercial banks regarding minimum capital requirements. This regulatory capital consists of Tier I and Tier II capital. All commercial banks must maintain a minimum total capital of 8% from risk weighted assets (RWAs) of the bank (Basel 2001). Under this arrangement, Tier I percent must exceed at least 4% of the risk weighted assets and 3% of total assets. In Tier II, the amount must not exceed the amount of Tier I. This system therefore requires at least 50% of the amount of total capital to be supplied by TIER 1 capital. In November 2010, the capital ratio (CR) definition was changed based on the Basel-III Capital Framework. Under Basel-III, the calculation of CR is stricter in regard to the definition of capital (Hannoun 2010)[5].

Empirical studies provide mixed evidence on the relationship between regulatory capital ratio and credit risk. Berger and DeYoung (1997) suggest that CR has a negative relationship with credit risk whereas Ahmad and Ariff (2007) found a positive relationship between regulatory capital and credit risk in Japan, Malaysia and Mexico. Godlewski (2005) discussed CR in a different perspective and noted that banks with different levels of regulatory capitals react differently to credit risk. Banks with low regulatory capital will have a significant negative relationship with credit risk. This explains why undercapitalized banks may not be able to deal with risky loans and in turn will face the problem of higher credit risk.

The other important variable is capital buffer. In previous studies, capital buffer is a proxy for the ratio of total equity to total assets ratio. Capital buffer is expected to have a negative relationship with credit risk level. Cebenoyan and Strahan (2004) found a negative relationship between capital buffer and credit risk in United States (US) commercial banks for 1988 to 1993. Berger and DeYoung (1997) documented mixed results regarding the relationship between CR and non-performance loans. They suggested that banks with a low CR will have a negative relationship between the capital and credit risk. This situation may happen due to moral hazard issues. With regard to Islamic banks, Abedifar et al. (2013) in their study reported a negative relationship between capital asset ratio and credit risk. However, they failed to prove any significant relationship between the understudy variables. Rahman and Shahimi (2010) used data from the Malaysian Islamic banks and windows[6] and observed a significant negative relationship between capital buffer and credit risk. Most Islamic banks in Malaysia are new as they began their operation between 2005 and 2010 and consequently IBs may only have small amounts of capital as compared to CBs.

The ability to generate income based on given assets is one of the important factors when measuring efficiency. Net interest margin (NIM)[7] is one of the indicators that can be used to proxy efficiency in credit risk analysis for CBs. NIM is defined as the spread between interest income and expenses over the total assets invested by the bank. Angbazo (1997) explained that when a bank's NIM decreases, the bank may change its credit risk policy by accepting more risky loans and indirectly increase credit risk. It means that banks with a smaller NIM tend to have higher credit risk levels. This may be due to a bank's decision to increase the margin and practice a more liberal credit policy. In a study by Maudos and De Guevara (2004), NIM had a positive significant effect on credit risk. As IBs are free from interest provisions, the effect of NIM on credit risk may be different. Rahman and Shahimi (2010) used interest expenses instead of the NIM and found a positive and significant relationship between interest expenses and credit risk.

---

5 Under Basel III, the minimum capital adequacy ratio that banks must maintain is 8%. The capital adequacy ratio measures a bank's capital in relation to its risk-weighted assets.

6 The Bank Negara Malaysia introduced the IB system when it launched the Skim Perbankan Tanpa Faedah (Interest–free banking Scheme) in 1993. Since then, commercial banks have offered IB products through a specialized service called the 'Islamic window'.

7 In IB it's called Net Profit Margin (NPM), hereafter we assume that NIM for CBs and NPM for IBs.

Louzis et al. (2012) suggested that the too-big-to-fail theory is important in determining credit risk. They claim that banks which believe in such a theory have a higher propensity to expose themselves to excessive risk-taking activities, for example, by giving loans to lower quality of borrowers and having a high leverage ratio. Theoretically, larger banks can absorb more risk-taking activities compared to smaller banks. Saunders et al. (1990) concluded that size and risk should be negatively related, as larger banks have more diversification in assets to mitigate risk. A similar result was observed by How et al. (2005) in their study of analysing Islamic financing and risk in Malaysia. They concluded that the larger banks have significantly less credit risk compared to smaller banks. Other studies which support this finding of similar bank's size and credit risk relationship are Rahman and Shahimi (2010); Ahmad and Ahmad (2004); Konishi and Yasuda (2004); Gulati et al. (2019) among others. Gulati et al.'s (2019) paper empirically showed that the size of banks in India influence their credit risk. The authors indicated that larger banks in the industry are exposed to greater credit risk. Additional to large volumes of financing, these banks also provide financing to various types of businesses, resulting in an increased exposure to individual business risks.

Moreover, size also helps banks contain adverse effects of a financial crisis. Abdelrahim (2013) found that the size of Saudi banks during the GFC had a significant negative relationship with their credit risk. This implies that the larger the bank, the lower the credit risk. Beck et al. (2013) also reported a similar finding where size was significantly and negatively related to the NPL of CBs and Islamic banks during the GFC.

3. Data and Methodology

This section explains the details of the data selection from ASEAN and GCC regions, research methodology employed, importance of the variables used to interpret the data set and an appropriate model used to conduct empirical study. Let us begin with the data selection.

3.1. Data

The dataset in this empirical study consists of nine panels; four from ASEAN region and five from GCC countries, for a 12-year time period between 2000 to 2011. These sample countries are selected because they practice a dual banking system; conventional and Islamic banking. In total there are 72 IBs from nine selected countries of both regions. We face two complication in choosing unbalanced panel data model. Firstly, some IBs started operation in different years rather than the sampled period (i.e., 2000 to 2011) which resulted unequal operational periods. Secondly, some of the banks, 'bank characteristics' such as NPL, CR and loan loss provision (LLP) were missing. To overcome on this problem, we used unbalanced time and unbalanced panels in our model. So, the total number of observations used in the regression analysis is turned out to be 180, representing only 40 full-fledge Islamic banks out of 72 banks. The sample selection details of 180 observation with sampling distribution of time periods and the number of selected banks from 9 countries are given in Table A3 in Appendix B. All the data has been converted into the US dollar (US$) to maintain consistency for comparison purposes. The data were collected from the BankScope[8] database and other information sourced from each bank's website and respective country's Central Bank reports and website. Table 1 reports the details sample frame of the number of banks selected for specific country and regions.

In our empirical study, the credit risk is measured as the ratio of non-performance financing (loans) to the total financing outstanding. The credit risk is modelled at the microeconomic or BSV level from the consolidated financial statement of each selected bank. Several BSV are considered and are categorize into few groups to represent the financing quality, moral hazard, management efficiency

---

8 The total number of Islamic banks operating in each country is listed in Appendix A and the sampling ddistribution of the number of oobservations by years and ccountry are given in Tables A2 and A3 in Appendix B.

9 Just recently, this bank is closed in 2019 by the MAS.

and capital. We first used the proportion of loan loss provision to measure the quality of the loan. With regards to banks, increases in provision for loss justify the deterioration of the quality of loan in their banking book. This may lead to the higher NPL value resulting higher credit risk level. In early section, we noted some studies have confirmed that capital plays important role in managing credit risk in banks. Two variables are used to examine the effect of capital on credit risk. First is 'total equity to total assets' and the second is 'total capital to total risk weighted assets. We expected these two variables may show a positive or a negative effect on credit risk, as different level of regulatory capital reacts differently to the underlying credit risk.

The 'net interest margin' and 'earnings ratio' are another important aspect which need to be considered in examining the determinants of credit risk. Both variables will measure the efficiency of the bank in their daily operation. The inclusion of these variables is to see 'how bank decision on generating income will affect credit risk?'.

Table 1. Number of Sampled Islamic Banks (IBs) in Association of South East Asian Nations (ASEAN) and Gulf Cooperation Council (GCC).

No.	Country	Group	No. of IBs
1	Brunei	ASEAN	1
2	Indonesia	ASEAN	1
3	Malaysia	ASEAN	17
4	Singapore[9]	ASEAN	1
5	Bahrain	GCC	5
6	Kuwait	GCC	3
7	Qatar	GCC	3
8	UAE	GCC	6
9	Saudi Arabia	GCC	3
	Total		40

3.2. Research Methodology

This paper employs the unbalanced panel data technique to examine the determinants of credit risk of IBs from nine countries of ASEAN and the GCC regions. Unbalanced panel data is a technique that pools the unequal sample observations in the cross-section over a certain period. In panel data the observations are indexed through ($N \times T$) dimension. N is the number of firms (panels) and T is the dimension of a time series, such as years, months or daily data series; $t = 1, 2, \ldots, T$ of each $i = 1, 2, \ldots, N$ cross-section observations in the sample. The unbalanced panel data regression model fits this study because it can analyze changes at the bank level which cannot be done in either cross-section or time series models.

The panel data model is expressed as:

$$y_{it} = \beta_0 + \beta_{it}\, X_{it} + u_{it}\; j = 1, \ldots, m(i); t = 1, \ldots, T, i = 1, \ldots, n. \tag{1}$$

where in (1) above, the sample size consists of unbalanced panels such that $N = \sum_{i=1}^{n} m(i)$, where $m(i)$ is the number of banks in the ith country, y_{it}, u_{it} are $N \times 1$ vectors, X is $N \times k$ matrix, β is $k \times 1$ vector and β_0 is an unknown constant coefficient to be estimated, and X_{it} refers to the set of explanatory variable with $N \times k$ dimension representing selected Islamic bank.

The panel data model controls for the unobserved individual heterogeneity of firms (IBs) by incorporating firm-specific effects, which may be fixed or random. In this case u_{it} is a time-varying error term that can be written as $u_{it} = \alpha_i + v_{it}$. The α_i denotes the unobservable effects of the individual IB that are constant overtime and v_{it} is the remaining disturbance with a usual assumption that it is not correlated to the dependent variable. Therefore, the Equation (1) can be expressed as follows:

$$y_{it} = \beta_0 + \beta_{it}\, X_{it} + \alpha_i + v_{it} \tag{2}$$

The model (2) is based on the following set of assumptions:

i. α_i and v_{it} are normally distributed and they are mutually independent,

ii. $E(\alpha_i) = E(v_{ij}) = 0$, for $i = 1, \ldots, m, j = 1, 2, \ldots, m(i)$,

iii. $E(\alpha_j \alpha_{i'}) = \begin{cases} \sigma_1^2, & i = i' \\ 0, & otherwise, \end{cases}$

iv. $E(v_{ij} v_{i'j'}) = \begin{cases} \sigma_2^2, & i = i', j = j' \\ 0, & otherwise. \end{cases}$

In the scenario where the unobserved effects α_i is correlated with the explanatory variables, the fixed effects panel data is used. Alternatively, if it is proven that all explanatory variables are truly random, then random effects should be employed. Due to the nature of bank characteristics such as size of assets, risk and capital and market timing, the employment of unbalanced panel data regression assuming fixed effects is appropriated, and this choice can be tested using the Hausman test.

The estimated model of credit risk, under (1) and (2) can be expressed as:

$$\mathrm{CR}_{it} = \beta_0 + \beta_{it} X_{it} + \alpha_i + \nu_{it} \tag{3}$$

For $i = 1, \ldots, 15 = N, t = 1, \ldots, 12 = T, k = 1, \ldots, 7 =$ BSV's.

Where in (3) above, CR_{it} is the dependent variable of which represents credit risk of the ith IBs. X_{it} is a set of explanatory variables measured at time t, α_i is unobserved in all periods but constant over time i, ν_{it} is a time-varying idiosyncratic error and the total number of selected observations in our sample are 180. The detail sample selection is given in Tables A2 and A3 in Appendix B at the end of the paper.

Note that in Equation (3), CR_{it}—credit risk is proxy by the ratio of non-performance financing to the total financing outstanding. This is due to Lassoued (2018) approach to determine the key factors of credit risk in ASEAN and GCC Islamic banks. These are seven BSV's used as exploratory variables of credit risk. The BSV includes are financing, financing quality, capital buffer, capital ratio, net interest margin, management efficiency and log of total assets (SIZE). We test the following four hypotheses associated with RQ1 to RQ4, as discussed in Section 1.

Hypothesis 1 (H1). *Bank specific variables (BSV) are the key determinant of credit risk.*

Further, this current study also investigates if there is any significant different between two regions, the ASEAN and the GCC's Islamic banks in term of their credit risk level. To answer this question, a dummy variable is used to represent regional countries group. Group dummy is equal to '1' for GCC and '0' for the ASEAN. This study also controls for age factor in regard to the credit risk level. The objective is to examine if age of the banks also influences the IB's credit risk. We assume that older Islamic banks are likely to have more experience, knowledge and better operating systems for managing credit risk exposures. Thus, age is expected to have a negative relationship with the dependent variable.

Hypothesis 2 (H2). *Credit risk level is significantly different for ASEAN and GCC Islamic banks.*

Hypothesis 3 (H3). *Age factor gives impact on the credit risk.*

To capture the effects of macroeconomic factors, the models are controlled by some important dummy variables. A set of time dummy for each year of the observation is included, examining the changes in economic conditions and regulations concerning the Islamic banks over that time. The dummy for the base year (year = 2000) is excluded from the estimation model to avoid multicollinearity.[10] In addition, the analysis also investigates the effects of the global financial

---

10 Berger and DeYoung (1997) suggest that the dummy for base year should be excluded from the estimation model.

crisis (GFC) on credit risk across various countries. To achieve this objective, the dummy representing crisis period is introduced and the years 2008, 2009, and 2010 are defined as the crisis period. The GFC wrecked the financial system from mid-2008 to mid-2009. However, this study also included 2010 as crisis year to capture the delayed effect across countries. Crisis is a time period dummy variable representing 1 for 2008, 2009, and 2010 and zero for non-crisis period.

Hypothesis 4 (H4). *GFC do affects the credit risk of Islamic banks.*

The details of variables and their definitions are included in Table 2 below.

Table 2. Empirical Model Variables and Definitions.

Variables	Abbreviation	Proxy Measurement
Credit Risk	CR	Non-performing financing to total financing outstanding
Financing Expansion	Fin. Exp	Total financing to total assets
Quadratic Term of Financing Expansion	Fin. Exp^2	The squared value of Fin. expansion
Financing Quality	FLP	Financing loss provisions to total assets
Capital Buffer	Cap Buffer	Total equity to total assets
Capital Ratio	CAPR	Total capital (TIER 1 and TIER 2 capital) to Total RWA
Net Interest Margin	NIM	(Profit-Cost)/Average Invested Assets
Management efficiency	MGT	Total earning assets to total assets
Total Assets	SIZE	Natural logarithm of total assets
Group dummy	GROUP	Dummy variables; '1' for Islamic banks in GCC group and '0' for Islamic banks in ASEAN group.
Crisis Period	Crisis	Dummy variable; '1' for crisis period 2008, 2009, 2010 and '0' for other years.
Age of Banks	Age	How long the banks were established

4. Empirical Results

As discussed earlier that the aim of this paper is to examine the determinants of credit risk by examining a few bank specific variables and dummy variables. So, to this end we considered ten (10) explanatory variables and three (3) dummy variables representing countries group, age and financial crisis in a similar manner as Mansor et al. (2019) did for the case of Islamic Mutual fund[11]. The results are tabulated in Table 3 which summarize the summary statistics regarding credit risk and bank-specific characteristic variables for all 40 banks. It includes 20 Islamic banks from ASEAN member countries and the other 20 Islamic banks from GCC member countries. The average value of credit risk[12] for the 12-year period is 5.2% and the median is 3.5%. This figure indicates that about half of the Islamic banks in the study have a credit risk of less than 3.5%. This situation suggests that there are a few Islamic banks with higher credit risk which is increasing the average value of credit risk. The bank level average credit risk between Islamic banks differs dramatically, ranging from a minimum of 0.04% to a maximum of 22.11%.

For the composition of the Islamic banks' total assets, on average, 56.15% of assets are contributed by financing (loan) activities. Some banks that are exposed to a higher risk profile, have found rely heavily on financing activities with a maximum amount of 88.23% of ratio between total financing to total assets. More than 50% of the sample banks are exposed to this situation as the median value of the ratio of financing to total assets is 58.06%.

Capital is very important to buffer risk exposure faced by banks. The mean of the 40 banks' capital buffer is 13.16%. This variable ranges from a minimum of negative 1.7% to a maximum of 73.17%.

---

[11] Just recently, Mansor et al. (2019) studied the return performance and persistence of Islamic and conventional mutual funds during financial crises periods in the presence of spurious regression and noted misleading and controversial conclusions on the performance of funds.

[12] Credit risk is the ratio of non-performance financing to total financing.

A similar situation involves the important capital indicator called CR (capital ratio). The mean value for CR is 19.53% ranging from a negative 2.47% to 92.02%. After further investigation of the dataset, the biggest negative value of capital buffer and CR derives from Malaysian Islamic banks[13].

To evaluate the efficiency of Islamic banks in generating profits, two bank-specific characteristics are included in the analysis. The NIM which is referring to margin between cost and profit of financing activities shows a mean value of 4%. The most efficient Islamic banks can generate a margin of 13.53% and the smallest ones are able to generate 0.52%. This very low margin is due to some sample banks in the dataset being very new and only have observations for one or two years[14]. The ratio of total earning assets to total assets is used to indicate management efficiency. On average, Islamic banks in ASEAN and GCC have a very high percentage of total earning assets with a mean value of 82.16%. The higher proportion of total earning assets to total assets is a good sign in that most Islamic banks have high earning assets rather than non-earning assets. Bank size is another important factor that should be included in the analysis of credit risk determinants. On average about 50% of the total assets is made up of financing amounts, and larger banks can afford higher levels of credit risk. The observations reveal that the average total assets are US$7,814,832. It is worth noting here that the size differs markedly ranging from a minimum of US$353,507 to a maximum of US$58,900,000. The huge variation may be caused by sampled banks having started at different times.

Table 3. Summary Statistics of Bank specific variables.

Variable	Mean	Median	Min	Max	Std. Dev	Kurtosis	Skewness
Cr	5.219	3.497	0.040	22.113	4.946	4.242	1.335
Fin. Exp	56.153	58.060	13.691	88.233	13.828	2.750	−0.320
FLP	1.380	0.926	−0.610	25.120	2.400	60.946	6.800
Cap. Buffer	13.161	11.296	−1.699	73.168	8.279	17.488	2.626
CAPR	19.530	17.405	−2.470	92.020	9.991	21.941	3.415
NIM	4.005	3.691	0.520	13.529	1.769	7.079	1.238
MGT	82.166	86.597	18.031	99.342	13.941	5.968	−1.598
SIZE (US$)	7,814,832	3,988,425	353,507	58,900,000	10,500,000	9.853	2.607

Notes: (i). Sample consists of 180 observations on fully-fledged Islamic banks (unbalanced data selected from 40 banks for 2000 to 2011). Sample data are not the same for all years due to banks being established in different years. The table presents the mean, median, minimum, maximum, standard deviation, kurtosis and skewness value of each variable. All the data are in ratio percentage value except for SIZE which is in thousand US$. (ii). CR is the ratio of non-performance financing to total financing; Fin. Exp, the ratio of total financing to total assets; FLP, the ratio of loan loss provision to total assets; Cap Buffer, the ratio of total equity to total assets; CAPR, the ratio of TIER 1 & TIER 2 to total risk-weighted assets; NIM, net interest margin; MGT, the ratio of total earning assets to total assets; size is the natural logarithm of borrowers' total assets.

4.1. *Correlation Analysis*

Pairwise correlation testing is conducted to provide statistical measures on the relationship between two variables. This test is also calculated to detect multicollinearity, which arises when two or more independent variables interact to a high degree. A high level of interaction may increase the standard errors of the estimated regression coefficients, thus resulting in bias in the empirical findings. Table 4 reports the correlation coefficient between the dependent and independent variables. The correlation coefficient indicates the magnitude and direction of the relationship. The correlation matrix reveals that there are two variables that have high inter-correlation with the correlation value above 0.5. Those variables are CAPR and Cap Buffer (0.725) and GROUP and MGT (0.526). To further test the high inter-correlations, the variance inflation test (VIF) is conducted. This test suggests that there is no serious multicollinearity occurring in the variables used.

---

13 This negative value of capital buffer and capital ratio was experienced by the Bank Islam Malaysia Berhad and resulted from a huge loss incurred in 2005.

14 Refer to Table A2 in Appendix B for details on how old each bank is and Table A3 in Appendix B show number of years and number of banks included in our sample of 180 observations.

Table 4. Pairwise Correlation Matrix of Bank-specific Variables.

	CR	Fin. Exp	FLP	Cap Buffer	CAPR	NIM	MGT	SIZE	Age	GROUP	Crisis
CR	1										
Fin. Exp	−0.224 ***	1									
FLP	0.329 ***	−0.046	1								
Cap. Buffer	−0.054	0.069	0.098	1							
CAPR	−0.049	−0.195 ***	0.132 *	0.725 ***	1						
NIM	−0.110	0.151 **	0.077	0.207 ***	0.247 ***	1					
MGT	−0.014	0.388 ***	−0.086	0.193 ***	−0.208 ***	−0.105	1				
SIZE	0.043	0.219 ***	−0.083	−0.012	−0.183 **	−0.003	0.181 **	1			
Age	−0.074	0.048	−0.085	−0.165 **	−0.114	−0.067	0.046	0.095	1		
GROUP	−0.147	0.175 **	−0.171	0.481 ***	0.217 ***	0.123	0.526 ***	0.415 ***	0.000	1	
Crisis	−0.179 **	0.069	0.105	0.088	0.107	0.067	−0.247 ***	0.047	−0.009	−0.075	1

Notes: CR is the ratio of non-performance financing to total financing; Fin. Exp, the ratio of total financing to total assets; FLP, the ratio of loan loss provision to total assets; Cap Buffer, the ratio of total equity to total assets; CAPR, the ratio of TIER 1 & TIER 2 to total assets; NIM, net interest margin; MGT, the ratio of total earning assets to total assets; SIZE, the natural logarithm of total assets; GROUP is a dummy '1' for GCC countries Islamic banks, '0' otherwise; Age refers to the age of the bank at time *t*; Crisis is equal '1' for 2008,2009 & 2010, '0' for other years. Note that ***, ** and * denotes significance at 1%, 5% and 10% levels, respectively.

4.2. Estimated Results of Whole Sample Islamic Banks

Table 5 reports the regression results for credit risk model about all possible samples. We used fixed effects and the random effect models to do the estimation. The decision to use these two models is based on a few econometric tests for panel data. We conducted the BPLM test to decide which model is appropriate for the estimation model. Based on results of the BPLM test, we reject the null hypothesis, and this indicates that significant differences exist between these banks. Therefore, simple OLS regression is not suitable for analyzing the data. Further, using the random effects generalized least square (RE-GLS) model, we estimate the determinants of credit risk of all samples. However, to acknowledge the variability in Islamic banks across the sample countries, we also run a fixed effects (FE) model. In using the FE model, we can control for all time-invariant differences between the individual Islamic banks which had not been observed by the model equation. Therefore, the FE model is expected to produce unbiased estimated coefficients.

To evaluate why the results between RE-GLS and FE models conflict, the Hausman test is used. This test has rejected the null hypothesis and suggests that the difference in coefficients is systematic, and therefore the FE model should be used to estimate the determinants of credit risk for whole samples Islamic banks. Column 1 of Table 5 presents the results of the FE model. It is important to note that we were unable to use the FE model for the column 2 estimation. A group dummy is included in this particular estimation to compare credit risk determinants across the ASEAN and GCC groups. GROUP dummy takes a value of '1' for GCC countries' Islamic banks and this dummy is time-invariant. In this case the RE-GLS model is used because it can estimate time invariant variables, whereas the FE model cannot. Note that dummies were included in both models and standard errors were calculated and adjusted for 40 clusters in the bank.

Table 5. Full Sample Regression Results.

Independent Variables	Dependent Variable: Credit Risk			
	(1) FE		(2) RE-GLS	
	Coefficient	S.E.	Coefficient	S.E.
C	69.550 ***	21.775	13.385	10.006
Fin. Exp	−0.007	0.037	−0.026	0.025
FLP	0.280 *	0.159	0.469 *	0.249
Cap. Buffer	0.080	0.097	0.108	0.086
CAPR	−0.057	0.047	−0.067	0.060
NIM	0.156	0.167	0.134	0.181
MGT	−0.057	0.053	−0.075	0.046
SIZE	−3.966 **	1.645	0.200	0.701
GROUP			0.169	1.640
R-squared	0.275		0.232	
No. of observation	180		180	
Time Dummy	Yes		Yes	

Notes: (i) The table presents estimation results using fixed effects and random effect GLS. Column (1) reports estimated results for firm and time FE. Column (2) reports estimated results for RE-GLS with time dummy. All column results report robust standard errors are adjusted for heteroskedasticity and covariance using White's cross-sections. ***, ** and * denotes significance at 1%, 5% and 10% levels, respectively. The estimations are conducted on unbalanced panel data of 180 observations from 2000–2011 for 40 Islamic banks of 9 countries. (ii) Dependent variable is the ratio of non-performance financing to total financing. The independent variables are Fin. Exp, the ratio of total financing to total assets; FLP, the ratio of loan loss provision to total assets; Cap Buffer, the ratio of total equity to total assets; CAPR, the ratio of TIER 1 & TIER 2 to total assets; NIM, net interest margin; MGT, the ratio of total earning assets to total assets; SIZE, the natural logarithm of total assets; GROUP is a dummy '1' for GCC countries Islamic banks, '0' otherwise.

The results of the financing expansion appear to have a negative sign in both models in columns 1 and 2 in Tables 4 and 5. This suggests that a higher ratio of financing to total assets reduces the credit risk level of Islamic banks. The negative coefficient between credit risk and financing expansion signals that Islamic financing types offer a low risk of default since this result contradicts that generally found in the literature. However, we failed to find any significant relationship between financing expansion and credit risk in all sample Islamic banks.

The coefficients for FLP are positive and statistically significant regardless of specification and estimation method used for all sample Islamic banks in Table 5. This demonstrates that the larger the provision allocated by the banks, then the credit risk will be higher. Theoretically, banks normally make a higher provision for loss to signal that the quality of financing portfolio held by the banks will deteriorate. Banks will make a larger provision to anticipate future losses reflected by the high-risk financing portfolio and any adverse external events. The results suggest that Islamic banks make higher provision to anticipate increases in future credit risk levels. It is consistent with studies by Eng and Nabar (2007) and Ahmad and Ariff (2007). Louhichi and Boujelbene (2016) claim that high quality loan will contribute to lower credit risk. As FLP proxy by the amount of loss provision made by the banks, the positive results signaling that the bank management should have better policy in giving loan or financing to control the quality of financing.

The results concerning the two capital variables illustrate the effects of capital composition on banks' credit risk levels. Capital buffer (Cap buffer) represents the leverage effect and CAPR represents how specific regulatory standard affects banks' credit risk exposures. Cap buffer is statistically insignificant, suggesting that leverage has little influence on credit risk behavior of all sample's Islamic banks. CAPR has a negative coefficient in all estimations and does not demonstrate any significant influence on credit risk. The objective of having high leverage and CAR is to reduce the level of problem loans. The descriptive statistics of all sample Islamic banks in the ASEAN and the GCC reveal that on average Islamic banks have large amounts of regulatory capital (CAPR).[15] Even under-capitalized banks held more than the regulatory minimum requirement. Therefore, the CAPR is insignificant in driving the credit risk level of all Islamic banks.

Regarding the relationship between credit risk and earnings, NIM appears to have a positive coefficient as expected. However, both models fail to find any statistically significant relationship between NIM and credit risk. Another measure of earning (the ratio of total earning assets to total assets) is also related to banks' management efficiency. MGT also appears to have no statistically significant effect on Islamic banks' credit risk. These findings are inconsistent with previous empirical findings on banks in the US and Europe. It is argued that better management efficiency should provide banks with less credit risk. We further investigate this issue by looking at a specific country or sub-group of country in the next section.

Examining the coefficients on assets size and credit risk shows that a negative and statistical significance at 5% appears when using the fixed effects model. This suggests an inverse relationship between bank size and credit risk. Larger banks can absorb more risk-taking activities because they are more diverse. Saunders et al. (1990) contend that size and risk should be negatively related because the larger the bank, the greater its ability to diversify assets risk. This conclusion is consistent with the studies on Malaysia and Japan (How et al. 2005; Konishi and Yasuda 2004; Rahman and Shahimi 2010).

The GROUP dummy takes on a value of 1 for Islamic banks in GCC countries. As observed from Table 1 that there are total 20 Islamic banks in 5 GCC countries and 20 Islamic banks from 4 ASEAN countries. The GROUP dummy was only included in the RE effect model.[16] Using the RE estimation, the GROUP dummy has demonstrated a positive coefficient. This indicates that Islamic banks in GCC countries are exposed to slightly higher credit risk compared to the Islamic banks in the ASEAN group. However, we fail to find statistically significant relationship between GROUP dummy and credit risk.

Time fixed effects are included in both models to control for macroeconomic changes. The inclusion of time FE is necessary after considering the result of the joint test. The joint test is conducted to see if

---

15 On average the Islamic banks in both ASEAN and the GCC countries have the CAPR above the standard as suggested by Basel-II. The suggested CAPR based on Basel-II is 8percent.

16 Note that FE regression is not able to derive the coefficient for the GROUP dummy. The GROUP variable will be omitted due to collinearity of the dummy variable.

the dummies of all years are equal to zero, if they are then no time fixed effects are needed. We have rejected the null hypothesis that all years' coefficients are jointly equal to zero. Therefore, time FE is required in the estimation.

4.3. Examination of the Quadratic Specification

The model specifications include financing expansion as a possible explanatory variable. In the previous estimation we found a negative coefficient between financing expansion and credit risk. We further investigate whether there is a non-linear relationship between financing expansion and credit risk and plotted the residual of the model without square term against financing expansion. The scatter plot shows a pattern of curving, a sign that the error term does correlate with financing expansion quadratically. We also examine linear fit and quadratic fit between credit risk and financing expansion. Comparing these two graphs suggests that quadratic seems to be the better fit. Therefore, we include quadratic specification for financing expansion in the next estimated model. The following equations were used to estimate the model:

$$\begin{aligned} \text{CR}_{it} = \beta_0 + \beta_1\text{Fin Exp}_{it} + \beta_2\text{Fin Exp}^2{}_{it} + \beta_3\text{FLP}_{it} + \beta_4\text{Cap Buffer}_{it} + \beta_5\text{CAPR}_{it} + \beta_6\text{NIM}_{it} \\ + \beta_7\text{MGT}_{it} + \beta_8\text{SIZE}_{it} + \alpha_{it} + v_{it} \end{aligned} \quad (4)$$

$$\begin{aligned} \text{CR}_{it} = \beta_0 + \beta_1\text{Fin Exp}_{it} + \beta_2\text{Fin Exp}^2{}_{it} + \beta_3\text{FLP}_{it} + \beta_4\text{Cap Buffer}_{it} + \beta_5\text{CAPR}_{it} + \beta_6\text{NIM}_{it} \\ + \beta_7\text{MGT}_{it} + \beta_8\text{SIZE}_{it} + \beta_9\text{GROUP}_{it} + u_{it} \end{aligned} \quad (5)$$

Table 6 reports the estimation results for the FE and RE-GLS with the quadratic term of financing expansion. The robust errors are reported. The negative coefficient of financing expansion^2 indicates that an inverted U-shaped quadratic relationship exists between financing expansion and credit risk. However, we find an insignificant relationship between financing expansion and credit risk for both models. This outcome suggests that financing activities do not statistically significantly influence the level of credit risk in all sample Islamic banks. The other explanatory variables' results are like the previous estimation results reported in Table 5. The quadratic specification for financing expansion will be used for the other estimation model in the next subsection.

Table 6. Estimated Results with Quadratic Term.

Independent Variables	Dependent Variable: Credit Risk			
	FE		RE-GLS	
	Coefficient	S.E.	Coefficient	S.E.
C	69.286 ***	23.960	11.996	10.376
Fin. Exp	0.002	0.185	0.062	0.152
Fin. Exp^2	−0.00008	0.001	−0.001	0.001
FLP	0.280 *	0.159	0.466 *	0.249
Cap. Buffer	0.079	0.100	0.096	0.092
CAPR	−0.056	0.041	−0.058	0.057
NIM	0.157	0.171	0.144	0.186
MGT	−0.057	0.055	−0.076	0.047
SIZE	−3.963 **	1.670	0.145	0.691
GROUP			0.218	1.648
R-squared	0.275		0.236	
No. of observation	180		180	
Time Dummy	Yes		Yes	

Notes: (i). The table presents estimation results using fixed effects and random effect GLS. Column (1) reports estimated results with firm and time FE. Column (2) reports estimated results for RE-GLS with time dummy. All column results robust the Standard errors are adjusted for40 clusters of banks. Note that ***, ** and * denotes significance at 1%, 5% and 10% level, respectively. The estimations are conducted on unbalanced panel data of 180 observations for 40 IB of ASEAN and GCC countries from 2000–2011. (ii). Dependent variable is the ratio of non-performance financing to total financing. The independent variables are Fin. Exp, the ratio of total financing to total assets; FLP, the ratio of loan loss provision to total assets; Cap Buffer, the ratio of total equity to total assets; CAPR, the ratio of TIER 1 & TIER 2 to total assets; NIM, net interest margin; MGT, the ratio of total earning assets to total assets; SIZE, the natural logarithm of total assets; GROUP is a dummy '1' for GCC countries IB, '0' otherwise; Age refers to the age of the bank up to the year 2011; Fin. Exp^2 is the squared value of Fin. Exp.

4.4. The Robustness Test on Age Specification

To accommodate the effect of Islamic banks longevity or age in determining level of credit risk, the age variable was added into the model estimations. The age variable is defined as the number of years since a bank's establishment. The ASEAN and GCC have a range of age value from 1 to 37 years. With different experiences in the industry, it is possible that age will influence the credit risk level of the sample Islamic banks.

Table 7 reports results from the FE and RE using GLS estimations with a robust standard error adjusted for 40 clusters banks. It is observed from the above table that age appears to have a positive relationship with credit risk. The FE estimation find an insignificant relationship between age and credit risk which is contradict with the RE-GLS model. The RE-GLS model suggests that the older the Islamic banks operating in terms of number of years, the more credit risk exposures they are likely to experience. This section also tests for a quadratic relationship between age and credit risk. However, the result failed to find significant effects when all sample Islamic banks in the dataset are included.

Table 7. Estimated Results for Model with Age Variable.

Independent Variables	Dependent Variable: Credit Risk			
	FE		RE-GLS	
	Coefficient	**S.E.**	**Coefficient**	**S.E.**
C	68.434 ***	22.908	23.832 **	11.509
Fin. Exp	0.002	0.185	0.064	0.161
Fin. Exp^2	−0.00008	0.001	−0.001	0.001
FLP	0.280 *	0.159	0.424 *	0.228
Cap. Buffer	0.079	0.100	0.082	0.089
CAPR	−0.056	0.041	−0.044	0.057
NIM	0.157	0.171	0.085	0.163
MGT	−0.057	0.055	−0.067	0.047
SIZE	−3.963 **	1.670	−0.800	0.722
GROUP			−0.715	1.720
Age	0.258	0.363	0.197 **	0.083
R-squared	0.274		0.259	
No. of observation	180		180	
Time Dummy	Yes		Yes	

Notes: (i). The table presents estimation results using fixed effects and random effect GLS. Column (1) reports estimated results with firm and time FE. Column (2) reports estimated results for RE-GLS with time dummy. All column results robust the Standard errors are adjusted for heteroskedasticity and covariance using White's cross-sections. ***, ** and * denotes significance at 1-percent, 5-percent and 10-percent level, respectively. The estimations are conducted on unbalanced panel data of 180 observations for 40 Islamic banks of ASEAN and GCC countries from 2000–2011. (ii). Dependent variable is the ratio of non-performance financing to total financing. The independent variables are Fin. Exp, the ratio of total financing to total assets; FLP, the ratio of loan loss provision to total assets; Cap Buffer, the ratio of total equity to total assets; CAPR, the ratio of TIER 1 & TIER 2 to total assets; NIM, net interest margin; MGT, the ratio of total earning assets to total assets; SIZE, the natural logarithm of total assets; GROUP is a dummy '1' for GCC countries Islamic banks, '0' otherwise; Age refers to the age of the bank up to the year 2011; Fin. Exp^2 is the squared value of Fin. Exp; Age is the number of years since the banks' establishment.

4.5. The Global Financial Crisis (GFC) and Credit Risk

This section investigates the effects of the GFC on credit risk of Islamic banks in the ASEAN and GCC countries. The GFC caused much harm to the banking industry. It is believed that the CBs were much more affected than the Islamic banks. Table 8 reports the regression results for the impact of the GFC on all sample Islamic banks for their credit risk in six separate estimation models. We use panel data FE and RE-GLS specifications, and the six separate estimations are calculated using different set of explanatory variables, for example, with or without group dummy and bank age. It is worth mentioning that we do not include the quadratic term of age for all sample estimations.

From Table 8; column 2, we see that the coefficients of crisis dummy are negative and only statistically significant when the group dummy is included in the estimation model. This variable is added in column 2 is RE-GLS model.

Table 8. Estimated Results for the global financial crisis (GFC).

Independent Variables	Dependent Variable: Credit Risk											
	FE(1)		RE-GLS(2)		RE-GLS(3)		FE(4)		RE-GLS(5)		RE-GLS(6)	
	Coeff.	S.E.	Coeff.	S.E.	Coeff.	S.E.	Coeff.	S.E.	Coeff.	S.E.	Coeff.	S.E.
C	73.521 ***	21.110	14.117	9.838	16.794 *	9.956	72.496 ***	20.155	25.676 **	11.357	27.646 **	11.013
Fin. Exp	0.044	0.171	0.106	0.136	0.106	0.138	0.044	0.171	0.110	0.144	0.110	0.145
Fin Exp^2	−0.0004	0.001	−0.001	0.001	−0.001	0.001	−0.0004	0.001	−0.001	0.001	−0.001	0.001
FLP	0.283 **	0.134	0.463 **	0.221	0.464 **	0.222	0.283 **	0.134	0.424 **	0.200	0.427 **	0.202
Cap. Buffer	0.061	0.100	0.067	0.085	0.056	0.089	0.061	0.100	0.052	0.083	0.049	0.088
CAPR	−0.045	0.038	−0.046	0.054	−0.047	0.054	−0.045	0.038	−0.031	0.055	−0.035	0.054
NIM	0.189	0.196	0.157	0.197	0.134	0.207	0.189	0.196	0.094	0.172	0.092	0.182
MGT	−0.069	0.056	−0.089 *	0.047	−0.094 **	0.047	−0.069	0.056	−0.080 *	0.047	−0.087 *	0.047
SIZE	−4.279 ***	1.533	0.018	0.671	−0.129	0.647	−4.279 ***	1.533	−0.910	0.719	−1.067	0.701
Crisis	−2.214	1.470	−2.387 *	1.348	−2.172	1.462	−2.214	1.470	−2.443	1.368	−2.290	1.478
Group			−0.631	1.719					−1.619	1.780		
Age							0.310	0.330	0.199 **	0.084	0.189 **	0.090
R-squared	0.306		0.271		0.240		0.306		0.303		0.269	
No. of observation	180		180		180		180		180		180	
Time Dummy	Yes		Yes		Yes		Yes		Yes		Yes	

Notes: (i) The table presents estimation results using the RE-GLS and FE regression models. All column results the Standard errors are adjusted for heteroskedasticity and covariance using White's cross-sections. ***, ** and * denotes significance at 1-percent, 5-percent and 10-percent level, respectively. The estimations are conducted on unbalanced panel data of 180 observations for 40 Islamic banks of ASEAN and GCC countries from 2000–2011. (ii) Dependent variable is the ratio of non-performance financing to total financing. The independent variables are Fin. Exp, the ratio of total financing to total assets; FLP, the ratio of loan loss provision to total assets; Cap Buffer, the ratio of total equity to total assets; CAPR, the ratio of TIER 1 & TIER 2 to total assets; NIM, net interest margin; MGT, the ratio of total earning assets to total assets; SIZE, the natural logarithm of total assets; REGION is a dummy '1' for GCC countries' IB, '0' otherwise; Crisis is a dummy '1' for 2008,2009,2010, '0' otherwise; DBM is a dummy '1' for Malaysian Islamic banks, '0' otherwise; Fin. Exp^2 is the squared value of Fin. Exp; Age refers to the age of banks since their establishment.

The group dummy for this purpose value of one for the GCC countries' Islamic banks. Islamic banks in the GCC had lower credit risk than those of the ASEAN during the crisis period of 2008 to 2010. This situation might be due to several factors: (i) strong economic and financial state of GCC countries during the GFC, (ii) Islamic banks in the GCC did not engage in high risk financing portfolios, and (iii) different financing contracts offered by the Islamic banks in the GCC. Overall, the results suggest that Islamic banks carry lower credit risk during crisis periods. Hasan and Dridi (2010) claim that the uniqueness of the IB business model helped nullify the GFC's severe impact on profitability and credit performance.

The coefficient of financing expansion has a negative insignificant coefficient relationship with credit risk. This is consistent with results explained in the previous section. It also explains that higher growth in financing does not cause an increase in credit risk level during the crisis period. This finding agrees with the one achieved by Abedifar et al. (2013). Regarding financing quality, the FLP coefficient shows a positive and significant result regardless of specification and estimation methods.

The management efficiency of Islamic banks was not significantly affected by the GFC. MGT had a negative and statistically significant effect on credit risk when the models are controlled for the group dummy. As for the size of the banks, it only appears to have a negative and significant relationship when the model uses the FE specification. Using RE-GLS, size is insignificant in all samples.

The dummy to proxy Malaysian Islamic banks is introduced in the model estimation. The DBM dummy takes the value of one for Islamic banks. The estimation results for columns 3 and 6 report that Islamic banks' credit risk did not act differently from the other 8 countries' Islamic banks during the GFC.

The inclusion of age as the explanatory variable together with the group dummy and crisis implies that older Islamic banks were exposed to higher credit risk than newer Islamic banks during the GFC. The coefficients of age are positive and statistically significant. This suggests that the GFC did affect the older Islamic banks.

5. Conclusions and Limitation

This paper analyses the determinants of credit risk in Islamic banks within the ASEAN and GCC regions. It uses financial data—consisting of 180 observations—from five GCC countries and four ASEAN countries, during the period 2000 to 2011. Previous studies argue that BSV significantly influences the credit risk level of commercial banks. However, only a few studies have focused so far on the credit risk determinants of Islamic banks. Therefore, this paper aims to compare the credit risk profiles of these countries, the main determinants of credit risk and uses subsample periods to assess the impact of the GFC on credit risk. Statistical and econometric methods such as descriptive statistics, mean difference t-test and panel data models were applied to achieve these objectives. The study did not control for country-specific environmental issues. Instead, the analysis was conducted using firm, country-specific samples for the ASEAN and GCC countries, and macroeconomic changes that were controlled through a time and crisis dummy.

The most important evidence arising from this paper concerns the main determinants of credit risk and how changing economic conditions affect the credit risk level of Islamic banks. The FE and RE-GLS panel data analysis models were applied to the unbalanced dataset for the whole sample and subsample Islamic banks. Regarding credit risk determinants in Islamic banks in the ASEAN and GCC, it can be concluded that financing quality demonstrates a positive significant relationship with credit risk level regardless of specification models and datasets. Similar results appear for the comparison of determinants in Islamic banks in the ASEAN and GCC groups. This result implies that Islamic banks should scrutinize their financing policy to ensure they can reduce the probability of default, and therefore mitigate provisions for loss.

The descriptive statistics indicate a significant difference in sizes between countries and sub-sample groups. Using the FE model specification, asset sizes appear to have a negative and statistically significant influence on credit risk across different countries and groups. This suggests that large banks have an advantage in terms of portfolio diversification and managerial skill to generate more finance with a lower credit risk than smaller banks. A large asset size is normally associated with how long a bank has operated. Older banks tend to have larger assets compared to newer banks. Therefore, bank age was included in the estimation models.

Macroeconomic condition changes, particularly the recent GFC, provide important evidence for the study. It is suggested that Islamic banks were not greatly affected by the GFC and performed better because they had lower credit risk during 2008 to 2010. The resilience of Islamic banks during crises implies that the Islamic banking is relatively safer compared to conventional banking. These results are consistent with the findings of Bhatti and Nguyen (2012) and Al Rahahleh et al. (2019). These findings are essential for policy makers, investors and other stakeholders including banks and central banks.

The findings of this study imply several policy and regulation implications. Firstly, this study suggests that there is a significant difference in terms of asset size between banks in ASEAN and GCC regions. This indicates that the regulators might consider suggesting Islamic banks which are smaller in size to have a strategic merger in order to become stronger and larger. In addition, the regulators may also emphasize that the bank's management maintain an adequate level of capital level, which plays an important role in managing credit risk. Secondly, there is evidence that Islamic banks are more resilient during the financial crisis. Therefore, policy makers can increase awareness and promote the advantages of Islamic banking in creating a sustainable and stable financial system.

This study concentrates only on a few Islamic banks in ASEAN and GCC countries. As the sample was selective, it imposes several limitations especially in terms of the choice of econometric models and model specifications. Employing a mixed methods analysis approach to examine the main issues of this proposition has enhanced the robustness of the investigation. The study only uses bank-specific characteristics as explanatory variables for the credit risk of Islamic banks. Therefore, the effects of macroeconomic variables on credit risk were not discussed except for the impact of the GFC. In summary, it can be concluded that the finding of this study may be interpreted as a policy paper for financiers, investors and other stakeholders including banks and central banks, identifying that Islamic banks may be better risk-protected during periods of financial distress and crises.

Author Contributions: Both authors are participated in this research as F.N.M. is the main investigator and M.I.B. is her supervisor. F.N.M. initiated the original manuscript, and then the revised draft and its changes into model specification, rewriting, updating literature review was incorporated by M.I.B. All authors have read and agreed to the published final revised version of the manuscript.

Acknowledgments: We are thankful to three anonymous reviewers for their constructive comments which have improved the paper and Taha Bhatti and Esha Zahid for valuable comments in proofreading the paper.

Conflicts of Interest: The authors declare no conflict of interest.

Appendix A

Table A1. Total Number of Islamic banks in ASEAN and GCC Countries.

No.	Country	Group	No. of Islamic Banks
1	Brunei	ASEAN	3
2	Indonesia	ASEAN	1
3	Malaysia	ASEAN	17
4	Singapore	ASEAN	1
5	Bahrain	GCC	22
6	Kuwait	GCC	9
7	Qatar	GCC	5
8	UAE	GCC	10
9	Saudi Arabia	GCC	4
	Total		72

Source: BankScope database.

Appendix B

Table A2. Details of the Sample Islamic banks.

No.	Bank Name	Country	Date of Establishment
1	Al-Salam Bank-Bahrain B.S.C.	Bahrain	3-May-2005
2	Albaraka Banking Group B.S.C.	Bahrain	6-Jan-1998
3	Khaleeji Commercial Bank B.S.C.	Bahrain	20-Oct-2003
4	Kuwait Finance House	Bahrain	9-Dec-2001
5	Shamil Bank of Bahrain B.S.C.	Bahrain	1982
6	Bank Islam Brunei	Brunei	2005
7	Bank Syariah Mandiri	Indonesia	1999
8	Boubyan Bank KSC	Kuwait	2004
9	Kuwait Finance House	Kuwait	1977
10	Kuwait International Bank	Kuwait	Jul-2007
11	Affin Islamic Bank Berhad	Malaysia	2006
12	Al Rajhi Banking & Inv Corp (Malaysia) Berhad	Malaysia	2006
13	Alliance Islamic Bank Berhad	Malaysia	2008
14	AmIslamic Bank Berhad	Malaysia	2006
15	Asian Finance Bank Berhad	Malaysia	2005
16	Bank Islam Malaysia Berhad	Malaysia	1983
17	Bank Muamalat Malaysia Berhad	Malaysia	1999
18	CIMB Islamic Bank Berhad	Malaysia	2006
19	EONCAP Islamic Bank Berhad	Malaysia	2006
20	HSBC Amanah Malaysia Berhad	Malaysia	2004
21	Hong Leong Islamic Bank Berhad	Malaysia	2005
22	Kuwait Finance House (Malaysia) Berhad	Malaysia	2005
23	Maybank Islamic Berhad	Malaysia	2008
24	OCBC Al-Amin Bank Berhad	Malaysia	2008
25	Public Islamic Bank Berhad	Malaysia	2008
26	RHB Islamic Bank Berhad	Malaysia	2005
27	Standard Chartered Saadiq Berhad	Malaysia	2008
28	Masraf Al Rayan (Q.S.C.)	Qatar	10-Sep-2006
29	Qatar International Islamic Bank	Qatar	1-Jan-1991
30	Qatar Islamic Bank SAQ	Qatar	7-Jan-1983
31	Al Rajhi Bank	Saudi Arabia	1978
32	Alinma Bank	Saudi Arabia	28-Mar-2006
33	Bank AlBilad	Saudi Arabia	4-Nov-2004
34	The Islamic Bank of Asia	Singapore	7-May-2007
35	Abu Dhabi Islamic Bank	UAE	20-May-1997
36	Ajman Bank	UAE	Feb-2008
37	Dubai Bank	UAE	2-Aug-2002
38	Dubai Islamic Bank	UAE	1975
39	Emirates Islamic Bank	UAE	2004
40	Sharjah Islamic Bank	UAE	2002

Table A3. The sampling Distribution of Observations by years and Country.

Banks/Years	Periods	2000	2001	2002	2003	2004	2005	2006	2007	2008	2009	2010	2011	Total
Bahrain	6							2	2	4	3	1	1	13
Kuwait	6							1	2	3	3	3	2	14
Qatar	11		1	2	2	2	2	2	2	1	3	3	3	23
Saudi Arabia	8					1	1	1	1	2	2	2	3	13
UAE	6							1	4	4	5	5	5	24
Malaysia	12	2	2	2	1	2	2	6	8	15	17	17	8	82
Brunei	4									1	1	1	1	4
Indonesia	6				1	1	1	1	1	1				6
Singapore	1											1		1
Total		2	3	4	4	6	6	14	20	31	34	33	23	180

Note: This table show that the selected banks in unbalanced time and panels from each country.

References

Abdelrahim, Khalil Elian. 2013. Effectiveness of Credit Risk Management of Saudi Banks in the Light of Global Financial Crisis: A Qualitative Study. *Asian Transaction on Basic and Applied Sciences* 3: 73–91.

Abedifar, Pejman, Philip Molyneux, and Amine Tarazi. 2013. Risk in Islamic Banking. *Review of Finance* 17: 2035–96. [CrossRef]

Ahmad, Nor Hayati, and Mohamed Ariff. 2007. Multi-Country Study of Bank Credit Risk Determinants. *The International Journal of Banking and Finance* 5: 135–52.

Ahmad, Nor Hayati, and Shahrul Nizam Ahmad. 2004. Key Factors Influencing Credit Risk of Islamic Bank: A Malaysian Case. *The Journal of Muamalat and Islamic Finance Research* 1: 65–80.

Ahmadyan, Azam. 2018. Measuring Credit Risk Management and Its Impact on Bank Performance in Iran. *Marketing and Branding Research* 5: 168–83. [CrossRef]

Ahmed, Anwer S., Carolyn Takeda, and Shawn Thomas. 1999. Bank Loan Loss Provisions: A Reexamination of Capital Management, Earning Management and Signalling Effects. *Journal of Accounting and Economics* 28: 1–25. [CrossRef]

Akkizidis, Ioannis, and Sunil Kumar Khandelwal. 2008. *Financial Risk Management for Islamic Banking and Finance*. New York: Palgrave Macmillan.

Al-Tamimi, Hussein A. Hassan, and Faris Mohammed Al-Mazrooei. 2007. Banks' Risk Management: A Comparison Study of UAE National and Forein Banks. *The Journal of Risk Finance* 8: 394–409. [CrossRef]

Alandejani, Maha, and Mehmet Asutay. 2017. Nonperforming loans in the GCC banking sectors: Does the Islamic finance matter? *Research in International Business and Finance* 42: 832–54. [CrossRef]

Al Rahahleh, Naseem, M. Ishaq Bhatti, and Faridah Najuna Misman. 2019. Developments in Risk Management in Islamic Finance: A Review. *Journal of Risk and Financial Management* 12: 37. [CrossRef]

Angbazo, Lazarus. 1997. Commercial Bank Net Interest Margins, Default Risk, Interest Rate Risk, and Off- Balance Sheet Banking. *Journal of Banking & Finance* 21: 55–87.

Azmat, Saad, ASM Sohel Azad, M. Ishaq Bhatti, and Hamza Ghaffar. 2020. Islamic Banking, Costly Religiosity and Competition. *Journal of Financial Research*. [CrossRef]

Basel. 1999. *Principles for The Management of Credit Risk*. Basel: Basel Committe on Banking Supervision.

Basel. 2001. *Basel II Consultative Document*. Basel: Basel Committee on Banking Supervision.

Beck, Thorsten, Asli Demirgüç-Kunt, and Ouarda Merrouche. 2013. Islamic vs. Conventional Banking: Business Model, Efficiency and Stability. *Journal of Banking & Finance* 37: 433–47. [CrossRef]

Berger, Allen N., and Robert DeYoung. 1997. Problem Loans and Cost Efficiency in Commercial Banks. *Journal of Banking & Finance* 21: 849–70.

Bhatti, M. Ishaq, and Cuong C. Nguyen. 2012. Diversification evidence from international equity markets using extreme values and stochastic copulas. *Journal of International Financial Markets Institutions & Money* 22: 622–46.

Bhatti, M. Ishaq, Naseem Al Rahahleh, and Hussain Mohi-ud-Din Qadri. 2019. Recent Development in Islamic Finance and financial products. In *The Growth of Islamic Finance and Banking: Innovation, Governance and Risk Mitigation*, 1st ed. Edited by Hussain Mohi-ud-Din Qadri and Ishaq Bhatti. Abingdon: Routledge, pp. 5–16.

Bonfim, Diana. 2009. Credit Risk Drivers: Evaluating the Contribution of Firm Level Information and of Macroeconomic Dynamics. *Journal of Banking & Finance* 33: 281–99.

Cebenoyan, A. Sinan, and Philip E. Strahan. 2004. Risk Management, Capital Structure and Lending at Banks. *Journal of Banking & Finance* 28: 19–43.

Cihák, Martin, and Heiko Hesse. 2008. *Islamic Banks and Financial Stability: An Empirical Analysis*. IMF Working Paper. WP 08/16. Washington, DC: International Monetary Fund, pp. 1–29.

Eng, Li Li, and Sandeep Nabar. 2007. Loan Loss Provisions by Banks in Hong Kong, Malaysia and Singapore. *Journal of International Financial Management & Accounting* 18: 18–38. [CrossRef]

Froot, Kenneth A., David S. Scharfstein, and Jeremy C. Stein. 1993. Risk Management: Coordinating Corporate Investment and Financing Policies. *The Journal of Finance* 48: 1629–58. [CrossRef]

Gallo, John G., Vincent P. Apilado, and James W. Kolari. 1996. Commercial Bank Mutual Fund Activities: Implications for Bank Risk and Profitability. *Journal of Banking & Finance* 20: 1775–91.

Godlewski, C. J. 2005. Bank Capital and Credit Risk Taking in Emerging Market Economies. *Journal of Banking Regulation* 6: 128–45. [CrossRef]

Gulati, Rachita, Anju Goswami, and Sunil Kumar. 2019. What drives credit risk in the Indian banking industry? An empirical investigation. *Economic Systems* 43: 42–62. [CrossRef]

Hannoun, Hervé. 2010. *The Basel III Capital Framework: A Decisive Breakthrough*. Basel: Bank for International Settlements.

Hasan, Maher, and Jemma Dridi. 2010. *The Effects of The Global Crisis on Islamic and Conventional Banks: A Comparative Study*. IMF Working Paper. Washington, DC: International Monetary Fund, pp. 1–46.

Hassan, Abul. 2009. Risk Management Practices of Islamic Banks of Brunei Darussalam. *The Journal of Risk Finance* 10: 23–37. [CrossRef]

Hassan, M. Kabir, Ashraf Khan, and Andrea Paltrinieri. 2018. Liquidity Risk, Credit Risk and Stability in Islamic and Conventional Banks. *Research in International Business and Finance* 48: 17–31. [CrossRef]

How, Janice C. Y., Melina Abdul Karim, and Peter Verhoeven. 2005. Islamic Financing and Bank Risks: The Case of Malaysia. *Thunderbird International Business Review* 47: 75–94. [CrossRef]

Imbierowicz, Björn, and Christian Rauch. 2014. The relationship between liquidity risk and credit risk in banks. *Journal of Banking & Finance* 40: 242–56.

İncekara, Ahmet, and Harun Çetinkaya. 2019. Credit Risk Management: A Panel Data Analysis on The Islamic Banks in Turkey. *Procedia Computer Science* 158: 947–54. [CrossRef]

Khawaja, Mohsin, M. Ishaq Bhatti, and Dawood Ashraf. 2020. Ownership and control in a double decision framework for raising capital. *Emerging Markets Review* 41: 100657. [CrossRef]

Konishi, Masaru, and Yukihiro Yasuda. 2004. Factors Affecting Bank Risk Taking: Evidence From Japan. *Journal of Banking & Finance* 28: 215–32.

Lassoued, Mongi. 2018. Comparative study on credit risk in Islamic banking institutions: The case of Malaysia. *The Quarterly Review of Economics and Finance* 70: 267–78. [CrossRef]

Louhichi, Awatef, and Younes Boujelbene. 2016. Credit risk, managerial behaviour and macroeconomic equilibrium within dual banking systems: Interest-free vs. interest-based banking industries. *Research in International Business and Finance* 38: 104–21. [CrossRef]

Louzis, Dimitrios P., Angelos T. Vouldis, and Vasilios L. Metaxas. 2012. Macroeconomic and bank-specific determinants of non-performing loans in Greece: A comparative study of mortgage, business and consumer loan portfolios. *Journal of Banking & Finance* 36: 1012–27.

Love, Inessa, and Rima Turk Ariss. 2014. Macro-financial linkages in Egypt: A panel analysis of economic shocks and loan portfolio quality. *Journal of International Financial Markets, Institutions and Money* 28: 158–81. [CrossRef]

Madura, Jeff, Anna D. Martin, and Don A. Taylor. 1994. Determinants of Implied Risk at Depository Institutions. *Applied Financial Economics* 4: 363–70. [CrossRef]

Mansor, Fadillah, Naseem Al Rahahleh, and M. Ishaq Bhatti. 2019. New Evidence on Fund Performance in Extreme Events. *International Journal of Managerial Finance* 15: 511–32. [CrossRef]

Maudos, Joaquín, and Juan Fernandez De Guevara. 2004. Factors Explaining the Interest Margin in the Banking Sectors of the European Union. *Journal of Banking and Finance* 28: 2259–81. [CrossRef]

McKibbin, Warwick J., and Roshen Fernando. 2020. *The Global Macroeconomic Impacts of COVID-19: Seven Scenarios*. CAMA Working Paper. Canberra: The Centre for Applied Macroeconomic Analysis (CAMA).

Misman, Faridah Najuna, Ishaq Bhatti, Weifang Lou, Syamsyul Samsudin, and Nor Hadaliza Abd Rahman. 2015. Islamic Banks Credit Risk: A Panel study. *Procedia Economics and Financec* 31: 75–82. [CrossRef]

Rahman, Aisyah Abdul, and Shahida Shahimi. 2010. Credit Risk and Financing Structure of Malaysian Islamic Banks. *Journal of Economic Cooperation and Development* 31: 83–105.

Reinhart, Carmen M, and Kenneth S Rogoff. 2011. From financial crash to debt crisis. *American Economic Review* 101: 1676–706. [CrossRef]

Saunders, Anthony, Elizabeth Strock, and Nickolaos G. Travlos. 1990. Ownership Structure, Deregulation, and Bank Risk Taking. *Journal of Finance* 45: 643–54. [CrossRef]

Zoubi, Taisier A., and Osamah Al-Khazali. 2007. Empirical Testing of the Loss Provisions of Banks in the GCC Region. *Managerial Finance* 33: 200–511. [CrossRef]

Zarei, Alireza, Mohamed Ariff, and M. Ishaq Bhatti. 2019. The impact of exchange rates on stock market returns: New evidence from seven free-floating currencies. *The European Journal of Finance* 25: 1277–88. [CrossRef]

3

A General Framework for Portfolio Theory—Part I: Theory and Various Models

Stanislaus Maier-Paape [1,*] and Qiji Jim Zhu [2]

[1] Institut für Mathematik, RWTH Aachen University, Templergraben 55, 52062 Aachen, Germany
[2] Department of Mathematics, Western Michigan University, 1903 West Michigan Avenue, Kalamazoo, MI 49008, USA; zhu@wmich.edu
[*] Correspondence: maier@instmath.rwth-aachen.de

Abstract: Utility and risk are two often competing measurements on the investment success. We show that efficient trade-off between these two measurements for investment portfolios happens, in general, on a convex curve in the two-dimensional space of utility and risk. This is a rather general pattern. The modern portfolio theory of Markowitz (1959) and the capital market pricing model Sharpe (1964), are special cases of our general framework when the risk measure is taken to be the standard deviation and the utility function is the identity mapping. Using our general framework, we also recover and extend the results in Rockafellar et al. (2006), which were already an extension of the capital market pricing model to allow for the use of more general deviation measures. This generalized capital asset pricing model also applies to e.g., when an approximation of the maximum drawdown is considered as a risk measure. Furthermore, the consideration of a general utility function allows for going beyond the "additive" performance measure to a "multiplicative" one of cumulative returns by using the log utility. As a result, the growth optimal portfolio theory Lintner (1965) and the leverage space portfolio theory Vince (2009) can also be understood and enhanced under our general framework. Thus, this general framework allows a unification of several important existing portfolio theories and goes far beyond. For simplicity of presentation, we phrase all for a finite underlying probability space and a one period market model, but generalizations to more complex structures are straightforward.

Keywords: convex programming; financial mathematics; risk measure; utility functions; efficient frontier; Markowitz portfolio theory; capital market pricing model; growth optimal portfolio; fractional Kelly allocation

MSC: 52A41; 90C25; 91G99

---

1. Introduction

The modern portfolio theory of Markowitz (1959) pioneered the quantitative analysis of financial economics. The most important idea proposed in this theory is that one should focus on the trade-off between expected return and the risk measured by the standard deviation. Mathematically, the modern portfolio theory leads to a quadratic optimization problem with linear constraints. Using this simple mathematical structure, Markowitz gave a complete characterization of the efficient frontier for trade-off of the return and risk. Tobin showed that the efficient portfolios are an affine function of the expected return Tobin (1958). Markowitz portfolio theory was later generalized by Lintner (1965), Mossin (1966), Sharpe (1964) and Treynor (1999) in the capital asset pricing model (CAPM) by involving a riskless bond. In the CAPM model, both the efficient frontier and the related efficient portfolios are affine in terms of the expected return (Sharpe 1964; Tobin 1958).

The nice structures of the solutions in the modern portfolio theory and the CAPM model afford many applications. For example, the CAPM model is designed to provide reasonable equilibrium prices for risky assets in the market place. Sharpe used the ratio of excess return to risk (called the Sharpe ratio) to provide a measurement for investment performance (Sharpe 1966). In addition, the affine structure of the efficient portfolio in terms of the expected return leads to the concept of a market portfolio as well as the two fund theorem (Tobin 1958) and the one fund theorem (Sharpe 1964; Tobin 1958). These results provided a theoretical foundation for passive investment strategies.

In many practical portfolio problems, however, one needs to consider more general pairs of reward and risk. For example, the growth portfolio theory can be viewed as maximizing the log utility of a portfolio. In order to address the issue that an optimal growth portfolio is usually too risky in practice, practitioners often have to impose additional restrictions on the risk (MacLean et al. 2009; Vince 2009; Vince and Zhu 2015). In particular, current drawdown (Maier-Paape 2016), maximum drawdown and its approximations (De Prado et al. 2013; Maier-Paape 2015; Vince and Zhu 2015), deviation measure (Rockafellar et al. 2006), as well as conditional value at risk (Rockafellar and Uryasev 2000) and more abstract coherent risk measures (Artzner et al. 1999) are widely used as risk measures in practice. Risk, as measured by such criteria, is reduced by diversification. Mathematically, it is to say these risk measures are convex. For these reasons, considering the trade-off between general risk measures and expected utilities are crucial in portfolio problems. In particular, including risk measures beyond positive homogeneous risk measures allows for measuring risk by drawdown (see Maier-Paape and Zhu (2017)), a concept to which many practitioners are sensitive.

The goal and main results of this paper are to extend the modern portfolio theory into a general framework under which one can analyze efficient portfolios that trade-off between a convex risk measure and a reward captured by a concave expected utility (see Section 3). We phrase our primal problem as a convex portfolio optimization problem of minimizing a convex risk measure subject to the constraint that the expected utility of the portfolio is above a certain level. Thus, convex duality plays a crucial role and the structure of the solutions to both the primal and dual problems often have significant financial implications. We show that, in the space of risk measure and expected utility, efficient trade-off happens on an increasing concave curve (cf. Proposition 8 and Theorem 4). We also show that the efficient portfolios continuously depend on the level of the expected utility (see Theorem 5), and moreover, we can describe the curve of efficient portfolios quantitatively in a precise manner (cf. Proposition 9 and Corollary 2).

To avoid technical complications, we restrict our analysis to the practical case in which the status of an underlying economy is represented by a finite sample space. Under this restriction, the Markowitz modern portfolio theory and the capital asset pricing model are special cases of this general theory. Markowitz determines portfolios of purely risky assets which provide an efficient trade-off between expected return and risk measured by the standard deviation (or equivalently the variance). Mathematically, this is a class of convex programming problems of minimizing the standard deviation of the portfolio parameterized by the level of the expected returns. The capital asset pricing model, in essence, extends the Markowitz modern portfolio theory by including a riskless bond in the portfolio. We observe that the space of the risk-expected return is, in fact, the space corresponding to the dual of the Markowitz portfolio problem. The shape of the famous Markowitz bullet is a manifestation of the well known fact that the optimal value function of a convex programming problem is convex with respect to the level of constraint. As mentioned above, the Markowitz portfolio problem is a quadratic optimization problem with linear constraint. This special structure of the problem dictates the affine structure of the optimal portfolio as a function of the expected return (see Theorem 6). This affine structure leads to the important two fund theorem (cf. Theorem 7) that provides a theoretical foundation for the passive investment method. For the capital asset pricing model, such an affine structure appears in both the primal and dual representation of the solutions, which leads to the one fund theorem in the portfolio space and the capital market line in the dual space of risk-return trade-off (cf. Theorems 8 and 9).

The flexibility in choosing different risk measures allows us to extend the analysis of the essentially quadratic risk measure pioneered by Markowitz to a wider range. For example, when a deviation measure (Rockafellar et al. 2006) is used as risk measure, which happens e.g., when an approximation of the current drawdown is considered (see Maier-Paape and Zhu (2017)), and the expected return is used to gauge the performance, we show that the affine structure of the efficient solution in the classical capital market pricing model is preserved (cf. Theorem 10 and Corollary 3), recovering and extending especially the results in Rockafellar et al. (2006). In particular, we can show that the condition in CAPM that ensures the existence of a market portfolio has a full generalization to portfolio problems with positive homogeneous risk measures (see Theorem 11). This is significant in that it shows that the passive investment strategy is justifiable in a wide range of settings.

The consideration of a general utility function, however, allows us to go beyond the "additive" performance measure in modern portfolio theory to a "multiplicative" one including cumulative returns when, for example, using the log utility. As a result, the growth optimal portfolio theory (Lintner 1965) and the leverage space portfolio theory (Vince 2009) can also be understood under our general framework. The optimal growth portfolio pursues to maximize the expected log utility that is equivalent to maximize the expected cumulative compound return. It is known that the growth optimal portfolio is usually too risky. Thus, practitioners often scale back the risky exposure from a growth optimal portfolio. In our general framework, we consider the portfolio that minimizes a risk measure given a fixed level of expected log utility. Under reasonable conditions, we show that such portfolios form a path parameterized by the level of expected log utility in the portfolio space that connects the optimal growth portfolio and the portfolio of a riskless bond (see Theorem 13). In general, for different risk measures, we will derive different paths. These paths provide justifications for risk reducing curves proposed in the leverage space portfolio theory (Vince 2009). The dual problem projects the efficient trade-off path into a concave curve in the risk-expected log utility space parallel to the role of Markowitz bullet in the modern portfolio theory and the capital market line in the capital asset pricing model. Under reasonable assumptions, the efficient frontier for log utility is a bounded increasing concave curve. The lower left endpoint of the curve corresponds to the portfolio of pure riskless bond and the upper right endpoint corresponds to the growth optimal portfolio. The increasing nature of the curve tells us that the more risk we take, the more cumulative return we can expect. The concavity of the curve indicates, however, that, with the increase of the risk, the marginal increase of the expected cumulative return will decrease.

Markowitz portfolio theory essentially maximizes a linear expected utility while the growth optimal portfolio focuses on the log utility. Other utility functions were also considered in portfolio problems. Our general framework brings them together in a unified way. Besides unifying the several important results laid out above, the general framework, furthermore, has many new applications. In this first installment of the paper, we layout the framework, derive the theoretical results of crucial importance and illustrate them with a few examples. More specific results on drawdown risk measures will appear in Maier-Paape and Zhu (2017). We arrange the paper as follows: first, we discuss necessary preliminaries in the next section. Section 3 is devoted to our main result: a framework to efficient trade-off between risk and utility of portfolios and its properties. In Section 4, we give a unified treatment of Markowitz portfolio theory and capital asset pricing model using our framework. Section 5 is devoted to a discussion of positive homogeneous risk measures under which the optimal trade-off portfolio possesses an affine structure. This situation fully generalizes Markowitz and CAPM theories and thus many of the conditions in Section 4 find an analog in Section 5. Section 6 discusses growth optimal portfolio theory and leverage portfolio theory. We conclude in Section 7 pointing to applications worthy of further investigation.

2. Preliminaries

2.1. A Portfolio Model

We consider a simple one period financial market model S on an economy with finite states represented by a sample space $\Omega = \{\omega_1, \omega_2, \ldots, \omega_N\}$. We use a probability space $(\Omega, 2^\Omega, P)$ to represent the states of the economy and their corresponding probability of occurring, where 2^Ω is the algebra of all subsets of Ω. The space of random variables on $(\Omega, 2^\Omega, P)$ is denoted $RV(\Omega, 2^\Omega, P)$ and it is used to represent the payoff of risky financial assets. Since the sample space Ω is finite, $RV(\Omega, 2^\Omega, P)$ is a finite dimensional vector space. We use $RV_+(\Omega, 2^\Omega, P)$ to represent of the cone of nonnegative random variables in $RV(\Omega, 2^\Omega, P)$. Introducing the inner product

$$\langle X, Y \rangle_{RV} = \mathbb{E}[XY], \quad X, Y \in RV(\Omega, 2^\Omega, P),$$

$RV(\Omega, 2^\Omega, P)$ becomes a (finite dimensional) Hilbert space.

Definition 1. (Financial Market) *We say that* $S_t = (S_t^0, S_t^1, \ldots, S_t^M)^\top, t = 0, 1$ *is a financial market in a one period economy provided that* $S_0 \in \mathbb{R}_+^{M+1}$ *and* $S_1 \in (0, \infty) \times RV_+(\Omega, 2^\Omega, P)^M$. *Here,* $S_0^0 = 1, S_1^0 = R > 0$ *represents a risk free bond with a positive return when* $R > 1$. *The rest of the components* $S_t^m, m = 1, \ldots, M$ *represent the price of the m-th risky financial asset at time t.*

We will use the notation $\widehat{S_t} = (S_t^1, \cdots, S_t^M)^\top$ when we need to focus on the risky assets. We assume that S_0 is a constant vector representing the prices of the assets in this financial market at $t = 0$. The risk is modeled by assuming $\widehat{S}_1 = (S_1^1, \ldots, S_1^M)^\top$ to be a nonnegative random vector on the probability space $(\Omega, 2^\Omega, P)$, that is $S_1^m \in RV_+(\Omega, 2^\Omega, P), m = 1, 2, \ldots, M$. A portfolio is a column vector $x \in \mathbb{R}^{M+1}$ whose components x_m represent the share of the m-th asset in the portfolio and $S_t^m x_m$ is the portion of capital invested in asset m at time t. Hence, x_0 corresponds to the investment in the risk free bond and $\widehat{x} = (x_1, \ldots, x_M)^\top$ is the risky part.

Remark 1. *Restricting to a finite sample space avoids the distraction of technical difficulties. This is also practical since, in the real world, one can only use a finite quantity of information. Furthermore, we restrict our presentation to the one period market model. However, more complex sample spaces and market models such as multi-period financial models should be treatable with a similar approach.*

We often need to restrict the selection of portfolios. For example, in many applications, we consider only portfolios with unit initial cost, i.e., $S_0^\top x = 1$. The following definition makes this precise.

Definition 2. (Admissible Portfolio) *We say that* $A \subset \mathbb{R}^{M+1}$ *is a set of* admissible portfolios *provided that A is a nonempty closed and convex set. We say that A is a set of* admissible portfolios with unit initial price *provided that A is a closed convex subset of* $\{x \in \mathbb{R}^{M+1} : S_0^\top x = 1\}$.

2.2. Convex Programming

The trade-off between convex risks and concave expected utilities yields essentially convex programming problems. For convenience of the reader, we collect notation and relevant results in convex analysis, which are important in the discussion below. We omit most of the proofs that can be found in Borwein and Zhu (2016); Carr and Zhu (forthcoming); Rockafellar (1970). Readers who know convex programming well can skip this section.

Let X be a finite dimensional Banach space. Recall that a set $C \subset X$ is convex if, for any $x, y \in C$ and $s \in [0, 1]$, $sx + (1-s)y \in C$. For an extended valued function $f : X \to \mathbb{R} \cup \{+\infty\}$, we define its domain by

$$\text{dom}(f) := \{x \in X : f(x) < \infty\}$$

and its epigraph by

$$\text{epi}(f) := \{(x, r) \in X \times \mathbb{R} : r \geq f(x)\}.$$

We say f is lower semi-continuous if epi(f) is a closed set. The following proposition characterizes an epigraph of a function.

Proposition 1. (Characterization of Epigraph) *Let F be a closed subset of* $X \times \mathbb{R}$ *such that* $\inf\{r : (x,r) \in F\} > -\infty$ *for all* $x \in \mathbb{R}$. *Then, F is the epigraph for a lower semi-continuous function* $f : X \to (-\infty, \infty]$, *i.e.,* $F = \text{epi}(f)$, *if and only if*

$$(x,r) \in F \Rightarrow (x, r+k) \in F, \ \forall k > 0. \tag{1}$$

Proof. The key is to observe that, for a set F with the structure in (1), a function

$$f(x) = \inf\{r : (x,r) \in F\} \tag{2}$$

is well defined and then $F = \text{epi}(f)$ holds. □

We say a function f is convex if $\text{epi}(f)$ is a convex set. Alternatively, f is convex if and only if, for any $x, y \in \text{dom}(f)$ and $s \in [0,1]$,

$$f(sx + (1-s)y) \le sf(x) + (1-s)f(y).$$

Consider $f : X \to [-\infty, +\infty)$. We say f is concave when $-f$ is convex and we say f is upper semi-continuous if $-f$ is lower semi-continuous. Define the hypograph of a function f by

$$\text{hypo}(f) = \{(x,r) \in X \times \mathbb{R} : r \le f(x)\}.$$

Then, a symmetric version of Proposition 1 is

Proposition 2. (Characterization of Hypograph) *Let F be a closed subset of* $X \times \mathbb{R}$ *such that* $\sup\{r : (x,r) \in F\} < +\infty$ *for all* $x \in \mathbb{R}$. *Then, F is the hypograph of an upper semi-continuous function* $f : X \to [-\infty, \infty)$, *i.e.,* $F = \text{hypo}(f)$, *if and only if*

$$(x,r) \in F \Rightarrow (x, r-k) \in F, \ \forall k > 0. \tag{3}$$

Moreover, the function f *can be defined by*

$$f(x) = \sup\{r : (x,r) \in F\}. \tag{4}$$

Remark 2. *The value of the function* f *in Proposition 1 (Proposition 2) at a given point* x *cannot assume* $-\infty$ *(*$+\infty$*) and therefore* $\{x\} \times \mathbb{R} \not\subset F$.

Since utility functions are concave and risk measures are usually convex, the analysis of a general trade-off between utility and risk naturally leads to a convex programming problem. The general form of such convex programming problems is

$$v(y,z) := \inf_{x \in X} [f(x) : g(x) \le y, h(x) = z], \text{ for } y \in \mathbb{R}^M, z \in \mathbb{R}^N, \tag{5}$$

where f, g and h satisfy the following assumption.

Assumption 1. *Assume that* $f : X \to \mathbb{R} \cup \{+\infty\}$ *is a lower semi-continuous extended valued convex function,* $g : X \to \mathbb{R}^M$ *is a vector valued function with convex components,* $\le$ *signifies componentwise minorization and* $h : X \to \mathbb{R}^N$ *is an affine mapping, for natural numbers* M, N. *Moreover, at least one of the components of* g *has compact sublevel sets.*

Convex programming problems have nice properties due to the convex structure. We briefly recall the pertinent results related to convex programming. First, the optimal value function v is convex.

This is a well-known result that can be found in standard books on convex analysis, e.g., Borwein and Zhu (2005).

Proposition 3. (Convexity of Optimal Value Function) *Let f, g and h satisfy Assumption 1. Then, the optimal value function v in the convex programming problem (5) is convex and lower semi-continuous.*

By and large, there are two (equivalent) general approaches to help solving a convex programming problem: by using the related dual problem and by using Lagrange multipliers. The two methods are equivalent in the sense that a solution to the dual problem is exactly a Lagrange multiplier (see Borwein and Zhu (2016)). Using Lagrange multipliers is more accessible to practitioners outside the special area of convex analysis. We will take this approach. The Lagrange multipliers method tells us that, under mild assumptions, we can expect there exists a Lagrange multiplier $\lambda = (\lambda_y, \lambda_z) \in \mathbb{R}^M \times \mathbb{R}^N$ with $\lambda_y \geq 0$ such that $\bar{x}$ is a solution to the convex programming problem (5) if and only if it is a solution to the unconstrained problem of minimizing

$$\begin{aligned} L(x,\lambda) &:= f(x) + \langle \lambda, (g(x) - y, h(x) - z) \rangle_{\mathbb{R}^M \times \mathbb{R}^N} \\ &= f(x) + \langle \lambda_y, g(x) - y \rangle_{\mathbb{R}^M} + \langle \lambda_z, h(x) - z \rangle_{\mathbb{R}^N}. \end{aligned} \tag{6}$$

The function $L(x, \lambda)$ is called the Lagrangian. To understand why and when a Lagrange multiplier exists, we need to recall the definition of the subdifferential.

Definition 3. (Subdifferential) *Let X be a finite dimensional Banach space and X^* its dual space. The subdifferential of a lower semi-continuous convex function $\phi : X \to \mathbb{R} \cup \{+\infty\}$ at $x \in \mathrm{dom}(\phi)$ is defined by*

$$\partial\phi(x) = \{x^* \in X^* : \phi(y) - \phi(x) \geq \langle x^*, y - x \rangle \ \forall y \in X\}.$$

Geometrically, an element of the subdifferential gives us the normal vector of a support hyperplane for the convex function at the relevant point. It turns out that Lagrange multipliers of problem (5) are simply the negative of elements of the subdifferential of v as summarized in the lemma below.

Theorem 1. (Lagrange Multiplier) *Let $v : \mathbb{R}^M \times \mathbb{R}^N \to \mathbb{R} \cup \{+\infty\}$ be the optimal value function of the constrained optimization problem (5) with f, g and h satisfying Assumption 1. Suppose that, for fixed $(y, z) \in \mathbb{R}^M \times \mathbb{R}^N$, $-\lambda = -(\lambda_y, \lambda_z) \in \partial v(y, z)$ and $\bar{x}$ is a solution of (5). Then,*

(i) $\lambda_y \geq 0$,
(ii) the Lagrangian $L(x, \lambda)$ defined in (6) attains a global minimum at $\bar{x}$, and
(iii) λ satisfies the complementary slackness condition

$$\langle \lambda, (g(\bar{x}) - y, h(\bar{x}) - z) \rangle = \langle \lambda_y, g(\bar{x}) - y \rangle = 0, \tag{7}$$

where $\langle \cdot, \cdot \rangle$ signifies the inner product.

Proof. See (Carr and Zhu forthcoming, Theorem 1.2.15). □

Remark 3. By Theorem 1 Lagrange multipliers exist when (5) has a solution $\bar{x}$ and $\partial v(y, z) \neq \emptyset$. Calculating $\partial v(y, z)$ requires to know the value of v in a neighborhood of (y, z) and is not realistic. Fortunately, the well-known Fenchel–Rockafellar theorem (see e.g., Borwein and Zhu (2005)) tells us when (y, z) belongs to the relative interior of $\mathrm{dom}(v)$, then $\partial v(y, z) \neq \emptyset$. This is a very useful sufficient condition. A particularly useful special case is the Slater condition (see also Borwein and Zhu (2005)): there exists $x \in \mathrm{dom}(f)$ such that $g(x) < y$. Under this condition, $\partial v(y) \neq \emptyset$ holds.

3. Efficient Trade-Off between Risk and Utility

We consider the financial market described in Definition 1 and consider a set of admissible portfolios $A \subset \mathbb{R}^{M+1}$ (see Definition 2). The payoff of each portfolio $x \in A$ at time $t = 1$ is $S_1^\top x$. The merit of a portfolio x is often judged by its expected utility $\mathbb{E}[u(S_1^\top x)]$, where u is an increasing concave utility function. The increasing property of u models the more payoff the better. The concavity reflects the fact that, with the increase of payoff, its marginal utility to an investor decreases. On the other hand, investors are often sensitive to the risk of a portfolio that can be gauged by a risk measure. Because diversification reduces risk, the risk measure should be a convex function.

3.1. Technical Assumptions

Some standard assumptions on the utility and risk functions are often needed in the more technical discussion below. We collect them here.

Assumption 2. (Conditions on Risk Measure) *Consider a continuous risk function $\mathfrak{r} : A \to [0, +\infty)$ where A is a set of admissible portfolios according to Definition 2. We will often refer to some of the following assumptions:*

(r1) (Riskless Asset Contributes No risk) *The risk measure $\mathfrak{r}(x) = \widehat{\mathfrak{r}}(\widehat{x})$ is a function of only the risky part of the portfolio, where $x^\top = (x_0, \widehat{x}^\top)$.*

(r1n) (Normalization) *There is at least one portfolio of purely bonds in A. Furthermore, $\mathfrak{r}(x) = 0$ if and only if x contains only riskless bonds, i.e., $x^\top = (x_0, \widehat{0}^\top)$ for some $x_0 \in \mathbb{R}$.*

(r2) (Diversification Reduces Risk) *The risk function $\mathfrak{r}$ is convex.*

(r2s) (Diversification Strictly Reduces Risk) *The risk function $\widehat{\mathfrak{r}}$ is strictly convex.*

(r3) (Positive homogeneous) *For $t > 0, \widehat{\mathfrak{r}}(t\widehat{x}) = t\widehat{\mathfrak{r}}(\widehat{x})$.*

(r3s) (Diversification Strictly Reduces Risk on Level Sets) *The risk function $\widehat{\mathfrak{r}}$ satisfies (r3) and, for all $\widehat{x} \neq \widehat{y}$ with $\widehat{\mathfrak{r}}(\widehat{x}) = \widehat{\mathfrak{r}}(\widehat{y}) = 1$ and $\alpha \in (0, 1)$,*

$$\widehat{\mathfrak{r}}(\alpha\widehat{x} + (1-\alpha)\widehat{y}) < \alpha\widehat{\mathfrak{r}}(\widehat{x}) + (1-\alpha)\widehat{\mathfrak{r}}(\widehat{y}) = 1.$$

Condition (r3) precludes (r2s). Thus, condition (r3s) serves as a replacement for (r2s) when the risk measure satisfies (r3). Moreover, we have the following useful result.

Lemma 1. *Assuming a risk measure $\mathfrak{r}$ satisfies (r1), (r1n) and (r3s). Then,*

(a) *$\mathfrak{r}$ satisfies (r2), and*

(b) *$f(x) = \widehat{f}(\widehat{x}) = [\widehat{\mathfrak{r}}(\widehat{x})]^2$ satisfies (r1), (r1n) and (r2s).*

Proof. Let $\alpha \in (0, 1)$ and $\widehat{x} \neq \widehat{y}$ be given. If $\widehat{x}$ and $\widehat{y}$ lie on the same ray through $\widehat{0}$, say $\widehat{x} = c\widehat{y}$ for some $c \geq 0$, then convexity of $\widehat{\mathfrak{r}}$ there is clear due to (r3). For $\widehat{x}$ and $\widehat{y}$ not on the same ray and with $\widehat{x}/\widehat{\mathfrak{r}}(\widehat{x}) \neq \widehat{y}/\widehat{\mathfrak{r}}(\widehat{y})$, defining $\lambda := \frac{\alpha\widehat{\mathfrak{r}}(\widehat{x})}{\alpha\widehat{\mathfrak{r}}(\widehat{x})+(1-\alpha)\widehat{\mathfrak{r}}(\widehat{y})}$, we have $1 - \lambda = \frac{(1-\alpha)\widehat{\mathfrak{r}}(\widehat{y})}{\alpha\widehat{\mathfrak{r}}(\widehat{x})+(1-\alpha)\widehat{\mathfrak{r}}(\widehat{y})}$, and since $\widehat{\mathfrak{r}}(\widehat{x}/\widehat{\mathfrak{r}}(\widehat{x})) = \widehat{\mathfrak{r}}(\widehat{y}/\widehat{\mathfrak{r}}(\widehat{y})) = 1$, by (r3s), we have

$$1 > \widehat{\mathfrak{r}}(\lambda\widehat{x}/\widehat{\mathfrak{r}}(\widehat{x}) + (1-\lambda)\widehat{y}/\widehat{\mathfrak{r}}(\widehat{y})) = \widehat{\mathfrak{r}}\left(\frac{\alpha\widehat{x} + (1-\alpha)\widehat{y}}{\alpha\widehat{\mathfrak{r}}(\widehat{x}) + (1-\alpha)\widehat{\mathfrak{r}}(\widehat{y})}\right) = \frac{\widehat{\mathfrak{r}}(\alpha\widehat{x} + (1-\alpha)\widehat{y})}{\alpha\widehat{\mathfrak{r}}(\widehat{x}) + (1-\alpha)\widehat{\mathfrak{r}}(\widehat{y})}, \tag{8}$$

verifying (r2) for $\mathfrak{r}$ since $\mathfrak{r}(x) = \widehat{\mathfrak{r}}(\widehat{x})$ depends only on $\widehat{x}$ by (r1).

Clearly, $\widehat{f}(\widehat{x}) = [\widehat{\mathfrak{r}}(\widehat{x})]^2$ has the properties (r1) and (r1n). Squaring (8), we derive

$$[\widehat{\mathfrak{r}}(\alpha\widehat{x} + (1-\alpha)\widehat{y})]^2 < [\alpha\widehat{\mathfrak{r}}(\widehat{x}) + (1-\alpha)\widehat{\mathfrak{r}}(\widehat{y})]^2 \leq \alpha[\widehat{\mathfrak{r}}(\widehat{x})]^2 + (1-\alpha)[\widehat{\mathfrak{r}}(\widehat{y})]^2. \tag{9}$$

Furthermore, on rays $\{\widehat{x} \mid \widehat{x} = c\widehat{y}, c \geq 0\}$ due to (r3), we have $\widehat{f}(t\widehat{y}) = t^2\widehat{f}(\widehat{y})$ and the strict convexity of $\widehat{f}$ there is clear as well. Hence, the square of the risk measure satisfies (r2s). □

Remark 4. (Deviation measure) *Our risk measure is described in terms of the portfolio. Assumptions (r1), (r1n), (r2) and (r3) are equivalent to the axioms of a* deviation measure *in Rockafellar et al. (2006), which is described in terms of the random payoff variable generated by the portfolio. Assumption (r1) excludes the widely used coherent risk measure introduced in Artzner et al. (1999), which requires cash reserve, reduces risk.*

Assumption 3. (Conditions on Utility Function) *Utility functions* $u : \mathbb{R} \to \mathbb{R} \cup \{-\infty\}$ *are upper semi-continuous functions on their domain* $\mathrm{dom}(u) = \{t \in \mathbb{R} : u(t) > -\infty\}$ *and are usually assumed to satisfy some of the following properties:*

(u1) (Profit Seeking) *The utility function u is an increasing function.*
(u2) (Diminishing Marginal Utility) *The utility function u is concave.*
(u2s) (Strict Diminishing Marginal Utility) *The utility function u is strictly concave.*
(u3) (Bankrupcy Forbidden) *For* $t < 0$, $u(t) = -\infty$.
(u4) (Unlimited Growth) *For* $t \to +\infty$, *we have* $u(t) \to +\infty$.

Another important condition that often appears in the financial literature is no arbitrage (see (Carr and Zhu forthcoming, Definition 3.5)). In the sequel, it is also useful to have two other related concepts.

Definition 4. *Consider a portfolio* $x \in \mathbb{R}^{M+1}$ *on the financial market* S_t.

(a) (No Nontrivial Riskless Portfolio) *We say a portfolio x is* riskless *if*

$$\langle S_1 - RS_0, x \rangle \geq 0.$$

We say the market has no nontrivial riskless portfolio *if there does not exist a riskless portfolio x with* $\widehat{x} \neq \widehat{0}$.

(b) (No Arbitrage) *We say x is an* arbitrage *if it is riskless and there exists some* $\omega \in \Omega$ *such that*

$$\langle S_1(\omega) - RS_0, x \rangle \neq 0.$$

We say market S_t *has* no arbitrage *if there does not exist any arbitrage portfolio.*

(c) (Nontrivial Bond Replicating Portfolio) *We say that* $x^\top = (x_0, \widehat{x}^\top)$ *is a* nontrivial bond replicating portfolio *if* $\widehat{x} \neq \widehat{0}$ *and*

$$\langle S_1 - RS_0, x \rangle = 0.$$

An arbitrage is a way to make return above the risk free rate without taking any risk of losing money. If such an opportunity exists, then investors will try to take advantage of it. In this process, they will bid up the price of the risky assets and cause the arbitrage opportunity to disappear. For this reason, usually people assume a financial market does not contain any arbitrage. A trivial riskless portfolio of investing everything in the riskless asset S_t^0 always exists. A nontrivial riskless portfolio, however, is not to be expected and we will often use this assumption. It turns out that the difference between no nontrivial riskless portfolio and no arbitrage is exactly the existence of a nontrivial bond replicating portfolio. The three conditions in Definition 4 (a), (b) and (c) are related as follows:

Proposition 4. *Consider the financial market* S_t *of Definition 1. There is no nontrivial riskless portfolio in* S_t *if and only if* S_t *has no arbitrage portfolio and no nontrivial bond replicating portfolio. It follows that no nontrivial riskless portfolio implies no arbitrage portfolio.*

Proof. The conclusion follows directly from Definition 4. □

Assuming that the financial market has no arbitrage, then no nontrivial riskless portfolio is equivalent to no nontrivial bond replicating portfolio and has the following characterization.

Theorem 2. (Characterization of no Nontrivial Bond Replicating Portfolio) *Assuming the financial market S_t in Definition 1 has no arbitrage. Then, the following assertions are equivalent:*

(i) *There is no nontrivial bond replicating portfolio.*
(ii) *For every nontrivial portfolio x with $\widehat{x} \neq \widehat{0}$, there exists some $\omega \in \Omega$ such that*

$$\langle S_1(\omega) - RS_0, x\rangle < 0. \tag{10}$$

(ii*) *For every risky portfolio $\widehat{x} \neq \widehat{0}$, there exists some $\omega \in \Omega$ such that*

$$\langle \widehat{S}_1(\omega) - R\widehat{S}_0, \widehat{x}\rangle < 0. \tag{11}$$

(iii) *The matrix*

$$G := \begin{bmatrix} S_1^1(\omega_1) - RS_0^1 & S_1^2(\omega_1) - RS_0^2 & \dots & S_1^M(\omega_1) - RS_0^M \\ S_1^1(\omega_2) - RS_0^1 & S_1^2(\omega_2) - RS_0^2 & \dots & S_1^M(\omega_2) - RS_0^M \\ \vdots & \vdots & \vdots & \vdots \\ S_1^1(\omega_N) - RS_0^1 & S_1^2(\omega_N) - RS_0^2 & \dots & S_1^M(\omega_N) - RS_0^M \end{bmatrix} \in \mathbb{R}^{N\times M} \tag{12}$$

has rank M, in particular $N \geq M$.

Proof. We use a cyclic proof. (i)→ (ii): If (ii) fails, then $\langle S_1 - RS_0, x\rangle \geq 0$ for some nontrivial x. By (i), x must be an arbitrage, which is a contradiction. (ii)→ (ii*): obvious. (ii*)→ (iii): If (iii) is not true, then $G\widehat{x} = 0$ has a nontrivial solution that is a contradiction to (11). (iii)→ (i): Assume that there exists a portfolio x^* with $\widehat{x}^* \neq \widehat{0}$, which replicates the bond. Then, $\langle S_1 - RS_0, x^*\rangle = 0$. This implies that $\langle \widehat{S}_1 - R\widehat{S}_0, \widehat{x}^*\rangle = 0$ so that $G\widehat{x}^* = 0$, which contradicts (iii). □

A rather useful corollary of Theorem 2 is that any of the conditions (i)–(iii) of that theorem ensures the covariance matrix of the risky assets to be positive definite.

Corollary 1. (Positive Definite Covariance Matrix) *Assume the financial market S_t in Definition 1 has no nontrivial riskless portfolio. Then, the covariant matrix of the risky assets*

$$\Sigma := \mathbb{E}[(\widehat{S}_1 - \mathbb{E}(\widehat{S}_1))(\widehat{S}_1 - \mathbb{E}(\widehat{S}_1))^\top] = (\mathbb{E}[(S_1^i - \mathbb{E}(S_1^i))(S_1^j - \mathbb{E}(S_1^j))])_{i,j=1,\dots,M} \tag{13}$$

is positive definite.

Proof. We note that, under the assumption of the corollary, for any nontrivial risky portfolio $\widehat{x}$, $\widehat{S}_1^\top \widehat{x}$ cannot be a constant. Otherwise, $\langle \widehat{S}_1 - R\widehat{S}_0, \widehat{x}\rangle$ would be a constant, which contradicts S_t has no nontrivial riskless portfolio. It follows that, for any nontrivial risky portfolio $\widehat{x}$,

$$Var(\widehat{S}_1^\top \widehat{x}) = \widehat{x}^\top \Sigma \widehat{x} > 0.$$

Thus, Σ is positive definite. □

Corollary 1 shows that the standard deviation as a risk measure satisfies the properties (r1), (r1n), (r2) and (r3s) in Assumption 2.

3.2. Efficient Frontier for the Risk-Utility Trade-Off

We note that, to increase the utility, one often has to take on more risk and, as a result, the risk increases. The converse is also true. For example, if one allocates all the capital to the riskless bond, then there will be no risk, but the price to pay is that one has to forgo all the opportunities to get a high payoff on risky assets so as to reduce the expected utility. Thus, the investment decision of selecting an appropriate portfolio becomes one of trading-off between the portfolio's expected return and risk. To understand such a trade-off, we define, for a set of admissible portfolios $A \subset \mathbb{R}^{M+1}$ in Definition 2, the set

$$\mathcal{G}(\mathfrak{r}, u; A) := \{(r, \mu) : \exists x \in A \text{ s.t. } r \geq \mathfrak{r}(x), \mu \leq \mathbb{E}[u(S_1^\top x)]\} \subset \mathbb{R}^2, \tag{14}$$

on the two-dimensional risk-expected utility space for a given risk measure $\mathfrak{r}$ and utility u. Given a financial market S_t and a portfolio x, we often measure risk by observing $S_1^\top x$. The following simple proposition is useful in linking such observations to the risk measure in Assumption 2.

Proposition 5. (Induced Risk Measure) *(a) Fixing a financial market S_t as in Definition 1. Suppose that $\rho : RV(\Omega, 2^\Omega, P) \to [0, +\infty)$ is a lower semi-continuous, convex and positive homogeneous function. Moreover, assume that $\rho(S_1^\top x) = \rho(\widehat{S}_1^\top \widehat{x})$. Then, $\mathfrak{r} : A \to [0, +\infty)$, $\mathfrak{r}(x) := \rho(S_1^\top x)$ is a lower semi-continuous risk measure satisfying properties* (r1), (r2) *and* (r3) *in Assumption 2.*

The following are two sufficient conditions ensuring $\rho(S_1^\top x) = \rho(\widehat{S}_1^\top \widehat{x})$ that are easy to verify:

(1) *When ρ is invariant under adding constants, i.e., $\rho(X) = \rho(X + c)$, for any $X \in RV(\Omega, 2^\Omega, P)$ and $c \in \mathbb{R}$. A useful example is when ρ is the standard deviation.*
(2) *When ρ is restricted to a set of admissible portfolios A with unit initial cost. In this case, we can see that*

$$\widehat{\mathfrak{r}}(\widehat{x}) := \rho(R + (\widehat{S}_1 - R\widehat{S}_0)^\top \widehat{x}) = \rho(S_1^\top x). \tag{15}$$

(b) If the financial market S_t has no nontrivial riskless portfolio and ρ is strictly convex, then, for a set A of admissible portfolios with unit initial cost, $\widehat{\mathfrak{r}} : A \to [0, +\infty)$ satisfies (r2s) *in Assumption 2.*

Similarly, we are interested in when the expected utility $x \mapsto \mathbb{E}[u(S_1^\top x)]$ of $S_1^\top x$ is strictly concave in x. Below, we provide a set of sufficient conditions guaranteeing this. The easy proof is left to the reader.

Proposition 6. (Strict Concavity of Expected Utility) *Assume that*

(a) *the financial market S_t has no nontrivial riskless portfolio,*
(b) *the utility function u satisfies condition (u2s) in Assumption 3, and*
(c) *A is a set of admissible portfolios with unit initial cost as in Definition 2.*

Then, the expected utility $\mathbb{E}[u(S_1^\top x)]$ as a function of the portfolio x is upper semi-continuous and strictly concave on A.

When $\mathfrak{r}(x) = \rho(S_1^\top x)$ is induced by ρ as in Proposition 5 we also use the notation $\mathcal{G}(\rho, u, A)$. Clearly, if $A' \subset A$ then $\mathcal{G}(\mathfrak{r}, u; A') \subset \mathcal{G}(\mathfrak{r}, u; A)$. The following assumption will be needed in concrete applications.

Assumption 4. (Compact Level Sets) *Either (a) for each $\mu \in \mathbb{R}$, $\{x \in \mathbb{R}^{M+1} : \mu \leq \mathbb{E}[u(S_1^\top x)], x \in A\}$ is compact or (b) for each $r \in \mathbb{R}$, $\{x \in \mathbb{R}^{M+1} : r \geq \mathfrak{r}(x), x \in A\}$ is compact.*

Proposition 7. *Assume that A is a set of admissible portfolios as in Definition 2. We claim: (a) Assume that the risk measure $\mathfrak{r}$ satisfies (r2) in Assumption 2 and the utility function u satisfies (u2) in Assumption 3. Then, set $\mathcal{G}(\mathfrak{r}, u; A)$ is convex and $(r, \mu) \in \mathcal{G}(\mathfrak{r}, u; A)$ implies that, for any $k > 0$, $(r + k, \mu) \in \mathcal{G}(\mathfrak{r}, u; A)$ and $(r, \mu - k) \in \mathcal{G}(\mathfrak{r}, u; A)$. (b) Assume furthermore that Assumption 4 holds. Then, $\mathcal{G}(\mathfrak{r}, u; A)$ is closed.*

Proof. (a) The property $(r, \mu) \in \mathcal{G}(\mathfrak{r}, u; A)$ implies that, for any $k > 0$, $(r + k, \mu) \in \mathcal{G}(\mathfrak{r}, u; A)$ and $(r, \mu - k) \in \mathcal{G}(\mathfrak{r}, u; A)$ follows directly from the definition of $\mathcal{G}(\mathfrak{r}, u; A)$.

Suppose that $(r_1, \mu_1), (r_2, \mu_2) \in \mathcal{G}(\mathfrak{r}, u; A)$ and $s \in [0, 1]$. Then, there exists $x^1, x^2 \in A$ such that

$$r_i \geq \mathfrak{r}(x^i) \text{ and } \mu_i \leq \mathbb{E}[u(S_1^\top x^i)], i = 1, 2.$$

Then, convexity of $\mathfrak{r}$ in x yields

$$sr_1 + (1-s)r_2 \geq s\mathfrak{r}(x^1) + (1-s)\mathfrak{r}(x^2) \geq \mathfrak{r}(sx^1 + (1-s)x^2),$$

and (u2) gives

$$s\mu_1 + (1-s)\mu_2 \leq s\mathbb{E}[u(S_1^\top x^1)] + (1-s)\mathbb{E}[u(S_1^\top x^2)] \leq \mathbb{E}[u(S_1^\top (sx^1 + (1-s)x^2))].$$

Thus,

$$s(r_1, \mu_1) + (1-s)(r_2, \mu_2) \in \mathcal{G}(\mathfrak{r}, u; A)$$

so that $\mathcal{G}(\mathfrak{r}, u; A)$ is convex.

(b) Suppose that $(r_n, \mu_n) \to (r, \mu)$, for a sequence in $\mathcal{G}(\mathfrak{r}, u; A)$. Then, there exists a sequence $x^n \in A$ such that

$$r_n \geq \mathfrak{r}(x^n) \text{ and } \mu_n \leq \mathbb{E}[u(S_1^\top x^n)]. \tag{16}$$

By Assumption 4, a subsequence of x^n (denoted again by x^n) converges to, say, $\bar{x} \in A$. Taking limits in (16), by the upper semicontinuity of u, we arrive at

$$r \geq \mathfrak{r}(\bar{x}) \text{ and } \mu \leq \mathbb{E}[u(S_1^\top \bar{x})]. \tag{17}$$

Thus, $(r, \mu) \in \mathcal{G}(\mathfrak{r}, u; A)$ and hence $\mathcal{G}(\mathfrak{r}, u; A)$ is a closed set. □

Now, we can represent a portfolio $x \in A \subset \mathbb{R}^{M+1}$ as a point $(\mathfrak{r}(x), \mathbb{E}[u(S_1^\top x)]) \in \mathcal{G}(\mathfrak{r}, u; A)$ in the two-dimensional risk-expected utility space. Investors prefer portfolios with lower risk if the expected utility is the same or with higher expected utility given the same level of risk.

Definition 5. (Efficient Portfolio and Frontier) *We say that a portfolio $x \in A$ is* efficient *provided that there does not exist any portfolio $x' \in A$ such that either*

$$\mathfrak{r}(x') \leq \mathfrak{r}(x) \text{ and } \mathbb{E}[u(S_1^\top x')] > \mathbb{E}[u(S_1^\top x)]$$

or

$$\mathfrak{r}(x') < \mathfrak{r}(x) \text{ and } \mathbb{E}[u(S_1^\top x')] \geq \mathbb{E}[u(S_1^\top x)].$$

We call the set of images of all efficient portfolios in the two-dimensional risk-expected utility space the efficient frontier *and denote it by $\mathcal{G}_{eff}(\mathfrak{r}, u; A)$.*

The next theorem characterizes efficient portfolios in the risk-expected utility space.

Theorem 3. (Efficient Frontier) *Efficient portfolios represented in the two-dimensional risk-expected utility space are all located in the (non vertical or horizontal) boundary of the set $\mathcal{G}(\mathfrak{r}, u; A)$. Moreover, consider admissible portfolios A, B. If $B \subset A$, then*

$$\mathcal{G}_{eff}(\mathfrak{r}, u; A) \cap \mathcal{G}(\mathfrak{r}, u; B) \subset \mathcal{G}_{eff}(\mathfrak{r}, u; B). \tag{18}$$

Proof. If a portfolio x represented in the risk-expected utility space as (r, μ) is not on the (non vertical or horizontal) boundary of the $\mathcal{G}(\mathfrak{r}, u; A)$, then, for ε small enough, we have either $(r - \varepsilon, \mu) \in \mathcal{G}(\mathfrak{r}, u; A)$

or $(r, \mu + \varepsilon) \in \mathcal{G}(\mathfrak{r}, u; A)$. This means x can be improved. The inclusion (18) directly follows from $\mathcal{G}(\mathfrak{r}, u; B) \subset \mathcal{G}(\mathfrak{r}, u; A)$. □

Remark 5. (Empty Efficient Frontier) *If $(\alpha, \widehat{0}) \in A$ for all $\alpha \in \mathbb{R}$ and the increasing utility function u has no upper bound, then for any risk measure $\mathfrak{r}$ satisfying (r1) and (r1n) in Assumption 2, $\{0\} \times \mathbb{R} \subset \mathcal{G}(\mathfrak{r}, u; A)$. By Proposition 7 $[0, +\infty) \times \mathbb{R} \subset \mathcal{G}(\mathfrak{r}, u; A)$, which implies that $\mathcal{G}_{eff}(\mathfrak{r}, u; A) = \emptyset$. Thus, practically meaningful $\mathcal{G}(\mathfrak{r}, u; A)$ always correspond to sets of admissible portfolios A such that the initial cost $S_0 \cdot x$ for all $x \in A$ is limited. Moreover, if the initial cost has a range and riskless bonds are included in the portfolio, then we will see a vertical line segment on the μ axis and the efficient portfolio corresponds to the upper bound of this vertical line segments. Thus, it suffices to consider sets of portfolios A with unit initial cost.*

3.3. Representation of Efficient Frontier

In view of Remark 5, in this section, we will consider a set of admissible portfolios A with unit initial cost as in Definition 2. By Proposition 7, we can view the set $\mathcal{G}(\mathfrak{r}, u; A)$ as an epigraph on the expected utility-risk space or a hypograph on the risk-expected utility space. By Propositions 1 and 2, the set $\mathcal{G}(\mathfrak{r}, u; A)$ naturally defines two functions $\gamma : \mathbb{R} \to \mathbb{R} \cup \{+\infty\}$ and $\nu : \mathbb{R} \to \mathbb{R} \cup \{-\infty\}$:

$$\mu \mapsto \gamma(\mu) := \inf\{r : (r, \mu) \in \mathcal{G}(\mathfrak{r}, u; A)\} = \inf\{\mathfrak{r}(x) : \mathbb{E}[u(S_1^\top x)] \geq \mu, x \in A\} \geq 0, \tag{19}$$

and

$$r \mapsto \nu(r) := \sup\{\mu : (r, \mu) \in \mathcal{G}(\mathfrak{r}, u; A)\} = \sup\{\mathbb{E}[u(S_1^\top x)] : \mathfrak{r}(x) \leq r, x \in A\}, \tag{20}$$

where we assume Assumption 4 to ensure ν is well defined, i.e., $\nu(r) < \infty$ for all $r \in \mathbb{R}$.

Proposition 8. (Function Related to the Efficient Frontier) *Assume that the risk measure $\mathfrak{r}$ satisfies (r2) in Assumption 2 and the utility function u satisfies (u2) in Assumption 3. Furthermore, assume that Assumption 4 holds for a set of admissible portfolios A with unit initial cost. Then, the functions $\mu \mapsto \gamma(\mu)$ and $r \mapsto \nu(r)$ are increasing lower semi-continuous convex and increasing upper semi-continuous concave, respectively. Moreover, for any $(r_0, \mu_0) \in \mathcal{G}_{eff}(\mathfrak{r}, u; A)$, $(-\infty, \mu_0] \subset \mathrm{dom}(\gamma) := \{\mu \in \mathbb{R} : \gamma(\mu) < \infty\}$ and $[r_0, \infty) \subset \mathrm{dom}(\nu) := \{r \in \mathbb{R} : \nu(r) > -\infty\}$.*

Proof. The increasing property of γ and ν follows directly from the second representation in (19) and (20), respectively.

The properties for the domains of γ and ν follow directly from Proposition 7.

The other properties of γ and ν follow directly from Propositions 1 and 2 since $\mathcal{G}(\mathfrak{r}, u; A)$ is closed and convex according to Proposition 7.

Alternatively, we can also directly apply Proposition 3 to the second representation in (19) and (20) to derive the convexity and concavity of γ and ν, respectively. □

To describe a representation of the efficient frontier in the next theorem, we will use the *exchange operator* $\hat{P} : \mathbb{R}^2 \to \mathbb{R}^2$ defined by $\hat{P}(x_1, x_2) = (x_2, x_1)$.

Theorem 4. (Representation of the Efficient Frontier) *Assume that the risk measure $\mathfrak{r}$ satisfies (r2) in Assumption 2 and the utility function u satisfies (u2) in Assumption 3. Furthermore, assume that Assumption 4 holds for a set of admissible portfolios A with unit initial cost. Then, the efficient frontier has the following representation*

$$\mathcal{G}_{eff}(\mathfrak{r}, u; A) = \hat{P}[\mathrm{graph}(\gamma)] \cap \mathrm{graph}(\nu) \tag{21}$$

or equivalently

$$\mathcal{G}_{eff}(\mathfrak{r},u;A) = \{(\gamma(\mu),\mu) : \mu \in \text{dom}(\gamma) \subset \mathbb{R}\} \cap \{(r,\nu(r)) : r \in \text{dom}(\nu) \subset \mathbb{R}\}. \tag{22}$$

More specifically, setting

$$I := \text{dom}(\nu) \cap \text{range}(\gamma) = \{r \in \mathbb{R} : \exists \mu \text{ with } (r,\mu) \in \mathcal{G}_{eff}(\mathfrak{r},u;A)\} \tag{23}$$

and

$$J := \text{dom}(\gamma) \cap \text{range}(\nu) = \{\mu \in \mathbb{R} : \exists r \text{ with } (r,\mu) \in \mathcal{G}_{eff}(\mathfrak{r},u;A)\}, \tag{24}$$

we find that I *and* J *are intervals and the representation*

$$\mathcal{G}_{eff}(\mathfrak{r},u;A) = \hat{P}[\text{graph}(\gamma\mid_J)] = \text{graph}(\nu\mid_I) \tag{25}$$

holds, where $\gamma : J \to \mathbb{R}$ *and* $\nu : I \to \mathbb{R}$ *are continuous. Moreover,* $\gamma : J \to I$ *and* $\nu : I \to J$ *are strictly increasing, bijective and inverse to each other, i.e.,*

$$\gamma \circ \nu(r) = r \;\forall r \in I \text{ and } \nu \circ \gamma(\mu) = \mu \;\forall \mu \in J. \tag{26}$$

Proof. First, we show that the right-hand side of (21) is a subset of the left-hand side. Let $(r_0,\mu_0) \in \hat{P}[\text{graph}(\gamma)] \cap \text{graph}(\nu)$. Since $\hat{P}[\text{graph}(\gamma)] := \{(\gamma(\mu),\mu) : \mu \in \mathbb{R}\}$ and $\text{graph}(\nu) = \{(r,\nu(r)) : r \in \mathbb{R}\}$ necessarily $(r_0,\mu_0) \in \mathbb{R}^2$. Note that, in particular, (22) holds. Using $(r_0,\mu_0) \in \text{graph}(\nu)$, we get from (20)

$$\mu_0 = \nu(r_0) = \sup\{\mathbb{E}[u(S_1^\top x)] : \mathfrak{r}(x) \le r_0, x \in A\}. \tag{27}$$

Similarly, from (19)

$$r_0 = \gamma(\mu_0) = \inf\{\mathfrak{r}(x) : \mathbb{E}[u(S_\top x)] \ge \mu_0, x \in A\}. \tag{28}$$

With (27), we can select a sequence $x_n \in A$ such that $\mathfrak{r}(x_n) \le r_0$ and $\mathbb{E}[u(S_1^\top x_n)] \nearrow \mu_0$. By Assumption 4, either $\{x \in A : \mathfrak{r}(x) \le r_0\}$ or $\{x \in A : \mathbb{E}[u(S_1^\top x)] \ge \mu_0 - 1\}$ is compact. Hence, without loss of generality, we may assume that $x_n \to x^* \in A$ with $\mathfrak{r}(x^*) \le r_0$ and $\mathbb{E}[u(S_1^\top x^*)] \ge \mu_0$ by the upper semicontinuity of $x \mapsto \mathbb{E}[u(S_1^\top x)]$. Note that $\mathfrak{r}(x^*) < r_0$ would contradict (28). Thus, $\mathfrak{r}(x^*) = r_0$, so that $(r_0,\mu_0) \in \mathcal{G}(\mathfrak{r},u;A)$. Now, consider $(r_1,\mu_1) \in \mathcal{G}(\mathfrak{r},u;A)$. If $\mu_1 > \mu_0$ and $r_1 \le r_0$, then

$$\nu(r_1) := \sup\{\mu : (r_1,\mu) \in \mathcal{G}(\mathfrak{r},u;A)\} \ge \mu_1 > \mu_0 = \nu(r_0)$$

contradicting that ν is increasing. On the other hand, if $r_1 < r_0$ and $\mu_1 \ge \mu_0$, then

$$\gamma(\mu_1) := \inf\{r : (r,\mu_1) \in \mathcal{G}(\mathfrak{r},u;A)\} \le r_1 < r_0 = \gamma(\mu_0),$$

contradicting the increasing property of γ. Thus, $(r_0,\mu_0) \in \mathcal{G}_{eff}(\mathfrak{r},u;A)$.

To conclude (21), it remains to show that the left-hand side of (21) is a subset of the right-hand side. Let $(r_0,\mu_0) \in \mathcal{G}_{eff}(\mathfrak{r},u;A) \subset \mathcal{G}(\mathfrak{r},u;A) \subset \mathbb{R}^2$. Then, there exists some efficient $x^* \in A$ with $r_0 = \mathfrak{r}(x^*)$ and $\mu_0 = \mathbb{E}[u(S_1^\top x^*)]$. This means both the supremum in (27) and the infimum in (28) are attained at x^* so that $r_0 = \gamma(\mu_0)$ and $\mu_0 = \nu(r_0)$. It follows that

$$(r_0,\mu_0) \in \hat{P}[\text{graph}(\gamma)] \cap \text{graph}(\nu).$$

Since, by Proposition 8, ν and γ are convex and concave functions, respectively, they are continuous in the interior of its domain. When $\mathcal{G}_{eff}(\mathfrak{r},u;A)$ is not a single point, it is therefore a continuous curve except for the possible finite endpoints. By Proposition 8, if $\mathcal{G}_{eff}(\mathfrak{r}, u; A)$ contains (r, μ), then $(-\infty, \mu] \subset \mathrm{dom}(\gamma)$ and $[r, \infty) \subset \mathrm{dom}(\nu)$. Thus, if $\mathcal{G}_{eff}(\mathfrak{r}, u; A)$ has a finite left endpoint, we can represent it in the form $(\gamma(\mu_e), \mu_e)$ where μ_e is in the interior of $\mathrm{dom}(\gamma)$. Thus, for any $\mu \to \mu_e+$, $(\gamma(\mu), \mu) \to (\gamma(\mu_e), \mu_e)$ so that $\mathcal{G}_{eff}(\mathfrak{r}, u; A)$ is right continuous. Similarly, if $\mathcal{G}_{eff}(\mathfrak{r}, u; A)$ has a finite right endpoint, then it is left continuous at this endpoint. Finally, representation (22) implies that the projection of $\mathcal{G}_{eff}(\mathfrak{r}, u; A)$ onto the r and μ axises are intervals I and J, respectively, giving (23) and (24). Moreover, the representations in (25) follow immediately. Furthermore, since $\mathcal{G}_{eff}(\mathfrak{r}, u; A)$ contains no vertical or horizontal lines (see Theorem 3), $\gamma : J \to I$ and $\nu : I \to J$ are strictly increasing. Thus, both are injective, and surjectivity follows from (23) and (24). Finally, (26) follows from (22). □

3.4. Efficient Portfolios

We now turn to analyze how the corresponding efficient portfolios behave. Ideally, we would want that each point on the efficient trade-off frontier corresponds to exactly one portfolio. For this purpose, we need additional assumptions on risk measures and utility functions.

Theorem 5. (Efficient Portfolio Path) *Consider a financial market S_t as defined in Definition 1 and assume that A is a set of admissible portfolios with unit initial cost as in Definition 2. We also assume Assumption 4 holds and*

(c0) *there exists some $\bar{x} \in A$ with $\bar{\mu} := \mathbb{E}[u(S_1^\top \bar{x})]$ and $\bar{r} := \mathfrak{r}(\bar{x})$ finite.*

In addition, suppose that one of the following conditions holds:

(c1) *The risk measure $\mathfrak{r}$ satisfies conditions (r1) and (r2s) in Assumption 2 and the utility function satisfies conditions (u1) and (u2) in Assumption 3.*

(c2) *The risk measure $\mathfrak{r}$ satisfies conditions (r1) and (r2) in Assumption 2 and the utility function satisfies conditions (u1) and (u2s) in Assumption 3.*

(c3) *The risk measure $\mathfrak{r}$ satisfies conditions (r1), (r1n) and (r3s) in Assumption 2 and the utility function satisfies conditions (u1) and (u2) in Assumption 3.*

Then, each point $(r, \mu) \in \mathcal{G}_{eff}(\mathfrak{r}, u; A)$ corresponds to a unique efficient portfolio $x(r, \mu) \in A$ and the mapping $(r, \mu) \mapsto x(r, \mu)$ is continuous on $\mathcal{G}_{eff}(\mathfrak{r}, u; A)$ (onesided continuous at the finite endpoint(s)). Moreover, efficient portfolios have the continuous representation $r \mapsto x(r, \nu(r))$ and $\mu \mapsto x(\gamma(\mu), \mu)$ on intervals I defined in (23) and J defined in (24), respectively.

Proof. Note that Assumption 4 and condition (c0) ensures that $\mathcal{G}_{eff}(\mathfrak{r}, u; A)$ is nonempty.

We first show the uniqueness of the efficient portfolio. Suppose that portfolios $x^1 \neq x^2$ both correspond to $(r, \mu) \in \mathcal{G}_{eff}(\mathfrak{r}, u; A)$. We consider only the case when (c1) is satisfied (and the case when (c2) or (c3) is satisfied can be argued in a similar way). Then, by (r1) and (21), we must have $r = \hat{\mathfrak{r}}(\hat{x}^1) = \hat{\mathfrak{r}}(\hat{x}^2) = \mathfrak{r}(x^1) = \mathfrak{r}(x^2) = \gamma(\mu)$ and $\mathbb{E}[u(S_1^\top x^i)] = \mu, x^i \in A, i = 1, 2$. Note that because A has unit initial cost, $\hat{x}^1 \neq \hat{x}^2$. Since A is convex, $x^* = (x^1 + x^2)/2 \in A$. Conditions (r2s) and (u2) imply that $\mathbb{E}[u(S_1^\top x^*)] \geq \mu$ and due to the strict convexity of $\hat{\mathfrak{r}}$ by (r1), $\mathfrak{r}(x^*) = \hat{\mathfrak{r}}(\hat{x}^*) < \gamma(\mu)$, a contradiction. Thus, the efficient portfolio corresponding to $(r, \mu) \in \mathcal{G}_{eff}(\mathfrak{r}, u; A)$ is unique and we denote it by $x(r, \mu)$. The mapping $(r, \mu) \to x(r, \mu)$ is well defined.

Next, we show the continuity of the mapping $(r, \mu) \to x(r, \mu)$. If $\mathcal{G}_{eff}(\mathfrak{r}, u; A)$ is a single point, there is nothing to prove. When $\mathcal{G}_{eff}(\mathfrak{r}, u; A)$ is not a single point by Theorem 4, we can represent all the efficient portfolios either as the image of the mapping $r \mapsto x(r, \nu(r))$ on I or as the image of the mapping $\mu \mapsto x(\gamma(\mu), \mu)$ on J. Suppose that $x(r, \mu)$ is discontinuous at $(\bar{r}, \bar{\mu}) \in \mathcal{G}_{eff}(\mathfrak{r}, u; A)$. We first focus on the case when Assumption 4 (a) holds. Then, for a fixed positive number $\varepsilon_0 > 0$, there exist sequences $\mu_n \to \bar{\mu}$ ($\mu_n \nearrow \bar{\mu}$ if $\bar{\mu} = \max(J)$ or $\mu_n \searrow \bar{\mu}$ if $\bar{\mu} = \min(J)$) and such that $\|x(\gamma(\mu_n), \mu_n) - x(\gamma(\bar{\mu}), \bar{\mu})\| \geq \varepsilon_0$ where

$$\mathbb{E}[u(S_1^\top x(\gamma(\mu_n), \mu_n))] \geq \mu_n \text{ and } \mathfrak{r}(x(\gamma(\mu_n), \mu_n)) = \hat{\mathfrak{r}}(\hat{x}(\gamma(\mu_n), \mu_n)) = \gamma(\mu_n). \quad (29)$$

By Assumption 4 (a), we may assume without loss of generality that $x(\gamma(\mu_n), \mu_n)$ converges to some portfolio x^* with $\|x^* - x(\gamma(\bar{\mu}), \bar{\mu})\| \geq \varepsilon_0$. Furthermore, by Proposition 8, $\mu \mapsto \gamma(\mu)$ is concave, and by Theorem 4 continuous on J. Taking limits in (29) and using the upper semicontinuity of $x \mapsto \mathbb{E}[u(S_1^\top x)]$ yields

$$\mathbb{E}[u(S_1^\top x^*)] \geq \bar{\mu} \text{ and } \hat{\mathfrak{r}}(\hat{x}^*) = \gamma(\bar{\mu}) = \bar{r}. \tag{30}$$

However, the uniqueness of the efficient portfolio (30) implies that $x^* = x(\gamma(\bar{\mu}), \bar{\mu})$, which is a contradiction. If Assumption 4 (b) holds, we can use the mapping $r \mapsto x(r, \nu(r))$ on the interval I to obtain a similar contradiction. □

Remark 6. *Interval $I = \mathrm{dom}(\nu) \cap \mathrm{range}(\gamma)$ is always bounded from below by 0 because the risk measure is always none negative, other than that, both $I = \mathrm{dom}(\nu) \cap \mathrm{range}(\gamma)$ and $J = \mathrm{dom}(\gamma) \cap \mathrm{range}(\nu)$ can be open, closed, half open and half closed. They can be finite or infinite. Although various situations are possible, we do have a precise characterization of their endpoints in the next proposition.*

Proposition 9. *Under the conditions of Theorem 5, define*

$$r_{\min} := \inf[\mathrm{dom}(\nu) \cap \mathrm{range}(\gamma)] = \inf I,$$

$$r_{\max} := \sup[\mathrm{dom}(\nu) \cap \mathrm{range}(\gamma)] = \sup I,$$

$$\mu_{\min} := \inf[\mathrm{dom}(\gamma) \cap \mathrm{range}(\nu)] = \inf J,$$

and

$$\mu_{\max} := \sup[\mathrm{dom}(\gamma) \cap \mathrm{range}(\nu)] = \sup J.$$

Then,

$$r_{\min} = \inf\{\mathfrak{r}(x) : \mathbb{E}[u(S_1^\top x)] > -\infty, x \in A\} \geq 0, \tag{31}$$

$$\mu_{\max} = \sup\{\mathbb{E}[u(S_1^\top x)], x \in A\} > -\infty, \tag{32}$$

$$\mu_{\min} = \lim_{r \searrow r_{\min}} \sup\{\mathbb{E}[u(S_1^\top x)] : \mathfrak{r}(x) \leq r, x \in A\} \leq \mu_{\max}, \tag{33}$$

and

$$r_{\max} = \lim_{\mu \nearrow \mu_{\max}} \inf\{\mathfrak{r}(x) : \mathbb{E}[u(S_1^\top x)] \geq \mu, x \in A\} \geq r_{\min}. \tag{34}$$

Proof. We start with (31). Let $\bar{r} := \inf\{\mathfrak{r}(x) : \mathbb{E}[u(S_1^\top x)] > -\infty, x \in A\}$. It is clear that, for any μ, $\bar{r} \leq \gamma(\mu)$ so that $\bar{r}$ is a lower bound for $I = \mathrm{dom}(\nu) \cap \mathrm{range}(\gamma)$, i.e., $\bar{r} \leq r_{\min}$. For any $r > \bar{r}$, there exist some finite μ such that

$$S(\mu, r) := \{x \in A : \mathbb{E}[u(S_1^\top x)] \geq \mu > -\infty \text{ and } \mathfrak{r}(x) \leq r\} \neq \emptyset. \tag{35}$$

By Assumption 4, $S(\mu, r)$ is compact. Thus, $\gamma(\mu) \in [\bar{r}, r]$ is attained by some $x^* \in A$ with $\mathbb{E}[u(S_1^\top x^*)] \geq \mu$. It follows that $S(\mu, \gamma(\mu))$ defined in (35) is nonempty and, therefore, compact by Assumption 4. Thus, $\nu(\gamma(\mu)) > -\infty$ implying $\gamma(\mu) \in \mathrm{dom}(\nu) \cap \mathrm{range}(\gamma) = I$ and hence $\gamma(\mu) \geq r_{\min}$. However, since $r > \bar{r}$ was arbitrary, $\gamma(\mu)$ can be chosen close to $\bar{r}$ implying $\bar{r} \geq r_{\min}$ and in conclusion $\bar{r} = r_{\min}$.

Note that, since $\mathfrak{r}(x)$ is always finite, we have

$$\sup\{\mathbb{E}[u(S_1^\top x)], x \in A\} = \sup\{\mathbb{E}[u(S_1^\top x)], \mathfrak{r}(x) < \infty, x \in A\}.$$

Thus, the proof of (32) is parallel to that of (31). Having determined $r_{\min}$ and $\mu_{\max}$, we have $r_{\max} = \lim_{\mu \nearrow \mu_{\max}} \gamma(\mu)$ and $\mu_{\min} = \lim_{r \searrow r_{\min}} \nu(r)$. Hence, representations (33) and (34) directly follow from the definitions of ν and γ, respectively. □

Corollary 2. *Under the conditions of Theorem 5, we have*

(a) $r_{\min} \in I$ *if and only if* $\mu_{\min} \in J$, *and* $r_{\max} \in I$ *if and only if* $\mu_{\max} \in J$.
(b) *If* $r_{\min} \in I$ *then* $\mu_{\min} = \nu(r_{\min})$ *and* $\gamma(\mu_{\min}) = r_{\min}$.
(c) *If* $\mu_{\max} \in J$ *then* $r_{\max} = \gamma(\mu_{\max})$ *and* $\nu(r_{\max}) = \mu_{\max}$.
(d) (i) *If* $r_{\min} \in I$ *and* $\mu_{\max} \in J$ *then* $I = [r_{\min}, r_{\max}]$ *and* $J = [\mu_{\min}, \mu_{\max}]$.
(ii) *If* $r_{\min} \notin I$ *and* $\mu_{\max} \in J$ *then* $I = (r_{\min}, r_{\max}]$ *and* $J = (-\infty, \mu_{\max}]$.
(iii) *If* $r_{\min} \in I$ *and* $\mu_{\max} \notin J$ *then* $I = [r_{\min}, \infty)$ *and* $J = [\mu_{\min}, \mu_{\max})$.
(iv) *If* $r_{\min} \notin I$ *and* $\mu_{\max} \notin J$ *then* $I = (r_{\min}, \infty)$ *and* $J = (-\infty, \mu_{\max})$.

Proof. Let $r_{\min} \in I \subset \text{dom}(\nu)$. Then, $r_{\min} = \gamma(\bar{\mu})$ for some $\bar{\mu} \in J$ by Theorem 4. Since γ is an increasing function, we have $\bar{\mu} = \min J$. Hence, $\bar{\mu} = \mu_{\min}$ and $r_{\min} = \gamma(\mu_{\min})$. Then, $\nu(r_{\min}) = \bar{\mu} = \mu_{\min}$ follows since $\gamma \circ \nu = id$ is the identity mapping on I. The converse and the case for max can be proved analogously. This proves (a), (b) and (c). Moreover, (d)(i) directly follows from (b) and (c).

If $r_{\min} \notin I$, we show $\mu_{\min} = -\infty$. In fact, if $\mu_{\min} > -\infty$, then, for any natural number n, we can select $x^n \in A$ such that $\mathfrak{r}(x^n) \leq r_{\min} + 1/n$ and $\mathbb{E}[u(S_1^\top x^n)] \geq \mu_{\min}$. By Assumption 4, we may assume without loss of generality that $x^n \to x^* \in A$. Taking limits as $n \to \infty$, we conclude that $\mathfrak{r}(x^*) \leq r_{\min}$ and $\mathbb{E}[u(S_1^\top x^*)] \geq \mu_{\min}$ and both have to be equality. Thus, $(r_{\min}, \mu_{\min}) \in \mathcal{G}_{eff}(\mathfrak{r}, u; A)$, a contradiction. This shows (d)(ii).

Analogously, one gets that $\mu_{\max} \notin J$ implies $r_{\max} = \infty$, which shows (d)(iii) and (d)(iv). □

Remark 7. *Several interesting cases when* $\mathcal{G}_{eff}(\mathfrak{r}, u; A)$ *has finite endpoints are discussed below:*

(a) The quantity $r_{\min}$ *is always finite and* $\mu_{\min}$ *may be finite as well as illustrated in Figure 1. However,* $\mu_{\min}$ *may also be* $-\infty$, *as Example 1 shows. A typical efficient frontier corresponding to this case is illustrated in Figure 2.*

(b) Suppose $\mu_{\max}$ *is finite and attained at an efficient portfolio* $x(\gamma(\mu_{\max}), \mu_{\max})$. *Under the conditions of Theorem 5, the portfolio* $\kappa := x(\gamma(\mu_{\max}), \mu_{\max})$ *is unique and independent of the risk measure. A graphic illustration is given in Figure 3.*

(c) Trade-off between utility and risk is thus implemented by portfolios $x(\gamma(\mu), \mu)$ *that trace out a curve in the so-called leverage space introduced by Vince (2009). Note that the curve* $x(\gamma(\mu), \mu)$ *depends on the risk measure* $\mathfrak{r}$ *as well as the utility function* u. *This provides a method for systematically selecting portfolios in the leverage space to reduce risk exposure.*

(d) If, in addition, $\mathfrak{r}$ *satisfies (r1n) in Assumption 2 and* $u(R) > -\infty$ *then* $r_{\min} = 0$, $\mu_{\min} = u(R)$ *and* $x(r_{\min}, \mu_{\min}) = (1, \widehat{0}^\top)^\top$ *(see Figure 4).*

(e) Unlike in (b), $\mu_{\max}$ *finite can also happen when the efficient frontier is unbounded (see Example 2).*

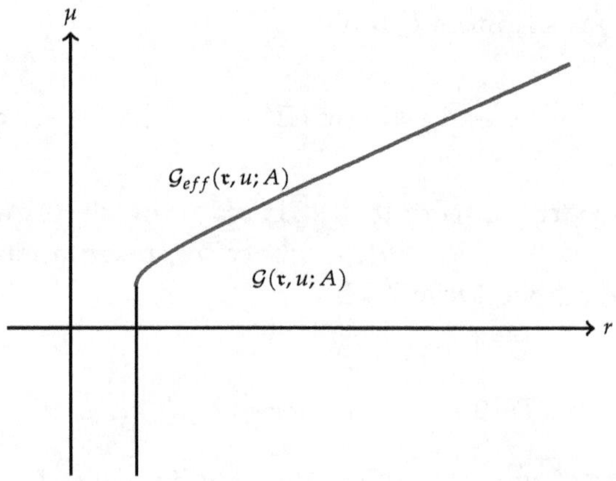

Figure 1. Efficient frontier with both $r_{\min}$ and $\mu_{\min}$ are finite and attained.

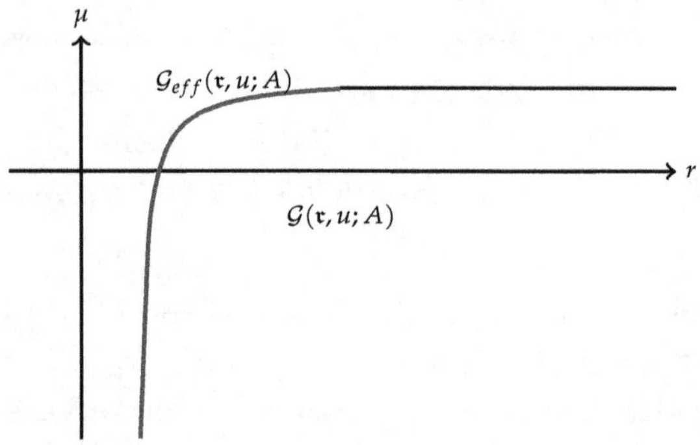

Figure 2. Efficient frontier with $\mu_{\min} = -\infty$.

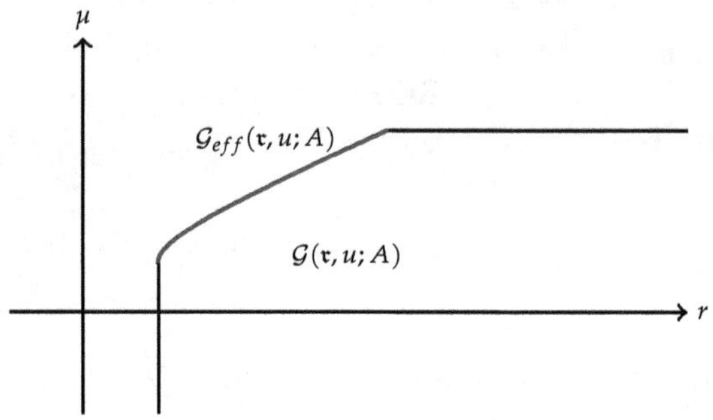

Figure 3. Efficient frontier when $r_{\min} > 0$ and $\mu_{\max}$ is finite and attained as maximum.

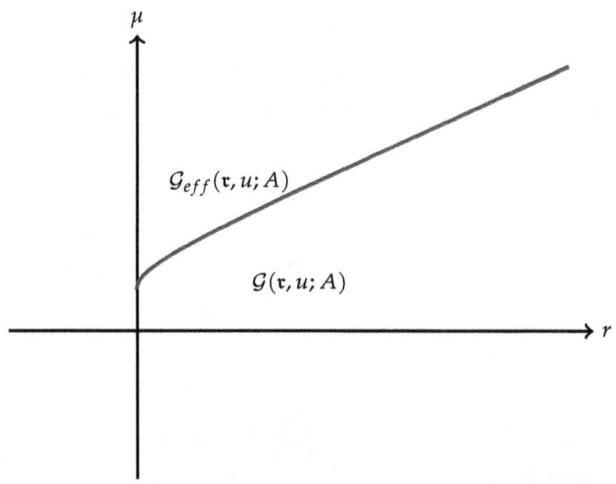

Figure 4. Efficient frontier with $(1, \widehat{0}^\top)^\top \in A$.

Example 1. (for $\mu_{\min} = -\infty$) *Consider a portfolio problem with the log utility on a financial market that contains no bond and two risky assests (i.e., $M = 2$)*

$$\nu(r) := \sup_{\widehat{x}\in\mathbb{R}^2} \{\mathbb{E}[\ln(\widehat{S}_1^\top \widehat{x})] : \mathfrak{r}(\widehat{x}) \le r, \widehat{S}_0^\top \widehat{x} = 1\}. \tag{36}$$

The financial market $\widehat{S}_t = (S_t^1, S_t^2)^\top$ (since the riskless asset is not involved in (36), it is irrelevant to the problem) is specified as follows: $\widehat{S}_0 = [1,1]^\top$, $\widehat{S}_1$ is a random vector on the sample space $\Omega = \{\omega_1, \omega_2, \omega_3\}$ with $P(\omega_1) = P(\omega_2) = P(\omega_3) = 1/3$ and a payoff matrix

$$[\widehat{S}_1(\omega_1), \widehat{S}_1(\omega_2), \widehat{S}_1(\omega_3)] = \begin{bmatrix} 1 & 3 & 0.5 \\ 0.5 & 0.8 & 1.2 \end{bmatrix}. \tag{37}$$

Note that, for instance with $R = 1$, this market has no nontrivial riskless portfolio. We use the risk measure

$$\mathfrak{r}(\widehat{x}) := \sqrt{(x_1 - 2x_2)^2 + 100(2x_1 + x_2)^2}, \tag{38}$$

which satisfies (r1), (r1n) and (r3s) and, therefore, Assumption 4(b) holds. Clearly, $\nu(\mathfrak{r}([1,0]^\top)) > 0$ and finite. Notice that on the feasible set $\widehat{S}_0^\top \widehat{x} = 1$, i.e., $x_2 = 1 - x_1$. It follows that the risk measure

$$\mathfrak{r}(\widehat{x}) := \sqrt{(3x_1 - 2)^2 + 100(x_1 + 1)^2}$$

attains a minimum $r_m = \frac{50}{109}\sqrt{109}$ at $\widehat{x}_m = (-94/109, 203/109)^\top$. Observing $\widehat{S}_1^\top(\omega_2)\widehat{x}_m < 0$, we must have $r_{\min} > r_m$ and

$$\mu_{\min} = \lim_{r \searrow r_{\min}} \nu(r) = -\infty.$$

Example 2. (for $\mu_{\max} < \infty$ and $r_{\max} = \infty$) *Consider the same risk measure as in the previous example, but use instead the utility function $u(t) = 1 - e^{-t}$. We analyze*

$$\nu(r) := \sup_{\widehat{x}\in\mathbb{R}^2} \{\mathbb{E}[u(\widehat{S}_1^\top \widehat{x})] : \mathfrak{r}(\widehat{x}) \le r, \widehat{S}_0^\top \widehat{x} = 1\}, \tag{39}$$

where the financial market is defined by

$$[\widehat{S}_1(\omega_1), \widehat{S}_1(\omega_2), \widehat{S}_1(\omega_3)] = \begin{bmatrix} 1 & 3.6 & 0.5 \\ 0.5 & 1.2 & 0.3 \end{bmatrix} \tag{40}$$

on the sample space $\Omega = \{\omega_1, \omega_2, \omega_3\}$ with $P(\omega_1) = P(\omega_2) = P(\omega_3) = 1/3$. Again, on the feasible set $\widehat{S}_0^\top \widehat{x} = 1$, i.e., $x_2 = 1 - x_1$. The portfolio as a function of x_1 implies

$$(\widehat{S}_1^\top(\omega_i)[x_1, 1 - x_1]^\top)_{i=1,2,3} = [0.5, 1.2, 0.3] + x_1[0.5, 2.4, 0.2].$$

As $x_1 \to \infty$, we can see that $\mathfrak{r}(\widehat{x}) \to \infty$ and $\mathbb{E}[u(\widehat{S}_1^\top \widehat{x})] \to 1$. Hence, $r_{\max} = \infty$ and $\mu_{\max} = 1 < \infty$. Notice that (40) with, e.g., $R = 1$, has an arbitrage portfolio $\widehat{x}^* = (1, -1)^\top$, but the existence of an arbitrage seems to be necessary in constructing such an example.

4. Markowitz Portfolio Theory and CAPM Model

Let us now turn to applications of the general theory. We show that the results in the previous section provide a general unified framework for several familiar portfolio theories. They are Markowitz portfolio theory, the CAPM model, growth optimal portfolio theory and leverage space portfolio theory. Of course, when dealing with concrete risk measures and expected utilities related to these concrete theories, an additional helpful structure in the solutions often emerge. Although many different expositions of these theories do already exist in the literature, for the convenience of readers, we include brief arguments using Lagrange multiplier methods. In this entire section, we will assume that the market S_t from Definition 1 has no nontrivial riskless portfolio.

4.1. Markowitz Portfolio Theory

Markowitz portfolio theory that considers only risky assets (see Markowitz (1959)), can be understood as a special case of the framework discussed in Section 3. The risk measure is the standard deviation σ and the utility function is the identity function. Thus, we face the problem

$$\begin{aligned} \min \quad & \sigma(\widehat{S}_1^\top \widehat{x}) \\ \text{Subject to} \quad & \mathbb{E}[\widehat{S}_1^\top \widehat{x}] \geq \mu,\ \widehat{S}_0^\top \widehat{x} = 1. \end{aligned} \tag{41}$$

We assume $\mathbb{E}[\widehat{S}_1]$ is not proportional to $\widehat{S}_0$, that is, for any $\alpha \in \mathbb{R}$,

$$\mathbb{E}[\widehat{S}_1] \neq \alpha \widehat{S}_0. \tag{42}$$

Since the variance is a monotone increasing function of the standard deviation, we can minimize half of the variance for convenience:

$$\begin{aligned} \min_{\widehat{x} \in \mathbb{R}^M} \quad & \widehat{\mathfrak{r}}(\widehat{x}) := \frac{1}{2}\mathrm{Var}(\widehat{S}_1^\top \widehat{x}) = \frac{1}{2}\sigma^2(\widehat{S}_1^\top \widehat{x}) = \frac{1}{2}\widehat{x}^\top \Sigma \widehat{x} \\ \text{Subject to} \quad & \mathbb{E}[\widehat{S}_1^\top \widehat{x}] \geq \mu,\ \widehat{S}_0^\top \widehat{x} = 1. \end{aligned} \tag{43}$$

Optimization problem (43) is already in the form (19) with $A = \{x \in \mathbb{R}^{M+1} : S_0^\top x = 1, x_0 = 0\}$. We can check if condition (c1) in Theorem 5 is satisfied. Moreover, Corollary 1 implies that Σ is positive definite since S_t has no nontrivial riskless portfolio. Hence, the risk function $\widehat{\mathfrak{r}}$ has compact level sets. Thus, Assumption 4 is satisfied and Theorem 5 is applicable. Let $\widehat{x}(\mu)$ be the optimal portfolio corresponding to μ. Consider the Lagrangian

$$L(\widehat{x}, \lambda) := \frac{1}{2}\widehat{x}^\top \Sigma \widehat{x} + \lambda_1(\mu - \widehat{x}^\top \mathbb{E}[\widehat{S}_1]) + \lambda_2(1 - \widehat{x}^\top \widehat{S}_0), \tag{44}$$

where $\lambda_1 \geq 0$. Thanks to Theorem 1, we have

$$0 = \nabla_{\widehat{x}} L = \Sigma \widehat{x}(\mu) - (\lambda_1 \mathbb{E}[\widehat{S}_1] + \lambda_2 \widehat{S}_0). \tag{45}$$

In other words,

$$\widehat{x}(\mu) = \Sigma^{-1}(\lambda_1 \mathbb{E}[\widehat{S}_1] + \lambda_2 \widehat{S}_0). \tag{46}$$

We must have $\lambda_1 > 0$ because otherwise $\widehat{x}(\mu)$ would be unrelated to the payoff $\widehat{S}_1$. The complementary slackness condition implies that $\mathbb{E}[\widehat{S}_1^\top \widehat{x}(\mu)] = \mu$. Left multiplying (45) by $\widehat{x}^\top(\mu)$, we have

$$\sigma^2(\mu) = \lambda_1 \mu + \lambda_2. \tag{47}$$

To determine the Lagrange multipliers, we need the numbers $\alpha = \mathbb{E}[\widehat{S}_1]^\top \Sigma^{-1} \mathbb{E}[\widehat{S}_1]$, $\beta = \mathbb{E}[\widehat{S}_1]^\top \Sigma^{-1} \widehat{S}_0$ and $\gamma = \widehat{S}_0^\top \Sigma^{-1} \widehat{S}_0$. Left multiplying (46) by $\mathbb{E}[\widehat{S}_1]^\top$ and $\widehat{S}_0^\top$, we have

$$\mu = \lambda_1 \alpha + \lambda_2 \beta \tag{48}$$

and

$$1 = \lambda_1\beta + \lambda_2\gamma. \tag{49}$$

Solving (48) and (49), we derive

$$\lambda_1 = \frac{\gamma\mu - \beta}{\alpha\gamma - \beta^2} \text{ and } \lambda_2 = \frac{\alpha - \beta\mu}{\alpha\gamma - \beta^2}, \tag{50}$$

where

$$\alpha\gamma - \beta^2 = \det\left([\mathbb{E}[\widehat{S}_1^\top], \widehat{S}_0^\top]\Sigma^{-1} \begin{bmatrix} \mathbb{E}[\widehat{S}_1] \\ \widehat{S}_0 \end{bmatrix} \right) > 0, \tag{51}$$

since Σ^{-1} is positive definite and condition (42) holds. Substituting (50) into (47), we see that the efficient frontier is determined by the curve

$$\sigma(\mu) = \sqrt{\frac{\gamma\mu^2 - 2\beta\mu + \alpha}{\alpha\gamma - \beta^2}} = \sqrt{\frac{\gamma}{\alpha\gamma - \beta^2}\left(\mu - \frac{\beta}{\gamma}\right)^2 + \frac{1}{\gamma}} \geq \frac{1}{\sqrt{\gamma}}, \tag{52}$$

usually referred to as the Markowitz bullet due to its shape. A typical Markowitz bullet is shown in Figure 5 with an asymptote

$$\mu = \frac{\beta}{\gamma} + \sigma(\mu)\sqrt{\frac{\alpha\gamma - \beta^2}{\gamma}}. \tag{53}$$

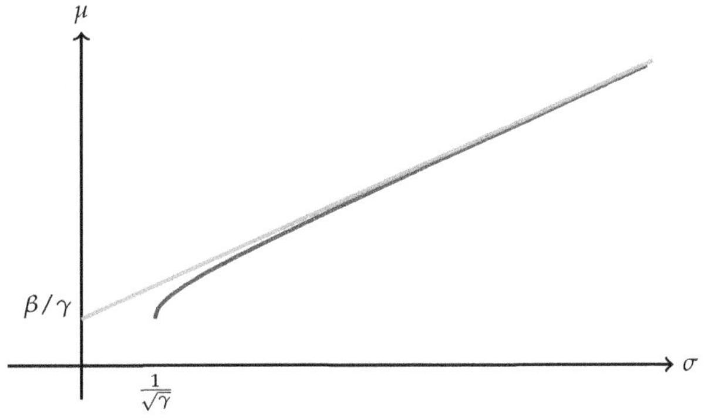

Figure 5. Markowitz Bullet.

Note that $\mathcal{G}(\frac{1}{2}\text{Var}, id, \{S_0^\top x = 1, x_0 = 0\}) = \mathcal{G}(\sigma, id, \{S_0^\top x = 1, x_0 = 0\})$. Thus, relationships (52) and (53) describe the efficient frontier $\mathcal{G}_{eff}(\sigma, id, \{S_0^\top x = 1, x_0 = 0\})$ as in Definition 5. In addition, note that (52) implies that $\mu_{\min} = \beta/\gamma$ and $r_{\min} = 1/\sqrt{\gamma}$. Thus, as a corollary of Theorem 5, we have

Theorem 6. (Markowitz Portfolio Theorem) *Assume that the financial market S_t has no nontrivial riskless portfolio and $\mathbb{E}[\widehat{S}_1]$ is not proportional to $\widehat{S}_0$ (see (42)). The Markowitz efficient portfolios of (41) represented in the (σ, μ)−plane are given by*

$$\mathcal{G}_{eff}(\sigma, id; \{S_0^\top x = 1, x_0 = 0\}).$$

They correspond to the upper boundary of the Markowitz bullet given by

$$\sigma(\mu) = \sqrt{\frac{\gamma\mu^2 - 2\beta\mu + \alpha}{\alpha\gamma - \beta^2}}, \ \mu \in \left[\frac{\beta}{\gamma}, +\infty\right).$$

The optimal portfolio $\widehat{x}(\mu)$ can be determined by (46) and (50) as

$$\widehat{x}(\mu) = \mu\frac{\Sigma^{-1}(\gamma\mathbb{E}[\widehat{S}_1] - \beta\widehat{S}_0)}{\alpha\gamma - \beta^2} + \frac{\Sigma^{-1}(\alpha\widehat{S}_0 - \beta\mathbb{E}[\widehat{S}_1])}{\alpha\gamma - \beta^2}, \tag{54}$$

which is affine in μ.

The structure of the optimal portfolio in (54) implies the well known two fund theorem derived by Tobin (1958).

Theorem 7. (Two Fund Theorem) *Select two distinct portfolios on the Markowitz efficient frontier. Then, any portfolio on the Markowitz efficient frontier can be represented as the linear combination of these two portfolios.*

4.2. Capital Asset Pricing Model

The capital asset pricing model (CAPM) is a theoretical equilibrium model independently proposed by Lintner (1965), Mossin (1966), Sharpe (1964) and Treynor (1999) for pricing a risky asset according to its expected payoff and market risk, often referred to as the beta. The core of the capital asset pricing model is including a riskless bond in the Markowitz mean-variance analysis. Thus, we can apply the general framework in Section 3 with the same setting as in Section 4.1. Similar to the previous section, we can consider the equivalent problem of

$$\begin{aligned} \min_{x \in \mathbb{R}^{M+1}} \quad & \frac{1}{2}\sigma^2(S_1^\top x) = \frac{1}{2}\widehat{x}^\top \Sigma \widehat{x} =: \mathfrak{r}(\widehat{x}) \\ \text{Subject to} \quad & \mathbb{E}[S_1^\top x] \geq \mu,\ S_0^\top x = 1. \end{aligned} \tag{55}$$

Similar to the last section problem (55) is in the form (19) with $A = \{x \in \mathbb{R}^{M+1} : S_0^\top x = 1\}$. We can check that condition (c1) in Theorem 5 is satisfied. Again, the risk function $\mathfrak{r}$ has compact level sets since Σ is positive definite. Thus, Assumption 4 is satisfied and Theorem 5 is applicable. The Lagrangian of this convex programming problem is

$$L(x, \lambda) := \frac{1}{2}\widehat{x}^\top \Sigma \widehat{x} + \lambda_1(\mu - x^\top \mathbb{E}[S_1]) + \lambda_2(1 - x^\top S_0), \tag{56}$$

where $\lambda_1 \geq 0$. Again, we have

$$0 = \nabla_x L = (0, \Sigma\widehat{x}(\mu)) - (\lambda_1 \mathbb{E}[S_1] + \lambda_2 S_0). \tag{57}$$

Using $S_1^0 = R$ and $S_0^0 = 1$, the first component of (57) implies

$$\lambda_2 = -\lambda_1 R, \tag{58}$$

so that (57) becomes

$$0 = \nabla_x L = (0, \Sigma\widehat{x}(\mu)) - \lambda_1(\mathbb{E}[S_1] - RS_0). \tag{59}$$

Clearly, $\lambda_1 > 0$ for $\widehat{x}(\mu) \neq 0$. Using the complementary slackness condition $\mathbb{E}[S_1^\top x(\mu)] = \mu$, we derive

$$\sigma^2(\mu) = \widehat{x}^\top(\mu)\Sigma\widehat{x}(\mu) = \lambda_1(\mu - R), \tag{60}$$

by left multiplying $x^\top(\mu)$ in (59). Solving $\widehat{x}(\mu)$ from (59), we have

$$\widehat{x}(\mu) = \lambda_1 \Sigma^{-1}(\mathbb{E}[\widehat{S}_1] - R\widehat{S}_0). \tag{61}$$

Left multiplying with $\mathbb{E}[\widehat{S}_1^\top]$ and $\widehat{S}_0^\top$ and using the α, β and γ introduced in the previous section, we derive

$$\mu - x_0(\mu)R = \lambda_1(\alpha - R\beta) \tag{62}$$

and

$$1 - x_0(\mu) = \lambda_1(\beta - R\gamma), \tag{63}$$

respectively. Multiplying (63) by R and subtracting it from (62), we get

$$\mu - R = \lambda_1(\alpha - 2\beta R + \gamma R^2). \tag{64}$$

Combining (60) and (64), we arrive at

$$\sigma^2(\mu) = \frac{(\mu - R)^2}{\alpha - 2\beta R + \gamma R^2}. \tag{65}$$

Clearly, efficient portfolios only occur for $\mu \geq R$, since, for $\mu = R$, the pure bond portfolio $(1, \widehat{0}^\top)^\top$ is the only efficient (and risk free) portfolio. Relation (65) defines a straight line on the (σ, μ)-plane

$$\sigma(\mu) = \frac{\mu - R}{\sqrt{\Delta}} \quad \text{or} \quad \mu = R + \sigma(\mu)\sqrt{\Delta}, \tag{66}$$

where $\Delta := \alpha - 2\beta R + \gamma R^2 > 0$ if

$$\mathbb{E}[\widehat{S}_1] - R\widehat{S}_0 \neq \widehat{0}, \tag{67}$$

since Σ is positive definite. The line given in (66) is called the *capital market line.*

In addition, combining (61), (63) and (64), we have

$$x^\top(\mu) = \Delta^{-1}[\alpha - \beta R - \mu(\beta - \gamma R), (\mu - R)(\mathbb{E}[\widehat{S}_1^\top] - R\widehat{S}_0^\top)\Sigma^{-1}]. \tag{68}$$

Again, we see the affine structure of the solution. Note that, although the computation is done in terms of the risk function $\widehat{\mathfrak{r}}(\widehat{x}) = \frac{1}{2}\widehat{x}^\top\Sigma\widehat{x}$, relationships in (66) are in terms the risk function $\sigma(S_1^\top x)$. Thus, they describe the efficient frontier $\mathcal{G}_{eff}(\sigma, id; \{S_0^\top x = 1\})$ as in Definition 5. In summary, we have

Theorem 8. (CAPM) *Assume that the financial market S_t of Definition 1 has no nontrivial riskless portfolio. Moreover, assume that condition (67) holds. The efficient portfolios for the CAPM model $\mathcal{G}_{eff}(\sigma, id; \{S_0^\top x = 1\})$ represented in the (σ, μ)-plane are a straight line passing through $(0, R)$ corresponding to the portfolio of pure risk free bond. The optimal portfolio $x(\mu)$ can be determined by (68), which is affine in μ and can be represented as points in the (σ, μ)-plane as located on the capital market line*

$$\mu = R + \sigma\sqrt{\Delta}, \ \sigma \geq 0.$$

In particular, when $\mu = R$ and $\mu = (\alpha - \beta R)/(\beta - \gamma R)$, we derive, respectively, the portfolio $(1, \widehat{0}^\top)^\top$ that contains only the riskless bond and the portfolio $(0, (\mathbb{E}[\widehat{S}_1^\top] - R\widehat{S}_0^\top)\Sigma^{-1}/(\beta - \gamma R))^\top$ that contains only risky assets. We call this portfolio the *market portfolio* and denote it x_M. The market portfolio corresponds to the coordinates

$$(\sigma_M, \mu_M) = \left(\frac{\sqrt{\Delta}}{\beta - \gamma R}, R + \frac{\Delta}{\beta - \gamma R}\right). \tag{69}$$

Since the risk σ is non negative, we see that the market portfolio exists only when

$$\beta - \gamma R > 0.$$

This condition is

$$\widehat{S}_0^\top \Sigma^{-1}(\mathbb{E}[\widehat{S}_1] - R\widehat{S}_0) > 0. \quad (70)$$

By Theorem 3,

$$\begin{aligned}(\sigma_M, \mu_M) &\in \mathcal{G}_{eff}(\sigma, id; \{S_0^\top x = 1\}) \cap \mathcal{G}(\sigma, id; \{S_0^\top x = 1, x_0 = 0\}) \\ &\subset \mathcal{G}_{eff}(\sigma, id; \{S_0^\top x = 1, x_0 = 0\}).\end{aligned} \quad (71)$$

Thus, the market portfolio has to reside on the Markowitz efficient frontier. Moreover, by (68), we can see that the market portfolio x_M is the only portfolio on the CAPM efficient frontier that consists of purely risky assets. Thus,

$$\mathcal{G}_{eff}(\sigma, id; \{S_0^\top x = 1\}) \cap \mathcal{G}(\sigma, id; \{S_0^\top x = 1, x_0 = 0\}) = \{(\sigma_M, \mu_M)\}, \quad (72)$$

so that the capital market line is tangent to the Markowitz bullet at (σ_M, μ_M) as illustrated in Figure 6.

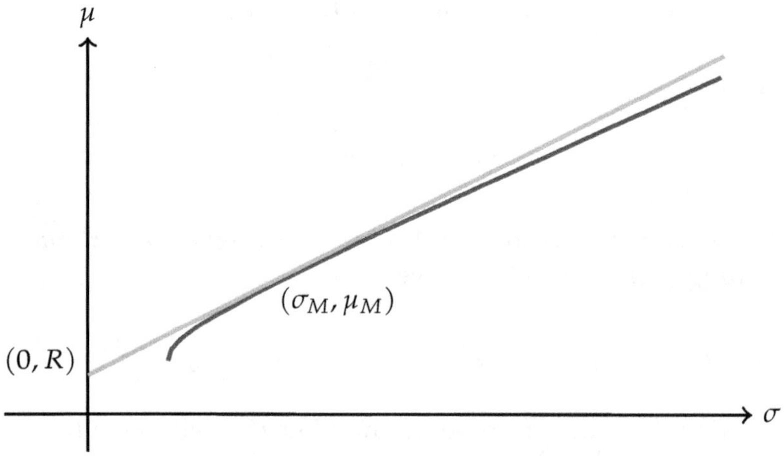

Figure 6. Capital Market Line and Markowitz Bullet.

Remark 8. *Observe that $\Sigma^{-1}(\mathbb{E}[\widehat{S}_1] - R\widehat{S}_0)$ is proportional to the optimal portfolio in (61). Thus, condition (70) means that any optimal portfolio should have an positive initial cost. Note that (70) also implies (67).*

The affine structure of the solutions is summarized in the following one fund theorem Sharpe (1964); Tobin (1958).

Theorem 9. (One Fund Theorem) *Assume that the financial market S_t has no nontrivial riskless portfolio. Moreover, assume that condition (70) holds. All the optimal portfolios in the CAPM model (55) are generalized convex combinations of the riskless bond and the market portfolio $x_M = (0, (\mathbb{E}[\widehat{S}_1^\top] - R\widehat{S}_0^\top)\Sigma^{-1}/(\beta - \gamma R))^\top$, which corresponds to (σ_M, μ_M). The capital market line is tangent to the boundary of the Markowitz bullet at the coordinates of the market portfolio (σ_M, μ_M) and intercepts the μ-axis at $(0, R)$ (see Figure 6).*

Alternatively, we can write the slope of the capital market line as

$$\sqrt{\Delta} = \frac{\mu_M - R}{\sigma_M}. \quad (73)$$

This quantity is called the *price of risk* and we can rewrite the equation for the capital market line (66) as

$$\mu = R + \frac{\mu_M - R}{\sigma_M}\sigma. \tag{74}$$

5. Affine Efficient Frontier for Positive Homogeneous Risk Measure

The affine dependence of the efficient portfolio on the return μ observed in the CAPM still holds when the standard deviation is replaced by the more general deviation measure (see Rockafellar et al. (2006)). In this section, we derive this affine structure using the general framework discussed in Section 3 and provide a proof different from that of Rockafellar et al. (2006). Moreover, we provide a sufficient condition for the existence of the master fund in the one fund theorem generalizing condition $\beta - R\gamma > 0$ (see (70)) for the existence of the market portfolio in the CAPM model. We also construct a counter-example showing that the two fund theorem (Theorem 7) fails in this setting. Let us consider a risk measure $\mathfrak{r}$ that satisfies (r1), (r1n), (r2) and (r3) in Assumption 2 and the related problem of finding efficient portfolios becomes

$$\begin{aligned} \min_{x \in \mathbb{R}^{M+1}} \quad & \mathfrak{r}(x) = \widehat{\mathfrak{r}}(\widehat{x}) \\ \text{Subject to} \quad & \mathbb{E}[S_1^\top x] \geq \mu,\ S_0^\top x = 1. \end{aligned} \tag{75}$$

Since, for $\mu = R$, there is an obvious solution $x(R) = (1, \widehat{0}^\top)^\top$ corresponding to $\mathfrak{r}(x(R)) = \widehat{\mathfrak{r}}(\widehat{0}) = 0$, we have $r_{\min} = 0$ and $\mu_{\min} = R$. In what follows, we will only consider $\mu > R$. Moreover, we note that for $\widehat{\mathfrak{r}}$ satisfying the positive homogeneous property (r3) in Assumption 2, $\widehat{y} \in \partial\widehat{\mathfrak{r}}(\widehat{x})$ implies that

$$\widehat{\mathfrak{r}}(\widehat{x}) = \langle \widehat{y}, \widehat{x} \rangle. \tag{76}$$

In fact, for any $t \in (-1, 1)$,

$$t\widehat{\mathfrak{r}}(\widehat{x}) = \widehat{\mathfrak{r}}((1+t)\widehat{x}) - \widehat{\mathfrak{r}}(\widehat{x}) \geq t\langle \widehat{y}, \widehat{x} \rangle, \tag{77}$$

and (76) follows. Now we can state and prove the theorem on affine dependence of the efficient portfolio on the return μ.

Theorem 10. (Affine Efficient Frontier for Positive Homogeneous Risk Measures) *Assume that the risk measure $\mathfrak{r}$ satisfies assumptions (r1), (r1n), (r2) and (r3) in Assumption 2 with $A = \{x \in \mathbb{R}^{M+1} : S_0^\top x = 1\}$ and Assumption 4 (b) holds. Furthermore, assume*

$$\mathbb{E}[\widehat{S}_1] - R\widehat{S}_0 \neq \widehat{0}. \tag{78}$$

Then, there exists an efficient portfolio x^1 corresponding to $(r_1, \mu_1) := (\mathfrak{r}(x^1), R+1)$ on the efficient frontier for problem (75) such that the efficient frontier for problem (75) in the risk-expected return space is a straight line that passes through the points (0,R) corresponding to a portfolio of pure bond $(1, \widehat{0}^\top)^\top$ and (r_1, μ_1) corresponding to the portfolio x^1, respectively. Moreover, the straight line connecting $(1, \widehat{0}^\top)^\top$ and x^1 in the portfolio space, namely for $\mu \geq R$,

$$x(\mu) = (\mu_1 - \mu)(1, \widehat{0}^\top)^\top + (\mu - R)x^1 \tag{79}$$

represents a set of efficient portfolios for (75) that corresponds to

$$(\gamma(\mu), \mu) = ((\mu - R)r_1, \mu) \tag{80}$$

in the risk-expected return space (see Definition 5 and (19)).

Proof. The Lagrangian of this convex programming problem (75) is

$$L(x,\lambda) := \mathfrak{r}(x) + \lambda_1(\mu - x^\top \mathbb{E}[S_1]) + \lambda_2(1 - x^\top S_0), \tag{81}$$

where $\lambda_1 \geq 0$ and $\lambda_2 \in \mathbb{R}$.

Condition (78) implies that there exists some $\bar{m} \in \{1,2,\dots,M\}$, such that $\mathbb{E}[S_1^{\bar{m}}] \neq RS_0^{\bar{m}}$. Hence, for any μ, there exists a portfolio of the form $y = (y_0, 0, \dots, 0, y_{\bar{m}}, 0, \dots, 0)^\top$ satisfying

$$\begin{bmatrix} \mathbb{E}[S_1^\top y] \\ S_0^\top y \end{bmatrix} = \begin{bmatrix} Ry_0 + \mathbb{E}[S_1^{\bar{m}}]y_{\bar{m}} \\ y_0 + S_0^{\bar{m}} y_{\bar{m}} \end{bmatrix} = \begin{bmatrix} R & \mathbb{E}[S_1^{\bar{m}}] \\ 1 & S_0^{\bar{m}} \end{bmatrix} \begin{bmatrix} y_0 \\ y_{\bar{m}} \end{bmatrix} = \begin{bmatrix} \mu \\ 1 \end{bmatrix} \tag{82}$$

because the matrix in (82) is invertible. Thus, for any $\mu \geq R$, Assumption 4 (b) with $A = \{x \in \mathbb{R}^{M+1} : S_0^\top x = 1\}$ and condition (78) ensure the existence of an optimal solution to problem (75).

Denoting one of those solutions by $x(\mu)$ (may not be unique), we have

$$\gamma(\mu) = \mathfrak{r}(x(\mu)) = \hat{\mathfrak{r}}(\hat{x}(\mu)). \tag{83}$$

Fixing $\mu_1 = R + 1 > R$, denote $x^1 = x(\mu_1)$. Then,

$$\lambda_1 \mathbb{E}[S_1] + \lambda_2 S_0 \in \partial \mathfrak{r}(x^1). \tag{84}$$

Since $\mathfrak{r}$ is independent of x_0, we have

$$\lambda_1 \mathbb{E}[S_1^0] + \lambda_2 S_0^0 = 0 \text{ or } \lambda_2 = -\lambda_1 R. \tag{85}$$

Substituting (85) into (84) we have

$$\lambda_1 \mathbb{E}[\hat{S}_1 - R\hat{S}_0] \in \partial \hat{r}(\hat{x}^1) \tag{86}$$

so that, for all $\hat{x} \in \mathbb{R}^M$,

$$\hat{\mathfrak{r}}(\hat{x}) - \hat{\mathfrak{r}}(\hat{x}^1) \geq \lambda_1 \mathbb{E}[(\hat{S}_1 - R\hat{S}_0)^\top (\hat{x} - \hat{x}^1)] = \lambda_1(\mathbb{E}[(\hat{S}_1 - R\hat{S}_0)^\top \hat{x}] - (\mu_1 - R)) \tag{87}$$

because, at the optimal solution $\hat{x}^1$, the constraint is binding. Using (r3), it follows from (76) and (86) that

$$\hat{\mathfrak{r}}(\hat{x}^1) = \lambda_1 \mathbb{E}[(\hat{S}_1 - R\hat{S}_0)^\top \hat{x}^1] = \lambda_1(\mu_1 - R) = \lambda_1. \tag{88}$$

Thus, we can write (87) as

$$\hat{\mathfrak{r}}(\hat{x}) \geq \hat{\mathfrak{r}}(\hat{x}^1) \mathbb{E}[(\hat{S}_1 - R\hat{S}_0)^\top \hat{x}]. \tag{89}$$

For $t \geq 0$, define the homotopy between $x^0 := (1, \hat{0}^\top)^\top$ and x^1

$$x^t := (tx_0^1 + (1-t), t\hat{x}^1). \tag{90}$$

We can verify that $S_0^\top x^t = 1$ and $\mathbb{E}[S_1^\top x^t] = R + t$ so that

$$\mathbb{E}[(S_1 - RS_0)^\top x^t] = t. \tag{91}$$

On the other hand, it follows from assumptions (r1) and (r3) that

$$\mathfrak{r}(x^t) = \widehat{\mathfrak{r}}(t\widehat{x}^1) = t\,\widehat{\mathfrak{r}}(\widehat{x}^1). \tag{92}$$

Thus, for any x satisfying $S_0^\top x = 1$ and $\mathbb{E}[S_1^\top x] \geq R + t$, it follows from (89) that

$$\widehat{\mathfrak{r}}(\widehat{x}) \geq \widehat{\mathfrak{r}}(\widehat{x}^1)t. \tag{93}$$

For any $\mu > R$, letting $t_\mu := \mu - R$, we have $\mu = R + t_\mu$ and hence $x^{t_\mu} = x(\mu)$. Thus, by inequality (93), we have $\widehat{\mathfrak{r}}(\widehat{x}(\mu)) \geq t_\mu \widehat{\mathfrak{r}}(\widehat{x}^1)$. On the other hand, $x(\mu)$ is an efficient portfolio implies that $\widehat{\mathfrak{r}}(\widehat{x}(\mu)) \leq \widehat{\mathfrak{r}}(\widehat{x}^{t_\mu}) = t_\mu \widehat{\mathfrak{r}}(\widehat{x}^1)$ yielding equality

$$\gamma(\mu) = \widehat{\mathfrak{r}}(\widehat{x}(\mu)) = \widehat{\mathfrak{r}}(\widehat{x}^{t_\mu}) = t_\mu \widehat{\mathfrak{r}}(\widehat{x}^1) = (\mu - R)\widehat{\mathfrak{r}}(\widehat{x}^1), \text{ for } \mu \geq R. \tag{94}$$

In other words, $\gamma(\mu)$ is an affine function in μ. In addition, we conclude that points $(\gamma(\mu), \mu)$ on this efficient frontier correspond to efficient portfolios

$$x(\mu) = x^{t_\mu} = \left((\mu - R)x_0^1 + \mu_1 - \mu, (\mu - R)\widehat{x}^1\right) = (\mu_1 - \mu)(1, \widehat{0}^\top)^\top + (\mu - R)x^1 \tag{95}$$

as an affine mapping of the parameter μ into the portfolio space showing (79).

In addition, using r_1, we can write (94) as

$$\gamma(\mu) = r_1(\mu - R). \tag{96}$$

That is to say, the efficient frontier of (75) in the risk-expected return space is given by the parameterized straight line (80). □

Corollary 3. *In Theorem 10, if instead of (r3) the stronger condition (r3s) holds, then the portfolio x^1 constructed there is unique and, therefore, for each fixed $\mu \geq R$, the efficient portfolio $x(\mu)$ in (79) is unique.*

Proof. Apply Theorem 5 with condition (c3). □

Theorem 10 and Corollary 3 manifest a full generalization of Theorem 8 on the capital market pricing model to positive homogeneous risk measures. Note that the necessary conditions on the financial market in (67) and (78) are the same.

Remark 9. *(a) Clearly, x^{t_R} corresponds to the portfolio $(1, \widehat{0}^\top)^\top$ with $\gamma(R) = \widehat{\mathfrak{r}}(\widehat{0}) = 0$. If $x_0^1 < 1$, setting $\mu_M := \frac{\mu_1 - Rx_0^1}{1 - x_0^1}$ and $r_M := \gamma(\mu_M) = \widehat{\mathfrak{r}}(\widehat{x}^1)/(1 - x_0^1)$, we see that (r_M, μ_M) on the efficient frontier corresponds to a purely risky efficient portfolio of (75)*

$$x_M := x^{t_{\mu_M}} = \left(0, \frac{1}{1 - x_0^1}(\widehat{x}^1)^\top\right)^\top. \tag{97}$$

Since x_M belongs to the image of the affine mapping in (95), the family of efficient portfolios as described by the affine mapping in (95) contains both the pure bond $(1, \widehat{0}^\top)^\top$ and the portfolio x_M that consists only of purely risky assets. In fact, we can represent the affine mapping in (95) as a parametrized line passing through $(1, \widehat{0}^\top)^\top$ and x_M as

$$x^{t_\mu} := \left(1 - \frac{\mu - R}{\mu_M - R}\right)(1, \widehat{0}^\top)^\top + \frac{\mu - R}{\mu_M - R}x_M, \text{ for } \mu \geq R, \tag{98}$$

which is a similar representation of the efficient portfolios as (79). The portfolio x_M is called a master fund *in Rockafellar et al. (2006). When $\mathfrak{r} = \sigma$, it is the* market portfolio *in the CAPM. For a general risk measure $\mathfrak{r}$*

satisfying conditions (r1), (r1n), (r2) and (r3) in Assumption 2, the master funds x_M are not necessarily unique. However, all master funds correspond to the same point (r_M, μ_M) in the risk-expected return space.

(b) We can also consider problem (75) on the set of admissible portfolios of purely risky assets, namely $\mathcal{G}_{eff}(\mathfrak{r}, id; \{S_0^\top x = 1, x_0 = 0\})$. Then, similar to the relationship between the Markowitz efficient frontier and the capital market line, it follows from Theorem 10 that

$$\mathcal{G}(\mathfrak{r}, id; \{S_0^\top x = 1, x_0 = 0\}) \cap \mathcal{G}_{eff}(\mathfrak{r}, id; \{S_0^\top x = 1\}) = \{(r_M, \mu_M)\}, \tag{99}$$

as illustrated in Figure 7.

(c) If $x_0^1 = 1$, then the efficient portfolios in (79) are related to μ in a much simpler fashion

$$(1, \widehat{0}^\top)^\top + (\mu - R)(0, (\widehat{x}^1)^\top)^\top. \tag{100}$$

There is no master fund as observed in Rockafellar et al. (2006) in this case. In the language of Rockafellar et al. (2006), the portfolio x^1 is called a basic fund. *Thus, Theorem 10 recovers the results in Theorem 2 and Theorem 3 in Rockafellar et al. (2006) with a different proof and a weaker condition (condition (78) is weaker than (A2) on page 752 of Rockafellar et al.). However, Corollary 3 is a significant improvement yielding uniqueness in case (r3s) holds. This will help below when we derive a sufficient condition for the existence of a master fund, which is solely depending on the risk measure and the financial market.*

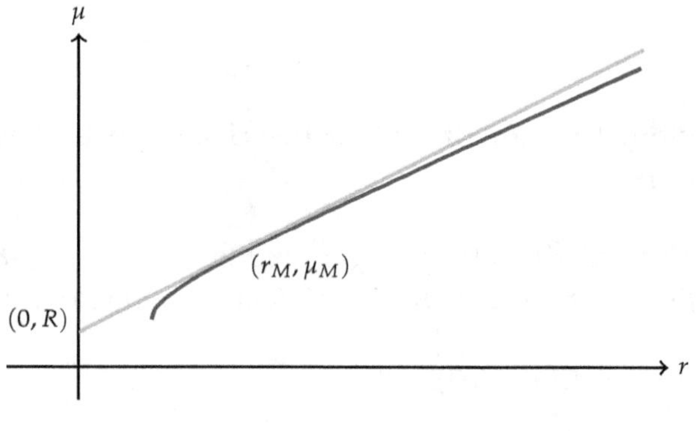

Figure 7. Capital Market Line for (75) when $1 - x_0^1 > 0$.

We see in Remark 9 that the existence of a master fund depends on whether or not $x_0^1 < 1$. Below, we characterize this condition in terms of $f(\widehat{x}) := [\widehat{\mathfrak{r}}(\widehat{x})]^2/2$ and its Fenchel conjugate $f^* : \mathbb{R}^M \to \mathbb{R}$, defined by $f^*(\widehat{y}) := \sup_{\widehat{x} \in \mathbb{R}^M}\{\langle \widehat{y}, \widehat{x}\rangle - f(\widehat{x})\}$.

Theorem 11. *Under the conditions of Corollary 3, assuming that f^* is differentiable at $\mathbb{E}[\widehat{S}_1 - R\widehat{S}_0]$, a master fund exists if and only if $\widehat{S}_0^\top \nabla f^*(\mathbb{E}[\widehat{S}_1 - R\widehat{S}_0]) > 0$.*

Proof. Combining (86) and (88) and using the chain rule, we can see that

$$[\widehat{\mathfrak{r}}(\widehat{x}^1)]^2 \mathbb{E}[\widehat{S}_1 - R\widehat{S}_0] \in \partial f(\widehat{x}^1). \tag{101}$$

By virtue of the Fenchel–Young equality (see (Carr and Zhu forthcoming, Proposition 1.3.1)), we have

$$f(\widehat{x}^1) + f^*([\widehat{\mathfrak{r}}(\widehat{x}^1)]^2 \mathbb{E}[\widehat{S}_1 - R\widehat{S}_0]) = \langle [\widehat{\mathfrak{r}}(\widehat{x}^1)]^2 \mathbb{E}[\widehat{S}_1 - R\widehat{S}_0], \widehat{x}^1\rangle, \tag{102}$$

and

$$\nabla f^*([\widehat{\mathfrak{r}}(\widehat{x}^1)]^2 \mathbb{E}[\widehat{S}_1 - R\widehat{S}_0]) = \widehat{x}^1. \tag{103}$$

It follows that $x_0^1 < 1$ is equivalent to

$$0 < 1 - x_0^1 = \widehat{S}_0^\top \widehat{x}^1 = \widehat{S}_0^\top \nabla f^*([\widehat{\mathfrak{r}}(\widehat{x}^1)]^2 \mathbb{E}[\widehat{S}_1 - R\widehat{S}_0]) = [\widehat{\mathfrak{r}}(\widehat{x}^1)]^4 \widehat{S}_0^\top \nabla f^*(\mathbb{E}[\widehat{S}_1 - R\widehat{S}_0]). \tag{104}$$

The last equality is because $f(t\widehat{x}) = t^2 f(\widehat{x})$ implies $f^*(t\widehat{y}) = t^2 f^*(\widehat{y})$. □

Remark 10. *We refer to Borwein and Vanderwerff (2009) for conditions ensuring the differentiability of f^* in Theorem 11. In the CAPM model $f(\widehat{x}) = \frac{1}{2}\widehat{x}^\top \Sigma \widehat{x}$ and $f^*(\widehat{y}) = \frac{1}{2}\widehat{y}^\top \Sigma^{-1}\widehat{y}$. Thus, the master fund exists if and only if*

$$\beta - R\gamma = \widehat{S}_0^\top \Sigma^{-1} \mathbb{E}[\widehat{S}_1 - R\widehat{S}_0] > 0,$$

which exactly recovers the condition in (70) for the existence of a market portfolio in the one fund theorem (cf. Theorem 9).

In general, for a risk measure with (r1), (r1n) and (r3s), if $f(\widehat{x}) = [\mathfrak{r}(\widehat{x})]^2/2$ is C^2, then $f(\widehat{x}) = \frac{1}{2}\widehat{x}^\top \widehat{\Sigma}\widehat{x}$ where $\widehat{\Sigma}$ is the Hessian of f at $\hat{0}$. Thus, a criterion for the existence of a master fund similar to (70) holds with Σ replaced by $\widehat{\Sigma}$.

Another very useful case is $\widehat{\mathfrak{r}}(\widehat{x}) = \|\widehat{x}\|_{\max}$. It is not hard to show that the conjugate of $f(\widehat{x}) = \|\widehat{x}\|_{\max}^2/2$ is $f^*(\widehat{y}) = \|\widehat{y}\|_1^2/2$. In fact, it follows from the Cauchy inequality that $\|\widehat{x}\|_{\max}^2/2 + \|\widehat{y}\|_1^2/2 \geq \langle \widehat{x}, \widehat{y}\rangle$. Thus,

$$\|\widehat{y}\|_1^2/2 \geq f^*(\widehat{y}). \tag{105}$$

On the other hand, for any $\widehat{y} = (y_1, \ldots, y_M)^\top$, defining $\widehat{x}_t := t(\mathrm{sgn}(y_1), \ldots, \mathrm{sgn}(y_M))^\top$, we have

$$\langle \widehat{x}_t, \widehat{y}\rangle - \|\widehat{x}_t\|_{\max}^2/2 = t\|\widehat{y}\|_1 - t^2/2. \tag{106}$$

The maximum of the expression in (106) as a function of t is $\|\widehat{y}\|_1^2/2$. It follows that

$$\|\widehat{y}\|_1^2/2 \leq f^*(\widehat{y}). \tag{107}$$

Combining (105) and (107), we arrive at $\|\widehat{y}\|_1^2/2 = f^*(\widehat{y})$. This example illustrates that using $\widehat{\mathfrak{r}}^2/2$ and its conjugate often helps. In fact, f^* is differentiable everywhere except for the coordinate axises. However, $\|\cdot\|_{\max}^*$ is an indicator function on the closed set $\{\widehat{y} : \|\widehat{y}\|_1 \leq 1\}$ (see (Carr and Zhu forthcoming, Proposition 2.4.2)), whose derivative is 0 at any differentiable point and, therefore, is not useful for our purpose.

Since the standard deviation satisfies Assumptions (r1), (r1n), (r2) and (r3s), the result above is a generalization of the relationship between the CAPM model and the Markowitz portfolio theory. We note that the standard deviation is not the only risk measure that satisfies these assumptions. For example, some forms of approximation to the expected drawdowns also satisfy these assumptions (cf. Maier-Paape and Zhu (2017)).

Theorem 10 and Corollary 3 are a full generalization of Theorem 8 on the CAPM and Theorem 11 is a generalization of the one fund theorem in Theorem 9. On the other hand, in Rockafellar et al. (2006), footnote 10, it has been noted that a similar generalization of the two fund theorem (Theorem 7) is not to be expected. We construct a concrete counter-example below.

Example 3. (Counter-example to a Generalized Two Fund Theorem) *Let us consider, for example,*

$$\min_{\widehat{x} \in \mathbb{R}^3} \quad \widehat{\mathfrak{r}}(\widehat{x}) \qquad \text{Subject to} \quad \mathbb{E}[\widehat{S}_1^\top \widehat{x}] \geq \mu, \; \widehat{S}_0^\top \widehat{x} = 1, \tag{108}$$

with $M = 3$.

Choose all $S_0^m = 1$*, so that* $\widehat{S}_0^\top \widehat{x} = 1$ *is* $x_1 + x_2 + x_3 = 1$*. Choose the payoff* S_1 *such that* $\mathbb{E}[\widehat{S}_1^\top \widehat{x}] = x_1$ *so that* $x_1 = \mu$ *at the optimal solution. Finally, let us construct* $\widehat{\mathfrak{r}}(\widehat{x})$ *so that the optimal solution* $\widehat{x}(\mu)$ *is not affine in* μ*.*

We do so by constructing a convex set G with $0 \in \text{int}G$ *(interior of G) and then set* $\widehat{\mathfrak{r}}(\widehat{x}) = 1$ *for* $\widehat{x} \in \partial G$ *(boundary of G) and extend* $\widehat{\mathfrak{r}}$ *to be positive homogeneous. Then, (r1), (r1n), (r2) and (r3) are satisfied.*

Now, let us specify G. Take the convex hull of the set $[-5,5] \times [-1,1] \times [-1,1]$ *and five other points. One point is* $E = (10,0,0)^\top$ *and the other four points A, B, C and D, are the corner points of a square that lies in the plane* $x_1 = 9$ *and has unit side length. To obtain that square, take the standard square with unit side length in* $x_1 = 9$*, i.e., the square with corner points* $(9, \pm 1/2, \pm 1/2)^\top$ *and rotate this square by 30 degrees counter clockwise in the* x_2x_3*-plane. Doing some calculation, one gets:*

$$\begin{aligned} A &= (9, (-1+\sqrt{3})/4, (1+\sqrt{3})/4)^\top,\ B = (9, (-1-\sqrt{3})/4, (-1+\sqrt{3})/4)^\top, \\ C &= (9, (1-\sqrt{3})/4, -(1+\sqrt{3})/4))^\top,\ D = (9, (1+\sqrt{3})/4), (1-\sqrt{3})/4))^\top. \end{aligned}$$

Obviously for $\mu = 1$*, the optimal solution is* $\widehat{x}(1) = (1,0,0)^\top$ *with* $\widehat{\mathfrak{r}}(\widehat{x}(1)) = 1/10$*. For* $\mu = 1 + \epsilon$ *with* $\epsilon > 0$ *small, we have* $\widehat{x}(1+\epsilon) = (1+\epsilon, \epsilon\sqrt{3}(+1-\sqrt{3})/6, \epsilon\sqrt{3}(-1-\sqrt{3})/6))^\top$ *(they lie on the ray through a point on the convex combination of C and* $(10,0,0)^\top$*), and, for* $\mu = 1 + d$ *with* $d > 0$ *large, we have* $\widehat{x}(1+d) = (1+d, -d/2, -d/2)^\top$ *(they lie on the ray through a point on the set* $\{(x_1, -1, -1)^\top : x_1 \in (2,5)\}$*. Therefore,* $\widehat{x}(\mu)$ *cannot be affine in* μ*.*

6. Growth Optimal and Leverage Space Portfolio

Growth portfolio theory is proposed by Lintner (1965) and is also related to the work of Kelly (1956). It is equivalent to maximizing the expected log utility:

$$\begin{aligned} \max_{x \in \mathbb{R}^{M+1}} \quad & \mathbb{E}[\ln(S_1^\top x)] \\ \text{Subject to} \quad & S_0^\top x = 1. \end{aligned} \tag{109}$$

Remark 11. *Problem (109) is equivalent to*

$$\max_{\widehat{x} \in \mathbb{R}^M} \mathbb{E}[\ln(R + (\widehat{S}_1 - R\widehat{S}_0)^\top \widehat{x})]. \tag{110}$$

The following theorem establishes the existence of the growth optimal portfolio as a corollary of our results in Section 3. This theorem reconfirms previous results in Hermes and Maier-Paape (2017) with somewhat different conditions and a shorter proof.

Theorem 12. (Growth Optimal Portfolio) *Assume that the financial market* S_t *of Definition 1 has no nontrivial riskless portfolio. Then, problem (109) has a unique optimal portfolio, which is often referred to as the* growth optimal portfolio *and is denoted* $\kappa \in \mathbb{R}^{M+1}$*.*

To prove Theorem 12, we need the following lemma.

Lemma 2. *Assume that the financial market* S_t *of Definition 1 has no nontrivial riskless portfolio. Let u be a utility function satisfying (u3) in Assumption 3. Then, for any* $\mu \in \mathbb{R}$*,*

$$\{x \in \mathbb{R}^{M+1} : \mathbb{E}[u(S_1^\top x)] \geq \mu, S_0^\top x = 1\} \tag{111}$$

is compact (and possibly empty in some cases).

Proof. Since, by Assumption 3, u is upper semi-continuous, the set in (111) is closed. Thus, we need only to show it is also bounded. Assume the contrary that there exists a sequence of portfolios x^n with

$$S_0^\top x^n = 1 \tag{112}$$

and $\|x^n\| \to \infty$ satisfying

$$\mathbb{E}[u(S_1^\top x^n)] \geq \mu. \tag{113}$$

Equation (112) implies that $\|\widehat{x}^n\| \to \infty$. Then, without loss of generality, we may assume $x^n/\|\widehat{x}^n\|$ converges to $x^* = (x_0^*, (\widehat{x}^*)^\top)^\top$ where $\|\widehat{x}^*\| = 1$. Condition (u3) and (113) for arbitrary $\mu \in \mathbb{R}$ imply that, for each natural number n,

$$S_1^\top x^n \geq 0. \tag{114}$$

Dividing (112) and (114) by $\|\widehat{x}^n\|$ and taking limits as $n \to \infty$, we derive $S_0^\top x^* = 0$ and $S_1^\top x^* \geq 0$. Thus, we have

$$(\widehat{S}_1 - R\widehat{S}_0)^\top \widehat{x}^* \geq 0, \tag{115}$$

and thus x^* is a nontrivial riskless portfolio, which is a contradiction. □

Proof of Theorem 12. We can verify that the utility function $u = \ln$ satisfies conditions (u1), (u2s), (u3) and (u4). In addition, $\{x : \mathbb{E}[\ln(S_1^\top x)] \geq \ln(R), S_0^\top x = 1\} \neq \emptyset$ because it contains $(1, \widehat{0}^\top)^\top$. Thus, Lemma 2 implies that problem (109) has at least one solution and

$$\mu_{\max} = \max_{x \in \mathbb{R}^{M+1}} \{\mathbb{E}[\ln(S_1^\top x)] : S_0^\top x = 1\}$$

is finite. By Proposition 6, $x \mapsto \mathbb{E}[\ln(S_1^\top x)]$ is strictly concave. Thus, problem (109) has a unique optimal portfolio. □

Assuming one repeatedly invests in the identical one period financial market, the growth optimal portfolio has the nice property that it provides the fastest compounded growth of the capital. By Remark 7(b), it is independent of any risk measures. In the special case that all the risky assets are representing a certain gaming outcome, κ is the Kelly allocation in Kelly (1956). However, the growth portfolio is seldomly used in investment practice for being too risky. The book (MacLean et al. 2009) provides an excellent collection of papers with chronological research on this subject. These observations motivated Vince (2009) to introduce his *leverage space portfolio* to scale back from the growth optimal portfolio. Recently, De Prado et al. (2013); Vince and Zhu (2015) further introduce systematical methods to scale back from the growth optimal portfolio by, among other ideas, explicitly accounting for limiting a certain risk measure. The analysis in Vince and Zhu (2015) and De Prado et al. (2013) can be phrased as solving

$$\gamma(\mu) := \inf\{\mathfrak{r}(x) = \widehat{\mathfrak{r}}(\widehat{x}) : \mathbb{E}[\ln(S_1^\top x)] \geq \mu, S_0^\top x = 1\}, \tag{116}$$

where $\mathfrak{r}$ is a risk measure that satisfies conditions (r1) and (r2). Alternatively, to derive the efficient frontier, we can also consider

$$\nu(r) := \sup\{\mathbb{E}[\ln(S_1^\top x)] : \mathfrak{r}(x) = \widehat{\mathfrak{r}}(\widehat{x}) \leq r, S_0^\top x = 1\}. \tag{117}$$

Applying Proposition 8, Theorem 5 and Remark 7 to the set of admissible portfolios $A = \{x \in \mathbb{R}^{M+1} : S_0^\top x = 1\}$, we derive:

Theorem 13. (Leverage Space Portfolio and Risk Measure) *We assume that the financial market S_t in Definition 1 has no nontrivial riskless portfolio and that the risk measure $\mathfrak{r}$ satisfies conditions (r1), (r1n) and (r2). Then, the problem*

$$\sup_{x \in \mathbb{R}^{M+1}} \quad \mathbb{E}[\ln(S_1^\top x)] \tag{118}$$
$$\text{subject to} \quad \mathfrak{r}(x) = \hat{\mathfrak{r}}(\hat{x}) \leq r, S_0^\top x = 1$$

has a bounded efficient frontier that can be parameterized as follows:

(a) problem (116) defines $\gamma(\mu) : [\ln(R), \mu_\kappa] \to \mathbb{R}$ as a continuous increasing convex function, where $\mu_\kappa := \mathbb{E}[\ln(S_1^\top \kappa)]$ and κ is the optimal growth portfolio. Moreover, problem (116) has a continuous path of unique solutions $z(\mu) := x(\gamma(\mu), \mu)$ that maps the interval $[\ln(R), \mu_\kappa]$ into a curve in the leverage portfolio space $\mathbb{R}^{M+1}$. Finally, $z(\ln(R)) = (1, \hat{0}^\top)^\top$, $z(\mu_\kappa)) = \kappa$, $\gamma(\ln(R)) = \hat{\mathfrak{r}}(\hat{0}) = 0$ and $\gamma(\mu_\kappa) = \mathfrak{r}(\kappa)$.

(b) problem (117) defines $\nu(r) : [0, \mathfrak{r}(\kappa)] \to \mathbb{R}$ as a continuous increasing concave function, where κ is the optimal growth portfolio. Moreover, problem (117) has a continuous path of unique solutions $y(r) := x(r, \nu(r))$ that maps the interval $[0, \mathfrak{r}(\kappa)]$ into a curve in the leverage portfolio space $\mathbb{R}^{M+1}$. Finally, $y(0) = (1, \hat{0}^\top)^\top$, $y(\mathfrak{r}(\kappa)) = \kappa$, $\nu(0) = \ln(R)$ and $\nu(\mathfrak{r}(\kappa)) = \mu_\kappa$.

Proof. Note that Assumption 4 (a) holds due to Lemma 2 and (c2) in Theorem 5 is also satisfied. Then, (a) follows straightforwardly from Theorem 5, where $\mu_{\max} = \mu_\kappa$ and $\mu_{\min} = \ln(R)$ are finite and attained and (b) follows from Theorem 5 with $r_{\min} = 0$ and $r_{\max} = \mathfrak{r}(\kappa)$. □

Remark 12. *Theorem 13 relates the leverage portfolio space theory to the framework setup in Section 3. It becomes clear that each risk measure satisfying conditions (r1), (r1n) and (r2) generates a path in the leverage portfolio space connecting the portfolio of a pure riskless bond to the growth optimal portfolio. Theorem 13 also tells us that different risk measures usually correspond to different paths in the portfolio space. Many commonly used risk measures satisfy conditions (r1) and (r2). The curve $z(\mu)$ provides a pathway to reduce risk exposure along the efficient frontier in the risk-expected log utility space. As observed in De Prado et al. (2013); Vince and Zhu (2015), when investments have only a finite time horizon, then there are additional interesting points along the path $z(\mu)$ such as the inflection point and the point that maximizes the return/risk ratio. Both of which provide further landmarks for investors.*

Similar to the previous sections, we can also consider the related problem of using only portfolios involving risky assets, i.e.,

$$\max_{\hat{x} \in \mathbb{R}^M} \quad \mathbb{E}[\ln(\hat{S}_1^\top \hat{x})] \tag{119}$$
$$\text{subject to} \quad \hat{S}_0^\top \hat{x} = 1.$$

Theorem 14. (Existence of Solutions) *Suppose that*

$$S_1^i(\omega) > 0, \ \forall \omega \in \Omega, i = 1, \ldots, M. \tag{120}$$

Then, problem (119) has a solution.

Proof. As in the proof of Theorem 13, we can see that Assumption 4 (a) holds due to Lemma 2. Observe that, for $\hat{x}^* = (1/M, 1/M, \ldots, 1/M)^\top$, we get from (120) that $\mathbb{E}[\ln(\hat{S}_1^\top \hat{x}^*)]$ is finite. Then, we can directly apply Theorem 5 with $A = \{x \in \mathbb{R}^{M+1} : S_0^\top x = 1, x_0 = 0\}$. □

With the help of Theorem 14, we can conclude that problem

$$\begin{aligned} \sup_{\hat{x}\in\mathbb{R}^M} \quad & \mathbb{E}[\ln(\hat{S}_1^\top \hat{x})] \\ \text{subject to} \quad & \hat{\mathfrak{r}}(\hat{x}) \le r, \hat{S}_0^\top \hat{x} = 1 \end{aligned} \tag{121}$$

generates an efficient frontier as well (comparable to the Markowitz bullet for $u = id$). However, due to the involvement of the log utility function, the relative location of efficient frontiers stemming from (118) and (121) may have several different configurations. The following is an example.

Example 4. *Let $M = 1$. Consider a sample space $\Omega = \{0,1\}$ with probability $P(0) = 0.45$ and $P(1) = 0.55$ and a financial market involving a riskless bond with $R = 1$ and one risky asset specified by $S_0^1 = 1$, $S_1^1(0) = 0.5$ and $S_1^1(1) = 1 + \alpha$ with $\alpha > 9/22$ so that $\mathbb{E}[S_1^1] > S_0^1$. Use the risk measure $\mathfrak{r}_1(x_0, x_1) = |x_1|$ (which is an approximation of the drawdown cf. Vince and Zhu (2015)). Then, it is easy to calculate that the efficient frontier corresponding to (118) is*

$$\nu(r) = 0.55\ln(1+\alpha r) + 0.45\ln(1-0.5r), r \in [0, r_{\max}^\alpha], \tag{122}$$

where $r_{\max}^\alpha = (22\alpha - 9)/20\alpha$. On the other hand, the efficient frontier stemming from (121) is a single point $\{(1, \nu(1))\}$, where $\nu(1) = 0.55\ln(1+\alpha) - 0.45\ln(2)$.

When $\alpha \in (9/22, 9/2)$, the two efficient frontiers corresponding to (118) and (121) have no common points (see Figure 8). However, when $\alpha \ge 9/2$, $\mathcal{G}_{eff}(\mathfrak{r}_1, \ln; \{S_0^\top x = 1, x_0 = 0\}) \subset \mathcal{G}_{eff}(\mathfrak{r}_1, \ln; \{S_0^\top x = 1\})$ (see Figure 9). In particular, when $\alpha = 9/2$, $\mathcal{G}_{eff}(\mathfrak{r}_1, \ln; \{S_0^\top x = 1, x_0 = 0\})$ coincides with the point on $\mathcal{G}_{eff}(\mathfrak{r}_1, \ln; \{S_0^\top x = 1\})$ corresponding to the growth optimal portfolio as illustrated in Figure 10.

In fact, a far more common restriction to the set of admissible portfolios are limits of risk. For this example, if, for instance, we restrict the risk by $\mathfrak{r}_1(x) \le 0.5$, then we will create a shared efficient frontier from (118) when $\mathfrak{r}$ is a priori restricted (see Figure 11).

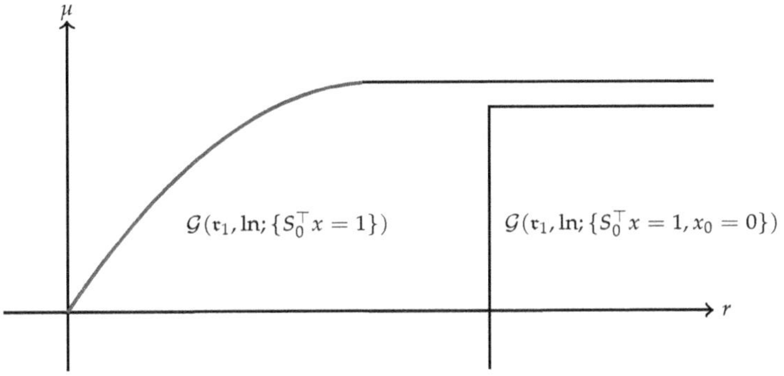

Figure 8. Separated efficient frontiers.

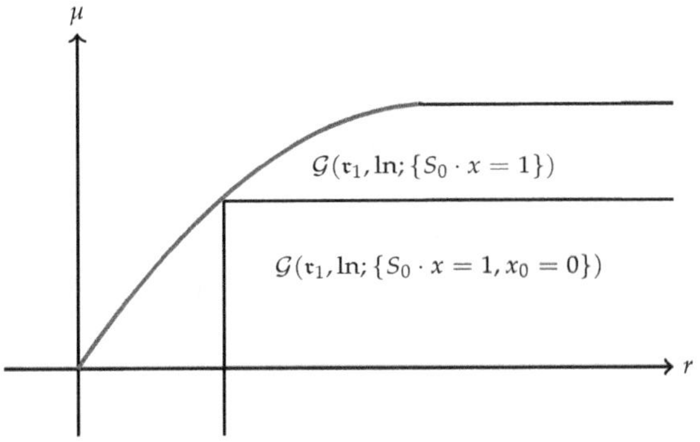

Figure 9. Touching efficient frontiers.

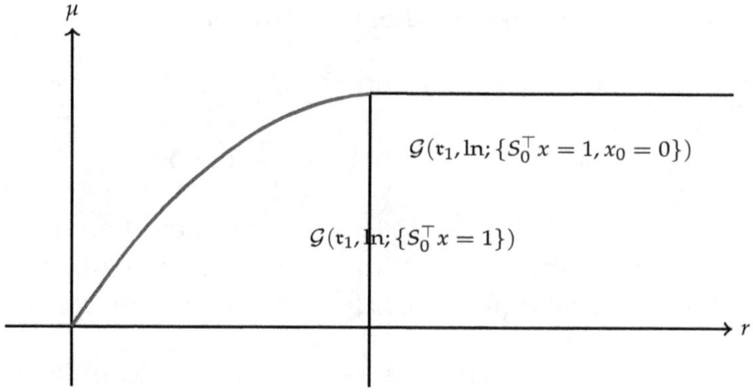

Figure 10. Touching efficient frontiers at growth optimal.

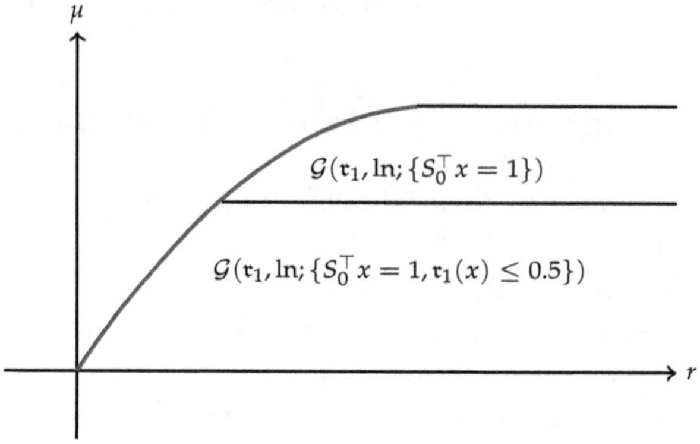

Figure 11. Shared efficient frontiers.

Remark 13. (Efficiency Index) *Although the growth optimal portfolio is usually not implemented as an investment strategy, the maximum utility $\mu_{\max}$ corresponding to the growth optimal portfolio κ, empirically estimated using historical performance data, can be used as a measure to compare different investment strategies. This is proposed in Zhu (2007) and called the efficiency index. When the only risky asset is the payoff of a game with two outcomes following a given playing strategy, the efficiency coefficient coincides with Shannon's information rate (see Kelly (1956); Shannon and Weaver (1949); Zhu (2007)). In this sense, the efficiency index gauges the useful information contained in the investment strategy it measures.*

7. Conclusions

Following the pioneering idea of Markowitz to trade-off the expected return and standard deviation of a portfolio, we consider a general framework to efficiently trade-off between a concave expected utility and a convex risk measure for portfolios. Under reasonable assumptions, we show that (i) the efficient frontier in such a trade-off is a convex curve in the expected utility-risk space, (ii) the optimal portfolio corresponding to each level of the expected utility is unique and (iii) the optimal portfolios continuously depend on the level of the expected utility. Moreover, we provide an alternative treatment and enhancement of the results in Rockafellar et al. (2006) showing that the one fund theorem (Theorem 9) holds in the trade-off between a deviation measure and the expected return (Theorem 11) and construct a counter-example illustrating that the two fund theorem (Theorem 7) fails in such a general setting. Furthermore, the efficiency curve in the leverage space is supposedly an economic way to scale back risk from the growth optimal portfolio (Theorem 13).

This general framework unifies a group of well known portfolio theories. They are Markowitz portfolio theory, capital asset pricing model, the growth optimal portfolio theory, and the leverage portfolio theory. It also extends these portfolio theories to more general settings.

The new framework also leads to many questions of practical significance worthy of further explorations. For example, quantities related to portfolio theories such as the Sharpe ratio and efficiency index can be used to measure investment performances. What other performance measurements can be derived using the general framework in Section 3? Portfolio theory can also inform us about pricing mechanisms such as those discussed in the capital asset pricing model and the fundamental theorem of asset pricing (see (Carr and Zhu forthcoming, Section 2.3). What additional pricing tools can be derived from our general framework?

Clearly, for the purpose of applications, we need to focus on certain special cases. Drawdown related risk measures coupled with the log utility attracts much attention in practice. In Part II of this series Maier-Paape and Zhu (2017), several drawdown related risk measures are constructed and analyzed.

Author Contributions: S.M.-P. and Q.J.Z. contributed equally to the work reported.

Acknowledgments: We thank Andreas Platen for his constructive suggestions after reading earlier versions of the manuscript.

References

Artzner, Philippe, Freddy Delbaen, Jean-Marc Eber, and Davia Heath. 1999. Coherent measures of risk. *Mathematical Finance* 9: 203–27. [CrossRef]

Borwein, Jonathan M., and Jon Vanderwerff. 2009. Differentiability of conjugate functions and perturbed minimization principles. *Journal of Convex Analysis* 16: 707–11.

Borwein, Jonathan M., and Qiji Jim Zhu. 2005. *Techniques of Variational Analysis*. New York: Springer.

Borwein, Jonathan M., and Qiji Jim Zhu. 2016. A variational approach to Lagrange multipliers. *Journal of Optimization Theory and Applications* 171: 727–56. [CrossRef]

Carr, Peter, and Qiji Jim Zhu. Forthcoming. *Convex Duality and Financial Mathematics*. Berlin: Springer.

De Prado, Marcos Lopez, Ralph Vince, and Qiji Jim Zhu. 2013. Optimal risk budgeting under a finite investment horizon. *SSRN Electronic Journal* 2364092. Available online: https://ssrn.com/abstract=2364092 (accessed on 29 March 2018).

Hermes, Andreas, and Stanislaus Maier-Paape. 2017. Existence and Uniqueness for the Multivariate Discrete Terminal Wealth Relative. *Risks* 5: 44. [CrossRef]

Kelly, John L. 1956. A new interpretation of information rate. *Bell System Technical Journal* 35: 917–26. [CrossRef]

Lintner, John. 1965. The valuation of risk assets and the selection of risky investments in stock portfolios and capital budgets. *Review of Economics and Statistics* 47: 13–37. [CrossRef]

MacLean, Leonard C., Edward O. Thorp, and William T. Ziemba, eds. 2009. *The Kelly Capital Growth Criterion: Theory and Practice*. Singapore: World Scientific.

Maier-Paape, Stanislaus. 2015. Optimal f and diversification. *International Federation of Technical Analysts Journal* 15: 4–7.

Maier-Paape, Stanislaus. 2016. *Risk Averse Fractional Trading Using the Current Drawdown*. Report No. 88. Aachen: Institut für Mathematik, RWTH Aachen.

Maier-Paape, Stanislaus, and Qiji Jim Zhu. 2017. *A General Framework for Portfolio Theory. Part II: Drawdown Risk Measures*. Report No. 92. Aachen: Institut für Mathematik, RWTH Aachen.

Markowitz, Harry. 1959. *Portfolio Selection*. Cowles Monograph, 16. New York: Wiley.

Mossin, Jan. 1966. Equilibrium in a Capital Asset Market. *Econometrica* 34: 768–83. [CrossRef]

Rockafellar, Ralph Tyrell. 1970. *Convex Analysis*. Vol. 28 Princeton Math. Series. Princeton: Princeton University Press.

Rockafellar, R. Tyrrell, and Stanislav Uryasev. 2000. Optimization of conditional value-at-risk. *Journal of Risk* 2: 21–42. [CrossRef]

Rockafellar, R. Tyrrell, Stan Uryasev, and Michael Zabarankin. 2006. Master funds in portfolio analysis with general deviation measures. *Journal of Banking and Finance* 30: 743–78. [CrossRef]

Shannon, Claude E., and Warren Weaver. 1949. *The Mathematical Theory of Communication*. Urbana: University of Illinois Press.

Sharpe, William F. 1964. Capital asset prices: A theory of market equilibrium under conditions of risk. *Journal of Finance* 19: 425–42.

Sharpe, William F. 1966. Mutual fund performance. *Journal of Business* 1: 119–38. [CrossRef]

Tobin, James. 1958. Liquidity preference as behavior towards risk. *The Review of Economic Studies* 26: 65–86. [CrossRef]

Treynor, Jack L. 1999. Toward a theory of market value of risky assets. In *Asset Pricing and Portfolio Performance: Models, Strategy and Performance Metrics*. Edited by Robert A. Korajczyk. London: Risk Books, pp. 15–22.

Vince, Ralph. 2009. *The Leverage Space Trading Model*. Hoboken: John Wiley and Sons.

Vince, Ralph, and Qiji Jim Zhu. 2015. Optimal betting sizes for the game of blackjack. *Risk Journals: Portfolio Management* 4: 53–75. [CrossRef]

Zhu, Qiji Jim. 2007. Mathematical analysis of investment systems. *Journal of Mathematical Analysis and Applications* 326: 708–20. [CrossRef]

4

A General Framework for Portfolio Theory—Part II: Drawdown Risk Measures

Stanislaus Maier-Paape [1,*] and Qiji Jim Zhu [2]

1 Institut für Mathematik, RWTH Aachen University, 52062 Aachen, Germany
2 Department of Mathematics, Western Michigan University, Kalamazoo, MI 49008, USA; qiji.zhu@wmich.edu
* Correspondence: maier@instmath.rwth-aachen.de

Abstract: The aim of this paper is to provide several examples of convex risk measures necessary for the application of the general framework for portfolio theory of Maier-Paape and Zhu (2018), presented in Part I of this series. As an alternative to classical portfolio risk measures such as the standard deviation, we, in particular, construct risk measures related to the "current" drawdown of the portfolio equity. In contrast to references Chekhlov, Uryasev, and Zabarankin (2003, 2005), Goldberg and Mahmoud (2017), and Zabarankin, Pavlikov, and Uryasev (2014), who used the absolute drawdown, our risk measure is based on the relative drawdown process. Combined with the results of Part I, Maier-Paape and Zhu (2018), this allows us to calculate efficient portfolios based on a drawdown risk measure constraint.

Keywords: admissible convex risk measures; current drawdown; efficient frontier; portfolio theory; fractional Kelly allocation, growth optimal portfolio; financial mathematics

MSC: 52A41; 91G10; 91G70; 91G80; 91B30

---

1. Introduction

Modern portfolio theory due to Markowitz (1959) has been the state of the art in mathematical asset allocation for over 50 years. Recently, in Part I of this series (see Maier-Paape and Zhu (2018)), we generalized portfolio theory such that efficient portfolios can now be considered for a wide range of utility functions and risk measures. The so found portfolios provide an efficient trade-off between utility and risk, just as in the Markowitz portfolio theory. Besides the expected return of the portfolio, which was used by Markowitz, general concave utility functions are now allowed, e.g., the log utility used for growth optimal portfolio theory (cf. Kelly (1956); Vince (1992, 1995); Vince and Zhu (2015); Zhu (2007, 2012); Hermes and Maier-Paape (2017); Hermes (2016)). Growth optimal portfolios maximize the expected log returns of the portfolio yielding fastest compounded growth.

Besides the generalization in the utility functions, as a second breakthrough, more realistic risk measures are now allowed. Whereas Markowitz and also the related capital asset pricing model (CAPM) of Sharpe (1964) use the standard deviation of the portfolio return as risk measure, the new theory of Part I in Maier-Paape and Zhu (2018) is applicable to a large class of convex risk measures.

Convex risk measures have a long tradition in mathematical finance. Besides the standard deviation, for example, the conditional value at risk (CVaR) provides a nontrivial convex risk measure (see Rockafellar and Uryasev (2002); and Rockafellar et al. (2006)), whereas the classical value at risk is not convex, and therefore cannot be used within this framework.

Thus, in Part II, our focus is to provide and analyze several such convex risk measures related to the expected log drawdown of the portfolio returns. In practice, drawdown related risk measures are superior in yielding risk averse strategies when compared to the standard deviation risk measure. Furthermore, the empirical simulations of Maier-Paape (2015) showed that (drawdown) risk averse strategies are also in great need when growth optimal portfolios are considered, since using them regularly generates tremendous drawdowns (see also Tharp (2008)). Therefore, the here-constructed drawdown related risk measures should be relevant for application in portfolio optimization, although a thorough real-world test is not part of this paper.

Several other authors have also introduced drawdown risk measures. For instance, Chekhlov et al. (2003, 2005) introduced the conditional drawdown at risk (CDaR) which is an application of the conditional value at risk on absolute drawdown processes. They showed properties like convexity and positive homogeneity for the CDaR. Later, Zabarankin et al. (2014) again used the conditional value at risk, but this time, on the absolute drawdown on a rolling time frame, to construct a new variant of the CDaR. Goldberg and Mahmoud (2017) introduced the so-called conditional expected drawdown (CED), a variant of a general deviation measure which again uses the conditional value risk, but now on pathwise maximum absolute drawdowns.

In contrast to the above literature, we here use the relative drawdown process to construct the so-called "current drawdown log series" in Section 5 which, in turn, yields the current drawdown related convex risk measures $\mathfrak{r}_{\text{cur}}$ and $\mathfrak{r}_{\text{cur}X}$, the latter being positive homogeneous.

The results in Part II are a natural generalization of Maier-Paape (2013, 2018), where drawdown related risk measures for a portfolio with only one risky asset were constructed. In these paper, as well as here, the construction of randomly drawn equity curves, which allows the measurement of drawdowns, is given in the framework of the growth optimal portfolio theory (see Section 3 and furthermore Vince (2009)). Therefore, we use Section 2 to provide the basics of the growth optimal theory and introduce our setup.

In Section 4, we introduce the concept of admissible convex risk measures, discuss some of their properties and show that the "risk part" of the growth optimal goal function provides such a risk measure. Then, in Section 5, we apply this concept to the expected log drawdown of the portfolio returns. Some of the approximations of these risk measures even yield positively homogeneous risk measures, which are strongly related to the concept of the deviation measures of Rockafellar et al. (2006). According to the theory of Part I Maier-Paape and Zhu (2018), such positively homogeneous risk measures provide—as in the CAPM model—an affine structure of the efficient portfolios when the identity utility function is used. Moreover, often in this situation, even a market portfolio, i.e., a purely risky efficient portfolio, related to drawdown risks can be provided as well.

Finally, we note that the main assumption of our market setup (Assumption 1 on the trade return matrix T of (1)) is equivalent to a one period financial market having no nontrivial riskless portfolios (which is a classical setup in mathematical finance since it combines the standard "no arbitrage condition" and the "no nontrivial bond-replicating portfolio condition"—see Definition A1, Definition A2 (a) and Theorem A2). This equivalence is a consequence of a generalized version of Theorem 2 of Maier-Paape and Zhu (2018) and is shown in the Appendix A (Corollary A1). In fact, the appendix provides the basic market setup for application of the generalized portfolio theory of Part I Maier-Paape and Zhu (2018), and it is therefore used as a link between Part I and Part II. It furthermore shows how the theory of Part I can be used with the risk measures constructed in this paper. Nonetheless, Parts I and II can be read independently.

2. Setup

In the following text, we use a market which is given by trade returns of several investment processes as described, for instance, in reference Vince (2009). As we will show in the appendix, such a situation can be obtained in the classical one period market model of financial mathematics (see Definition A1 and (A5)). For $1 \leq k \leq M$, $M \in \mathbb{N}$, we denote the k-th trading system by "system k". A trading system is an investment strategy applied to a financial instrument. Each system generates periodic trade returns, e.g., monthly, daily or the like. The net trade return of the i-th period of the k-th system is denoted by $t_{i,k}$, $1 \le i \le N, 1 \le k \le M$. Thus, we have the joint return matrix

period	(system 1)	(system 2)	$\cdots$	(system M)
1	$t_{1,1}$	$t_{1,2}$	$\cdots$	$t_{1,M}$
2	$t_{2,1}$	$t_{2,2}$	$\cdots$	$t_{2,M}$
$\vdots$	$\vdots$	$\vdots$	$\ddots$	$\vdots$
N	$t_{N,1}$	$t_{N,2}$	$\cdots$	$t_{N,M}$

and we denote

$$T := \left(t_{i,k}\right)_{\substack{1\le i\le N\\ 1\le k\le M}} \in \mathbb{R}^{N\times M}. \tag{1}$$

For better readability, we define the rows of T, which represent the returns of the i-th period of our systems, as

$$\boldsymbol{t_{i\bullet}} := (t_{i,1}, \ldots, t_{i,M}) \in \mathbb{R}^{1\times M}.$$

Following Vince (1992), for a vector of portions $\boldsymbol{\varphi} := (\varphi_1, \ldots, \varphi_M)^\top$, where φ_k stands for the portion of our capital invested in system k, we define the Holding Period Return (HPR) of the i-th period as

$$\mathrm{HPR}_i(\boldsymbol{\varphi}) := 1 + \sum_{k=1}^{M} \varphi_k\, t_{i,k} = 1 + \langle\, \boldsymbol{t}_{i\bullet}^\top, \boldsymbol{\varphi}\,\rangle, \tag{2}$$

where $\langle\cdot,\cdot\rangle$ is the scalar product in $\mathbb{R}^M$. The Terminal Wealth Relative (TWR) representing the gain (or loss) after the given N periods, when the vector $\boldsymbol{\varphi}$ is invested over all periods, is then given as

$$\mathrm{TWR}^{(N)}(\boldsymbol{\varphi}) := \prod_{i=1}^{N} \mathrm{HPR}_i(\boldsymbol{\varphi}) = \prod_{i=1}^{N} \left(1 + \langle\, \boldsymbol{t}_{i\bullet}^\top, \boldsymbol{\varphi}\,\rangle\right). \tag{3}$$

Since a Holding Period Return of zero for a single period means a total loss of our capital, we restrict $\mathrm{TWR}^{(N)} : \mathfrak{G} \to \mathbb{R}$ to the domain $\mathfrak{G}$ given by the following definition:

Definition 1. *A vector of portions $\boldsymbol{\varphi} \in \mathbb{R}^M$ is called* ***admissible*** *if $\boldsymbol{\varphi} \in \mathfrak{G}$ holds, where*

$$\begin{aligned}\mathfrak{G} &:= \left\{\boldsymbol{\varphi} \in \mathbb{R}^M \mid \mathrm{HPR}_i(\boldsymbol{\varphi}) \ge 0 \quad \textit{for all} \quad 1 \le i \le N\right\}\\ &= \left\{\boldsymbol{\varphi} \in \mathbb{R}^M \mid \langle\, \boldsymbol{t}_{i\bullet}^\top, \boldsymbol{\varphi}\rangle \ge -1 \quad \textit{for all} \quad 1 \le i \le N\right\}.\end{aligned} \tag{4}$$

Moreover, we define

$$\mathfrak{R} := \{\boldsymbol{\varphi} \in \mathfrak{G} \mid \exists 1 \le i_0 \le N \ s.t.\ \mathrm{HPR}_{i_0}(\boldsymbol{\varphi}) = 0\}. \tag{5}$$

Note that, in particular, $0 \in \overset{\circ}{\mathfrak{G}}$ (the interior of $\mathfrak{G}$) and $\mathfrak{R} = \partial\mathfrak{G}$, the boundary of $\mathfrak{G}$. Furthermore, negative φ_k are, in principle, allowed for short positions.

Lemma 1. *The set $\mathfrak{G}$ in Definition 1 is polyhedral and thus convex, as is $\overset{\circ}{\mathfrak{G}}$.*

Proof. For each $i \in \{1, \dots, N\}$, the condition

$$\mathrm{HPR}_i(\boldsymbol{\varphi}) \geq 0 \quad \Longleftrightarrow \quad \langle \boldsymbol{t}_{i\bullet}^{\top}, \boldsymbol{\varphi} \rangle \geq -1$$

defines a half space (which is convex). Since $\mathfrak{G}$ is the intersection of a finite set of half spaces, it is itself convex, in fact, it is even polyhedral. A similar reasoning yields that $\mathring{\mathfrak{G}}$ is convex, too. □

In the following text, we denote $\mathbb{S}_1^{M-1} := \{\boldsymbol{\varphi} \in \mathbb{R}^M\colon \|\boldsymbol{\varphi}\| = 1\}$ as the unit sphere in $\mathbb{R}^M$, where $\|\cdot\|$ denotes the Euclidean norm.

Assumption 1. ***(no risk free investment)*** *We assume that the trade return matrix T in* (1) *satisfies*

$$\forall\, \boldsymbol{\theta} \in \mathbb{S}_1^{M-1} \ \exists\, i_0 = i_0(\boldsymbol{\theta}) \in \{1, \dots, N\} \quad \text{such that } \langle \boldsymbol{t}_{i_0\bullet}^{\top}, \boldsymbol{\theta} \rangle < 0. \tag{6}$$

In other words, Assumption 1 states that no matter what "allocation vector" $\boldsymbol{\theta} \neq 0$ is used, there will always be a period i_0 resulting in a loss for the portfolio.

Remark 1.

(a) *Since $\boldsymbol{\theta} \in \mathbb{S}_1^{M-1}$ implies that $-\boldsymbol{\theta} \in \mathbb{S}_1^{M-1}$, Assumption 1 also yields the existence of a period j_0 resulting in a gain for each $\boldsymbol{\theta} \in \mathbb{S}_1^{M-1}$, i.e.,*

$$\forall\, \boldsymbol{\theta} \in \mathbb{S}_1^{M-1} \ \exists\, j_0 = j_0(\boldsymbol{\theta}) \in \{1, \dots, N\} \quad \text{such that } \langle \boldsymbol{t}_{j_0\bullet}^{\top}, \boldsymbol{\theta} \rangle > 0. \tag{7}$$

(b) *Note that with Assumption 1* $\ker(T) = \{\mathbf{0}\}$ *automatically follows, i.e., all trading systems are linearly independent.*

(c) *It is not important whether or not the trading systems are "profitable", since we allow short positions (cf. Assumption 1 in Hermes and Maier-Paape (2017)).*

Remark 2. *It is worthwhile noting that for a trade return matrix T stemming from a classical one period financial market (cf. Definition A1 and* (A5) *in the Appendix A), our Assumption 1 is equivalent to the "no nontrivial riskless portfolio condition" of the market (see Definition A2 (a) and Corollary A1).*

Lemma 2. *Let the return matrix $T \in \mathbb{R}^{N \times M}$ (as in* (1)*) satisfy Assumption 1. Then, the set $\mathfrak{G}$ in* (4) *is compact.*

Proof. Since $\mathfrak{G}$ is closed, the lemma follows from (6) yielding $\mathrm{HPR}_{i_0}(s\boldsymbol{\theta}) < 0$ for all $s > 0$ which are sufficiently large. A simple argument using the compactness of $\mathbb{S}_1^{M-1}$ yields that $\mathfrak{G}$ is bounded as well. □

3. Randomly Drawing Trades

The ultimate goal of this paper is to construct a risk measure which is somehow related to the drawdown risk of our financial market. It is clear how to measure the drawdown of a given equity curve between two different time points, but so far, we only have a trade return matrix representing a large number N of one period trade returns.

So, in order to generate equity curves, we assume that we can draw randomly and independently from the given trade returns. Note that, in practice, the trade returns will not be perfectly independent, but this is a good start; multi-period dependent trade returns could be investigated with a multi-period financial market which, of course, would complicate matters even more.

Thus, we construct equity curves by randomly drawing trades from the given trade return matrix.

Setup 1. ***(trading game)*** *Assume the trading systems have the trade return matrix T from* (1)*. In a trading game, the rows of T are drawn randomly. Each row $\boldsymbol{t}_{i\bullet}$ has a probability of $p_i > 0$, with $\sum_{i=1}^{N} p_i = 1$.*

Drawing randomly and independently $K \in \mathbb{N}$ times from this distribution results in a probability space $\Omega^{(K)} := \{\omega = (\omega_1, \ldots, \omega_K) : \omega_i \in \{1, \ldots, N\}\}$ and a terminal wealth relative (for fractional trading with portion $\boldsymbol{\varphi}$ is used)

$$\mathrm{TWR}_1^K(\boldsymbol{\varphi}, \omega) := \prod_{j=1}^{K} \left(1 + \langle \boldsymbol{t}_{\omega_j \bullet}^\top, \boldsymbol{\varphi} \rangle\right), \quad \boldsymbol{\varphi} \in \mathring{\mathfrak{G}}. \tag{8}$$

The natural discrete equity curve related to Setup 1 is

$$\mathrm{TWR}_1^k(\boldsymbol{\varphi}, \omega) := \prod_{j=1}^{k} \left(1 + \langle \boldsymbol{t}_{\omega_j \bullet}^\top, \boldsymbol{\varphi} \rangle\right)$$

for times $k = 1, \ldots, K$, which will become important in Section 5. For the time being, we work with (8).

In the rest of the paper we will use the natural logarithm, ln.

Theorem 1. *For each $\boldsymbol{\varphi} \in \mathring{\mathfrak{G}}$, the random variable $\mathcal{Z}^{(K)}(\boldsymbol{\varphi}, \cdot) : \Omega^{(K)} \to \mathbb{R}$, $\mathcal{Z}^{(K)}(\boldsymbol{\varphi}, \omega) := \ln\big(\mathrm{TWR}_1^K(\boldsymbol{\varphi}, \omega)\big)$, $K \in \mathbb{N}$, has the expected value*

$$\mathbb{E}\left[\mathcal{Z}^{(K)}(\boldsymbol{\varphi}, \cdot)\right] = K \cdot \ln \Gamma(\boldsymbol{\varphi}), \tag{9}$$

where $\Gamma(\boldsymbol{\varphi}) := \prod_{i=1}^{N} \left(1 + \langle \boldsymbol{t}_{i \bullet}^\top, \boldsymbol{\varphi} \rangle\right)^{p_i}$ is the weighted geometric mean of the holding period returns $\mathrm{HPR}_i(\boldsymbol{\varphi}) = 1 + \langle \boldsymbol{t}_{i \bullet}^\top, \boldsymbol{\varphi} \rangle > 0$ (see (2)) for all $\boldsymbol{\varphi} \in \mathring{\mathfrak{G}}$.

Proof. For a fixed $K \in \mathbb{N}$,

$$\begin{aligned}
\mathbb{E}\left[\mathcal{Z}^{(K)}(\boldsymbol{\varphi}, \cdot)\right] &= \sum_{\omega \in \Omega^{(K)}} \mathbb{P}(\{\omega\}) \left[\ln \prod_{j=1}^{K} \left(1 + \langle \boldsymbol{t}_{\omega_j \bullet}^\top, \boldsymbol{\varphi} \rangle\right)\right] \\
&= \sum_{j=1}^{K} \sum_{\omega \in \Omega^{(K)}} \mathbb{P}(\{\omega\}) \left[\ln \left(1 + \langle \boldsymbol{t}_{\omega_j \bullet}^\top, \boldsymbol{\varphi} \rangle\right)\right]
\end{aligned}$$

holds. For each $j \in \{1, \ldots, K\}$

$$\sum_{\omega \in \Omega^{(K)}} \mathbb{P}(\{\omega\}) \left[\ln \left(1 + \langle \boldsymbol{t}_{\omega_j \bullet}^\top, \boldsymbol{\varphi} \rangle\right)\right] = \sum_{i=1}^{N} p_i \cdot \ln\left(1 + \langle \boldsymbol{t}_{i \bullet}^\top, \boldsymbol{\varphi} \rangle\right)$$

is independent of j because each ω_j is an independent drawing. We thus obtain

$$\begin{aligned}
\left[\mathcal{Z}^{(K)}(\boldsymbol{\varphi}, \cdot)\right] &= K \cdot \sum_{i=1}^{N} p_i \cdot \ln\left(1 + \langle \boldsymbol{t}_{i \bullet}^\top, \boldsymbol{\varphi} \rangle\right) \\
&= K \cdot \ln \left[\prod_{i=1}^{N} \left(1 + \langle \boldsymbol{t}_{i \bullet}^\top, \boldsymbol{\varphi} \rangle\right)^{p_i}\right] = K \cdot \ln \Gamma(\boldsymbol{\varphi}).
\end{aligned}$$

□

Next, we want to split up the random variable $\mathcal{Z}^{(K)}(\boldsymbol{\varphi}, \cdot)$ into "chance" and "risk" parts. Since $\mathrm{TWR}_1^K(\boldsymbol{\varphi}, \omega) > 1$ corresponds to a winning trade series $t_{\omega_1 \bullet}, \ldots, t_{\omega_K \bullet}$ and $\mathrm{TWR}_1^K(\boldsymbol{\varphi}, \omega) < 1$ analogously corresponds to a losing trade series, we define the random variables corresponding to up trades and down trades:

Definition 2. *For $\boldsymbol{\varphi} \in \mathring{\mathfrak{G}}$ we set*

Up-trade log series:

$$\mathcal{U}^{(K)}(\boldsymbol{\varphi},\omega) := \ln\big(\max\{1, \mathrm{TWR}_1^K(\boldsymbol{\varphi},\omega)\}\big) \geq 0. \tag{10}$$

Down-trade log series:

$$\mathcal{D}^{(K)}(\boldsymbol{\varphi},\omega) := \ln\big(\min\{1, \mathrm{TWR}_1^K(\boldsymbol{\varphi},\omega)\}\big) \leq 0. \tag{11}$$

Clearly $\mathcal{U}^{(K)}(\boldsymbol{\varphi},\omega) + \mathcal{D}^{(K)}(\boldsymbol{\varphi},\omega) = \mathcal{Z}^{(K)}(\boldsymbol{\varphi},\omega)$. Hence, by Theorem 1 we get

Corollary 1. *For* $\boldsymbol{\varphi} \in \mathring{\mathfrak{G}}$

$$\mathbb{E}\left[\mathcal{U}^{(K)}(\boldsymbol{\varphi},\cdot)\right] + \mathbb{E}\left[\mathcal{D}^{(K)}(\boldsymbol{\varphi},\cdot)\right] = K \cdot \ln\Gamma(\boldsymbol{\varphi}) \tag{12}$$

holds.

Remark 3. *Since in the down-trade log series, all losing trades result in a negative value (and the rest is ignored), the expected value* $\mathbb{E}\left[\mathcal{D}^{(K)}(\boldsymbol{\varphi},\cdot)\right]$ *can be viewed as a "measure" of how much one will lose in a fixed time horizon of K periods on average, given the condition that it is a losing trade. Clearly this is not yet measuring drawdowns. However, it is simpler to start with this situation, and in Section 5, when we discuss drawdowns, we benefit from our investigations here.*

As in reference Maier-Paape (2018) we next search for explicit formulas for $\mathbb{E}\left[\mathcal{U}^{(K)}(\boldsymbol{\varphi},\cdot)\right]$ and $\mathbb{E}\left[\mathcal{D}^{(K)}(\boldsymbol{\varphi},\cdot)\right]$, respectively. By definition,

$$\mathbb{E}\left[\mathcal{U}^{(K)}(\boldsymbol{\varphi},\cdot)\right] = \sum_{\omega:\mathrm{TWR}_1^K(\boldsymbol{\varphi},\omega)>1} \mathbb{P}(\{\omega\}) \cdot \ln\Big(\mathrm{TWR}_1^K(\boldsymbol{\varphi},\omega)\Big). \tag{13}$$

Assume $\omega = (\omega_1,\ldots,\omega_K) \in \Omega^{(K)} := \{1,\ldots,N\}^K$ is for the moment fixed, and the random variable X_1 counts how many of the ω_j are equal to 1, i.e., $X_1(\omega) = x_1$ if in total x_1 of the ω_j's in ω are equal to 1. With similar counting of random variables $X_2,\ldots,X_N$, we obtain integer counts $x_i \geq 0$ and thus,

$$X_1(\omega) = x_1,\ X_2(\omega) = x_2,\ \ldots,\ X_N(\omega) = x_N \tag{14}$$

with $\sum_{i=1}^N x_i = K$. Hence, for this fixed ω, we obtain

$$\mathrm{TWR}_1^K(\boldsymbol{\varphi},\omega) = \prod_{j=1}^{K}\Big(1 + \langle\, \boldsymbol{t}_{\omega_j\bullet}^\top, \boldsymbol{\varphi}\,\rangle\Big) = \prod_{i=1}^{N}\Big(1 + \langle\, \boldsymbol{t}_{i\bullet}^\top, \boldsymbol{\varphi}\,\rangle\Big)^{x_i}. \tag{15}$$

Therefore, the condition on ω in the sum (13) is equivalently expressed as

$$\mathrm{TWR}_1^K(\boldsymbol{\varphi},\omega) > 1 \iff \ln\mathrm{TWR}_1^K(\boldsymbol{\varphi},\omega) > 0 \iff \sum_{i=1}^{N} x_i \ln\Big(1 + \langle\, \boldsymbol{t}_{i\bullet}^\top, \boldsymbol{\varphi}\,\rangle\Big) > 0. \tag{16}$$

To better understand the last sum, Taylor expansion may be used exactly as in Lemma 4.5 of Maier-Paape (2018) to obtain

Lemma 3. *Let integers* $x_i \geq 0$ *with* $\sum_{i=1}^N x_i = K > 0$ *be given. Furthermore, let* $\boldsymbol{\varphi} = s\,\boldsymbol{\theta} \in \mathring{\mathfrak{G}}$ *be a vector of admissible portions where* $\boldsymbol{\theta} \in \mathbb{S}_1^{M-1}$ *is fixed and* $s > 0$.

Then, $\varepsilon > 0$ exists (depending on $x_1, \ldots, x_N$ and $\boldsymbol{\theta}$) such that for all $s \in (0, \varepsilon]$, the following holds:

(a) $\sum_{i=1}^{N} x_i \langle \boldsymbol{t}_{i\bullet}^{\top}, \boldsymbol{\theta} \rangle > 0 \iff h(s, \boldsymbol{\theta}) := \sum_{i=1}^{N} x_i \ln\left(1 + s\langle \boldsymbol{t}_{i\bullet}^{\top}, \boldsymbol{\theta} \rangle\right) > 0$

(b) $\sum_{i=1}^{N} x_i \langle \boldsymbol{t}_{i\bullet}^{\top}, \boldsymbol{\theta} \rangle \leq 0 \iff h(s, \boldsymbol{\theta}) = \sum_{i=1}^{N} x_i \ln\left(1 + s\langle \boldsymbol{t}_{i\bullet}^{\top}, \boldsymbol{\theta} \rangle\right) < 0.$

Proof. The conclusions follow immediately from $h(0, \boldsymbol{\theta}) = 0$, $\frac{\partial}{\partial s} h(0, \boldsymbol{\theta}) = \sum_{i=1}^{N} x_i \langle \boldsymbol{t}_{i\bullet}^{\top}, \boldsymbol{\theta} \rangle$ and $\frac{\partial^2}{\partial s^2} h(0, \boldsymbol{\theta}) < 0$. □

With Lemma 3 we hence can restate (16). For $\boldsymbol{\theta} \in \mathbb{S}_1^{M-1}$ and all $s \in (0, \varepsilon]$, the following holds

$$\mathrm{TWR}_1^K(s\boldsymbol{\theta}, \omega) > 1 \iff \sum_{i=1}^{N} x_i \langle \boldsymbol{t}_{i\bullet}^{\top}, \boldsymbol{\theta} \rangle > 0. \tag{17}$$

Note that since $\Omega^{(K)}$ is finite and $\mathbb{S}_1^{M-1}$ is compact, a (maybe smaller) $\varepsilon > 0$ can be found such that (17) holds for all $s \in (0, \varepsilon]$, $\boldsymbol{\theta} \in \mathbb{S}_1^{M-1}$ and $\omega \in \Omega^{(K)}$.

Remark 4. *In the situation of Lemma 3, furthermore,*

$$(b)^* \qquad \sum_{i=1}^{N} x_i \langle \boldsymbol{t}_{i\bullet}^{\top}, \boldsymbol{\theta} \rangle \leq 0 \implies h(s, \boldsymbol{\theta}) < 0 \quad \textit{for all} \quad s > 0 \tag{18}$$

holds true since h is a concave function in s.

After all these preliminaries, we may now state the first main result. To simplify the notation, we set $\mathbb{N}_0 := \mathbb{N} \cup \{0\}$ and introduce

$$H^{(K,N)}(x_1, \ldots, x_N) := p_1^{x_1} \cdots p_N^{x_N} \binom{K}{x_1\ x_2 \cdots x_N} \tag{19}$$

for further reference, where $\binom{K}{x_1\ x_2 \cdots x_N} = \frac{K!}{x_1! x_2! \cdots x_N!}$ is the multinomial coefficient for $(x_1, \ldots, x_N) \in \mathbb{N}_0^N$ with $\sum_{i=1}^{N} x_i = K$ fixed and $p_1, \ldots, p_N$ are the probabilities from Setup 1.

Theorem 2. *Let a trading game as in Setup 1 with fixed $N, K \in \mathbb{N}$ be given and $\boldsymbol{\theta} \in \mathbb{S}_1^{M-1}$. Then, an $\varepsilon > 0$ exists such that for all $s \in (0, \varepsilon]$, the following holds:*

$$\mathbb{E}\left[\mathcal{U}^{(K)}(s\boldsymbol{\theta}, \cdot)\right] = u^{(K)}(s, \boldsymbol{\theta}) := \sum_{n=1}^{N} U_n^{(K,N)}(\boldsymbol{\theta}) \cdot \ln\left(1 + s\,\langle \boldsymbol{t}_{n\bullet}^{\top}, \boldsymbol{\theta} \rangle\right) \geq 0, \tag{20}$$

where

$$U_n^{(K,N)}(\boldsymbol{\theta}) := \sum_{\substack{(x_1, \ldots, x_N) \in \mathbb{N}_0^N \\ \sum_{i=1}^{N} x_i = K,\ \sum_{i=1}^{N} x_i \langle \boldsymbol{t}_{i\bullet}^{\top}, \boldsymbol{\theta} \rangle > 0}} H^{(K,N)}(x_1, \ldots, x_N) \cdot x_n \geq 0 \tag{21}$$

and with $H^{(K,N)}$ from (19).

Proof. $\mathbb{E}\left[\mathcal{U}^{(K)}(s\boldsymbol{\theta},\cdot)\right] \geq 0$ is clear from (10) even for all $s \geq 0$. The rest of the proof is along the lines of the proof of the univariate case Theorem 4.6 in reference Maier-Paape (2018), but will be given for convenience. Starting with (13) and using (14) and (17), we get for $s \in (0,\varepsilon]$

$$\mathbb{E}\left[\mathcal{U}^{(K)}(s\boldsymbol{\theta},\cdot)\right] = \sum_{\substack{(x_1,\dots,x_N)\in\mathbb{N}_0^N \\ \sum_{i=1}^N x_i = K}} \sum_{\substack{\omega: X_1(\omega)=x_1,\dots,X_N(\omega)=x_N \\ \sum_{i=1}^N x_i \langle \boldsymbol{t}_{i\bullet}^\top, \boldsymbol{\theta}\rangle > 0}} \mathbb{P}(\{\omega\}) \cdot \ln\left(\mathrm{TWR}_1^K(s\boldsymbol{\theta},\omega)\right).$$

Since there are $\binom{K}{x_1\, x_2 \cdots x_N} = \frac{K!}{x_1! x_2! \cdots x_N!}$ many $\omega \in \Omega^{(K)}$ for which $X_1(\omega) = x_1, \dots, X_N(\omega) = x_N$ holds, we furthermore get using (15)

$$\begin{aligned}\mathbb{E}\left[\mathcal{U}^{(K)}(s\boldsymbol{\theta},\cdot)\right] &= \sum_{\substack{(x_1,\dots,x_N)\in\mathbb{N}_0^N \\ \sum_{i=1}^N x_i = K,\ \sum_{i=1}^N x_i \langle \boldsymbol{t}_{i\bullet}^\top, \boldsymbol{\theta}\rangle > 0}} H^{(K,N)}(x_1,\dots,x_N) \sum_{n=1}^N x_n \cdot \ln\left(1 + s\cdot \langle \boldsymbol{t}_{n\bullet}^\top, \boldsymbol{\theta}\rangle\right) \\ &= \sum_{n=1}^N U_n^{(K,N)}(\boldsymbol{\theta}) \cdot \ln\left(1 + s\cdot \langle \boldsymbol{t}_{n\bullet}^\top, \boldsymbol{\theta}\rangle\right)\end{aligned}$$

as claimed. □

A similar result holds for $\mathbb{E}\left[\mathcal{D}^{(K)}(s\boldsymbol{\theta},\cdot)\right]$.

Theorem 3. *We assume that the conditions of Theorem 2 hold. Then,*

(a) *For $\boldsymbol{\theta} \in \mathbb{S}_1^{M-1}$ and $s \in (0,\varepsilon]$*

$$\mathbb{E}\left[\mathcal{D}^{(K)}(s\boldsymbol{\theta},\cdot)\right] = d^{(K)}(s,\boldsymbol{\theta}) := \sum_{n=1}^N D_n^{(K,N)}(\boldsymbol{\theta}) \cdot \ln\left(1 + s\,\langle \boldsymbol{t}_{n\bullet}^\top, \boldsymbol{\theta}\rangle\right) \leq 0 \tag{22}$$

holds, where

$$D_n^{(K,N)}(\boldsymbol{\theta}) := \sum_{\substack{(x_1,\dots,x_N)\in\mathbb{N}_0^N \\ \sum_{i=1}^N x_i = K,\ \sum_{i=1}^N x_i \langle \boldsymbol{t}_{i\bullet}^\top, \boldsymbol{\theta}\rangle \leq 0}} H^{(K,N)}(x_1,\dots,x_N) \cdot x_n \geq 0. \tag{23}$$

(b) *For all $s > 0$ and $\boldsymbol{\theta} \in \mathbb{S}_1^{M-1}$ with $s\boldsymbol{\theta} \in \overset{\circ}{\mathfrak{G}}$*

$$\mathbb{E}\left[\mathcal{D}^{(K)}(s\boldsymbol{\theta},\cdot)\right] \leq d^{(K)}(s,\boldsymbol{\theta}) \leq 0, \tag{24}$$

i.e., $d^{(K)}(s,\boldsymbol{\theta})$ is always an upper bound for the expectation of the down-trade log series.

Remark 5. *For large $s > 0$, either $\mathbb{E}\left[\mathcal{D}^{(K)}(s\boldsymbol{\theta},\cdot)\right]$ or $d^{(K)}(s,\boldsymbol{\theta})$ or both shall assume the value $-\infty$ in cases where at least one of the logarithms in their definition is not defined. Then, (24) holds for all $s\boldsymbol{\theta} \in \mathbb{R}^M$.*

Proof of Theorem 3.

ad (a): $\mathbb{E}\left[\mathcal{D}^{(K)}(s\boldsymbol{\theta},\cdot)\right] \leq 0$ follows from (11) again for all $s \geq 0$. Furthermore, by definition,

$$\mathbb{E}\left[\mathcal{D}^{(K)}(s\boldsymbol{\theta},\cdot)\right] = \sum_{\omega:\mathrm{TWR}_1^K(s\boldsymbol{\theta},\omega)<1} \mathbb{P}(\{\omega\}) \cdot \ln\left(\mathrm{TWR}_1^K(s\boldsymbol{\theta},\omega)\right). \tag{25}$$

The arguments given in the proof of Theorem 2 apply similarly, where, instead of (17), we use Lemma 3 (b) to get $s \in (0, \varepsilon]$

$$\mathrm{TWR}_1^K(s\boldsymbol{\theta}, \omega) < 1 \iff \sum_{i=1}^{N} x_i \langle \boldsymbol{t}_{i\bullet}^\top, \boldsymbol{\theta} \rangle \leq 0 \tag{26}$$

for all ω with

$$X_1(\omega) = x_1\,,\; X_2(\omega) = x_2, \ldots,\; X_N(\omega) = x_N\,. \tag{27}$$

ad (b): According to the extension of Lemma 3 in Remark 4, we also get

$$\sum_{i=1}^{N} x_i \langle \boldsymbol{t}_{i\bullet}^\top, \boldsymbol{\theta} \rangle \leq 0 \quad \Longrightarrow \quad \mathrm{TWR}_1^K(s\boldsymbol{\theta}, \omega) < 1 \quad \text{for all} \quad s > 0 \tag{28}$$

for all ω with (27). Therefore, no matter how large $s > 0$ is, the summands of $d^{(K)}(s, \boldsymbol{\theta})$ in (22) will always contribute to $\mathbb{E}\left[\mathcal{D}^{(K)}(s\boldsymbol{\theta}, \cdot)\right]$ in (25), but—at least for large $s > 0$—there may be even more (negative) summands from other ω. Hence, (24) follows for all $s > 0$. □

Remark 6. *Using multinomial distribution theory and* (19),

$$\sum_{\substack{(x_1,\ldots,x_N)\in\mathbb{N}_0^N \\ \sum_{i=1}^{N} x_i = K}} H^{(K,N)}(x_1, \ldots, x_N)\; x_n = p_n \cdot K \quad \textit{for all } n = 1, \ldots, N$$

holds and yields (again) with Theorems 2 and 3 for $s \in (0, \varepsilon]$

$$\mathbb{E}\left[\mathcal{U}^{(K)}(s\boldsymbol{\theta}, \cdot)\right] + \mathbb{E}\left[\mathcal{D}^{(K)}(s\boldsymbol{\theta}, \cdot)\right] = \sum_{n=1}^{N} p_n \cdot K \cdot \ln\Big(1 + s\langle \boldsymbol{t}_{n\bullet}^\top, \boldsymbol{\theta} \rangle\Big) = K \cdot \ln\Gamma(s\boldsymbol{\theta}).$$

Remark 7. *Using Taylor expansion in* (22) *we, therefore, obtain a first order approximation in s of the expected down-trade log series $\mathcal{D}^{(K)}(s\boldsymbol{\theta}, \cdot)$ (11), i.e., for $s \in (0, \varepsilon]$ and $\boldsymbol{\theta} \in \mathbb{S}_1^{M-1}$, the following holds:*

$$\mathbb{E}\left[\mathcal{D}^{(K)}(s\boldsymbol{\theta}, \cdot)\right] \approx \tilde{d}^{(K)}(s, \boldsymbol{\theta}) := s \cdot \sum_{n=1}^{N} D_n^{(K,N)}(\boldsymbol{\theta}) \cdot \langle \boldsymbol{t}_{n\bullet}^\top, \boldsymbol{\theta} \rangle\,. \tag{29}$$

In the sequel, we call $d^{(K)}$ the **first** and $\tilde{d}^{(K)}$ the **second approximation** of the expected down-trade log series. Noting that $\ln(1 + x) \leq x$ for $x \in \mathbb{R}$, when we extend $\ln\big|_{(-\infty,0]} := -\infty$, we can improve part **(b)** of Theorem 3:

Corollary 2. *In the situation of Theorem 3 for all $s \geq 0$ and $\boldsymbol{\theta} \in \mathbb{S}_1^{M-1}$ such that $s\boldsymbol{\theta} \in \mathring{\mathfrak{G}}$, we get:*

(a)

$$\mathbb{E}\left[\mathcal{D}^{(K)}(s\boldsymbol{\theta}, \cdot)\right] \leq d^{(K)}(s, \boldsymbol{\theta}) \leq \tilde{d}^{(K)}(s, \boldsymbol{\theta}). \tag{30}$$

(b) *Furthermore, $\tilde{d}^{(K)}$ is continuous in s and $\boldsymbol{\theta}$ (in s even positive homogeneous) and*

$$\tilde{d}^{(K)}(s, \boldsymbol{\theta}) \leq 0\,. \tag{31}$$

Proof. **(a)** is already clear from the statement above. To show **(b)**, the continuity in s of the second approximation,

$$\widetilde{d}^{(K)}(s,\boldsymbol{\theta}) = s \cdot \sum_{n=1}^{N} D_n^{(K,N)}(\boldsymbol{\theta}) \cdot \langle \boldsymbol{t}_{n\bullet}^{\top}, \boldsymbol{\theta} \rangle, \; s > 0,$$

in (29) is clear. However, even continuity in $\boldsymbol{\theta}$ follows with a short argument. Using (23),

$$\begin{aligned} \widetilde{d}^{(K)}(s,\boldsymbol{\theta}) &= s \cdot \sum_{n=1}^{N} \sum_{\substack{(x_1,\ldots,x_N) \in \mathbb{N}_0^N \\ \sum_{i=1}^N x_i = K, \; \sum_{i=1}^N x_i \langle \boldsymbol{t}_{i\bullet}^{\top}, \boldsymbol{\theta} \rangle \le 0}} H^{(K,N)}(x_1,\ldots,x_N) \cdot x_n \cdot \langle \boldsymbol{t}_{n\bullet}^{\top}, \boldsymbol{\theta} \rangle \\ &= s \cdot \sum_{\substack{(x_1,\ldots,x_N) \in \mathbb{N}_0^N \\ \sum_{i=1}^N x_i = K, \; \sum_{i=1}^N x_i \langle \boldsymbol{t}_{i\bullet}^{\top}, \boldsymbol{\theta} \rangle \le 0}} H^{(K,N)}(x_1,\ldots,x_N) \cdot \underbrace{\sum_{n=1}^{N} x_n \langle \boldsymbol{t}_{n\bullet}^{\top}, \boldsymbol{\theta} \rangle}_{\le 0} \\ &= s \cdot \sum_{\substack{(x_1,\ldots,x_N) \in \mathbb{N}_0^N \\ \sum_{i=1}^N x_i = K}} H^{(K,N)}(x_1,\ldots,x_N) \cdot \min\left\{ \sum_{n=1}^{N} x_n \langle \boldsymbol{t}_{n\bullet}^{\top}, \boldsymbol{\theta} \rangle, 0 \right\} \\ &=: s \cdot L^{(K,N)}(\boldsymbol{\theta}) \le 0 . \end{aligned} \tag{32}$$

Since $\sum_{n=1}^{N} x_n \langle \boldsymbol{t}_{n\bullet}^{\top}, \boldsymbol{\theta} \rangle$ is continuous in $\boldsymbol{\theta}$, $L^{(K,N)}(\boldsymbol{\theta})$ is continuous, too, and clearly $\widetilde{d}^{(K)}$ is non-positive. □

4. Admissible Convex Risk Measures

Various different approaches have been proposed to measure risks (see, for instance, Föllmer and Schied (2002), Chapter 4, for an introduction). For simplicity, we collect several important properties of risk measures in the following three definitions. How these risk measures can be embedded in the framework of a one period financial market, as used in Part I Maier-Paape and Zhu (2018), is discussed in Appendix A.

Definition 3. ***(admissible convex risk measure)*** *Let $\mathcal{Q} \subset \mathbb{R}^M$ be a convex set with $0 \in \mathcal{Q}$. A function $\mathfrak{r}\colon \mathcal{Q} \to \mathbb{R}_0^+$ is called an* ***admissible convex risk measure (ACRM)*** *if the following properties are satisfied:*

(a) $\mathfrak{r}(0) = 0$, $\mathfrak{r}(\boldsymbol{\varphi}) \ge 0$ *for all* $\boldsymbol{\varphi} \in \mathcal{Q}$.

(b) $\mathfrak{r}$ *is a convex and continuous function.*

(c) *For any $\boldsymbol{\theta} \in \mathbb{S}_1^{M-1}$ the function $\mathfrak{r}$ restricted to the set $\{s\boldsymbol{\theta} : s > 0\} \cap \mathcal{Q} \subset \mathbb{R}^M$ is strictly increasing in s, and hence, in particular, $\mathfrak{r}(\boldsymbol{\varphi}) > 0$ for all $\boldsymbol{\varphi} \in \mathcal{Q} \setminus \{0\}$.*

Definition 4. ***(admissible strictly convex risk measure)*** *If, in the situation of Definition 3, the function $\mathfrak{r}\colon \mathcal{Q} \to \mathbb{R}_0^+$ satisfies only (a) and (b), but is moreover strictly convex, then $\mathfrak{r}$ is called an* ***admissible strictly convex risk measure (ASCRM).***

Some of the here-constructed risk measures are moreover positive homogeneous.

Definition 5. ***(positive homogeneous)*** *The risk function $\mathfrak{r}\colon \mathbb{R}^M \to \mathbb{R}_0^+$ is* ***positive homogeneous*** *if*

$$\mathfrak{r}(s\boldsymbol{\varphi}) = s\mathfrak{r}(\boldsymbol{\varphi}) \;\; \textit{for all} \;\; s > 0 \;\; \textit{and} \;\; \boldsymbol{\varphi} \in \mathbb{R}^M.$$

Remark 8.

(a) *Note that the risk measures from the above are functions of a portfolio vector $\boldsymbol{\varphi}$, whereas in classical financial mathematics, usually the risk measure is a function of a random variable. For instance, the deviation measure of Rockafellar et al. (2006) is described in terms of the random payoff variable generated by the portfolio vector. However, viewed as a function of the portfolio vector, it is equivalent to a convex risk measure, as defined here (satisfying only (a) and (b) of Definition 3, but which is moreover positive homogeneous).*

(b) *Another nontrivial example of a convex risk measure is the conditional value at risk (CVaR), cf. references Rockafellar and Uryasev (2002) and Rockafellar et al. (2006).*

Remark 9. *It is easy to see that an admissible strictly convex risk measure automatically satisfies (c) in Definition 3, and thus, it is also an admissible convex risk measure. In fact, if $u > s > 0$ then $s = \lambda u$ for some $\lambda \in (0,1)$ and we obtain for $\boldsymbol{\theta} \in \mathbb{S}_1^{M-1}$*

$$\mathfrak{r}(s\boldsymbol{\theta}) = \mathfrak{r}(\lambda\, u\boldsymbol{\theta} + (1-\lambda)\cdot 0 \cdot \boldsymbol{\theta}) \leq \lambda\, \mathfrak{r}(u\boldsymbol{\theta}) + (1-\lambda)\mathfrak{r}(0\cdot\boldsymbol{\theta}) = \lambda\, \mathfrak{r}(u\boldsymbol{\theta}) < \mathfrak{r}(u\boldsymbol{\theta}) .$$

Example 1.

(a) *The function $\mathfrak{r}_1$ with $\mathfrak{r}_1(\boldsymbol{\varphi}) := \boldsymbol{\varphi}^\top \Lambda \boldsymbol{\varphi}$, $\boldsymbol{\varphi} \in \mathbb{R}^M$, for some symmetric positive definite matrix $\Lambda \in \mathbb{R}^{M\times M}$ is an admissible strictly convex risk measure (ASCRM).*

(b) *$\mathfrak{r}_2(\boldsymbol{\varphi}) := \sqrt{\mathfrak{r}_1(\boldsymbol{\varphi})}$ with $\mathfrak{r}_1$ from (a) is an admissible convex risk measure which is moreover positive definite. For instance, the standard deviation of the payoff variable generated by the portfolio return is of that form (cf. Maier-Paape and Zhu (2018), Corollary 1).*

(c) *For a fixed vector $c = (c_1, \ldots, c_M) \in \mathbb{R}^M$, with $c_j > 0$ for $j = 1, \ldots, M$, both,*

$$\mathfrak{r}_3(\boldsymbol{\varphi}) := \|\boldsymbol{\varphi}\|_{1,c} := \sum_{j=1}^{M} c_j|\varphi_j| \quad \text{and} \quad \mathfrak{r}_4(\boldsymbol{\varphi}) := \|\boldsymbol{\varphi}\|_{\infty,c} := \max_{1\leq j\leq M} \{c_j|\varphi_j|\} ,$$

define admissible convex risk measures (ACRM).

The structure of the ACRM implies nice properties about their level sets:

Lemma 4. *Let $\mathfrak{r} : \mathcal{Q} \to \mathbb{R}_0^+$ be an admissible convex risk measure. Then, the following holds:*

(a) *The set $\mathcal{M}(\alpha) := \{\boldsymbol{\varphi} \in \mathcal{Q} : \mathfrak{r}(\boldsymbol{\varphi}) \leq \alpha\}$, $\alpha \geq 0$, is convex and contains $0 \in \mathcal{Q}$.*

Furthermore, if $\overline{\mathcal{M}(\alpha)}$ is bounded and $\overline{\mathcal{M}(\alpha)} \subset \mathcal{Q}$, we have

(b1) *The boundary of $\mathcal{M}(\alpha)$ is characterized by $\partial\mathcal{M}(\alpha) = \{\boldsymbol{\varphi} \in \mathcal{Q} : \mathfrak{r}(\boldsymbol{\varphi}) = \alpha\} \neq \emptyset$.*

(b2) *$\partial\mathcal{M}(\alpha)$ is a codimension one manifold which varies continuously in α.*

Proof. $\mathcal{M}(\alpha)$ is a convex set, because $\mathfrak{r}$ is a convex function on the convex domain $\mathcal{Q}$. Thus, *(a)* is already clear.

ad (b): Assuming $\overline{\mathcal{M}(\alpha)} \subset \mathcal{Q}$ is bounded immediately yields $\mathring{\mathcal{M}}(\alpha) = \{\boldsymbol{\varphi} \in \mathcal{Q} : \mathfrak{r}(\boldsymbol{\varphi}) < \alpha\}$ and $\partial\mathcal{M}(\alpha) = \{\boldsymbol{\varphi} \in \mathcal{Q} : \mathfrak{r}(\boldsymbol{\varphi}) = \alpha\} \neq \emptyset$, the latter being a codimension one manifold and continuously varying in α due to Definition 3(c). □

In order to define a nontrivial ACRM, we use the down-trade log series of (11).

Theorem 4. *For a trading game, as in Setup 1, satisfying Assumption 1 the function $\mathfrak{r}_{\text{down}} : \mathring{\mathfrak{G}} \to \mathbb{R}_0^+$,*

$$\mathfrak{r}_{\text{down}}(\boldsymbol{\varphi}) = \mathfrak{r}_{\text{down}}^{(K)}(\boldsymbol{\varphi}) := -\mathbb{E}\left(\mathcal{D}^{(K)}(\boldsymbol{\varphi},\cdot)\right) \geq 0, \tag{33}$$

stemming from the down-trade log series in (11), *is an admissible convex risk measure (ACRM).*

Proof. We show that $\mathfrak{r}_{\text{down}}$ has the three properties, (a), (b), and (c), from Definition 3.

ad (a): $\mathcal{Q} = \mathring{\mathfrak{G}}$ is a convex set with $0 \in \mathring{\mathfrak{G}}$ according to Lemma 1. Since for all $\omega \in \Omega^{(K)}$ and $\boldsymbol{\varphi} \in \mathring{\mathfrak{G}}$

$$\mathcal{D}^{(K)}(\boldsymbol{\varphi},\omega) = \ln\Big(\min\big\{1, \text{TWR}_1^K(\boldsymbol{\varphi},\omega)\big\} \Big) = \min\big\{0, \ln \text{TWR}_1^K(\boldsymbol{\varphi},\omega)\big\} \leq 0$$

and $\text{TWR}_1^K(0,\omega) = 1$ we obtain Definition 3(a).

ad (b): For each fixed $\omega = (\omega_1,\ldots,\omega_K) \in \Omega^{(K)}$ the function $\boldsymbol{\varphi} \mapsto \text{TWR}_1^K(\boldsymbol{\varphi},\omega)$ is continuous in $\boldsymbol{\varphi}$, and therefore, the same holds true for $\mathfrak{r}_{\text{down}}$. Moreover, again for $\omega \in \Omega^{(K)}$ fixed, $\boldsymbol{\varphi} \mapsto \ln\, \text{TWR}_1^K(\boldsymbol{\varphi},\omega) = \sum_{j=1}^K \ln\Big(1 + \langle \boldsymbol{t}_{\omega_j\bullet}^\top, \boldsymbol{\varphi}\rangle\Big)$ is a concave function of $\boldsymbol{\varphi}$, since all summands are composed of the concave ln–function with an affine function. Thus, $\mathcal{D}^{(K)}(\boldsymbol{\varphi},\omega)$ is concave as well since the minimum of two concave functions is still concave, and therefore, $\mathfrak{r}_{\text{down}}$ is convex.

ad (c): It is sufficient to show that

$$\begin{aligned}&\mathfrak{r}_{\text{down}} \text{ from (33) is strictly convex along the line } \big\{s\boldsymbol{\theta}_0 : s > 0\big\} \cap \mathring{\mathfrak{G}} \subset \mathbb{R}^M \\ &\text{for any fixed } \boldsymbol{\theta}_0 \in \mathbb{S}_1^{M-1}.\end{aligned} \tag{34}$$

Therefore, let $\boldsymbol{\theta}_0 \in \mathbb{S}_1^{M-1}$ be fixed. In order to show (34), we need to find at least one $\overline{\omega} \in \Omega^{(K)}$ such that $\mathcal{D}^{(K)}(s\boldsymbol{\theta}_0, \overline{\omega})$ is strictly concave in $s > 0$. Using Assumption 1 we obtain some $i_0 = i_0(\boldsymbol{\theta}_0)$ such that $\langle \boldsymbol{t}_{i_0\bullet}^\top, \boldsymbol{\theta}_0 \rangle < 0$. Hence, for $\boldsymbol{\varphi}_s = s \cdot \boldsymbol{\theta}_0 \in \mathring{\mathfrak{G}}$ and $\overline{\omega} = (i_0, i_0, \ldots, i_0)$, we obtain

$$\mathcal{D}^{(K)}(s\boldsymbol{\theta}_0,\overline{\omega}) = K \cdot \ln\Big(1 + s\,\underbrace{\langle \boldsymbol{t}_{i_0\bullet}^\top, \boldsymbol{\theta}_0 \rangle}_{<0}\Big) < 0$$

which is a strictly concave function in $s > 0$. □

Example 2. *In order to illustrate* $\mathfrak{r}_{\text{down}}$ *of* (33) *and the other risk measures to follow, we introduce a simple trading game with* $M = 2$. *Set*

$$T = \begin{pmatrix} 1 & 1 \\ -\frac{1}{2} & 1 \\ 1 & -2 \\ -\frac{1}{2} & -2 \end{pmatrix} \in \mathbb{R}^{4\times 2} \quad \textit{with} \quad p_1 = p_2 = 0.375, \quad p_3 = p_4 = 0.125. \tag{35}$$

It is easy to see that bets in the first system (win 1 *with probability* 0.5 *or lose* $-\frac{1}{2}$*) and bets in the second system (win* 1 *with probability* 0.75 *or lose* -2*) are stochastically independent and have the same expectation value:* $\frac{1}{4}$. *The contour levels of* $\mathfrak{r}_{\text{down}}$ *for* $K = 5$ *are shown in Figure 1.*

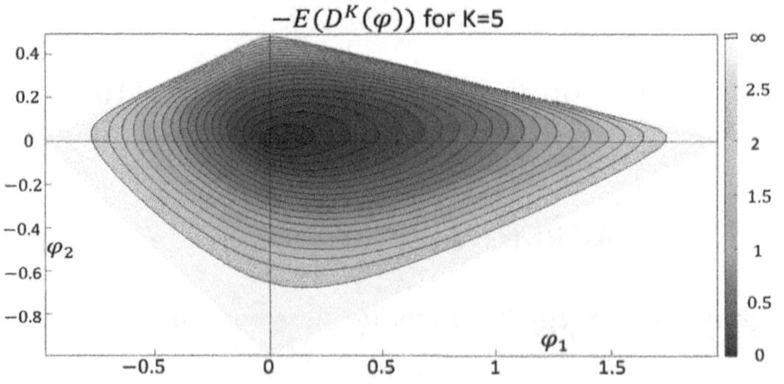

Figure 1. Contour levels for $\mathfrak{r}^{(K)}_{\text{down}}$ from (33) with $K = 5$ for T from Example 2.

Remark 10. *The function $\mathfrak{r}_{\text{down}}$ in (33) may or may not be an admissible strictly convex risk measure. To show this, we give two examples:*

(a) For

$$T = \begin{pmatrix} 1 & 2 \\ 2 & 1 \\ -1 & -1 \end{pmatrix} \in \mathbb{R}^{3\times 2} \quad (N = 3\,,\, M = 2),$$

the risk measure $\mathfrak{r}_{\text{down}}$ in (33) for $K = 1$ is not strictly convex. Consider, for example, $\boldsymbol{\varphi}_0 = \alpha \cdot (1,1)^\top \in \mathring{\mathfrak{G}}$ for some fixed $\alpha > 0$. Then, for $\boldsymbol{\varphi} \in B_\varepsilon(\boldsymbol{\varphi}_0)$, $\varepsilon > 0$ small, in the trading game, only the third row results in a loss, i.e.,

$$\mathbb{E}\left(\mathcal{D}^{(K=1)}(\boldsymbol{\varphi},\boldsymbol{\cdot})\right) = p_3 \ln\!\left(1 + \langle\, \boldsymbol{t}_{3\boldsymbol{\cdot}}^\top, \boldsymbol{\varphi}\,\rangle\right)$$

which is constant along the line $\boldsymbol{\varphi}_s = \boldsymbol{\varphi}_0 + s \cdot (1,-1)^\top \in B_\varepsilon(\boldsymbol{\varphi}_0)$ for small s and thus, ***not*** *strictly convex.*

(b) We refrain from giving a complete characterization for trade return matrices T for which (33) results in a strictly convex function, but only note that if besides Assumption 1, the condition

$$\text{span}\left\{\boldsymbol{t}_{i\boldsymbol{\cdot}}^\top : \langle\, \boldsymbol{t}_{i\boldsymbol{\cdot}}^\top, \boldsymbol{\theta}\,\rangle < 0\right\} = \mathbb{R}^M \quad \text{holds} \quad \forall\, \boldsymbol{\theta} \in \mathbb{S}_1^{M-1}, \tag{36}$$

then this is sufficient to give strict convexity of (33) and hence, in this case, $\mathfrak{r}_{\text{down}}$ in (33) is actually an ASCRM.

Now that we have seen that the negative expected down-trade log series of (33) is an admissible convex risk measure, it is natural to ask whether or not the same is true for the two approximations of the expected down-trade log series given in (22) and (29) as well. Starting with

$$d^{(K)}(s,\boldsymbol{\theta}) \;=\; \sum_{n=1}^{N} D_n^{(K,N)}(\boldsymbol{\theta}) \ln\!\left(1 + s\,\langle\, \boldsymbol{t}_{n\boldsymbol{\cdot}}^\top, \boldsymbol{\theta}\,\rangle\right)$$

from (22), the answer is negative. The reason is simply that $D_n^{(K,N)}(\boldsymbol{\theta})$ from (23) is, in general, not continuous for such $\boldsymbol{\theta} \in \mathbb{S}_1^{M-1}$ for which $(x_1,\ldots,x_N) \in \mathbb{N}_0^N$ with $\sum_{i=1}^{N} x_i = K$ exist and which satisfy $\sum_{i=1}^{N} x_i \,\langle\, \boldsymbol{t}_{i\boldsymbol{\cdot}}^\top, \boldsymbol{\theta}\,\rangle = 0$, but unlike in (32), for $\tilde{d}^{(K)}$, the sum over the log terms may not vanish.

Therefore, $d^{(K)}(s,\boldsymbol{\theta})$ is, in general, also not continuous. A more thorough discussion of this discontinuity can be found after Theorem 5. On the other hand, $\tilde{d}^{(K)}$ of (29) was proved to be continuous and nonpositive in Corollary 2. In fact, we can obtain

Theorem 5. *For the trading game of Setup 1, satisfying Assumption 1, the function $\mathfrak{r}_{\text{downX}}\colon \mathbb{R}^M \to \mathbb{R}_0^+$,*

$$\mathfrak{r}_{\text{downX}}(\boldsymbol{\varphi}) = \mathfrak{r}_{\text{downX}}^{(K)}(s\boldsymbol{\theta}) := -\,\tilde{d}^{(K)}(s,\boldsymbol{\theta}) = -s \cdot L^{(K,N)}(\boldsymbol{\theta}) \geq 0\,,\ \text{for } s \geq 0 \text{ and } \boldsymbol{\theta} \in \mathbb{S}_1^{M-1} \tag{37}$$

with $L^{(K,N)}(\boldsymbol{\theta})$ from (32) being an admissible convex risk measure (ACRM) according to Definition 3 and furthermore, positive homogeneous.

Proof. Clearly $\mathfrak{r}_{\text{downX}}$ is positive homogeneous, since $\mathfrak{r}_{\text{downX}}(s\boldsymbol{\theta}) = s \cdot \mathfrak{r}_{\text{downX}}(\boldsymbol{\theta})$ for all $s \geq 0$. So, we only need to check the ACRM properties in Definition 3.

ad (a) & ad (b): The only thing left to argue is the convexity of $\mathfrak{r}_{\mathrm{downX}}$ or the concavity of $\widetilde{d}^{(K)}(s,\boldsymbol{\theta}) = s \cdot L^{(K,N)}(\boldsymbol{\theta}) \leq 0$. To see this, according to Theorem 3

$$d^{(K)}(s,\boldsymbol{\theta}) = \mathbb{E}\left[\mathcal{D}^{(K)}(s\boldsymbol{\theta},\cdot)\right], \quad \text{for} \quad \boldsymbol{\theta} \in \mathbb{S}_1^{M-1} \quad \text{and} \quad s \in [0,\varepsilon],$$

is concave, because the right hand side is concave (see Theorem 4). Hence,

$$d_\alpha^{(K)}(s,\boldsymbol{\theta}) := \frac{\alpha}{\varepsilon}\, d^{(K)}\left(\frac{s\varepsilon}{\alpha},\boldsymbol{\theta}\right), \quad \text{for } \boldsymbol{\theta} \in \mathbb{S}_1^{M-1} \text{ and } s \in [0,\alpha]$$

is also concave. Note that right from the definition of $d^{(K)}(s,\boldsymbol{\theta})$ in (22) and of $L^{(K,N)}(\boldsymbol{\theta})$ in (32), it can readily be seen that for a fixed $\boldsymbol{\theta} \in \mathbb{S}_1^{M-1}$,

$$\frac{d^{(K)}(s,\boldsymbol{\theta})}{s} = \frac{d^{(K)}(s,\boldsymbol{\theta}) - d^{(K)}(0,\boldsymbol{\theta})}{s} \longrightarrow L^{(K,N)}(\boldsymbol{\theta}) \quad \text{for} \quad s \searrow 0.$$

Therefore, some further calculation yields uniform convergence

$$d_\alpha^{(K)}(s,\boldsymbol{\theta}) \longrightarrow s \cdot L^{(K,N)}(\boldsymbol{\theta}) \quad \text{for} \quad \alpha \to \infty$$

on the unit ball $B_1(0) := \{(s,\boldsymbol{\theta}) : s \in [0,1],\, \boldsymbol{\theta} \in \mathbb{S}_1^{M-1}\}$. Now, assuming $\widetilde{d}^{(K)}$ is not concave somewhere would immediately contradict the concavity of $d_\alpha^{(K)}$.

ad (c): In order to show that for any $\boldsymbol{\theta} \in \mathbb{S}_1^{M-1}$, the function $s \mapsto \mathfrak{r}_{\mathrm{downX}}(s\boldsymbol{\theta}) = -s\, L^{(K,N)}(\boldsymbol{\theta})$ is strictly increasing in s, it suffices to show $L^{(K,N)}(\boldsymbol{\theta}) < 0$. Since $L^{(K,N)}(\boldsymbol{\theta}) \leq 0$ is already clear, we only have to find one negative summand in (32). According to Assumption 1, for all $\boldsymbol{\theta} \in \mathbb{S}_1^{M-1}$, there is some $i_0 \leq N$, such that $\langle \boldsymbol{t}_{i_0\bullet}^{\top}, \boldsymbol{\theta} \rangle < 0$. Now, let

$$(x_1,\ldots,x_N) := (0,\ldots,0,\underset{\substack{\uparrow \\ i_0\text{-th place,}}}{K},0,\ldots,0)$$

then, $\sum_{i=1}^{N} x_i \langle \boldsymbol{t}_{i\bullet}^{\top}, \boldsymbol{\theta} \rangle = K \langle \boldsymbol{t}_{i_0\bullet}^{\top}, \boldsymbol{\theta} \rangle < 0$ giving $L^{(K,N)}(\boldsymbol{\theta}) < 0$ as claimed. □

We illustrate the contour levels of $\mathfrak{r}_{\mathrm{downX}}$ for Example 2 in Figure 2. As expected, the approximation of $\mathfrak{r}_{down}$ is best near $\boldsymbol{\varphi} = 0$ (cf. Figure 1).

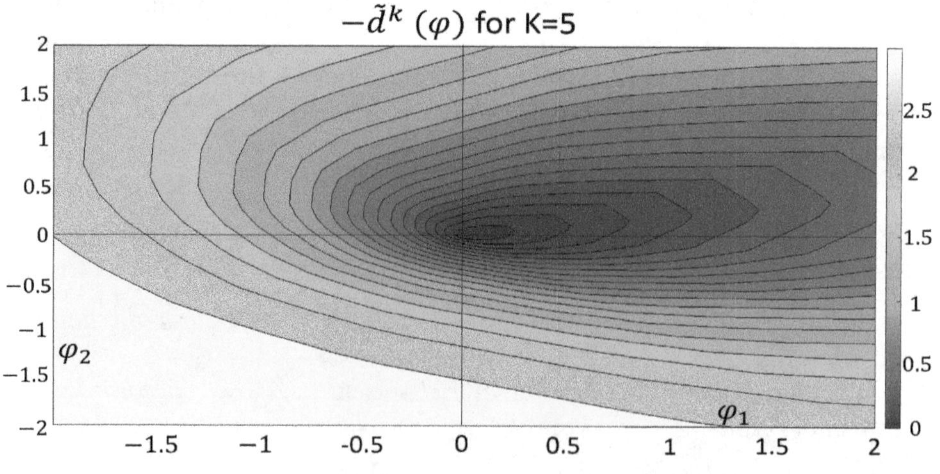

Figure 2. Contour levels for $\mathfrak{r}_{downX}^{(K)}$ with $K = 5$ for T from Example 2.

In conclusion, Theorems 4 and 5 yield two ACRM stemming from expected down-trade log series $\mathcal{D}^{(K)}$ of (11) and its second approximation $\widetilde{d}^{(K)}$ from (29). However, the first approximation $d^{(K)}$ from (22) is not an ACRM since the coefficients $D_n^{(K,N)}$ in (23) are not continuous. At first glance, however, this is puzzling since $\mathbb{E}\left(\mathcal{D}^{(K)}(s\boldsymbol{\theta},\cdot)\right)$ is clearly continuous and equals $d^{(K)}(s,\boldsymbol{\theta})$ for sufficiently small $s>0$ according to Theorem 3, $d^{(K)}(s,\boldsymbol{\theta})$ has to be continuous for small $s>0$, too. So, what have we missed? In order to unveil that "mystery", we give another representation for the expected down-trade log series again using $H^{(K,N)}$ of (19).

Lemma 5. *In the situation of Theorem 3, for all $s>0$ and $\boldsymbol{\theta}\in\mathbb{S}_1^{M-1}$ with $s\boldsymbol{\theta}\in\overset{\circ}{\mathfrak{G}}$ the following holds:*

$$\mathbb{E}\left[\mathcal{D}^{(K)}(s\boldsymbol{\theta},\cdot)\right] = \sum_{\substack{(x_1,\dots,x_N)\in\mathbb{N}_0^N\\ \sum_{i=1}^N x_i=K}} H^{(K,N)}(x_1,\dots,x_N)\cdot\ln\left(\min\left\{1,\prod_{n=1}^N\left(1+s\langle \boldsymbol{t}_{n\bullet}^\top,\boldsymbol{\theta}\rangle\right)^{x_n}\right\}\right). \tag{38}$$

Proof. (38) can be derived from the definition in (11) as follows: For $\omega\in\Omega^{(K)}$ with (14), clearly

$$\mathrm{TWR}_1^K(s\boldsymbol{\theta},\omega) = \prod_{n=1}^N\left(1+s\langle \boldsymbol{t}_{n\bullet}^\top,\boldsymbol{\theta}\rangle\right)^{x_n}$$

holds. Introducing for $s>0$ the set

$$\begin{aligned}\Xi_{x_1,\dots,x_N}(s) &:= \left\{\boldsymbol{\theta}\in\mathbb{S}_1^{M-1}:\prod_{j=1}^N\left(1+s\langle \boldsymbol{t}_{j\bullet}^\top,\boldsymbol{\theta}\rangle\right)^{x_j}<1\right\}\\ &= \left\{\boldsymbol{\theta}\in\mathbb{S}_1^{M-1}:\sum_{j=1}^N x_j\ln\left(1+s\langle \boldsymbol{t}_{j\bullet}^\top,\boldsymbol{\theta}\rangle\right)<0\right\}\end{aligned} \tag{39}$$

and using the characteristic function of a set A, χ_A, we obtain for all $s\boldsymbol{\theta}\in\overset{\circ}{\mathfrak{G}}$,

$$\mathbb{E}\left[\mathcal{D}^{(K)}(s\boldsymbol{\theta},\cdot)\right] = \sum_{\substack{(x_1,\dots,x_N)\in\mathbb{N}_0^N\\ \sum_{i=1}^N x_i=K}} H^{(K,N)}(x_1,\dots,x_N)\cdot\chi_{\Xi_{x_1,\dots,x_N}(s)}(\boldsymbol{\theta})\cdot\sum_{n=1}^N x_n\cdot\ln\left(1+s\langle \boldsymbol{t}_{n\bullet}^\top,\boldsymbol{\theta}\rangle\right) \tag{40}$$

giving (38). □

Observe that $d^{(K)}(s,\boldsymbol{\theta})$ has a similar representation, namely, using

$$\widehat{\Xi}_{x_1,\dots,x_N} := \left\{\boldsymbol{\theta}\in\mathbb{S}_1^{M-1}:\sum_{j=1}^N x_j\langle \boldsymbol{t}_{j\bullet}^\top,\boldsymbol{\theta}\rangle\le 0\right\}, \tag{41}$$

we get from the definition in (22) that for all $s\boldsymbol{\theta}\in\overset{\circ}{\mathfrak{G}}$,

$$d^{(K)}(s,\boldsymbol{\theta}) = \sum_{\substack{(x_1,\dots,x_N)\in\mathbb{N}_0^N\\ \sum_{i=1}^N x_i=K}} H^{(K,N)}(x_1,\dots,x_N)\cdot\chi_{\widehat{\Xi}_{x_1,\dots,x_N}}(\boldsymbol{\theta})\cdot\sum_{n=1}^N x_n\ln\left(1+s\langle \boldsymbol{t}_{n\bullet}^\top,\boldsymbol{\theta}\rangle\right) \tag{42}$$

holds. So, the only difference between (40) and (42) is that $\Xi_{x_1,\ldots,x_N}(s)$ is replaced by $\widehat{\Xi}_{x_1,\ldots,x_N}$ (with the latter being a half-space restricted to $\mathbb{S}_1^{M-1}$). Observing furthermore that due to (28)

$$\widehat{\Xi}_{x_1,\ldots,x_N} \subset \Xi_{x_1,\ldots,x_N}(s) \quad \forall\, s > 0\,, \tag{43}$$

the discontinuity of $d^{(K)}$ clearly comes from the discontinuity of the indicator function $\chi_{\widehat{\Xi}_{x_1,\ldots,x_N}}$, because

$$\sum_{j=1}^{N} x_j \cdot \langle \boldsymbol{t}_{j\bullet}^{\top}, \boldsymbol{\theta} \rangle = 0 \not\Leftrightarrow \sum_{n=0}^{N} x_n \ln\left(1 + s\langle \boldsymbol{t}_{n\bullet}^{\top}, \boldsymbol{\theta} \rangle\right) = 0$$

and the "mystery" is solved since Lemma 3(b) implies equality in (43) only for sufficiently small $s > 0$. Finally note that for large $s > 0$, not only the continuity gets lost, but moreover, $d^{(K)}(s, \boldsymbol{\theta})$ is no longer concave. The discontinuity can even be seen in Figure 3.

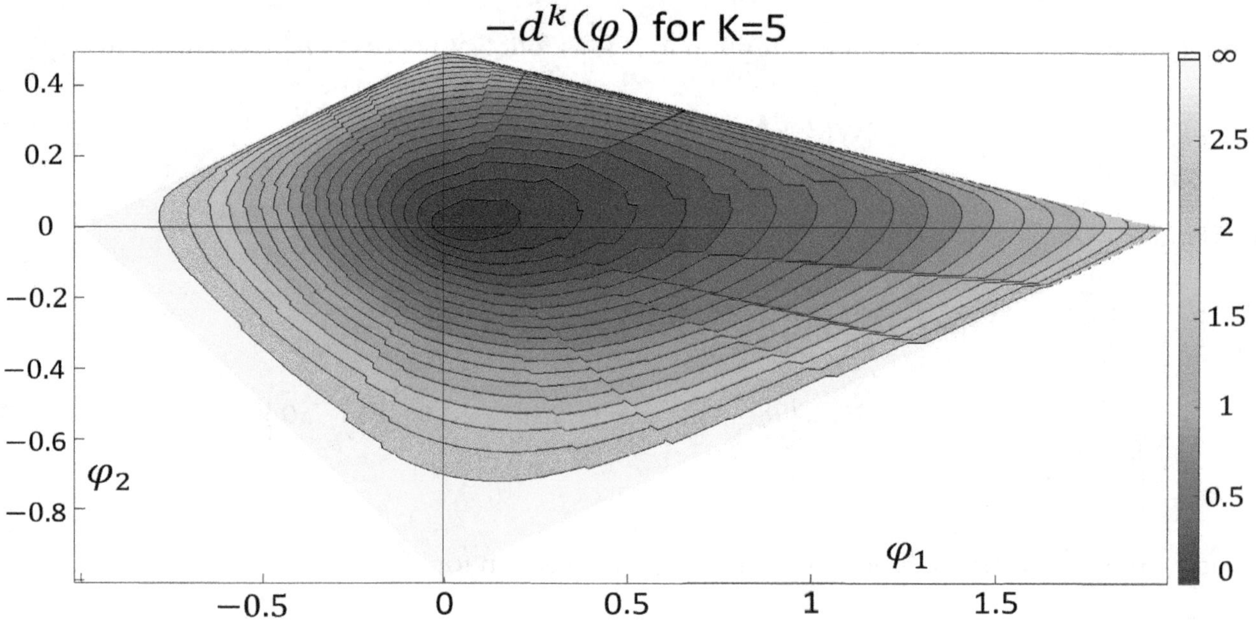

Figure 3. Discontinuous contour levels for $-d^{(K)}$ with $K = 5$ for T from Example 2.

5. The Current Drawdown

Several authors have already investigated drawdown related risk measures, focusing mostly on the absolute drawdown (see references Chekhlov et al. (2003, 2005); Goldberg and Mahmoud (2017); Zabarankin et al. (2014)). However, absolute drawdowns are problematic, in particular when long time series are observed, because then prices often vary over big ranges. We, therefore, took a different approach and constructed a drawdown related risk measure from relative drawdowns. Whereas the absolute drawdown measures the absolute price difference between the historic high points and the current price, the relative drawdown measures the percentage loss between the these two prices.

We keep discussing the trading return matrix T from (1) and probabilities $p_1, \ldots, p_N$ from Setup 1 for each row $\boldsymbol{t}_{i\bullet}$ of T. Drawing randomly and independently $K \in \mathbb{N}$ times such rows from that distribution results in a terminal wealth relative for fractional trading

$$\mathrm{TWR}_1^K(\boldsymbol{\varphi}, \omega) = \prod_{j=1}^{K}\left(1 + \langle \boldsymbol{t}_{\omega_j \bullet}^{\top}, \boldsymbol{\varphi} \rangle\right), \quad \boldsymbol{\varphi} \in \mathring{\mathfrak{G}}\,, \; \omega \in \Omega^{(K)} = \{1, \ldots, N\}^K\,,$$

depending on the betted portions, $\boldsymbol{\varphi} = (\varphi_1, \ldots, \varphi_M)$ (see Equation (8)). In order to investigate the *current drawdown* realized after the K-th draw, we more generally use the notation

$$\mathrm{TWR}_m^n(\boldsymbol{\varphi}, \omega) := \prod_{j=m}^{n} \left(1 + \langle \boldsymbol{t}_{\omega_j \bullet}^{\top}, \boldsymbol{\varphi} \rangle\right) . \tag{44}$$

The idea here is that $\mathrm{TWR}_1^n(\boldsymbol{\varphi}, \omega)$ is viewed as a discrete "equity curve" at time n (with $\boldsymbol{\varphi}$ and ω fixed). The current drawdown log series is defined as the logarithm of the drawdown of this equity curve realized from the maximum of the curve till the end (time K). We show below that this series is the counterpart of the *run–up* (cf. Figure 4).

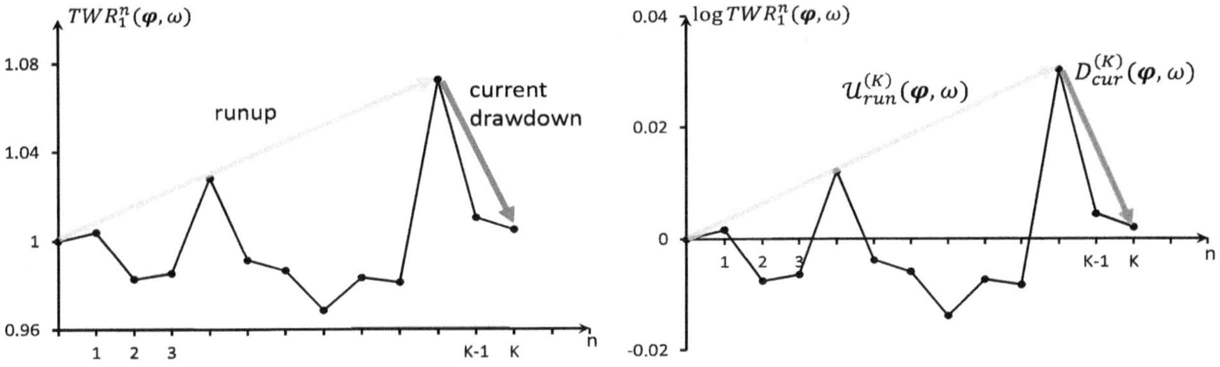

Figure 4. In the left figure, the run-up and the current drawdown are plotted for a realization of the TWR "equity"-curve and, to the right, are their log series.

Definition 6. *The* ***current drawdown log series*** *is set to*

$$\mathcal{D}_{\mathrm{cur}}^{(K)}(\boldsymbol{\varphi}, \omega) := \ln\left(\min_{1 \le \ell \le K} \min\{1, \mathrm{TWR}_\ell^K(\boldsymbol{\varphi}, \omega)\}\right) \le 0 , \tag{45}$$

and the ***run-up log series*** *is defined as*

$$\mathcal{U}_{\mathrm{run}}^{(K)}(\boldsymbol{\varphi}, \omega) := \ln\left(\max_{1 \le \ell \le K} \max\{1, \mathrm{TWR}_1^\ell(\boldsymbol{\varphi}, \omega)\}\right) \ge 0 .$$

The corresponding trade series are connected because the current drawdown starts after the run-up has stopped. To make this more precise, we fix ℓ where the run-up reaches its top.

Definition 7. ***(first*** **TWR** ***topping point)*** *For fixed* $\omega \in \Omega^{(K)}$ *and* $\boldsymbol{\varphi} \in \mathring{\mathfrak{G}}$, *define* $\ell^* = \ell^*(\boldsymbol{\varphi}, \omega) \in \{0, \ldots, K\}$ *with*

(a) $\ell^* = 0$ *in case* $\max_{1 \le \ell \le K} \mathrm{TWR}_1^\ell(\boldsymbol{\varphi}, \omega) \le 1$

(b) *and otherwise, choose* $\ell^* \in \{1, \ldots, K\}$ *such that*

$$\mathrm{TWR}_1^{\ell^*}(\boldsymbol{\varphi}, \omega) = \max_{1 \le \ell \le K} \mathrm{TWR}_1^\ell(\boldsymbol{\varphi}, \omega) > 1 , \tag{46}$$

where ℓ^* *should be minimal with that property.*

By definition, one easily gets

$$\mathcal{D}_{\mathrm{cur}}^{(K)}(\boldsymbol{\varphi}, \omega) = \begin{cases} \ln \mathrm{TWR}_{\ell^*+1}^K(\boldsymbol{\varphi}, \omega), & \text{in case } \ell^* < K, \\ 0, & \text{in case } \ell^* = K, \end{cases} \tag{47}$$

and

$$\mathcal{U}_{\text{run}}^{(K)}(\boldsymbol{\varphi}, \omega) = \begin{cases} \ln \mathrm{TWR}_1^{\ell^*}(\boldsymbol{\varphi}, \omega), & \text{in case } \ell^* \geq 1, \\ 0, & \text{in case } \ell^* = 0. \end{cases} \tag{48}$$

As in Section 3, we immediately obtain $\mathcal{D}_{\text{cur}}^{(K)}(\boldsymbol{\varphi}, \omega) + \mathcal{U}_{\text{run}}^{(K)}(\boldsymbol{\varphi}, \omega) = \mathcal{Z}^{(K)}(\boldsymbol{\varphi}, \omega)$ and therefore, by Theorem 1,

Corollary 3. *For* $\boldsymbol{\varphi} \in \mathring{\mathfrak{G}}$,

$$\mathbb{E}\left[\mathcal{D}_{\text{cur}}^{(K)}(\boldsymbol{\varphi}, \cdot)\right] + \mathbb{E}\left[\mathcal{U}_{\text{run}}^{(K)}(\boldsymbol{\varphi}, \cdot)\right] = K \cdot \ln \Gamma(\boldsymbol{\varphi}) \tag{49}$$

holds.

Explicit formulas for the expectation of $\mathcal{D}_{\text{cur}}^{(K)}$ and $\mathcal{U}_{\text{run}}^{(K)}$ are again of interest. By definition and with (47),

$$\mathbb{E}\left[\mathcal{D}_{\text{cur}}^{(K)}(\boldsymbol{\varphi}, \cdot)\right] = \sum_{\ell=0}^{K-1} \sum_{\substack{\omega \in \Omega^{(K)} \\ \ell^*(\boldsymbol{\varphi}, \omega) = \ell}} \mathbb{P}(\{\omega\}) \cdot \ln \mathrm{TWR}_{\ell+1}^{K}(\boldsymbol{\varphi}, \omega). \tag{50}$$

Before we proceed with this calculation, we need to discuss $\ell^* = \ell^*(\boldsymbol{\varphi}, \omega)$ further for some fixed ω. From Definition 7, in case $\ell^* \geq 1$, we get

$$\mathrm{TWR}_k^{\ell^*}(\boldsymbol{\varphi}, \omega) > 1 \quad \text{for } k = 1, \ldots, \ell^*, \tag{51}$$

since ℓ^* is the first time the run-up is topped, and, in case $\ell^* < K$,

$$\mathrm{TWR}_{\ell^*+1}^{\tilde{k}}(\boldsymbol{\varphi}, \omega) \leq 1 \quad \text{for } \tilde{k} = \ell^* + 1, \ldots, K. \tag{52}$$

Similarly to Section 3, we write $\boldsymbol{\varphi} \neq 0$ as $\boldsymbol{\varphi} = s\boldsymbol{\theta}$ for $\boldsymbol{\theta} \in \mathbb{S}_1^{M-1}$ and $s > 0$. The last inequality then may be rephrased for $s \in (0, \varepsilon]$ and some sufficiently small $\varepsilon > 0$ as

$$\begin{aligned} \mathrm{TWR}_{\ell^*+1}^{\tilde{k}}(s\boldsymbol{\theta}, \omega) \leq 1 \quad &\Longleftrightarrow \quad \ln \mathrm{TWR}_{\ell^*+1}^{\tilde{k}}((s\boldsymbol{\theta}, \omega) \leq 0 \\ &\Longleftrightarrow \quad \sum_{j=\ell^*+1}^{\tilde{k}} \ln\Big(1 + s\,\langle \boldsymbol{t}_{\omega_j \bullet}^{\top}, \boldsymbol{\theta} \rangle\Big) \leq 0 \\ &\Longleftrightarrow \quad \sum_{j=\ell^*+1}^{\tilde{k}} \langle \boldsymbol{t}_{\omega_j \bullet}^{\top}, \boldsymbol{\theta} \rangle \leq 0 \end{aligned} \tag{53}$$

by an argument similar to Lemma 3. Analogously, one finds for all $s \in (0, \varepsilon]$

$$\mathrm{TWR}_k^{\ell^*}(s\boldsymbol{\theta}, \omega) > 1 \Longleftrightarrow \sum_{j=k}^{\ell^*} \langle \boldsymbol{t}_{\omega_j \bullet}^{\top}, \boldsymbol{\theta} \rangle > 0. \tag{54}$$

This observation will become crucial to proof the next result on the expectation of the current drawdown.

Theorem 6. *Let a trading game as in Setup 1 with $N, K \in \mathbb{N}$ be fixed. Then, for $\boldsymbol{\theta} \in \mathbb{S}_1^{M-1}$ and $s \in (0, \varepsilon]$, the following holds:*

$$\mathbb{E}\left[\mathcal{D}_{\text{cur}}^{(K)}(s\boldsymbol{\theta}, \cdot)\right] = d_{cur}^{(K)}(s, \boldsymbol{\theta}) := \sum_{n=1}^{N} \left(\sum_{\ell=0}^{K} \Lambda_n^{(\ell,K,N)}(\boldsymbol{\theta}) \right) \cdot \ln\Big(1 + s\,\langle \boldsymbol{t}_{n\bullet}^{\top}, \boldsymbol{\theta} \rangle\Big) \tag{55}$$

where $\Lambda_n^{(K,K,N)} := 0$ is independent of $\boldsymbol{\theta}$ and for $\ell \in \{0, 1, \ldots, K-1\}$, the functions $\Lambda_n^{(\ell,K,N)}(\boldsymbol{\theta}) \geq 0$ are defined by

$$\Lambda_n^{(\ell,K,N)}(\boldsymbol{\theta}) := \sum_{\substack{\omega \in \Omega^{(K)} \\ \sum_{j=k}^{\ell} \langle \boldsymbol{t}_{\omega_j \bullet}^{\top}, \boldsymbol{\theta} \rangle > 0 \text{ for } k = 1, \ldots, \ell \\ \sum_{j=\ell+1}^{\tilde{k}} \langle \boldsymbol{t}_{\omega_j \bullet}^{\top}, \boldsymbol{\theta} \rangle \leq 0 \text{ for } \tilde{k} = \ell+1, \ldots, K}} \mathbb{P}(\{\omega\}) \cdot \#\{i \,|\, \omega_i = n,\, i \geq \ell + 1\}. \tag{56}$$

Proof. Again, the proof is very similar to the proof in the univariate case (see Theorem 5.4 in Maier-Paape (2018)). Starting with (50), we get

$$\mathbb{E}\left[\mathcal{D}_{\text{cur}}^{(K)}(s\boldsymbol{\theta}, \cdot)\right] = \sum_{\ell=0}^{K-1} \sum_{\substack{\omega \in \Omega^{(K)} \\ \ell^*(s\boldsymbol{\theta}, \omega) = \ell}} \mathbb{P}(\{\omega\}) \cdot \sum_{i=\ell+1}^{K} \ln\Big(1 + \langle \boldsymbol{t}_{\omega_i \bullet}^{\top}, s\boldsymbol{\theta} \rangle\Big)$$

and by (53) and (54) for all $s \in (0, \varepsilon]$,

$$\begin{aligned}
\mathbb{E}\left[\mathcal{D}_{\text{cur}}^{(K)}(s\boldsymbol{\theta}, \cdot)\right] &= \sum_{\ell=0}^{K-1} \sum_{\substack{\omega \in \Omega^{(K)} \\ \sum_{j=k}^{\ell} \langle \boldsymbol{t}_{\omega_j \bullet}^{\top}, \boldsymbol{\theta} \rangle > 0 \text{ for } k = 1, \ldots, \ell \\ \sum_{j=\ell+1}^{\tilde{k}} \langle \boldsymbol{t}_{\omega_j \bullet}^{\top}, \boldsymbol{\theta} \rangle \leq 0 \text{ for } \tilde{k} = \ell+1, \ldots, K}} \mathbb{P}(\{\omega\}) \cdot \sum_{i=\ell+1}^{K} \ln\Big(1 + s\,\langle \boldsymbol{t}_{\omega_i \bullet}^{\top}, \boldsymbol{\theta} \rangle\Big) \\
&= \sum_{\ell=0}^{K-1} \sum_{\substack{\omega \in \Omega^{(K)} \\ \sum_{j=k}^{\ell} \langle \boldsymbol{t}_{\omega_j \bullet}^{\top}, \boldsymbol{\theta} \rangle > 0 \text{ for } k = 1, \ldots, \ell \\ \sum_{j=\ell+1}^{\tilde{k}} \langle \boldsymbol{t}_{\omega_j \bullet}^{\top}, \boldsymbol{\theta} \rangle \leq 0 \text{ for } \tilde{k} = \ell+1, \ldots, K}} \mathbb{P}(\{\omega\}) \cdot \sum_{n=1}^{N} \#\{i \,|\, \omega_i = n,\, i \geq \ell+1\} \cdot \ln\Big(1 + s\,\langle \boldsymbol{t}_{n \bullet}^{\top}, \boldsymbol{\theta} \rangle\Big) \qquad (57) \\
&= \sum_{n=1}^{N} \sum_{\ell=0}^{K-1} \Lambda_n^{(\ell,K,N)}(\boldsymbol{\theta}) \cdot \ln\Big(1 + s\,\langle \boldsymbol{t}_{n \bullet}^{\top}, \boldsymbol{\theta} \rangle\Big) = d_{\text{cur}}^{(K)}(s, \boldsymbol{\theta})
\end{aligned}$$

since $\Lambda_n^{(K,K,N)} = 0$. □

In order to simplify the notation, we formally introduce the "linear equity curve" for $1 \leq m \leq n \leq K$, $\omega \in \Omega^{(K)} = \{1, \ldots, N\}^K$ and $\boldsymbol{\theta} \in \mathbb{S}_1^{M-1}$:

$$\text{linEQ}_m^n(\boldsymbol{\theta}, \omega) := \sum_{j=m}^{n} \langle \boldsymbol{t}_{\omega_j \bullet}^{\top}, \boldsymbol{\theta} \rangle \tag{58}$$

Then, we obtain, similarly to the first topping point $\ell^* = \ell^*(\boldsymbol{\varphi}, \omega)$ of the TWR-equity curve (44) (cf. Definition 7), the first topping point for the linear equity:

Definition 8. ***(first linear equity topping point)*** *For fixed $\omega \in \Omega^{(K)}$ and $\boldsymbol{\theta} \in \mathbb{S}_1^{M-1}$ define $\widehat{\ell}^* = \widehat{\ell}^*(\boldsymbol{\theta}, \omega) \in \{0, \ldots, K\}$ with*

(a) $\widehat{\ell}^* = 0$ *in case* $\max_{1 \le \ell \le K} \operatorname{linEQ}_1^{\ell}(\boldsymbol{\theta}, \omega) \le 0$

(b) *and otherwise, choose $\widehat{\ell}^* \in \{1, \ldots, K\}$ such that*

$$\operatorname{linEQ}_1^{\widehat{\ell}^*}(\boldsymbol{\theta}, \omega) = \max_{1 \le \ell \le K} \operatorname{linEQ}_1^{\ell}(\boldsymbol{\theta}, \omega) > 0, \tag{59}$$

where $\widehat{\ell}^*$ should be minimal with that property.

Let us discuss $\widehat{\ell}^* = \widehat{\ell}^*(\boldsymbol{\theta}, \omega)$ further for some fixed ω. From Definition 8, in case $\widehat{\ell}^* \ge 1$, we get

$$\operatorname{linEQ}_k^{\widehat{\ell}^*}(\boldsymbol{\theta}, \omega) > 0 \quad \text{for} \quad k = 1, \ldots, \widehat{\ell}^* \tag{60}$$

since $\widehat{\ell}^*$ is the first time that the run-up of the linear equity has been topped and, in case $\widehat{\ell}^* < K$

$$\operatorname{linEQ}_{\widehat{\ell}^*+1}^{\widetilde{k}}(\boldsymbol{\theta}, \omega) \le 0 \quad \text{for} \quad \widetilde{k} = \widehat{\ell}^* + 1, \ldots, K. \tag{61}$$

Hence, we conclude that $\omega \in \Omega^{(K)}$ satisfies $\widehat{\ell}^*(\boldsymbol{\theta}, \omega) = \ell$ if and only if

$$\sum_{j=k}^{\ell} \langle \boldsymbol{t}_{\omega_j \bullet}^{\top}, \boldsymbol{\theta} \rangle > 0 \text{ for } k = 1, \ldots, \ell \quad \text{and} \quad \sum_{j=\ell+1}^{\tilde{k}} \langle \boldsymbol{t}_{\omega_j \bullet}^{\top}, \boldsymbol{\theta} \rangle \le 0 \text{ for } \tilde{k} = \ell + 1, \ldots, K. \tag{62}$$

Therefore, (56) simplifies to

$$\Lambda_n^{(\ell,K,N)}(\boldsymbol{\theta}) = \sum_{\substack{\omega \in \Omega^{(K)} \\ \widehat{\ell}^*(\boldsymbol{\theta}, \omega) = \ell}} \mathbb{P}(\{\omega\}) \cdot \#\{i \,|\, \omega_i = n, \, i \ge \ell + 1\}. \tag{63}$$

Furthermore, according to (53) and (54), for small $s > 0$, ℓ^* ad $\widehat{\ell}^*$ coincide, i.e.,

$$\widehat{\ell}^*(\boldsymbol{\theta}, \omega) = \ell^*(s\boldsymbol{\theta}, \omega) \quad \text{for all} \quad s \in (0, \varepsilon]. \tag{64}$$

A very similar argument to the proof of Theorem 6 yields

Theorem 7. *In the situation of Theorem 6, for $\boldsymbol{\theta} \in \mathbb{S}_1^{M-1}$ and all $s \in (0, \varepsilon]$,*

$$\mathbb{E}\left[\mathcal{U}_{\text{run}}^{(K)}(s\boldsymbol{\theta}, \cdot)\right] = u_{\text{run}}^{(K)}(s, \boldsymbol{\theta}) := \sum_{n=1}^{N} \left(\sum_{\ell=0}^{K} \Upsilon_n^{(\ell,K,N)}(\boldsymbol{\theta}) \right) \cdot \ln\Big(1 + s \langle \boldsymbol{t}_{n\bullet}^{\top}, \boldsymbol{\theta} \rangle\Big) \tag{65}$$

holds, where $\Upsilon_n^{(0,K,N)} := 0$ is independent from $\boldsymbol{\theta}$ and for $\ell \in \{1, \ldots, K\}$, the functions $\Upsilon_n^{(\ell,K,N)}(\boldsymbol{\theta}) \ge 0$ are given as

$$\Upsilon_n^{(\ell,K,N)}(\boldsymbol{\theta}) := \sum_{\substack{\omega \in \Omega^{(K)} \\ \widehat{\ell}^*(\boldsymbol{\theta}, \omega) = \ell}} \mathbb{P}(\{\omega\}) \cdot \#\{i \,|\, \omega_i = n, \, i \le \ell\}. \tag{66}$$

Remark 11. *Again, we immediately obtain a first-order approximation for the expected current drawdown log series. For $s \in (0, \varepsilon]$,*

$$\mathbb{E}\left[\mathcal{D}_{\text{cur}}^{(K)}(s\boldsymbol{\theta}, \cdot)\right] \approx \tilde{d}_{\text{cur}}^{(K)}(s, \boldsymbol{\theta}) := s \cdot \sum_{n=1}^{N} \left(\sum_{\ell=0}^{K} \Lambda_n^{(\ell,K,N)}(\boldsymbol{\theta}) \right) \cdot \langle \boldsymbol{t}_{n\bullet}^{\top}, \boldsymbol{\theta} \rangle \tag{67}$$

holds. Moreover, since $\mathcal{D}_{\text{cur}}^{(K)}(\boldsymbol{\varphi},\omega) \leq \mathcal{D}^{(K)}(\boldsymbol{\varphi},\omega) \leq 0$, $d_{\text{cur}}^{(K)}(s,\boldsymbol{\theta}) \leq d^{(K)}(s,\boldsymbol{\theta}) \leq 0$ *and* $\tilde{d}_{\text{cur}}^{(K)}(s,\boldsymbol{\theta}) \leq \tilde{d}^{(K)}(s,\boldsymbol{\theta}) \leq 0$ *holds as well.*

As discussed in Section 4 for the down-trade log series, we also want to study the current drawdown log series (45) with respect to admissible convex risk measures.

Theorem 8. *For a trading game as in Setup 1 satisfying Assumption 1, the function* $\mathfrak{r}_{\text{cur}}: \mathring{\mathfrak{G}} \to \mathbb{R}_0^+$,

$$\mathfrak{r}_{\text{cur}}(\boldsymbol{\varphi}) = \mathfrak{r}_{\text{cur}}^{(K)}(\boldsymbol{\varphi}) := -\mathbb{E}\left[\mathcal{D}_{\text{cur}}^{(K)}(\boldsymbol{\varphi},\cdot)\right] \geq 0, \quad \boldsymbol{\varphi} \in \mathring{\mathfrak{G}}, \tag{68}$$

is an admissible convex risk measure (ACRM).

Proof. It is easy to see that the proof of Theorem 4 can almost literally be adapted to the current drawdown case. □

Regard Figure 5 for an illustration of $\mathfrak{r}_{\text{cur}}$. Compared to $\mathfrak{r}_{\text{down}}$ in Figure 1 the contour plot looks quite similar, but near $0 \in \mathbb{R}^M$, obviously, $\mathfrak{r}_{\text{cur}}$ grows faster. Similarly, we obtain an ACRM for the first-order approximation $\tilde{d}_{\text{cur}}^{(K)}(s,\boldsymbol{\theta})$ in (67):

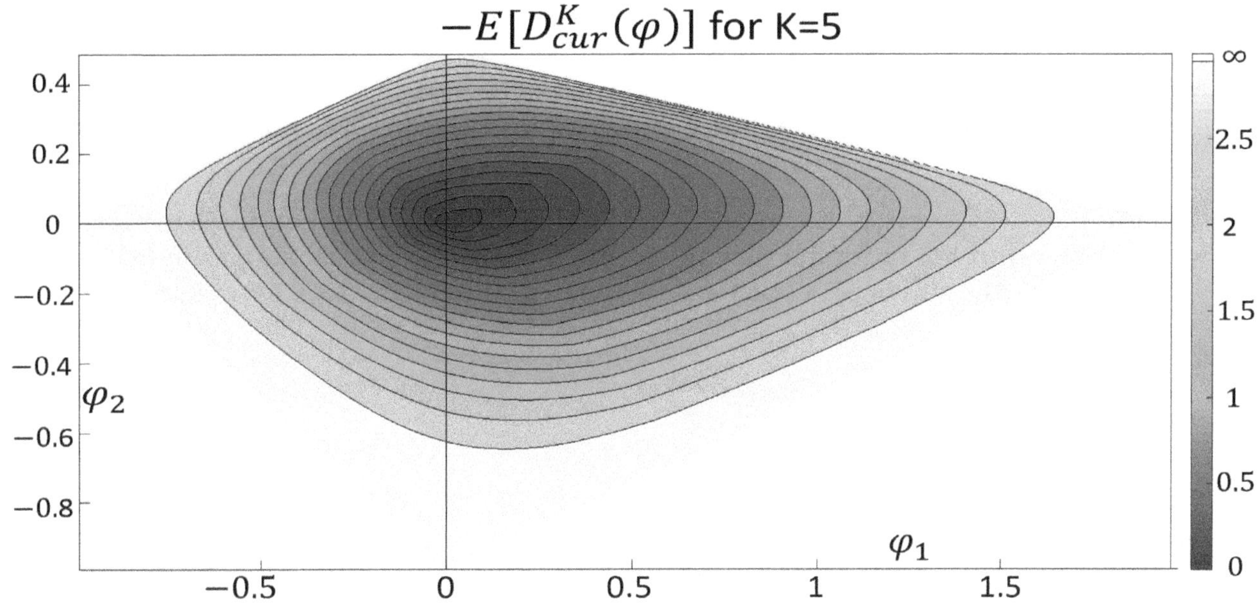

Figure 5. Contour levels for $\mathfrak{r}_{cur}^{(K)}$ from (68) with $K = 5$ for Example 2.

Theorem 9. *For the trading game of Setup 1 satisfying Assumption 1, the function* $\mathfrak{r}_{\text{cur}X}: \mathbb{R}^M \to \mathbb{R}_0^+$,

$$\mathfrak{r}_{\text{cur}X}(\boldsymbol{\varphi}) = \mathfrak{r}_{\text{cur}X}^{(K)}(s\boldsymbol{\theta}) := -\tilde{d}_{\text{cur}}^{(K)}(s,\boldsymbol{\theta}) = -s \cdot L_{\text{cur}}^{(K,N)}(\boldsymbol{\theta}) \geq 0, \; \textit{for} \quad s \geq 0 \quad \textit{and} \quad \boldsymbol{\theta} \in \mathbb{S}_1^{M-1}$$

with

$$L_{\text{cur}}^{(K,N)}(\boldsymbol{\theta}) := \sum_{\ell=0}^{K-1} \sum_{\substack{\omega \in \Omega^{(K)} \\ \widehat{\ell}^*(\boldsymbol{\theta},\omega)=\ell}} \mathbb{P}(\{\omega\}) \cdot \sum_{i=\ell+1}^{K} \langle \, \boldsymbol{t}_{\omega_i \bullet}^{\top}, \, \boldsymbol{\theta} \, \rangle \tag{69}$$

is an admissible convex risk measure (ACRM) according to Definition 3 which is moreover positive homogeneous.

Proof. We use (57) to derive the above formula for $L_{\text{cur}}^{(K,N)}(\boldsymbol{\theta})$. Now, most of the arguments of the proof of Theorem 5 work here as well, once we know that $L_{\text{cur}}^{(K,N)}(\boldsymbol{\theta})$ is continuous in $\boldsymbol{\theta}$. To see that, we remark once more that for the first topping point, $\widehat{\ell}^* = \widehat{\ell}^*(\boldsymbol{\theta},\omega) \in \{0,\ldots,K\}$, of the linearized equity curve $\sum_{j=1}^{n} \langle \boldsymbol{t}_{\omega_j \bullet}^{\top}, \boldsymbol{\theta} \rangle$, $n = 1,\ldots,K$, the following holds (cf. Definition 8 and (61)):

$$\text{linEQ}_{\widehat{\ell}^*+1}^{K}(\boldsymbol{\theta},\omega) = \sum_{i=\widehat{\ell}^*+1}^{K} \langle \boldsymbol{t}_{\omega_i \bullet}^{\top}, \boldsymbol{\theta} \rangle \leq 0\,.$$

Thus,

$$L_{\text{cur}}^{(K,N)}(\boldsymbol{\theta}) = \sum_{\ell=0}^{K-1} \sum_{\substack{\omega\in\Omega^{(K)} \\ \widehat{\ell}^*(\boldsymbol{\theta},\omega)=\ell}} \mathbb{P}(\{\omega\}) \cdot \underbrace{\sum_{i=\ell+1}^{K} \langle \boldsymbol{t}_{\omega_i \bullet}^{\top}, \boldsymbol{\theta} \rangle}_{\leq 0} \leq 0\,.$$

Although the topping point $\widehat{\ell}^*(\boldsymbol{\theta},\omega)$ for $\omega \in \Omega^{(K)}$ may jump when $\boldsymbol{\theta}$ is varied in case $\sum_{i=\widehat{\ell}^*+1}^{j} \langle \boldsymbol{t}_{\omega_i \bullet}^{\top}, \boldsymbol{\theta} \rangle = 0$ for some $j \geq \widehat{\ell}^* + 1$, i.e.,

$$\sum_{i=\widehat{\ell}^*+1}^{K} \langle \boldsymbol{t}_{\omega_i \bullet}^{\top}, \boldsymbol{\theta} \rangle = \sum_{i=j}^{K} \langle \boldsymbol{t}_{\omega_i \bullet}^{\top}, \boldsymbol{\theta} \rangle\,,$$

the continuity of $L_{\text{cur}}^{(K,N)}(\boldsymbol{\theta})$ is still granted since the summation is over all $\ell = 0,\ldots,K-1$. Hence, all claims are proved. □

A contour plot of $\mathfrak{r}_{\text{curX}}$ can be seen in Figure 6. The first topping point of the linearized equity curve will also be helpful to order the risk measures $\mathfrak{r}_{\text{cur}}$ and $\mathfrak{r}_{\text{curX}}$. Reasoning as in (53) (see also Lemma 3) and using (61), we obtain, in case $\widehat{\ell}^* < K$ for $s \in (0,\varepsilon]$ and $\widetilde{k} = \widehat{\ell}^* + 1,\ldots,K$, that

$$\text{linEQ}_{\widehat{\ell}^*+1}^{\widetilde{k}}(\boldsymbol{\theta},\omega) = \sum_{j=\widehat{\ell}^*+1}^{\widetilde{k}} \langle \boldsymbol{t}_{\omega_j \bullet}^{\top}, \boldsymbol{\theta} \rangle \leq 0 \implies \sum_{j=\widehat{\ell}^*+1}^{\widetilde{k}} \ln\Big(1 + s\,\langle \boldsymbol{t}_{\omega_j \bullet}^{\top}, \boldsymbol{\theta} \rangle\Big) \leq 0\,. \tag{70}$$

However, since ln is concave, the above implication holds true even for all $s > 0$ with $\boldsymbol{\varphi} = s\boldsymbol{\theta} \in \mathring{\mathfrak{G}}$. Hence, for $\widetilde{k} = \widehat{\ell}^* + 1,\ldots,K$ and $\boldsymbol{\varphi} = s\boldsymbol{\theta} \in \mathring{\mathfrak{G}}$

$$\text{linEQ}_{\widehat{\ell}^*+1}^{\widetilde{k}}(\boldsymbol{\theta},\omega) \leq 0 \implies \ln \text{TWR}_{\widehat{\ell}^*+1}^{\widetilde{k}}(s\boldsymbol{\theta},\omega) \leq 0\,. \tag{71}$$

Looking at (52) once more, we observe that the first topping point of the TWR equity curve ℓ^* necessarily is less than or equal to $\widehat{\ell}^*$. Thus, we have shown

Lemma 6. *For all $\omega \in \Omega^{(K)}$ and $\boldsymbol{\varphi} = s\boldsymbol{\theta} \in \mathring{\mathfrak{G}}$ the following holds (see also (64)):*

$$\ell^*(s\boldsymbol{\theta},\omega) \leq \widehat{\ell}^*(\boldsymbol{\theta},\omega)\,. \tag{72}$$

This observation helps to order $\mathbb{E}\left[\mathcal{D}_{\text{cur}}^{(K)}(s\boldsymbol{\theta},\bullet)\right]$ and $d_{\text{cur}}^{(K)}(s,\boldsymbol{\theta})$:

Theorem 10. *For all $\boldsymbol{\varphi} = s\boldsymbol{\theta} \in \mathring{\mathfrak{G}}$, with $s > 0$ and $\boldsymbol{\theta} \in \mathbb{S}_1^{M-1}$, we have*

$$\mathbb{E}\left[\mathcal{D}_{\text{cur}}^{(K)}(s\boldsymbol{\theta},\bullet)\right] \leq d_{\text{cur}}^{(K)}(s,\boldsymbol{\theta}) \leq \widetilde{d}_{\text{cur}}^{(K)}(s,\boldsymbol{\theta}) \leq 0\,. \tag{73}$$

Proof. Using (50) for $\boldsymbol{\varphi} = s\boldsymbol{\theta} \in \overset{\circ}{\mathfrak{G}}$,

$$\begin{aligned}
\mathbb{E}\left[\mathcal{D}_{\text{cur}}^{(K)}(s\boldsymbol{\theta},\boldsymbol{\cdot})\right] &= \sum_{\ell=0}^{K-1} \sum_{\substack{\omega\in\Omega^{(K)}\\ \ell^*(s\boldsymbol{\theta},\omega)=\ell}} \mathbb{P}(\{\omega\}) \cdot \ln \mathrm{TWR}_{\ell+1}^{K}(s\boldsymbol{\theta},\omega) \\
&\overset{\text{Lemma 6}}{\leq} \sum_{\ell=0}^{K-1} \sum_{\substack{\omega\in\Omega^{(K)}\\ \tilde{\ell}^*(\boldsymbol{\theta},\omega)=\ell}} \mathbb{P}(\{\omega\}) \cdot \sum_{i=\ell+1}^{K} \ln\Big(1 + s\,\langle \boldsymbol{t}_{\omega_i\bullet}^{\top}, \boldsymbol{\theta}\rangle\Big) \\
&\overset{(62)}{=} \sum_{\ell=0}^{K-1} \sum_{\substack{\omega\in\Omega^{(K)}\\ \sum_{j=k}^{\ell}\langle \boldsymbol{t}_{\omega_j\bullet}^{\top},\boldsymbol{\theta}\rangle > 0 \text{ for } k=1,\dots,\ell \\ \sum_{j=\ell+1}^{\tilde{k}}\langle \boldsymbol{t}_{\omega_j\bullet}^{\top},\boldsymbol{\theta}\rangle \leq 0 \text{ for } \tilde{k}=\ell+1,\dots,K}} \mathbb{P}(\{\omega\}) \cdot \sum_{i=\ell+1}^{K} \ln\Big(1 + s\,\langle \boldsymbol{t}_{\omega_i\bullet}^{\top}, \boldsymbol{\theta}\rangle\Big) \overset{(57)}{=} d_{\text{cur}}^{(K)}(s,\boldsymbol{\theta})\,.
\end{aligned}$$

The second inequality in (73) follows, as in Section 3, from $\ln(1+x) \leq x$ (see (55) and (67)) and the third inequality is already clear from Remark 11. □

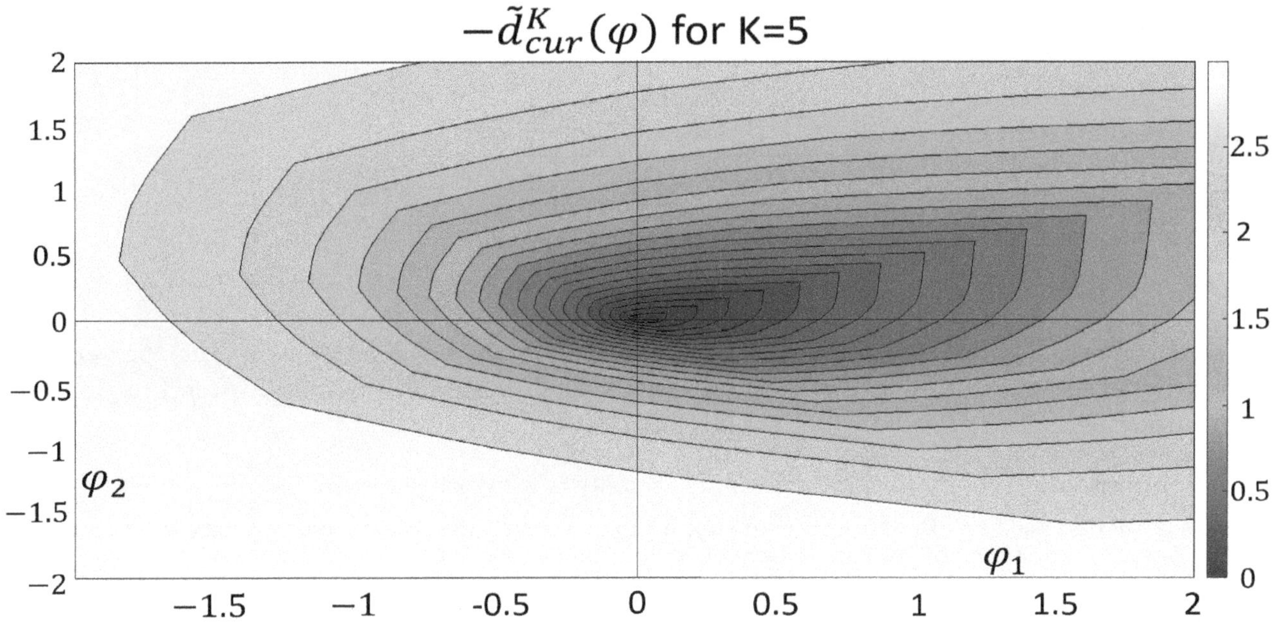

Figure 6. Contour levels for $\mathfrak{r}_{curX}^{(K)}$ from Theorem 9 with $K = 5$ for Example 2.

6. Conclusions

Let us summarize the results of the last sections. We obtained two down-trade log series related admissible convex risk measures (ACRM) according to Definition 3, namely

$$\mathfrak{r}_{\text{down}}(\boldsymbol{\varphi}) \geq \mathfrak{r}_{\text{down}X}(\boldsymbol{\varphi}) \geq 0 \quad \text{for all} \quad \boldsymbol{\varphi} \in \overset{\circ}{\mathfrak{G}}$$

(see Corollary 2 and Theorems 4 and 5). Similarly, we obtained two current drawdown-related (ACRM), namely,

$$\mathfrak{r}_{\text{cur}}(\boldsymbol{\varphi}) \geq \mathfrak{r}_{\text{cur}X}(\boldsymbol{\varphi}) \geq 0 \quad \text{for all} \quad \boldsymbol{\varphi} \in \overset{\circ}{\mathfrak{G}}$$

(cf. Theorems 8 and 9 as well as Theorem 10). Furthermore, due to Remark 11, we have the ordering

$$\mathfrak{r}_{\text{cur}}(\boldsymbol{\varphi}) \geq \mathfrak{r}_{\text{down}}(\boldsymbol{\varphi}) \quad \text{and} \quad \mathfrak{r}_{\text{cur}X}(\boldsymbol{\varphi}) \geq \mathfrak{r}_{\text{down}X}(\boldsymbol{\varphi}), \; \boldsymbol{\varphi} \in \mathring{\mathfrak{G}}. \tag{74}$$

All four risk measures can be used in order to apply the general framework for the portfolio theory of reference Maier-Paape and Zhu (2018). Since the two approximated risk measures $\mathfrak{r}_{\text{down}X}$ and $\mathfrak{r}_{\text{cur}X}$ are positive homogeneous, according to reference Maier-Paape and Zhu (2018), the efficient portfolios will have an affine linear structure. Although we were able to prove a lot of results for these for practical applications relevant risk measures, there are still open questions. To state only one of them, we note that convergence of these risk measures for $K \to \infty$ is unclear, but empirical evidence seems to support such a statement (see Figure 7).

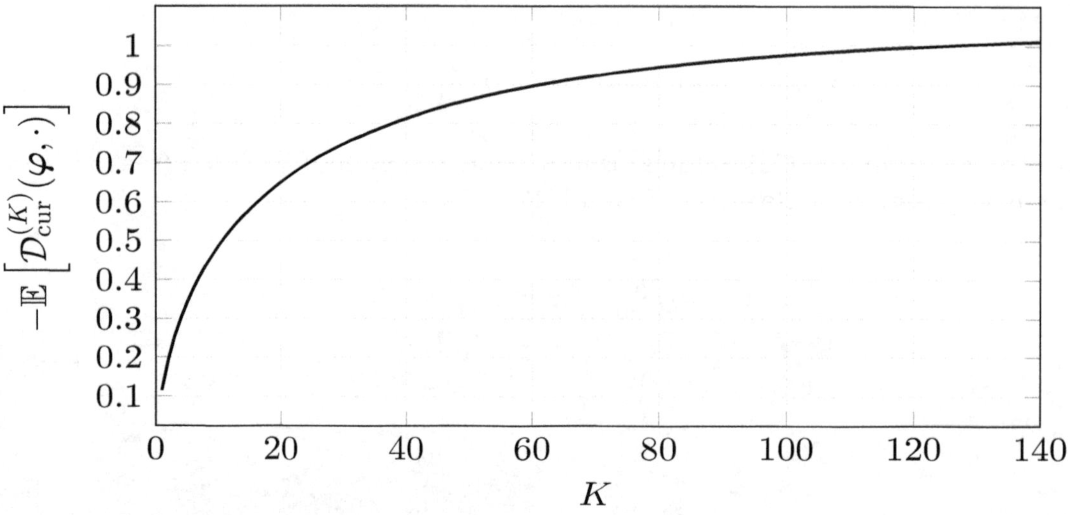

Figure 7. Convergence of $\mathfrak{r}_{\text{cur}}^{(K)}$ with fixed $\boldsymbol{\varphi}^* = (\varphi_1^*, \varphi_2^*)^T = \left(\frac{1}{5}, \frac{1}{5}\right)^\top$ for Example 2 .

Furthermore, a variety of real-world applications should be discussed in order to verify the practical benefit of portfolios constructed with drawdown risk measures. We intend to do this in future work.

Author Contributions: S.M.-P. and Q.J.Z. contributed equally to the work reported.

Acknowledgments: We thank René Brenner for support in generating the contour plots of the risk measures and Andreas Platen for careful reading of an earlier version of the manuscript.

Abbreviations

The following abbreviations are used in this manuscript:

ACRM	Admissible Convex Risk Measure
ASCRM	Admissible Strictly Convex Risk Measure
TWR	Terminal Wealth Relative
HPR	Holding Period Return

Appendix A. Transfer of a One Period Financial Market to the TWR Setup

The aim of this appendix is to show that a one period financial market can be transformed into the Terminal Wealth Relative (TWR) setting of Vince (1992, 2009). In particular, we show how the trade return matrix T of (1) has to be defined in order to apply the risk measure theory for current drawdowns of Section 4 and 5 to the general framework for portfolio theory of Part I, Maier-Paape and Zhu (2018).

Definition A1. *(one period financial market) Let $S_t = (S_t^0, S_t^1, \ldots, S_t^M)^\top$, $t \in \{0,1\}$ be a financial market in a one period economy. Here, $S_0^0 = 1$ and $S_1^0 = R \geq 1$ represents a risk free bond, whereas the other components, $S_t^m, m = 1, \ldots, M$ represent the price of the m-th risky asset at time t and $\widehat{S}_t = (S_t^1, \ldots, S_t^M)^\top$ is the column vector of all risky assets. S_0 is assumed to be a constant vector whose components are the prices of the assets at $t = 0$. Furthermore, $\widehat{S}_1 = (S_1^1, \ldots, S_1^M)^\top$ is assumed to be a random vector in a finite probability space $\mathcal{A} = \mathcal{A}_N = \{\alpha_1, \ldots, \alpha_N\}$, i.e., $\widehat{S}_1 : \mathcal{A}_N \to \mathbb{R}^M$ represents the new price at $t = 1$ for the risky assets, with probabilities $\mathbb{P}(\{\alpha_i\}) = q_i$ for $i = 1, \ldots, N$.*

A portfolio is a column vector $x \in \mathbb{R}^{M+1}$ whose components x_m represent the investments in the m-th asset, $m = 0, \ldots, M$. Hence, $\widehat{x} = (x_1, \ldots, x_M)^\top \in \mathbb{R}^M$ represents the risky assets and x_0 represents the bond. In order to normalize that situation, we consider portfolios with unit initial cost, i.e.,

$$S_0^\top x = 1. \tag{A1}$$

Since $S_0^0 = 1$ this implies

$$x_0 + \widehat{S}_0^\top \widehat{x} = x_0 + \sum_{m=1}^{M} S_0^m x_m = 1. \tag{A2}$$

Therefore, the interpretation in Table A1 is obvious.

Table A1. Invested capital portions.

x_0	portion of capital invested in bond
$S_0^m x_m$	portion of capital invested in m-th risky asset, $m = 1, \ldots, M$

So, if an investor has an initial capital of C_{ini} in his depot, the invested money in the depot is divided as in Table A2.

Table A2. Invested money in depot for a portfolio $x = (x_0, \ldots, x_M)^T$.

$C_{ini}\, x_0$	cash position of the depot
$C_{ini}\, S_0^m\, x_m$	invested money in m-th asset, $m = 1, \ldots, M$
$C_{ini}\, x_m$	amount of shares of m-th asset to be bought at $t = 0$, $m = 1, \ldots, M$

Clearly $(S_1 - R\, S_0)^\top x = S_1^\top x - R$ is the (random) gain of the unit initial cost portfolio relative to the riskless bond. In such a situation, the merit of a portfolio x is often measured by its expected utility $\mathbb{E}\left[u\left(S_1^\top x\right)\right]$, where $u\colon \mathbb{R} \to \mathbb{R} \cup \{-\infty\}$ is an increasing concave utility function (see reference Maier-Paape and Zhu (2018), Assumption 3). In growth optimal portfolio theory, the natural logarithm $u = \ln$ (cf. e.g., reference Maier-Paape and Zhu (2018), sct. 6) is used to yield the optimization problem:

$$\begin{aligned} \mathbb{E}\left[\ln(S_1^\top x)\right] &\overset{!}{=} \max, \qquad x \in \mathbb{R}^{M+1}, \\ \text{s.t.} \qquad S_0^\top x &= 1. \end{aligned} \tag{A3}$$

The following discussion aims to show that the above optimization problem (A3) is an alternative way of stating the Terminal Wealth Relative optimization problem of Vince (cf. Hermes and Maier-Paape (2017); Vince (1995)). Using $S_1^0 = R$, we obtain $S_1^\top x = R\,x_0 + \widehat{S}_1^\top \widehat{x}$ and hence with (A2),

$$\begin{aligned}\mathbb{E}\left[\ln(S_1^\top x)\right] &= \mathbb{E}\left[\ln\left(R(1-\widehat{S}_0^\top \widehat{x}) + \widehat{S}_1^\top \widehat{x}\right)\right] \\ &= \sum_{\alpha \in \mathcal{A}_N} \mathbb{P}(\{\alpha\}) \cdot \ln\left(R + \left[\widehat{S}_1(\alpha) - R\,\widehat{S}_0\right]^\top \widehat{x}\right).\end{aligned}$$

Using the probabilities for $\alpha \in \mathcal{A}_N$ in Definition A1, we furthermore get

$$\begin{aligned}\mathbb{E}\left[\ln(S_1^\top x)\right] - \ln(R) &= \sum_{i=1}^N q_i \ln\left(1 + \left[\frac{\widehat{S}_1(\alpha_i) - R\widehat{S}_0}{R}\right]^\top \widehat{x}\right) \\ &= \sum_{i=1}^N q_i \ln\left(1 + \sum_{m=1}^M \underbrace{\left[\frac{S_1^m(\alpha_i) - R\,S_0^m}{R\,S_0^m}\right]}_{=:\,t_{i,m}} \cdot \underbrace{S_0^m\,x_m}_{=:\,\varphi_m}\right).\end{aligned} \tag{A4}$$

This results in a "trade return" matrix,

$$T = (t_{i,m})_{\substack{1\le i\le N\\ 1\le m\le M}} \in \mathbb{R}^{N\times M}, \tag{A5}$$

whose entries represent discounted relative returns of the m-th asset for the i-th realization α_i. Furthermore, the column vector $\boldsymbol{\varphi} = (\varphi_m)_{1\le m\le M} \in \mathbb{R}^M$ with components $\varphi_m = S_0^m\,x_m$ has, according to Table A1, the interpretation given in Table A3.

Table A3. Investment vector $\boldsymbol{\varphi} = (\varphi_1, \ldots, \varphi_M)^T$ for the TWR model.

φ_m	portion of capital invested in m-th risky asset, $m = 1, \ldots, M$

Thus, we get

$$\mathbb{E}\left[\ln(S_1^\top x)\right] - \ln(R) = \sum_{i=1}^N \ln\left(\left[1 + \left\langle \mathbf{t}_{i,\bullet}^\top, \boldsymbol{\varphi}\right\rangle_{\mathbb{R}^M}\right]^{q_i}\right) \tag{A6}$$

which is a geometrically weighted version of the TWR. For $q_i = \frac{1}{N}$ (Laplace assumption), this involves the usual Terminal Wealth Relative (TWR) of Vince (1995), that was already introduced in (3), i.e.,

$$\mathbb{E}\left[\ln\left(S_1^\top x\right)\right] - \ln(R) = \ln\left(\left[\prod_{i=1}^N \left(1 + \left\langle \mathbf{t}_{i,\bullet}^\top, \boldsymbol{\varphi}\right\rangle_{\mathbb{R}^M}\right)\right]^{q_i}\right) = \ln\left(\left[\mathrm{TWR}^{(N)}(\boldsymbol{\varphi})\right]^{1/N}\right). \tag{A7}$$

Therefore, under the assumption of a Laplace situation, the optimization problem (A3) is equivalent to

$$\mathrm{TWR}^{(N)}(\boldsymbol{\varphi}) \overset{!}{=} \max, \quad \boldsymbol{\varphi} \in \mathbb{R}^M. \tag{A8}$$

Furthermore, the trade return matrix T in (A5) may be used to define admissible convex risk measures, as introduced in Definition 3, which, in turn, give nontrivial applications to the general framework for the portfolio theory in Part I Maier-Paape and Zhu (2018). To see this, note again that according to (A4), any portfolio vector $x = \left(x_0, \widehat{x}^\top\right)^\top \in \mathbb{R}^{M+1}$ of a unit cost portfolio (A1) has a one to one correspondence with an investment vector

$$\boldsymbol{\varphi} = (\boldsymbol{\varphi}_m)_{1 \le m \le M} = (S_0^m \cdot x_m)_{1 \le m \le M} =: \Lambda \cdot \widehat{x} \tag{A9}$$

for a diagonal matrix $\Lambda \in \mathbb{R}^{M \times M}$ with only positive diagonal entries $\Lambda_{m,m} = S_0^m$. Then, we obtain the following:

Theorem A1. *Let $\mathfrak{r} : \operatorname{Def}(\mathfrak{r}) \to \mathbb{R}_0^+$ be any of our four down-trade or drawdown related risk measures, $\mathfrak{r}_{\text{down}}, \mathfrak{r}_{\text{downX}}, \mathfrak{r}_{\text{cur}}$ and $\mathfrak{r}_{\text{curX}}$, (see (74)) for the trading game of Setup 1 satisfying Assumption 1. Then,*

$$\widehat{\mathfrak{r}}\,(\widehat{x}) := \mathfrak{r}\,(\Lambda\widehat{x}) = \mathfrak{r}(\boldsymbol{\varphi})\,, \quad \widehat{x} \in \operatorname{Def}\,(\widehat{\mathfrak{r}}) := \Lambda^{-1}\operatorname{Def}(\mathfrak{r}) \subset \mathbb{R}^M \tag{A10}$$

has the following properties:

(r1) $\widehat{\mathfrak{r}}$ *depends only on the risky part* $\widehat{x}$ *of the portfolio* $x = \left(x_0, \widehat{x}^\top\right)^\top \in \mathbb{R}^{M+1}$.
(r1n) $\widehat{\mathfrak{r}}\,(\widehat{x}) = 0$ *if and only if* $\widehat{x} = \widehat{0} \in \mathbb{R}^M$.
(r2) $\widehat{\mathfrak{r}}$ *is convex in* $\widehat{x}$.
(r3) *The two approximations* $\mathfrak{r}_{\text{downX}}$ *and* $\mathfrak{r}_{\text{curX}}$ *furthermore yield positive homogeneous* $\widehat{\mathfrak{r}}$, *i.e.,* $\widehat{\mathfrak{r}}\,(t\widehat{x}) = t\,\widehat{\mathfrak{r}}\,(\widehat{x})$ *for all* $t > 0$.

Proof. See the respective properties of $\mathfrak{r}$ (cf. Theorems 4, 5, 8 and 9). In particular, $\mathfrak{r}_{\text{down}}, \mathfrak{r}_{\text{downX}}, \mathfrak{r}_{\text{cur}}$ and $\mathfrak{r}_{\text{curX}}$ are admissible convex risk measures according to Definition 3 and thus *(r1)*, *(r1n)*, and *(r2)* follow. □

Remark A1. *It is clear that $\widehat{\mathfrak{r}} = \widehat{\mathfrak{r}}_{\text{down}}, \widehat{\mathfrak{r}}_{\text{downX}}, \widehat{\mathfrak{r}}_{\text{cur}}$ or $\widehat{\mathfrak{r}}_{\text{curX}}$ can be evaluated on any set of admissible portfolios $A \subset \mathbb{R}^{M+1}$ according to Definition 2 of Maier-Paape and Zhu (2018) if*

$$\mathit{Proj}_{\mathbb{R}^M}\, A \subset \operatorname{Def}\,(\widehat{\mathfrak{r}})\,, \text{ where } \mathit{Proj}_{\mathbb{R}^M}(x) := \widehat{x} \in \mathbb{R}^M\,,$$

and the properties (r1), (r1n), (r2) (and only for $\mathfrak{r}_{\text{downX}}$ and $\mathfrak{r}_{\text{curX}}$ also (r3)) in Assumption 2 of Maier-Paape and Zhu (2018) follow from Theorem A1. In particular, $\widehat{\mathfrak{r}}_{\text{downX}}$ and $\widehat{\mathfrak{r}}_{\text{curX}}$ satisfy the conditions of a deviation measure in Rockafellar et al. (2006) (which is defined directly on the portfolio space).

Remark A2. *The application of the theory of Part I Maier-Paape and Zhu (2018) to the risk measures $\mathfrak{r} = \mathfrak{r}_{\text{cur}}$ or $\mathfrak{r} = \mathfrak{r}_{\text{down}}$ is somewhat more involved because due to Theorems 4 and 8, $\mathfrak{r}\colon \overset{\circ}{\mathfrak{G}} \to \mathbb{R}_0^+$ is defined on the convex and bounded but open set $\overset{\circ}{\mathfrak{G}}$, (cf. Definition 1). However, in order to apply, for instance, Theorems 4 and 5 of Maier-Paape and Zhu (2018), the risk measure has to be defined on a set of admissible portfolios $A \subset \mathbb{R}^{M+1}$ which have moreover unit initial cost (see again Definition 2 of Maier-Paape and Zhu (2018)). In particular, A has to be closed, convex and nonempty. To get around that problem, Theorems 4 and 5 of Maier-Paape and Zhu (2018) can be applied to the admissible sets with unit initial cost*

$$A_n := \left\{ x = (x_0, \widehat{x}) \in \mathbb{R}^{M+1} \,\middle|\, S_0^\top x = 1, \quad 0 \le \widehat{\mathfrak{r}}\,(\widehat{x}) \le n \right\}, \quad \textit{for } n \in \mathbb{N} \textit{ fixed},$$

with $\mathfrak{r} = \mathfrak{r}_{\text{cur}}$ or $\mathfrak{r} = \mathfrak{r}_{\text{down}}$ and $\widehat{\mathfrak{r}}$ according to (A10), and to the convex risk measure

$$\mathfrak{r}^{(n)}\colon A_n \longrightarrow [0,\infty)\,, \quad x = (x_0, \widehat{x}) \longmapsto \mathfrak{r}^{(n)}(x) := \widehat{\mathfrak{r}}\,(\widehat{x})\,.$$

Again, all $\mathfrak{r}^{(n)}$ satisfy (r1), (r1n) and (r2) in Assumption 2 of Maier-Paape and Zhu (2018), but now with

$$\mathit{Proj}_{\mathbb{R}^M}\, A_n \subset\subset \operatorname{Def}\,(\widehat{\mathfrak{r}}) = \overset{\circ}{\mathfrak{G}}\,,$$

i.e., the projection of A_n lies compactly in $\overset{\circ}{\mathfrak{G}}$. Note that Assumption 4 in Maier-Paape and Zhu (2018) is satisfied, because for arbitrary, but fixed $n \in \mathbb{N}$,

$$\left\{ x \in \mathbb{R}^{M+1} \,\middle|\, \mathfrak{r}^{(n)}(x) \le r, \quad x \in A_n \right\}$$

is obviously compact for all $r \in \mathbb{R}$. So together with any upper semi-continuous and concave utility function $u\colon \mathbb{R} \to \mathbb{R} \cup \{-\infty\}$ satisfying (u1) and (u2s) of Assumption 3 in Maier-Paape and Zhu (2018), Theorems 4 and 5 (c2) in Maier-Paape and Zhu (2018) can be applied and yield, for instance, an efficiency frontier in risk utility space

$$\mathcal{G}_{eff}^{(n)} := \mathcal{G}_{eff}\left(\mathfrak{r}^{(n)}, u;\, A_n\right) \subset \mathcal{G}^{(n)},$$

where

$$\mathcal{G}^{(n)} := \mathcal{G}\left(\mathfrak{r}^{(n)}, u;\, A_n\right) = \left\{ (r,\mu) \in \mathbb{R}^2 \,\middle|\, \exists x \in A_n \text{ s.t. } \mu \le \mathbb{E}\left[u\left(S_1^\top x\right)\right], \quad \mathfrak{r}^{(n)}(x) \le r \right\} \subset \mathbb{R}^2$$

and each point $(r,\mu) \in \mathcal{G}_{eff}^{(n)}$ corresponds to a unique efficient portfolio $x = x^{(n)}(r,\mu) \in A_n$. Since $\mathcal{G}_{eff}^{(n)} \subset \mathcal{G}_{eff}^{(n+1)}$ for all $n \in \mathbb{N}$, it is not difficult to show that

$$\mathcal{G}_{eff}^{(\infty)} := \bigcup_{n\in\mathbb{N}} \mathcal{G}_{eff}^{(n)} \subset \bigcup_{n\in\mathbb{N}} \mathcal{G}^{(n)} \subset \mathbb{R}^2$$

corresponds to an efficiency frontier with still unique efficient portfolios $x = x(r,\mu) \subset \bigcup_{n\in\mathbb{N}} A_n$ whenever $(r,\mu) \in \mathcal{G}_{eff}^{(\infty)}$, but now for the problem

$$\begin{aligned} &\min_{x = (x_0,\hat{x}) \in \mathbb{R}^{M+1}} \hat{\mathfrak{r}}(\hat{x}) \\ &\text{Subject to } \mathbb{E}\left[u\left(S_1^\top x\right)\right] \ge \mu \text{ and } S_0^\top x = 1, \end{aligned} \tag{A11}$$

where $\hat{\mathfrak{r}} = \hat{\mathfrak{r}}_{cur}$ or $\hat{\mathfrak{r}} = \hat{\mathfrak{r}}_{down}$ can be extended by ∞ for $\hat{x} \notin \overset{\circ}{\mathfrak{G}}$. In that sense, we can without loss of generality apply the general framework of Part I Maier-Paape and Zhu (2018) to $\mathfrak{r}_{cur}$ and $\mathfrak{r}_{down}$.

Remark A3. *Formally our drawdown or down-trade is a function of a TWR equity curve of a K period financial market. However, since this equity curve is obtained by drawing K times stochastic independently from one and the same market in Definition A1, we still can work with a one period market model.*

We want to close this section with some remarks on the "no nontrivial riskless portfolio" condition of the one period financial market that is often used in reference Maier-Paape and Zhu (2018). Below, we will see that this condition is equivalent to Assumption 1 (cf. Corollary A1) which was necessary to construct admissible convex risk measures in this paper. To see this, we rephrase Theorem 2 of reference Maier-Paape and Zhu (2018) slightly. Let us begin with the relevant market conditions (see Definition 4 of Maier-Paape and Zhu (2018)).

Definition A2. *Consider a portfolio $x \in \mathbb{R}^{M+1}$ on the one period financial market S_t as in Definition A1.*

(a) (No Nontrivial Riskless Portfolio) We say a portfolio x is ***riskless*** *if*

$$(S_1 - RS_0)^\top x \ge 0 .$$

We say the market has ***no nontrivial riskless portfolio*** *if a riskless portfolio x with $\hat{x} \neq \hat{0}$ does not exist.*

(b) *(No Arbitrage) We say x is an* ***arbitrage*** *if it is riskless and there exists some $\alpha \in \mathcal{A}_N$ such that*

$$(S_1(\alpha) - RS_0)^\top x \neq 0 .$$

We say market S_t has ***no arbitrage*** *if an arbitrage portfolio does not exist.*

(c) *(Nontrivial Bond Replicating Portfolio) We say that $x^\top = (x_0, \widehat{x}^\top)$ is a* ***nontrivial bond replicating portfolio*** *if $\widehat{x} \neq \widehat{0}$ and*

$$(S_1 - RS_0)^\top x = 0 .$$

Using this notation, we can extend Theorem 2 of Maier-Paape and Zhu (2018).

Theorem A2. ***(Characterization of no Nontrivial Riskless Portfolio)*** *Assume a one period financial market as in Setup A1 is given. Then, the following assertions are equivalent:*

(i) *The market has no arbitrage portfolio and there is no nontrivial bond replicating portfolio.*

(i)* *The market has no nontrivial riskless portfolio.*

(ii) *For every nontrivial portfolio $x \in \mathbb{R}^{M+1}$ (i.e., with $\widehat{x} \neq \widehat{0}$), there exists some $\alpha \in \mathcal{A}_N$ such that*

$$(S_1(\alpha) - RS_0)^\top x < 0 . \tag{A12}$$

(ii)* *For every risky portfolio $\widehat{x} \neq \widehat{0}$, some $\alpha \in \mathcal{A}_N$ exists such that*

$$\left(\widehat{S}_1(\alpha) - R\widehat{S}_0\right)^\top \widehat{x} < 0 . \tag{A13}$$

(iii) *The market has no arbitrage and the matrix*

$$T_S := \begin{bmatrix} S_1^1(\alpha_1) - R\, S_0^1 & S_1^2(\alpha_1) - R\, S_0^2 & \dots & S_1^M(\alpha_1) - R\, S_0^M \\ S_1^1(\alpha_2) - R\, S_0^1 & S_1^2(\alpha_2) - R\, S_0^2 & \dots & S_1^M(\alpha_2) - R\, S_0^M \\ \vdots & \vdots & & \vdots \\ S_1^1(\alpha_N) - R\, S_0^1 & S_1^2(\alpha_N) - R\, S_0^2 & \dots & S_1^M(\alpha_N) - R\, S_0^M \end{bmatrix} \in \mathbb{R}^{N \times M} \tag{A14}$$

has rank M, in particular, $N \geq M$.

Proof. Clearly, *(i)* and *(i)** as well as *(ii)* and *(ii)** are equivalent by definition. Therefore, the main difference of the assertion here to Theorem 2 of reference Maier-Paape and Zhu (2018) is that in the cited theorem, the no arbitrage property is a general assumption on the market, whereas here, we explicitly use it in the statements *(i)* and *(iii)*, but not in *(ii)*. Since by Theorem 2 of reference Maier-Paape and Zhu (2018), for a no arbitrage market *(i)*, *(ii)* and *(iii)* are equivalent, it only remains to show the implication

$$(ii) \overset{!}{\Longrightarrow} \text{the market } S_t \text{ has no arbitrage} .$$

To see this, we assume S_t has an arbitrage portfolio $x^* \in \mathbb{R}^{M+1}$, although *(ii)* holds. Then, by definition, x^* is riskless, and there is some $\alpha \in \mathcal{A}_N$ such that

$$\left(\widehat{S}_1(\alpha) - R\widehat{S}_0\right)^\top \widehat{x}^* = (S_1(\alpha) - RS_0)^\top x^* \neq 0 .$$

Hence, $\widehat{x}^* \neq \widehat{0}$ and by assumption, *(ii)* x^* cannot be riskless, a contradiction. □

We come back to Assumption 1 which is a condition on the trade return matrix T in (1) and crucial in all our applications to construct new drawdown related risk measures. If the trade return matrix T is constructed as in reference (A4) and (A5) from a one period financial market S_t, then it is easy to see that Assumption 1 is indeed nothing but the property *(ii)** of Theorem A2. Therefore, we have

Corollary A1. *Consider a one period financial market S_t as in Setup A1. Then, there is no nontrivial riskless portfolio in S_t if and only if the trade return matrix T from* (A4) *and* (A5) *satisfies Assumption 1.*

To conclude, in the situation of a one period financial market, the main condition in Part I Maier-Paape and Zhu (2018) (no nontrivial riskless portfolio) and the main condition here (Assumption 1) are equivalent. Thus, together with the results of Part I, it is possible to define and calculate efficient portfolios based on a risk measure using relative drawdowns.

References

Chekhlov, Alexei, Stanislav Uryasev, and Michael Zabarankin. 2003. Portfolio optimization with drawdown constraints. In *Asset and Liability Management Tools*. Edited by Bernd Scherer. London: Risk Books, pp. 263–78.

Chekhlov, Alexei, Stanislav Uryasev, and Michael Zabarankin. 2005. Drawdown measure in portfolio optimization. *International Journal of Theoretical and Applied Finance* 8: 13–58. [CrossRef]

Föllmer, Hans, and Alexander Schied. 2002. *Stochastic Finance*, 1st ed. Berlin: De Gruyter.

Goldberg, Lisa R., and Ola Mahmoud. 2017. Drawdown: from Practice to Theory and Back Again. *Mathematics and Financial Economics* 11: 275–97. [CrossRef]

Hermes, Andreas. 2016. A Mathematical Approach to Fractional Trading: Using the Terminal Wealth Relative with Discrete and Continuous Distributions. Ph.D. thesis, RWTH Aachen University, Aachen, Germany. [CrossRef]

Hermes, Andreas, and Stanislaus Maier-Paape. 2017. Existence and uniqueness for the multivariate discrete terminal wealth relative. *Risks*, 5: 44. [CrossRef]

Kelly, John L., Jr. 1956. A new interpretation of information rate. *Bell System Technical Journal* 35: 917–26. [CrossRef]

Maier-Paape, Stanislaus. 2013. *Existence Theorems for Optimal Fractional Trading*. Report No. 67. Aachen: Institut für Mathematik, RWTH Aachen University. Available online: https://www.instmath.rwth-aachen.de/Preprints/maierpaape20131008.pdf (accessed on 6 August 2018).

Maier-Paape, Stanislaus. 2015. Optimal f and diversification. *International Federation of Technical Analysts Journal* 15: 4–7.

Maier-Paape, Stanislaus. 2018. Risk averse fractional trading using the current drawdown. *Journal of Risk* 20: 1–25. [CrossRef]

Maier-Paape, Stanislaus, and Qiji Jim Zhu. 2018. A general framework for portfolio theory. Part I: Theory and various models. *Risks*, 6: 53. [CrossRef]

Markowitz, Harry M. 1959. *Portfolio Selection: Efficient Diversification of Investment*. New York: John Wiley & Sons.

Rockafellar, Ralph T., and Stanislav Uryasev. 2002. Conditional value–at–risk for general loss distributions. *Journal of Banking and Finance* 26: 1443–71. [CrossRef]

Rockafellar, Ralph T., Stanislav Uryasev, and Michael Zabarankin. 2006. Generalized deviations in risk analysis. *Finance and Stochastics* 10: 51–74. [CrossRef]

Rockafellar, Ralph T., Stanislav Uryasev, and Michael Zabarankin. 2006. Master funds in portfolio analysis with general deviation measures. *Journal of Banking and Finance* 30: 743–78. [CrossRef]

Sharpe, William F. 1964. Capital asset prices: A theory of market equilibrium under conditions of risk. *Journal of Finance* 19: 425–42.

Vince, Ralph. 1992. *The Mathematics of Money Management, Risk Analysis Techniques for Traders*. New York: John Wiley & Sons.

Vince, Ralph. 1995. *The New Money Management: A Framework for Asset Allocation*. New York: John Wiley & Sons.

Vince, Ralph. 2009. *The Leverage Space Trading Model: Reconciling Portfolio Management Strategies and Economic Theory*. New York: John Wiley & Sons.

Vince, Ralph, and Qiji Jim Zhu. 2015. Optimal betting sizes for the game of blackjack. *Risk Journals: Portfolio Management* 4: 53–75.

Tharp, Van K. 2008. *Van Tharp's Definite Guide to Position Sizing.* Cary: The International Institute of Trading Mastery.

Zabarankin, Michael, Konstantin Pavlikov, and Stanislav Uryasev. 2014. Capital asset pricing model (capm) with drawdown measure. *European Journal of Operational Research* 234: 508–17. [CrossRef]

Zhu, Qiji Jim. 2007. Mathematical analysis of investment systems. *Journal of Mathematical Analysis and Applications* 326: 708–20. [CrossRef]

Zhu, Qiji Jim. 2012. Convex analysis in financial mathematics. *Nonlinear Analysis, Theory Method and Applications* 75: 1719–36. [CrossRef]

5

Markov Chain Monte Carlo Methods for Estimating Systemic Risk Allocations

Takaaki Koike * and Marius Hofert

Department of Statistics and Actuarial Science, University of Waterloo, 200 University Avenue West, Waterloo, ON N2L 3G1, Canada; marius.hofert@uwaterloo.ca

* Correspondence: tkoike@uwaterloo.ca

Abstract: In this paper, we propose a novel framework for estimating systemic risk measures and risk allocations based on Markov Chain Monte Carlo (MCMC) methods. We consider a class of allocations whose jth component can be written as some risk measure of the jth conditional marginal loss distribution given the so-called crisis event. By considering a crisis event as an intersection of linear constraints, this class of allocations covers, for example, conditional Value-at-Risk (CoVaR), conditional expected shortfall (CoES), VaR contributions, and range VaR (RVaR) contributions as special cases. For this class of allocations, analytical calculations are rarely available, and numerical computations based on Monte Carlo (MC) methods often provide inefficient estimates due to the rare-event character of the crisis events. We propose an MCMC estimator constructed from a sample path of a Markov chain whose stationary distribution is the conditional distribution given the crisis event. Efficient constructions of Markov chains, such as the Hamiltonian Monte Carlo and Gibbs sampler, are suggested and studied depending on the crisis event and the underlying loss distribution. The efficiency of the MCMC estimators is demonstrated in a series of numerical experiments.

Keywords: systemic risk measures; conditional Value-at-Risk (CoVaR); capital allocation; copula models; quantitative risk management

---

1. Introduction

In portfolio risk management, *risk allocation* is an essential step to quantifying the risk of each unit of a portfolio by decomposing the total risk of the whole portfolio. One of the most prevalent rules to determine risk allocations is the *Euler princple*, proposed by Tasche (1995) and justified from various viewpoints, such as the RORAC compatibility (Tasche (1995) and Tasche (2008)) and cooperative game theory (Denault (2001)). For the popular risk measures, such as VaR, RVaR, and ES, Euler allocations take the form of conditional expectations of the underlying loss random vector given a certain rare event on the total loss of the portfolio; see Tasche (2001) for derivations. We call this rare event the *crisis event*.The decomposition of risks is also required in the context of systemic risk measurement. *Systemic risk* is the risk of financial distress of an entire economy as a result of the failure of individual components of the financial system. To quantify such risks, various *systemic risk measures* have been proposed in the literature, such as *conditional VaR (CoVaR)* (Adrian and Brunnermeier (2016)), *conditional expected shortfall (CoES)* (Mainik and Schaanning (2014)), and *marginal expected shortfall (MES)* (Acharya et al. (2017)). These three measures quantify the risk of individuals by taking the VaR, ES, and expectation of the individual loss, respectively, under some stressed scenario—that is, given the crisis event. Chen et al. (2013), Hoffmann et al. (2016), and Kromer et al. (2016) proposed an axiomatic characterization of systemic risk measures, where the risk of the aggregated loss in a financial system is first measured and then decomposed into the individual economic entities. Due to the similarity of risk allocations with the derivation of systemic risk measures, we refer to both of them as *systemic risk allocations*. In fact, MES coincides with the Euler allocation of ES, and other Euler allocations can be regarded as special cases of systemic risk measures considered in Gourieroux and Monfort (2013).

Calculating systemic risk allocations given an unconditional joint loss distribution is generally challenging, since analytical calculations often require knowledge of the joint distribution of the marginal and aggregated loss. Furthermore, MC estimation suffers from the rare-event character of the crisis event. For computing CoVaR, CoES, and MES, Mainik and Schaanning (2014), Bernardi et al. (2017), and Jaworski (2017) derived formulas based on the copula of the marginal and aggregated loss; Asimit and Li (2018) derived asymptotic formulas based on the extreme value theory; and Girardi and Ergün (2013) estimated CoVaR under a multivariate GARCH model. Vernic (2006), Chiragiev and Landsman (2007), Dhaene et al. (2008), and Furman and Landsman (2008) calculated Euler allocations for specific joint distributions. Asimit et al. (2011) derived asymptotic formulas for risk allocations. Furman and Zitikis (2009) and Furman et al. (2018) calculated weighted allocations, which include Euler allocations as special cases, under a Stein-type assumption. Concerning the numerical computation of Euler allocations, Glasserman (2005), Glasserman and Li (2005), and Kalkbrener et al. (2004) considered importance sampling methods, and Siller (2013) proposed the Fourier transform Monte Carlo method, all specifically for credit portfolios. For general copula-based dependence models, analytical calculations of systemic risk allocations are rarely available, and an estimation method is, to the best of our knowledge, only addressed in Targino et al. (2015), where sequential Monte Carlo (SMC) samplers are applied.

We address the problem of estimating systemic risk allocations under general copula-based dependent risks in the case where the copula between the marginal and aggregated losses are not necessarily available. We consider a general class of systemic risk allocations in the form of risk measures of a conditional loss distribution given a crisis event, which includes CoVaR, CoES, MES, and Euler allocations as special cases. In our proposed method, the conditional loss distribution, called the *target distribution* π, is simulated by a Markov chain whose stationary distribution is the desired distribution π by sequentially updating the sample path based on the available information from π. While this MCMC method resembles the SMC in Targino et al. (2015), the latter requires a more complicated implementation involving the choice of forward and backward kernels, resampling and move steps, and even MCMC in the move steps. Our suggested approach directly constructs a single sophisticated Markov chain depending on the target distribution of interest. Applications of MCMC to estimating risk allocations have been studied in Koike and Minami (2019), specifically for VaR contributions. Our paper explores and demonstrates the applicability of MCMC methods to a more general class of systemic risk allocations.

Almost all MCMC methods used in practice are of the *Metropolis–Hastings (MH)* type (Metropolis et al. (1953) and Hastings (1970)), where the so-called *proposal distribution* q generates a candidate of the next state based on the current state. This candidate is then accepted or rejected according to the so-called *acceptance probability* to adjust the stationary distribution to be the target distribution π. As explained in Section 3.1 below, the resulting Markov chain has serial correlation, which adversarially affects the efficiency of the estimator. An efficient MCMC of MH type is such that the proposal distribution generates a candidate which exhibits low correlation with the current state with sufficiently large acceptance probability. The main difficulty in constructing such an efficient MCMC estimator for systemic risk allocations is that the support of the target distribution π is subject to constraints determined by the crisis event. For such target distributions, simple MCMC methods, such as random walk MH, are not efficient since a candidate is immediately rejected if it violates the constraints; see Section 3.2 for details.

To tackle this problem, we consider two specific MCMC methods, *Hamiltonian Monte Carlo (HMC)* (Duane et al. (1987)) and the *Gibbs sampler (GS)* (Geman and Geman (1984) and Gelfand and Smith (1990)). In the HMC method, a candidate is generated according to the so-called Hamiltonian dynamics, which leads to a high acceptance probability and low correlation with the current state by accurately simulating the dynamics of sufficiently long length; see Neal et al. (2011) and Betancourt (2017) for an introduction to HMC. Moreover, the HMC candidates always belong to the crisis event by reflecting the dynamics when the chain hits the boundary of the constraints; see Ruján (1997), Pakman and Paninski (2014), Afshar and Domke (2015), Yi and Doshi-Velez (2017), and Chevallier et al. (2018) for this reflection property of the HMC method. An alternative method to handle the constraints is the GS, in which the chain is updated in each component. Since all the components except the updated one remain fixed, a componentwise update is typically subject to weaker constraints. As long as such componentwise updates are feasible, the GS candidates belong to the crisis event, and the acceptance probability is always 1; see Geweke (1991), Gelfand et al. (1992), and Rodriguez-Yam et al. (2004) for the application of the GS to constrained target distributions, and see Gudmundsson and Hult (2014) and Targino et al. (2015) for applications to estimating risk contributions.

Our findings include efficient MCMC estimators of systemic risk allocations achieved via HMC with reflection and GSs. We assume that the unconditional joint loss density is known, possibly through its marginal densities and copula density. Depending on the supports of the marginal loss distributions and the crisis event, different MCMC methods are applicable. We find that if the marginal loss distributions are one-sided, that is, the supports are bounded from the left, then the crisis event is typically a bounded set and HMC shows good performance. On the other hand, if the marginal losses are two-sided, that is, they have both right and left tails, the crisis event is often unbounded and the GSs perform better, provided that the random number generators of the conditional copulas are available. Based on the samples generated by the MC method, we propose heuristics to determine the parameters of the HMC and GS methods, for which no manual interaction is required. Since, in the MCMC method, the conditional loss distribution of interest is directly simulated, in contrast to MC where rejection is applied based on the unconditional loss distribution, the MCMC method generally outperforms the MC method in terms of the sample size, and thus the standard error. This advantage of MCMC becomes more pronounced as the probability of the crisis event becomes smaller. We demonstrate this efficiency of the MCMC estimators of systemic risk allocations by a series of numerical experiments.

This paper is organized as follows. The general framework of the estimation problem of systemic risk allocations is introduced in Section 2. Our class of systemic risk allocations is proposed in Section 2.1, and their estimation via the MC method is presented in Section 2.2. Section 3 is devoted to MCMC methods for estimating systemic risk allocations. After a brief review of MCMC methods in Section 3.1, we formulate our problem of estimating systemic risk allocations in terms of MCMC in Section 3.2. HMC and GS for constrained target distributions are then investigated in Sections 3.3 and 3.4, respectively. In Section 4, numerical experiments are conducted, including simulation and empirical studies, and a detailed comparison of MC and our introduced MCMC methods is provided. Section 5 concludes with practical guidance and limitations of the presented MCMC methods. An R script reproducing the numerical experiments is available as Supplementary Material.

2. Systemic Risk Allocations and Their Estimation

In this section, we define a broad class of systemic risk allocations, including Euler allocations, CoVaR, and CoES as special cases. Then, the MC method is described to estimate systemic risk allocations.

2.1. A Class of Systemic Risk Allocations

Let $(\Omega, \mathcal{F}, \mathbb{P})$ be an atomless probability space, and let $X_1, \ldots, X_d$, $d \geq 2$ be random variables on this space. The random vector $\boldsymbol{X} = (X_1, \ldots, X_d)$ can be interpreted as losses of a portfolio of size d, or losses of d economic entities in an economy over a fixed time period. Throughout the paper, a positive value of a loss random variable represents a financial loss, and a negative loss is interpreted as a profit. Let $F_{\boldsymbol{X}}$ denote the joint cumulative distribution function (cdf) of $\boldsymbol{X}$ with marginal distributions $F_1, \ldots, F_d$. Assume that $F_{\boldsymbol{X}}$ admits a probability density function (pdf) $f_{\boldsymbol{X}}$ with marginal densities $f_1, \ldots, f_d$. Sklar's theorem (Nelsen (2006)) allows one to write

$$F_{\mathbf{X}}(\boldsymbol{x}) = C(F_1(x_1), \dots, F_d(x_d)), \quad \boldsymbol{x} = (x_1, \dots, x_d) \in \mathbb{R}^d, \tag{1}$$

where $C : [0,1]^d \to [0,1]$ is a *copula* of $\mathbf{X}$. Assuming the density c of the copula C to exist, $f_{\mathbf{X}}$ can be written as

$$f_{\mathbf{X}}(\boldsymbol{x}) = c(F_1(x_1), \dots, F_d(x_d)) f_1(x_1) \cdots f_d(x_d), \quad \boldsymbol{x} \in \mathbb{R}^d.$$

An *allocation* $A = (A_1, \dots, A_d)$ is a map from a random vector $\mathbf{X}$ to $(A_1(\mathbf{X}), \dots, A_d(\mathbf{X})) \in \mathbb{R}^d$. The sum $\sum_{j=1}^d A_j(\mathbf{X})$ can be understood as the capital required to cover the total loss of the portfolio or the economy. The jth component $A_j(\mathbf{X})$, $j = 1, \dots, d$ is then the contribution of the jth loss to the total capital $\sum_{j=1}^d A_j(\mathbf{X})$. In this paper, we consider the following class of allocations

$$A^{\varrho_1, \dots, \varrho_d, \mathcal{C}} = (A_1^{\varrho_1, \mathcal{C}}, \dots, A_d^{\varrho_d, \mathcal{C}}), \quad A_j^{\varrho_j, \mathcal{C}}(\mathbf{X}) = \varrho_j(X_j \mid \mathbf{X} \in \mathcal{C}),$$

where ϱ_j is a map from a random variable to $\mathbb{R}$ called the jth *marginal risk measure* for $j = 1, \dots, d$, and $\mathcal{C} \subseteq \mathbb{R}^d$ is a set called the *crisis event*. The conditioning set $\{\mathbf{X} \in \mathcal{C}\}$ is simply written as $\mathcal{C}$ if there is no confusion. As we now explain, this class of allocations covers well-known allocations as special cases. For a random variable $X \sim F$, we define the *Value-at-Risk (VaR)* of X at confidence level $\alpha \in (0,1]$ by

$$\mathrm{VaR}_\alpha(X) := \inf\{x \in \mathbb{R} : F(x) \geq \alpha\}.$$

Range Value-at-Risk (RVaR) at confidence levels $0 < \alpha_1 < \alpha_2 \leq 1$ is defined by

$$\mathrm{RVaR}_{\alpha_1, \alpha_2}(X) = \frac{1}{\alpha_2 - \alpha_1} \int_{\alpha_1}^{\alpha_2} \mathrm{VaR}_\gamma(X) \, \mathrm{d}\gamma,$$

and, if it exists, *expected shortfall (ES)* at confidence level $\alpha \in (0,1)$ is defined by $\mathrm{ES}_\alpha(X) = \mathrm{RVaR}_{\alpha,1}(X)$. Note that ES is also known as C(onditional)VaR, T(ail)VaR, A(verage)VaR and C(onditional)T(ail)E(xpectation). These risk measures are law-invariant in the sense that they depend only on the distribution of X. Therefore, we sometimes write $\varrho(F)$ instead of $\varrho(X)$.

We now define various crisis events and marginal risk measures. A typical form of the crisis event is an intersection of a set of linear constraints

$$\mathcal{C} = \bigcap_{m=1}^{M} \left\{ \boldsymbol{h}_m^\top \boldsymbol{x} \geq v_m \right\}, \quad \boldsymbol{h}_m \in \mathbb{R}^d, \quad v_m \in \mathbb{R}, \quad m = 1, \dots, M, \quad M \in \mathbb{N}. \tag{2}$$

Several important special cases of the crisis event of Form (2) are provided in the following.

Definition 1 (VaR, RVaR, and ES crisis events). *For $S = \sum_{j=1}^d X_j$, the* VaR, RVaR *and* ES *crisis events are defined by*

$$\mathcal{C}_\alpha^{\mathrm{VaR}} = \{\boldsymbol{x} \in \mathbb{R}^d \mid \mathbf{1}_d^\top \boldsymbol{x} = \mathrm{VaR}_\alpha(S)\}, \quad \alpha \in (0,1),$$
$$\mathcal{C}_{\alpha_1,\alpha_2}^{\mathrm{RVaR}} = \{\boldsymbol{x} \in \mathbb{R}^d \mid \mathrm{VaR}_{\alpha_1}(S) \leq \mathbf{1}_d^\top \boldsymbol{x} \leq \mathrm{VaR}_{\alpha_2}(S)\}, \quad 0 < \alpha_1 < \alpha_2 \leq 1,$$
$$\mathcal{C}_\alpha^{\mathrm{ES}} = \{\boldsymbol{x} \in \mathbb{R}^d \mid \mathrm{VaR}_\alpha(S) \leq \mathbf{1}_d^\top \boldsymbol{x}\}, \quad 0 < \alpha < 1, \quad \alpha \in (0,1),$$

respectively, where $\mathbf{1}_d$ is the d-dimensional vector of ones.

Definition 2 (Risk contributions and conditional risk measures). *For $j \in \{1, \dots, d\}$, we call $A_j^{\varrho_j, \mathcal{C}}$ of*

1. *risk contribution-type if $\varrho_j = \mathbb{E}$;*

2. *CoVaR type if* $\varrho_j = \mathrm{VaR}_{\beta_j}$ *for* $\beta_j \in (0,1)$;
3. *CoRVaR type if* $\varrho_j = \mathrm{RVaR}_{\beta_{j,1},\beta_{j,2}}$ *for* $0 < \beta_{j,1} < \beta_{j,2} \leq 1$; *and*
4. *CoES-type if* $\varrho_j = \mathrm{ES}_{\beta_j}$ *for* $\beta_j \in (0,1)$.

The following examples show that $A_j^{\varrho_j,\mathcal{C}}$ coincides with popular allocations for some specific choices of marginal risk measure and crisis event.

Example 1 (Special cases of $A^{\varrho_1,\dots,\varrho_d,\mathcal{C}}$).

(1) *Risk contributions. If the crisis event is chosen to be* $\mathcal{C}_\alpha^{\mathrm{VaR}}$, $\mathcal{C}_{\alpha_1,\alpha_2}^{\mathrm{RVaR}}$ *or* $\mathcal{C}_\alpha^{\mathrm{ES}}$, *the allocations of the risk contribution type* $\varrho_j = \mathbb{E}$ *reduce to the* VaR, RVaR, *or* ES *contributions defined by*

$$\begin{aligned}\mathrm{VaR}_\alpha(\boldsymbol{X}, S) &= \mathbb{E}[\boldsymbol{X} \mid S = \mathrm{VaR}_\alpha(S)],\\ \mathrm{RVaR}_{\alpha_1,\alpha_2}(\boldsymbol{X}, S) &= \mathbb{E}[\boldsymbol{X} \mid \mathrm{VaR}_{\alpha_1}(S) \leq S \leq \mathrm{VaR}_{\alpha_2}(S)],\\ \mathrm{ES}_\alpha(\boldsymbol{X}, S) &= \mathbb{E}[\boldsymbol{X} \mid S \geq \mathrm{VaR}_\alpha(S)],\end{aligned}$$

respectively. These results are derived by allocating the total capital $\mathrm{VaR}_\alpha(S)$, $\mathrm{RVaR}_{\alpha_1,\alpha_2}(S)$ *and* $\mathrm{ES}_\alpha(S)$ *according to the Euler principle; see Tasche (1995). The ES contribution is also called the MES and used as a systemic risk measure; see Acharya et al. (2017).*

(2) *Conditional risk measures. CoVaR and CoES are systemic risk measures defined by*

$$\begin{aligned}\mathrm{CoVaR}^{=}_{\alpha,\beta}(X_j, S) &= \mathrm{VaR}_\beta(X_j|S = \mathrm{VaR}_\alpha(S)), \quad \mathrm{CoVaR}_{\alpha,\beta}(X_j, S) = \mathrm{VaR}_\beta(X_j|S \geq \mathrm{VaR}_\alpha(S)),\\ \mathrm{CoES}^{=}_{\alpha,\beta}(X_j, S) &= \mathrm{ES}_\beta(X_j|S = \mathrm{VaR}_\alpha(S)), \quad \mathrm{CoES}_{\alpha,\beta}(X_j, S) = \mathrm{ES}_\beta(X_j|S \geq \mathrm{VaR}_\alpha(S)),\end{aligned}$$

for $\alpha, \beta \in (0,1)$; *see Mainik and Schaanning (2014) and Bernardi et al. (2017). Our CoVaR and CoES-type allocations with crisis events* $\mathcal{C} = \mathcal{C}^{\mathrm{VaR}_\alpha}$ *or* $\mathcal{C}^{\mathrm{ES}_\alpha}$ *coincide with those defined in the last displayed equations.*

Remark 1 (Weighted allocations). *For a measurable function* $w : \mathbb{R}^d \to \mathbb{R}_+ := [0,\infty)$, *Furman and Zitikis (2008) proposed the* weighted allocation $\varrho_w(\boldsymbol{X})$ *with the* weight function w *being defined by* $\varrho_w(\boldsymbol{X}) = \mathbb{E}[\boldsymbol{X}w(\boldsymbol{X})]/\mathbb{E}[w(\boldsymbol{X})]$. *By taking an indicator function as weight function* $w(\boldsymbol{x}) = \mathbf{1}_{[\boldsymbol{x}\in\mathcal{C}]}$ *and provided that* $\mathbb{P}(\boldsymbol{X} \in \mathcal{C}) > 0$, *the weighted allocation coincides with the risk contribution-type systemic allocation* $A^{\mathbb{E},\dots,\mathbb{E},\mathcal{C}}$.

2.2. Monte Carlo Estimation of Systemic Risk Allocations

Even if the joint distribution $F_{\boldsymbol{X}}$ of the loss random vector $\boldsymbol{X}$ is known, the conditional distribution of $\boldsymbol{X}$ given $\boldsymbol{X} \in \mathcal{C}$, denoted by $F_{\boldsymbol{X}|\mathcal{C}}$, is typically too complicated to analytically calculate the systemic risk allocations $A^{\varrho_1,\dots,\varrho_d,\mathcal{C}}$. An alternative approach is to numerically estimate them by the MC method, as is done in Yamai and Yoshiba (2002) and Fan et al. (2012). To this end, assume that one can generate i.i.d. samples from $F_{\boldsymbol{X}}$. If $\mathbb{P}(\boldsymbol{X} \in \mathcal{C}) > 0$, the MC estimator of $A_j^{\varrho_j,\mathcal{C}}$, $j = 1,\dots,d$ is constructed as follows:

(1) *Sample from* $\boldsymbol{X}$: For a sample size $N \in \mathbb{N}$, generate $\boldsymbol{X}^{(1)},\dots,\boldsymbol{X}^{(N)} \overset{\text{ind.}}{\sim} F_{\boldsymbol{X}}$.

(2) *Estimate the crisis event*: If the crisis event $\mathcal{C}$ contains unknown quantities, replace them with their estimates based on $\boldsymbol{X}^{(1)},\dots,\boldsymbol{X}^{(N)}$. Denote by $\hat{\mathcal{C}}$ the estimated crisis event.

(3) *Sample from the conditional distribution of* $\boldsymbol{X}$ *given* $\hat{\mathcal{C}}$: Among $\boldsymbol{X}^{(1)},\dots,\boldsymbol{X}^{(N)}$, determine $\tilde{\boldsymbol{X}}^{(n)}$ such that $\tilde{\boldsymbol{X}}^{(n)} \in \hat{\mathcal{C}}$ for all $n = 1,\dots,N$.

(4) *Construct the MC estimator*: The MC estimate of $A_j^{\varrho_j,\mathcal{C}}$ is $\varrho_j(\hat{F}_{\tilde{\boldsymbol{X}}})$ where $\hat{F}_{\tilde{\boldsymbol{X}}}$ is the empirical cdf (ecdf) of the $\tilde{\boldsymbol{X}}^{(n)}$'s.

For an example of (2), if the crisis event is $\mathcal{C}^{\mathrm{RVaR}_{\alpha_1,\alpha_2}} = \{\boldsymbol{x} \in \mathbb{R}^d \mid \mathrm{VaR}_{\alpha_1}(S) \leq \mathbf{1}_d^\top \boldsymbol{x} \leq \mathrm{VaR}_{\alpha_2}(S)\}$, then $\mathrm{VaR}_{\alpha_1}(S)$ and $\mathrm{VaR}_{\alpha_2}(S)$ are unknown parameters, and thus they are replaced by $\mathrm{VaR}_{\alpha_1}(\hat{F}_S)$ and

$\mathrm{VaR}_{\alpha_2}(\hat{F}_S)$, where $\hat{F}_S$ is the ecdf of the total loss $S^{(n)} := X_1^{(n)} + \cdots + X_d^{(n)}$ for $n = 1, \ldots, N$. By the *law of large numbers (LLN)* and the *central limit theorem (CLT)*, the MC estimator of $A^{\varrho_1,\ldots,\varrho_d,\mathcal{C}}$ is consistent, and the approximate confidence interval of the true allocation can be constructed based on the asymptotic normality; see Glasserman (2005).

The MC cannot handle VaR crisis events if S admits a pdf, since $\mathbb{P}(\boldsymbol{X} \in \mathcal{C}^{\mathrm{VaR}_\alpha}) = \mathbb{P}(S = \mathrm{VaR}_\alpha(S)) = 0$, and thus, no subsample is picked in (3) above. A possible remedy (although the resulting estimator suffers from an inevitable bias) is to replace $\mathcal{C}_\alpha^{\mathrm{VaR}}$ with $\mathcal{C}_{\alpha-\delta,\alpha+\delta}^{\mathrm{RVaR}}$ for sufficiently small $\delta > 0$, so that $\mathbb{P}(S \in \mathcal{C}_{\alpha-\delta,\alpha+\delta}^{\mathrm{RVaR}}) = 2\delta > 0$.

The main advantage of MC for estimating systemic risk allocations $A^{\varrho_1,\ldots,\varrho_d,\mathcal{C}}$ is that only a random number generator for $F_{\boldsymbol{X}}$ is required for implementing the method. Furthermore, MC is applicable for any choice of the crisis event $\mathcal{C}$ as long as $\mathbb{P}(\boldsymbol{X} \in \mathcal{C}) > 0$. Moreover, the main computational load is simulating $F_{\boldsymbol{X}}$ in (1) above, which is typically not demanding. The disadvantage of the MC method is its inefficiency concerning the rare-event characteristics of $\varrho_1, \ldots, \varrho_d$ and $\mathcal{C}$. To see this, consider the case where $\mathcal{C} = \mathcal{C}_{\alpha_1,\alpha_2}^{\mathrm{RVaR}}$ and $\varrho_j = \mathrm{RVaR}_{\beta_1,\beta_2}$ for $\alpha_1 = \beta_1 = 0.95$ and $\alpha_2 = \beta_2 = 0.975$. If the MC sample size is $N = 10^5$, there are $N \times (\alpha_2 - \alpha_1) = 2500$ subsamples resulting from (3). To estimate $\mathrm{RVaR}_{\beta_1,\beta_2}$ in (4) based on this subsample, only $2500 \times (\beta_2 - \beta_1) = 62.5$ samples contribute to computing the estimate, which is generally not enough for statistical inference. This effect of sample size reduction is relaxed if ES and/or ES crisis events are considered, but is more problematic for the VaR crisis event since there is a trade-off concerning reducing bias and MC error when choosing δ; see Koike and Minami (2019).

3. MCMC Estimation of Systemic Risk Allocations

To overcome the drawback of the MC method for estimating systemic risk allocations, we introduce MCMC methods, which simulate a given distribution by constructing a Markov chain whose stationary distribution is $F_{\boldsymbol{X}|\mathcal{C}}$. In this section, we first briefly review MCMC methods, including the MH algorithm as a major subclass of MCMC methods, and then study how to construct an efficient MCMC estimator for the different choices of crisis events.

3.1. A Brief Review of MCMC

Let $E \subseteq \mathbb{R}^d$ be a set and $\mathcal{E}$ be a σ-algebra on E. A *Markov chain* is a sequence of E-valued random variables $(\boldsymbol{X}^{(n)})_{n\in\mathbb{N}_0}$ satisfying the Markov property $\mathbb{P}(\boldsymbol{X}^{(n+1)} \in A \mid \boldsymbol{X}^{(k)} = \boldsymbol{x}^{(k)}, k \leq n) = \mathbb{P}(\boldsymbol{X}^{(n+1)} \in A \mid \boldsymbol{X}^{(n)} = \boldsymbol{x}^{(n)})$ for all $n \geq 1$, $A \in \mathcal{E}$, and $\boldsymbol{x}^{(1)}, \ldots, \boldsymbol{x}^{(n)} \in E$. A Markov chain is characterized by its *stochastic kernel* $K : E \times \mathcal{E} \to [0,1]$ given by $\boldsymbol{x} \times A \mapsto K(\boldsymbol{x}, A) := \mathbb{P}(\boldsymbol{X}^{(n+1)} \in A \mid \boldsymbol{X}^{(n)} = \boldsymbol{x})$. A probability distribution π satisfying $\pi(A) = \int_E \pi(\mathrm{d}\boldsymbol{x}) K(\boldsymbol{x}, A)$ for any $\boldsymbol{x} \in E$ and $A \in \mathcal{E}$ is called *stationary distribution*. Assuming $K(\boldsymbol{x}, \cdot)$ has a density $k(\boldsymbol{x}, \cdot)$, the *detailed balance condition* (also known as the *reversibility*) with respect to π is given by

$$\pi(\boldsymbol{x})k(\boldsymbol{x}, \boldsymbol{y}) = \pi(\boldsymbol{y})k(\boldsymbol{y}, \boldsymbol{x}), \quad \boldsymbol{x}, \boldsymbol{y} \in E, \tag{3}$$

and is known as a sufficient condition for the corresponding kernel K to have the stationary distribution π; see Chib and Greenberg (1995). MCMC methods simulate a distribution as a sample path of a Markov chain whose stationary distribution π is the desired one. For a given distribution π, also known as *target distribution*, and a functional ϱ, the quantity of interest $\varrho(\pi)$ is estimated by the MCMC estimator $\varrho(\hat{\pi})$ where $\hat{\pi}$ is the empirical distribution constructed from a sample path $\boldsymbol{X}^{(1)}, \ldots, \boldsymbol{X}^{(N)}$ of the Markov chain whose stationary distribution is π. Under regularity conditions, the MCMC estimator is consistent and asymptotically normal; see Nummelin (2002), Nummelin (2004), and Meyn and Tweedie (2012). Its asymptotic variance can be estimated from $(\boldsymbol{X}^{(1)}, \ldots, \boldsymbol{X}^{(N)})$ by, for instance, the *batch means estimator*; see Jones et al. (2006), Geyer (2011) and Vats et al. (2015) for more details. Consequently, one can construct approximate confidence intervals for the true quantity $\varrho(\pi)$ based on a sample path of the Markov chain.

Since the target distribution π is determined by the problem at hand, the problem is to find the stochastic kernel K having π as the stationary distribution such that the corresponding Markov chain can be easily simulated. One of the most prevalent stochastic kernels is the *Metropolis–Hastings (MH) kernel*, defined by $K(\boldsymbol{x}, \mathrm{d}\boldsymbol{y}) = k(\boldsymbol{x}, \boldsymbol{y})\mathrm{d}\boldsymbol{y} + r(\boldsymbol{x})\delta_{\boldsymbol{x}}(\mathrm{d}\boldsymbol{y})$, where $\delta_{\boldsymbol{x}}$ is the Dirac delta function; $k(\boldsymbol{x}, \boldsymbol{y}) = q(\boldsymbol{x}, \boldsymbol{y})\alpha(\boldsymbol{x}, \boldsymbol{y})$; $q : E \times E \to \mathbb{R}_+$ is a function called a *proposal density* such that $\boldsymbol{x} \mapsto q(\boldsymbol{x}, \boldsymbol{y})$ is measurable for any $\boldsymbol{y} \in E$ and $\boldsymbol{y} \mapsto q(\boldsymbol{x}, \boldsymbol{y})$ is a probability density for any $\boldsymbol{x} \in E$;

$$\alpha(\boldsymbol{x}, \boldsymbol{y}) = \begin{cases} \min\left\{\frac{\pi(\boldsymbol{y})q(\boldsymbol{y},\boldsymbol{x})}{\pi(\boldsymbol{x})q(\boldsymbol{x},\boldsymbol{y})}, 1\right\}, & \text{if } \pi(\boldsymbol{x})q(\boldsymbol{x}, \boldsymbol{y}) > 0, \\ 0, & \text{otherwise;} \end{cases}$$

and $r(\boldsymbol{x}) = 1 - \int_E k(\boldsymbol{x}, \boldsymbol{y})\mathrm{d}\boldsymbol{y}$. It can be shown that the MH kernel has stationary distribution π; see Tierney (1994). Simulation of the Markov chain with this MH kernel is conducted by the *MH algorithm* given in Algorithm 1.

Algorithm 1 Metropolis–Hastings (MH) algorithm.

Require: Random number generator of the proposal density $q(\boldsymbol{x}, \cdot)$ for all $\boldsymbol{x} \in E$, $\boldsymbol{x}^{(0)} \in \mathrm{supp}(\pi)$ and the ratio $\pi(\boldsymbol{y})/\pi(\boldsymbol{x})$ for $\boldsymbol{x}, \boldsymbol{y} \in E$, where π is the density of the stationary distribution.
Input: Sample size $N \in \mathbb{N}$, proposal density q, and initial value $\boldsymbol{X}^{(0)} = \boldsymbol{x}^{(0)}$.
Output: Sample path $\boldsymbol{X}^{(1)}, \ldots, \boldsymbol{X}^{(N)}$ of the Markov chain.

for $n := 0, \ldots, N-1$ **do**
(1) Generate $\tilde{\boldsymbol{X}}^{(n)} \sim q(\boldsymbol{X}^{(n)}, \cdot)$.
(2) Calculate the *acceptance probability*

$$\alpha_n := \alpha(\boldsymbol{X}^{(n)}, \tilde{\boldsymbol{X}}^{(n)}) = \min\left\{\frac{\pi(\tilde{\boldsymbol{X}}^{(n)})q(\tilde{\boldsymbol{X}}^{(n)}, \boldsymbol{X}^{(n)})}{\pi(\boldsymbol{X}^{(n)})q(\boldsymbol{X}^{(n)}, \tilde{\boldsymbol{X}}^{(n)})}, 1\right\}. \tag{4}$$

(3) Generate $U \sim \mathcal{U}(0,1)$ and set $\boldsymbol{X}^{(n+1)} := 1_{[U \le \alpha_n]}\tilde{\boldsymbol{X}}^{(n)} + 1_{[U > \alpha_n]}\boldsymbol{X}^{(n)}$.
end for

An advantage of the MCMC method is that a wide variety of distributions can be simulated as a sample path of a Markov chain even if generating i.i.d. samples is not directly feasible. The price to pay is an additional computational cost to calculate the acceptance probability (4), and a possibly higher standard deviation of the estimator $\varrho(\hat{\pi})$ compared to the standard deviation of estimators constructed from i.i.d. samples. This attributes to the serial dependence among MCMC samples, which can be seen as follows. Suppose first that the candidate $\tilde{\boldsymbol{X}}^{(n)}$ is rejected (so $\{U > \alpha_n\}$ occurs). Then $\boldsymbol{X}^{(n+1)} = \boldsymbol{X}^{(n)}$, and thus, the samples are perfectly dependent. The candidate $\tilde{\boldsymbol{X}}^{(n)}$ is more likely to be accepted if the acceptance probability α_n is close to 1. In this case, $\pi(\boldsymbol{X}^{(n)})$ and $\pi(\tilde{\boldsymbol{X}}^{(n)})$ are expected to be close to each other (otherwise, $\pi(\tilde{\boldsymbol{X}}^{(n)})/\pi(\tilde{\boldsymbol{X}}^{(n)})$ and thus α_n can be small). Under the continuity of π, $\tilde{\boldsymbol{X}}^{(n)}$ and $\boldsymbol{X}^{(n)}$ are expected to be close and thus dependent with each other. An efficient MCMC method is such that the candidate $\tilde{\boldsymbol{X}}^{(n)}$ is sufficiently far from $\boldsymbol{X}^{(n)}$ with the probability $\pi(\tilde{\boldsymbol{X}}^{(n)})$ being as close to $\pi(\boldsymbol{X}^{(n)})$ as possible. The efficiency of MCMC can indirectly be inspected through the *acceptance rate (ACR)* and the *autocorrelation plot (ACP)*; ACR is the percentage of times a candidate $\tilde{\boldsymbol{X}}$ is accepted among the N iterations, and ACP is the plot of the autocorrelation function of the generated sample path. An efficient MCMC method shows high ACR and steady decline in ACP; see Chib and Greenberg (1995) and Rosenthal et al. (2011) for details. Ideally, the proposal density q is constructed only based on π, but typically, q is chosen among a parametric family of distributions. For such cases, simplicity of the choice of tuning parameters of q is also important.

3.2. MCMC Formulation for Estimating Systemic Risk Allocations

Numerous choices of proposal densities q are possible to construct an MH kernel. In this subsection, we consider how to construct an efficient MCMC method for estimating systemic risk allocations $A^{\varrho_1,\dots,\varrho_d,\mathcal{C}}$ depending on the choice of the crisis event $\mathcal{C}$. Our goal is to directly simulate the conditional distribution $\boldsymbol{X}|\mathcal{C}$ by constructing a Markov chain whose stationary distribution is

$$\pi(\boldsymbol{x}) = f_{\boldsymbol{X}|\boldsymbol{X}\in\mathcal{C}}(\boldsymbol{x}) = \frac{f_{\boldsymbol{X}}(\boldsymbol{x})}{\mathbb{P}(\boldsymbol{X}\in\mathcal{C})}\mathbf{1}_{[\boldsymbol{x}\in\mathcal{C}]}, \quad \boldsymbol{x}\in E\subseteq\mathbb{R}^d, \tag{5}$$

provided $\mathbb{P}(\boldsymbol{X}\in\mathcal{C}) > 0$. Samples from this distribution can directly be used to estimate systemic risk allocations with crisis event $\mathcal{C}$ and arbitrary marginal risk measures $\varrho_1,\dots,\varrho_d$. Other potential applications are outlined in Remark 2.

Remark 2 (Gini shortfall allocation). *Samples from the conditional distribution* $F_{\boldsymbol{X}|\mathcal{C}_\alpha^{\mathrm{ES}}}$ *can be used to estimate, for example, the* tail-Gini coefficient $\mathrm{TGini}_\alpha(X_j,S) = \frac{4}{1-\alpha}\mathrm{Cov}(X_j,F_S(S)\mid S\geq \mathrm{VaR}_\alpha(S))$ *for* $\alpha\in(0,1)$, *and the* Gini shortfall allocation *(Furman et al. (2017))* $\mathrm{GS}_\alpha(X_j,S) = \mathbb{E}[X_j\mid S\geq\mathrm{VaR}_\alpha(S)] + \lambda\cdot\mathrm{TGini}_\alpha(X_j,S)$, $\lambda\in\mathbb{R}_+$ *more efficiently than by applying the MC method. Another application is to estimate risk allocations derived by optimization, given a constant economic capital; see Laeven and Goovaerts (2004) and Dhaene et al. (2012).*

We now construct an MH algorithm with target distribution (5). To this end, we assume that

1. the ratio $f_{\boldsymbol{X}}(\boldsymbol{y})/f_{\boldsymbol{X}}(\boldsymbol{x})$ can be evaluated for any $\boldsymbol{x},\boldsymbol{y}\in\mathcal{C}$, and that
2. the support of $f_{\boldsymbol{X}}$ is $\mathbb{R}^d$ or $\mathbb{R}_+^d$.

Regarding Assumption 1, the normalization constant of $f_{\boldsymbol{X}}$ and the probability $\mathbb{P}(\boldsymbol{X}\in\mathcal{C})$ are not necessary to be known, since they cancel out in the numerator and the denominator of $\pi(\boldsymbol{y})/\pi(\boldsymbol{x})$. In Assumption 2, the loss random vector $\boldsymbol{X}$ refers to the *profit&loss (P&L)* if $\mathrm{supp}(f_{\boldsymbol{X}}) = \mathbb{R}^d$, and to *pure losses* if $\mathrm{supp}(f_{\boldsymbol{X}}) = \mathbb{R}_+^d$. Note that the case $\mathrm{supp}(f_{\boldsymbol{X}}) = [c_1,\infty]\times\cdots\times[c_d,\infty]$, $c_1,\dots,c_d\in\mathbb{R}$ is essentially included in the case of pure losses as long as the marginal risk measures $\varrho_1,\dots,\varrho_d$ are law invariant and translation invariant, and the crisis event is the set of linear constraints of Form (2). To see this, define $\tilde{X}_j = X_j - c_j$, $j=1,\dots,d$, $\tilde{\boldsymbol{X}} = (\tilde{X}_1,\dots,\tilde{X}_d)$ and $\boldsymbol{c} = (c_1,\dots,c_d)$. Then $\mathrm{supp}(f_{\tilde{\boldsymbol{X}}}) = \mathbb{R}_+^d$ and $\boldsymbol{X}|(\boldsymbol{X}\in\mathcal{C}) \overset{\mathrm{d}}{=} \tilde{\boldsymbol{X}}|(\tilde{\boldsymbol{X}}\in\tilde{\mathcal{C}}) + \boldsymbol{c}$, where $\tilde{\mathcal{C}}$ is the set of linear constraints with parameters $\tilde{\boldsymbol{h}}_m = \boldsymbol{h}_m$ and $\tilde{v}_m = v_m - \boldsymbol{h}_m^\top\boldsymbol{c}$. By law invariance and translation invariance of $\varrho_1,\dots,\varrho_d$,

$$\varrho_j(X_j|\boldsymbol{X}\in\mathcal{C}) = c_j + \varrho_j(\tilde{X}_j|\tilde{\boldsymbol{X}}\in\tilde{\mathcal{C}}), \quad j=1,\dots,d.$$

Therefore, the problem of estimating $A^{\varrho_1,\dots,\varrho_d,\mathcal{C}}(\boldsymbol{X})$ reduces to that of estimating $A^{\varrho_1,\dots,\varrho_d,\tilde{\mathcal{C}}}(\tilde{\boldsymbol{X}})$ for the shifted loss random vector $\tilde{\boldsymbol{X}}$ (such that $\mathrm{supp}(f_{\tilde{\boldsymbol{X}}}) = \mathbb{R}_+^d$) and the modified crisis event of the same form.

For the P&L case, the RVaR and ES crisis events are the set of linear constraints of Form (2) with the number of constraints $M=2$ and 1, respectively. In the case of pure losses, additional d constraints $\boldsymbol{e}_{j,d}^\top\boldsymbol{x}\geq 0$, $j=1,\dots,d$ are imposed, where $\boldsymbol{e}_{j,d}$ is the jth d-dimensional unit vector. Therefore, the RVaR and ES crisis events are of Form (2) with $M=d+2$ and $d+1$, respectively. For the VaR crisis event, $\mathbb{P}(\boldsymbol{X}\in\mathcal{C}) = 0$, and thus, (5) cannot be properly defined. In this case, the allocation $A^{\varrho_1,\dots,\varrho_d,\mathcal{C}^{\mathrm{VaR}}}$ depends on the conditional joint distribution $\boldsymbol{X}|\mathcal{C}_\alpha^{\mathrm{VaR}}$, but is completely determined by its first $d' := d-1$ variables $(X_1,\dots,X_{d'})|\mathcal{C}_\alpha^{\mathrm{VaR}}$, since $X_d|\mathcal{C}_\alpha^{\mathrm{VaR}} \overset{\mathrm{d}}{=} (\mathrm{VaR}_\alpha(S) - \sum_{j=1}^{d'}X_j)|\mathcal{C}_\alpha^{\mathrm{VaR}} \overset{\mathrm{d}}{=} \mathrm{VaR}_\alpha(S) - \sum_{j=1}^{d'}X_j|\mathcal{C}_\alpha^{\mathrm{VaR}}$. Estimating systemic risk allocations under the VaR crisis event can thus be achieved by simulating the target distribution

$$\pi^{\mathrm{VaR}_\alpha}(\boldsymbol{x}') = f_{\boldsymbol{X}'|S=\mathrm{VaR}_\alpha(S)}(\boldsymbol{x}) = \frac{f_{(\boldsymbol{X}',S)}(\boldsymbol{x}', \mathrm{VaR}_\alpha(S))}{f_S(\mathrm{VaR}_\alpha(S))}$$
$$= \frac{f_{\boldsymbol{X}}(\boldsymbol{x}', \mathrm{VaR}_\alpha(S) - \boldsymbol{1}_{d'}^\top \boldsymbol{x}')}{f_S(\mathrm{VaR}_\alpha(S))} \boldsymbol{1}_{[\mathrm{VaR}_\alpha(S) - \boldsymbol{1}_{d'}^\top \boldsymbol{x}' \in \mathrm{supp}(f_d)]}, \quad \boldsymbol{x}' \in \mathbb{R}^{d'}, \tag{6}$$

where $\boldsymbol{X}' = (X_1, \ldots, X_{d'})$ and the last equation is derived from the linear transformation $(\boldsymbol{X}', S) \mapsto \boldsymbol{X}$ with unit Jacobian. Note that other transformations are also possible; see Betancourt (2012). Under Assumption 1, the ratio $\pi^{\mathrm{VaR}_\alpha}(\boldsymbol{y})/\pi^{\mathrm{VaR}_\alpha}(\boldsymbol{x})$ can be evaluated and $f_S(\mathrm{VaR}_\alpha(S))$ is not required to be known. In the case of pure losses, the target distribution $\pi^{\mathrm{VaR}_\alpha}$ is subject to d linear constraints $\boldsymbol{e}_{j,d'}^\top \boldsymbol{x}' \geq 0$, $j = 1, \ldots, d'$ and $\boldsymbol{1}_{d'}^\top \boldsymbol{x}' \geq \mathrm{VaR}_\alpha(S)$, where the first d' constraints come from the non-negativity of the losses and the last one is from the indicator in (6). Therefore, the crisis event C^{VaR} for $(X_1, \ldots, X_{d'})$ is of Form (2). In the case of P&L, $\mathrm{supp}(f_d) = \mathbb{R}$ and $\mathrm{VaR}_\alpha(S) - \boldsymbol{1}_{d'}^\top \boldsymbol{x}' \in \mathrm{supp}(f_d)$ holds for any $\boldsymbol{x}' \in \mathbb{R}^{d'}$. Therefore, the target distribution (6) is free from any constraints and the problem reduces to constructing an MCMC method with target distribution $\pi(\boldsymbol{x}') \propto f_{\boldsymbol{X}}(\boldsymbol{x}', \mathrm{VaR}_\alpha(S) - \boldsymbol{1}_{d'}^\top \boldsymbol{x}')$, $\boldsymbol{x}' \in \mathbb{R}^{d'}$. In this paper, the P&L case with VaR crisis event is not investigated further, since our focus is the simulation of constrained target distributions; see Koike and Minami (2019) for an MCMC estimation in the P&L case.

MCMC methods to simulate constrained target distributions require careful design of the proposal density q. A simple MCMC method is *Metropolis–Hastings with rejection* in which the support of the proposal density q may not coincide with that of the target distribution, which is the crisis event C, and a candidate is immediately rejected when it violates the constraints. This construction of MCMC is often inefficient due to a low acceptance probability, especially around the boundary of C. In this case, an efficient MCMC method can be expected only when the probability mass of π is concentrated near the center of C. In the following sections, we introduce two alternative MCMC methods for the constrained target distributions $F_{\boldsymbol{X}|C}$ of interest, the HMC method and the GS. Each of them is applicable and can be efficient for different choices of the crisis event and underlying loss distribution functions $F_{\boldsymbol{X}}$

3.3. *Estimation with Hamiltonian Monte Carlo*

We find that if the HMC method is applicable, it is typically the most preferable method to simulate constrained target distributions because of its efficiency and ease of handling constraints. In Section 3.3.1, we briefly present the HMC method with a reflection for constructing a Markov chain supported on the constrained space. In Section 3.3.2, we propose a heuristic for determining the parameters of the HMC method based on the MC presamples.

3.3.1. Hamiltonian Monte Carlo with Reflection

For the possibly unnormalized target density π, consider the *potential energy* $U(\boldsymbol{x})$, *kinetic energy* $K(\boldsymbol{p})$, and the *Hamiltonian* $H(\boldsymbol{x}, \boldsymbol{p})$ defined by

$$U(\boldsymbol{x}) = -\log \pi(\boldsymbol{x}), \quad K(\boldsymbol{p}) = -\log f_K(\boldsymbol{p}) \quad \text{and} \quad H(\boldsymbol{x}, \boldsymbol{p}) = U(\boldsymbol{x}) + K(\boldsymbol{p}),$$

with *position variable* $\boldsymbol{x} \in E$, *momentum variable* $\boldsymbol{p} \in \mathbb{R}^d$, and *kinetic energy density* $f_K(\boldsymbol{p})$ such that $f_K(-\boldsymbol{p}) = f_K(\boldsymbol{p})$. In this paper, the kinetic energy distribution F_K is set to be the multivariate standard normal with $K(\boldsymbol{p}) = \frac{1}{2}\boldsymbol{p}^\top \boldsymbol{p}$ and $\nabla K(\boldsymbol{p}) = \boldsymbol{p}$; other choices of F_K are discussed in Appendix B.2. In the HMC method, a Markov chain augmented on the state space $E \times \mathbb{R}^d$ with the stationary distribution $\pi(\boldsymbol{x}) f_K(\boldsymbol{p})$ is constructed and the desired samples from π are obtained as the first $|E|$-dimensional margins. A process $(\boldsymbol{x}(t), \boldsymbol{p}(t))$, $t \in \mathbb{R}$ on $E \times \mathbb{R}^d$ is said to follow the *Hamiltonian dynamics* if it follows the ordinary differential equation (ODE)

$$\frac{\mathrm{d}}{\mathrm{d}t}\boldsymbol{x}(t) = \nabla K(\boldsymbol{p}), \quad \frac{\mathrm{d}}{\mathrm{d}t}\boldsymbol{p}(t) = -\nabla U(\boldsymbol{x}). \tag{7}$$

Through the Hamiltonian dynamics, the Hamiltonian H and the volume are conserved, that is, $\mathrm{d}H(\boldsymbol{x}(t), \boldsymbol{p}(t))/\mathrm{d}t = 0$ and the map $(\boldsymbol{x}(0), \boldsymbol{p}(0)) \mapsto (\boldsymbol{x}(t), \boldsymbol{p}(t))$ has a unit Jacobian for any $t \in \mathbb{R}$; see Neal et al. (2011). Therefore, the value of the joint target density $\pi \cdot f_K$ remains unchanged by the Hamiltonian dynamics, that is,

$$\pi(\boldsymbol{x}(0))f_K(\boldsymbol{p}(0)) = \exp(-H(\boldsymbol{x}(0), \boldsymbol{p}(0))) = \exp(-H(\boldsymbol{x}(t), \boldsymbol{p}(t))) = \pi(\boldsymbol{x}(t))f_K(\boldsymbol{p}(t)), \quad t \geq 0.$$

In practice, the dynamics (7) are discretized for simulation by, for example, the so-called *leapfrog method* summarized in Algorithm 2; see Leimkuhler and Reich (2004) for other discretization methods.

Algorithm 2 Leapfrog method for Hamiltonian dynamics.

Input: Current states $(\boldsymbol{x}(0), \boldsymbol{p}(0))$, stepsize $\epsilon > 0$, gradients ∇U and ∇K.
Output: Updated position $(\boldsymbol{x}(\epsilon), \boldsymbol{p}(\epsilon))$.

(1) $\boldsymbol{p}\left(\frac{\epsilon}{2}\right) = \boldsymbol{p}(0) - \frac{\epsilon}{2}\nabla U(\boldsymbol{x}(0))$.
(2) $\boldsymbol{x}(\epsilon) = \boldsymbol{x}(0) + \epsilon \nabla K(\boldsymbol{p}\left(\frac{\epsilon}{2}\right))$.
(3) $\boldsymbol{p}(\epsilon) = \boldsymbol{p}(\epsilon/2) + \frac{\epsilon}{2}\nabla U(\boldsymbol{x}(\epsilon))$.

Note that the evaluation of ∇U does not require the normalization constant of π to be known, since $\nabla U = -(\nabla\pi)/\pi$. By repeating the leapfrog method T times with stepsize ϵ, the Hamiltonian dynamics are approximately simulated with length $T\epsilon$. Due to the discretization error, the Hamiltonian is not exactly preserved, while it is expected to be almost preserved for ϵ which is small enough. The discretization error $H(\boldsymbol{x}(T\epsilon), \boldsymbol{p}(T\epsilon)) - H(\boldsymbol{x}(0), \boldsymbol{p}(0))$ is called the *Hamiltonian error*.

All the steps of the HMC method are described in Algorithm 3. In Step (1), the momentum variable is first updated from $\boldsymbol{p}(0)$ to $\boldsymbol{p}$, where $\boldsymbol{p}$ follows the kinetic energy distribution F_K so that the value of the Hamiltonian $H = -\log(\pi \cdot f_K)$ changes. In Step (3), the current state $(\boldsymbol{x}(0), \boldsymbol{p})$ is moved along the level curve of $H(\boldsymbol{x}(0), \boldsymbol{p})$ by simulating the Hamiltonian dynamics.

Algorithm 3 Hamiltonian Monte Carlo to simulate π.

Require: Random number generator of F_K, $\boldsymbol{x}^{(0)} \in \mathrm{supp}(\pi)$, $\pi(\boldsymbol{y})/\pi(\boldsymbol{x})$, $\boldsymbol{x}, \boldsymbol{y} \in E$ and $f_K(\boldsymbol{p}')/f_K(\boldsymbol{p})$, $\boldsymbol{p}, \boldsymbol{p}' \in \mathbb{R}^d$.
Input: Sample size $N \in \mathbb{N}$, kinetic energy density f_K, target density π, gradients of the potential and kinetic energies ∇U and ∇K, stepsize $\epsilon > 0$, integration time $T \in \mathbb{N}$ and initial position $\boldsymbol{X}^{(0)} = \boldsymbol{x}^{(0)}$.
Output: Sample path $\boldsymbol{X}^{(1)}, \ldots, \boldsymbol{X}^{(N)}$ of the Markov chain.

for $n := 0, \ldots, N-1$ **do**
(1) Generate $\boldsymbol{p}^{(n)} \sim F_K$.
(2) Set $(\tilde{\boldsymbol{X}}^{(n)}, \tilde{\boldsymbol{p}}^{(n)}) = (\boldsymbol{X}^{(n)}, \boldsymbol{p}^{(n)})$.
(3) **for** $t := 1, \ldots, T$,

$$(\tilde{\boldsymbol{X}}^{(n+t/T)}, \tilde{\boldsymbol{p}}^{(n+t/T)}) = \textbf{Leapfrog}(\tilde{\boldsymbol{X}}^{(n+(t-1)/T)}, \tilde{\boldsymbol{p}}^{(n+(t-1)/T)}, \epsilon, \nabla U, \nabla K).$$

end for
(4) $\tilde{\boldsymbol{p}}^{(n+1)} = -\boldsymbol{p}^{(n+1)}$.
(5) Calculate $\alpha_n = \min\left\{\frac{\pi(\tilde{\boldsymbol{X}}^{(n+1)})f_K(\tilde{\boldsymbol{p}}^{(n+1)})}{\pi(\boldsymbol{X}^{(n)})f_K(\boldsymbol{p}^{(n)})}, 1\right\}$.
(6) Set $\boldsymbol{X}^{(n+1)} := 1_{[U \leq \alpha_n]}\tilde{\boldsymbol{X}}^{(n+1)} + 1_{[U > \alpha_n]}\boldsymbol{X}^{(n)}$ for $U \sim \mathrm{U}(0,1)$.
end for

By flipping the momentum in Step (4), the HMC method is shown to be reversible w.r.t. π (c.f. (3)) and thus to have the stationary distribution π; see Neal et al. (2011) for details. Furthermore, by the conservation property of the Hamiltonian dynamics, the acceptance probability in Step (5) is expected to be close to 1. Moreover, by taking T as sufficiently large, the candidate $\tilde{\boldsymbol{X}}^{(n+1)}$ is expected to be sufficiently decorrelated from the current position $\boldsymbol{X}^{(n)}$. Consequently, the resulting Markov chain is expected to be efficient.

The remaining challenge for applying the HMC method to our problem of estimating systemic risk allocations is how to handle the constraint $\mathcal{C}$. As we have seen in Sections 2.1 and 3.2, $\mathcal{C}$ is assumed to be an intersection of linear constraints with parameters $(\boldsymbol{h}_m, v_m)$, $m = 1, \ldots, M$ describing hyperplanes. Following the ordinary leapfrog method, a candidate is immediately rejected when the trajectory of the Hamiltonian dynamics penetrates one of these hyperplanes. To avoid it, we modify the leapfrog method according to the reflection technique introduced in Afshar and Domke (2015) and Chevallier et al. (2018). As a result, the trajectory is reflected when it hits a hyperplane and the Markov chain moves within the constrained space with probability one. Details of the HMC method with the reflection for our application are described in Appendix A.

3.3.2. Choice of Parameters for HMC

HMC requires as input two parameters, the *stepsize* ϵ, and the *integration time* T. As we now explain, neither of them should be chosen too large nor too small. Since the stepsize ϵ controls the accuracy of the simulation of the Hamiltonian dynamics, ϵ needs to be small enough to approximately conserve the Hamiltonian; otherwise, the acceptance probability can be much smaller than 1. On the other hand, an ϵ which is too small requires the integration time T to be large enough for the trajectory to reach a farther distance, which is computationally costly. Next, the integration time T needs to be large enough to decorrelate the candidate state with the current state. Meanwhile, the trajectory of the Hamiltonian dynamics may make a U-turn and come back to the starting point if the integration time T is too long; see Neal et al. (2011) for an illustration of this phenomenon.

A notable characteristic of our problem of estimating systemic risk allocations is that the MC sample from the target distribution π is available but its sample size may not be sufficient for statistical inference, and, in the case of the VaR crisis event, the samples only approximately follow the target distribution. We utilize the information of this *MC presample* to build a heuristic for determining the parameters (ϵ, T); see Algorithm 4.

In this heuristic, the initial stepsize is set to be $\epsilon = c_\epsilon d^{-1/4}$ for some constant $c_\epsilon > 0$, say, $c_\epsilon = 1$. This scale was derived in Beskos et al. (2010) and Beskos et al. (2013) under certain assumptions on the target distribution. We determine ϵ through the relationship with the acceptance probability. In Step (2-2-2-1) of Algorithm 4, multiple trajectories are simulated, starting from each MC presample with the current stepsize ϵ. In the next Step (2-2-2-2), we monitor the acceptance probability and the distance between the starting and ending points while extending the trajectories. Based on the asymptotic optimal acceptance probability 0.65 (c.f. Gupta et al. (1990) and Betancourt et al. (2014)) as $d \to \infty$, we set the *target acceptance probability* as

$$\underline{\alpha} = \frac{1 + (d-1) \times 0.65}{d} \in (0.65, 1].$$

The stepsize is gradually decreased in Step (2-1) of Algorithm 4 until the minimum acceptance probability calculated in Step (2-3) exceeds $\underline{\alpha}$. To prevent the trajectory from a U-turn, in Step (2-2-2-3), each trajectory is immediately stopped when the distance begins to decrease. The resulting integration time is set to be the average of these turning points, as seen in Step (3). Note that other termination conditions of extending trajectories are possible; see Hoffman and Gelman (2014) and Betancourt (2016).

Algorithm 4 Heuristic for determining the stepsize ϵ and integration time T.

Input: MC presample $\mathbf{X}_1^{(0)}, \dots, \mathbf{X}_{N_0}^{(0)}$, gradients ∇U and ∇K, target acceptance probability $\underline{\alpha}$, initial constant $c_\epsilon > 0$ and the maximum integration time $T_{\max}$ ($c_\epsilon = 1$ and $T_{\max} = 1000$ are set as default values).
Output: Stepsize ϵ and integration time T.

(1) Set $\alpha_{\min} = 0$ and $\epsilon = c_\epsilon d^{-1/4}$.
(2) **while** $\alpha_{\min} < \underline{\alpha}$
  (2-1) Set $\epsilon = \epsilon/2$.
  (2-2) **for** $n := 1, \dots, N_0$
    (2-2-1) Generate $\boldsymbol{p}_n^{(0)} \sim F_K$.
    (2-2-2) **for** $t := 1, \dots, T_{\max}$
      (2-2-2-1) Set $\mathbf{Z}_n^{(t)} = \textbf{Leapfrog}(\mathbf{Z}_n^{(t-1)}, \epsilon, \nabla U, \nabla K)$ for $\mathbf{Z}_n^{(t-1)} = (\mathbf{X}_n^{(t-1)}, \boldsymbol{p}_n^{(t-1)})$.
      (2-2-2-2) Calculate

$$\alpha_{n,t} = \alpha(\mathbf{Z}_n^{(t-1)}, \mathbf{Z}_n^{(t)}) \quad \text{and} \quad \Delta_t = ||\mathbf{X}_n^{(t)} - \mathbf{X}_n^{(0)}|| - ||\mathbf{X}_n^{(t-1)} - \mathbf{X}_n^{(0)}||.$$

      (2-2-2-3) **if** $\Delta_t < 0$ and $\Delta_{t-1} > 0$, **break** and set $T_n^* = t - 1$.
      end for
    end for
  (2-3) Compute $\alpha_{\min} = \min(\alpha_{n,t} \mid t = 1, 2, \dots, T_n^*, \ n = 1, \dots, N_0)$.
end while
(3) Set $T = \lfloor \frac{1}{N_0} \sum_{n=1}^{N_0} T_n^* \rfloor$.

At the end of this section, we briefly revisit the choice of the kinetic energy distribution F_K, which is taken to be a multivariate standard normal throughout this work. As discussed in Neal et al. (2011), applying the HMC method with target distribution π and kinetic energy distribution $\mathrm{N}(\mathbf{0}, \Sigma^{-1})$ is equivalent to applying HMC with the standardized target distribution $\boldsymbol{x} \to \pi(L\boldsymbol{x})$ and $F_K = \mathrm{N}(\mathbf{0}, \boldsymbol{I})$, where L is the *Cholesky factor* of Σ such that $\Sigma = LL^\top$. By taking Σ to be the covariance matrix of π, the standardized target distribution becomes uncorrelated with unit variances. In our problem, the sample covariance matrix $\hat{\Sigma} = \hat{L}\hat{L}^\top$ calculated based on the MC presample is used alternatively. The new target distribution $\tilde{\pi}(\boldsymbol{y}) = \pi(\hat{L}\boldsymbol{y})|\hat{L}|$ where $|\hat{L}|$ denotes the Jacobian of $\hat{L}$, is almost uncorrelated with unit variances, and thus the standard normal kinetic energy fits well; see Livingstone et al. (2019). If the crisis event consists of the set of linear constraints $(\boldsymbol{h}_m, v_m)$, $m = 1, \dots, M$, then the standardized target density is also subject to the set of linear constraints $(\hat{L}^\top \boldsymbol{h}_m, v_m)$, $m = 1, \dots, M$. Since the ratio $f_{\mathbf{X}}(\hat{L}\boldsymbol{y})/f_{\mathbf{X}}(\hat{L}\boldsymbol{x})$ can still be evaluated under Assumption 1, we conclude that the problem remains unchanged after standardization.

Theoretical results of the HMC method with normal kinetic energy are available only when C is bounded (Cances et al. (2007) and Chevallier et al. (2018)), or when C is unbounded and the tail of π is roughly as light as that of the normal distribution (Livingstone et al. (2016) and Durmus et al. (2017)). Boundedness of C holds for VaR and RVaR crisis events with pure losses; see Koike and Minami (2019). As is discussed in this paper, convergence results of MCMC estimators are accessible when the density of the underlying joint loss distribution is bounded from above on C, which is typically the case when the underlying copula does not admit lower tail dependence. For other cases where C is unbounded or the density explodes on C, no convergence results are available. Potential remedies for the HMC method to deal with heavy-tailed target distributions are discussed in Appendix B.2.

3.4. Estimation with Gibbs Sampler

As discussed in Section 3.3.2, applying HMC methods to heavy-tailed target distributions on unbounded crisis events is not theoretically supported. To deal with this case, we introduce the GS in this section.

3.4.1. True Gibbs Sampler for Estimating Systemic Risk Allocations

The GS is a special case of the MH method in which the proposal density q is completely determined by the target density π via

$$q_{GS}(\boldsymbol{x}, \boldsymbol{y}) = \sum_{\boldsymbol{i}=(i_1,\ldots,i_d)\in\mathcal{I}_d} p_{\boldsymbol{i}}\pi(y_{i_1}|\boldsymbol{x}_{-i_1})\pi(y_{i_2}|y_{i_1}, \boldsymbol{x}_{-(i_1,i_2)})\cdots\pi(y_{i_d}|\boldsymbol{y}_{-i_d}), \tag{8}$$

where $\boldsymbol{x}_{-(j_1,\ldots,j_l)}$ is the $(d-l)$-dimensional vector that excludes the components $j_1, \ldots, j_l$ from $\boldsymbol{x}$, $\pi(x_j|\boldsymbol{x}_{-j}) = \pi_{j|-j}(x_j|\boldsymbol{x}_{-j})$ is the conditional density of the jth variable of π given all the other components, $\mathcal{I}_d \subseteq \{1,\ldots,d\}^d$ is the so-called *index set*, and $(p_{\boldsymbol{i}} \in [0,1],\ \boldsymbol{i} \in \mathcal{I}_d)$ is the *index probability distribution* such that $\sum_{\boldsymbol{i}\in\mathcal{I}_d} p_{\boldsymbol{i}} = 1$. For this choice of q, the acceptance probability is always equal to 1; see Johnson (2009). The GS is called *deterministic scan (DSGS)* if $\mathcal{I}_d = \{(1,\ldots,d)\}$ and $p_{(1,\ldots,d)} = 1$. When the index set is the set of permutations of $(1,\ldots,d)$, the GS is called *random permulation (RPGS)*. Finally, the *random scan GS (RSGS)* has the proposal (8) with $\mathcal{I}_d = \{1,\ldots,d\}^d$ and $p_{(i_1,\ldots,i_d)} = p_{i_1}\cdots p_{i_d}$ with probabilities $(p_1,\ldots,p_d) \in (0,1)^d$ such that $\sum_{j=1}^d p_j = 1$. These three GSs can be shown to have π as stationary distribution; see Johnson (2009).

Provided that the *full conditional distributions* $\pi_{j|-j}$, $j = 1,\ldots,d$ can be simulated, the proposal distribution (8) can be simulated by first selecting an index $\boldsymbol{i} \in \mathcal{I}_d$ with probability $p_{\boldsymbol{i}}$ and then replacing the jth component of the current state with a sample from $\pi_{j|-j}$ sequentially for $j = i_1,\ldots,i_d$. The main advantage of the GS is that the tails of π are naturally incorporated via full conditional distributions, and thus the MCMC method is expected to be efficient even if π is heavy-tailed. On the other hand, the applicability of the GS is limited to target distributions such that $\pi_{j|-j}$ is available. Moreover, fast simulators of $\pi_{j|-j}$, $j = 1,\ldots,d$, are required, since the computational time linearly increases w.r.t. the dimension d.

In our problem of estimating systemic risk allocations, we find that the GS is applicable when the crisis event is of the form

$$C = \{\boldsymbol{x} \in \mathbb{R}^d \text{ or } \mathbb{R}_+^d \mid v_1 \le \boldsymbol{h}^\top \boldsymbol{x} \le v_2\}, \quad v_1, v_2 \in \mathbb{R}\cup\{\pm\infty\}, \quad \boldsymbol{h} = (h_1,\ldots,h_d) \in \mathbb{R}^d \backslash \{\boldsymbol{0}_d\}. \tag{9}$$

The RVaR crisis event is obviously a special case of (9), and the ES crisis event is included as a limiting case for $v_2 \to \infty$. Furthermore, the full conditional copulas of the underlying joint loss distribution and their inverses are required to be known as we now explain. Consider the target density $\pi = f_{\boldsymbol{X}|v_1\le\boldsymbol{h}^\top\boldsymbol{X}\le v_2}$. For its jth full conditional density $\pi_{j|-j}(x_j|\boldsymbol{x}_{-j})$, notice that

$$\{v_1 \le \boldsymbol{h}^\top \boldsymbol{X} \le v_2,\ \boldsymbol{X}_{-j} = \boldsymbol{x}_{-j}\} = \left\{\frac{v_1 - \boldsymbol{h}_{-j}^\top \boldsymbol{x}_{-j}}{h_j} \le X_j \le \frac{v_2 - \boldsymbol{h}_{-j}^\top \boldsymbol{x}_{-j}}{h_j},\ \boldsymbol{X}_{-j} = \boldsymbol{x}_{-j}\right\}$$

and thus, for $v_{i,j}(\boldsymbol{x}_{-j}) = (v_i - \boldsymbol{h}_{-j}^\top \boldsymbol{x}_{-j})/h_j$, $i = 1,2$, we obtain the cdf of $\pi_{j|-j}$ as

$$F_{X_j|(v_1\le\boldsymbol{h}^\top\boldsymbol{X}\le v_2,\ \boldsymbol{X}_{-j}=\boldsymbol{x}_{-j})}(x_j) = \frac{F_{X_j|\boldsymbol{X}_{-j}=\boldsymbol{x}_{-j}}(x_j) - F_{X_j|\boldsymbol{X}_{-j}=\boldsymbol{x}_{-j}}(v_{1,j}(\boldsymbol{x}_{-j}))}{F_{X_j|\boldsymbol{X}_{-j}=\boldsymbol{x}_{-j}}(v_{2,j}(\boldsymbol{x}_{-j})) - F_{X_j|\boldsymbol{X}_{-j}=\boldsymbol{x}_{-j}}(v_{1,j}(\boldsymbol{x}_{-j}))} \tag{10}$$

for $v_{1,j}(\boldsymbol{x}_{-j}) \leq x_j \leq v_{2,j}(\boldsymbol{x}_{-j})$. Denoting the denominator of (10) by $\Delta_j(\boldsymbol{x}_{-j})$, we obtain the quantile function

$$F^{-1}_{X_j|(v_1\leq \boldsymbol{h}^\top \boldsymbol{X}\leq v_2,\ \boldsymbol{X}_{-j}=\boldsymbol{x}_{-j})}(u) = F^{-1}_{X_j|\boldsymbol{X}_{-j}=\boldsymbol{x}_{-j}}\left(\Delta_j(\boldsymbol{x}_{-j})\cdot u + F_{X_j|\boldsymbol{X}_{-j}=\boldsymbol{x}_{-j}}(v_{1,j}(\boldsymbol{x}_{-j}))\right).$$

Therefore, if $F_{X_j|\boldsymbol{X}_{-j}=\boldsymbol{x}_{-j}}$ and its quantile function are available, one can simulate the full conditional target densities $\pi_{j|-j}$ with the inversion method; see Devroye (1985). Availability of $F_{X_j|\boldsymbol{X}_{-j}=\boldsymbol{x}_{-j}}$ and its inverse typically depends on the copula of $\boldsymbol{X}$. By Sklar's theorem (1), the jth full conditional distribution of $F_{\boldsymbol{X}}$ can be written as

$$F_{X_j|\boldsymbol{X}_{-j}=\boldsymbol{x}_{-j}}(x_j) = C_{j|-j}(F_j(x_j) \mid \boldsymbol{F}_{-j}(\boldsymbol{x}_{-j})),$$

where $\boldsymbol{F}_{(j_1,\dots,j_l)}(\boldsymbol{x}_{(j_1,\dots,j_l)}) = (F_{j_1}(x_{j_1}),\dots,F_{j_l}(x_{j_l}))$, $-(j_1,\dots,j_l) = \{1,\dots,d\}\backslash(j_1,\dots,j_l)$ and $C_{j|-j}$ is the jth *full conditional copula* defined by

$$C_{j|-j}(u_j|\boldsymbol{u}_{-j}) = \mathbb{P}(U_j \leq u_j \mid \boldsymbol{U}_{-j} = \boldsymbol{u}_{-j}) = \frac{D_{-j}C(\boldsymbol{u})}{D_{-j}C(u_1,\dots,u_{j-1},1,u_{j+1},\dots,u_d)},$$

where D denotes the operator of partial derivatives with respect to the components given as subscripts and $\boldsymbol{U} \sim C$. Assuming the full conditional copula $C_{j|-j}$ and its inverse $C^{-1}_{j|-j}$ are available, one can simulate $\tilde{X}_j \sim \pi_{j|-j}$ via

$$\begin{aligned}
&U \sim \mathrm{U}(0,1),\\
&\tilde{U} = U + (1-U)C_{j|-j}(F_j(v_1(\boldsymbol{x}_{-j}) \mid \boldsymbol{F}_{-j}(\boldsymbol{x}_{-j})),\\
&\tilde{X}_j = F_j^{-1} \circ C^{-1}_{j|-j}(\tilde{U} \mid \boldsymbol{F}_{-j}(\boldsymbol{x}_{-j})).
\end{aligned}$$

Examples of copulas for which the full conditional distributions and their inverses are available include normal, Student t, and Clayton copulas; see Cambou et al. (2017). In this case, the GS is also applicable to the corresponding survival (π-rotated) copula $\hat{C}$, since

$$\hat{C}_{j|-j}(\boldsymbol{u}) = 1 - C_{j|-j}(1-u_j \mid \boldsymbol{1}_{d'} - \boldsymbol{u}_{-j}),\quad \hat{C}^{-1}_{j|-j}(\boldsymbol{u}) = 1 - C^{-1}_{j|-j}(1-u_j \mid \boldsymbol{1}_{d'} - \boldsymbol{u}_{-j}),\quad j=1,\dots,d,$$

by the relationship $\tilde{\boldsymbol{U}} = \boldsymbol{1} - \boldsymbol{U} \sim \hat{C}$ for $\boldsymbol{U} \sim C$. In a similar way, one can also obtain full conditional copulas and their inverses for other rotated copulas; see Hofert et al. (2018) Section 3.4.1 for rotated copulas.

In the end, we remark that even if the full conditional distributions and their inverses are not available, $\pi_{j|-j}$ can be simulated by, for example, the acceptance and rejection method, or even the MH algorithm; see Appendix B.3.

3.4.2. Choice of Parameters for GS

As discussed in Section 3.3.2, we use information from the MC presamples to determine the parameters of the Gibbs kernel (8). Note that standardization of the variables as applied in the HMC method in Section 3.3.2 is not available for the GS, since the latter changes the underlying joint loss distribution, and since the copula after rotating variables is generally not accessible, except for in the elliptical case; see Christen et al. (2017). Among the presented variants of GSs, we adopt RSGS, since determining d probabilities $(p_1,\dots,p_d)$ is relatively easy, whereas RPGS requires $d!$ probabilities to be determined. To this end, we consider the RSGS with the parameters $(p_1,\dots,p_d)$ determined by a heuristic described in Algorithm 5.

Algorithm 5 Random scan Gibbs sampler (RSGS) with heuristic to determine $(p_1, \ldots, p_d)$.

Require: Random number generator of $\pi_{j|-j}$ and $\boldsymbol{x}^{(0)} \in \text{supp}(\pi)$.
Input: MC presample $\tilde{\boldsymbol{X}}_1^{(0)}, \ldots, \tilde{\boldsymbol{X}}_{N_0}^{(0)}$, sample size $N \in \mathbb{N}$, initial state $\boldsymbol{x}^{(0)}$, sample size of the pre-run N_{pre} and the target autocorrelation ρ ($N_{\text{pre}} = 100$ and $\rho = 0.15$ are set as default values).
Output: N sample path $\boldsymbol{X}^{(1)}, \ldots, \boldsymbol{X}^{(N)}$ of the Markov chain.

(1) Compute the sample covariance matrix $\hat{\Sigma}$ based on $\tilde{\boldsymbol{X}}_1^{(0)}, \ldots, \tilde{\boldsymbol{X}}_{N_0}^{(0)}$.
(2) Set $p_j \propto \hat{\Sigma}_{j,j} - \hat{\Sigma}_{j,-j}\hat{\Sigma}_{-j,-j}^{-1}\hat{\Sigma}_{-j,j}$ and $\boldsymbol{X}^{(0)} = \boldsymbol{X}_{\text{pre}}^{(0)} = \boldsymbol{x}^{(0)}$.
(3) **for** $n := 1, \ldots, N_{\text{pre}}$
   (3-1) Generate $J = j$ with probability p_j.
   (3-2) Update $X_{\text{pre},J}^{(n)} \sim \pi_{J|-J}(\cdot|\boldsymbol{X}_{\text{pre}}^{(n-1)})$ and $\boldsymbol{X}_{\text{pre},-J}^{(n)} = \boldsymbol{X}_{\text{pre},-J}^{(n-1)}$.
end for
(4) Set

$$T = \text{argmin}_{h \in \mathbb{N}_0} \left\{ \text{estimated autocorrelations of } \boldsymbol{X}_{\text{pre}}^{(1)}, \ldots, \boldsymbol{X}_{\text{pre}}^{(N_{\text{pre}})} \text{ with lag } h \leq \rho \right\}.$$

(5) **for** $n := 1, \ldots, N, t := 1, \ldots, T$
   (5-1) Generate $J = j$ with probability p_j.
   (5-2) Update $X_J^{(n-1+t/T)} \sim \pi_{J|-J}(\cdot|\boldsymbol{X}^{(n-1+(t-1)/T)})$ and $\boldsymbol{X}_{-J}^{(n-1+t/T)} = \boldsymbol{X}_{-J}^{(n-1+(t-1)/T)}$.
end for

The RSGS kernel is simulated in Steps (3) and (5) of Algorithm 5. To determine the selection probabilities $p_1, \ldots, p_d$, consider a one-step update of the RSGS from $\boldsymbol{X}^{(n)}$ to $\boldsymbol{X}^{(n+1)}$ with $\boldsymbol{X}^{(n)} \sim \pi$ and the one-step kernel

$$K_{\text{RSGS}}(\boldsymbol{x}, \boldsymbol{y}) = \sum_{j=1}^{d} p_j \pi_{j|-j}(y_j|\boldsymbol{x}_{-j}) \mathbf{1}_{[\boldsymbol{y}_{-j} = \boldsymbol{x}_{-j}]}.$$

Liu et al. (1995, Lemma 3) implies that

$$\text{Cov}(X_j^{(n)}, X_j^{(n+1)}) = \sum_{i=1}^{d} p_i \mathbb{E}[\mathbb{E}[X_j \mid \boldsymbol{X}_{-i}]] = \sum_{i=1}^{d} p_i \{m_j^{(2)} - \mathbb{E}[\text{Var}(X_j \mid \boldsymbol{X}_{-i})]\} \propto -\sum_{i=1}^{d} p_i \mathbb{E}[\text{Var}(X_j \mid \boldsymbol{X}_{-i})]),$$

where $m_j^{(k)}$ is the kth moment of π_j.

For the objective function $\sum_{j=1}^{d} \text{Cov}(X_j^{(n)}, X_j^{(n+1)})$, its minimizer $(p_1^*, \ldots, p_d^*)$ under the constraint $\sum_{j=1}^{d} p_j = 1$ satisfies

$$p_j^* \propto \mathbb{E}[\text{Var}(X_j \mid \boldsymbol{X}_{-j})]. \tag{11}$$

While this optimizer can be computed based on the MC presamples, we observed that its stable estimation is as computationally demanding as estimating the risk allocations themselves. Alternatively, we calculate (11) under the assumption that π follows an elliptical distribution. Under this assumption, (11) is given by

$$p_j \propto \Sigma_{j,j} - \Sigma_{j,-j}\Sigma_{-j,-j}^{-1}\Sigma_{-j,j},$$

where Σ is the covariance matrix of π and Σ_{J_1,J_2}, $J_1, J_2 \subseteq \{1, \ldots, d\}$ is the submatrix of Σ with indices in $J_1 \times J_2$. As seen in Step (2) of Algorithm 5, Σ is replaced by its estimate based on the MC presamples.

As shown in Christen et al. (2017), Gibbs samplers require a large number of iterations to lower the serial correlation when the target distribution has strong dependence. To reduce serial correlations, we take every Tth sample in Step (5-2), where $T \in \mathbb{N}$ is called the *thinning interval of times*. Note that we use the same notation T as that of the integration time in HMC, since they both represent a repetition time of some single step. Based on the preliminary run with length N_{pre} in Step (3) in Algorithm 5, T is determined as the smallest lag h such that the marginal autocorrelations with lag h are all smaller than the target autocorrelation ρ; see Step (4) in Algorithm 5.

4. Numerical Experiments

In this section, we demonstrate the performance of the MCMC methods for estimating systemic risk allocations by a series of numerical experiments. We first conduct a simulation study in which true allocations or their partial information are available. Then, we perform an empirical study to demonstrate that our MCMC methods are applicable to a more practical setup. Finally, we make more detailed comparisons between the MC and MCMC methods in various setups. All experiments were run on a MacBook Air with 1.4 GHz Intel Core i5 processor and 4 GB 1600 MHz of DDR3 RAM.

4.1. Simulation Study

In this simulation study, we compare the estimates and standard errors of the MC and MCMC methods under the low-dimensional risk models described in Section 4.1.1. The results and discussions are summarized in Section 4.1.2.

4.1.1. Model Description

We consider the following three-dimensional loss distributions:

(M1) *generalized Pareto distributions (GPDs)* with parameters $(\xi_j, \beta_j) = (0.3, 1)$ and survival Clayton copula with parameter $\theta = 2$ so that Kendall's tau equals $\tau = \theta/(\theta + 2) = 0.5$;

(M2) multivariate Student t distribution with $\nu = 5$ degrees of freedom, location vector $\mathbf{0}$, and dispersion matrix $\Sigma = (\rho_{i,j})$, where $\rho_{j,j} = 1$ and $\rho_{i,j} = |i - j|/d$ for $i, j = 1, \ldots, d$, $i \neq j$.

Since the marginals are homogeneous and the copula is exchangeable, the systemic risk allocations under the loss distribution (M1) are all equal, provided that the crisis event is invariant under the permutation of the variables. For the loss distribution (M2), by ellipticality of the joint distribution, analytical formulas of risk contribution-type systemic risk allocations are available; see McNeil et al. (2015) Corollary 8.43. The parameters of the distributions (M1) and (M2) take into account the stylized facts that the loss distribution is heavy-tailed and extreme losses are positively dependent.

We consider the VaR, RVaR, and ES crisis events with confidence levels $\alpha^{\text{VaR}} = 0.99$, $(\alpha_1^{\text{RVaR}}, \alpha_2^{\text{RVaR}}) = (0.975, 0.99)$ and $\alpha^{\text{ES}} = 0.99$, respectively. For each crisis event, the risk contribution, VaR, RVaR, and ES-type systemic risk allocations are estimated by the MC and MCMC methods, where the parameters of the marginal risk measures VaR, RVaR, and ES are set to be $\beta^{\text{VaR}} = 0.99$, $(\beta_1^{\text{RVaR}}, \beta_2^{\text{RVaR}}) = (0.975, 0.99)$ and $\beta^{\text{ES}} = 0.99$, respectively.

We first conduct the MC simulation for the distributions (M1) and (M2). For the VaR crisis event, the modified event $\mathcal{C}^{\text{mod}} = \{\text{VaR}_{\alpha-\delta}(S) \leq \mathbf{1}_d^\top \boldsymbol{x} \leq \text{VaR}_{\alpha+\delta}(S)\}$ with $\delta = 0.001$ is used to ensure that $\mathbb{P}(\boldsymbol{X} \in \mathcal{C}^{\text{mod}}) > 0$. Based on these MC presamples, the Markov chains are constructed as described in Sections 3.3 and 3.4. For the MCMC method, (M1) is the case of pure losses and (M2) is the case of P&L. Therefore, the HMC method is applied to the distribution (M1) for the VaR and RVaR crisis events, the GS is applied to (M1) for the ES crisis event and the GS is applied to the distribution (M2) for the RVaR and ES crisis events. The target distribution of (M2) with VaR constraint is free from constraints and was already investigated in Koike and Minami (2019); we thus omit this case and consider the five remaining cases.

Note that 99.8% of the MC samples from the unconditional distribution are discarded for the VaR crisis event and a further 97.5% of them are wasted to estimate the RVaR contributions. Therefore, $1/(0.002 \times 0.025) = 10^5/5 = 20{,}000$ MC samples are required to obtain one MC sample from the conditional distribution. Taking this into account, the sample size of the MC estimator is set to be $N_{\text{MC}} = 10^5$. The sample size of the MCMC estimators is free from such constraints and thus is chosen to be $N_{\text{MCMC}} = 10^4$. Initial values x_0 for the MCMC methods are taken as the mean vector calculated from the MC samples. Biases are computed only for the contribution-type allocations in the distribution (M2) since the true values are available in this case. For all the five cases, the MC and the MCMC standard errors are computed according to Glasserman (2013) Chapter 1, for MC, and Jones et al. (2006) for MCMC. Asymptotic variances of the MCMC estimators are estimated by the batch means estimator with batch length $L_N := \lceil N^{\frac{1}{2}} \rceil = 100$ and batch size $B_N := \lceil N/L_N \rceil = 100$. The results are summarized in Tables 1 and 2.

Table 1. Estimates and standard errors for the MC and HMC estimators of risk contribution, RVaR, VaR, and ES-type systemic risk allocations under (I) the VaR crisis event, and (II) the RVaR crisis event for the loss distribution (M1). The sample size of the MC method is $N_{\text{MC}} = 10^5$, and that of the HMC method is $N_{\text{MCMC}} = 10^4$. The acceptance rate (ACR), stepsize ϵ, integration time T, and run time are ACR $= 0.996$, $\epsilon = 0.210$, $T = 12$, and run time $= 1.277$ mins in Case (I), and ACR $= 0.984$, $\epsilon = 0.095$, $T = 13$, and run time $= 1.649$ mins in Case (II).

	MC			HMC		
Estimator	$A_1^{\varrho,\mathcal{C}}(X)$	$A_2^{\varrho,\mathcal{C}}(X)$	$A_3^{\varrho,\mathcal{C}}(X)$	$A_1^{\varrho,\mathcal{C}}(X)$	$A_2^{\varrho,\mathcal{C}}(X)$	$A_3^{\varrho,\mathcal{C}}(X)$
(I) GPD + survival Clayton with VaR crisis event: $\{S = \text{VaR}_{0.99}(S)\}$						
$\mathbb{E}[\boldsymbol{X}\|\mathcal{C}^{\text{VaR}}]$	9.581	9.400	9.829	9.593	9.599	9.619
Standard error	0.126	0.118	0.120	0.007	0.009	0.009
$\text{RVaR}_{0.975,0.99}(\boldsymbol{X}\|\mathcal{C}^{\text{VaR}})$	12.986	12.919	13.630	13.298	13.204	13.338
Standard error	0.229	0.131	0.086	0.061	0.049	0.060
$\text{VaR}_{0.99}(\boldsymbol{X}\|\mathcal{C}^{\text{VaR}})$	13.592	13.235	13.796	13.742	13.565	13.768
Standard error	0.647	0.333	0.270	0.088	0.070	0.070
$\text{ES}_{0.99}(\boldsymbol{X}\|\mathcal{C}^{\text{VaR}})$	14.775	13.955	14.568	14.461	14.227	14.427
Standard error	0.660	0.498	0.605	0.192	0.176	0.172
(II) GPD + survival Clayton with RVaR crisis event: $\{\text{VaR}_{0.975}(S) \le S \le \text{VaR}_{0.99}(S)\}$						
$\mathbb{E}[\boldsymbol{X}\|\mathcal{C}^{\text{RVaR}}]$	7.873	7.780	7.816	7.812	7.802	7.780
Standard error	0.046	0.046	0.046	0.012	0.012	0.011
$\text{RVaR}_{0.975,0.99}(\boldsymbol{X}\|\mathcal{C}^{\text{RVaR}})$	11.790	11.908	11.680	11.686	11.696	11.646
Standard error	0.047	0.057	0.043	0.053	0.055	0.058
$\text{RVaR}_{0.99}(\boldsymbol{X}\|\mathcal{C}^{\text{VaR}})$	12.207	12.382	12.087	12.102	12.053	12.044
Standard error	0.183	0.197	0.182	0.074	0.069	0.069
$\text{ES}_{0.99}(\boldsymbol{X}\|\mathcal{C}^{\text{RVaR}})$	13.079	13.102	13.059	12.859	12.791	12.713
Standard error	0.182	0.173	0.188	0.231	0.218	0.187

Table 2. Estimates and standard errors for the MC and the GS estimators of risk contribution, VaR, RVaR, and ES-type systemic risk allocations under (III) distribution (M1) and the ES crisis event, (IV) distribution (M2), and the RVaR crisis event, and (V) distribution (M2) and ES crisis event. The sample size of the MC method is $N_{\mathrm{MC}} = 10^5$ and that of the GS is $N_{\mathrm{MCMC}} = 10^4$. The thinning interval of times T, selection probability $\boldsymbol{p}$ and run time are $T = 12$, $\boldsymbol{p} = (0.221, 0.362, 0.416)$ and run time = 107.880 secs in Case (III), $T = 10$, $\boldsymbol{p} = (0.330, 0.348, 0.321)$ and run time = 56.982 secs in Case (IV) and $T = 4$, $\boldsymbol{p} = (0.241, 0.503, 0.255)$ and run time = 22.408 secs in Case (V).

	MC			**GS**		
Estimator	$A_1^{\varrho,\mathcal{C}}(X)$	$A_2^{\varrho,\mathcal{C}}(X)$	$A_3^{\varrho,\mathcal{C}}(X)$	$A_1^{\varrho,\mathcal{C}}(X)$	$A_2^{\varrho,\mathcal{C}}(X)$	$A_3^{\varrho,\mathcal{C}}(X)$
(III) GPD + survival Clayton with ES crisis event: $\{\mathrm{VaR}_{0.99}(S) \leq S\}$						
$\mathbb{E}[\boldsymbol{X}\|\mathcal{C}^{\mathrm{ES}}]$	15.657	15.806	15.721	15.209	15.175	15.190
Standard error	0.434	0.475	0.395	0.257	0.258	0.261
$\mathrm{RVaR}_{0.975,0.99}(\boldsymbol{X}\|\mathcal{C}^{\mathrm{ES}})$	41.626	41.026	45.939	45.506	45.008	45.253
Standard error	1.211	1.065	1.615	1.031	1.133	1.256
$\mathrm{VaR}_{0.99}(\boldsymbol{X}\|\mathcal{C}^{\mathrm{ES}})$	49.689	48.818	57.488	55.033	54.746	54.783
Standard error	4.901	4.388	4.973	8.079	5.630	3.803
$\mathrm{ES}_{0.99}(\boldsymbol{X}\|\mathcal{C}^{\mathrm{ES}})$	104.761	109.835	97.944	71.874	72.588	70.420
Standard error	23.005	27.895	17.908	4.832	4.584	4.313
(IV) Multivariate t with RVaR crisis event: $\{\mathrm{VaR}_{0.975}(S) \leq S \leq \mathrm{VaR}_{0.99}(S)\}$						
$\mathbb{E}[\boldsymbol{X}\|\mathcal{C}^{\mathrm{RVaR}}]$	2.456	1.934	2.476	2.394	2.060	2.435
Bias	0.019	−0.097	0.038	−0.043	0.029	−0.002
Standard error	0.026	0.036	0.027	0.014	0.023	0.019
$\mathrm{RVaR}_{0.975,0.99}(\boldsymbol{X}\|\mathcal{C}^{\mathrm{RVaR}})$	4.670	4.998	4.893	4.602	5.188	4.748
Standard error	0.037	0.042	0.031	0.032	0.070	0.048
$\mathrm{RVaR}_{0.99}(\boldsymbol{X}\|\mathcal{C}^{\mathrm{VaR}})$	5.217	5.397	5.240	4.878	5.717	5.092
Standard error	0.238	0.157	0.145	0.049	0.174	0.100
$\mathrm{ES}_{0.99}(\boldsymbol{X}\|\mathcal{C}^{\mathrm{RVaR}})$	5.929	5.977	5.946	5.446	6.517	6.063
Standard error	0.204	0.179	0.199	0.156	0.248	0.344
(V) Multivariate t with ES crisis event: $\{\mathrm{VaR}_{0.99}(S) \leq S\}$						
$\mathbb{E}[\boldsymbol{X}\|\mathcal{C}^{\mathrm{ES}}]$	3.758	3.099	3.770	3.735	3.126	3.738
Bias	0.017	−0.018	0.029	-0.005	0.009	−0.003
Standard error	0.055	0.072	0.060	0.031	0.027	0.030
$\mathrm{RVaR}_{0.975,0.99}(\boldsymbol{X}\|\mathcal{C}^{\mathrm{ES}})$	8.516	8.489	9.051	8.586	8.317	8.739
Standard error	0.089	0.167	0.161	0.144	0.156	0.158
$\mathrm{VaR}_{0.99}(\boldsymbol{X}\|\mathcal{C}^{\mathrm{ES}})$	9.256	9.754	10.327	9.454	9.517	9.890
Standard error	0.517	0.680	0.698	0.248	0.293	0.327
$\mathrm{ES}_{0.99}(\boldsymbol{X}\|\mathcal{C}^{\mathrm{ES}})$	11.129	12.520	12.946	11.857	12.469	12.375
Standard error	0.595	1.321	0.826	0.785	0.948	0.835

4.1.2. Results and Discussions

Since a fast random number generators are available for the joint loss distributions (M1) and (M2), the MC estimators are computed almost instantly. On the other hand, the MCMC methods cost around 1.5 min for simulating the $N = 10^4$ MCMC samples, as reported in Tables 1 and 2. For the HMC method, the main computational cost consists of calculating gradients $N \times T$ times for the leapfrog method, and calculating the ratio of target densities N times in the acceptance/rejection step, where N is the length of the sample path and T is the integration time. For the GS, simulating an N-sample path requires $N \times T \times d$ random numbers from the full conditional distributions, where T here is the thinning interval of times. Therefore, the computational time of the GS linearly increases w.r.t. the dimension d, which can become prohibitive for the GS in high dimensions. To save computational time, MCMC methods generally require careful implementations of calculating the gradients and the ratio of the target densities for HMC, and of simulating the full conditional distributions for GS.

Next, we inspect the performance of the HMC and GS methods. We observed that the autocorrelations of all sample paths steadily decreased below 0.1 if lags were larger than 15. Together with the high ACRs, we conclude that the Markov chains can be considered to be converged. According to the heuristic in Algorithm 4, the stepsize and integration time for the HMC method are selected to be $(\epsilon, T) = (0.210, 12)$ in Case (I) and $(\epsilon, T) = (0.095, 13)$ in Case (II). As indicated by the small Hamiltonian errors in Figure 1, the acceptance rates in both cases are quite close to 1.

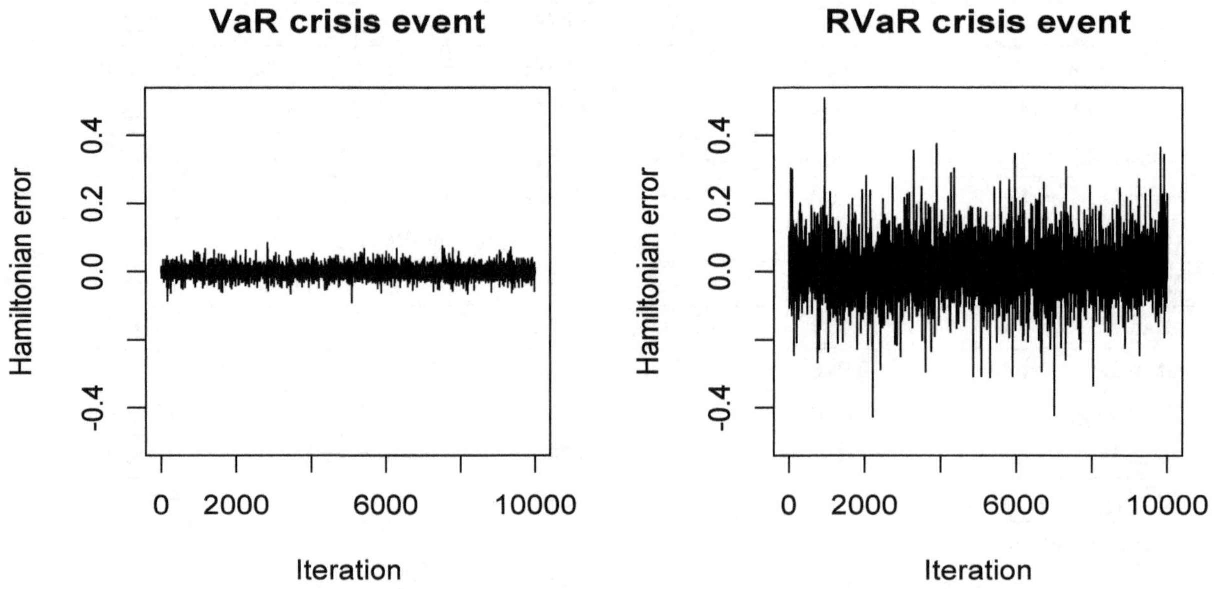

Figure 1. Hamiltonian errors of the HMC methods for estimating systemic risk allocations with VaR (**left**) and RVaR (**right**) crisis events for the loss distribution (M1). The stepsize and integration time are set to be $(\epsilon, T) = (0.210, 12)$ in Case (I) and $(\epsilon, T) = (0.095, 13)$ in Case (II).

For the GS, the thinning interval of times T and the selection probability $\boldsymbol{p}$ are determined as $T = 12$ and $\boldsymbol{p} = (0.221, 0.362, 0.416)$ in Case (III), $T = 10$ and $\boldsymbol{p} = (0.330, 0.348, 0.321)$ in Case (IV) and $T = 4$ and $\boldsymbol{p} = (0.241, 0.503, 0.255)$ in Case (V). For biases of the estimators, observe that in all cases ((I) to (V)), the estimates of the MC method and the MCMC method are close to each other. In Cases (I), (II), and (III), the true allocations are the homogeneous allocations, whereas their exact values are not known. From the estimates in Tables 1 and 2, the MCMC estimates are, on average, more equally allocated compared to those of the MC method, especially in Case (III) where heavy-tailedness may lead to quite slow convergence rates of the MC method. Therefore, lower biases of the MCMC estimators are obtained, compared to those of the MC estimators. In the case of risk contributions in Case (IV) and (V), exact biases are computed based on ellipticality, and they show that the GS estimator has a smaller bias than the one of the MC estimator.

Although the MC sample size is 10 times larger than that of the MCMC method, the standard error of the latter is, in most cases, smaller than the MC standard error. This improvement becomes larger as the probability of the crisis event becomes smaller. The largest improvement is observed in Case (I) with the VaR crisis event, and the smallest one is in Cases (III) and (V) with the ES crisis event. MCMC estimates of the risk contribution-type allocations have consistently smaller standard errors than the MC ones. For the RVaR, VaR, and ES-type allocations, the improvement of standard error varies according to the loss models and the crisis event. A notable improvement is observed for ES-type allocation in Case (III), although a stable statistical inference is challenging due to the heavy-tailedness of the target distribution.

Overall, the simulation study shows that the MCMC estimators outperform the MC estimators due to the increased effective sample size and its insusceptibility to the probability of the crisis event. The MCMC estimators are especially recommended when the probability of the crisis event is too small for the MC method to sufficiently simulate many samples for a meaningful statistical analysis.

Remark 3 (Joint loss distributions with negative dependence in the tail). *In the above simulation study, we only considered joint loss distributions with positive dependence. Under the existence of positive dependence, the target density $f_{\mathbf{X}|v_\alpha \le S \le v_\beta}$ puts more probability mass around its mean, and the probability decays as the point moves away from the mean, since positive dependence among $X_1, \ldots, X_d$ prevents them from going in opposite directions (i.e., one component increases and another one decreases) under the sum constraint; see* Koike and Minami (2019) *for details. This phenomenon leads to the target distributions being more centered and elliptical, which in turn facilitates efficient moves of Markov chains. Although it may not be realistic, joint loss distributions with negative dependence in the tail are also possible. In this case, the target distribution has more variance, heavy tails, and is even multimodal, since two components can move in opposite directions under the sum constraint. For such cases, constructing efficient MCMC methods becomes more challenging; see* Lan et al. (2014) *for a remedy for multimodal target distributions with Riemannian manifold HMC.*

4.2. Empirical Study

In this section, we illustrate our suggested MCMC methods for estimating risk allocations from insurance company indemnity claims. The dataset consists of 1500 liability claims provided by the Insurance Services Office. Each claim contains an indemnity payment X_1 and an allocated loss adjustment expense (ALAE) X_2; see Hogg and Klugman (2009) for a description. The joint distribution of losses and expenses is studied, for example, in Frees and Valdez (1998) and Klugman and Parsa (1999). Based on Frees and Valdez (1998), we adopt the following parametric model:

(M3) univariate marginals are $X_1 \sim \text{Par}(\lambda_1, \theta_1)$ and $X_2 \sim \text{Par}(\lambda_2, \theta_2)$ with $(\lambda_1, \theta_1) = (14,036, 1.122)$ and $(\lambda_2, \theta_2) = (14,219, 2.118)$, and the copula is the survival Clayton copula with parameter $\theta = 0.512$ (which corresponds to Spearman's rho $\rho_S = 0.310$).

Note that in the loss distribution (M3), the Gumbel copula used in Frees and Valdez (1998) is replaced by the survival Clayton copula, since both of them have the same type of tail dependence and the latter possesses more computationally tractable derivatives. The parameter of the survival Clayton copula is determined so that it reaches the same Spearman's rho observed in Frees and Valdez (1998). Figure 2 illustrates the data and samples from the distribution (M3). Our goal is to calculate the VaR, RVaR, and ES-type allocations with VaR, RVaR, and ES crisis events for the same confidence levels as in Section 4.1.1. We apply the HMC method to all three crisis events since, due to the infinite and finite variances of X_1 and X_2, respectively, the optimal selection probability of the second variable calculated in Step 2 of Algorithm 5 is quite close to 0, and thus the GS did not perform well. The simulated HMC samples are illustrated in Figure 2. The results of estimating the systemic risk allocations are summarized in Table 3.

The HMC samples shown in Figure 2 indicate that the conditional distributions of interest are successfully simulated from the desired regions. As displayed in Figure 3, the Hamiltonian errors of all three HMC methods are sufficiently small, which led to the high ACRs of 0.997, 0.986, and 0.995, as listed in Table 3. We also observed that autocorrelations of all sample paths steadily decreased below 0.1 if lags were larger than 80. Together with the high ACRs, we conclude that the Markov chains can be considered to be converged. Due to the heavy-tailedness of the target distribution in the case of the ES crisis event, the stepsize is very small and the integration time is very large compared to the former two cases of the VaR and RVaR crisis events. As a result, the HMC algorithm in this case has a long run time.

The estimates of the MC and HMC methods are close in all cases, except Case (III). In Case (III), the HMC estimates are smaller than the MC ones in almost all cases. Based on the much smaller standard errors of HMC, one could infer that the MC estimates are likely overestimating the allocations due to a small number of extremely large losses, although the corresponding conditional distribution is extremely heavy-tailed, and thus no estimation method might be reliable. In terms of the standard error, the estimation of systemic risk allocations by the HMC method were improved in Cases (I) and (III) compared to that of the MC method; the MC standard errors are slightly smaller than those of HMC in Case (II). All results considered, we conclude from this empirical study that the MCMC estimators outperform the MC estimators in terms of standard error. On the other hand, as indicated by the theory of HMC with normal kinetic energy, the HMC method is not recommended for heavy-tailed target distributions due to the long computational time caused by a small stepsize and large integration time determined by Algorithm 5.

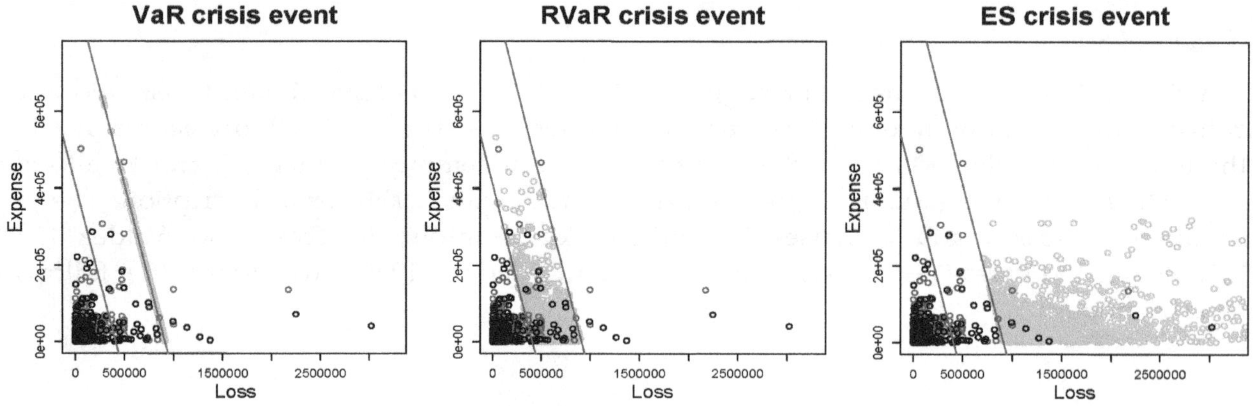

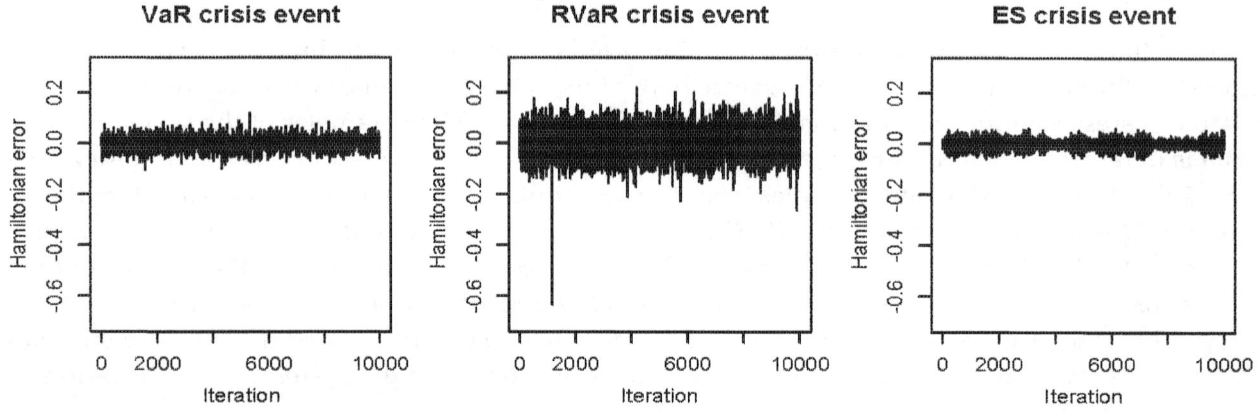

Table 3. Estimates and standard errors for the MC and HMC estimators of RVaR, VaR, and ES-type systemic risk allocations under the loss distribution (M3) with the (I) VaR crisis event, (II) RVaR crisis event, and (III) ES crisis event. The MC sample size is $N_{MC} = 10^5$, and that of the HMC method is $N_{MCMC} = 10^4$. The acceptance rate (ACR), stepsize ϵ, integration time T, and run time are ACR $= 0.997$, $\epsilon = 0.015$, $T = 34$ and run time $= 2.007$ min in Case (I), ACR $= 0.986$, $\epsilon = 0.026$, $T = 39$ and run time $= 2.689$ min in Case (II), ACR $= 0.995$, $\epsilon = 5.132 \times 10^{-5}$, $T = 838$ and run time $= 44.831$ min in Case (III).

	MC		HMC	
Estimator	$A_1^{\varrho,\mathcal{C}}(X)$	$A_2^{\varrho,\mathcal{C}}(X)$	$A_1^{\varrho,\mathcal{C}}(X)$	$A_2^{\varrho,\mathcal{C}}(X)$
(I) VaR crisis event: $\{S = \mathrm{VaR}_{0.99}(S)\}$				
$\mathbb{E}[\boldsymbol{X}\mid\mathcal{C}^{\mathrm{VaR}}]$	842465.497	73553.738	844819.901	71199.334
Standard error	7994.573	7254.567	6306.836	6306.836
$\mathrm{RVaR}_{0.975,0.99}(\boldsymbol{X}\mid\mathcal{C}^{\mathrm{VaR}})$	989245.360	443181.466	915098.833	428249.307
Standard error	307.858	24105.163	72.568	20482.914
$\mathrm{VaR}_{0.99}(\boldsymbol{X}\mid\mathcal{C}^{\mathrm{VaR}})$	989765.514	500663.072	915534.362	615801.118
Standard error	4670.966	54576.957	669.853	96600.963
$\mathrm{ES}_{0.99}(\boldsymbol{X}\mid\mathcal{C}^{\mathrm{VaR}})$	990839.359	590093.887	915767.076	761038.843
Standard error	679.055	75024.692	47.744	31211.908
(II) RVaR crisis event: $\{\mathrm{VaR}_{0.975}(S) \le S \le \mathrm{VaR}_{0.99}(S)\}$				
$\mathbb{E}[\boldsymbol{X}\mid\mathcal{C}^{\mathrm{RVaR}}]$	528455.729	60441.368	527612.751	60211.561
Standard error	3978.477	2119.461	4032.475	2995.992
$\mathrm{RVaR}_{0.975,0.99}(\boldsymbol{X}\mid\mathcal{C}^{\mathrm{RVaR}})$	846956.570	349871.745	854461.670	370931.946
Standard error	1866.133	6285.523	2570.997	9766.697
$\mathrm{VaR}_{0.99}(\boldsymbol{X}\mid\mathcal{C}^{\mathrm{RVaR}})$	865603.369	413767.829	871533.550	437344.509
Standard error	5995.341	29105.059	12780.741	21142.135
$\mathrm{ES}_{0.99}(\boldsymbol{X}\mid\mathcal{C}^{\mathrm{RVaR}})$	882464.968	504962.099	885406.811	529034.580
Standard error	3061.110	17346.207	3134.144	23617.278
(III) ES crisis event: $\{\mathrm{VaR}_{0.99}(S) \le S\}$				
$\mathbb{E}[\boldsymbol{X}\mid\mathcal{C}^{\mathrm{ES}}]$	8663863.925	137671.653	2934205.458	140035.782
Standard error	3265049.590	10120.557	165794.772	14601.958
$\mathrm{RVaR}_{0.975,0.99}(\boldsymbol{X}\mid\mathcal{C}^{\mathrm{ES}})$	35238914.131	907669.462	17432351.450	589309.196
Standard error	2892208.689	31983.660	443288.649	3471.641
$\mathrm{VaR}_{0.99}(\boldsymbol{X}\mid\mathcal{C}^{\mathrm{ES}})$	56612082.905	1131248.055	20578728.307	615572.940
Standard error	1353975.612	119460.411	1364899.752	12691.776
$\mathrm{ES}_{0.99}(\boldsymbol{X}\mid\mathcal{C}^{\mathrm{ES}})$	503537848.192	2331984.181	25393466.446	649486.810
Standard error	268007317.199	468491.127	1138243.137	7497.200

4.3. Detailed Comparison of MCMC with MC

In the previous numerical experiments, we fixed the dimensions of the portfolios and confidence levels of the crisis events. Comparing the MC and MCMC methods after balancing against computational time might be more reasonable, although one should keep in mind that run time depends on various external factors, such as the implementation, hardware, workload, programming language, or compiler options (and our implementation was not optimized for any of these factors). In this section, we compare the MC and MCMC methods with different dimensions, confidence levels, and parameters of the HMC methods in terms of bias, standard error, and the mean squared error (MSE), adjusted by run time.

In this experiment, we fix the sample size of the MC and MCMC methods as $N_{\text{MC}} = N_{\text{MCMC}} = 10^4$. In addition, we assume $\boldsymbol{X} \sim t_\nu(\boldsymbol{0}, P)$, that is, the joint loss follows the multivariate Student t distribution with $\nu = 6$ degrees of freedom, location vector $\boldsymbol{0}$, and dispersion matrix P, which is the correlation matrix with all off-diagonal entries equal to $1/12$. The dimension d of the loss portfolio will vary for comparison. We consider only risk contribution-type systemic risk allocations under VaR, RVaR, and ES crisis events, as true values of these allocations are available to compare against; see McNeil et al. (2015), Corollary 8.43. If b and σ denote the bias and standard deviation of the MC or MCMC estimator and S the run time, then (under the assumption that run time linearly increases by sample size) we define the *time-adjusted MSEs* by

$$\text{MSE}_{\text{MC}} = b_{\text{MC}}^2 + \frac{\sigma_{\text{MC}}^2}{\frac{S_{\text{MCMC}}}{S_{\text{MC}}} \times N_{\text{MCMC}}} \quad \text{and} \quad \text{MSE}_{\text{MCMC}} = b_{\text{MCMC}}^2 + \frac{\sigma_{\text{MCMC}}^2}{N_{\text{MCMC}}}.$$

We can then compare the MC and MCMC estimators in terms of bias, standard error, and time-adjusted MSE under the following three scenarios:

(A) $\text{VaR}_{0.99}$, $\text{RVaR}_{0.95,0.99}$, and $\text{ES}_{0.99}$ contributions are estimated by the MC, HMC, and GS methods for dimensions $d \in \{4, 6, 8, 10\}$. Note that the GS is applied only to RVaR and ES contributions, not to VaR contributions (same in the other scenarios).

(B) For $d = 5$, $\text{VaR}_{\alpha^{\text{VaR}}}$, $\text{RVaR}_{\alpha_1^{\text{RVaR}},\alpha_2^{\text{RVaR}}}$ and $\text{ES}_{\alpha^{\text{ES}}}$ contributions are estimated by the MC, HMC, and GS methods for confidence levels $\alpha^{\text{VaR}} \in \{0.9, 0.99, 0.999, 0.9999\}$, $(\alpha_1^{\text{RVaR}}, \alpha_2^{\text{RVaR}}) \in \{(0.9, 0.9999), (0.9, 0.99), (0.99, 0.999), (0.999, 0.9999)\}$ and $\alpha^{\text{ES}} \in \{0.9, 0.99, 0.999, 0.9999\}$.

(C) For $d = 5$, $\text{VaR}_{0.9}$, $\text{RVaR}_{0.9,0.99}$ and $\text{ES}_{0.9}$ contributions are estimated by the MC and HMC methods with the parameters $(\epsilon_{\text{opt}}, T_{\text{opt}})$ (determined by Algorithm 4) and $(\epsilon, T) \in \{(10\epsilon_{\text{opt}}, 2T_{\text{opt}}), (10\epsilon_{\text{opt}}, T_{\text{opt}}/2), (\epsilon_{\text{opt}}/10, 2T_{\text{opt}}), (\epsilon_{\text{opt}}/10, T_{\text{opt}}/2)\}$.

In the MC method, the modified VaR contribution $\mathbb{E}[\boldsymbol{X}|C_{\alpha-\delta,\alpha+\delta}^{\text{RVaR}}]$ with $\delta = 0.01$ is computed. Moreover, if the size of the conditional sample for estimating RVaR and ES contributions is less than 100, then the lower confidence level of the crisis event is subtracted by 0.01, so that at least 100 MC presamples are guaranteed. For the sample paths of the MCMC methods, ACR, ACP, and Hamiltonian errors for the HMC methods were inspected and the convergences of the chains were checked, as in Sections 4.1 and 4.2.

The results of the comparisons of (A), (B), and (C) are summarized in Figures 4–6. In Figure 4, the performance of the MC, HMC, and GS estimators is roughly similar across dimensions from 4 to 10. For all crisis events, the HMC and GS estimators outperform MC in terms of bias, standard error, and time-adjusted MSE. From (A5) and (A8), standard errors of the GS estimators are slightly higher than those of the HMC ones, which result in slightly improved performance of the HMC estimator over the GS in terms of MSE. In Figure 5, bias, standard error, and MSE of the MC estimator tend to increase as the probability of the conditioning set decreases. This is simply because the size of the conditional samples in the MC method decreases proportionally to the probability of the crisis event. On the other hand, the HMC and GS estimators provide a stably better performance than MC since such sample size reduction does not occur. As seen in (B4) to (B9) in the cases of $\text{RVaR}_{0.999,0.9999}$ and $\text{ES}_{0.9999}$, however, if the probability of the conditioning event is too small and/or the distribution of the MC presample is too different from the original conditional distribution of interest, then the parameters of the HMC method determined by Algorithm 4 can be entirely different from the optimal, which leads to a poor performance of the HMC method, as we will see in the next scenario (C). In Figure 6, the HMC method with optimally determined parameters from Algorithm 4 is compared to non-optimal parameter choices. First, the optimal HMC estimator outperforms MC in terms of bias, standard error, and time-adjusted MSE. On the other hand, from the plots in Figure 6, we see that some of the non-optimal HMC estimators are significantly worse than MC. Therefore, a careful choice of the parameters of the HMC method is required to obtain an improved performance of the HMC method compared to MC.

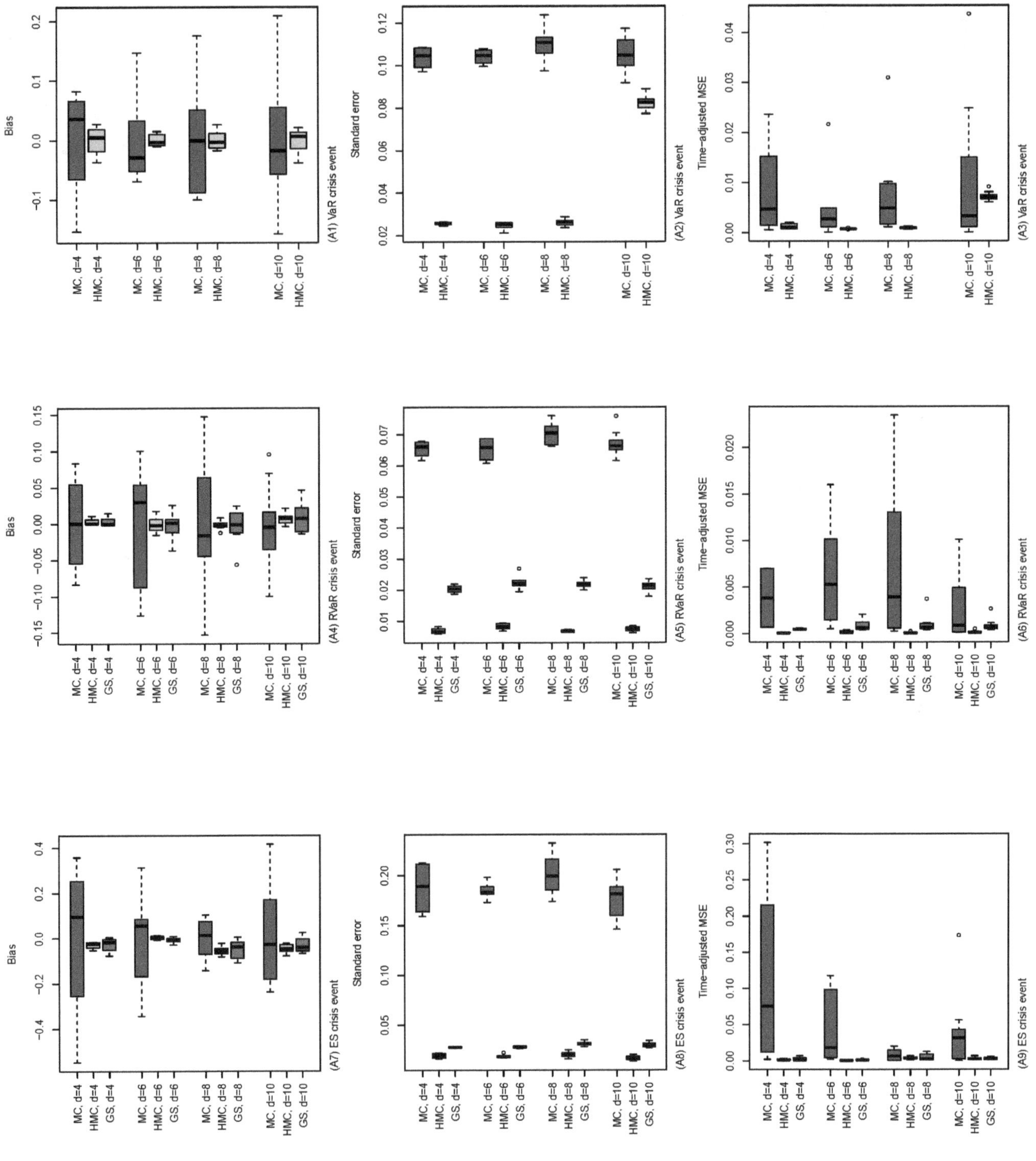

Figure 4. Bias (**left**), standard error (**middle**) and time-adjusted mean squared error (**right**) of the MC, HMC, and GS estimators of risk contribution-type systemic risk allocations under $\mathrm{VaR}_{0.99}$ (**top**), $\mathrm{RVaR}_{0.95,0.99}$ (**middle**), and $\mathrm{ES}_{0.99}$ (**bottom**) crisis events. The underlying loss distribution is $t_\nu(\boldsymbol{\mu}, P)$, where $\nu = 6$, $\boldsymbol{\mu} = \mathbf{0}$ and $P = 1/12 \cdot \mathbf{1}_d \mathbf{1}_d^\top + \mathrm{diag}_d(11/12)$ for portfolio dimensions $d \in \{4, 6, 8, 10\}$. Note that the GS method is applied only to RVaR and ES contributions.

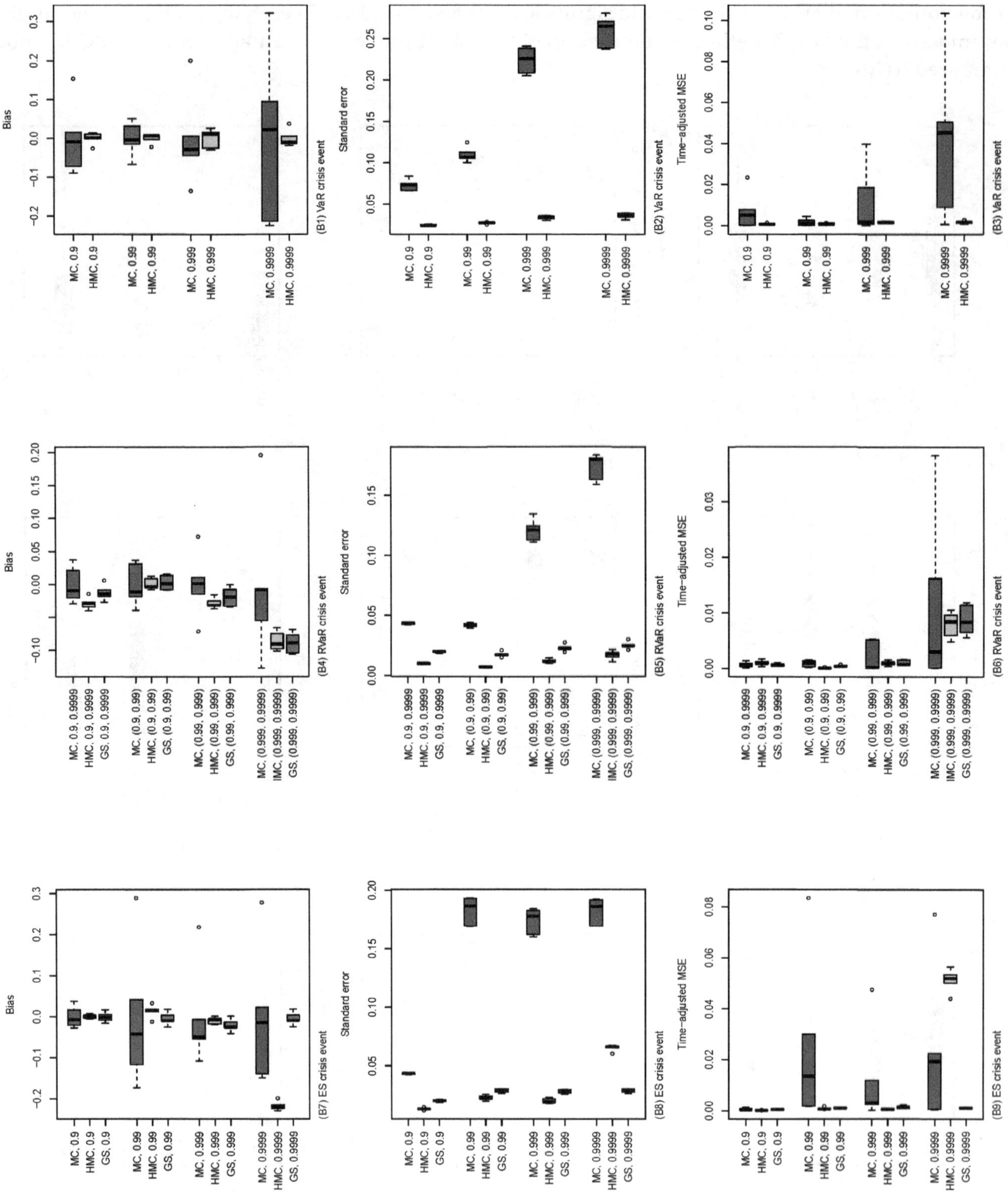

Figure 5. Bias (**left**), standard error (**middle**), and time-adjusted mean squared error (**right**) of the MC, HMC, and GS estimators of risk contribution-type systemic risk allocations with the underlying loss distribution $t_\nu(\boldsymbol{\mu}, P)$, where $\nu = 6$, $\boldsymbol{\mu} = \mathbf{0}$, $P = 1/12 \cdot \mathbf{1}_d \mathbf{1}_d^\top + \mathrm{diag}_d(11/12)$ and $d = 5$. The crisis event is taken differently, as $\mathrm{VaR}_{\alpha^{\mathrm{VaR}}}$ (**top**), $\mathrm{RVaR}_{\alpha_1^{\mathrm{RVaR}}, \alpha_2^{\mathrm{RVaR}}}$ (**middle**) and $\mathrm{ES}_{\alpha^{\mathrm{ES}}}$ (**bottom**) for confidence levels $\alpha^{\mathrm{VaR}} \in \{0.9, 0.99, 0.999, 0.9999\}$, $(\alpha_1^{\mathrm{RVaR}}, \alpha_2^{\mathrm{RVaR}}) \in \{(0.9, 0.9999), (0.9, 0.99), (0.99, 0.999), (0.999, 0.9999)\}$, and $\alpha^{\mathrm{ES}} \in \{0.9, 0.99, 0.999, 0.9999\}$. Note that the GS method is applied only to RVaR and ES contributions.

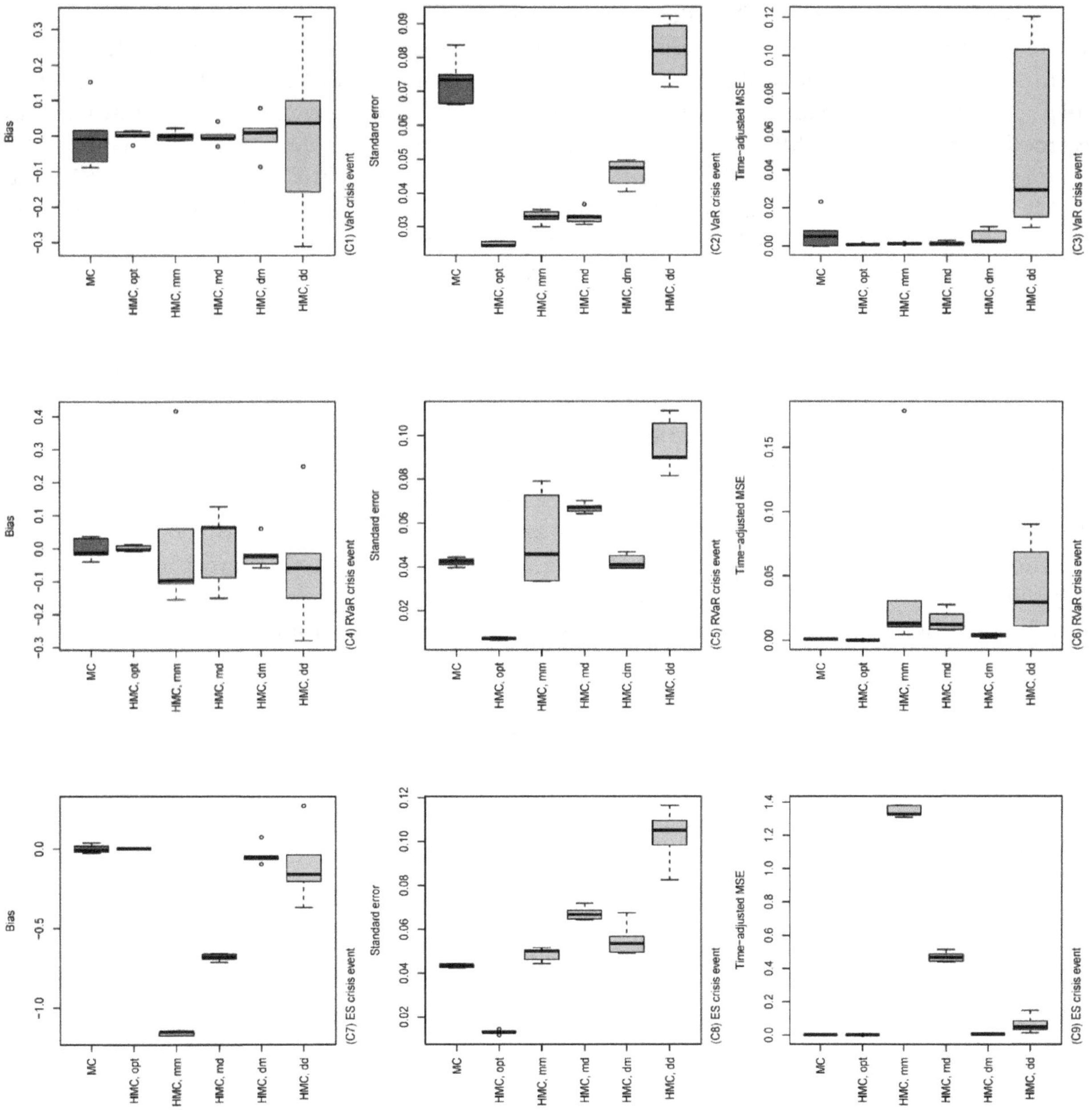

Figure 6. Bias (**left**), standard error (**middle**), and time-adjusted mean squared error (**right**) of the MC and HMC estimators of risk contribution-type systemic risk allocations under $\mathrm{VaR}_{0.9}$, $\mathrm{RVaR}_{0.9,0.99}$, and $\mathrm{ES}_{0.9}$ crisis events. The underlying loss distribution is $t_\nu(\boldsymbol{\mu}, P)$, where $\nu = 6$, $\boldsymbol{\mu} = \mathbf{0}$, $P = 1/12 \cdot \mathbf{1}_d \mathbf{1}_d^\top + \mathrm{diag}_d(11/12)$ and $d = 5$. The parameters of the HMC method are taken as $(\epsilon_{\mathrm{opt}}, \epsilon_{\mathrm{opt}})$ determined by Algorithm 4 and $(\epsilon, T) \in \{(10\epsilon_{\mathrm{opt}}, 2T_{\mathrm{opt}}),\ (10\epsilon_{\mathrm{opt}}, T_{\mathrm{opt}}/2),\ (\epsilon_{\mathrm{opt}}/10, 2T_{\mathrm{opt}}),\ (\epsilon_{\mathrm{opt}}/10, T_{\mathrm{opt}}/2)\}$. In the labels of the x-axes, each of the five cases $(\epsilon_{\mathrm{opt}}, \epsilon_{\mathrm{opt}})$, $(10\epsilon_{\mathrm{opt}}, 2T_{\mathrm{opt}})$, $(10\epsilon_{\mathrm{opt}}, T_{\mathrm{opt}}/2)$, $(\epsilon_{\mathrm{opt}}/10, 2T_{\mathrm{opt}})$ and $(\epsilon_{\mathrm{opt}}/10, T_{\mathrm{opt}}/2)$ is denoted by HMC.opt, HMC.mm, HMC.md, HMC.dm, and HMC.dd, respectively.

5. Conclusion, Limitations and Future Work

Efficient calculation of systemic risk allocations is a challenging task, especially when the crisis event has a small probability. To solve this problem for models where a joint loss density is available, we proposed MCMC estimators where a Markov chain is constructed with the conditional loss distribution, given the crisis event as the target distribution. By using HMC and GS, efficient simulation methods from the constrained target distribution were obtained and the resulting MCMC estimator was expected to have a smaller standard error compared to that of the MC estimator. Sample efficiency is significantly improved, since the MCMC estimator is computed from samples generated directly from the conditional distribution of interest. Another advantage of the MCMC method is that its performance is less sensitive to the probability of the crisis event, and thus to the confidence levels of the underlying risk measures. We also proposed a heuristic for determining the parameters of the HMC method based on the MC presamples. Numerical experiments demonstrated that our MCMC estimators are more efficient than MC in terms of bias, standard error, and time-adjusted MSE. Stability of the MCMC estimation with respect to the probability of the crisis event and efficiency of the optimal parameter choice of the HMC method were also investigated in the experiments.

Based on the results in this paper, our MCMC estimators can be recommended when the probability of the crisis event is too small for MC to sufficiently simulate many samples for a statistical analysis and/or when unbiased systemic risk allocations under the VaR crisis event are required. The MCMC methods are likely to perform well when the dimension of the portfolio is less than or around 10, losses are bounded from the left, and the crisis event is of VaR or RVaR type; otherwise, heavy-tailedness and computational time can become challenging. Firstly, a theoretical convergence result of the HMC method is typically not available when the target distribution is unbounded and heavy-tailed, which is the case when the losses are unbounded and/or the crisis event is of ES type; see the case of the ES crisis event in the empirical study in Section 4.2. Secondly, both the HMC and GS methods suffer from high-dimensional target distributions since the algorithms contain parts of steps where the computational cost linearly increases in dimension. We observed that, in this case, although the MCMC estimator typically improves bias and standard error compared to MC, the improvement vanishes in terms of time-adjusted MSE due to the long computational time of the MCMC method. Finally, multimodality of joint loss distributions and/or the target distribution is also an undesirable feature since full conditional distributions and their inverses (which are required to implement the GS) are typically unavailable in the former case, and the latter case prevents the HMC method from efficiently exploring the entire support of the target distribution. Potential remedies for heavy-tailed and/or high-dimensional target distributions are the HMC method with a non-normal kinetic energy distribution and roll-back HMC; see Appendix B for details. Further investigation of HMC methods and faster methods for determining the HMC parameters are left for future work.

Author Contributions: Conceptualization, T.K.; methodology, T.K.; formal analysis, T.K.; investigation, T.K. and M.H.; resources, T.K.; data curation, T.K.; writing—original draft preparation, T.K.; writing—review and editing, M.H.; visualization, T.K. and M.H.; supervision, M.H.; project administration, T.K.; funding acquisition, M.H. All authors have read and agreed to the published version of the manuscript.

Acknowledgments: We wish to thank to an associate editor and anonymous referees for their careful reading of the manuscript and their insightful comments.

Abbreviations

The following abbreviations are used in this manuscript:

i.i.d.	Independent and identically distributed
pdf	Probability distribution function
cdf	Cumulative distribution function
ecdf	Empirical cdf
GPD	Generalized Pareto distribution
MSE	Mean squared error
LLN	Law of large numbers
CLT	Central limit theorem
VaR	Value-at-Risk

RVaR	Range VaR
ES	Expected shortfall
MES	Marginal expected shortfall
CoVaR	Conditional VaR
CoES	Conditional ES
MC	Monte Carlo
SMC	Sequential Monte Carlo
MCMC	Markov chain Monte Carlo
ACR	Acceptance rate
ACP	Autocorrelation plot
MH	Metropolis–Hastings
GS	Gibbs sampler
MGS	Metropolized Gibbs sampler
DSGS	Deterministic scan GS
RPGS	Random permutation GS
RSGS	Random scan GS
HMC	Hamiltonian Monte Carlo
RBHMC	Roll-back HMC
RMHMC	Riemannian manifold HMC
ALAE	Allocated loss adjustment expense
P&L	Profit and loss

Appendix A. Hamiltonian Dynamics with Boundary Reflection

In this appendix, we describe details of the HMC method with boundary reflection, as mentioned in Section 3.3.1. Let $(\boldsymbol{h}, v)$ be the hyperplane which the trajectory of the Hamiltonian dynamics hit at $(\boldsymbol{x}(t), \boldsymbol{p}(t))$. At this time, $(\boldsymbol{x}(t), \boldsymbol{p}(t))$ is immediately replaced by $(\boldsymbol{x}(t), \boldsymbol{p}_r(t))$ where $\boldsymbol{p}_r(t)$ is the *reflected momentum* defined by

$$\boldsymbol{p}_r(t) = \boldsymbol{p}_{\parallel}(t) - \boldsymbol{p}_{\perp}(t),$$

where $\boldsymbol{p}_{\parallel}(t)$ and $\boldsymbol{p}_{\perp}(t)$ are such that $\boldsymbol{p}(t) = \boldsymbol{p}_{\parallel}(t) + \boldsymbol{p}_{\perp}(t)$ and $\boldsymbol{p}_{\parallel}(t)$ and $\boldsymbol{p}_{\perp}(t)$ are parallel and perpendicular to the hyperplane $(\boldsymbol{h}, v)$, respectively. Afshar and Domke (2015) and Chevallier et al. (2018) showed that the map $(\boldsymbol{x}(t), \boldsymbol{p}(t)) \mapsto (\boldsymbol{x}(t), \boldsymbol{p}_r(t))$ preserves the volume and the Hamiltonian, and that this modified HMC method has the stationary distribution π. As long as the initial position $\boldsymbol{x}^{(0)}$ belongs to $\mathcal{C}$, the trajectory of the HMC method never violates the constraint $\mathcal{C}$. The algorithm of this HMC method with reflection is obtained by replacing the **Leapfrog** function call in Step (3) of Algorithm 3 by Algorithm A1. Accordingly, the parameters of the hyperplanes need to be passed as input to Algorithm 3.

In Step (3-1) of Algorithm A1 the time t_m at which the trajectory hits the boundary $(\boldsymbol{h}_m, v_m)$ is computed. If $0 < t_m < 1$ for some $m \in \{1, \ldots, M\}$, then the chain hits the boundary during the dynamics with length ϵ. At the smallest time t_{m^*} among such hitting times, the chain reflects from $(\boldsymbol{x}^*, \boldsymbol{p})$ to $(\boldsymbol{x}_r^*, \boldsymbol{p}_r)$ against the corresponding boundary $(\boldsymbol{h}_{m^*}, v_{m^*})$ as described in Step (3-2-1) of Algorithm A1. The remaining length of the dynamics is $(1 - t_{m^*})\epsilon_{\text{temp}}$ and Step (3) is repeated until the remaining length becomes zero. Other techniques of reflecting the dynamics are discussed in Appendix B.1.

Algorithm A1 Leapfrog method with boundary reflection.

Input: Current state $(\boldsymbol{x}(0), \boldsymbol{p}(0))$, stepsize $\epsilon > 0$, gradients ∇U and ∇K, and constraints $(\boldsymbol{h}_m, v_m)$, $m = 1, \ldots, M$.

Output: Updated state $(\boldsymbol{x}(\epsilon), \boldsymbol{p}(\epsilon))$.

(1) Update $\boldsymbol{p}(\epsilon/2) = \boldsymbol{p}(0) + \epsilon/2\nabla U(\boldsymbol{x}(0))$.

(2) Set $(\boldsymbol{x}, \boldsymbol{p}) = (\boldsymbol{x}(0), \boldsymbol{p}(\epsilon/2))$, $\epsilon_{\text{temp}} = \epsilon$.

(3) **while** $\epsilon_{\text{temp}} > 0$

(3-1) Compute

$$\boldsymbol{x}^* = \boldsymbol{x} + \epsilon_{\text{temp}} \nabla K(\boldsymbol{p}),$$
$$t_m = (v_m - \boldsymbol{h}_m^\top \boldsymbol{x})/(\epsilon \boldsymbol{h}_m^\top \boldsymbol{p}), \quad m = 1, \ldots, M.$$

(3-2) **if** $t_m \in [0, 1]$ for any $m = 1, \ldots, M$,

(3-2-1) Set

$$m^* = \operatorname{argmin}\{t_m \mid 0 \leq t_m \leq 1,\ m = 1, \ldots, M\},$$
$$\boldsymbol{x}_r^* = \boldsymbol{x}^* - 2\frac{\boldsymbol{h}_{m^*}^\top \boldsymbol{x}^* - v_{m^*}}{\boldsymbol{h}_{m^*}^\top \boldsymbol{h}_{m^*}} \boldsymbol{h}_{m^*},$$
$$\boldsymbol{p}_r = \frac{\boldsymbol{x}^* - \boldsymbol{x} - t_{m^*}\epsilon \boldsymbol{p}}{\epsilon(1 - t_{m^*})}.$$

(3-2-2) Set $(\boldsymbol{x}, \boldsymbol{p}) = (\boldsymbol{x}_r^*, \boldsymbol{p}_r)$ and $\epsilon_{\text{temp}} = (1 - t_{m^*})\epsilon_{\text{temp}}$.

else

(3-2-3) Set $(\boldsymbol{x}, \boldsymbol{p}) = (\boldsymbol{x}^*, \boldsymbol{p})$ and $\epsilon_{\text{temp}} = 0$.

end if

end while

(4) Set $\boldsymbol{x}(\epsilon) = \boldsymbol{x}$ and $\boldsymbol{p}(\epsilon) = \boldsymbol{p} + \frac{\epsilon}{2}\nabla U(\boldsymbol{x})$.

Appendix B. Other MCMC Methods

In this appendix, we introduce some advanced MCMC techniques potentially applicable to the problem of estimating systemic risk allocations.

Appendix B.1. Roll-Back HMC

Yi and Doshi-Velez (2017) proposed *roll-back HMC (RBHMC)*, in which the indicator function $\mathbf{1}_{[\boldsymbol{x} \in \mathcal{C}]}$ in the target distribution (5) is replaced by a smooth sigmoid function so that the Hamilotonian dynamics naturally move back inwards when the trajectory violates the constraints. HMC with reflection presented in Section 3.3.1 requires to check M boundary conditions at every iteration of the Hamiltonian dynamics. In our problem the number M linearly increases with the dimension d in the case of pure losses, which leads to a linear increase in the computational cost. The RBHMC method avoids such explicit boundary checks, and thus can reduce the computational cost of the HMC method with constrained target distributions. Despite saving computational time, we observed that the RBHMC method requires a careful choice of the stepsize $\epsilon > 0$ and the smoothness parameter of the sigmoid function involved, and we could not find any guidance on how to choose them to guarantee a stable performance.

Appendix B.2. Riemannian Manifold HMC

Livingstone et al. (2019) indicated that non-normal kinetic energy distributions can potentially deal with heavy-tailed target distributions. In fact, the kinetic energy distribution F_K can even be dependent on the position variable $\boldsymbol{x}$. For example, when $F_K(\cdot|\boldsymbol{x}) = \mathrm{N}(\mathbf{0}, G(\boldsymbol{x}))$ for a positive definite matrix $G(\boldsymbol{x}) > 0$ and $\boldsymbol{x} \in E$, the resulting HMC method is known as *Riemannian manifold HMC (RMHMC)* since this case is equivalent to applying HMC on the Riemannian manifold with metric $G(\boldsymbol{x})$; see Girolami and Calderhead (2011). Difficulties in implementing RMHMC are in the choice of metric G and in the simulation of the Hamiltonian dynamics. Due to the complexity of the Hamiltonian dynamics, simple discretization schemes such as the leapfrog method are not applicable, and the trajectory is updated implicitly by solving some system of equations; see Girolami and Calderhead (2011). Various choices of the metric G are studied in Betancourt (2013), Lan et al. (2014) and Livingstone and Girolami (2014) for different purposes. Simulation of RMHMC is studied, for example, in Byrne and Girolami (2013).

Appendix B.3. Metropolized Gibbs Samplers

Müller (1992) introduced the *Metropolized Gibbs sampler (MGS)* in which the proposal density q in the MH kernel is set to be $q = f_{\boldsymbol{Y}|v_1 \le \boldsymbol{h}^\top \boldsymbol{Y} \le v_2}$ where $\boldsymbol{Y}$ has the same marginal distributions as $\boldsymbol{X}$ but a different copula C^q for which $C^q_{j|-j}$ and $C^{q,-1}_{j|-j}$ are available so that the GS can be applied to simulate this proposal. This method can be used when the inversion method is not feasible since $C_{j|-j}$ or $C^{-1}_{j|-j}$ are not available. Following the MH algorithm, the candidate is accepted with the acceptance probability (4), which can be simply written as

$$\alpha(\boldsymbol{x}, \tilde{\boldsymbol{x}}) = \min\left\{ \frac{c(\boldsymbol{F}(\tilde{\boldsymbol{x}}))c^q(\boldsymbol{F}(\boldsymbol{x}))}{c(\boldsymbol{F}(\boldsymbol{x}))c^q(\boldsymbol{F}(\tilde{\boldsymbol{x}}))}, 1 \right\}.$$

As an example of the MGS, suppose C is the Gumbel copula, for which the full conditional distributions cannot be inverted analytically. One could then choose the survival Clayton copula as the proposal copula C^q above. For this choice of copula, $q_{j|-j}$ is available by the inversion method as discussed in Section 3.4.1. Furthermore, the acceptance probability is expected to be high especially on the upper tail part because the upper threshold copula of C defined as $\mathbb{P}(\boldsymbol{U} > \boldsymbol{v} \mid \boldsymbol{U} > \boldsymbol{u})$, $\boldsymbol{v} \in [\boldsymbol{u}, \boldsymbol{1}]$, $\boldsymbol{u} \in [0,1]^d$, $\boldsymbol{U} \sim C$ is known to converge to that of a survival Clayton copula when $\lim u_j \to \infty$, $j = 1, \ldots, d$; see Juri and Wüthrich (2002), Juri and Wüthrich (2003), Charpentier and Segers (2007) and Larsson and Nešlehová (2011).

References

Acharya, Viral V., Lasse H. Pedersen, Thomas Philippon, and Matthew Richardson. 2017. Measuring systemic risk. *The Review of Financial Studies* 30: 2–47. [CrossRef]

Adrian, Tobias, and Markus K. Brunnermeier. 2016. Covar. *The American Economic Review* 106: 1705. [CrossRef]

Afshar, Hadi Mohasel, and Justin Domke. 2015. Reflection, refraction, and hamiltonian monte carlo. In *Advances in Neural Information Processing Systems*. Cambridge: The MIT Press, pp. 3007–15.

Asimit, Alexandru V., Edward Furman, Qihe Tang, and Raluca Vernic. 2011. Asymptotics for risk capital allocations based on conditional tail expectation. *Insurance: Mathematics and Economics* 49: 310–24. [CrossRef]

Asimit, Alexandru V., and Jinzhu Li. 2018. Systemic risk: An asymptotic evaluation. *ASTIN Bulletin: The Journal of The IAA* 48: 673–98. [CrossRef]

Bernardi, Mauro, Fabrizio Durante, and Piotr Jaworski. 2017. Covar of families of copulas. *Statistics & Probability Letters* 120: 8–17.

Beskos, Alexandros, Natesh Pillai, Gareth Roberts, Jesus-Maria Sanz-Serna, and Andrew Stuart. 2010. The acceptance probability of the hybrid monte carlo method in high-dimensional problems. *AIP Conference Proceedings* 1281: 23–6.

Beskos, Alexandros, Natesh Pillai, Gareth Roberts, Jesus-Maria Sanz-Serna, and Andrew Stuart. 2013. Optimal tuning of the hybrid monte carlo algorithm. *Bernoulli* 19: 1501–34. [CrossRef]

Betancourt, Michael. 2012. Cruising the simplex: Hamiltonian monte carlo and the dirichlet distribution. *AIP Conference Proceedings* 1443: 157–64.

Betancourt, Michael. 2013. A general metric for riemannian manifold hamiltonian monte carlo. In *International Conference on Geometric Science of Information*. New York: Springer, pp. 327–34.

Betancourt, Michael. 2016. Identifying the optimal integration time in hamiltonian monte carlo. *arXiv*. [CrossRef]

Betancourt, Michael. 2017. A conceptual introduction to hamiltonian monte carlo. *arXiv*. [CrossRef]

Betancourt, Michael, Simon Byrne, and Mark Girolami. 2014. Optimizing the integrator step size for hamiltonian monte carlo. *arXiv*. [CrossRef]

Byrne, Simon, and Mark Girolami. 2013. Geodesic monte carlo on embedded manifolds. *Scandinavian Journal of Statistics* 40: 825–45. [CrossRef] [PubMed]

Cambou, Mathieu, Marius Hofert, and Christiane Lemieux. 2017. Quasi-random numbers for copula models. *Statistics and Computing* 27: 1307–29. [CrossRef]

Cances, Eric, Frédéric Legoll, and Gabriel Stoltz. 2007. Theoretical and numerical comparison of some sampling methods for molecular dynamics. *ESAIM: Mathematical Modelling and Numerical Analysis* 41: 351–89. [CrossRef]

Charpentier, Arthur, and Johan Segers. 2007. Lower tail dependence for archimedean copulas: Characterizations and pitfalls. *Insurance: Mathematics and Economics* 40: 525–32. [CrossRef]

Chen, Chen, Garud Iyengar, and Ciamac C. Moallemi. 2013. An axiomatic approach to systemic risk. *Management Science* 59: 1373–88. [CrossRef]

Chevallier, Augustin, Sylvain Pion, and Frédéric Cazals. 2018. Hamiltonian Monte Carlo With Boundary Reflections, and Application To Polytope Volume Calculations. Available online: https://hal.archives-ouvertes.fr/hal-01919855/ (accessed on 8 January 2020).

Chib, Siddhartha, and Edward Greenberg. 1995. Understanding the Metropolis–Hastings algorithm. *The American Statistician* 49: 327–35.

Chiragiev, Arthur, and Zinoviy Landsman. 2007. Multivariate pareto portfolios: Tce-based capital allocation and divided differences. *Scandinavian Actuarial Journal* 2007: 261–80. [CrossRef]

Christen, J. Andrés, Colin Fox, and Mario Santana-Cibrian. 2017. Optimal direction gibbs sampler for truncated multivariate normal distributions. *Communications in Statistics-Simulation and Computation* 46: 2587–600. [CrossRef]

Denault, Michel. 2001. Coherent allocation of risk capital. *Journal of Risk* 4: 1–34. [CrossRef]

Devroye, Luc. 1985. *Non-Uniform Random Variate Generation*. New York: Springer.

Dhaene, Jan, Luc Henrard, Zinoviy Landsman, Antoine Vandendorpe, and Steven Vanduffel. 2008. Some results on the cte-based capital allocation rule. *Insurance: Mathematics and Economics* 42: 855–63. [CrossRef]

Dhaene, Jan, Andreas Tsanakas, Emiliano A. Valdez, and Steven Vanduffel. 2012. Optimal capital allocation principles. *Journal of Risk and Insurance* 79: 1–28. [CrossRef]

Duane, Simon, Anthony D. Kennedy, Brian J. Pendleton, and Duncan Roweth. 1987. Hybrid monte carlo. *Physics Letters B* 195: 216–22. [CrossRef]

Durmus, Alain, Eric Moulines, and Eero Saksman. 2017. On the convergence of hamiltonian monte carlo. *arXiv* arXiv:1705.00166.

Fan, Guobin, Yong Zeng, and Woon K. Wong. 2012. Decomposition of portfolio var and expected shortfall based on multivariate copula simulation. *International Journal of Management Science and Engineering Management* 7: 153–60. [CrossRef]

Frees, Edward W., and Emiliano A. Valdez. 1998. Understanding relationships using copulas. *North American Actuarial Journal* 2: 1–25. [CrossRef]

Furman, Edward, Alexey Kuznetsov, and Ričardas Zitikis. 2018. Weighted risk capital allocations in the presence of systematic risk. *Insurance: Mathematics and Economics* 79: 75–81. [CrossRef]

Furman, Edward, and Zinoviy Landsman. 2008. Economic capital allocations for non-negative portfolios of dependent risks. *ASTIN Bulletin: The Journal of the IAA* 38: 601–19. [CrossRef]

Furman, Edward, Ruodu Wang, and Ričardas Zitikis. 2017. Gini-type measures of risk and variability: Gini shortfall, capital allocations, and heavy-tailed risks. *Journal of Banking & Finance* 83: 70–84.

Furman, Edward, and Ričardas Zitikis. 2008. Weighted risk capital allocations. *Insurance: Mathematics and Economics* 43: 263–9. [CrossRef]

Furman, Edward, and Ričardas Zitikis. 2009. Weighted pricing functionals with applications to insurance: An overview. *North American Actuarial Journal* 13: 483–96. [CrossRef]

Gelfand, Alan E., and Adrian F. M. Smith. 1990. Sampling-based approaches to calculating marginal densities. *Journal of the American Statistical Association* 85: 398–409. [CrossRef]

Gelfand, Alan E., Adrian F. M. Smith, and Tai-Ming Lee. 1992. Bayesian analysis of constrained parameter and truncated data problems using gibbs sampling. *Journal of the American Statistical Association* 87: 523–32. [CrossRef]

Geman, Stuart, and Donald Geman. 1984. Stochastic relaxation, gibbs distributions, and the bayesian restoration of images. *IEEE Transactions on Pattern Analysis and Machine Intelligence* 6: 721–41. [CrossRef]

Geweke, John. 1991. Efficient simulation from the multivariate normal and student-t distributions subject to linear constraints and the evaluation of constraint probabilities. In *Computing Science and Statistics: Proceedings of the 23rd Symposium on the Interface*. Fairfax: Interface Foundation of North America, Inc., pp. 571–8.

Geyer, Charles. 2011. Introduction to markov chain monte carlo. In *Handbook of Markov Chain Monte Carlo*. New York: Springer, pp. 3–47.

Girardi, Giulio, and A. Tolga Ergün. 2013. Systemic risk measurement: Multivariate garch estimation of covar. *Journal of Banking & Finance* 37: 3169–80.

Girolami, Mark, and Ben Calderhead. 2011. Riemann manifold langevin and hamiltonian monte carlo methods. *Journal of the Royal Statistical Society: Series B (Statistical Methodology)* 73: 123–214. [CrossRef]

Glasserman, Paul. 2005. Measuring marginal risk contributions in credit portfolios. *Journal of Computational Finance* 9: 1–41. [CrossRef]

Glasserman, Paul. 2013. *Monte Carlo Methods in Financial Engineering*. New York: Springer.

Glasserman, Paul, and Jingyi Li. 2005. Importance sampling for portfolio credit risk. *Management Science* 51: 1643–56. [CrossRef]

Gourieroux, Christian, and Alain Monfort. 2013. Allocating systemic risk in a regulatory perspective. *International Journal of Theoretical and Applied Finance* 16: 1350041. [CrossRef]

Gudmundsson, Thorbjörn, and Henrik Hult. 2014. Markov chain monte carlo for computing rare-event probabilities for a heavy-tailed random walk. *Journal of Applied Probability* 51: 359–76. [CrossRef]

Gupta, Sourendu, A. Irbäc, Frithjof Karsch, and Bengt Petersson. 1990. The acceptance probability in the hybrid monte carlo method. *Physics Letters B* 242: 437–43. [CrossRef]

Hastings, W. Keith. 1970. Monte carlo sampling methods using markov chains and their applications. *Biometrika* 57: 97–109. [CrossRef]

Hofert, Marius, Ivan Kojadinovic, Martin Mächler, and Jun Yan. 2018. *Elements of Copula Modeling with R*. New York: Springer Use R! Series. [CrossRef]

Hoffman, Matthew D., and Andrew Gelman. 2014. The no-u-turn sampler: Adaptively setting path lengths in hamiltonian monte carlo. *Journal of Machine Learning Research* 15: 1593–623.

Hoffmann, Hannes, Thilo Meyer-Brandis, and Gregor Svindland. 2016. Risk-consistent conditional systemic risk measures. *Stochastic Processes and Their Applications* 126: 2014–37. [CrossRef]

Hogg, Robert V., and Stuart A. Klugman. 2009. *Loss Distributions*. Hoboken: John Wiley & Sons, Volume 249.

Jaworski, Piotr. 2017. On conditional value at risk (covar) for tail-dependent copulas. *Dependence Modeling* 5: 1–19. [CrossRef]

Johnson, Alicia A. 2009. Geometric Ergodicity of Gibbs Samplers. Available online: https://conservancy.umn.edu/handle/11299/53661 (accessed on 8 January 2020).

Jones, Galin L., Murali Haran, Brian S. Caffo, and Ronald Neath. 2006. Fixed-width output analysis for markov chain monte carlo. *Journal of the American Statistical Association* 101: 1537–47. [CrossRef]

Juri, Alessandro, and Mario V. Wüthrich. 2002. Copula convergence theorems for tail events. *Insurance: Mathematics and Economics* 30: 405–20. [CrossRef]

Juri, Alessandro, and Mario V. Wüthrich. 2003. Tail dependence from a distributional point of view. *Extremes* 6: 213–46. [CrossRef]

Kalkbrener, Michael, Hans Lotter, and Ludger Overbeck. 2004. Sensible and efficient capital allocation for credit portfolios. *Risk* 17: S19–S24.

Klugman, Stuart A., and Rahul Parsa. 1999. Fitting bivariate loss distributions with copulas. *Insurance: Mathematics and Economics* 24: 139–48. [CrossRef]

Koike, Takaaki, and Mihoko Minami. 2019. Estimation of risk contributions with mcmc. *Quantitative Finance* 19: 1579–97. [CrossRef]

Kromer, Eduard, Ludger Overbeck, and Konrad Zilch. 2016. Systemic risk measures on general measurable spaces. *Mathematical Methods of Operations Research* 84: 323–57. [CrossRef]

Laeven, Roger J. A., and Marc J. Goovaerts. 2004. An optimization approach to the dynamic allocation of economic capital. *Insurance: Mathematics and Economics* 35: 299–319. [CrossRef]

Lan, Shiwei, Jeffrey Streets, and Babak Shahbaba. 2014. Wormhole hamiltonian monte carlo. In *Twenty-Eighth AAAI Conference on Artificial Intelligence*. Available online: https://www.aaai.org/ocs/index.php/AAAI/AAAI14/paper/viewPaper/8437 (accessed on 8 January 2020).

Larsson, Martin, and Johanna Nešlehová. 2011. Extremal behavior of archimedean copulas. *Advances in Applied Probability* 43: 195–216. [CrossRef]

Leimkuhler, Benedict, and Sebastian Reich. 2004. *Simulating Hamiltonian Dynamics*. Cambridge: Cambridge University Press, Volume 14.

Liu, Jun S., Wing H. Wong, and Augustine Kong. 1995. Covariance structure and convergence rate of the gibbs sampler with various scans. *Journal of the Royal Statistical Society: Series B (Methodological)* 57: 157–69. [CrossRef]

Livingstone, Samuel, Michael Betancourt, Simon Byrne, and Mark Girolami. 2016. On the geometric ergodicity of hamiltonian monte carlo. *arXiv*. arXiv:1601.08057.

Livingstone, Samuel, Michael F. Faulkner, and Gareth O. Roberts. 2019. Kinetic energy choice in hamiltonian/hybrid monte carlo. *Biometrika* 106: 303–19. [CrossRef]

Livingstone, Samuel, and Mark Girolami. 2014. Information-geometric markov chain monte carlo methods using diffusions. *Entropy* 16: 3074–102. [CrossRef]

Mainik, Georg, and Eric Schaanning. 2014. On dependence consistency of covar and some other systemic risk measures. *Statistics & Risk Modeling* 31: 49–77.

McNeil, Alexander J., Rüdiger Frey, and Paul Embrechts. 2015. *Quantitative Risk Management: Concepts, Techniques and Tools*. Princeton: Princeton University Press.

Metropolis, Nicholas, Arianna W. Rosenbluth, Marshall N. Rosenbluth, Augusta H. Teller, and Edward Teller. 1953. Equation of state calculations by fast computing machines. *The Journal of Chemical Physics* 21: 1087–92. [CrossRef]

Meyn, Sean P., and Richard L. Tweedie. 2012. *Markov Chains and Stochastic Stability*. New York: Springer.

Müller, Peter. 1992. Alternatives to the Gibbs Sampling Scheme. Available online: http://citeseerx.ist.psu.edu/viewdoc/summary?doi=10.1.1.48.5613 (accessed on 8 January 2020).

Neal, Radford M. 2011. Mcmc using hamiltonian dynamics. *Handbook of Markov Chain Monte Carlo* 2: 2.

Nelsen, Roger B. 2006. *An Introduction to Copulas*. New York: Springer.

Nummelin, Esa. 2002. Mc's for mcmc'ists. *International Statistical Review* 70: 215–40. [CrossRef]

Nummelin, Esa. 2004. *General Irreducible Markov Chains and Non-Negative Operators*. Cambridge: Cambridge University Press.

Pakman, Ari, and Liam Paninski. 2014. Exact hamiltonian monte carlo for truncated multivariate gaussians. *Journal of Computational and Graphical Statistics* 23: 518–42. [CrossRef]

Rodriguez-Yam, Gabriel, Richard A. Davis, and Louis L. Scharf. 2004. Efficient gibbs sampling of truncated multivariate normal with application to constrained linear regression. Unpublished manuscript.

Rosenthal, Jeffrey S. 2011. Optimal proposal distributions and adaptive mcmc. In *Handbook of Markov Chain Monte Carlo*. Edited by Steve Brooks, Andrew Gelman, Galin Jones and Xiao-Li Meng. Boca Raton: CRC Press.

Rujån, Pål. 1997. Playing billiards in version space. *Neural Computation* 9: 99–122. [CrossRef]

Siller, Thomas. 2013. Measuring marginal risk contributions in credit portfolios. *Quantitative Finance* 13: 1915–23. [CrossRef]

Targino, Rodrigo S., Gareth W. Peters, and Pavel V. Shevchenko. 2015. Sequential monte carlo samplers for capital allocation under copula-dependent risk models. *Insurance: Mathematics and Economics* 61: 206–26. [CrossRef]

Tasche, Dirk. 1995. *Risk Contributions and Performance Measurement;* Working Paper; München: Techische Universität München.

Tasche, Dirk. 2001. Conditional expectation as quantile derivative. *arXiv*. arXiv:math/0104190.

Tasche, Dirk. 2008. Capital allocation to business units and sub-portfolios: The euler principle. In *Pillar II in the New Basel Accord: The Challenge of Economic Capital*. Edited by Andrea Resti. London: Risk Books, pp. 423–53.

Tierney, Luke. 1994. Markov chains for exploring posterior distributions. *The Annals of Statistics* 1994: 1701–28. [CrossRef]

Vats, Dootika, James M. Flegal, and Galin L. Jones. 2015. Multivariate output analysis for markov chain monte carlo. *arXiv*. arXiv:1512.07713.

Vernic, Raluca. 2006. Multivariate skew-normal distributions with applications in insurance. *Insurance: Mathematics and Economics* 38: 413–26. [CrossRef]

Yamai, Yasuhiro, and Toshinao Yoshiba. 2002. Comparative analyses of expected shortfall and value-at-risk: Their estimation error, decomposition, and optimization. *Monetary and Economic Studies* 20: 87–121.

Yi, Kexin, and Finale Doshi-Velez. 2017. Roll-back hamiltonian monte carlo. *arXiv*. [CrossRef]

6

Modelling and Forecasting Stock Price Movements with Serially Dependent Determinants

Rasika Yatigammana [1], Shelton Peiris [2,3], Richard Gerlach [4] and David Edmund Allen [2,5,6,*]

1 Central Bank of Sri-Lanka, Colombo 01, Sri Lanka; yatigammanar@hotmail.com
2 School of Mathematics and Statistics, The University of Sydney, Sydney 2006, Australia; shelton.peiris@sydney.edu.au
3 Department of Statistics, The University of Colombo, Colombo 03, Sri-Lanka
4 Discipline of Business Analytics, The University of Sydney, Sydney 2006, Australia; richard.gerlach@sydney.edu.au
5 Department of Finance, Asia University, Taichung 41354, Taiwan
6 School of Business and Law, Edith Cowan University, Joondalup 6027, Australia
* Correspondence: profallen2007@gmail.com

Abstract: The direction of price movements are analysed under an ordered probit framework, recognising the importance of accounting for discreteness in price changes. By extending the work of Hausman et al. (1972) and Yang and Parwada (2012),This paper focuses on improving the forecast performance of the model while infusing a more practical perspective by enhancing flexibility. This is achieved by extending the existing framework to generate short term multi period ahead forecasts for better decision making, whilst considering the serial dependence structure. This approach enhances the flexibility and adaptability of the model to future price changes, particularly targeting risk minimisation. Empirical evidence is provided, based on seven stocks listed on the Australian Securities Exchange (ASX). The prediction success varies between 78 and 91 per cent for in-sample and out-of-sample forecasts for both the short term and long term.

Keywords: ordered probit; stock prices; auto-regressive; multi-step ahead forecasts

---

1. Introduction

There has been a significant growth in market micro-structure research, which is concerned with the study of the underlying process that translates the latent demands of investors into transaction prices and volumes (Madhavan 2000). The study of the time series properties of security prices has been central to market micro-structure research for many years. Madhavan (2000) asserts that frictions and departures from symmetric information do affect the trading process. Furthermore, insights into future price trends provides additional information useful in strategy formulation. As per financial economic theory, the asset returns cannot be easily predicted by employing statistical or other techniques and incorporating publicly available information. Nevertheless, recent literature bears evidence of successful forecasting of asset return signs; see for example, Breen et al. (1989); Leung et al. (2000); White (2000); Pesaran and Timmermann (2004) and Cheung et al. (2005). While having mean independence, it is statistically probable to have sign and volatility dependence in asset returns (Christoffersen and Diebold 2006).

The knowledge of the future direction of the stock price movement provides valuable guidance in developing profitable trading strategies. However, there is no clear consensus on the stochastic behaviour of prices or on the major factors determining the change in prices. In this context, theories of information asymmetry stating that private information deduced from trading causes market price fluctuations (See Kyle 1985) became important propositions. Consequently, many market attributes have been employed as substitutes for information in the study of security price behaviour. Price changes occur in discrete increments, which are denoted in multiples of ticks. It is well recognised today that failing to treat the price process as a discrete series could adversely affect prediction results. Initially the modeling of discrete transaction prices was done by Gottlieb and Kalay (1985). The generalisation and variation of such a modeling framework can be found in Ball (1988); Glosten and Harris (1988); Harris (1990); Dravid (1991) and Hasbrouck (1999). Most often, earlier studies have treated price change as a continuous variable, primarily focusing on the unconditional distribution, ignoring the timing of transactions, which is irregular and random. The "ordered probit model", which was initially proposed by Aitchison and Silvey (1957) is a useful model for discrete dependent variables, which can take only a finite number of values with a natural ordering. Gurland et al. (1960) developed it further and later it was introduced into the social sciences by McKelvey and Zavoina (1975), which became an analytical tool in the financial market security price dynamics of micro-structure research. This could be used to quantify the effects of various factors on stock price movements, whilst accounting for discreteness in price changes and the irregular spacing of trades.

In an ordered probit analysis of the conditional distribution of price changes, Hausman et al. (1972) recognised the importance of accounting for discreteness, especially in intraday price movements. In such fine samples, the extent of price change is limited to a few distinct values, which may not be well approximated by a continuous state space. Their paper investigated the impact of several explanatory variables in capturing the transaction price changes. Importantly, the clock-time effect, measured in terms of duration between two consecutive trades, bid-ask spread, trade size and market-wide or systematic movements in prices based on a market index on conditional distribution of price changes were modeled under this framework. In a more recent study, Yang and Parwada (2012) extended the existing empirical literature on the impact of market attributes on price dynamics, utilising an ordered probit model. Their study explored the price impact of variables such as market depth and trade imbalance (also referred to as order imbalance in quote driven markets), in addition to trade size, trade indicator, bid-ask spread and duration which were found to be significant in similar studies. The model thus estimated by Yang and Parwada (2012), was able to forecast the direction of price change for about 72% of the cases, on average.

The in-sample and out-of-sample forecasts provided by the authors were based on the observed values of the regressors in the forecast horizon. However, in generating out-of-sample forecasts beyond one-step ahead incorporating observed values for regressors is of limited practical use, as they are not observed priori. Developing multi-step ahead forecasts, at least for a few transactions ahead is much more beneficial from a practical perspective, for effective decision making. However, such forecasting evidence under this framework is seemingly absent in the literature. Therefore, in addressing this shortcoming, this paper introduces a forecasting mechanism to generate forecasts beyond the one-step ahead level. Towards this end, disaggregated forecasts are generated first, for each of the explanatory variables for the period concerned. In order to generate forecasts for the regressors included, the serial dependence structure of each of the variables is investigated and appropriate forecasting models are fitted. Sign forecasts are subsequently generated, based on those predicted regressor values, rather than on observed values and the estimated coefficients of the ordered probit model. These prediction results are compared with those of the existing literature. Through the introduction of dynamic variables into the forecasting system, the predictive capability of this approach is investigated through a study based on the stocks of seven major companies listed in the Australian Securities Exchange (ASX).

In summary, the primary motivation of this paper is to introduce a method to enhance the flexibility and adaptability of the ordered probit model to generate multi-step ahead forecasts of stock price changes. Identifying and estimating appropriate univariate models for forecasting each explanatory variable, taking their serial dependence structure into account, towards this endeavour, is the second motivation. The third motivation is to improve on the results of Yang and Parwada (2012) in model estimation and forecast accuracy, by reducing noise in the data used and suitably formulating variables. Therefore, this exercise features the same stocks and almost the same independent variables that were employed by Yang and Parwada (2012). We were able to achieve an 88 per cent plus rate of accuracy, on average, in the out of-sample forecasts of the direction of price changes using observed regressor values. In addition, more than 91 per cent of in-sample estimates, on average, correctly predicted the direction of price change. This is in comparison to the 72 per cent achieved by Yang and Parwada (2012). It is between 78-80 per cent when predictied regressor values were incorporated.

The remainder of the paper is organized as follows. Section 2 provides a review of the ordered probit model while Section 3 gives a description of the data and the variables used in the analysis. This section reports the summary statistics for each variable for the chosen stocks and introduces the relevant models for estimation and forecasting of durations, residuals and regressors. The empirical evidence is reported in Section 4 including model estimation and diagnostics. The results of the forecasting exercise for both in-sample and out-of-sample are presented in Section 5 and finally, the concluding remarks are provided in Section 6.

2. A Review of the Ordered Probit Model

In a sequence of transaction prices, $P_{t_0}, P_{t_1}, P_{t_2}, \ldots, P_{t_T}$ occurring at times $t_0, t_1, t_2, \ldots, t_T$ the resulting price changes multiplied by 100 is represented as an integer multiple of a tick and denoted by $Y_1, Y_2, \ldots, Y_T$, where $Y_k \equiv \{P_{t_k} - P_{t_{k-1}}\} \times 100$. The ordered probit model analyses discrete dependent variables with responses that are ordinal but not continuous. Underlying the indexing in such models, there exists a latent continuous metric and the thresholds partition the real line into a series of different regions corresponding to these ordinal categories. Therefore, the unobserved latent continuous variable Y^* is related to the observed discrete variable Y. It is assumed that the conditional mean of Y^* is described as a linear combination of observed explanatory variables, X and a disturbance term that has a Normal distribution.

The ordered probit specification takes the following form:

$$Y_k^* = X_k'\beta + \varepsilon_k, \quad \text{where} \quad \varepsilon_k|X_k \sim i.n.i.d.N(0, \sigma_k^2), \tag{1}$$

where i.n.i.d denotes that the errors are independently but not identically distributed. X_k is a $q \times 1$ vector of predetermined explanatory variables that govern the conditional mean, Y_k^* and β is a $q \times 1$ vector of parameters to be estimated. Here, the subscript denotes the transaction time. The observed price change Y_k is related to the latent continuous variable Y_k^* according to the following scheme:

$$Y_k = \begin{cases} s_1 & \text{if } Y_k^* \in A_1 \\ s_2 & \text{if } Y_k^* \in A_2 \\ \vdots & \vdots \\ s_m & \text{if } Y_k^* \in A_m \end{cases}, \tag{2}$$

where the sets A_k are comprised of non overlapping ranges of values, partitioning the continuous state space of Y_k^* and the s_j are the corresponding discrete values containing the state space of Y_k, which are called states. Let s_j's be the price change in ticks $-2, -1, 0, 1, \ldots$. Suppose that the threshold values of A are given as follows:

$$\begin{cases} A_1 \equiv (-\infty, \alpha_1], \\ A_2 \equiv (\alpha_1, \alpha_2], \\ \vdots \\ A_k \equiv (\alpha_{k-1}, \alpha_k], \\ \vdots \\ A_m \equiv (\alpha_{m-1}, \infty). \end{cases} \tag{3}$$

The number of states, m is kept finite, though in reality price change could take any value in cents to avoid the explosion of an unknown number of parameters. As per Hausman et al. (1972), the only requirement in this framework is the conditional independence of the ε_k's, where all the serial dependence would be captured by the regressors. Further, there are no restrictions on the temporal dependence of the X_k's. The conditional distribution of Y_k , conditioned upon X_k depends on the partition boundaries and the distributional assumption of ε_k. The conditional distribution in the case of Gaussian ε_k is

$$P(Y_k = s_i|X_k) = P(X_k'\beta + \varepsilon_k \in A_i|X_k)$$

$$= \begin{cases} P(X_k'\beta + \varepsilon_k \leq \alpha_1|X_k) & \text{if } i = 1, \\ P(\alpha_{i-1} < X_k'\beta + \varepsilon_k \leq \alpha_i|X_k) & \text{if } 1 < i < m, \\ P(\alpha_{m-1} < X_k'\beta + \varepsilon_k|X_k) & \text{if } i = m, \end{cases} \tag{4}$$

$$= \begin{cases} \Phi\left(\frac{\alpha_1 - X_k'\beta}{\sigma_k}\right) & \text{if } i = 1, \\ \Phi\left(\frac{\alpha_i - X_k'\beta}{\sigma_k}\right) - \Phi\left(\frac{\alpha_{i-1} - X_k'\beta}{\sigma_k}\right) & \text{if } 1 < i < m, \\ 1 - \Phi\left(\frac{\alpha_{m-1} - X_k'\beta}{\sigma_k}\right) & \text{if } i = m, \end{cases} \tag{5}$$

where $\Phi(\cdot)$ denotes the standard Normal cumulative distribution function. Since the distance between the conditional mean $X_k'\beta$ and the partition boundaries determines the probability of any observed price change, the probabilities of attaining each state, given the conditional mean, could be changed by shifting the partition boundaries appropriately. The explanatory variables capture the marginal effects of various economic factors that influence the likelihood of a given state as opposed to another. Therefore, the ordered probit model determines the empirical relation between the unobservable continuous state space and the observed discrete state space as a function of the explanatory variables, X_k, by estimating all the system parameters, including β coefficients, the conditional variance σ_k^2 and the partition boundaries α, from the data itself.

Let U_{ik} be an indicator variable, which takes the value 1 if the realisation of the kth observation, Y_k is the ith state s_i and 0 otherwise. The log likelihood function L for the price changes $Y = [Y_1, Y_2, \ldots, Y_T]$, conditional on the regressors, $X = [X_1, X_2, \ldots, X_T]$, takes the following form:

$$\begin{gathered} L(Y|X) = \Sigma_{k=1}^{T} \left\{ U_{1k}.log\Phi\left(\frac{\alpha_1 - X_k'\beta}{\sigma_k}\right) \right. \\ + \Sigma_{i=2}^{m-1} U_{ik}.log\left[\Phi\left(\frac{\alpha_i - X_k'\beta}{\sigma_k}\right) - \Phi\left(\frac{\alpha_{i-1} - X_k'\beta}{\sigma_k}\right)\right] \\ \left. + U_{mk}.log\left[1 - \Phi\left(\frac{\alpha_{m-1} - X_k'\beta}{\sigma_k}\right)\right] \right\} \end{gathered} \tag{6}$$

Hausman et al. (1972) has reparameterised the conditional variance σ_k^2 based on the time between trades and lagged spread.

Models for Correlated Errors and Explanatory Variables

As mentioned in the above subsection, models with an appropriate autoregressive structure are used as forecasting models for the explanatory variables. Autoregressive integrated moving average (ARIMA) models of order (p,d,q) or ARIMA (p,d,q) models are used tomodel the autocorrelation in a time series and are used to predict behaviour based on past values alone. However, certain variables warranted the application of a simple ARIMA type model while others exhibit long range dependence, which require autoregressive fractionally integrated moving average (ARFIMA) (p,d,q) type models to describe their behaviour. On the other hand, forecasts of indicator variables with more than two categories are based on multinomial logistic regressions, where the responses are nominal categories. The heteroscedasticity in the residuals is captured by the generalised autoregressive conditional heteroscedasticity GARCH(p, q) model (Bollerslev 1986), following (Yang and Parwada 2012). A brief description of each of these models are given in the Appendix.

3. Data, Variables and ACD Model

3.1. Data Description and ACD Model

The relevant data for this analysis was obtained from the Securities Industry Research Centre of Asia-Pacific (SIRCA) in Australia. The dataset consists of time stamped tick-by-tick trades, to the nearest millisecond and other information pertaining to trades and quotes for the chosen stocks listed in the Australian Securities Exchange (ASX). This study is based on a sample of stock prices collected during a three month period from 16 January 2014 to 15 April 2014. The stocks that were not subjected to any significant structural change, representing seven major industry sectors, are included in the sample. The selected stocks are Australian Gas Light Company (AGL), BHP Billiton (BHP), Commonwealth Bank (CBA), News Corporation (NCP), Telstra (TLS), Westfarmers (WES) and Woodside Petroleum (WPL) from Utilities, Materials, Financials, Consumer Discretionary, Telecommunication services, Consumer Staples and Energy sectors respectively. All seven of these stocks are included in the study by Yang and Parwada (2012), consisting of both liquid and less liquid assets, to minimise sample selection biases. However, the sampling period and the sample size differ between studies. Two stocks are not included in this paper due to the absence of transactions during the study period. Intraday price changes extracted from tick by tick trade data forms the basic time series under consideration. Overnight price changes are excluded as their properties differ significantly from those of intraday price changes (See Amihud and Mendelson 1987; Stoll and Whaley 1990). The trading hours of ASX are from 10.00 a.m. to 4.00 p.m. Due to the possibility of contamination of the trading process by including opening and closing trades (Engle and Russell 1998), the trades during the initial 30 min of opening and the final 30 min prior to closing are disregarded.

The following information with respect to each transaction is collected for each stock: Trade data comprising of date, time, transaction price and trade size, quote data such as bid price and ask price, market depth data comprising of volume at the highest bid price (best bid) and volume at the lowest ask price (best ask) and market index (ASX200). HFD generally contains erroneous transactions and outliers that do not correspond to plausible market activity. This is mainly attributed to the high velocity of transactions (Falkenberry 2002). Among others Hansen and Lunde (2006); Brownlees and Gallo (2006) and Barndorff-Nielsen et al. (2009) have paid special attention to the importance of data cleaning. A rigorous cleaning procedure is used here in obtaining a reliable data series for the analysis, mainly in accordance with the procedure outlined in Barndorff-Nielsen et al. (2009). To generate a time series at unique time points, during the instances of simultaneous multiple trades (quotes), the median transaction price (bid/ask prices) of those trades (quotes) is considered. Correspondingly, cumulative volume of those trades (quotes) are taken as the trade volume (bid/ask volume).

In the ordered probit model, the dependent variable Y_k is the price change between the kth and $k-1$th trade multiplied by 100. This records Y_k in cents, which however is equivalent to ticks as the tick size of the ASX for stocks with prices of the chosen magnitude is 1 cent. In this analysis, several different explanatory variables are included to measure their association with direction of price movement, following Yang and Parwada (2012). Bid and ask quotes are reported as and when quotes are updated, which necessitates the matching of quotes to transaction prices. Each transaction price is matched to the quote reported immediately prior to that transaction. Similarly, aggregate volumes at the best bid and best ask prices together with the ASX200 index representing the market are also matched in a similar fashion. The bid-ask spread $Sprd_{k-1}$, is given in cents, while $LBAV_{k-1}$ & $LBBV_{k-1}$ denote the natural log of number of shares at best ask and bid prices respectively. $LVol_{k-1}$ gives the natural logarithm of $(k-1)$th trade size. Conditional duration, ψ_{k-1} and standardised transaction duration ϵ_{k-1} are derived estimates by fitting an autoregressive conditional duration model (ACD (1,1)) to diurnally adjusted duration data. A brief description of the model introduced by Engle and Russell (1998) is presented in Appendix A. The initial record of each day is disregarded as it is linked to the previous day's prices and results in negative durations. TI_{k-1} denotes the trade indicator of $(k-1)$th trade, which classifies a trade as buyer-initiated, seller-initiated or other type of trade. Trade imbalance TIB_{k-1}, based on the preceding 30 trades that occurred on the same day (Yang and Parwada 2012) (YP hereafter) is calculated as follows:

$$TIB_{k-1} = \frac{\sum_{j=1}^{30}\left(TI_{(k-1)-j} \times Vol_{(k-1)-j}\right)}{\sum_{j=1}^{30} Vol_{(k-1)-j}} \tag{7}$$

The first 30 observations of trade imbalance (TIB) is set to zero as TIB also depends on the previous day's trade imbalance for these transactions.

Market index return $RIndx_{k-1}$, prevailing immediately prior to transaction k is computed as given below:

$$RIndx_{k-1} = \ln(INDX_{k-1}) - \ln(INDX_{k-2}) \tag{8}$$

The sampling period and the use and categorisation of certain variables in this analysis differ from YP. ASX200 is applied here instead of specific sector indexes as the impact of the performance of the overall economy tends to be more significant on stock price behaviour than of a specific sector. On the other hand, the reference point for grouping the price changes is the 'one tick' threshold vis a vis the 'zero' change. This provides a more meaningful classification of the groups, as the categorisation of price change is based on a range of values rather than a fixed value for a certain group.

3.2. Sample Statistics

The main characteristics of the chosen variables in the analysis and how those characteristics differ between stocks could be ascertained from the several summary statistics that are provided in Table 1. There is considerable variation in the price level among the stocks considered in the sample. The highest price during this period ranged between AUD 4.96 for TLS and AUD 77.87 for CBA. The volatility of prices as indicated by the standard deviation of the percentage price change is not very high, with the TLS recording the highest value of 7.65 per cent. For most other stocks, it is less than 5 per cent. Average trade volume also records a substantial dispersion between the stocks, which varied from 161 for NCP and 6983 for TLS during the period. An indication of whether a transaction is buyer-initiated or seller-initiated is required for the empirical analysis. This measure is useful in identifying the party most anxious to execute the trade and the actions of whom would be reflected in terms of the bid/ask spread. The trades fall into these two categories in more or less equal proportions across stocks and are very similar in value except for TLS. The indeterminate trades form around 8–18% of trades, while it is 45% for TLS. The absence of asymmetric pressure from the buying or selling side suggests that there were no events with major news impact that would have resulted in abnormal trades and returns. This is further highlighted by zero mean returns.

The trading frequency as measured by the average duration between two consecutive trades also varies across stocks significantly. For more liquid stocks such as BHP, CBA and WES, trades tend to occur every 5 s or less on average. The other stocks are generally traded within 10 s. However, NCP is traded every 25 s on average. The observed large dispersions is a characteristic inherent in trade durations. Next, the estimation of the duration dynamics under an ACD model is considered, since the expected and standardised durations enter the orderd probit model as two separate variables.

The estimated coefficients of the ACD (1,1) model fitted to diurnally adjusted durations is presented in Table 2. The multiplicative error component is assumed to follow a Standardised Weibull distribution. All the coefficients are highly significant for each of the stocks, indicating the dependence of the expected duration on its past behaviour. It is straightforward to estimate the conditional expected durations, ψ_k utilising the parameter estimates from the ACD model. The diurnal component was estimated using a cubic spline with knots at each half hour between 10:30 a.m. and 15:30 p.m. The standardised durations or the unexpected durations, ϵ_k are then obtained by dividing the diurnally adjusted durations by the conditional expected durations, which is an i.i.d. process. The parameter estimates are based on the conditional maximum likelihood approach, using the standardised Weibull distribution for ϵ_k. The Weibull distribution is a better choice here as opposed to exponential since the shape parameter is statistically significant and different from unity for all the stocks. Refer to the Appendix for the corresponding log-likelihood function.

Table 1. Descriptive statistics of the variables considered in the ordered probit model for all the stocks, for the period from 16 January 2014 to 15 April 2014.

Statistic	AGL	BHP	CBA	NCP	TLS	WES	WPL
Price (AUD)							
Max price	16.15	39.79	77.87	20.17	5.29	43.93	39.5
Min price	14.71	35.06	72.15	16.92	4.96	40.88	36.54
Price Change (%)							
Mean	0.0000	0.0000	0.0000	0.0000	0.0000	0.0000	0.0000
Std.dev	0.0376	0.0197	0.0124	0.0728	0.0765	0.0181	0.0183
Duration (Seconds)							
Mean	9.59	3.51	3.49	24.76	8.04	4.26	5.30
Std.dev	19.01	7.37	7.56	49.91	12.47	9.08	11.08
Trade Volume							
Mean	395	710	285	161	6983	281	318
Std.dev	2206	3622	2183	711	39,379	1370	1290
Shares at the Best Bid Price							
Mean	4451	5498	1579	877	941,002	1841	1983
Std.dev	5027	6464	2899	1994	603,015	2504	2406
Shares at the Best Ask Price							
Mean	4399	5513	1808	977	992,906	1945	2100
Std.dev	5409	7544	5053	1649	642,204	2775	2719
Market Index Returns, *ASX200*							
Mean	0.0000	0.0000	0.0000	0.0000	0.0000	0.0000	0.0000
Std.dev	0.0001	0.0001	0.0001	0.0001	0.0001	0.0001	0.0001
Trade Imbalance							
Mean	−0.0268	−0.0119	0.0094	−0.0623	0.0094	0.0224	0.0004
Std.dev	0.4653	0.4590	0.4401	0.4863	0.5082	0.4564	0.4446
Trade Direction (%)							
Buyer initiated	40.9	41.0	44.7	43.9	27.0	44.2	44.6
Seller initiated	41.6	41.0	42.2	48.1	27.6	40.6	41.9

The standardised durations are deemed weakly exogenous in the case of Australian stocks, according to the regression results of YP. They have regressed the standardised residuals on trades, volumes and returns for each of the stocks, which included the seven stocks of our study. On the other hand, both these studies consider the lagged measures of duration, addressing the problem of endogeneity to some extent. Furthermore, Dufour and Engle (2000) have treated durations as a strongly exogeneous variable in assessing the role of time on price dynamics.

The volumes at the best bid and ask prices prevailing prior to a transaction gives a measure of market depth. TLS has the deepest market, minimising the price impact cost for its trades. The trade imbalance (TIB) attempts to capture the cumulative demand side and supply side discrepancy over the last 30 trades. TIB < 0, if seller-initiated cumulative trading volume exceeded the buyer-initiated cumulative trading volume, during the immediately preceeding 30 trades prior to the current transaction. On the other hand, TIB > 0, if the buyer-initiated volume was more than the seller-initiated volume. The zero indicates either all indeterminate trades or an exact matching of selling and buying volumes during the period. In any case, zeros are very rare. Overall, there is a insignificant trade imbalance across all stocks. However, three stocks have a negative sign implying the selling volume marginally exceeded the buying volume while the other four stocks have a positive sign indicating the reverse phenomenon.

Table 2. The coefficient estimates of an ACD (1,1) model with Standardised Weibull errors fitted for the stocks. The conditional expected duration where x_k is the adjusted duration. α is the shape parameter of the Weibull distribution.

Parameter	AGL	BHP	CBA	NCP	TLS	WES	WPL
α_0	0.3177 (21.92 *)	0.0024 (10.16 *)	0.3178 (32.47 *)	0.0348 (10.03 *)	0.0291 (28.82 *)	0.3349 (23.33 *)	0.0030 (6.65 *)
α_1	0.3113 (27.91 *)	0.0110 (20.61 *)	0.2195 (41.03 *)	0.1476 (15.53 *)	0.2180 (59.84 *)	0.1652 (29.71 *)	0.0201 (18.48 *)
β	0.4764 (26.80 *)	0.9865 (1371.66 *)	0.4949 (40.08 *)	0.8524 (89.69 *)	0.7820 (214.64 *)	0.5220 (30.26 *)	0.9785 (747.16 *)
α	0.2523 (427.88 *)	0.4295 (726.73 *)	0.4258 (731.49 *)	0.4369 (255.94 *)	0.5756 (476.06 *)	0.4194 (672.39 *)	0.4046 (582.99 *)

* Significant at 99% level.

It is noticed that most of the variables exhibit serial correlation, with variables such as $LVol$, $LBBV$, $LBAV$, $Sprd$, TI and TIB showing strong serial dependence, for all stocks. For illustration, Figures 1–3 present the time series behaviour together with the acf and pacf for a few selected variables for a random stock, AGL.

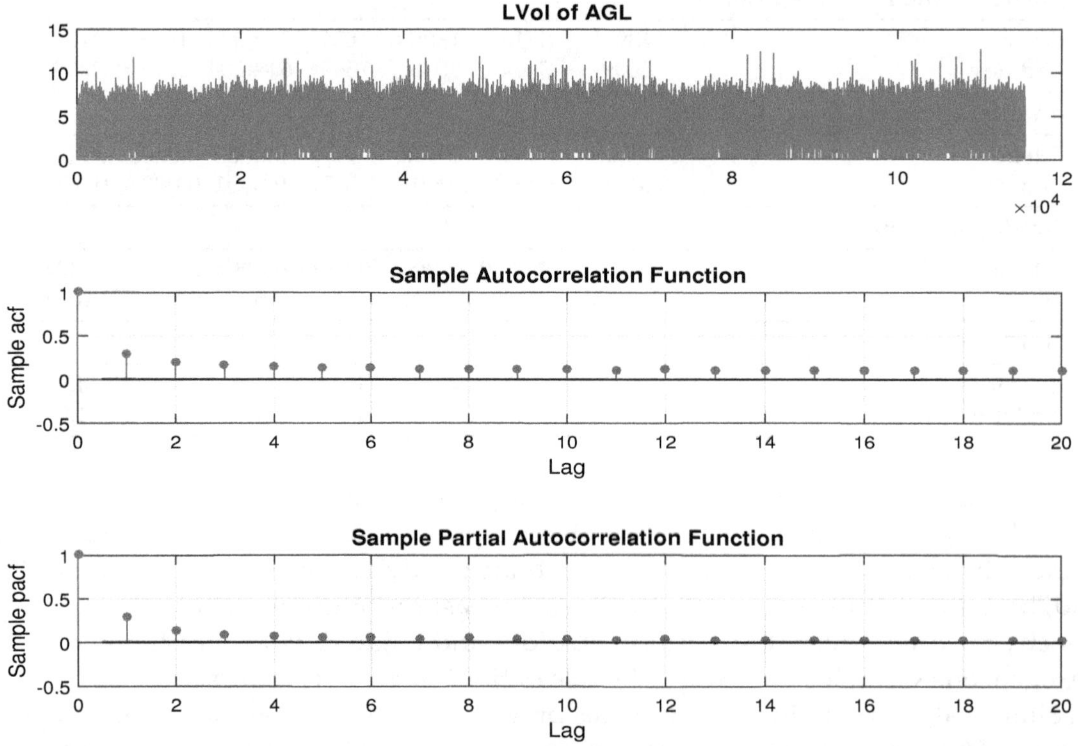

Figure 1. Time series, acf and pacf for LVol of AGL.

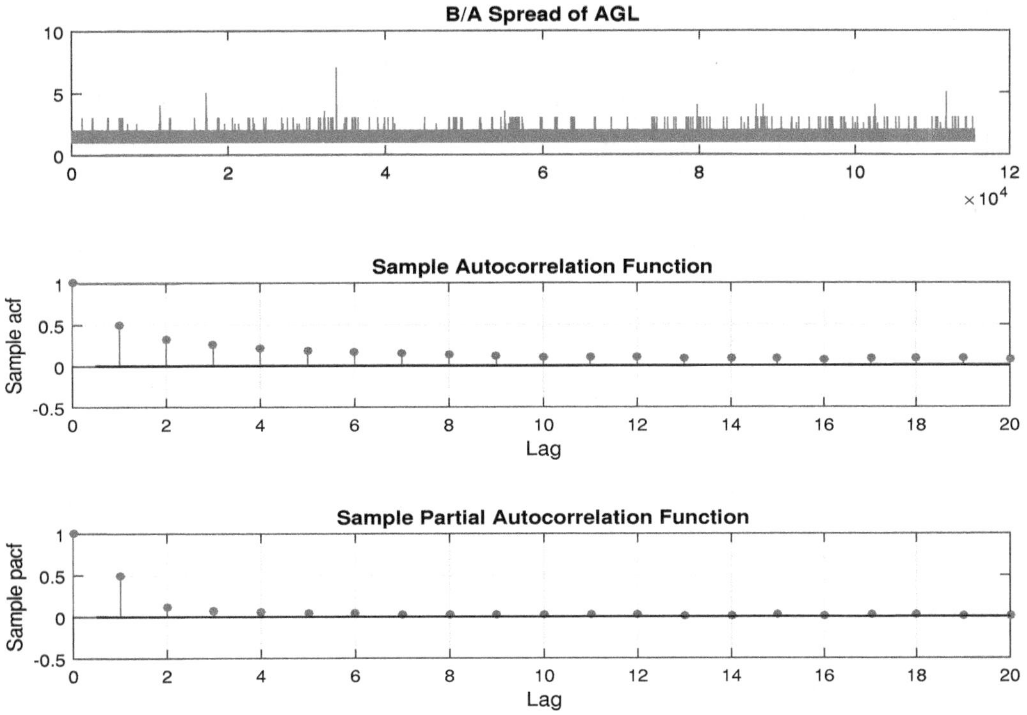

Figure 2. Time series, acf and pacf for spread of AGL.

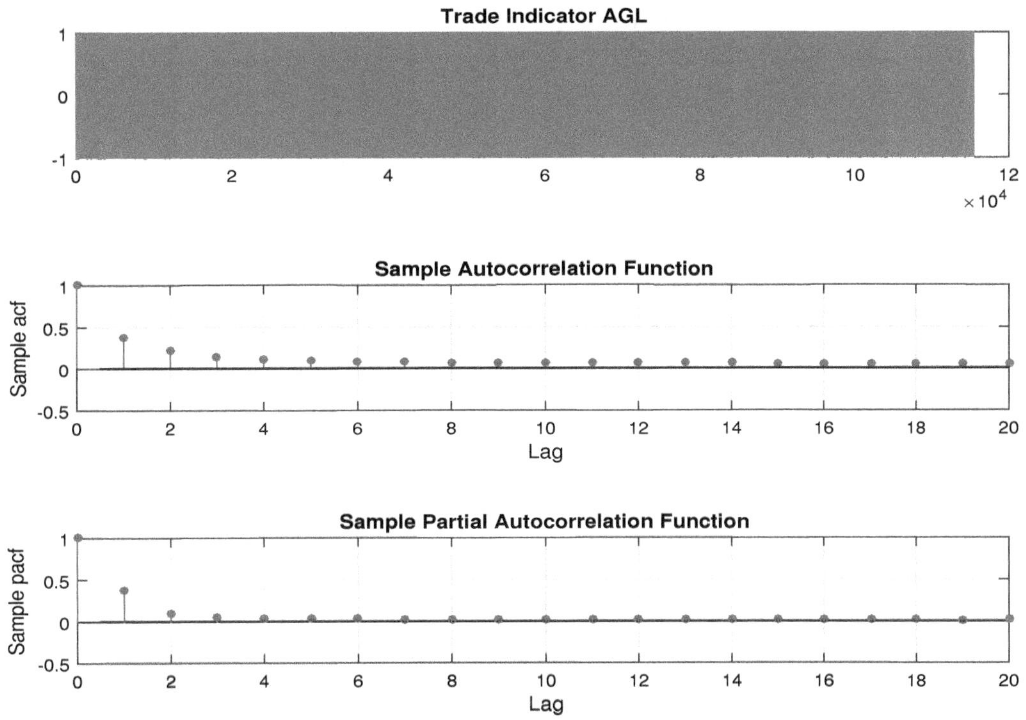

Figure 3. Time series, acf and pacf for trade indicator of AGL.

A novel feature of this study is that unlike in YP's study, we incorporate this feature by developing forecasting models for each explanatory variable based on the serial dependence structure. Therefore, Section 2 reports some useful models for capturing this feature in X_k's and σ_k^2, while details of the forecasting exercise is discussed later in Section 5.1

4. Empirical Evidence

The model estimation for the direction of price change is carried out for these stocks for the period 16 January to 14 April 2014. Out of sample forecasts are generated for the last day of the sample, on 15 April 2014 from 10:30 a.m. to 15:30 p.m.

Y_k denotes the price changes between the k and $(k-1)$th trades in terms of integer multiples of ticks. The price change here is representative of the change in the observed transaction prices. The number of states that could be assumed by the observed price changes Y_k is set to 3, under the ordered probit framework. Price increases of at least 1 tick being grouped as +1, price decreases of at least 1 tick as -1, while price changes falling in $(-1,1)$, taking the value 0. The choice of m is based on achieving the balance between price resolution and minimising states with zero or very few observations. The decision to restrict m to 3 was mainly influenced by the fact that the observed price changes exceeding ± 2 ticks was below 0.05% for most stocks. The distribution of observed price changes in terms of ticks, over the transactions, is presented in Figure 4. Prices tend to remain stable in more than 80 per cent of the transactions, in general. For the rest of the time, rises and falls are more or less equally likely.

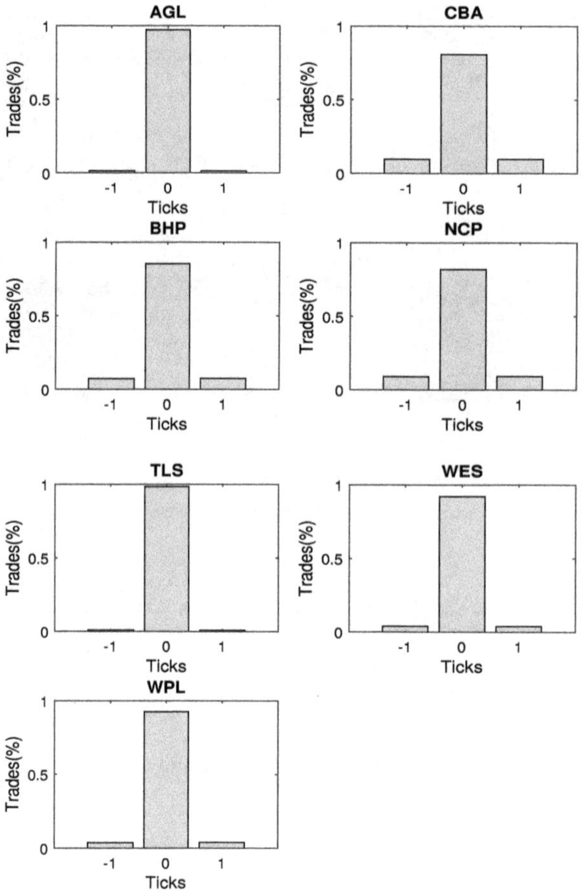

Figure 4. Distribution of the number of trades over the three categories of price change in terms of ticks, for all stocks during the period.

4.1. Ordered Probit Model Estimation

Prior to model estimation, all variables considered in the analysis was tested for stationarity using an Augmented Dickey-Fuller (ADF) test, which confirmed the same, which is in agreement with previous findings. The Ordered probit model specification depends on the underlying distribution of the price series. The model can assume any suitable arbitrary multinomial distribution, by shifting the partition boundaries accordingly. However, the assumption of Gaussianity here has no major impact in deriving the state probabilities, though it is relatively easier to capture conditional heteroscedasticity.

The dependent variable in Equation (11) below is the price change in ticks. (An explanation of the latent continuous version of the price change was given in Section 2). The variables used in Equation (11) were described in Section 3. Just to recap, the first three variables on the R.H.S. of Equation (11) are three lags of the dependent variable. TI_{k-1} is the trade indicator; which classifies a trade as a buyer-initiated, seller-initiated or other type of trade. $SPRD_{k-1}$, is the Bid-Ask spread, measured in cents. $LVol_{k-1}$ gives the natural logarithm of $(k-1)$th trade size. $LBAV_{k-1}$ and $LBABV$ denote the natural log of number of shares at best ask and bid prices respectively. TIB_{k-1} is the trade imbalance, based on the preceding 30 trades on the same day. Conditional duration, ψ_{k-1} and standardised transaction duration ϵ_{k-1} are derived estimates by fitting an autoregressive conditional duration model (ACD (1,1)) to diurnally adjusted duration data. The ACD (1,1) model is described in the appendix. $RIndx_{k-1}$, prevailing immediately prior to transaction k, is calculated as the continuously compounded return on the ASX 200.

The mean equation under the ordered probit specification takes the following form:

$$\begin{aligned} X_k'\beta = \beta_1 Y_{k-1} + \beta_2 Y_{k-2} + \beta_3 Y_{k-3} + \beta_4 TI_{k-1} + \beta_5 Sprd_{k-1} + \beta_6 LVol_{k-1} \\ +\beta_7 LBAV_{k-1} + \beta_8 LBBV_{k-1} + \beta_9 TIB_{k-1} + \beta_{10} TI_{k-1} * \psi_{k-1} \\ +\beta_{11} TI_{k-1} * \epsilon_{k-1} + \beta_{12} RIndx_{k-1} \end{aligned} \tag{9}$$

The maximum likelihood estimates of the ordered probit model on price changes were computed based on BHHH algorithm of Berndt et al. (1974). The estimated coefficients of the above ordered probit system are presented in Table 3 while the corresponding z statistics are recorded within parentheses. Most of the regressors are highly significant to the model for all seven stocks, based on the asymptotically normally distributed z statistic (Hausman et al. 1972). The pseudo-R^2 values given at the bottom of the table show an improvement, irrespective of the number of observations, in comparison to those of YP. A relatively higher number of significant coefficients across all stocks is another improvement.

The first three lags of the dependent variable comes under scrutiny, first. All the lags are significant with a 95% confidence level, with a negative coefficient for each stock. This inverse relationship with past price changes is consistent with the existing literature, indicating a reversal in the price compared to its past changes. Consider a one tick rise in price over the last three trades in the case of AGL, for example, keeping the other variables constant. The subsequent fall in the conditional mean (Y_k^*) would be 3.9448, which is less than the lower threshold, resulting in -1 for Y_k. The coefficients of the traditional variables such as the bid ask spread ($Sprd$), trade volume (LVol) and the market index returns are significant for all stocks but one, in each case. The $Sprd$ and $LVol$ has a positive impact on the price change across all stocks. The market index returns, based on the ASX200, as a measure of the overall economy, generally has a significant positive impact on price changes. Overall, this is in line with the conventional wisdom. Meanwhile, the coefficients of the trade indicator, the number of shares at the best bid price and the number of shares at the best ask price are significant for all stocks.

The trade imbalance (TIB) between buyers and sellers has a positive impact on price change and is statistically significant across all stocks. This phenomenon agrees well with the general inference that more buyer-initiated trades tend to exert pressure from the demand-side, resulting in a subsequent rise in price and vice versa. The impact of the time duration between trades is measured separately via the two constituent components of an ACD model. One is the conditional expected duration (signed), $TI_{k-1} * \psi_{k-1}$ and the other isthe standardised innovations (signed), also referred to as unexpected durations, $TI_{k-1} * \epsilon_{k-1}$. The signed conditional expected duration is significant for all stocks while the unexpected component is significant for all but one. This highlights the informational impact of time between trades in price formation. The interpretation of these measures of duration is not straightforward as they are comprised of two components. The kind of impact those variables have on price change will depend on the significance of the trade initiation as well as on the durations.

One striking feature is that either both the components have a positive impact or both have a negative impact for a given stock. Wald tests were performed to investigate the significance of duration on price changes. The tests were conducted under the null hypotheses in which either the coefficient of the conditional duration is zero or the coefficient of standardised duration is zero or both are jointly zero. The resultant F statistics suggest that both the components of duration are significant for all the stocks considered. The test results are not presented here for the sake of brevity.

The partition boundaries produced below the coefficient estimates determine the partition points of the direction of change in the latent variable. There are three possible directions the price change can take in terms of ticks, $Y_k \leq -1$, $Y_k = 0$ and $Y_k \geq +1$. By comparing these boundary values with the estimated continuous variable Y_k^*, values −1, 0 or +1 are assigned to the observed variable $\hat{Y}_k$.

Table 3. Coefficient estimates β_i, of ordered probit model on direction of price change based on 12 explanatory variables for the selected stocks. The sampling period was 16 January 2014 to 15 January 2014. Z statistics are given within parentheses for each parameter.

Parameter	AGL	BHP	CBA	NCP	TLS	WES	WPL
Obs.	*114,318*	*316,547*	*317,761*	*41,085*	*137,323*	*260,954*	*205,651*
Y_{k-1}	−2.2281 (−72.21 *)	−1.0240 (−130.16 *)	−0.7915 (−119.64 *)	−0.7637 (−54.32 *)	−1.7745 (−53.16 *)	−1.4750 (−143.59 *)	−1.6261 (−113.69 *)
Y_{k-2}	−1.1262 (−37.38 *)	−0.3614 (−50.67 *)	−0.3247 (−52.35 *)	−0.2554 (−18.92 *)	−0.9070 (−21.15 *)	−0.7413 (−72.42 *)	−0.8578 (−62.50 *)
Y_{k-3}	−0.5905 (−19.79 *)	−0.1142 (−16.65 *)	−0.1153 (−19.56 *)	−0.1405 (−10.50 *)	−0.4252 (−12.21 *)	−0.3533 (−33.69 *)	−0.4137 (−30.20 *)
TI	0.9572 (67.69 *)	1.2730 (285.32*)	−0.2832 (−88.07 *)	−0.1256 (−8.95 *)	−1.2319 (−38.61 *)	0.8899 (165.00 *)	0.9831 (146.16 *)
$Sprd$	0.0479 (3.16 *)	0.0342 (6.71 *)	0.0078 (2.60 *)	0.0117 (1.85 **)	0.0703 (1.21)	0.0238 (0.95)	0.0261 (4.83 *)
$LVol$	0.0047 (1.16)	0.0090 (6.13 *)	0.0050 (3.67 *)	0.0167 (4.92 *)	0.0118 (3.04 *)	0.0060 (3.03 *)	0.0043 (1.85 **)
$LBAV$	0.0801 (12.36 *)	0.1019 (48.39 *)	0.0337 (20.31 *)	−0.0312 (−6.94 *)	−0.0515 (−4.76 *)	0.0398 (15.25 *)	0.0607 (19.05 *)
$LBBV$	−0.0760 (−12.03 *)	−0.1097 (−53.04 *)	−0.0397 (−23.81 *)	0.0252 (5.66 *)	0.0425 (3.32 *)	−0.0575 (−21.15 *)	−0.0744 (−21.51 *)
TIB	0.0488 (2.52 *)	0.0647 (9.70 *)	0.0929 (15.89 *)	0.0457 (3.04 *)	0.1916 (9.47 *)	0.0986 (11.50 *)	0.0696 (6.77 *)
$TI * \psi$	−0.2246 (−31.79 *)	−0.3764 (−119.95 *)	0.7304 (203.38 *)	0.0353 (4.24 *)	−0.0546 (−3.91 *)	−0.2506 (−62.24 *)	−0.2631 (−56.41 *)
$TI * \epsilon$	−0.0535 (−11.51 *)	−0.0608 (−37.49 *)	0.0706 (55.74 *)	0.0013 (0.40)	−0.0213 (−4.01 *)	−0.0314 (−14.58 *)	−0.0328 (−12.73 *)
$RIndx$	262.0988 (3.30 *)	110.1514 (2.47 *)	194.2312 (3.71 *)	307.72 (7.49 *)	−107.5324 (−0.87)	342.8466 (6.52 *)	139.1455 (2.72 *)
α_1	−2.8628	−2.1469	−1.6552	−1.5723	−4.5651	−2.3399	−2.4639
α_2	2.9999	2.1869	1.6699	1.7676	5.1375	2.2403	2.3768
$Pseudo - R^2$	0.3203	0.3339	0.2226	0.2068	0.3223	0.2589	0.2833

* Significant at 95% level. ** Significant at 90% level.

In parameterising the conditional variance, an ARMA specification was used following YP. Therefore, a GARCH (p, q) specification including up to two lags was used on the residual series of the ordered probit model across all stocks. The orders p, q were selected on the basis of Akaike information criterion (AIC). The selected parameter estimates of the fitted GARCH models are reported in Table 4. Only some of the parameters appear to be significant with less persistence in conditional volatility for some stocks.

Table 4. Coefficient estimates of GARCH parameters of the conditional variance of the residuals for all stocks. ω, constant; κ, GARCH parameters; δ, ARCH parameters

Parameter	AGL	BHP	CBA	NCP	TLS	WES	WPL
Obs.	*114,318*	*316,547*	*317,761*	*41,085*	*137,323*	*260,954*	*205,651*
ω	0.4081 (0.3419)	0.0468 (0.5782)	0.0022 (0.4748)	0.0598 (0.3415)	0.0204 (0.1226)	0.3242 (0.5995)	0.3282 (0.4998)
κ_1	0.3194 (0.2182)	0.3803 (0.3205)	0.9723 (46.8638)	0.8255 (2.4207)	0.9175 (2.9561)	0.2445 (0.2668)	0.2406 (0.2209)
κ_2		0.5157 (0.4516)				0.2045 (0.2272)	0.2172 (0.2019)
δ_1	0.2523 (0.6870)	0.0429 (0.9682)	0.0244 (1.4103)	0.0873 (0.6766)	0.0615 (0.0.2994)	0.1735 (1.3347)	0.1660 (1.1188)

4.2. Price Impact of a Trade

Price impact measures the effect of a current trade of a given volume on the conditional distribution of the subsequent price movement. In order to derive this, $X_k\beta$ has to be conditioned on trade size and other relevant explanatory variables. The volumes, durations and the spread were kept at their median values while the index was fixed at 0.001 whereas trade indicator and trade imbalance were kept at zero to minimise any bias. It is observed that the coefficients of the three lags of Y_k are not identical, implying path dependence of the conditional distribution of price changes (Hausman et al. 1972). Consequently, the conditioning has to be based on a particular sequence of price changes as well, as a change in the order will affect the final result. These conditioning values of X_k's specify the market conditions under which the price impact is to be evaluated.

The conditional probabilities were estimated under five scenarios of path dependence keeping the other quantities at the specified values. These are falling prices $(-1/-1/-1)$, rising prices $(1/1/1)$, constant prices $(0/0/0)$ and alternative price changes, $(-1/+1/-1)$ and $(+1/-1/+1)$. Figures 5 and 6 exhibit the plots of estimated probabilities under the first three scenarios for all the seven stocks. The shifts in the distribution are clearly evident for the first two cases as against the third case of constant prices. Under the falling price scenario, the shift is more towards the right while for the rising price scenario, it is more towards the left indicating an increased chance of price reversal after three consecutive rises or falls. In the case of alternating prices it was revealed that prices tend to remain stable in the subsequent trade.

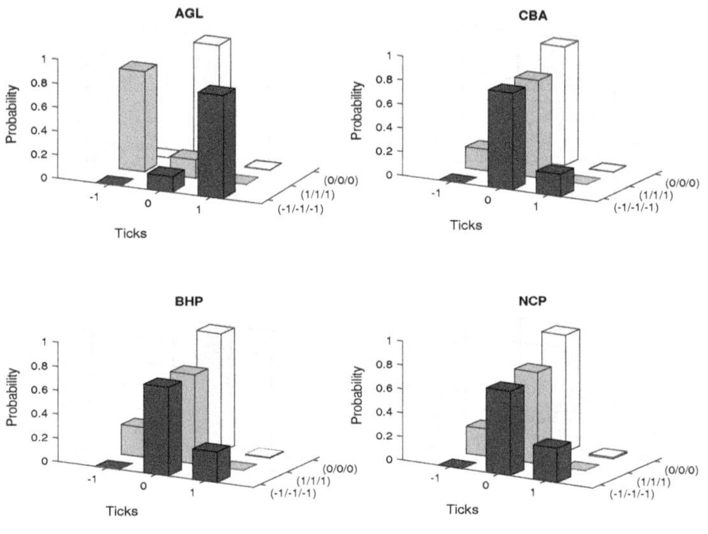

Figure 5. Distribution of estimated probabilities of direction of price change conditioned on constant, increasing and decreasing past price changes.

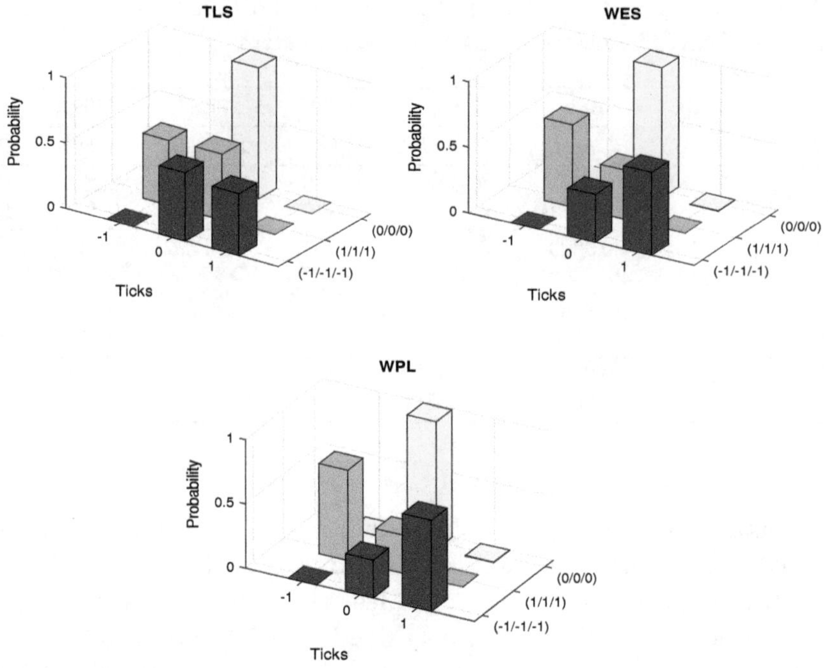

Figure 6. Distribution of estimated probabilities of direction of price change conditioned on constant, increasing and decreasing past price changes.

4.3. Diagnostics

A well specified ordinary least squares (OLS) regression would exhibit little serial correlation in the residuals. A similar kind of test could be performed on the generalised residuals in the case of ordered probit to test its validity, as it is not possible to obtain residuals directly (Hausman et al. 1972). Table 5 contains the sample cross-correlation coefficients of generalised residuals with the lagged generalised fitted values, $\hat{Y}_{k-j}$, computed up to 12 lags. Under the null hypothesis of no serial correlation, the theoretical cross-correlation coefficients should be zero or close to zero. The reported values are quite small, varying in the range from -0.01 to 6.19×10^{-6}.

Table 5. Cross-autocorrelation coefficents $\hat{\vartheta}_j, j = 1, \ldots, 12$ of generalised residuals with lagged generalised fitted price changes.

Parameter	AGL	BHP	CBA	NCP	TLS	WES	WPL
$\hat{\vartheta}_1$	−0.0025	−0.0002	−0.0015	−0.0004	0.0004	−0.0015	−0.0004
$\hat{\vartheta}_2$	−0.0057	0.0012	−0.0015	−0.0002	−0.0012	−0.0003	0.0009
$\hat{\vartheta}_3$	−0.0103	−0.0005	−0.0016	0.0008	−0.0008	0.0010	0.0015
$\hat{\vartheta}_4$	−0.0058	6.19×10^{-6}	−0.0018	−0.0029	−0.0028	−0.0004	0.0013
$\hat{\vartheta}_5$	−0.0045	0.0006	−0.0018	−0.0022	−0.0039	0.0005	−0.0017
$\hat{\vartheta}_6$	−0.0056	−0.0001	−0.0020	−0.0025	0.0016	0.0031	0.0018
$\hat{\vartheta}_7$	0.0009	−0.0008	−0.0018	0.0002	−0.0015	0.0034	0.0001
$\hat{\vartheta}_8$	0.0029	0.0001	−0.0017	0.0043	−0.0039	0.0010	0.0003
$\hat{\vartheta}_9$	0.0001	-7.76×10^{-5}	−0.0017	0.0057	−0.0023	0.0036	−0.0023
$\hat{\vartheta}_{10}$	0.0047	0.0003	−0.0015	0.0039	−0.0021	0.0030	0.0042
$\hat{\vartheta}_{11}$	0.0076	0.0020	−0.0013	0.0025	−0.0033	0.0009	0.0017
$\hat{\vartheta}_{12}$	0.0011	0.0014	−0.0011	0.0014	−0.0041	0.0024	−0.0002

5. Forecasting the Direction of Price Change

The forecasting performance of the ordered probit model fitted to the stocks is investigated. The tests of in-sample and out of-sample forecasts provide some basis to gauge the model's ability to accurately forecast the future direction of price changes. Forecasts are generated under three scenarios. In-sample probability estimates are based on the last week of the training sample from 8 April to 14 April 2014. Meanwhile, out-of-sample forecasts are based on the final day of the data series, 15 April.

Only one day is considered for the out-of-sample performance as it is not feasible to project price changes beyond one day with any degree of accuracy as a normal trading day contains more than 1000 transactions for all the stocks, with the exception of NCP which had only 417. Out-of-sample forecasts are computed in two ways. One is one-step ahead forecasts based on the observed, recorded values of the regressors and the other is the multi-step ahead, using their predicted values. The next subsection discusses the forecast generation under the second scenario in more detail. The commonly observed measures of forecast performance are not so relevant in this case, since the dependent variable is categorical. However, some measures such as root mean square error (RMSE) and mean absolute deviation (MAD) were calculated for both in-sample and out-of-sample forecasts, though they are not reported here for the sake of brevity.

5.1. Out-of-Sample Multi-Step Ahead Forecasts with Disaggregated Predictions of Individual Explanatory Variables

In real life, the values of the regressors are not observed priori, to forecast at least a few transactions ahead. Unlike in YP's study this paper develops out-of-sample multi-step ahead forecasts based on disaggregated predictions of the regressors. Under this scenario, multi-step ahead forecasts are generated for the entire forecast horizon, based on the estimated models, as well as 100-step ahead rolling basis. The rolling forecasts of price change are based on similar forecasts of explanatory variables. Towards this end, we first predict the future values of the regressors based on models that are fitted to capture the autoregressive behaviour of each variable in the sample. Under this setup, forecasts of price change are derived for the estimated transactions occurring on the last day of the series, 15 April 2014. The relevant models are fitted after a careful inspection of the autocorrelation function (acf) and the partial autocorrelation function (pacf) of the individual series, as discussed in Section 2. The model selection among several competing models is based on the AIC for a given regressor. In most instances, the time series of $LVol$ shows a hyperbolic decay in their acfs and pacfs, similar to Figure 1. Therefore, an ARFIMA type model is the preferred choice for $LVol$. The fractional differencing parameter, d is always within the range of 0 to 0.5, indicating the presence of long memory. On the other hand, most other variables such as $LBBV$, $LBAV$, TIB and $Sprd$ have slow decaying autocorrelations and partial autocorrelations, with the majority falling short of a hyperbola. Figure 2 gives a general perception on the behaviour observed in these variables. For these regressors, an ARMA type model suffices for most stocks, in general. Forecasts of trade indicator are based on a multinomial logistic regression on $LBAV$, $LBBV$, lags of Y and lags of TI, as the common contenders for the explanatory variables. Parameter estimates of predictive models for selected variables are illustrated in Tables 6 and 7 for the stock, AGL. The expected and unexpected durations are forecasted by the estimated ACD model.

Table 6. Coefficient estimates of autoregressive model parameters fitted to selected independent variables. The t statistics are given within parentheses. Illustrative examples include a long memory and a short memory model for $LVol$ and $Sprd$ for the stock AGL. d, long memory parameter; ϕ, AR parameters; θ, MA parameters.

Parameter	LVol	Spread
	(ARFIMA)	(ARMA)
c		0.0030 (7.30)
d	0.1867 (68.50)	
ϕ_1	0.0082 (15.72)	1.7555 (160.732)
ϕ_2		−0.7581 (−71.06)
θ_1	−0.0079 (−35.59)	−1.3455 (−123.55)
θ_2		0.2774 (41.16)
θ_3		0.0621 (15.35)
θ_4		0.0136 (3.67)
θ_5		0.0052 (1.80)

Table 7. Coefficient estimates of multinomial logistic regression model parameters fitted to Trade indicator (TI) of AGL. The base category is 1. Z statistics are given in parentheses.

Independent Variable	Category −1	Category 0
c	0.1449 (2.63)	−1.9155 (−26.87)
dp_{k-1}	0.2095 (5.08)	0.1128 (1.98)
$lbbv_{k-1}$	−0.3146 (−60.57)	−0.0746 (−10.41)
$lbav_{k-1}$	0.3001 (60.42)	0.2302 (35.96)
TI_{k-1}	−0.9664 (−119.26)	−0.4632 (−42.96)

5.2. *Forecast Performance of the Ordered Probit Model*

The basic test of forecast errors is mainly based on the number of correct forecasts as a percentage of total forecasts. The fitted directions of price change, $\hat{Y}_k$, based on the estimated coefficients are compared with their actual counterparts for each transaction in the forecasting sample. The number of exact tallies provide the number of correct forecasts. The in-sample forecast results illustrated in Table 8 reports a 91% accuracy, which is a very high percentage, by any means, vouching for the significant forecasting ability of the model. In comparison, YP achieved a percentage of 72. On the other hand, out-of sample results are provided in Table 9. For one-step ahead forecasts based on observed regressor values, the direction could be accurately predicted 88 per cent of the time, on average, across all stocks. The percentage achieved by YP again is 72 per cent. Meanwhile, the performance of the multi-step ahead forecasts based on the fitted regressor values is not as striking as in the other two cases, as expected. Notwithstanding, percentages of 78 and 85, on average, are highly noteworthy and are still higher than the 72 per cent of YP. The comparatively dismal performance of TLS under the first scenario given in panel 2 (a) of Table 9 may have been influenced by a relatively small number of price changes recorded during the period. However, the rolling forecasts show a remarkable improvement. The ex-post forecast of this stock is slightly better than the ex-ante forecast, which is quite contrary to the other stocks. The reverse is observed for five of the other stocks, as anticipated, while for one stock, it is similar.

The predictions of regressors based on serial correlation structures do not provide very good long term multi-step ahead forecasts, due to mean reversion. As a result of this, the forecasts of price change direction, based on those fitted values may also not provide reliable long term forecasts. A single day is referred to as longterm as the average daily transactions exceed 1000 for most stocks in the sample. Therefore, under these circumstances, the forecast horizon is restricted to the 100 transactions of the last day on a rolling basis, which resulted in a much better accuracy percentage of 85, in comparison to the one incorporating all the transactions of that day. It is worthwhile mentioning that from an individual stock's perspective, the short term performance is better than the long term. The worst case scenario gives around 75 per cent of out-of-sample correct forecasts, whereas it is around 85 per cent for the in-sample predictions.

Based on predicted price movements, investors can adjust their trading positions accordingly in formulating trading strategies, risk management, portfolio allocations etc. However, the most risky position under these forecast scenarios would be the adverse selection (see Yang and Parwada 2012, for more details). It is where the actual occurrence is the opposite of the predicted price movement, with possible adverse effects on the investor's networth. Therefore, it is worthwhile examining the extent of the possibility of this risk of adverse selection taking place. The percentages of predictions in the opposite direction for actual rise/fall are given in Tables 8 and 9 for in-sample predictions and out-of-sample forecasts respectively. Generally, this risk is very small and not more than 1 per cent across all stocks, except TLS, under all the forecast scenarios. In the case of out-of-sample forecasts, TLS records a 50 per cent risk of adverse selection, mainly as a result of only two recorded price falls in the forecast sample. Furthermore, altogether there are only three rises/falls in the price, giving rise to zero correct classifications for those categories for TLS.

The predicted conditional probabilities of the three categories of forecast price change $\hat{Y}_k$, -1, 0 and 1 are generated under the ordered probit system for in-sample as well as out-of-sample forecasts. $\hat{Y}_k$ is assigned the value of the category with the highest probability for a given transaction. These probabilities obtained for the stock, CBA, are illustrated for 100 observations during the forecast period, in Figures 7 and 8 to represent all the stocks, which show similar behaviour. For a given observation, the vertical sum of the three conditional probabilities is one. In the case of both in-sample and out-of-sample scenarios, the probabilities tend to fluctuate. However, for the majority of observations, no price change category tends to have a probability greater than 50 per cent, in general, resulting in lower percentages of correct classifications for rises and falls in prices. This does not indicate a deviation from the real life behavior in prices, with respect to the overall distribution across the three categories. Nevertheless, this phenomenon highlights a slight over prediction in that category. A similar pattern of behaviour is observed for the forecasts with predicted regressors as well.

As discussed earlier, most of the trades do not witness heavy movements in prices. Nevertheless, if a rise/fall in price could be foreseen in advance, investors are in a better position to create profitable strategies or to manage risk appropriately. Since multi-step ahead predictions of opposite price movements are rare, a forecast rise/fall would provide useful signals of future price directions. This, when combined with the knowledge of past price paths, will aid the investor in making a more informed decision in strategy formulation in his favour, especially towards minimising risk. However, improving the individual forecasts of the explanatory variables will be beneficial in realising better predictions of future price movements under this framework.

Table 8. In-sample predictions of direction of price change for the last one week period of the training sample from 8 April 2014 to 14 April 2014.

Parameter		AGL	BHP	CBA	NCP	TLS	WES	WPL
One Week—08/04–14/04								
Observations		114,318	316,547	317,761	41,085	137,323	260,954	205,651
accuracy(%)		97.80	86.20	85.11	85.24	98.75	92.19	94.76
−1		40.00	23.79	36.03	25.48	39.29	27.11	38.45
0		99.79	98.67	98.14	98.64	99.65	99.51	99.78
+1		45.40	24.29	35.73	32.01	36.00	33.57	37.09
Actual	Forecast	No. %	No. %	No. %	No. %	No. %	No. %	No. %
−1	+1	0 0	1 0.05	6 0.32	1 0.42	0 0	0 0	0 0
+1	−1	0 0	0 0	3 0.17	0 0	0 0	0 0	0 0

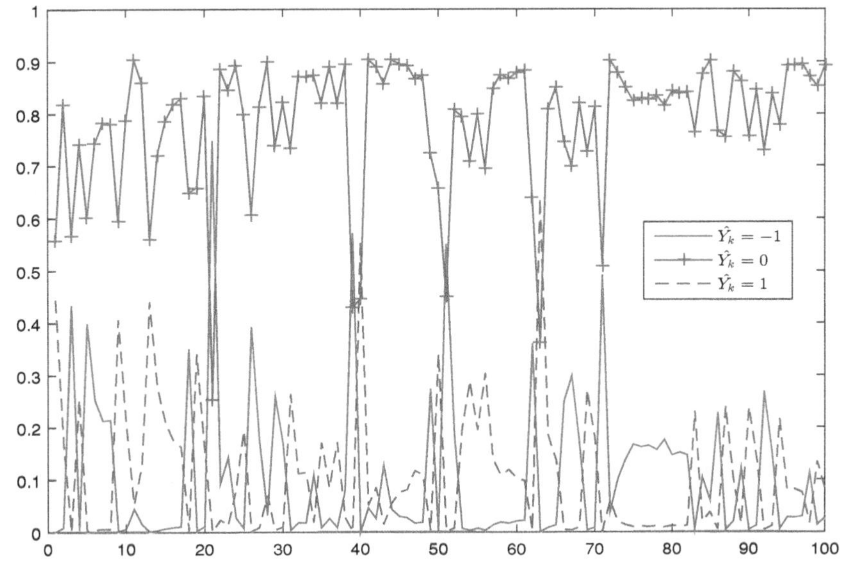

Figure 7. In-sample estimated probabilities of direction of price change for 100 observations of CBA.

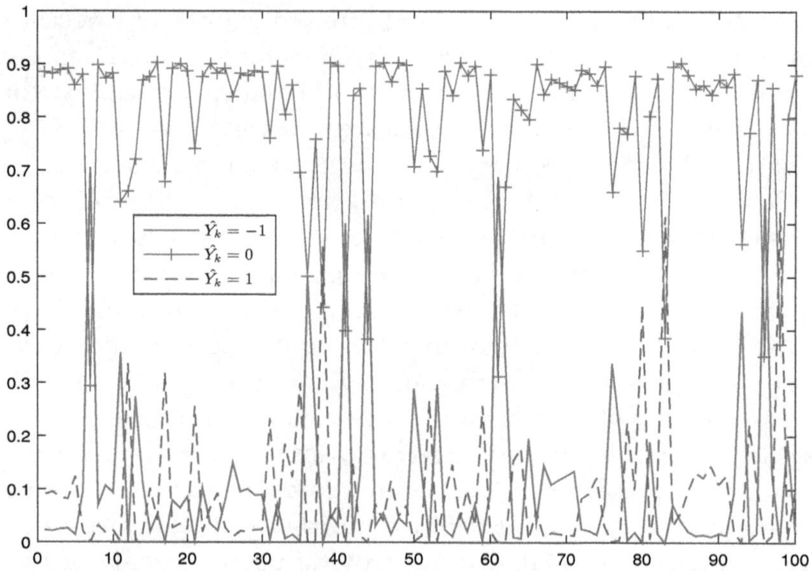

Figure 8. Out of-sample estimated probabilities of direction of price change for 100 observations of CBA, based on actual regressor values.

Table 9. Out-of sample forecasts of direction of price change for the last day of the sample, 15 April 2014. First panel contains one-step ahead forecasts based on actual explanatory variables and the second panel, muti-step ahead with predicted variables.

Parameter		AGL	BHP	CBA	NCP	TLS	WES	WPL
One-Step Ahead—15/04								
Observations		1151	3319	4073	417	1218	2518	3638
accuracy (%)		97.83	85.90	79.65	75.30	99.67	88.28	91.70
−1		35.29	27.40	26.80	21.54	0.00	32.54	32.77
0		99.73	98.47	97.31	96.82	99.92	98.95	99.47
+1		38.89	23.84	26.88	37.68	0.00	38.03	35.53
Actual	Forecast	No. %	No. %	No. %	No. %	No. %	No. %	No. %
−1	+1	0 0	0 0	6 1.2	0 0	0 0	2 1.2	0 0
+1	−1	0 0	0 0	1 0.2	0 0	0 0	0 0	0 0
Multi-Step Ahead—15/04								
(a) All transactions								
Observations		1151	3319	4073	417	1218	2518	3638
accuracy (%)		97.74	82.74	74.93	67.87	47.46	87.41	90.07
(b) 100-step ahead								
accuracy (%)		97.48	83.25	80.55	74.82	79.97	89.87	92.25
−1		30.77	25.34	21.94	20.00	0.00	23.78	20.43
0		98.93	94.94	99.87	100.00	80.16	99.14	99.88
+1		38.46	29.18	23.72	23.19	0.00	27.45	25.71
Actual	Forecast	No. %	No. %	No. %	No. %	No. %	No. %	No. %
−1	+1	0 0	2 0.68	3 0.58	0 0	1 50	0 0	0 0
+1	−1	0 0	0 0	0 0	0 0	0 0	0 0	0 0

6. Conclusions

The future direction of stock price movements are predicted through the estimation of an ordered probit model under an empirical setup. The study comprises of intra-day transaction data of seven stocks representing seven industry sectors, listed on the ASX. The ordered probit specification seems to adequately capture the price changes. All the explanatory variables are highly significant for the majority of the stocks. Diagnostics indicate lack of serial correlation in residuals with the implication of the model providing a good fit. The sequence of trades has an impact on the conditional distribution of price changes, while the trade size too is important with larger volumes putting more pressure on prices.

In improving forecast accuracy of the model, our study differs from that of YP in certain respects. Percentage of success in predicting future direction of price movements is used as a yardstick to measure the forecasting strength of the model. The success rate of the in-sample predictions is around 91 per cent and out-of sample one-step ahead forecasts happens to be 88 per cent. These percentages are much higher than the respective percentage of 72 per cent achieved by YP, for both cases. Overall, our forecasts outperform those of YP for each common stock.

Another main contribution of this study is to forecast price changes within a more practical perspective. In real life, the values of the regressors are not known a-priori to forecast at least a few transactions ahead. In addressing this drawback, we first predict the future values of the regressors based on their serial correlation structures by way of appropriate models. This resulted in several Autoregressive Moving Average (ARMA) and Autoregressive Fractionally Integrated Moving Average (ARFIMA) type models. In a subsequent step, these disaggregated forecasts are incorporated into the ordered probit model to generate future price change forecasts. Obviously, the 100-steps ahead short term forecasts perform better than the longterm ones including all transactions in the forecast horizon for most stocks. On average, the successful percentage in the long term is still a reasonable 78 per cent, which is affected by a poorly performing stock. On the other hand, the average success rate in the short term is around 85 per cent, which is quite remarkable.

Given the considerably high percentage of constant prices in real life, the model captures this phenomenon, albeit with a slight bias towards predicting no change. However, the risk of adverse selection is minimised. Nevertheless, this predictive model is useful for investors in developing successful trading strategies, particularly towards minimising risk as this provides valuable signals towards the future directions of price movements. The usefulness of this model to growth driven investors could be enhanced by improving the forecasting accuracy of the independent variables by adopting more sophisticated econometric techniques within a unified framework. In addition, the investigation of the adequacy of the conditional variance specification may also prove useful in improving the forecast probabilities.

Author Contributions: R.Y., R.G., S.P. and D.E.A. conceived and designed the experiments. R.Y. performed the experiments and analysed the data. R.Y., R.G., S.P. and D.E.A. wrote the paper.

Acknowledgments: The authors thank the reviewers for helpful comments.

Appendix A. Models for Errors and Explanatory Variables

Appendix A.1. ACD Specification to Model Transaction Durations

The Autoregressive Conditional Duration (ACD) model analyses transaction duration, identifying it as a conditional point process.The temporal dependence of the diurnally adjusted duration process is captured by the conditional expected duration, $\psi_k = E(x_k|x_{k-1}, \ldots, x_1)$, under a linear ACD$(p, q)$ specification and has the following form:

$$\psi_k = \alpha_0 + \sum_{i=1}^{p} \alpha_i x_{k-i} + \sum_{j=1}^{q} \beta_j \psi_{k-j}, \tag{A1}$$

where $p \geq 0$; $q \geq 0$. The standardized durations

$$\epsilon_k = \frac{x_k}{\psi_k}$$

are i.i.d. with $E(\epsilon_i) = 1$. The log likelihood function for the Std. Weibull errors, is

$$L(x|\theta) = \sum_{k=2}^{T} \alpha \ln \left[\Gamma\left(1 + \frac{1}{\alpha}\right)\right] + \ln\left(\frac{\alpha}{x_k}\right) + \alpha \ln\left(\frac{x_k}{\psi_k}\right) - \left[\Gamma\left(1 + \frac{1}{\alpha}\right)\frac{x_k}{\psi_k}\right]^{\alpha}, \tag{A2}$$

where α is the shape parameter of the density.

Appendix A.2. GARCH Specification to Model Heteroscedasticity

Conditional variance in the residuals (ε_k) of the orderd probit model, σ_k^2 can be estimated from this model.

$$\varepsilon_k = \sigma_k \eta_k, \quad \varepsilon_k | X_k \sim (o, \sigma_k^2)$$

where σ_k^2 is the conditional volatility of ε_k given the past historical information, η_k is a sequence of independently and identically distributed (i.i.d.) random variables with zero mean and variance 1 such that

$$\sigma_k^2 = \omega + \sum_{i=1}^{p'} \kappa_i \sigma_{k-i}^2 + \sum_{j=1}^{q'} \delta_j \varepsilon_{k-j}^2.$$

Appendix A.3. ARIMA Model

A series $\{X_k\}$ that could be modeled as a stationary ARMA(p'', q'') process after being differenced d times is denoted as ARIMA(p'', d, q'') with the following form:

$$\phi(B)(1-B)^d X_k = c + \theta(B) a_k, \tag{A3}$$

where $\phi(B) = 1 - \phi_1 - \ldots - \phi_p, \theta(B) = 1 + \theta_1 + \ldots + \theta_q$ and $a_k \sim WN(0, \sigma_a^2)$ and B is the backshift operator.

Appendix A.4. Long Memory ARFIMA Model

ARFIMA is designed to capture the long range dependence in time series. This model extends the ARIMA model in (A3) allowing d to lie between -0.5 and + 0.5 yielding a fractionally integrated series. ARFIMA process is said to exhibit stationary long memory if $d \in (0, 0.5)$. See Granger and Joyeux (1980) for details.

An ARFIMA(p'', d, q'') process has the same form as in (A3) and the operator $(1-B)^d$ is given by

$$(1-B)^d = \sum_{k=0}^{\infty} \frac{\Gamma(k-d)B^k}{\Gamma(-d)\Gamma(k+1)}; \quad d \notin \{1, 2, \ldots\}$$

Appendix A.5. Multinomial Logistic Regression

Multinomial logistic regression is an extension of binary logistic regression, that handles polytomous responses. This is used to predict the response category or the probability of category membership of a nominal outcome variable. The log odds of the outcome are modeled as a linear combination of multiple explanatory variables.

If $x_k = (x_{k1}, x_{k2}, \ldots, x_{kr})'$ follows a multinomial distribution with r response categories and parameter $\pi_k = (\pi_{k1}, \pi_{k2}, \ldots, \pi_{kr})'$, then

$$log\left(\frac{\pi_{kj}}{\pi_{kj}^*}\right) = y_k^T \beta_j', j \neq j^*$$

considering j^* as the baseline category. Assuming that mth category is the baseline category ($j^* = m$), the coefficient vector is

$$\beta' = (\beta_1', \beta_2', \ldots, \beta_{m-1}', \beta_{m+1}', \ldots, \beta_r')$$

References

Aitchison, John, and Samuel D. Silvey. 1957. The generalization of probit analysis to the case of multiple responses. *Biometrika* 44: 131–40. [CrossRef]

Amihud, Yakov, and Haim Mendelson. 1987. Trading mechanisms and stock returns: An empirical investigation. *The Journal of Finance* 42: 533–53. [CrossRef]

Ball, Clifford A. 1988. Estimation bias induced by discrete security prices. *The Journal of Finance* 43: 841–65. [CrossRef]

Barndorff-Nielsen, Ole E., P. Reinhard Hansen, Asger Lunde, and Neil Shephard. 2009. Realized kernels in practice: Trades and quotes. *The Econometrics Journal* 12: C1–32. [CrossRef]

Berndt, Ernst R., Bronwyn H. Hall, Robert E. Hall, and Jerry A. Hausman. 1974. Estimation and inference in nonlinear structural models. *Annals of Economic and Social Measurement* 3: 653–65.

Bollerslev, Tim. 1986. Generalized autoregressive conditional heteroskedasticity. *Journal of Econometrics* 31: 307–27. [CrossRef]

Breen, William, Lawrence R. Glosten, and Ravi Jagannathan. 1989. Economic significance of predictable variations in stock index returns. *Journal of Finance* 44: 1177–89. [CrossRef]

Brownlees, Christian T., and Giampiero M. Gallo. 2006. Financial econometric analysis at ultra-high frequency: Data handling concerns. *Computational Statistics & Data Analysis* 51: 2232–45.

Cheung, Yin-Wong, Menzie D. Chinn, and Antonio Garcia Pascual. 2005. Empirical exchange rate models of the nineties: Are any fit to survive? *Journal of International Money and Finance* 24: 1150–75. [CrossRef]

Christoffersen, Peter F., and Francis X. Diebold. 2006. Financial asset returns, direction-of-change forecasting, and volatility dynamics. *Management Science* 52: 1273–87. [CrossRef]

Dravid, Ajay R. 1991. *Effects of Bid-Ask Spreads and Price Discreteness on Stock Returns*. Technical Report. Philadelphia: Wharton School Rodney L. White Center for Financial Research.

Dufour, Alfonso, and Robert F. Engle. 2000. Time and the price impact of a trade. *Journal of Finance* 55: 2467–98. [CrossRef]

Engle, Robert F., and Jeffrey R. Russell. 1998. Autoregressive conditional duration: A new model for irregularly spaced transaction data. *Econometrica* 66: 1127–62. [CrossRef]

Falkenberry, Thomas N. 2002. *High Frequency Data Filtering*. Great Falls: Tick Data Inc.

Glosten, Lawrence R., and Lawrence E. Harris. 1988. Estimating the components of the bid/ask spread. *Journal of Financial Economics* 21: 123–42. [CrossRef]

Gottlieb, Gary, and Avner Kalay. 1985. Implications of the discreteness of observed stock prices. *The Journal of Finance* 40: 135–53. [CrossRef]

Granger, Clive W. J., and Roselyne Joyeux. 1980. An introduction to long-memory time series models and fractional differencing. *Journal of Time Series Analysis* 1: 15–29. [CrossRef]

Gurland, John, Ilbok Lee, and Paul A. Dahm. 1960. Polychotomous quantal response in biological assay. *Biometrics* 16: 382–98. [CrossRef]

Hansen, Peter R., and Asger Lunde. 2006. Realized variance and market microstructure noise. *Journal of Business & Economic Statistics* 24: 127–61.

Harris, Lawrence. 1990. Estimation of stock price variances and serial covariances from discrete observations. *Journal of Financial and Quantitative Analysis* 25: 291–306. [CrossRef]

Hasbrouck, Joel. 1999. The dynamics of discrete bid and ask quotes. *The Journal of Finance* 54: 2109–42. [CrossRef]

Hausman, Jerry A., Andrew W. Lo, and A. Craig MacKinlay. 1992. An ordered probit analysis of transaction stock prices. *Journal of Financial Economics* 31: 319–79. [CrossRef]

Kyle, Albert S. 1985. Continuous auctions and insider trading. *Econometrica: Journal of the Econometric Society* 53: 1315–35. [CrossRef]

Leung, Mark T., Hazem Daouk, and An-Sing Chen. 2000. Forecasting stock indices: A comparison of classification and level estimation models. *International Journal of Forecasting* 16: 173–90. [CrossRef]

Madhavan, Ananth. 2000. Market microstructure: A survey. *Journal of Financial Markets* 3: 205–58. [CrossRef]

McKelvey, Richard D., and William Zavoina. 1975. A statistical model for the analysis of ordinal level dependent variables. *Journal of Mathematical Sociology* 4: 103–20. [CrossRef]

Pesaran, M. Hashem, and Allan Timmermann. 2004. How costly is it to ignore breaks when forecasting the direction of a time series? *International Journal of Forecasting* 20: 411–25. [CrossRef]

Stoll, Hans R., and Robert E. Whaley. 1990. Stock market structure and volatility. *Review of Financial Studies* 3: 37–71. [CrossRef]

White, Halbert. 2000. A reality check for data snooping. *Econometrica* 68: 1097–126. [CrossRef]

Yang, Joey Wenling, and Jerry Parwada. 2012. Predicting stock price movements: An ordered probit analysis on the Australian Securities Exchange. *Quantitative Finance* 12: 791–804. [CrossRef]

7

Credit Risk Meets Random Matrices: Coping with Non-Stationary Asset Correlations

Andreas Mühlbacher * and Thomas Guhr

Fakultät für Physik, Universität Duisburg-Essen, Lotharstraße 1, 47048 Duisburg, Germany; thomas.guhr@uni-due.de

* Correspondence: andreas.muehlbacher@uni-due.de

Abstract: We review recent progress in modeling credit risk for correlated assets. We employ a new interpretation of the Wishart model for random correlation matrices to model non-stationary effects. We then use the Merton model in which default events and losses are derived from the asset values at maturity. To estimate the time development of the asset values, the stock prices are used, the correlations of which have a strong impact on the loss distribution, particularly on its tails. These correlations are non-stationary, which also influences the tails. We account for the asset fluctuations by averaging over an ensemble of random matrices that models the truly existing set of measured correlation matrices. As a most welcome side effect, this approach drastically reduces the parameter dependence of the loss distribution, allowing us to obtain very explicit results, which show quantitatively that the heavy tails prevail over diversification benefits even for small correlations. We calibrate our random matrix model with market data and show how it is capable of grasping different market situations. Furthermore, we present numerical simulations for concurrent portfolio risks, i.e., for the joint probability densities of losses for two portfolios. For the convenience of the reader, we give an introduction to the Wishart random matrix model.

Keywords: credit risk; financial markets; non-stationarity; random matrices; structural models; Wishart model

---

1. Introduction

To assess the impact of credit risk on the systemic stability of the financial markets and the economy as a whole is of considerable importance as the subprime crisis of 2007–2009 and the events following the collapse of Lehman Brothers drastically demonstrated (Hull 2009). Better credit risk estimation is urgently called for. A variety of different approaches exists, see (Bielecki and Rutkowski 2013; Bluhm et al. 2016; Crouhy et al. 2000; Duffie and Singleton 1999; Glasserman and Ruiz-Mata 2006; Heitfield et al. 2006; Ibragimov and Walden 2007; Lando 2009; Mainik and Embrechts 2013; McNeil et al. 2005) for an overview. Most of them fall into the reduced-form (Chava et al. 2011; Duffie and Singleton 1999; Schönbucher 2003) or structural-approach class (Elizalde 2005; Merton 1974); a comprehensive review is given in (Giesecke 2004). The problem to be addressed becomes ultimately a statistical one, as loss distributions for large portfolios of credit contracts have to be estimated. Typically, they have a very heavy right tail, which is due to either unusually large single events such as the Enron bankruptcy or the simultaneous occurrence of many small events as seen during the subprime crisis. Reducing this tail would increase the stability of the financial system as a whole. Unfortunately, the claim that diversification can lower the risk of a portfolio is questionable or even wrong, because often, the correlations between the asset values are ignored. They are very important in a portfolio of credit contracts, e.g., in the form of collateralized debt obligations (CDOs). In detailed studies, it was shown that the presence of even weak positive correlation diversification fails to reduce the portfolio risk (Glasserman 2004; Schönbucher 2001) for first passage models and for the Merton model (Koivusalo and Schäfer 2012; Schäfer et al. 2007; Schmitt et al. 2014).

Recently, progress has been made to analytically solve the Merton model (Merton 1974) in a most general setting of a correlated market and even in the realistic case of fluctuating correlations between the assets. The covariance and correlation matrix of asset values changes in time (Münnix et al. 2012; Sandoval and Franca 2012; Song et al. 2011; Zhang et al. 2011), exhibiting an important example of the non-stationarity, which is always present in financial markets. The approach we review here (Schmitt et al. 2013, 2014, 2015; Sicking et al. 2018) uses the fact that the set of different correlation matrices measured in a smaller time window that slides through a longer dataset can be modeled by an ensemble of random correlation matrices. The asset values are found to be distributed according to a correlation averaged multivariate distribution (Chetalova et al. 2015; Schmitt et al. 2013, 2014, 2015). This assumption is confirmed by detailed empirical studies. Applied to the Merton model, this ensemble approach drastically reduces, as a most welcome side effect, the number of relevant parameters. We are left with only two, an average correlation between asset values and a measure for the strength of the fluctuations. The special case of zero average correlation has been previously considered (Münnix et al. 2014). The limiting distribution for a portfolio containing an infinite number of assets is also given, providing a quantitative estimate for the limits of diversification benefits. We also report the results of Monte Carlo simulations for the general case of empirical correlation matrices that yield the value at risk (VaR) and expected tail loss (ETL).

Another important aspect is comprised of concurrent losses of different portfolios. Concurrent extreme losses might impact the solvencies of major market participants, considerably enlarging the systemic risks. From an investor's point of view, buying CDOs allows on to hold a "slice" of each contract within a given portfolio (Benmelech and Dlugosz 2009; Duffie and Garleanu 2001; Longstaff and Rajan 2008). Such an investor might be severely affected by significant concurrent credit portfolio losses. It is thus crucial to assess in which way and how strongly the losses of different portfolios are coupled. In the framework of the Merton model and the ensemble average, losses of two credit portfolios are studied, which are composed of statistically-dependent credit contracts. Since correlation coefficients only give full information in the case of Gaussian distributions, the statistical dependence of these portfolio losses is investigated by means of copulas (Nelsen 2007). The approach discussed here differs from the one given in (Li 2000), as Monte Carlo simulations of credit portfolio losses with empirical input from S&P 500 and Nikkei 225 are run and the resulting empirical copulas are analyzed in detail. There are many other aspects causing systemic risk such as fire sales spillover (Di Gangi et al. 2018).

We review our own work on how to take into account the non-stationarity of asset correlations into credit risk (Schmitt et al. 2013, 2014, 2015; Sicking et al. 2018). To make the paper self-contained, this review is preceded by a brief sketch of the Wishart model and a discussion of its re-interpretation to model non-stationary correlations.

This review paper is organized as follows: In Section 2, we introduce random matrix theory for non-stationary asset correlations, including a sketch of the Wishart model for readers not familiar with random matrices. This approach is used in Section 3 to account for fluctuating asset correlations in credit risk. In Section 4, concurrent credit portfolio losses are discussed. Conclusions are given in Section 5.

2. Random Matrix Theory for Non-Stationary Asset Correlations

We sketch the salient features of the Wishart model for correlation and covariance matrices in Section 2.1. In Section 2.2, we discuss a new interpretation of the Wishart model as a model to describe the non-stationarity of the correlations.

2.1. Wishart Model for Correlation and Covariance Matrices

Financial markets are highly correlated systems, and risk assessment always requires knowledge of correlations or, more generally, mutual dependencies. We begin with briefly summarizing some of the facts needed in the sequel. To be specific, we consider stock prices and returns, but correlations can be measured in the same way for all observables that are given as time series. We are interested in, say, K companies with stock prices $S_k(t)$, $k = 1, \ldots, K$ as functions of time t. The relative price changes over a fixed time interval Δt, i.e., the returns:

$$r_k(t) = \frac{S_k(t+\Delta t) - S_k(t)}{S_k(t)} \tag{1}$$

are well known to have distributions with heavy tails; the smaller the Δt, the heavier. The sampled Pearson correlation coefficients are defined as:

$$\begin{aligned} C_{kl} &= \langle M_k(t) M_l(t) \rangle_T \\ M_k(t) &= \frac{r_k(t) - \langle r_k(t) \rangle_T}{\sigma_k} \end{aligned} \tag{2}$$

between the two companies k and l in the time window of length T. The time series $M_k(t)$ are obtained from the return time series $r_k(t)$ by normalizing (in some communities referred to as standardizing) to zero mean and to unit variance, where the sample standard deviation σ_k is evaluated in the above-mentioned time window. We define the $K \times T$ rectangular data matrix M whose k-th row is the time series $M_k(t)$. The correlation matrix with entries C_{kl} is the given by:

$$C = \frac{1}{T} M M^{\dagger}, \tag{3}$$

where † indicates the transpose. By definition, C is real symmetric and has non-negative eigenvalues. We will also use the covariance matrix $\Sigma = \sigma C \sigma$ where the diagonal matrix σ contains the standard deviations $\sigma_k, k = 1, \ldots, K$. Setting $A = \sigma M$, we may write:

$$\Sigma = \frac{1}{T} A A^{\dagger} \tag{4}$$

for the covariance matrix. We have to keep in mind that correlations or covariances only fully grasp the mutual dependencies if the multivariate distributions are Gaussian, which is not the case for returns if Δt is too small. We come back to this point.

Correlation or covariance matrices can be measured for arbitrary systems in which the observables are time series. About ninety years ago, Wishart (Muirhead 2005; Wishart 1928) put forward a random matrix model to assess the statistical features of the correlation or covariance matrices by comparing to a Gaussian null hypothesis. Consider the K values $A_k(t)$, $k = 1, \ldots, K$ at a fixed time t, which form the K component data vector $A(t)A(t) = (A_1(t), \ldots, A_K(t))^{\dagger}$. Now, suppose that we draw the entries of this vector from a multivariate Gaussian distribution with some covariance matrix Σ_0, say, meaning that:

$$\widetilde{w}(A(t)|\Sigma_0) = \frac{1}{\det^{1/2}(2\pi\Sigma_0)} \exp\left(-\frac{1}{2} A^{\dagger}(t) \Sigma_0^{-1} A(t)\right) \tag{5}$$

is the probability density function. We now make the important assumptions that, first, the data vectors are statistically independent for different times t and, second, the distribution (5) has exactly the same form for all times $t = 1, \ldots, T$ with the same covariance matrix Σ_0. Put differently, we assume that the data are from a statistical viewpoint, Markovian and stationary in time. The probability density function for the entire model data matrix A is then simply the product:

$$\begin{aligned} w(A|\Sigma_0) &= \prod_{t=1}^{T} \widetilde{w}(A(t)|\Sigma_0) \\ &= \frac{1}{\det^{T/2}(2\pi\Sigma_0)} \exp\left(-\frac{1}{2}\mathrm{tr}A^\dagger\Sigma_0^{-1}A\right) . \end{aligned} \tag{6}$$

This is the celebrated Wishart distribution for the data matrix A, which predicts the statistical features of random covariance matrices. By construction, we find for the average of the model covariance matrix $AA^\dagger/T$:

$$\langle\frac{1}{T}AA^\dagger\rangle = \int d[A]w(A|\Sigma_0)\frac{1}{T}AA^\dagger = \Sigma_0 , \tag{7}$$

where the angular brackets indicate the average over the Wishart random matrix ensemble (6) and where $d[A]$ stands for the flat measure, i.e., for the product of the differentials of all independent variables:

$$d[A] = \prod_{k,t} dA_k(t) . \tag{8}$$

We notice that in the random matrix model, each $A_k(t)$ is one single random variable; both the index k and the argument t are discrete. Hence, the $dA_k(t)$ is not the differential of a function, rather it is simply the differential of the random variable $A_k(t)$. The Wishart ensemble is based on the assumptions of statistical independence for different times, stationarity and a multivariate Gaussian functional form. The covariance matrix Σ_0 is the input for the mean value of the Wishart ensemble about which the individual random covariance matrices fluctuate in a Gaussian fashion. The strength of the fluctuations is intimately connected with the length T of the model time series. Taking the formal limit $T \to \infty$ reduces the fluctuations to zero, and all random covariance matrices are fixed to Σ_0. It is worth mentioning that the Wishart model for random correlation matrices has the same form. If we replace A with M and Σ_0 with C_0, we find the Wishart distribution that yields the statistical properties of random correlation matrices.

The Wishart model serves as a benchmark and a standard tool in statistical inference (Muirhead 2005) by means of an ergodicity argument: the statistical properties of individual covariance or correlation matrices may be estimated by an ensemble of such matrices, provided their dimension K is large. Admittedly, this ergodicity argument does not necessarily imply that the probability density functions are multivariate Gaussians. Nevertheless, arguments similar to those that lead to the central limit theorem corroborate the Gaussian assumption, and empirically, it was seen to be justified in a huge variety of applications. A particularly interesting application of the Wishart model for correlations in the simplified form with $C_0 = 1_K$ was put forward by the Paris and Boston econophysics groups (Laloux et al. 1999; Plerou et al. 1999) who compared the eigenvalue distributions (marginal eigenvalue probability density functions) of empirical financial correlation matrices with the theoretical prediction. They found good agreement in the bulk of the distributions, which indicates a disturbing amount of noise-dressing in the data due to the relatively short lengths of the empirical time series with considerable consequences for portfolio optimization methods (Bouchaud and Potters 2003; Giada and Marsili 2002; Guhr and Kälber 2003; Pafka and Kondor 2004; Plerou et al. 2002; Tumminello et al. 2005).

2.2. New Interpretation and Application of the Wishart Model

Financial markets are well known to be non-stationary, i.e., the assumption of stationarity is only meaningful on short time scales and is bound to fail on longer ones. Non-stationary complex systems pose fundamental challenges (Bernaola-Galván et al. 2001; Gao 1999; Hegger et al. 2000;

Rieke et al. 2002) for empirical analysis and for mathematical modeling (Zia and Rikvold 2004; Zia and Schmittmann 2006). An example from finance is comprised of the strong fluctuations of the sample standard deviations σ_k, measured in different time windows of the same length T (Black 1976; Schwert 1989), as shown in Figure 1. Financial markets demonstrated their non-stationarity in a rather drastic way during the recent years of crisis. Here, we focus on the non-stationarity of the correlations. Their fluctuations in time occur, e.g., because the market expectations of the traders change, the business relations between the companies change, particularly in a state of crisis, and so on. To illustrate how strongly the $K \times K$ correlation matrix C as a whole changes in time, we show it for subsequent time windows in Figure 2. The dataset used here consists of $K = 306$ continuously-traded companies in the S&P 500 index between 1992 and 2012 (Yahoo n.d.). Each point represents a correlation coefficient between two companies. The darker the color, the larger the correlation. The companies are sorted according to industrial sectors. The inter-sector correlation is visible in the off-diagonal blocks, whereas the intra-sector correlation is visible in the blocks on the diagonal. For later discussion, we emphasize that the stripes in these correlation matrices indicate the structuring of the market in industrial sectors; see, e.g., (Münnix et al. 2012).

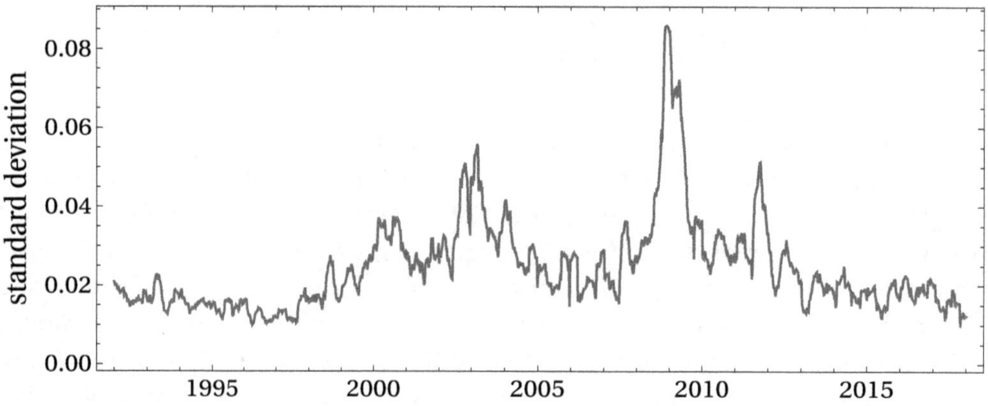

Figure 1. Standard deviation time series for Goodyear from 1992–2018. The return interval is $\Delta t = 1$ trading day, and the time window has a length of $T = 60$ trading days.

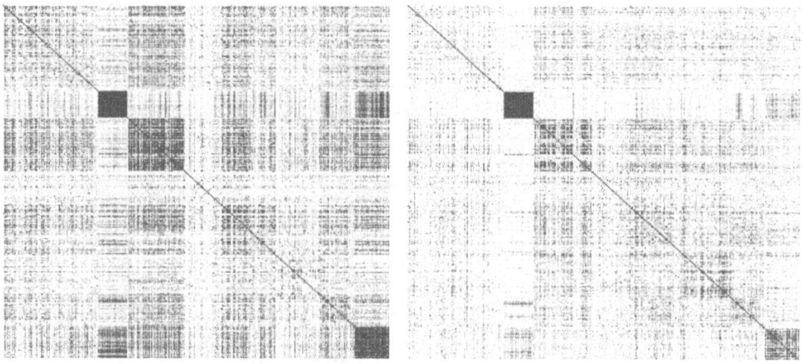

Figure 2. Correlation matrices of $K = 306$ companies for the fourth quarter of 2005 and the first quarter of 2006; the darker, the stronger the correlation. The companies are sorted according to industrial sectors. Reproduced with permission from (Schmitt et al. 2013), EPLA.

Clearly, the non-stationary fluctuations of the correlations influence all deduced economic observables, and it is quite plausible that this effect will be strong for the statistics of rare, correlated events. In the sequel, we will show that the tails of the loss distributions in credit risks will be particularly sensitive to the non-stationarity of the correlations. We will also extend the Merton model (Merton 1974) of credit risk to account for the non-stationarity. To this end, we will now put forward a re-interpretation of the Wishart random matrix model for correlation matrices (Schmitt et al. 2013). As mentioned in Section 2.1, the Wishart model in its original and widely-used form is based on the assumption of stationarity. Using ergodicity, it predicts statistical properties of large individual correlation and covariance matrices with the help of a fictitious ensemble of random matrices. Ergodicity means that averages of one single system over a very long time can be replaced by an average over an ensemble of matrices or other mathematical structures, which represent all possible systems of the same kind. We now argue that the Wishart model may be viewed as an ensemble of random matrices that models a truly existing ensemble of non-stationary covariance matrices. The elements of this ensemble model are in a statistical sense a set of covariance matrices, which result from a measurement. In the re-interpretation of the Wishart model the issue of ergodicity does not arise. Two elements in this latter ensemble are shown in Figure 2; the whole ensemble consists of all correlation matrices measured with a window of length T sliding through a set of much longer time series of length T_{tot}. The size of the truly existing ensemble is thus T_{tot}/T if the windows do not overlap. The average correlation or covariance matrices C_0 or Σ_0 are simply the sample averages over the whole time series of length T_{tot}. We have K time series divided into pieces of length T that yield the truly existing ensemble. To model it with an ensemble of random matrices, we have to employ data matrices A with K rows, representing the model time series, but we are free to choose their length N. As argued above, the length of the time series controls the strength of the fluctuations around the mean. Thus, we use $K \times N$ random data matrices A and write:

$$w(A|\Sigma_0) = \frac{1}{\det^{N/2}(2\pi\Sigma_0)} \exp\left(-\frac{1}{2}\text{tr}A^\dagger\Sigma_0^{-1}A\right) \tag{9}$$

for the probability density function. The $K \times K$ mean covariance matrix Σ_0 is the input and given by the sample mean using the whole time series of length T_{tot}. This is our re-interpreted Wishart model to describe fluctuating, non-stationary covariance or correlation matrices. Importantly, ergodicity reasoning is not evoked here, and it would actually be wrong. It is also worth mentioning that we are not restricted to large matrix dimensions.

Next, we demonstrate that the non-stationarity in the correlations induces generic, i.e., universal features in financial time series of correlated markets. We begin with showing that the returns are to a good approximation multivariate Gaussian distributed, if the covariance matrix Σ is fixed. We begin with assuming that the distribution of the K dimensional vectors $r(t) = (r_1(t), \ldots, r_K(t))$ for a fixed return interval Δt while t is running through the dataset is given by:

$$g(r|\Sigma) = \frac{1}{\sqrt{\det(2\pi\Sigma)}} \exp\left(-\frac{1}{2}r^\dagger\Sigma^{-1}r\right) , \tag{10}$$

where we suppress the argument t of r in our notation. We test this assumption with the daily S&P 500 data. We divide the time series in windows of length $T = 25$ trading days, which is short enough to ensure that the sampled covariances can be viewed as constant within these windows. We aggregate the data, i.e., we rotate the return vector into the eigenbasis of Σ and normalize with the corresponding eigenvalues. As seen in Figure 3, there is good agreement with a Gaussian over at least four orders of magnitude; details of the analysis can be found in (Schmitt et al. 2013). To account for the non-stationarity of the covariance matrices, we replace them with random matrices:

$$\Sigma \longrightarrow \frac{1}{N}AA^\dagger , \tag{11}$$

drawn form the distribution (9). We emphasize that the random matrices A have dimension $K \times N$. The larger the N, the more terms contribute to the individual matrix elements of $AA^\dagger/N$, eventually fixing them for $N \to \infty$ to the mean Σ_0. The fluctuating covariances alter the multivariate Gaussian (10). We model this by the ensemble averaged return distribution:

$$\langle g \rangle (r|\Sigma_0, N) = \int d[A] g\left(r \middle| \frac{1}{N} AA^\dagger\right) w(A|\Sigma_0) , \tag{12}$$

which parametrically depends on the fixed empirical covariance matrix Σ_0, as well as on N. The ensemble average can be done analytically (Schmitt et al. 2013) and results in:

$$\langle g \rangle (r|\Sigma_0, N) = \frac{1}{2^{N/2+1}\Gamma(N/2)\sqrt{\det(2\pi\Sigma_0/N)}} \frac{\mathcal{K}_{(K-N)/2}\left(\sqrt{Nr^\dagger\Sigma_0^{-1}r}\right)}{\sqrt{Nr^\dagger\Sigma_0^{-1}r}^{(K-N)/2}} , \tag{13}$$

where $\mathcal{K}_\nu$ is the modified Bessel function of the second kind of order ν. In the data analysis below, we will find $K > N$. Since the empirical covariance matrix Σ_0 is fixed, N is the only free parameter in the distribution (13). For large N, it approaches a Gaussian. The smaller N, the heavier the tails, for $N = 2$ the distribution is exponential. Importantly, the returns enter $\langle g \rangle (r|\Sigma_0, N)$ only via the bilinear form $r^\dagger\Sigma^{-1}r$.

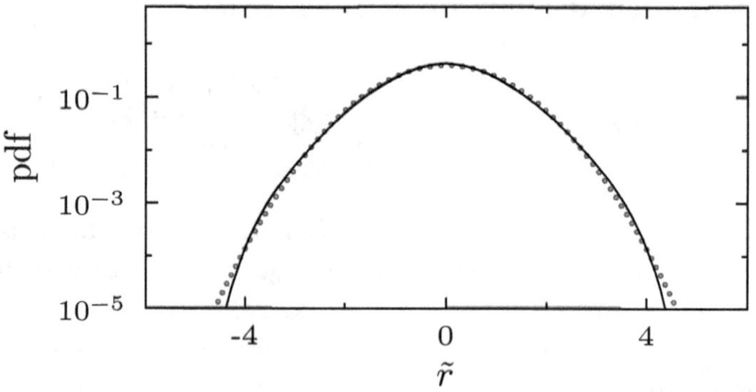

Figure 3. Aggregated distribution of normalized returns $\tilde{r}$ for fixed covariances from the S&P 500 dataset, $\Delta t = 1$ trading day and window length $T = 25$ trading days. The circles show a normal distribution. Reproduced with permission from (Schmitt et al. 2013), EPLA.

To test our model, we again have to aggregate the data, but now for the entire S&P 500 dataset from 1992–2012, i.e., $T_{\text{tot}} = 5275$ days; see Figure 4. We find $N = 5$ for daily returns, i.e., $\Delta t = 1$ trading day and $N = 14$ for $\Delta t = 20$ trading days. Furthermore, a more detailed comparison with larger datasets for monthly returns is provided in Figure 5. Here, stocks taken from the S&P 500 index and stocks taken from NASDAQ are used. In the top left corner, the dataset consists of 307 stocks taken from the S&P 500 index, which are continuously traded in the period 1992–2012. The other datasets following clockwise are: 439 stocks from S&P 500 index in the time period 2002–2012, 2667 stocks from NASDAQ in the time period 2002–2012 and 708 stocks from NASDAQ in the time period 1992–2012. We find values around $N = 20$ for monthly returns. Both datasets are available at (Yahoo n.d.). There is a good agreement between the model and data. Importantly, the distributions have heavy tails, which result from the fluctuations of the covariances; the smaller the N, the heavier. For small N, there are deviations between theory and data in the tails. Three remarks are in order. First, one should clearly distinguish this multivariate analysis from the stylized facts of individual stocks, which are well known to have heavy-tailed distributions. This is to some extent accounted for in our model, as seen in the bottom part of Figure 4. In the top part, the tails are heavier because the time interval Δt is much shorter. To further account for this, we need to modify the Wishart model by using a distribution different from a Gaussian one (Meudt et al. 2015). Second, Figure 2 clearly shows that the empirical ensemble of correlation matrices has inner structures, which are also contained in our model, because the mean Σ_0 enters. Third, an important issue for portfolio management is that the random matrix approach reduces the effect of fluctuating correlations to one single parameter characterizing its strength. Hence, the fluctuation strength of correlations in a given time interval can directly be estimated from the empirical return distribution without having to estimate the correlations on shorter time intervals (Chetalova et al. 2015).

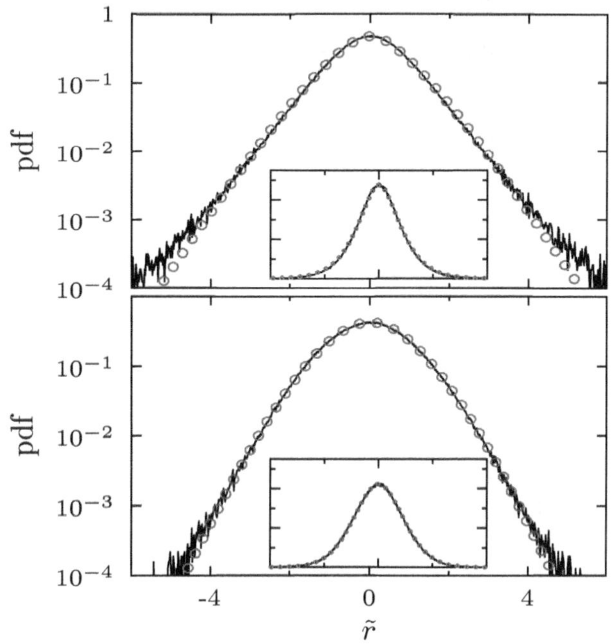

Figure 4. Aggregated distribution of the rotated and scaled returns $\tilde{r}$ for $\Delta t = 1$ (**top**) and $\Delta t = 20$ (**bottom**) trading days. The circles correspond to the aggregation of the distribution (13). Reproduced with permission from (Schmitt et al. 2013), EPLA.

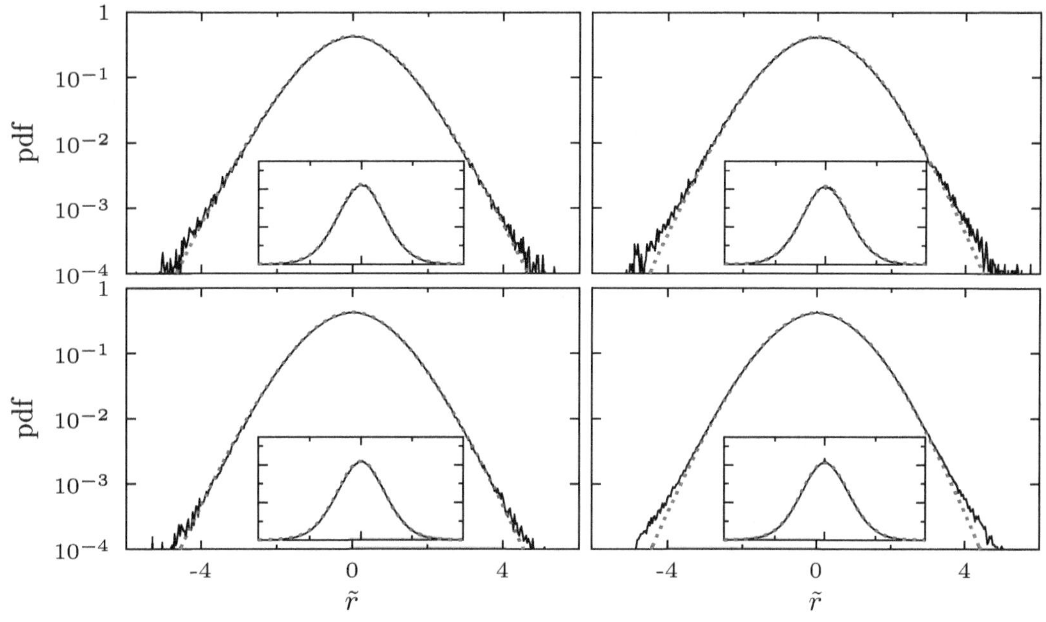

Figure 5. Aggregated distribution for the normalized monthly returns with the empirical covariance matrix on a logarithmic scale. The black line shows the empirical distribution; the red dotted line shows the theoretical results. The insets show the corresponding linear plots. **Top** left/right: S&P 500 (1992–2012)/(2002–2012); **bottom** left/right: NASDAQ (1992–2012)/(2002–2012). Reproduced with permission from (Schmitt et al. 2015), Infopro Digital.

In the mathematics and economics literature, dynamic models based on Wishart processes were introduced, involving multivariate stochastic volatilities (Gouriéroux and Sufana 2004; Gouriéroux et al. 2009). Various quantities such as leverage, risk premia, prices of options and Wishart autoregressive processes are calculated and discussed. These studies are related to ours, although our focus is not on the processes, rather on the resulting distributions, because we wish to directly model multivariate return distributions in a non-stationary setting.

3. Modeling Fluctuating Asset Correlations in Credit Risk

Structural credit risk models employ the asset value at maturity to derive default events and their ensuing losses. Thus, the distribution that describes the asset values has to be chosen carefully. One major requirement is that the distribution is in good accordance with empirical data. This goal can be achieved by using the random matrix approach for the asset correlations, discussed in Section 2. Based on (Schmitt et al. 2014, 2015), we discuss the Merton model together with the random matrix approach in Section 3.1. In Section 3.2, we reveal the results for the average loss distribution of a credit portfolio. The adjustability of the model is shown in Section 3.3. In Section 3.4, we discuss the impact of the random matrix approach on VaR and ETL.

3.1. Random Matrix Approach

We start out from the Merton model (Merton 1974) and extend it considering a portfolio of K credit contracts. Each obligor in the portfolio is assumed to be a publicly-traded company. The basic idea is that the asset value $V_k(t)$ of company k is the sum of time-independent liabilities F_k and equity $E_k(t)$, i.e., $V_k(t) = F_k + E_k(t)$. The stochastic process $V_k(t)$ represents the unobservable asset (firm) value. This is indeed a weakness of the Merton model, which has often been discussed (Duan 1994; Elizalde 2005). Here, we proceed by assuming that $V_k(t)$ can be estimated by the observable equity values (Eom et al. 2004) . In the spirit of the Merton model, $V_k(t)$ is modeled by a geometric Brownian motion. Therefore, one can trace back the changes in asset values to stock price returns and estimate the parameters of the stochastic process like volatility and drift by empirical stock price data. The liabilities mature after some time T_{M}, and the obligor has to fulfill his/her obligations and make a required payment. Thus, he/she has to pay back the face value F_k without any coupon payments in between. This is related to a zero coupon bond, and the equity of the company can be viewed as an European call option on its asset value with strike price F_k. A default occurs only if at maturity, the asset value $V_k(T_{\mathrm{M}})$ is below the face value F_k. The corresponding normalized loss is:

$$L_k = \frac{F_k - V_k(T_{\mathrm{M}})}{F_k} \Theta(F_k - V_k(T_{\mathrm{M}})) \, . \tag{14}$$

The Heaviside step function $\Theta(x)$ guarantees that a loss is always larger than zero. This is necessary, because in the case $V_k(T_{\mathrm{M}}) > F_k$, the company is able to make the promised payment, and no loss occurs. In other words, the default criterion can be affiliated with the leverage at maturity $F_k/V_k(T_{\mathrm{M}})$. If the leverage is larger than one, a default occurs, and if the leverage is below one, no default occurs. The total portfolio loss L is a sum over the individual losses weighted by their fractions f_k in the portfolio:

$$L = \sum_{k=1}^{K} f_k L_k \quad , \quad f_k = \frac{F_k}{\sum_{i=1}^{K} F_i} \, . \tag{15}$$

The aim is to describe the average portfolio loss distribution $p(L)$, which can be expressed by means of a filter integral:

$$p(L) = \int\limits_{[0,\infty)^K} d[V] g(V|\Sigma) \delta\left(L - \sum_{k=1}^{K} f_k L_k\right) \, , \tag{16}$$

where $g(V|\Sigma)$ is the multivariate distribution of all asset values at maturity time T_M and Σ is the covariance matrix, and the measure $d[V]$ is the product of all differentials:

$$d[V] = \prod_{k=1}^{K} dV_k \, . \tag{17}$$

This is equivalent to a $K-1$-fold convolution, which is expressed in terms of a filter integral by means of the Dirac delta function $\delta(x)$. We notice the complexity of the integral (16) as the losses (14) involve Heaviside functions. The distribution $g(V|\Sigma)$ is obtained by the more easily accessible distribution $g(r|\Sigma)$ where r is the return vector consisting of the returns:

$$r_k(t) = \frac{V_k(t+\Delta t) - V_k(t)}{V_k(t)} \, , \tag{18}$$

defined analogously to (1). Here, Δt is the return horizon, which corresponds to the maturity time, i.e.,

$$\Delta t = T_M \tag{19}$$

because we are interested in changes of the asset values over the time period T_M.

The crucial problem is that the asset values show fluctuating correlations in the course of time. This non-stationarity has to be taken into account by the distribution $g(r|\Sigma)$ when larger time scales like one year or more are considered. As described in Section 2, the random matrix approach can be used to cope with the non-stationary asset correlations. The average asset value distribution $\langle g \rangle \, (V|\Sigma_0, N)$ is obtained by averaging a multivariate normal distribution over an ensemble of Wishart distributed correlation matrices. Thus, we calculate the loss distribution as an ensemble average. From (16), we find:

$$\langle p \rangle (L|\Sigma_0, N) = \int\limits_{[0,\infty)^K} d[V] \langle g \rangle (V|\Sigma_0, N) \delta \left(L - \sum_{k=1}^{K} f_k L_k \right) \, . \tag{20}$$

Again, we emphasize that the ensemble truly exists as a consequence of the non-stationarity. As a side effect of the random matrix approach, the resulting distribution depends only on two parameters: the $K \times K$ average covariance matrix Σ and the free parameter N, which controls the strength of the fluctuations around the average covariance matrix. N behaves like an inverse variance of the fluctuations; the smaller the N, the larger the fluctuations become. Both parameters have to be determined by historical stock price data.

The average asset value distribution depends on the $K \times K$ mean covariance matrix Σ_0. To circumvent the ensuing complexity and to make analytical progress, we assume an effective average correlation matrix:

$$C_0 = \begin{bmatrix} 1 & c & c & \dots \\ c & 1 & c & \dots \\ c & c & 1 & \dots \\ \vdots & \vdots & \vdots & \ddots \end{bmatrix} \tag{21}$$

where all off-diagonal elements are equal to c. The average correlation is calculated over all assets for the selected time horizon. We emphasize that only the effective average correlation matrix C_0 is fixed; the correlations in the random matrix approach fluctuate around this mean value. In the sequel, whenever we mention a covariance matrix with an effective correlation matrix, we denote it as an effective covariance matrix, and whenever we mention a fully-empirical covariance matrix where all off-diagonal elements differ from another, we denote it as an empirical covariance matrix or a covariance matrix with a heterogeneous correlation structure. Using the assumption (21), analytical tractability is achieved, but it also raises the question whether the data can still be described well. To compare the result with the data, one has to rotate and scale the returns again, but instead of using the empirical covariance matrix the covariance matrix with the effective average correlation structure has to be applied. The results for monthly returns, using the same dataset as in Figure 5, are shown in Figure 6. Still, there is a good agreement between the average asset value distribution with the assumption (21) and the data. This leads to the conclusion that the approximation is reasonable. Considering the parameter N_{eff}, which is needed to describe the fluctuations around the effective average correlation matrix, values around $N_{\text{eff}} = 4$ are found. In contrast to the larger values around $N = 20$, which describe the distributions best in the case of an empirical correlation matrix, the lower values in the case of an effective correlation matrix with average correlation c are needed to describe the larger fluctuations around this average. This result corroborates the interpretation of N as an inverse variance of the fluctuations. Now, the correlation structure of a financial market is captured solely by two parameters: the average correlation coefficient c and parameter N, which indicates the strength of the fluctuations around this average.

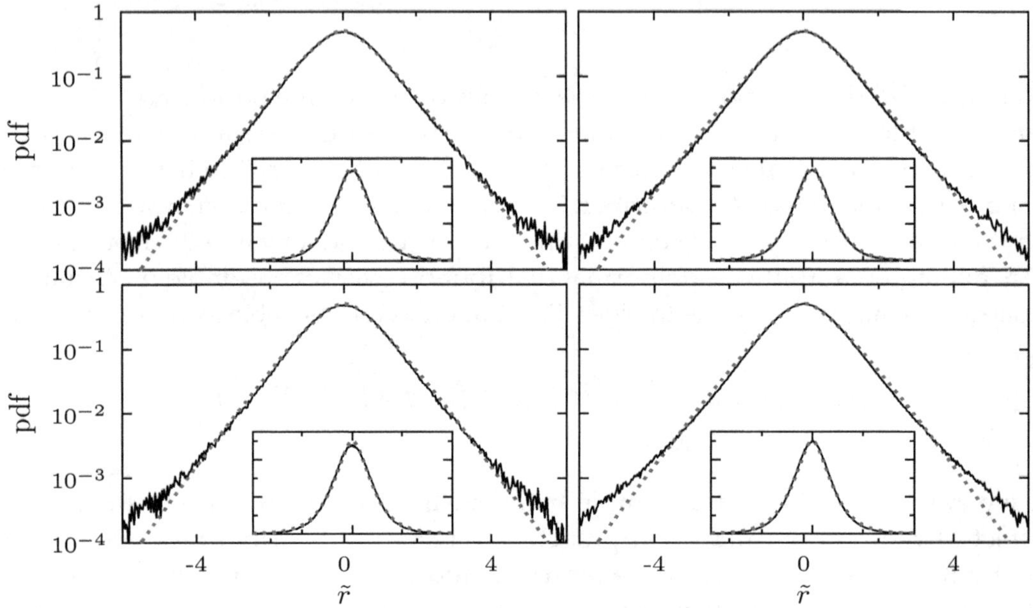

Figure 6. Aggregated distribution for the normalized monthly returns with the effective correlation matrix on a logarithmic scale. The black line shows the empirical distribution; the red dotted line shows the theoretical results. The insets show the corresponding linear plots. **Top** left/right: S&P 500 (1992–2012)/(2002–2012); **bottom** left/right: NASDAQ (1992–2012)/(2002–2012). The average correlation coefficients are $c = 0.26, 0.35, 0.21$ and 0.25, respectively. Reproduced with permission from (Schmitt et al. 2015), Infopro Digital.

3.2. Average Loss Distribution

Having shown the quality of the random matrix approach, we may now proceed in calculating the average portfolio loss distribution (20). We deduce the average distribution for the asset values $\langle g \rangle (V|\Sigma_0, N)$ from the result (13) for the returns. In the Merton model, it is assumed that the asset values $V_k(t)$ follow a geometric Brownian motion with drift and volatility constants μ_k and ρ_k, respectively. This leads to a multivariate Gaussian of the form (10) for the returns, which is consistent with the random matrix approach. Therefore, according to Itô's Lemma (Itô 1944), we perform a change of variables:

$$r_k \longrightarrow \ln \frac{V_k(T_{\text{M}})}{V_{k0}} - \left(\mu_k - \frac{\rho_k^2}{2} \right) T_{\text{M}} \,, \tag{22}$$

with $V_{k0} = V_k(0)$ and the volatilities:

$$\rho_k = \frac{\sigma_k}{\sqrt{T_M}}, \tag{23}$$

where σ_k is the standard deviation in connection with (2). Furthermore, we assume a large portfolio in which all face values F_k are of the same order and carry out an expansion for large K. The analytical result is:

$$\begin{aligned}\langle p\rangle(L|c,N) = & \frac{1}{\sqrt{2\pi}2^{N/2}\Gamma(N/2)}\int_0^\infty dz\, z^{N/2-1}e^{-z/2}\sqrt{\frac{N}{2\pi}} \\ & \times\int_{-\infty}^{+\infty} du \exp\left(-\frac{N}{2}u^2\right)\frac{1}{\sqrt{M_2(z,u)}}\exp\left(-\frac{(L-M_1(z,u))^2}{2M_2(z,u)}\right)\end{aligned} \tag{24}$$

for the average loss distribution with:

$$M_1(z,u) = \sum_{k=1}^{K} f_k m_{1k}(z,u) \tag{25}$$

and:

$$M_2(z,u) = \sum_{k=1}^{K} f_k^2\left(m_{2k}(z,u) - m_{1k}^2(z,u)\right). \tag{26}$$

The j-th moments $m_{jk}(z,u)$ are:

$$\begin{aligned}m_{jk}(z,u) = & \frac{\sqrt{N}}{\rho_k\sqrt{2\pi T_M(1-c)}}\int_{-\infty}^{\hat{F}_k} d\hat{V}_k\left(1-\frac{V_{k0}}{F_k}\exp\left(\sqrt{z}\hat{V}_k + \left(\mu_k - \frac{\rho_k^2}{2}\right)T_M\right)\right)^j \\ & \times\exp\left(-\frac{\left(\hat{V}_k + \sqrt{cT_M}u\rho_k\right)^2}{2T_M(1-c)\rho_k^2/N}\right),\end{aligned} \tag{27}$$

see (Schmitt et al. 2014). The changed variable is $\hat{V}_k = (\ln(V_k(T_M)/V_{k0}) - (\mu_k - \rho_k^2/2)T_M)/\sqrt{z}$ with the upper bound for the integral (27):

$$\hat{F}_k = \frac{1}{\sqrt{z}}\left(\ln\frac{F_k}{V_{k0}} - \left(\mu_k - \frac{\rho_k^2}{2}\right)T_M\right). \tag{28}$$

The integrals in (24) have to be evaluated numerically.

To further illustrate the results, we assume homogeneous credit portfolios. A portfolio is said to be homogeneous when all contracts have the same face value $F_k = F$ and start value $V_k(0) = V_0$ and the same parameters for the underlying stochastic processes like volatility $\rho_k = \rho$ and drift $\mu_k = \mu$. Of course, this does not mean that all asset values follow the same path from $t = 0$ to maturity T_M because underlying processes are stochastic.

It is often argued that diversification significantly reduces the risk in a credit portfolio. In the context mentioned here, diversification solely means the increase of the number K of credit contracts in the credit portfolio on the same market. The limit distribution for an infinitely large portfolio provides information about whether this argument is right or wrong. We thus consider a portfolio of size $K \to \infty$ and find the limiting distribution:

$$\langle p\rangle(L|c,N)\Big|_{K\to\infty} = \frac{1}{2^{N/2}\Gamma(N/2)}\sqrt{\frac{N}{2\pi}}\int_0^\infty dz\, z^{N/2-1}e^{-z/2}\exp\left(-\frac{N}{2}u_0^2\right)\frac{1}{|\partial m_1(z,u)/\partial u|_{z,u_0}}, \tag{29}$$

where $u_0(L, z)$ is the implicit solution of the equation:

$$L = m_1(z, u_0) \ . \tag{30}$$

We drop the second argument of the first moment $m_1(z, u_0)$ from (27), since we consider a homogeneous portfolio. To arrive at the result (29), we use standard methods of the theory of generalized functions and distributions (Lighthill 1958). We now display the average loss distribution for different K. The model depends on four parameters, which can be calibrated by empirical data. Three of them, the average drift μ, the average volatility ρ and the average correlation coefficient c, can be directly calculated from the data. The fourth parameter N, controlling the strength of the fluctuations, has to be determined by fitting the average asset value distribution onto the data. The resulting average portfolio loss distribution $\langle p \rangle (L|c, N)$ for correlation averaged asset values is shown in Figure 7. Different portfolio sizes $K = 10, 100$ and $K \to \infty$ and two different maturity times $T_{\text{M}} = 20$ trading days and $T_{\text{M}} = 252$ trading days are shown. For the estimation of the empirical parameters, the S&P 500 dataset in the time period 1992–2012 is used. The parameters for $T_{\text{M}} = 20$ trading days are $N = 4.2$, $\mu = 0.013$ month^{-1}, $\rho = 0.1$ month$^{-1/2}$ and an average correlation coefficient of $c = 0.26$, shown on the top, and for a maturity time of $T_{\text{M}} = 1$ year $N = 6.0$, $\mu = 0.17$ year^{-1}, $\rho = 0.35$ year$^{-1/2}$ and an average correlation coefficient of $c = 0.28$, shown on the bottom. Moreover, a face value of $F = 75$ and an initial asset value of $V_0 = 100$ are used. There is always a slowly decreasing heavy-tail. A significant decrease of the risk of large losses cannot be achieved by increasing the size of the credit portfolio. Instead, the distribution quickly converges to the limiting distribution $K \to \infty$. This drastically reduces the effect of diversification. In a quantitative manner, it is thus shown that diversification does not work for credit portfolios with correlated asset values. Speaking pictorially, the correlations glue the obligors together and let them act to some extent like just one obligor.

The values of the average correlation coefficient c and the parameter N also influence the average loss distribution. The larger the average correlation c and the smaller the parameter N, the heavier are the tails of the distribution and the more likely is the risk of large losses.

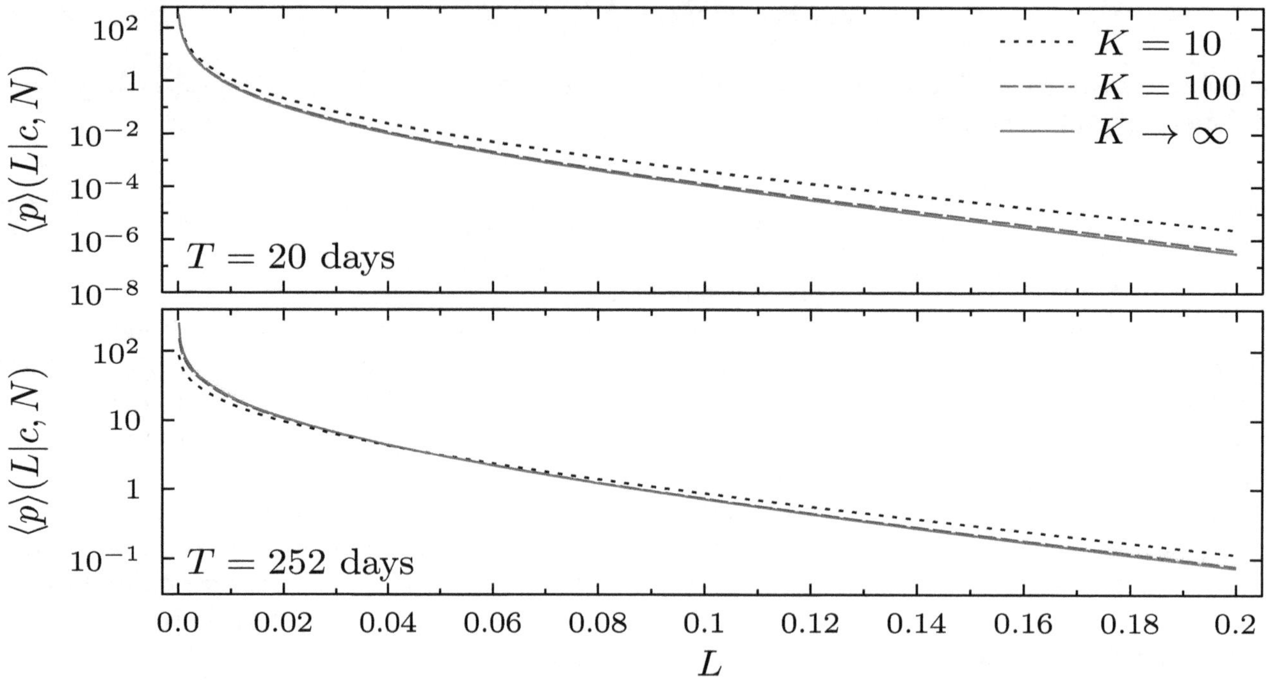

Figure 7. Average portfolio loss distribution for different portfolio sizes of $K = 10$, $K = 100$ and the limiting case $K \to \infty$. At the **top**, the maturity time is one month; at the **bottom**, it is one year. Reproduced with permission from (Schmitt et al. 2015), Infopro Digital.

3.3. *Adjusting to Different Market Situations*

The non-stationarity of financial markets implies that there are calm periods where the markets are stable, as well as periods of crisis as in the period 2008–2010; see, e.g., for the volatility in Figure 1. Observables describing the market behavior in different periods vary significantly. Consequently, the loss distribution, particularly its tail, strongly changes in different market situations. Our model fully grasps this effect. The parameters, i.e., drift, volatility, average correlation coefficient and parameter N, can be adjusted to different periods. To demonstrate the adjustability of our model based on the random matrix approach, we consider the two periods 2002–2004 and 2008–2010. The first period is rather calm, whereas the second includes the global financial crisis. We determine the average parameters for monthly returns of continuously-traded S&P 500 stocks, shown in Table 1. For each period, we take the corresponding parameters and calculate the average portfolio loss distribution; see Figure 8. As expected, we find a much more pronounced tail risk in times of crisis. This is mainly due to the enlarged average correlation coefficient in times of crisis. Consequently, we are able to adjust the model to various periods. It even is possible to adjust the parameters and hence the tail behavior dynamically.

The setting discussed here includes avalanche or contagion effects only indirectly when calibrated to a market situation in the state of crisis. Direct modeling of contagion is provided in (Hatchett and Kühn 2009; Heise and Kühn 2012).

Table 1. Average parameters used for two different time horizons. Taken from (Schmitt et al. 2015).

Time Horizon for Estimation	K	N_{eff}	ρ in Month$^{-1/2}$	μ in Month^{-1}	c
2002–2004	436	5	0.10	0.015	0.30
2008–2010	478	5	0.12	0.01	0.46

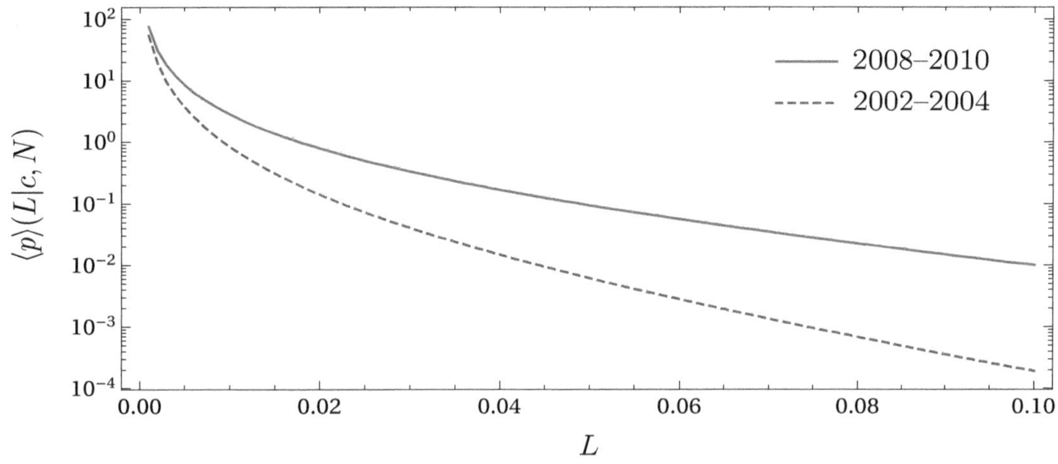

Figure 8. Average loss distribution for different parameters taken from Table 1. The dashed line corresponds to the calm period 2002–2004; the solid line corresponds to the global financial crisis 2008–2010.

3.4. *Value at Risk and Expected Tail Loss*

The approximation of an effective correlation matrix facilitated analytical progress, but importantly, the average asset return distribution still fits empirical data well when using this approximation. We now show that this approximation is also capable of estimating the value at risk (VaR) and the expected tail loss (ETL), also referred to as expected shortfall. We compare the results obtained in this approximation with the results obtained for an empirical covariance matrix. This is also interesting from the risk management perspective because it is common to estimate the covariance matrix over a long period of time and use it as an input for various risk estimation methods. Put differently, we are interested in the quality of risk estimation using an effective correlation matrix and taking fluctuating correlations into account.

The comparison of the effective correlation matrix with the empirical covariance matrix cannot be done analytically. Hence, Monte Carlo simulations to calculate the VaR and ETL are carried out. For each asset, its value at maturity time T_M is simulated and the portfolio loss according to (15) is calculated. All assets have the same fraction in the portfolio. For different time horizons, the empirical covariance matrix, volatilities and drifts for monthly returns of the S&P 500 stocks are calculated. In addition, the parameter N is determined as described above. In the calm period 2002–2004, we find for the empirical covariance matrix a rather large parameter value of $N = 14$, whereas during the financial crisis in 2008–2010, we find $N = 7$. This once more illustrates the meaning of N as an inverted variance of the fluctuations.

The relative deviations of the VaR and ETL for different quantiles of the effective covariance matrix from the empirical covariance matrix are calculated. This is done in two different ways. First, one may assume a fully-homogeneous portfolio where the average values for volatility and drift for each stock are used. Second, one may use the empirically-obtained values for each stock. It turns out that in most cases, the effective covariance matrix together with homogeneous volatility and drift underestimates the risk. In contrast, if one uses heterogeneous volatilities and drifts and the effective covariance matrix, one finds a satisfactory agreement compared to the full empirical covariance matrix; see (Schmitt et al. 2015). In the latter case, the effective covariance matrix slightly overestimates the VaR and ETL in most cases. Hence, the structure of the correlation matrix does not play a decisive role in the risk estimation. This is so because the loss distribution is always a multiply-averaged quantity. A good estimation of the volatilities, however, is crucial.

The benefit of the random matrix approach is shown by comparing the VaR calculated for $N \to \infty$ and for different values of N. The case $N \to \infty$ does not allow fluctuations of the covariance matrix. This means that we use stationary correlations, which turn the distribution $\langle g \rangle (V|\Sigma_0, N)$ of the asset values at maturity into a multivariate log-normal distribution. Thus, for $N \to \infty$, the benefits of the random matrix approach are disabled. The underestimation of the VaR by using stationary correlations, i.e., $N \to \infty$, is measured in terms of the relative deviation from the VaR calculated for empirical values of N. The empirical covariance matrix and the empirical, i.e., heterogeneous, volatilities and drifts calculated in the period 2006–2010 are used. The results are shown in Figure 9. Here, different quantiles $\alpha = 0.99, 0.995, 0.999$ are used. For the empirically-observed parameter $N = 12$, the VaR is underestimated between 30% and 40%. Hence, to avoid a massive underestimation of risk, the fluctuations of the asset correlations must be accounted for.

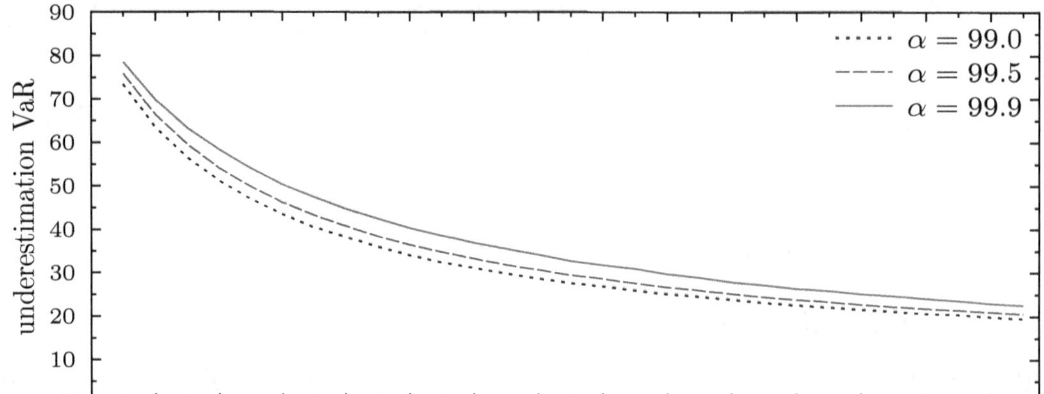

Figure 9. Underestimation of the VaR if fluctuating asset correlations are not taken into account. The empirical covariance matrix is used and compared for different values of N. Reproduced with permission from (Schmitt et al. 2015), Infopro Digital.

4. Concurrent Credit Portfolio Losses

In the previous section, solely one single portfolio on a financial market was considered. Here, based on (Sicking et al. 2018), we consider the problem of concurrent portfolio losses where two non-overlapping credit portfolios are taken into account. In Section 4.1, we discuss copulas of homogeneous portfolios. The dependence of empirical S&P 500- and Nikkei-based credit portfolios is discussed in Section 4.2.

4.1. Simulation Setup

We consider two non-overlapping credit portfolios, which are set up according to Figure 10, in which the financial market is illustrated by means of its correlation matrix. The color indicates the strength of the correlation of two companies in the market. Hence, the diagonal is red as the diagonal of a correlation matrix is one by definition. The two portfolios are marked in Figure 10 as black rimmed squares. Both portfolios include K contracts, which means they are of equal size and no credit contract is contained in either portfolio. Despite the fact that the portfolios are non-overlapping, they are correlated due to non-zero correlations in the off-diagonal squares.

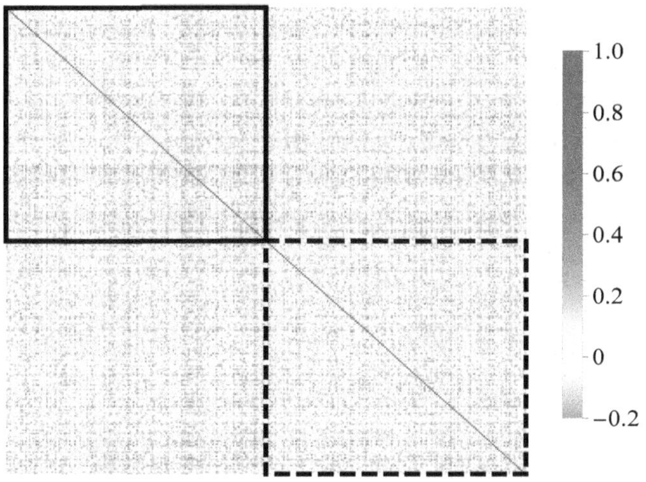

Figure 10. Heterogeneous correlation matrix illustrating a financial market. The two rimmed squares correspond to two non-overlapping credit portfolios. Taken from (Sicking et al. 2018).

The joint bivariate distribution of the losses $L^{(1)}$ and $L^{(2)}$ of two credit portfolios:

$$p(L^{(1)}, L^{(2)}) = \int\limits_{[0,\infty)^K} d[V] g(V|\Sigma) \delta\left(L^{(1)} - \sum_{k=1}^{K} f_k^{(1)} L_k^{(1)}\right) \delta\left(L^{(2)} - \sum_{k=1}^{K} f_k^{(2)} L_k^{(2)}\right) \quad (31)$$

is defined analogously to (16). Here, the upper index indicates the corresponding portfolio. The normalized losses $L_k^{(b)}$ and portfolio losses $L^{(b)}$, as well as the fractions $f_k^{(b)}$ for $b = 1,2$ are defined analogously to (14) and (15), respectively. The total face value $F_k = F_k^{(1)} + F_k^{(2)}$ is the sum over the face values for both portfolios. We remark that for two non-overlapping portfolios, one of the addends is always zero.

With this simulation setup, the correlated asset values $V_k(T_M)$ for each contract are simulated several thousand times to calculate the portfolio losses and out of them the empirical portfolio loss copula. A copula is the joint distribution of a bivariate random variable expressed as a function of the quantiles for the two marginal distributions. The basic idea of copulas is to separate the mutual dependence of a bivariate random variable from the two marginal distributions to analyze the statistical dependencies. In particular, we will analyze the copula density, which is illustrated by means of a normalized two-dimensional histogram. Hence, when speaking of a copula, we rather mean its density. To obtain a better understanding of the mutual dependencies, which are expressed by the empirical copula, it is compared to a Gaussian copula. This Gaussian copula is fully determined by the correlation coefficient of the portfolio losses.

To systematically study the influence of different parameters on the portfolio loss copula, it is helpful to analyze homogeneous portfolios first. The most generic features can be found by focusing on asset correlations and drifts. The simulation is run in two different ways. First, we consider Gaussian dynamics for the stock price returns. This means that the asset values at maturity time T_{M} are distributed according to a multivariate log-normal distribution. We notice that in the case of Gaussian dynamics, the fluctuations of the random correlations around the average correlation coefficient are zero. This corresponds to the case $N \to \infty$. Second, we use fluctuating asset correlations, employing a parameter value of $N_{\mathrm{eff}} = 5$ in accordance with the findings of (Schmitt et al. 2015) for an effective correlation matrix; see Table 1. For the simulation, the parameters $\mu = 10^{-3}\,\mathrm{day}^{-1}$, $\rho = 0.03\,\mathrm{day}^{-1/2}$ and leverages $F/V_0 = 0.75$ are chosen. The portfolios are of size $K = 50$; the maturity time is $T_{\mathrm{M}} = 1$ year; and a market with vanishing asset correlation, i.e., $c = 0$, is considered. The resulting copulas are shown in Figure 11. For $N \to \infty$, the loss copula is constant. This result is quite obvious. Due to the Gaussian dynamics and $c = 0$, the asset values are uncorrelated and statistically independent. Therefore, the portfolio losses, which are derived from those independent quantities, do not show mutual dependencies either. The resulting copula is an independence copula, which agrees with a Gaussian loss copula for a portfolio loss correlation of $\mathrm{Corr}(L_1, L_2) = 0$. In the color code, only white appears. The difference of the empirical copula and the Gaussian copula within each bin is illustrated by means of a color code. The color bar on the right-hand side indicates the difference between the two copulas. The colors yellow to red imply a stronger dependence by the empirical copula in the given (u, v)-interval than predicted by the Gaussian copula. The colors turquoise to blue imply a weaker dependence of the empirical copula than by a Gaussian copula. White implies that the local dependence is equal. The empirical average loss correlation calculated from the simulation outcomes is zero and corroborates this result.

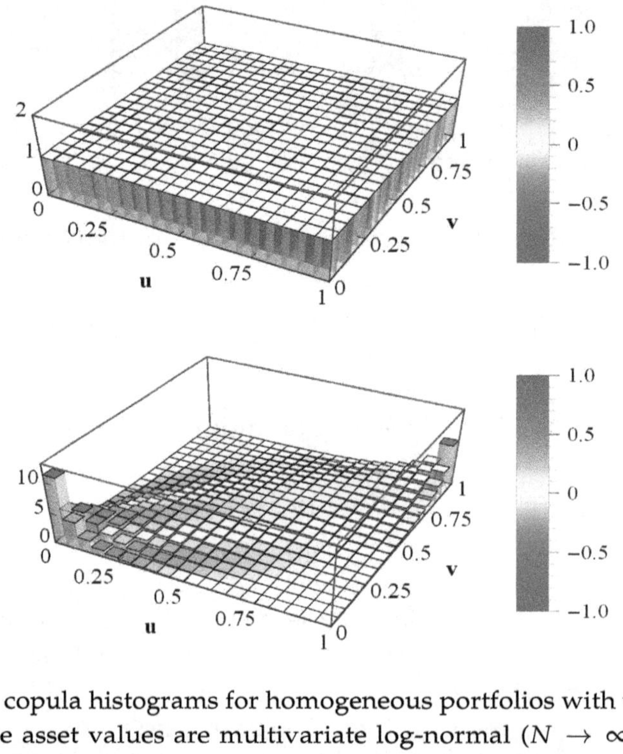

Figure 11. Average loss copula histograms for homogeneous portfolios with vanishing average asset correlations $c = 0$. The asset values are multivariate log-normal ($N \to \infty$) in the top figure and multivariate heavy-tailed ($N_{\mathrm{eff}} = 5$) in the bottom figure. The color bar indicates the local deviations from the corresponding Gaussian copula. Taken from (Sicking et al. 2018).

In the bottom panel of Figure 11, the combination of $c = 0$ and $N_{\mathrm{eff}} = 5$ is shown. The deviations from the independence copula are striking. They emerge because we included according to the random matrix approach fluctuating asset correlations around the average correlation $c = 0$. In that way, positive. as well as negative correlations are equally likely. Having a look at the copula histograms, we find a significant deviation from a Gaussian copula. A Gaussian copula is always symmetric regarding the line spanning from $(0,1)$ to $(1,0)$. Nevertheless, the portfolio loss correlation is $\mathrm{Corr}(L_1, L_2) = 0.752$. The deviations from the Gaussian copula, which is determined by the calculated correlation coefficient, can be seen in Figure 11. Especially in the $(1,1)$ corner, which is related to concurrent extreme losses, we see that the empirical copula shows a weaker dependence than the Gaussian copula. We still have to answer the question why the portfolio losses exhibit such a strong positive correlation, although the average asset correlation is set to zero in the simulation. First, as explained above, credit risk is highly asymmetric. For example, if in a credit portfolio, one single contract generates a loss, it is already sufficient enough that the whole portfolio generates a loss. The company defaulting may just cause a small portfolio loss, but still, it dominates all other non-defaulting and maybe prospering companies. In other words, there is no positive impact of non-defaulting companies on the portfolio losses. All those non-defaults are projected onto zero. Second, the fluctuating asset correlations imply a division of the companies into two blocks. The companies show positive correlations within the blocks and negative correlations across them. Due to the aforementioned fact that non-defaulting companies have no positive impact on the loss distribution, the anti-correlations contribute to the portfolio loss correlation in a limited fashion. They would act as a risk reduction, which is limited according to the asymmetry of credit risk. On the other side, positive correlations within the blocks imply a high risk of concurrent defaults.

We now investigate the impact of the drift. All non-defaulting companies are projected onto a portfolio loss equal to zero. The influence of these projections onto zero and therefore the default-non-default ratio can be analyzed in greater detail by varying the drift of the asset values. For example, if a strong negative drift is chosen, it is highly likely that all companies will default at maturity.

We consider Gaussian dynamics with an average asset correlation of $c = 0.3$ and a volatility of $\rho = 0.02\,\mathrm{day}^{-1/2}$ and different values of μ. Figure 12 shows the resulting copulas for three different drift parameters. In the top panel, a drift of $\mu = 10^{-3}\,\mathrm{day}^{-1}$ was chosen, which leads to a non-default ratio of 39.1% and an estimated portfolio loss correlation of $\mathrm{Corr}(L_1, L_2) = 0.851$. One finds a significant deviation from a symmetric Gaussian copula. In the middle and bottom panel, a drift of $\mu = 3 \times 10^{-4}\,\mathrm{day}^{-1}$ and $\mu = -3 \times 10^{-3}\,\mathrm{day}^{-1}$ was chosen, which leads to non-default ratios of 12.8% and zero, respectively. The estimated portfolio loss correlations increase as the non-default ratios decrease, and one finds a correlation of $\mathrm{Corr}(L_1, L_2) = 0.904$ and $\mathrm{Corr}(L_1, L_2) = 0.954$, respectively. Moreover, we see that the empirical copula turns ever more Gaussian if the percentage of non-defaults decreases. Finally, at a default probability of 100%, the empirical loss copula is a Gaussian copula. This is seen in the bottom panel where no color except for white appears. In the middle and top panel, we see deviations from the Gaussian copula. Especially in the $(1,1)$ corner, we see that the empirical copula exhibits a stronger dependence than predicted by the corresponding Gaussian copula. In both cases, the statistical dependence of large concurrent portfolio losses is underestimated by the Gaussian copula.

We infer that an increase in default probability yields an increase in portfolio loss correlation. In addition, we conclude that the loss of information, which is caused by the projections onto zero, is responsible for the observed deviations of the statistical dependencies from Gaussian copulas.

4.2. *Empirical Credit Portfolios*

Now, more realistic portfolios with heterogeneous parameters are considered. To systematically study the influence of heterogeneity only, the volatility is initially chosen to be heterogeneous. Afterwards, we will proceed with the analysis of fully-heterogeneous portfolios. The empirical parameters like asset correlation, drift and volatility are determined by historical datasets from S&P 500 and Nikkei 225.

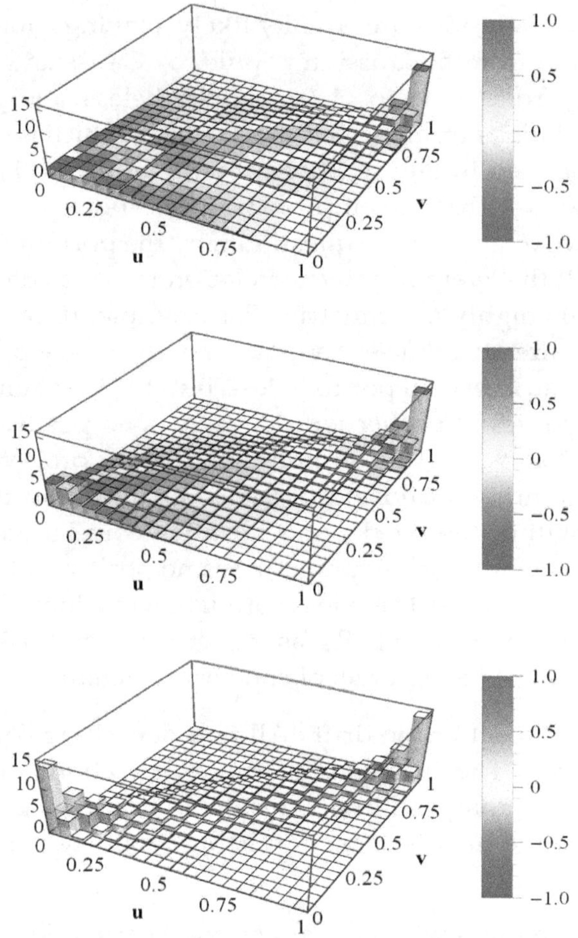

Figure 12. Average loss copula histograms for homogeneous portfolios with asset correlations $c = 0.3$. The asset values are multivariate log-normal ($N \to \infty$). The drifts are $\mu = 10^{-3}$ day^{-1} (**top**), 3×10^{-4} day^{-1} (**middle**) and -3×10^{-3} day^{-1} (**bottom**). The color bar indicates the local deviations from the corresponding Gaussian copula. Taken from (Sicking et al. 2018).

In order to avoid any effect due to a specific parameter choice, the average over thousands of simulations run with different parameter values is calculated.

We begin with investigating the heterogeneity of single parameters. Gaussian dynamics with an average asset correlation $c = 0.3$ and a homogeneous large negative drift of $\mu = -3 \times 10^{-3}$ day^{-1} is considered. Due to the large negative drift, we have seen that in the case of an additional homogeneous volatility, the resulting dependence structure is a Gaussian copula. A rather simple heterogeneous portfolio is constructed when only the daily volatilities are considered random. For each contract, the volatility is drawn from a uniform distribution in the open interval $(0, 0.25)$. The resulting average portfolio loss copula is shown in Figure 13. We again compare the average copula calculated by the simulation outcomes with the average over the corresponding Gaussian copulas determined by the portfolio loss correlation. Surprisingly, the single parameter heterogeneity is sufficient to cause deviations from the Gaussian copula. The coloring shows deviations of the empirical copula from the Gaussian copula especially in the vicinity of the $(0, 0)$ and $(1, 1)$ corners. We come to the conclusion that a choice of one or more heterogeneous parameters, i.e., a large variety in different parameters for each portfolio, alters the dependence structure from an ideal Gaussian copula. The more heterogeneous the portfolios become, the larger the deviations from the symmetric Gaussian copula.

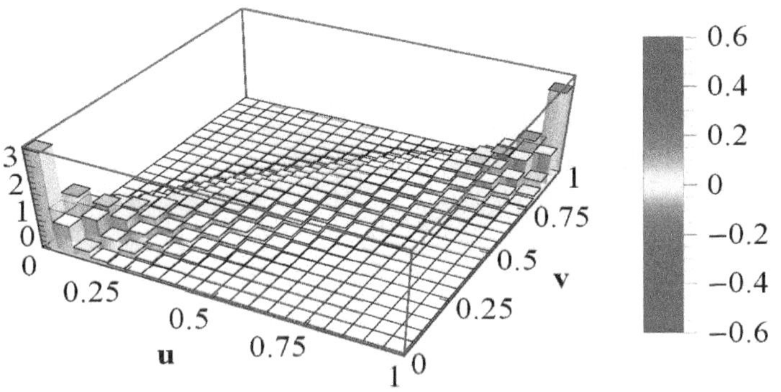

Figure 13. Average loss copula histograms for two portfolios with heterogeneous volatilities drawn from a uniform distribution in the interval $(0, 0.25)$. The color bar indicates the local deviations from the corresponding Gaussian copula. Taken from (Sicking et al. 2018).

So far, there are two causes for non-Gaussian empirical copulas: the loss of information, induced by the projections of non-defaults onto zero, as well as parameter heterogeneity.

We now turn to empirical portfolios. Before starting the simulation, the empirical parameters have to be defined. The dataset consists of stock return data from 272 companies listed on the S&P 500 index and from 179 companies listed on the Nikkei 225 index. It is sampled in a 21-year interval, which covers the period January 1993–April 2014. To set up a realistic, fully-homogeneous portfolio, drifts, volatilities and correlations are calculated from this empirical dataset. Moreover, in (Schmitt et al. 2013), it was shown that annual returns behave normally for empirical asset values. To match these findings, the Gaussian dynamics for the stock price returns is applied. To obtain an average empirical portfolio loss copula, one first averages over different pairs of portfolios and then averages over randomly chosen annual time intervals taken out of the 21-year period. By averaging over different pairs of portfolios, results that are due to specific features of two particular portfolios are avoided. We consider three different cases, which are shown in Figure 14. In the first case, which is shown in the top panel, one portfolio is drawn from S&P 500 and the other is drawn from Nikkei 225. In the second case (middle panel), both portfolios are drawn from S&P 500, and in the third case (bottom panel) both are drawn from Nikkei 225.

In all three cases, we find deviations of the empirical copula from the Gaussian copula. Especially the dependence of the extreme events is much more pronounced than by the prediction of a Gaussian copula. This can be seen in the $(1, 1)$ corner, where the colors indicate that the tails are much more narrow and pointed compared to the Gaussian copula. On the other side, the tails in the $(0, 0)$ corner are flatter compared to a Gaussian copula. The asymmetry regarding the line spanned by $(1, 0)$ and $(0, 1)$ leads to the conclusion that extreme portfolio losses occur more often simultaneously than in the case of small portfolio losses. Hence, an extreme loss of one portfolio is very likely to also yield an extreme loss of the other portfolio. This dependence is much stronger than predicted by a Gaussian copula. Thus, modeling portfolio loss dependencies by means of Gaussian copulas is deeply flawed and might cause severe underestimations of the actual credit risk.

Another important aspect of credit risk can be analyzed by considering different portfolio sizes. So far, only rather small portfolios of size $K = 50$ were chosen. Increasing the size of the portfolios leads to a rise in portfolio loss correlation. This behavior can be explained by the decrease of the idiosyncrasies of large portfolios. Moreover, it explains why the empirical loss copulas in Figure 14 are almost perfectly symmetric regarding the line spanned by $(0, 0)$ and $(1, 1)$. Portfolios based on the S&P 500 dataset with a size of $K = 50$ each reveal an significant average loss correlation of $\mathrm{Corr}(L_1, L_2) = 0.779$. Even if we decrease the size to $K = 14$ companies, an average portfolio loss correlation of $\mathrm{Corr}(L_1, L_2) > 0.5$ is found. This reveals that high dependencies among banks are not only limited to "big players", which hold portfolios of several thousand contracts. Furthermore, small institutions show noticeable dependencies even though their portfolios are non-overlapping.

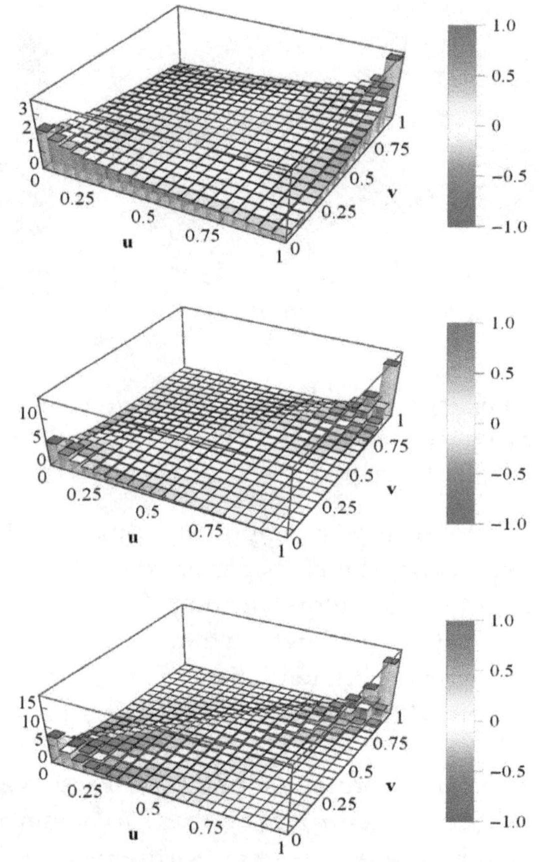

Figure 14. Time averaged loss copula histograms for two empirical copulas of size $K = 50$. The asset values are multivariate log-normal ($N \to \infty$). **Top**: Portfolio 1 is always drawn from S&P 500 and Portfolio 2 from Nikkei 225; **middle**: both portfolios are drawn from S&P 500; **bottom**: both portfolios are drawn from Nikkei 225. The color bar indicates the local deviations from the corresponding Gaussian copula. Taken from (Sicking et al. 2018).

5. Discussion

The motivation for the studies that we reviewed here was two-fold. First, the massive perturbations that shook the financial markets starting with the subprime crisis of 2007–2009 sharpened the understanding of how crucial the role of credits is for the stability of the economy as a whole in view of the strong interdependencies. Better credit risk estimation is urgently called for, particularly for rare, but drastic events, i.e., for the tails of the loss distributions. Particularly, the often claimed benefit of diversification has to be critically investigated. Second, the ubiquitous non-stationarity in financial markets has to be properly accounted for in the models. The financial crisis illustrates in a painful way that decisive economic quantities strongly fluctuate in time, ruling out elegant, but too simplistic equilibrium approaches, which fail to grasp the empirical situation.

This two-fold motivation prompted a random matrix approach to tackle and eventually solve the Merton model of credit risk for fully-correlated assets. A proper asset value distribution can be calculated by an ensemble average of random correlation matrices. The main ingredient is a new interpretation of the Wishart model for correlation or covariance matrices. While it was originally meant to describe generic statistical features resulting from stationary time series, i.e., eigenvalue densities and other quantities for large correlation matrices, the new interpretation grasps non-stationary correlation matrices by modeling a truly existing, measured set of such correlation matrices with an ensemble of random correlation matrices. Contrary to the original interpretation of the Wishart model, ergodicity reasoning is not applied, and a restriction to large matrices is not needed, either.

According to the Merton model, stock price data instead of data on asset values can be used to calibrate the required parameters. This is quite valuable because empirical data on asset values are not easy to obtain, whereas stock price data are commonly available. Considering long time horizons, the sample statistics of returns can be described by a multivariate mixture of distributions. The resulting distribution is the average of a multivariate normal distribution over an ensemble of Wishart-distributed covariance matrices. This random matrix approach takes the fluctuating asset correlations into account. As a very nice side effect, the random matrix approach reduces the number of parameters that describe the correlation structure of the financial market to two. Both of them can be considered as macroscopic. One parameter is a mean correlation coefficient of the asset values, and the other parameter describes the strength of the fluctuations around this average. Furthermore, the random matrix approach yields analytical tractability, which allows one to derive an analytical expression for the loss distribution of a portfolio of credit contracts, taking fluctuating asset correlations into account. In a quantitative manner, it is shown that in the presence of asset correlations, diversification fails to reduce the risk of large losses. This is substantial quantitative support and corroboration for qualitative reasoning in the economic literature. Furthermore, it is demonstrated that the random matrix approach can describe very different market situations. For example, in a crisis, the mean correlation coefficient is higher, and the parameter governing the strength of the fluctuations is smaller than in a quite period, with considerable impact on the loss distribution.

In addition, Monte Carlo simulations were run to calculate VaR and ETL. The results support the approximation of an effective average correlation matrix if heterogeneous average volatilities are taken into account. Moreover, the simulations show the benefit of the random matrix approach. If the fluctuations between the asset correlations are neglected, the VaR is underestimated by up to 40%. This underestimation could yield dramatic consequences. Therefore, the results strongly support a conservative approach to capital reserve requirements.

Light is shed on intrinsic instabilities of the financial sector. Sizable systemic risks are present in the financial system. These were revealed in the financial crisis of 2007–2009. Up to that point, tail-dependencies between credit contracts were underestimated, which emerged as a big problem in credit risk assessment. This is another motivation for models like ours that take asset fluctuations into account.

The dependence structure of credit portfolio losses was analyzed within the framework of the Merton model. Importantly, the two credit portfolios operate on the same correlated market, no matter if they belong to a single creditor or bank or to different banks. The instruments to analyze the joint risk are correlations and copulas. Correlations break down the dependence structure into one parameter and represent only a rough approximation for the coupling of portfolio losses. In contrast, copulas reveal the full dependence structure. For two non-overlapping credit portfolios, we found concurrent large portfolio losses to be more likely than concurrent small ones. This observation is in contrast to a symmetric Gaussian behavior as described by correlation coefficients. Risk estimation by solely using standard correlation coefficients yields a clear underestimation of concurrent large portfolio losses. Hence, from a systemic viewpoint, it is really necessary to incorporate the full dependence structure of joint risks.

Acknowledgments: Andreas Mühlbacher acknowledges support from Studienstiftung des deutschen Volkes.

References

Benmelech, Efraim, and Jennifer Dlugosz. 2009. The alchemy of CDO credit ratings. *Journal of Monetary Economics* 56: 617–34. [CrossRef]

Bernaola-Galván, Pedro, Plamen Ch. Ivanov, Luís A. Nunes Amaral, and H. Eugene Stanley. 2001. Scale invariance in the nonstationarity of human heart rate. *Physical Review Letters* 87: 168105. [CrossRef]

Bielecki, Tomasz R., and Marek Rutkowski. 2013. *Credit Risk: Modeling, Valuation and Hedging*. Berlin: Springer Science & Business Media.

Black, Fisher. 1976. Studies of stock price volatility changes. In *Proceedings of the 1976 Meetings of the American Statistical Association, Business and Economics Statistics Section*. Alexandria: American Statistical Association, pp. 177–81.

Bluhm, Christian, Ludger Overbeck, and Christoph Wagner. 2016. *Introduction to Credit Risk Modeling*. Boca Raton: CRC Press.

Bouchaud, Jean-Philippe, and Marc Potters. 2003. *Theory of Financial Risk and Derivative Pricing: From Statistical Physics to Risk Management*. Cambridge: Cambridge University Press.

Chava, Sudheer, Catalina Stefanescu, and Stuart Turnbull. 2011. Modeling the loss distribution. *Management Science* 57: 1267–87.[CrossRef]

Chetalova, Desislava, Thilo A. Schmitt, Rudi Schäfer, and Thomas Guhr. 2015. Portfolio return distributions: Sample statistics with stochastic correlations. *International Journal of Theoretical and Applied Finance* 18: 1550012.[CrossRef]

Crouhy, Michel, Dan Galai, and Robert Mark. 2000. A comparative analysis of current credit risk models. *Journal of Bank. & Finance* 24: 59–117.

Di Gangi, Domenico, Fabrizio Lillo, and Davide Pirino. 2018. Assessing Systemic Risk due to Fire Sales Spillover through Maximum Entropy Network Reconstruction. Available online: https://ssrn.com/abstract=2639178 (accessed on 27 February 2018).

Duan, Jin-Chuan. 1994. Maximum likelihood estimation using price data of the derivative contract. *Mathematical Finance* 4: 155–67. [CrossRef]

Duffie, Darrell, and Nicolae Garleanu. 2001. Risk and valuation of collateralized debt obligations. *Financial Analysts Journal* 57: 41–59. [CrossRef]

Duffie, Darrell, and Kenneth J. Singleton. 1999. Modeling term structures of defaultable bonds. *The Review of Financial Studies* 12: 687–720. [CrossRef]

Elizalde, Abel. 2005. *Credit Risk Models II: Structural Models*. Documentos de Trabajo CEMFI. Madrid: CEMFI.

Eom, Young H., Jean Helwege, and Jing-zhi Huang. 2004. Structural models of corporate bond pricing: An empirical analysis. *The Review of Financial Studies* 17: 499–544. [CrossRef]

Gao, Jinbao. 1999. Recurrence time statistics for chaotic systems and their applications. *Physical Review Letters* 83: 3178. [CrossRef]

Giada, Lorenzo, and Matteo Marsili. 2002. Algorithms of maximum likelihood data clustering with applications. *Physica A* 315: 650–64. [CrossRef]

Giesecke, Kay. 2004. Credit risk modeling and valuation: An introduction. In *Credit Risk: Models and Management*, 2nd ed. Edited by David Shimko. London: RISK Books, pp. 487–526.

Glasserman, Paul. 2004. Tail approximations for portfolio credit risk. *The Journal of Derivatives* 12: 24–42. [CrossRef]

Glasserman, Paul, and Jesus Ruiz-Mata. 2006. Computing the credit loss distribution in the Gaussian copula model: A comparison of methods. *Journal of Credit Risk* 2: 33–66. [CrossRef]

Gouriéroux, Christian, and Razvan Sufana. 2004. *Derivative Pricing with Multivariate Stochastic Volatility: Application to Credit Risk*. Working Papers 2004-31. Palaiseau, France: Center for Research in Economics and Statistics.

Gouriéroux, Christian, Joann Jasiak, and Razvan Sufana. 2009. The Wishart autoregressive process of multivariate stochastic volatility. *Journal of Econometrics* 150: 167–81. [CrossRef]

Guhr, Thomas, and Bernd Kälber. 2003. A new method to estimate the noise in financial correlation matrices. *Journal of Physics A* 36: 3009. [CrossRef]

Hatchett, Jon P. L., and Reimer Kühn. 2009. Credit contagion and credit risk. *Quantitative Finance* 9: 373–82. [CrossRef]

Hegger, Rainer, Holger Kantz, Lorenzo Matassini, and Thomas Schreiber. 2000. Coping with nonstationarity by overembedding. *Physical Review Letters* 84: 4092. [CrossRef]

Heitfield, Eric, Steve Burton, and Souphala Chomsisengphet. 2006. Systematic and idiosyncratic risk in syndicated loan portfolios. *Journal of Credit Risk* 2: 3–31. [CrossRef]

Heise, Sebastian, and Reimer Kühn. 2012. Derivatives and credit contagion in interconnected networks. *The European Physical Journal B* 85: 115. [CrossRef]

Hull, John C. 2009. The credit crunch of 2007: What went wrong? Why? What lessons can be learned? *Journal of Credit Risk* 5: 3–18. [CrossRef]

Ibragimov, Rustam, and Johan Walden. 2007. The limits of diversification when losses may be large. *Journal of Bank. & Finance* 31: 2551–69.

Itô, Kiyosi. 1944. Stochastic integral. *Proceedings of the Imperial Academy* 20: 519–24. [CrossRef]

Koivusalo, Alexander F. R., and Rudi Schäfer. 2012. Calibration of structural and reduced-form recovery models. *Journal of Credit Risk* 8: 31–51. [CrossRef]

Laloux, Laurent, Pierre Cizeau, Jean-Philippe Bouchaud, and Marc Potters. 1999. Noise dressing of financial correlation matrices. *Physical Review Letters* 83: 1467. [CrossRef]

Lando, David. 2009. *Credit Risk Modeling: Theory and Applications*. Princeton: Princeton University Press.

Li, David X. 2000. On default correlation: A copula function approach. *The Journal of Fixed Income* 9: 43–54. [CrossRef]

Lighthill, Michael J. 1958. *An introduction to Fourier Analysis and Generalised Functions*. Cambridge: Cambridge University Press.

Longstaff, Francis A., and Arvind Rajan. 2008. An empirical analysis of the pricing of collateralized debt obligations. *The Journal of Finance* 63: 529–63. [CrossRef]

Mainik, Georg, and Paul Embrechts. 2013. Diversification in heavy-tailed portfolios: Properties and pitfalls. *Annals of Actuarial Science* 7: 26–45. [CrossRef]

McNeil, Alexander J., Rüdiger Frey, and Paul Embrechts. 2005. *Quantitative Risk Management: Concepts, Techniques and Tools*. Princeton: Princeton University Press.

Merton, Robert C. 1974. On the pricing of corporate debt: The risk structure of interest rates. *The Journal of finance* 29: 449–70.

Meudt, Frederik, Martin Theissen, Rudi Schäfer, and Thomas Guhr. 2015. Constructing analytically tractable ensembles of stochastic covariances with an application to financial data. *Journal of Statistical Mechanics* 2015: P11025. [CrossRef]

Muirhead, Robb J. 2005. *Aspects of Multivariate Statistical Theory*, 2nd ed. Hoboken: John Wiley & Sons.

Münnix, Michael C., Rudi Schäfer, and Thomas Guhr. 2014. A random matrix approach to credit risk. *PLoS ONE* 9: e98030. [CrossRef]

Münnix, Michael C., Takashi Shimada, Rudi Schäfer, Francois Leyvraz, Thomas H. Seligman, Thomas Guhr, and H. Eugene Stanley. 2012. Identifying states of a financial market. *Scientific Reports* 2: 644. [CrossRef]

Nelsen, Roger B. 2007. *An Introduction to Copulas*. New York: Springer Science & Business Media.

Pafka, Szilard, and Imre Kondor. 2004. Estimated correlation matrices and portfolio optimization. *Physica A* 343: 623–34. [CrossRef]

Plerou, Vasiliki, Parameswaran Gopikrishnan, Bernd Rosenow, Luís A. Nunes Amaral, and H. Eugene Stanley. 1999. Universal and nonuniversal properties of cross correlations in financial time series. *Physical Review Letters* 83: 1471. [CrossRef]

Plerou, Vasiliki, Parameswaran Gopikrishnan, Bernd Rosenow, Luís A. Nunes Amaral, Thomas Guhr, and H. Eugene Stanley. 2002. Random matrix approach to cross correlations in financial data. *Physical Review E* 65: 066126. [CrossRef]

Rieke, Christoph, Karsten Sternickel, Ralph G. Andrzejak, Christian E. Elger, Peter David, and Klaus Lehnertz. 2002. Measuring nonstationarity by analyzing the loss of recurrence in dynamical systems. *Physical Review Letters* 88: 244102. [CrossRef]

Sandoval, Leonidas, and Italo De Paula Franca. 2012. Correlation of financial markets in times of crisis. *Physica A* 391: 187–208. [CrossRef]

Schäfer, Rudi, Markus Sjölin, Andreas Sundin, Michal Wolanski, and Thomas Guhr. 2007. Credit risk—A structural model with jumps and correlations. *Physica A* 383: 533–69. [CrossRef]

Schmitt, Thilo A., Desislava Chetalova, Rudi Schäfer, and Thomas Guhr. 2013. Non-stationarity in financial time series: Generic features and tail behavior. *Europhysics Letters* 103: 58003. [CrossRef]

Schmitt, Thilo A., Desislava Chetalova, Rudi Schäfer, and Thomas Guhr. 2014. Credit risk and the instability of the financial system: An ensemble approach. *Europhysics Letters* 105: 38004. [CrossRef]

Schmitt, Thilo A., Desislava Chetalova, Rudi Schäfer, and Thomas Guhr. 2015. Credit risk: Taking fluctuating asset correlations into account. *Journal of Credit Risk* 11: 73–94. [CrossRef]

Schönbucher, Philipp J. 2001. Factor models: Portfolio credit risks when defaults are correlated. *The Journal of Risk Finance* 3: 45–56. [CrossRef]

Schönbucher, Philipp J. 2003. *Credit Derivatives Pricing Models: Models, Pricing and Implementation*. Hoboken: John Wiley & Sons.

Schwert, G. William. 1989. Why does stock market volatility change over time? *The Journal of Finance* 44: 1115–53. [CrossRef]

Sicking, Joachim, Thomas Guhr, and Rudi Schäfer. 2018. Concurrent credit portfolio losses. *PLoS ONE* 13: e0190263.[CrossRef]

Song, Dong-Ming, Michele Tumminello, Wei-Xing Zhou, and Rosario N. Mantegna. 2011. Evolution of worldwide stock markets, correlation structure, and correlation-based graphs. *Physical Review E* 84: 026108. [CrossRef]

Tumminello, Michele, Tomaso Aste, Tiziana Di Matteo, and Rosario N. Mantegna. 2005. A tool for filtering information in complex systems. *Proceedings of the National Academy of Sciences USA* 102: 10421–26. [CrossRef]

Wishart, John. 1928. The generalised product moment distribution in samples from a normal multivariate population. *Biometrika* 20A: 32–52. [CrossRef]

Yahoo! n.d. Finance. Available online: http://finance.yahoo.com (accessed on 9 February 2018).

Zhang, Yiting, Gladys Hui Ting Lee, Jian Cheng Wong, Jun Liang Kok, Manamohan Prusty, and Siew Ann Cheong. 2011. Will the US economy recover in 2010? A minimal spanning tree study. *Physica A* 390: 2020–50. [CrossRef]

Zia, Royce K. P., and Per Arne Rikvold. 2004. Fluctuations and correlations in an individual-based model of biological coevolution. *Journal of Physics A* 37: 5135. [CrossRef]

Zia, Royce K. P., and Beate Schmittmann. 2006. A possible classification of nonequilibrium steady states. *Journal of Physics A* 39: L407. [CrossRef]

8

On Identifying the Systemically Important Tunisian Banks: An Empirical Approach based on the ΔCoVaR Measures

Wided Khiari [1,2,*] and Salim Ben Sassi [1,3]

1 Institut Supérieur de Gestion, University of Tunis, Le Bardo 2000, Tunisia; salimbensassi@yahoo.fr
2 GEF-2A Laboratory, University of Tunis, Le Bardo 2000, Tunisia
3 LAREQUAD, FSEG of Tunis, University of Tunis El Manar, Tunis 1068, Tunisia
* Correspondence: khiariwided@yahoo.fr

Abstract: The aim of this work is to assess systemic risk of Tunisian listed banks. The goal is to identify the institutions that contribute the most to systemic risk and that are most exposed to it. We use the CoVaR that considered the systemic risk as the value at risk (VaR) of a financial institution conditioned on the VaR of another institution. Thus, if the CoVaR increases with respect to the VaR, the spillover risk also increases among the institutions. The difference between these measurements is termed ΔCoVaR, and it allows for estimating the exposure and contribution of each bank to systemic risk. Results allow classifying Tunisian banks in terms of systemic risk involvement. They show that public banks occupy the top places, followed by the two largest private banks in Tunisia. These five banks are the main systemic players in the Tunisian banking sector. It seems that they are the least sensitive to the financial difficulties of existing banks and the most important contributors to the distress of the other banks. This work aims to add a broader perspective to the micro prudential application of regulation, including contagion, proposing a macro prudential vision and strengthening of regulatory policy. Supervisors could impose close supervision for institutions considered as potentially systemic banks. Furthermore, regulations should consider the systemic contribution when defining risk requirements to minimize the consequences of possible herd behavior.

Keywords: systemic risk; value at risk; quantile regression; CoVaR; cartography

---

1. Introduction

Ever since the genesis of the discipline, the quest for comprehending and measuring risk has been of paramount importance among academics. But in light of the large number of crises that have occurred in recent years, greater emphasis has been placed on understanding and managing the systemic risk measure. While this multidimensional concept is widely discussed in an increasing number of papers, there is still no consensus on a unique definition of systemic risk.

Tunisia had always been considered one of the best performers in the Middle East and North Africa (MENA) region, economically and humanely, in the run-up to the 2011 revolution. It was one of the first countries in the region to implement a set of early structural reforms, contributing to the success of the economy in the mid-1990s.

The Tunisian banking sector is composed of 11 deposit banks listed in the Tunisian Stock Exchange. Three of them are public and the participation of the government in their capital is more than 36%. No changes in the number of market players have occurred during the last five years, except for the implementation of a second Islamic bank.

No financial institution, in the Middle East and North Africa region (MENA), has a market share greater than 14% of total assets or loans and 16% of deposits, which is the case of Tunisian financial institutions. These percentages are generally much higher. BIAT, BNA and STB, the three largest banks, hold nearly 50% of total assets, with approximately equal weight. In contrast, for example, in Morocco, the top three banks granted 62% of loans to the economy, and the top five accounted for 81% in 2012 (Khiari and Nachnouchi 2018).

Now Tunisian's economy is suffering from exceptionally difficult conditions. The debts crises of the European Union have created a slowing down in goods exports, and the 14 January revolution gave rise to a long period of instability, not to mention institutional and political uncertainty. This worsening security situation caused a considerable drop in income in foreign currency from tourism. The Tunisian economy has also been affected by the adverse consequences associated with the Libyan revolution. All Tunisian's sectors had, and are still undergoing, a challenging transition phase. This post-revolutionary context has especially affected the banking sector, as the ability of Tunisian banks to overcome the financial instability has become a great concern. Indeed, they have become extremely fragile to any adverse shocks.

Improving the efficiency of the banking system and competition in the sector is based on a set of reforms focused on the restructuring of state-owned banks, accounting for 39% of total bank assets, strictly applying banking regulations and revising procedures to deal with the financial problems of banks in financial difficulties.

The determination of systemically implicated financial institutions is a major concern for academics and regulators. Although in the past systemic importance has been associated with the size of the institution as part of the problem of being "too big to fail", recent financial crises suggest that the situation is more complex. The interconnection of a systemically implicated financial institution is also identified by its interbank market links, and its effects are magnified by a strong leverage effect.

As a result, various empirical measures have been proposed to provide a more realistic view of the systemic importance of a financial institution (Bisias et al. 2012). For example, the Conditional Value at Risk (CoVaR) is the value at risk (VaR) of the financial system contingent on a specific event affecting a given financial institution. The contribution of a company to systemic risk (ΔCoVaR) can be explained intuitively by the difference between CoVaR when the company is in financial difficulty and when the company is not.

In recent years, there has been much research on these measures of systemic risk. The studies first show that definitions of systemic risk measures are not neutral so as to measure the impact of an institution on the overall system. Second, some of these measures are similar to traditional quantile and co-volatility measures. In addition, the primary measures of systemic risk are based primarily on the accuracy of special extreme quantiles of the future yield distribution. In addition, the magnitude of the model is largely underestimated when calculating VaR and other quantities related to the quantile (Boucher et al. 2013), so it is difficult to put in place a correct and reliable risk ranking system (Hurlin et al. 2012).

In this context, as an indicator of the risk level in financial institutions, VaR is widely used because of its simplicity and transparency. However, it only measures the individual risk of financial institutions rather than the contagion and degree of risk spread between financial institutions or financial markets. In 2011, Adrian and Brunnermeier proposed the CoVaR method to measure the condition risk value.

This method can, not only identify the risks of financial institutions, but also solve the problem of quantitative association between two financial institutions, so as to measure the risk spillover of financial institutions to other financial institutions. *VaR* is generally known as "risk value" or "in risk value", which refers to the maximum possible loss of a certain financial asset (or portfolio) in a certain period of time under a certain confidence level. If a stochastic variable R represents the return rates of assets, $VaRq$ is defined as the quantile q of the yield R. At present, the simplified method of financial market data (such as stock price, CDS price difference, credit default swap, etc.) is the most commonly used method to measure systemic risk in financial institutions, in which the Marginal Expected Shortfall (*MES*) and the CoVaR are the most popular and representative methods in the present simplified method.

However, studies on systemic risk measures are still rare in developing economies. Our research seeks to fill this gap by empirically analyzing systemic risk in the Tunisian banking sector in order to determine the most systemically important banks. The principle objective is to propose a classification that expresses, for each bank, its contribution and sensitivity to the risk of the banking system, based on the work of Adrian and Brunnermeier (2011), in which they used CoVaR as a measure for systemic risk. This can provide information about how banks can be subject to stricter supervision and also which banks to prioritize for rescuing, in the event of a financial crisis.

Adrian and Brunnermeier (2011) define the CoVaR as the value at risk (VaR) of a financial institution subordinated to the VaR of another institution. Thereby, if the CoVaR increases with respect to the VaR, the risk of overflow also increases between the institutions. By computing the difference between the two measures as ΔCoVaR, we will be able to assess the contribution and exposure of every financial institution to systemic risk.

The innovation of this work lies in applying conditional value risk (CoVaR) to the banking field and combining the model CoVaR with the quantile regression model. Taking the 11 listed banking companies in Tunisia as the sample, we combine the CoVaR model and quantile regression model to measure the spillover effect and the level of systemic risk contribution of Tunisian listed banks, so as to provide relevant countermeasures and suggestions for preventing systemic risk.

The rest of the paper is organized as follows. Section 2 serves as a brief literature review. In Section 3, we describe the methodology's framework and lay out our systemic risk measures: VaR, COVaR and ΔCoVaR estimates. In Section 4, we analyze the principal results and discussions. Lastly, Section 5 has the conclusions, as well as the limitations of our work and future research perspectives.

2. Literature Review

Systemic risk research is mainly from the perspective of crisis, and the systemic risk which is caused by bank run to bank operation is analyzed. Before and after the 1980s, a series of bank crises and high contagion during the crises made the spillover effect of systemic risk widely recognized.

Several researchers have tried to develop more appropriate empirical tools to better measure systemic risk. They believe that the classical measures used, such as beta and value-at-risk, are not effective in assessing global contagion, as has been demonstrated in the recent financial crisis. Indeed, many researchers believe that the most well-known classical risk measure, value at risk, is unable to capture the systemic nature of risk, as it focuses on a single institution. It does not take into account that an institution is part of a complex system that can generate new risks (Danielsson et al. 2011). As a result, it does not take into account the negative impacts associated with decisions made by other institutions.

Thus, the literature shows the emergence of new quantification measures. However, there is still no consensus between academics and regulators on an effective tool that can be used to estimate systemic risk more accurately.

After the financial crisis, there have been many works that have demonstrated deep research on systemic risk and have measured systemic risk by using the CoVaR, *MES*, *CCA* and other models. Acharya et al. (2010) used systemic expected shortfall (SES) to measure systemic risk. Their measurement focuses on the propensity of the company to be undercapitalized when the entire financial sector is on the left tail. The marginal expected shortfall (MES), is developed to measure financial institutions' contributions to systemic risk. Girardi and Ergün (2013) defined the systemic risk of an organization as its change of CoVaR in financial distress, and estimated the links between the system risk contributions and their characteristics of the four financial industry groups. Banulescu and Dumitrescu (2015) used the component expected shortfall (CES) to determine systemically important financial institutions in the United States. They break down the expected deficit and take into account the characteristics of the company. The study covers the period from June 2007 to June 2010 and covers the global financial crisis. The result shows that companies such as AIG, Lehman Brothers and Merrill Lynch, which suffered important losses during the financial crisis, are systemically important institutions. Derbali and Hallara (2015) used the MES model to measure the systemic risk of European financial institutions. Grieb (2015) applied the model of nonlinear factors, and logistic regression model to measure the potential impact of hedge funds on systemic risk. Her results show that the systemic risk of hedge fund is increasing. Reboredo and Ugolini (2015) used CoVaR method to measure the systemic risk of the European sovereign debt markets after the Greek debt crisis, and found that systemic risks are similar in all countries before the crisis, and the decoupling of the debt market and the systemic risk were reduced on the whole in the European debt market after the outbreak of the crisis. Brownlees and Engle (2017) used *SRISK* to measure the system risk contribution of financial firms. They offered a ranking of institutions in the different crisis stages.

To study the exposure and contribution of systemic risk in financial institutions to financial market, Lin et al. (2016) utilized different risk measures such as *SRISK*, *MES*, *CoVaR* and other methods. Karimalis and Nomikos (2017) researched the contribution of systemic risk in European large banks by adopting the model of *Copula* and *CoVaR*. More recently, Di Clemente (2018) adopted a model based on extreme value theory (EVT) to analyze the contribution of individual financial institution to the risk of the system, and showed the connection between a single financial institution and the financial system

Some Chinese scholars use CoVaR of the introduction of state variables to make an empirical analysis for the systemic risk in 14 Chinese listed banks, and the results show that there is significant systemic risk spillover in the listed commercial banks of China; some use the method CoVaR to measure the systemic risk of the banking industry, and put forward the corresponding suggestions for risk supervision; some have adopted the method CES to measure the systematic risk of the 14 listed Chinese banks and have investigated the relationship between income of non interest and systemic risk; and others use the quantile regression model of risk spillover effect to calculate and compare the CoVaR value of 15 commercial banks, and find that the banking industry will have a systemic risk spillover ffect in the event of a crisis.

In addition, $\triangle$CoVaR is not perforce symmetrical (i.e., the institution's VaR contribution to the institution's market risk *j* does not necessarily correspond to the VaR contribution of *j*'s *VaR* to *i*'s *VaR*), as shown by Adrian and Brunnermeier (2011). CoVaR's advantage is that it can be used with any other tail measure to assess other risks. For example, Chan-Lau (2009) follows a similar approach and evaluates systemic credit risk by measuring the dependency of financial institutions on default risk through a CDS spread analysis of 25 financial institutions in Europe, in Japan and the United States. Likewise, Gauthier et al. (2010) compare some other approaches to $\triangle$CoVaR to determine banks systemic capital requirements with reference to every bank's contribution to systemic risk. They conclude that financial stability can be significantly improved by implementing a banking regulatory system.

Table 1 below presents a summary of the various works cited above. Thus, it indicates for each author the context treated as well as the systemic risk measures adopted and the results obtained.

Table 1. A comparative table: Literature review on systemic risk measures.

Authors	Context	Systemic Risk Measures	Results
Chan-Lau (2009)	Financial institutions in Europe, Japan, and the United States.	ΔCoVaR	The results indicate that risk codependence is stronger during distress periods.
Gauthier et al. (2010)	Canadian banks	A network-based framework and a Merton model	The authors conclude that financial stability can be substantially enhanced by implementing a system perspective on bank regulation.
Acharya et al. (2010)	European and American contexts	SRISK and stress tests	They show that regulatory capital shortfalls measured relative to total assets provide similar rankings to SRISK for U.S. stress tests. On the contrary, rankings are substantially different when the regulatory capital shortfalls are measured relative to risk–weighted assets. Greater differences are observed in the European stress tests.
Reboredo and Ugolini (2015)	European sovereign debt markets	CoVaR	The systemic risks are similar in all countries before the crisis and the decoupling of debt market and systematic risk were globally reduced in the European market after the onset of the Greek debt crisis.
Grieb (2015)	Asian and Russian context	The model of nonlinear factors, and Logistic regression model	The authors show that the systemic risk of hedge fund is increasing.
Kupiec and Güntay (2016)	Different countries	MES and CoVar	They conclude that CoVaR and MES are not reliable measures of systemic risk.
Lin et al. (2016)	Taiwan financial institutions	Different risk measures like *SRISK, MES, CoVaR*	The main results indicate that although these three measures differ in their definition of the contributions to systemic risk, all are quite similar in identifying systemically important financial institutions (SIFIs).
Karimalis and Nomikos (2017)	European large banks	*Copula* and *CoVaR*	They highlight the importance of liquidity risk at the outset of the financial crisis in summer 2007 and find that changes in major macroeconomic variables can contribute significantly to systemic risk.
Brownlees and Engle (2017)	Top international financial firms	*SRISK*	They offered a ranking of institutions in the different crisis stages.
Hmissi et al. (2017)	Tunisian context	CES measure	They find that Tunisian public banks (STB, BNA and BH) are the riskiest systemically banking sector.
Di Clemente (2018)	European banking system	Extreme value theory (EVT)	They showed the connection between a single financial institution and the financial system.
Khiari and Nachnouchi (2018)	Tunisian context	*CoES* and MDS methodologies	They show that public banks respectively along with the two most important private banks hold the leading positions in the systemic risk rankings
Duan (2019)	Chinese context	CoVar	Authors find that the risk spillover value of China Pacific Insurance Company is the largest, followed by China Life Insurance Company, Ping'an Insurance Company of China is the last.

3. Material and Methods

This section presents the methodology used in this paper. Our main objective is to classify the Tunisian banks according to their involvement in the systemic risk. The first part presents an overview on the Tunisian banking sector. In the second part, we present the filtered historical simulation that we use to compute the VaR. The second part explains conditional value at risk (CoVaR) that we use to measure systemic risk and briefly discuss the quantile regression employed to estimate our systemic risk measure. In the last part, thanks to CoVaR, we assess the contribution of the bank to the overall risk ($\Delta CoVaR_q^{sys/i}$) as well as its exposure to aggregate shocks ($\Delta CoVaR_q^{i/system}$). Second, based on CoVaR's estimates we construct systemic risk cartography that allowed for putting forward the Tunisian banks systemic risk involvement.

3.1. Overview of Tunisian Banking Sector

According to Hammami and Boubaker (2015), the banking sector is the lung of economic activity. This is the case of Tunisia, where the economy is a debt-based economy. Indeed, the equilibrium of the banking system is a health status barometer of the whole economy. Tunisian banks occupy a considerable place in the financial sphere, as seen by the strong synchronization of the evolution of the TUNINDEX index with that of the TUNBANK[1], as shown in the following Figure 1.

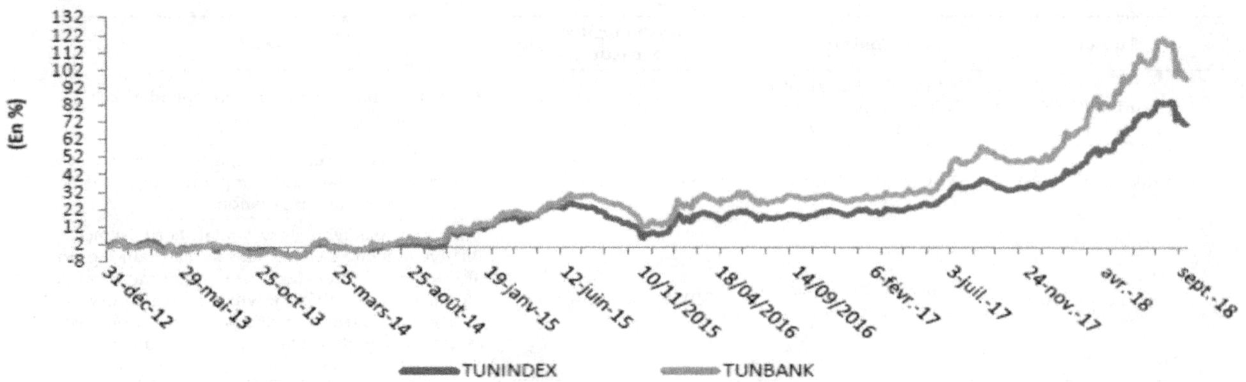

Figure 1. Evolution of the TUNINDEX and TUNBANK during the period 31 December 2012–September 2018. Source: Periodic Conjuncture Report N°121–October 2018, Tunisian Central Bank (Banque Centrale de Tunisie 2018).

In recent years, the banking sector has shown a disengagement from the state because of the introduction of foreign banks to the local banking market and the entry of foreign investors into the shareholding of local banks. The report of the Tunisian Central Bank (Banque Centrale de Tunisie 2012) classifies the bulk of banks into three categories: Banks with a strong participation of the State (Banque Nationale Agricole (BNA) for financing of agricultural sector, Société Tunisienne des Banques (STB) which finances the touristic sector and the Small and Medium Enterprises and Banque de l'Habitat (BH) for housing finance) (Blanco et al. 2014); Tunisian private-owned banks (Banque Internationale Arabe de Tunisie (BIAT) Banque de Tunisie (BT), Amen Bank and Banque de Tunisie et des Emirats (BTE)) and foreign-owned banks (Union Internationale de Banques (UIB), Union Bancaire pour le Commerce et l'Industrie-(UBCI) BNP Paribas, Attijari Bank and Arab Tunisian Bank (ATB)). Private and mixed-capital banks account for 70% of the Tunisian banking sector, although the role of public banks in financing the economy remains pre-emptive. In this banking network, there are 11 banks enjoying a certain popularity among Tunisians and are thus listed on the Tunisian stock market.

The central bank of Tunisia remains the only one responsible for the regulation of the banking activity. It has a role in overseeing monetary policy, supervising credit institutions as well as preserving the stability and security of the financial system. The Tunisian banking system is continuous, well-planned, well-developed and dynamic. At the beginning of the 1990s, the Tunisian banking sector had opened up on an international scale. This idea of liberalization, disintermediation, and disclosure among development banks; and between the deposit banks and the development banks to set up the universal bank, known as the "do-it-all" bank, was held on 10 July 2001.

With the political and economic uncertainty since January 2011, the Tunisian banking sector has undergone certain development, which has affected the situation of the Tunisian market. In this sense, Blanco et al. (2014) argue that this disturbance situation has threatened the viability of the banking sector, which has penalized Tunisian banks.

The rating assigned to Tunisia by the global rating agencies has a downward trend. In fact, just four days after the outbreak of the revolution, the rating agency "Fitch" located 6 Tunisian banks (ATB, BH, STB, BNA, BH, BIAT, and AB) under supervision with a negative implication. Then, in February 2013, "Standard and Poor's" lowered the rating of two banks: ATB from BB to BB– (no longer speculative) and BH went from BB– to B+ (BH went from speculative to very speculative). Then, in

[1] TUNBANK (Tunis Bank) is the stock market index exclusively for the Tunisian banking sector which contains the 11 banks listed on the stock market.

March 2013, "Moody's" dropped the ratings of five Tunisian banks: AB went from Ba2 to Ba3, ATB lost two notches to move from Baa3 to Ba2, BT and BIAT became more speculative by being awarded Ba2 instead of Ba1, and the STB went from Ba2 to B1. Finally, in 2018, the "Moody's" rating agency degraded the five Tunisian banks: AB, ATB, BT, BIAT and STB, with prospects going from stable to negative.

This decline was explained by deterioration in the macroeconomic environment of the banks, which supports not only the quality of their assets, their benefits, but also their capitalization. This situation emerged as a major dilemma in the banking sector called "Banking Run". Jouini and Saidane (2014) described the phenomena experienced by Tunisian banks as a panic crisis that represents massive liquidity withdrawals. In fact, the banking sector has remained frozen in a period of risk acceleration. For this reason, Blanco et al. (2014) believe that Tunisian authorities have been forced to intervene in the system to improve banking supervision, where 38% of bank assets are held by state-owned banks and bankruptcies leading to the appearance of systemic risk.

3.2. Data Description

The sample used includes publicly listed Tunisian banks which represent 92.51 % of total assets of the banking sector in Tunisia. Our panel contains a total of 11 banks. Unlike previous studies, which used weekly data (Khiari and Nachnouchi 2018), the daily closing price data of eleven listed banks and the banking industry index were selected to measure the systemic risk of Tunisian's bank industry from 2 January 2010 to 31 December 2018.

Tunisian's economy is suffering from exceptionally difficult conditions. The debts crises of the European Union have created a slowing down in goods exports, and the January 14th revolution gave rise to a long period of instability, not to mention institutional and political uncertainty. This worsening security situation caused a considerable drop in income in foreign currency from tourism. The Tunisian economy has also been affected by the adverse consequences associated with the Libyan revolution. All Tunisian's sectors had, and are still undergoing, a challenging transition phase. This post-revolutionary context has especially affected the banking sector, as the ability of Tunisian banks to overcome the financial instability has become a great concern. Indeed, they have become extremely fragile to any adverse shocks.

The sample period covers the whole period of subprime crisis, the January 14th revolution and the macroeconomic regulation and control of Tunisian government.

The closing price of each bank is converted to the form of logarithmic yield. The formula is:

$$R_{i,t} = Ln\ P_{i,t} - Ln\ P_{i,t-1}$$

Figure 2 and Table 2 show, respectively, the time series of stock return of the TUNBANK index and descriptive statistics of the 11 Tunisian banks of our panel.

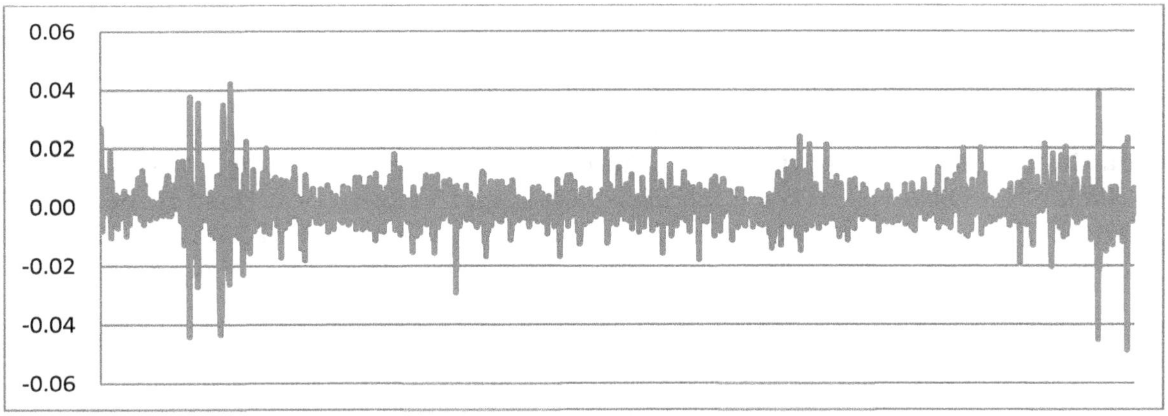

Figure 2. Time series of stock return of the TUNBANK index.

Table 2. Descriptive statistics of stock returns.

	N	Mean	Standard Deviation	Skewness	Kurtosis
AB	2235	−0.029	1.895	−21.775	797.500
ATB	2235	−0.035	1.254	−0.238	4.565
Attijari	2235	0.028	1.188	−0.098	7.265
BH	2235	−0.034	1.789	−5.047	105.419
BT	2235	−0.112	5.024	−41.939	1895.974
BTE	2235	−0.045	1.402	0.176	13.287
BNA	2235	0.009	1.551	0.452	4.082
UBCI	2235	−0.036	1.810	−6.527	158.577
BIAT	2235	0.028	1.249	0.199	4.339
STB	2235	−0.062	1.781	0.300	2132
UIB	2235	0.011	1.170	−0.948	22.974
TUNBANK	2235	0.022	0.645	−0.368	10.108

The majority of banks have negative means, with the exception of four banks: BNA, ATTIJARI, BIAT and UIB. This perfectly reflects the financial difficulties encountered by Tunisian banks. Since this centrally trending statistical measure is very sensitive to extreme values and can be highly contaminated by outliers, we have computed the adjusted mean. The latter compensates this measurement by omitting a predetermined percentage of values on the tails and computes the mean using the other observations.

The asymmetric coefficients show the asymmetry of the yield distributions. Indeed, four banks (BIAT, BNA, STB and BTE) are skewed to the right because they have a positive asymmetry. However, BT, UBCI, TIJARI, BH, AB, AB, UIB and ATB have a negative bias. They are therefore skewed to the left. These banks tend to have extreme negative values. All banks have high kurtosis values, which show the non-normality of their yield series. For UBCI, AB, BH and BT, an examination of their standard deviation, asymmetry and kurtosis shows that these banks have the highest values for these three indicators. They are therefore the most asymmetrical and have the widest gap between the lowest and highest yields. We can therefore conclude that their returns are very far from the average.

This conclusion shows the importance of the third and fourth moments of the distributions. For this reason, we have been tempted to go beyond the limited use of VaR and go further in the calculation of CoVaR, since it provides more information on the distribution of yields in the tail.

3.3. *VaR Estimation*

We use the filtered historical simulation for the calculation of the value at risk (VaR) as it ensures a good estimates quality. According to Paolella and Taschini (2008) this method is highly effective. Indeed, it adapts perfectly to non-normal distributions, and hence, deals with asymmetric distributions and volatility clustering. It is relatively simple to apply and requires no hypothesis regarding the distribution of returns. This semi-parametric method was presented for the first time by Adesi et al. in 1999. It is a combination of parametric models of conditional volatilities and nonparametric methods of simulations.

The residuals are processed using the GARCH filter in order to deal with heteroscedasticity. Then, the standardized residual returns from the dataset are scaled in an ascending order. Here, we are interested mainly in the 5% and 50% quantiles. $VaR_{95\%}$ and $VaR_{50\%}$ correspond respectively to the worst 112 days and the worst 1117 days over the course of the sample. The VaR of bank i at quantile q is

$$VaR^{i}{}_{q,t} = \mu_t + VaR_q \sqrt{ht} \tag{1}$$

where in μ_t is the expected returns and h_t refers to the standardized variances.

Applying (1) we get a series of weekly $VaR^{i}{}_{q}$. The average $VaR^{i}{}_{q,t}$ estimates are presented in Table 3.

Table 3. Banks average $VaR^i{}_{q,t}$.

Banks	BT	BIAT	UBCI	TIJARI	BH	UIB	AB	STB	ATB	BNA	BTE
Average VaRiq,t	−0.017454	−0.020229	−0.039537	−0.015918	−0.026186	−0.015632	−0.022018	−0.029432	−0.020185	−0.023813	−0.022569

It appears that the bank with the largest VaR is the UBCI. Conversely, UIB exhibits the lowest expected losses.

3.4. *CoVaR Estimation*

To measure market risk codependence, we use quantile regression since it offers a deeper analysis than ordinary least squares. It is also known for its simplicity and robustness in exploring relationships between variables evaluated in extreme quantiles. In fact, it takes into consideration the non-linearity of the dependencies between the yields. Furthermore, quantile regression does not require assumptions about the distribution of variables because it is a non-parametric method. Therefore, it avoids the inherent bias in the assumptions of the distributions on parametric methods.

We compute the regression coefficient $\alpha_q{}^i$ and $\beta_q{}^i$ using the following equation:

$$X_q{}^{i,sys} = \alpha_q{}^{sys} + \beta_q{}^{sys} X^{sys} \tag{2}$$

With $X_q{}^{i,sys}$: the return of the bank I at quantile q conditional to the return of the banking system X^i: the return of the banking sector.

Applied to the CoVaR, this method leads to the estimation of the loss of bank i when the system is facing an extreme event using the following expression:

$$CoVAR_{q,t}^{i/Xsys=VaRq} = VaR_q^i / Var_q^{sys} = \alpha_q^{\hat{s}ys} + \beta_q^{\hat{s}ys}\, Var_{q,t}^{sys} \tag{3}$$

where $VaRq,t^i$: VaR of institution i at q%.

The average $CoVaRq,t\ ^{sys/Xi=VaRq}$ is shown in Table 4.

Table 4. Banks average $CoVaRq,t\ ^{sys/Xi=VaRq}$.

Banks	BT	BIAT	UBCI	TIJARI	BH	UIB	AB	STB	ATB	BNA	BTE
COVaR i/sys	−0.039081	−0.042360	−0.067702	−0.040310	−0.050530	−0.037090	−0.037834	−0.052711	−0.042089	−0.053175	−0.056501

As seen in Table 4 the bank that faces the largest losses if the banking sector is in financial distress is the UBCI.

The contribution of bank i to systemic risk is:

$$\Delta CoVaR_q{}^{sys/i} = CoVaR\ {}_{q^{sys}}{}^{/Xi=VaR\ q} - CoVaR\ {}_{q^{sys}}{}^{/Xi=\ Mdian}$$

Finally, the exposure of a financial institution to system wide distress is:

$$\Delta CoVaR_q{}^{i/system} = CoVaR_q{}^{i/Xsystem=VaRq} - CoVaR\ {}_q\ {}^{i/Xsystem=Med}$$

We estimated the average ΔCoVaR to identify the most exposed and systemic entities in terms of market risk, across the sample. Table 5 presents the results obtained for the ΔCOVaR's measures. Values included in the first column are the average contribution of each bank to systemic market risk whereas the second represents the opposite relation as it corresponds to the average exposure of the system's stress to individual bank. In this sense, the former identifies the most contributor banks to the systemic market risk, while the latter allows us to recognize the most exposed banks to the system's risk.

Table 5. Banks average ΔCoVaR.

	Expoure $\Delta CoVaR_q^{i/sys}$	Contribution $\Delta CoVaR^{sys/i}$
AB	−0.032594	−0.021378
ATB	−0.036435	−0.02148
ATTIJARI	−0.028878	−0.018332
BH	−0.045772	−0.020545
BIAT	−0.021259	−0.018508
BNA	−0.036213	−0.020529
BT	−0.022813	−0.015852
BTE	−0.056501	−0.021164
STB	−0.035057	−0.021463
UIB	−0.029841	−0.019827
UBCI	−0.028356	−0.022987

According to these results, it appears that UBCI is the most important contributor to system's risk, since it has the most negative $\Delta CoVaR^{sys/i}$. Hence, it can be claimed that this bank has a significant influence on the banking system. Moreover, BTE is the most vulnerable bank to sector's risk. It is closely followed by the BH, ATB, BNA and the STB. Thus, it can be asserted that public banks are the most vulnerable to the banking sector's financial distress. Also, it is important to note that the least exposed entity is the one among those presenting the lowest contribution (the second lowest contribution) to the sector's systemic risk, namely the BIAT.

3.5. Back Testing

The calculation of the CoVaR depends on the VaR of the different institutions. Thus, to ensure the accuracy of the CoVaR, it is essential to test the VaR of all banks before calculating the CoVaR. The next step in our work is to evaluate the accuracy of the model specification in the estimation of the VaR. According to the Basel Committee on Banking Supervision (2010), the back-test is a statistical means allowing for validating a model by simply comparing actual results to expected results. According to Philippe (2007) a model of VaR must allow us to anticipate the future with precision. The most common tests used to test the VAR model are the ones of Kupiec (1995) and Christoffersen (1998). Kupiec (1995) uses the unconditional coverage test to check whether the numbers of exceptions in the VaR model conform to the confidence interval on which the VaR is defined. An exception is a case where the actual loss is greater than the estimated VaR. According to the Kupiec test, a perfect model of VaR is the one where the expected number of exceptions is equal to the real exceptions. In addition to the number of exceptions, Christoffersen (1998) has also tested the dispersion of exceptions. He shows that a VaR model with clustered exceptions is not considered as an exact model because it will not consider correlations and market volatility. In this work, we compute Kupiec (1995)'s Likelihood Ratio (LR) tests on the empirical failure rates in order to assess the performance of our model.

Results are presented in Table 6 below:

Table 6. Value-at-risk back testing.

		Short Positions		
Quantile	**Success Rate**	**Kupiec LRS** [1]	***p*-Value**	**ESF** [2]
0.9500	0.95302	0.43762	0.50827	0.035825
0.9750	0.97002	2.1380	0.14369	0.039317
0.9900	0.98613	3.0178	0.082353	0.045175
0.9950	0.99060	6.8889	0.0086733	0.046838
0.9975	0.99284	12.890	0.00033043	0.048614
		Long Positions		
Quantile	**Failure Rate**	**Kupiec LRS**	***p*-Value**	**ESF**
0.0500	0.033110	15.162	9.8682×10^{-5}	−0.040975
0.0250	0.019239	3.3011	0.069235	−0.049888
0.0100	0.009396	0.084060	0.77187	−0.068311
0.0050	0.0062640	0.66418	0.41509	−0.085305
0.0025	0.0044743	2.8248	0.092818	−0.10279

[1] LR refers to the likelihood ratio statistic. [2] ESF refers to the expected shortfall.

As shown in this table, the computed values are the Kupiec LR test, the failure/success rate, p-values and the expected shortfall (ESF) with significance level, $\alpha = 0.0025, 0.005, 0.01, 0.025, 0.05$ and $\alpha = 0.95, 97.5, 0.99, 99.5, 99.75$ for long and short positions respectively. The objective is to check whether the failure/success rate of the model is statistically equal to the expected one. The success rate for short position refers to the percentage of positive returns larger than the VaR prediction, while the failure rate for the long position is the percentage of negative returns smaller than the VAR prediction.

The results show that the model performs very well. Indeed, the Kupiec LR test's p-values show that the model accurately predicts VaR for all cases (long and short positions and at all confidence levels). This result clearly shows that the model is able to capture the reality of the Tunisian banking sector.

4. Discussion: The Positioning of Tunisian Banks Based on Their Systemic Risks' Implication

The CoVaRs, as calculated in the previous section, are used to provide a comprehensive and unified statistical profile of all Tunisian Banks according to their implication level (contribution and exposure) in systemic risk. Thus, we set a detailed map to show the relative positioning of all banks according to their implication into systemic risk.

In our case, we choose two dimensions that express the implication of each bank in systemic risk. As shown in the Table 7, The first dimension (horizontal axis) indicates the bank's exposure ($\Delta CoVaR^{i/sys}$) and the second (vertical axis) points to the contribution of banks to the system risk.

Table 7. Dimensions reflecting level of involvement of Tunisian Banks in the systemic risk.

	First Dimension Horizontal Axis (Bank's Exposure)	Second Dimension Vertical Axis (Bank's Contribution)
Axis	$\Delta CoVaR^{sys/i}$	$\Delta CoVaRq^{i/system}$

From the point of view of the graphical representation, this leads to a space where each bank is marked by a dot and scaled according to its involvement in systemic risk. Figure 3 is the map that has been recovered from the confrontation of the two axis (dimensions).

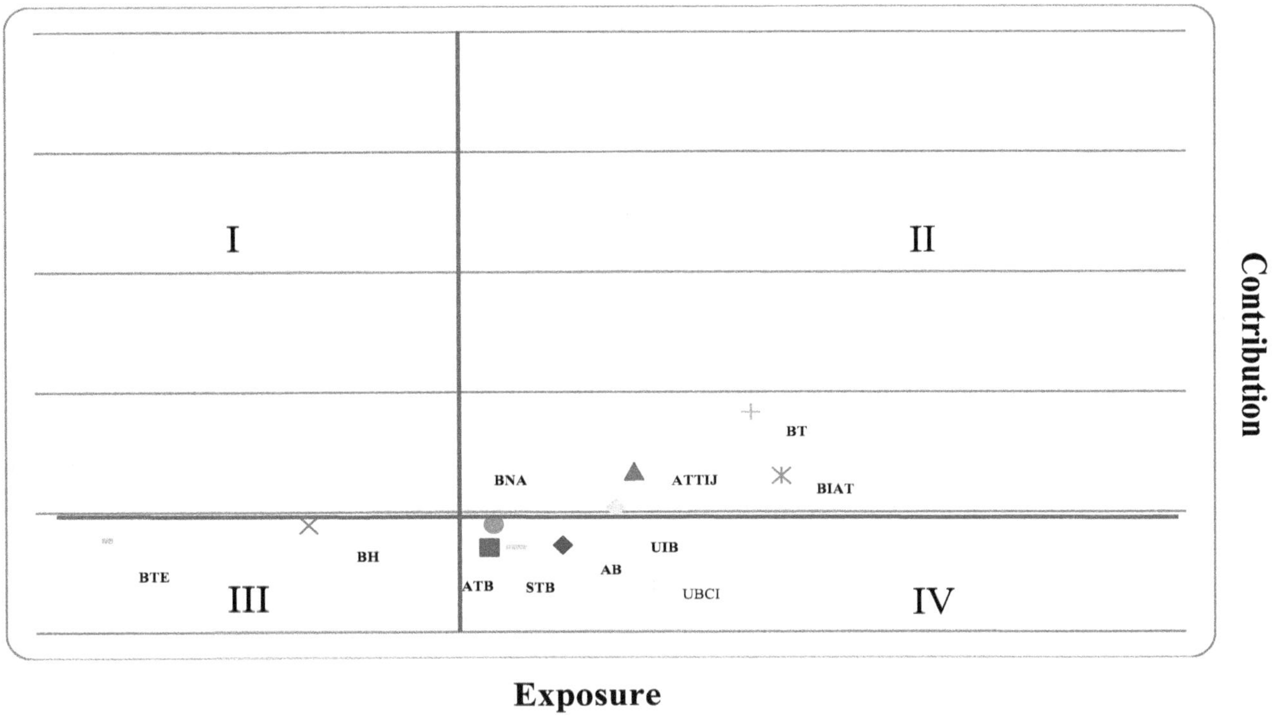

Figure 3. The positioning of Tunisian banks based on their systemic risks' implication.

In order to interpret this map, we choose to divide it into four zones according to the implication degree of each bank in the systemic risk. This repartition is established using the mean of each series of ΔCoVaR calculated for all the banks of the sample. The Formula used is: *(min ΔCOVaR + max ΔCoVaR)/2 Or: ∑ ΔCoVaR/11.*

The results for the two formulas are given by the following Table 8. As shown in this table, the two methods give approximately the same results:

Zone I: The lowest contributor and the highest exposed;
Zone II: The lowest contributor, the lowest exposed;
Zone III: The highest contributor and the highest exposed;
Zone IV: The highest contributor and the lowest exposed;

Table 8. Total means of ΔCoVaR.

	Exposure $\Delta CoVaR_q^{i/system}$	Contribution $\Delta CoVaR^{sys/i}$
(min ΔCOVaR + max ΔCOVaR)/2	−0.0194195	−0.03888
∑ ΔCOVaR/11	−0.02018773	−0.03397445

A first look on this cartography shows the existence of two dimensions. The first dimension represents the banks' contribution to systemic risk. It indicates the systemic potential of the bank. The second dimension is related to banks' sensitivity to systemic risk.

It seems that the banks located in Zones III and IV are the most productive banks of systemic risk. This implies that they contribute more to systemic risk than those in other areas. We can also conclude that banks in Zones II and IV face less loss in the event of default by banks other than those in Zones I and III. This particular reading makes it possible to conclude from the existence of the notion of domination. Indeed, the graph shows two groups of banks. Banks belonging to the zones I and III can be considered as dominated banks as they have the highest exposure levels. These banks seem to be very sensitive to the systemic risk of other banks. Banks belonging to Zones III and IV are the dominating banks as they have the highest contributor levels. These banks seem to impose important systemic risk to others banks.

The results of this mapping (Figure 3) allows us to divide banks according to their involvement in systemic risk.

The results from this cartography (Figure 3) allowed us to establish a distribution of banks based on their involvement in systemic risk. According to this figure, the public banks (STB, ATB and BNA), located in Zone IV, occupy the first three places because they are closest to the vertical axis. They are followed closely by the two main Tunisian private banks, UBCI and AM. These five banks are the main systemic players in the Tunisian banking sector. It seems that they are the least sensitive to the financial difficulties of other banks and the biggest contributors to the distress of existing banks. Then there is the public bank BH (located in Zone III). It should also be noted that BH and BTE are the most involved banks, as they are located furthest to the left. According to this map the BTE and BH are substantially involved in systemic risk as they represent the important $\Delta CoVaR^{sys/i}$ and $\Delta CoVaR_q^{i/system}$ measures.

On the other hand, BIAT and BT exhibit, relatively, the smallest contribution and exposure measures as they are situated the most to the right and top; hence they are less concerned by systemic risk.

What emerges from these results, is that those banks are the largest systemic players among the Tunisian banks. These results involve, among other things, a rethinking of risk management practices of these banks.

Indeed, regulators not only lack effective risk control measures for individual banks, but also lack an effective regulatory framework to detect and measure the spread of the overall risk spillover of the banking sector. Consequently, this shows the limits of regulation and supervisory practices to effectively manage risks to financial system soundness. Indeed, systemic risk and spillover of the banking sector have had an impact on the stability of the banking sector in the country and all over the financial system. To avoid any systemic risk, it is essential that regulators strictly supervise the banking sector in terms of micro and macro design.

First, there is a systemic risk contagion effect in the Tunisian banking sector, which has a significant impact on the financial market and the economy as a whole. There is a need to monitor risks and prevent them from micro and macro perspectives. Macro prudential surveillance should be strengthened and the systemic financial crisis caused by the increase of the risk contagion effect should be avoided. Differentiated management should be carried out according to the impact of Tunisian banks, and stricter supervision should be imposed to ensure the stability of the entire banking sector and thus prevent the spread of financial risks in the event of a crisis.

Then accelerate the daily risk management. Regulators should pay particular attention to the systemic risk contagion effect of Tunisian banks, focus on monitoring the operational risk of systemically important banks and strictly protect themselves from extreme risks, then pass them on to other secondary financial markets. For individual banks, they should not only focus on their own internal risks, but also be concerned about their risk being passed on to other financial institutions and constantly improve their risk control capabilities. Listed banks should optimize their portfolios and minimize the spillovers of systemic risk with reference to scientific judgment of the macroeconomic situation.

The distribution of Tunisian banks in terms of systemic risk involvement provided by this map adds a broader perspective to the micro prudential application of regulation that includes contagion and then formulates a macro prudential vision and strengthens regulatory policy. Supervisors could impose close supervision for institutions considered to be potentially systemic banks. In addition, regulations should take into account the systemic contribution when designing risk requirements in order to minimize the adverse consequences of possible herd behavior.

5. Conclusions

This work aims to analyze systemic risk among Tunisian listed banks to determine the most contributors and exposed institutions to the systemic risk.

In this paper, we use filtered historical simulation to estimate the VaR to compute the CoVaR using quantile regressions. These CoVaR estimates are selected to measure the contribution of the bank to the overall risk ($\Delta \text{CoVaR}_q{}^{sys/i}$) as well as its exposure to aggregate shocks ($\Delta CoVaR_q{}^{i/\text{system}}$). Based on CoVaR estimates, we set a perceptual map that allows us to explain and revise banks systemic risk in the Tunisian context.

Results suggest that the BTE and BH are substantially involved in systemic risk as they represent the important $\Delta \text{CoVaR}^{sys/i}$ and $\Delta CoVaR_q{}^{i/\text{system}}$ measures. On the other hand, BT and BIAT exhibit the smallest contribution and exposure measures, and hence they are the less concerned by systemic risk.

According to CoVaR estimates, public banks occupy the top positions, followed by the two largest private banks in Tunisia. These five banks are the main systemic players in the Tunisian banking sector. It seems that they are the least sensitive to the financial difficulties of other banks and the most important contributors to the distress of existing banks.

This study proposes a distribution of Tunisian banks in terms of systemic risk involvement. It aims to add a broader perspective to the micro prudential application of regulation including contagion, proposing a macro prudential vision that strengthens regulatory policy. Supervisors could impose close supervision for institutions considered to be potentially systemic banks. Furthermore, regulations should consider the systemic contribution when defining risk requirements to minimize the consequences of possible herd behavior.

However, it is important to mention that some shortcomings must be considered. First, the estimation error of the quantile regression increases substantially in the extreme quantile of the distribution. In addition, it is impossible to measure VaR accurately, which makes CoVaR estimates less accurate. Furthermore, CoVaR as regulatory policy tool is not able to differentiate between contagious and infected banks. Second, this measure is very sensitive to current changes in VaR estimates. As a result, companies that have portfolio returns that change more, seem to be more systemic than those with more stable yield and higher positions in these investments. Improvements in estimation are needed to address these gaps and can be considered as an interesting future avenue of research.

Author Contributions: Conceptualization, W.K.; methodology, W.K.; software, S.B.S.; validation, S.B.S.; formal analysis, W.K.; investigation, S.B.S.; resources, W.K. and S.B.S.; data curation, W.K. and S.B.S.; writing—original draft preparation, W.K.; writing—review and editing, W.K.

References

Acharya, Viral V., Lasse H. Pedersen, and Thomas Philippon. 2010. *Measuring Systemic Risk*. Working paper. New York, NY, USA: New York University.

Adrian, Tobis, and Markus Brunnermeier. 2011. *CoVaR*. Federal Reserve Bank of New York Staff Report, No. 348. New York: FRBNY.

Banque Centrale de Tunisie. 2012. Rapport Annuel. Rapport de la Banque Centrale de Tunisie, Tunisie. Available online: https://www.bct.gov.tn/bct/siteprod/documents/rapport2012.pdf (accessed on 11 December 2019).

Banque Centrale de Tunisie. 2018. Périodique de Conjoncture. Rapport de la Banque Centrale de Tunisie, No. 121. Tunisie. Available online: https://www.bct.gov.tn/bct/siteprod/documents/Conjoncture_fr.pdf (accessed on 11 December 2019).

Banulescu, Georgiana-Denisa, and Elena-Ivona Dumitrescu. 2015. Which are the SIFIs? A Component Expected Shortfall approach to systemic risk. *Journal of Banking & Finance* 50: 575–88.

Basel Committee on Banking Supervision. 2010. *Basel III: A Global Regulatory Framework for more Resilient Banks and Banking Systems*. Basel: Bank for International Settlements, Available online: https://www.bis.org/publ/bcbs189_dec2010.pdf (accessed on 11 December 2019).

Bisias, Dimitrios, Mark Flood, and Stavros Valavanis. 2012. A Survey of Systemic Risk Analytics. *Annual Review of Financial Economics* 4: 255–96. [CrossRef]

Blanco, Karim, Belgheith Haifa, Neira Kaouach, and Ines Khouaja. 2014. *Le Secteur Bancaire Tunisien: Evolution, Perspectives et Défis*. Tunis: La revue bancaire Amen Invest, intermédiaire en bourse.

Boucher, Christophe, Jon Danielsson, Patrick Kouontchou, and Bertrand Maillet. 2013. Risk Model-at-Risk. *Journal of Banking and Finance* 44: 72–92. [CrossRef]

Brownlees, Christian, and Robert F. Engle. 2017. SRISK: A Conditional Capital Shortfall Measure of Systemic Risk. *The Review of Financial Studies* 30: 48–79. [CrossRef]

Chan-Lau, Jorge. 2009. Default Risk Codependence in the Global Financial System: Was the Bear Stearns Bailout Justified? In *The Banking Crisis Handbook*. Edited by Greg N. Gregoriou. New York: McGraw Hill.

Christoffersen, Peter F. 1998. Evaluating interval forecasts. *International Economic Review* 39: 841–62. [CrossRef]

Di Clemente, Annalisa. 2018. Estimating the Marginal Contribution to Systemic Risk by a CoVaR-model Based on Copula Functions and Extreme Value Theory. *Economic Notes* 47: 1–44. [CrossRef]

Danielsson, Jon, Kevin R. James, Marcela Valenzuela, and Ilknur Zer. 2011. *Model Risk of Systemic Risk Models*. Working paper. London, UK: London School of Economics.

Derbali, Abdelkader, and Slaheddine Hallara. 2015. Systemic risk of European financial institutions: Estimation and ranking by the Marginal Expected Shortfall. *Research in International Business & Finance* 37: 32–40.

Duan, Xiaohua. 2019. Systematic Risk Measurement Based on CoVaR Model. *International Journal Of Circuits, Systems And Signal Processing* 13: 243–50.

Gauthier, Céline, Alfred Lehar, and Moez Souissi. 2010. *Macroprudential Regulation and Systemic Capital Requirements*. Working Paper 2010-4. Ottawa, ON, Canada: Bank of Canada.

Girardi, Giulio, and A. Tolga Ergün. 2013. Systemic risk measurement: Multivariate GARCH estimation of CoVaR. *Journal of Banking & Finance* 37: 3169–80.

Grieb, Frederik. 2015. Systemic Risk and Hedge Funds. *Social Science Electronic Publishing* 49: 235–340. [CrossRef]

Hammami, Yosra, and Adel Boubaker. 2015. Ownership structure and Bank Risk-Taking: Empirical Evidence fron the Middle East and North Africa. *International Business Research* 18: 271. [CrossRef]

Hmissi, Bochra, Azza Bejaoui, and Wafa Snoussi. 2017. On identifying the domestic systemically important banks: The case of Tunisia. *Research in International Business and Finance* 42: 1343–54. [CrossRef]

Hurlin, Christophe, Sébastien Laurent, Rogier Quaedvlieg, and Stephan Smeekes. 2012. *Ranking the Systemic Risk Measures*. New York: Mimeo.

Jouini, Elyes, and Dhafer Saidane. 2014. *Système bancaire en Tunisie: État des lieux et perspective. contribution à l'ouvrage dirigé par Elyès Jouini: Tunisie L'espoir: mode d'emploi pour une reprise*. Tunis: Cérès éditions.

Karimalis, Emmanouil N., and Nikos K. Nomikos. 2017. Measuring Systemic Risk in the European Banking Sector: A Copula CoVaR Approach. *European Journal of Finance* 24: 944–75. [CrossRef]

Khiari, Wided, and Jamila Nachnouchi. 2018. Banks' systemic risk in the Tunisian context: Measures and Determinants. *Research in International Business & Finance* 45: 620–31.

Kupiec, Paul, and Levent Güntay. 2016. Testing for Systemic Risk Using Stock Returns. *Journal of Financial Services Research* 49: 203–27. [CrossRef]

Kupiec, Paul. 1995. Techniques for verifying the accuracy of risk measurement models. *The Journal of Derivatives* 3: 73–84. [CrossRef]

Lin, Edward M. H., Sun Edward, and Yu Min Teh. 2016. Systemic Risk, Interconnectedness, and Non-core Activities in Taiwan Insurance Industry. *Annals of Operations Research* 12: 1–25.

Paolella, Marc S., and Luca Taschini. 2008. An Econometric Analysis of emission Allowances Prices. *Journal of Banking and Finance* 32: 2022–32. [CrossRef]

Philippe, Jorion. 2007. *Value at Risk: The New Benchmark for Managing Financial Risk*. New York: McGraw-Hill, p. 3.

Reboredo, Juan C., and Andrea Ugolini. 2015. Systemic risk in European sovereign debt markets: A CoVaR-copula approach. *Journal of International Money & Finance* 51: 214–44.

9

Target Matrix Estimators in Risk-Based Portfolios

Marco Neffelli

Department of Economics and Business Studies, University of Genova, Via Vivaldi, 5, 16126 Genova, Italy; marco.neffelli@edu.unige.it

Abstract: Portfolio weights solely based on risk avoid estimation errors from the sample mean, but they are still affected from the misspecification in the sample covariance matrix. To solve this problem, we shrink the covariance matrix towards the Identity, the Variance Identity, the Single-index model, the Common Covariance, the Constant Correlation, and the Exponential Weighted Moving Average target matrices. Using an extensive Monte Carlo simulation, we offer a comparative study of these target estimators, testing their ability in reproducing the *true* portfolio weights. We control for the dataset dimensionality and the shrinkage intensity in the Minimum Variance (MV), Inverse Volatility (IV), Equal-Risk-Contribution (ERC), and Maximum Diversification (MD) portfolios. We find out that the Identity and Variance Identity have very good statistical properties, also being well conditioned in high-dimensional datasets. In addition, these two models are the best target towards which to shrink: they minimise the misspecification in risk-based portfolio weights, generating estimates very close to the population values. Overall, shrinking the sample covariance matrix helps to reduce weight misspecification, especially in the Minimum Variance and the Maximum Diversification portfolios. The Inverse Volatility and the Equal-Risk-Contribution portfolios are less sensitive to covariance misspecification and so benefit less from shrinkage.

Keywords: estimation error; shrinkage; target matrix; risk-based portfolios

---

1. Introduction

The seminal contributions of Markowitz (1952, 1956) laid the foundations for his well-known portfolio building technique. Albeit elegant in its formulation and easy to be implemented in real-world applications, the Markowitz model relies on securities returns sample mean and sample covariance as inputs to estimate the optimal allocation. However, there is a large consensus on the fact that sample estimators perpetuate large estimation errors; this directly affects portfolio weights that often exhibit extreme values, fluctuating over time with very poor performance out-of-sample (De Miguel et al. 2009).

This problem has been tackled from different perspectives: Jorion (1986) and Michaud (1989) suggested Bayesian alternatives to the sample estimators; Jagannathan and Ma (2003) added constraints to the Markowitz model limiting the estimation error; Black and Litterman (1992) derived an alternative portfolio construction technique exclusively based on the covariance matrix among asset returns, avoiding estimating the mean value for each security and converging to the Markowitz Minimum Variance portfolio with no short-sales. This latter technique is supported by results in Merton (1980) and Chopra and Ziemba (1993), who clearly demonstrated how the mean estimation process can lead to more severe distortions than those in the case of the covariance matrix.

Following this perspective, estimation error can be reduced by considering risk-based portfolios: findings suggest they have good out-of-sample performance without much turnover (De Miguel et al. 2009). There is a recent research strand focused on deriving risk-based portfolios other than the Minimum Variance one. In this context, Qian (2006) designed a way to select assets by assigning to each of them the same contribution to the overall portfolio risk; Choueifaty and Coignard (2008) proposed a portfolio where diversification is the key criterion in asset selection; Maillard et al. (2010) offered a novel portfolio construction technique where weights perpetuate an equal risk contribution while maximising diversification. These portfolios are largely popular among practitioners[1]: they highlight the importance of diversification, risk budgeting; moreover, they put risk management in a central role, offering a low computational burden to estimate weights. They are perceived as "robust" models since they do not require the explicit estimation of the mean. Unfortunately, limiting the estimation error in this way poses additional problems related to the ill-conditioning of the covariance matrix that occurs when the number of securities becomes sensitively greater than the number of observations. In this case, the sample eigenvalues become more dispersed than the population ones (Marčenko and Pastur 1967), and the sample covariance matrix directly affects weight estimation. This means that for a high-dimensional dataset, the sample covariance matrix is not a reliable estimator.

To reduce misspecification effects on portfolio weights, more sophisticated estimators than the sample covariance have been proposed, for example the Bayes-Stein shrinkage technique (James and Stein 1961), henceforth shrinkage stems for its practical implementation and related portfolio performance. This technique reduces the misspecification in the sample covariance matrix by shrinking it towards an alternative estimator. Here, the problem is to select a convenient target estimator as well as to find the optimal intensity at which to shrink towards the sample covariance matrix. The latter is usually derived by minimising a predefined loss function to obtain the minimum distance between the *true* and the shrunk covariance matrices (Ledoit and Wolf 2003). A comprehensive overview on shrinkage intensity parameters can be found in (De Miguel et al. 2013), where the authors proposed an alternative way of deriving the optimal intensity based on the smoothed bootstrap approach. On the other hand, the target matrix is often selected among the class of structured covariance estimators (Briner and Connor 2008), especially because the matrix which shrinks is the sample one. As noted in (Candelon et al. 2012), the sample covariance matrix is the Maximum Likelihood Estimator (MLE) under the Normality of asset returns, hence it lets the data speak without imposing any structure. This naturally suggests it might be pulled towards a more structured alternative. Dealing with financial data, the shrinkage literature proposes six different models for the target matrix: the Single-Index market model (Ledoit and Wolf 2003; Briner and Connor 2008; Candelon et al. 2012; Ardia et al. 2017); the Identity matrix (Ledoit and Wolf 2004a; Candelon et al. 2012); the Variance Identity matrix (Ledoit and Wolf 2004a); the Scaled Identity matrix (De Miguel et al. 2013); the Constant Correlation model (Ledoit and Wolf 2004b) and (Pantaleo et al. 2011); the Common Covariance (Pantaleo et al. 2011). All these targets belong to the class of more structured covariance estimators than the sample one, thus implying the latter is the matrix to shrink.

Despite the great improvements in portfolio weight estimation under the Markowitz portfolio building framework, the shrinkage technique has only been applied in one work involving risk-based portfolios: that of Ardia et al. (2017), who comprehensively described the impacts of variance and covariance misspecifications in risk-portfolio weights. Ardia et al. (2017) tested four alternative covariance estimators to reduce weight misspecification; among those, only one refers to shrinkage as in (Ledoit and Wolf 2003), leaving room open for further research. In our work, we contribute to the existing literature, filling this gap and offering a comprehensive overview of shrinkage in risk-based portfolios. In particular, we study the effect of six target matrix estimators on the weights of four risk-based portfolios. To achieve this goal, we provide an extensive Monte Carlo simulation aimed at (1) assessing estimators' statistical properties and similarity with the *true* target matrix; (2) addressing the problem of how the selection of a specific target estimator affects the portfolio weights. We find out that the Identity and Variance Identity hold the best statistical properties, being well conditioned even in a high-dimensional dataset. These two estimators also represent the more efficient target

---

1 The majority of papers on risk-based portfolios are published in journal aimed at practitioners, as the Journal of Portfolio Management.

matrices towards which to shrink the sample one. In fact, portfolio weight derived shrinking towards the Identity and Variance Identity minimise the distance from their *true* counterparts, especially in the case of Minimum Variance and Maximum Diversification portfolios.

The rest of the paper is organised as follows. Section 2 introduces the risk-based portfolios employed in the study. Section 3 illustrates the shrinkage estimator, the moves to the six target matrix estimators and provides useful insights into misspecification when shrinkage is applied to risk-based portfolios. In Section 4, we run an extensive Monte Carlo analysis for describing how changes in the target matrix affect risk-based portfolio weights. Section 5 concludes.

2. Risk-Based Portfolios

Risk-based portfolios are particularly appealing since they rely only on the estimation of a proper measure of risk, i.e., the covariance matrix between asset returns. Assume an investment universe made by p assets:

$$X = (x_1, \ldots, x_p) \tag{1}$$

is a $n \times p$ containing a history of n log-returns for the i-th asset, where $i = 1, \ldots, p$. The covariance matrix among asset log-returns is the symmetric square matrix Σ[2] of dimension $p \times p$, and the unknown optimal weights form the vector ω of dimension $p \times 1$. Our working framework assumes to consider four risk-based portfolios: the Minimum Variance (MV), the Inverse Volatility (IV), the Equal-Risk-Contribution (ERC), and the Maximum Diversification (MD) upon two constraints; no short-selling ($\omega \in \Re^p_+$) and full allocation of the available wealth ($\omega'\mathbf{1}_p = 1$, where $\mathbf{1}_p$ is the vector of ones of length p).

The Minimum Variance portfolio (Markowitz 1952) derives the optimal portfolio weights by solving this minimization problem with respect to ω:

$$\omega_{MV} \equiv \underset{\omega}{\operatorname{argmin}} \left\{ \omega'\Sigma\omega \;\middle|\; \omega \in \Re^p_+, \omega'\mathbf{1}_p = 1 \right\} \tag{2}$$

where $\omega'\Sigma\omega$ is the portfolio variance.

In the Inverse Volatility portfolio, also known as the equal-risk-budget portfolio (Leote de Carvalho et al. 2012), a closed form solution is available. Each element of the vector ω is given by the inverse of the i-th asset variance (denoted by $\Sigma_{i,i}^{-1}$) divided by the inverse of the sum of all asset variances:

$$\omega_{IV} \equiv \left(\frac{\Sigma_{1,1}^{-1}}{\sum_{i=1}^{p} \Sigma_{i,i}^{-1}}, \ldots, \frac{\Sigma_{p,p}^{-1}}{\sum_{i=1}^{p} \Sigma_{i,i}^{-1}} \right)' \tag{3}$$

In the Equal-Risk-Contribution portfolio, as the name suggests, the optimal weights are calculated by assigning to each asset the same contribution to the whole portfolio volatility, thus originating a minimization procedure to be solved with respect to ω:

$$\omega_{ERC} \equiv \underset{\omega}{\operatorname{argmin}} \left\{ \sum_{i=1}^{p} \left(\%RC_i - \frac{1}{p} \right)^2 | \omega \in \Re^p_+, \omega'\mathbf{1}_p = 1 \right\} \tag{4}$$

Here, $\%RC_i \equiv \frac{\omega_i cov_{i,\pi}}{\sqrt{\omega'\Sigma\omega}}$ is the percentage risk contribution for the i-th asset, $\sqrt{\omega'\Sigma\omega}$ is the portfolio volatility as earlier defined, and $\omega_i cov_{i,\pi}$ provides a measure of the covariance of the i-th exposure to the total portfolio π, weighted by the corresponding ω_i.

Turning to the Maximum Diversification, as in Choueifaty and Coignard (2008) we preliminary define $DR(\omega)$ as the portfolio's diversification ratio:

---

2 With this we refer to the population covariance matrix, which by definition is not observable and then unfeasible. Hence, Σ is estimated taking into account the observations stored in X: we will deeply treat this in the next section.

$$DR(\omega) \equiv \frac{\omega' \sqrt{diag(\Sigma)}}{\sqrt{\omega' \Sigma \omega}}$$

where $diag(\Sigma)$ is a $p \times 1$ vector which takes all the asset variances $\Sigma_{i,i}$ and $\omega' \sqrt{diag(\Sigma)}$ is the weighted average volatility. By construction, it is $DR(\omega) \geq 1$, since the portfolio volatility is sub-additive (Ardia et al. 2017). Hence, the optimal allocation is the one with the highest DR:

$$\omega_{MD} \equiv \underset{\omega}{\operatorname{argmax}} \left\{ DR(\omega) \middle| \, \omega \in \Re^p_+, \omega' \mathbf{1}_p = 1 \right\}. \tag{5}$$

3. Shrinkage Estimator

The shrinkage technique relies upon three ingredients: the starting covariance matrix to shrink, the target matrix towards which the former is shrunk, and the shrinkage intensity, or roughly speaking the strength at which the starting matrix must be shrunk.

In financial applications, the starting matrix which is to shrink is always the sample covariance matrix. This is a very convenient choice that helps in the selection of a proper shrinkage target: being the sample covariance a model-free estimator that completely reflects the relationships among data[3], it becomes natural to select a target in the class of more structured covariance estimators (Briner and Connor 2008). In addition, this strategy allows direct control over the trade-off between estimation error and model error in the resulting shrinkage estimates. In fact, the sample covariance matrix is usually affected by a large amount of estimation error. This is reduced when shrinking towards a structured target which minimizes the sampling error at the cost of adding some misspecification by imposing a specific model. At this point, the shrinkage intensity is crucial because it must be set in such a way to minimize both errors.

To define the shrinkage estimator, we start from the definition of sample covariance matrix S. Recalling Equation (1), S is given by

$$S = \frac{1}{n-1} X'^{(I_n - \frac{1}{n}\mathbf{1}_n \mathbf{1}_n')} X, \tag{6}$$

where I_n denotes the $n \times n$ identity matrix and $\mathbf{1}_n$ is the ones column vector of length n. The shrinkage methodology enhances the sample covariance matrix estimation by shrinking S towards a specific target matrix T:

$$\Sigma_s = \delta T + (1 - \delta) S \tag{7}$$

where Σ_s is the shrinkage estimator; δ the shrinkage parameter and T the target matrix. In this work, we focus on the problem of selecting the target matrix. After a review of the literature on target matrices, in the following rows we present the target estimators considered in this study and we assess through a numerical illustration the impact of misspecification in the target matrix for the considered risk-based portfolios.

3.1. *Target Matrix Literature Review*

The target matrix should fit a desirable number of requirements: First, it should be structured much enough to lower the estimation error of the sample covariance matrix while not bringing too much error from model selection. Second, it should reflect the important features of the *true* covariance matrix (Ledoit and Wolf 2004b). The crucial question is: how much structure should we impose to fill in the requirements? Table 1 shows the target matrices employed so far in the literature, summarising information about the formula for the shrinkage intensity, the wealth allocation rule, and the addressed

---

[3] The sample covariance matrix is the Maximum Likelihood Estimator (MLE) under Normality, therefore it lets data speaks without imposing any structure.

research question. Not surprisingly, all the papers shrink the sample covariance matrix. What surprises is that only six target matrices have been examined: the one relying on the Single-Index market model, the Identity matrix, the Scaled Identity, and the Variance Identity, the Constant Correlation model and the Common Covariance model. Previously, four were proposed by Ledoit and Wolf in separate works (Ledoit and Wolf 2003, 2004a, 2004b) and were again proposed in subsequent works, while the Common Covariance appears only in (Pantaleo et al. 2011) and the Scaled Identity only in (De Miguel et al. 2013).

Table 1. Literature review of target matrices. "SCVm" = sample covariance matrix. "N.A." = not available. "GMVP" = Global Minimum Variance Portfolio.

Reference	Matrix to Shrink	Target Matrix	Shrinkage Intensity	Portfolio Selection Rule	Research Question
(Ledoit and Wolf 2003)	SCVm	Market Model and Variance Identity	Risk-function minimisation	Classical Markowitz problem	Portfolio Performance comparison
(Ledoit and Wolf 2004a)	SCVm	Identity	Risk-function minimisation	N.A.	Theoretical paper to gauge the shrinkage asymptotic properties
(Ledoit and Wolf 2004b)	SCVm	Constant Correlation Model	Optimal shrinkage constant	Classical Markowitz problem	Portfolio Performance comparison
(Briner and Connor 2008)	Demeaned SCVm	Market Model	Same as (Ledoit and Wolf 2004b)	N.A.	Analysis of the trade-off estimation error and model specification error
(Pantaleo et al. 2011)	SCVm	Market Model, Common Covariance and Constant Correlation Model	Unbiased estimator of (Schäfer and Strimmer 2005)	Classical Markowitz problem	Portfolio Performance comparison
(Candelon et al. 2012)	SCVm	Market Model and Identity	Same as (Ledoit and Wolf 2003, 2004b)	Black-Litterman GMVP	Portfolio Performance comparison
(De Miguel et al. 2013)	SCVm	Scaled Identity	Expected quadratic loss and bootstrapping approach	Classical Markowitz problem	Comprehensive investigation of shrinkage estimators
(Ardia et al. 2017)	SCVm	Market Model	Same as (Ledoit and Wolf 2003)	Risk-based portfolios	Theoretical paper to assess effect on risk-based weights

In Table 1, papers have been listed taking into account their contribution to the literature as regards the adoption of a novel target matrix estimator, the re-examination of a previously proposed target, and the comparison among different estimators. Ledoit and Wolf popularised the shrinkage methodology in portfolio selection: in Ledoit and Wolf (2003), they were also the first to compare the effects of shrinking towards different targets in portfolio performance. Shrinking towards the Variance Identity and shrinking towards the Market Model are two out of the eight estimators for the covariance matrix compared with respect to the reduction of estimation error in portfolio weights. They found significant improvements in portfolio performance when shrinking towards the Market Model. Briner and Connor (2008) well described the importance of selecting the target matrix among the class of structured covariance estimators, hence proposing to shrink the asset covariance matrix of demeaned returns towards the Market model as in Ledoit and Wolf (2003). Candelon et al. (2012) compared the effect of double shrinking the sample covariance either towards the Market Model and the Identity, finding that both estimators carry on similar out-of-sample performances. De Miguel et al. (2013) compared the effects of different shrinkage estimators on portfolio performance, highlighting the importance of the shrinkage intensity parameter and proposing a scaled version of the Identity Matrix as a target. Another important comparison among target matrices is that of Pantaleo et al. (2011), who compared the Market and Constant Correlation models as in Ledoit and Wolf (2003, 2004b) with the Common Covariance of Schäfer and Strimmer (2005) implemented as target matrix for the first time in finance. The authors assessed the effects on portfolio performances while controlling for the dimensionality of the dataset, finding that the Common Covariance should not be used when the number of observations is less than the number of assets. Lastly, Ardia et al. (2017) is the only work to implement shrinkage in risk-based portfolios. They shrunk the sample covariance matrix as in Ledoit and Wolf (2003), finding that the Minimum Variance and the Maximum Diversification portfolios are the most affected from covariance misspecification, hence they benefit the most from the shrinkage technique.

3.2. Estimators for the Target Matrix

We consider six estimators for the target matrix: the Identity and the Variance Identity matrix, the Single-index, the Common Covariance, the Constant Correlation and the Exponential Weighted Moving Average (EWMA) models. They are all structured estimators, in the sense that the number of parameters to be estimated is far less the $\frac{1}{2}p(p+1)$ required in the sample covariance case. Compared with the literature, we take into account all the previous target estimators,[4] adding to the analysis the EWMA: this estimator well addresses the problem of serial correlation and heteroskedasticity in asset returns.

The identity is a matrix with ones on the diagonal and zeros elsewhere. Choosing the Identity as the target is justified by the fact that is shows good statistical properties: it is always well conditioned and hence invertible (Ledoit and Wolf 2003). Besides the identity, we also consider a multiple of the identity, named the Identity Variance. This is given by:

$$T_{VId} \equiv I_p diag(S) I_p, \tag{8}$$

where $diag(S)$ is the main diagonal of the sample covariance matrix (hence the assets variances) and I_p the identity matrix of dimension p.

The Single Index Model (Sharpe 1963) assumes that the returns $\boldsymbol{r}_t$ can be described by a one-factor model, resembling the impact of the whole market:

$$\boldsymbol{r}_t = \boldsymbol{\alpha} + \boldsymbol{\beta} r_{mkt} + \varepsilon_t, \text{ with } t = 1, \ldots, n,$$

where r_{mkt} is the overall market returns; $\boldsymbol{\beta}$ is the vector of factor estimates for each asset; $\boldsymbol{\alpha}$ is the market mispricing, and ε_t the model error. The Single-Index market model represents a practical way of reducing the dimension of the problem, measuring how much each asset is affected by the market factor. The model implies the covariance structure among asset returns is given by:

$$T_{si} \equiv s^2_{mkt} \boldsymbol{\beta}\boldsymbol{\beta}' + \Omega, \tag{9}$$

where s^2_{mkt} is the sample variance of asset returns; $\boldsymbol{\beta}$ is the vector of beta estimates and Ω contains the residual variance estimates.

The Common Covariance model is aimed at minimizing the heterogeneity of assets variances and covariances by averaging both of them (Pantaleo et al. 2011). Let $\text{var}_{ij,i=j}$ and $\text{covar}_{ij,\, i\neq j}$ being the variances and covariances of the sample covariance matrix, respectively, their averages are given by:

$$\overline{\text{var}} = \frac{1}{p} \sum_{k=1}^{p} \text{var}_{k,i=j};$$

[4] In reality, we exclude the Scaled Identity of De Miguel et al. (2013) because of its great similarity with the Identity and Variance Identity implemented in our study.

$$\overline{\text{covar}} = \frac{1}{p(p-1)/2} \sum_{k=1}^{p(p-1)/2} \text{covar}_{k,\, i \neq j};$$

where p is the number of securities. The resulting target matrix T_{cv} has its diagonal elements all equal to the average of the sample covariance, while non-diagonal elements are all equal to the average of sample covariances.

In the Constant Correlation model the main diagonal is filled with sample variances, and elsewhere a constant covariance parameter which is equal for all assets. The matrix can be written according to the following decomposition:

$$T_{cc} \equiv P\, diag(S) P, \tag{10}$$

where P is the lower triangular matrix filled with the constant correlation parameter $\overline{\rho} = \frac{1}{p(p-1)/2} \sum_{i=1}^{p} \rho_{ij}$ for $i < j$ and ones in the main diagonal. Here, $diag(S)$ represents the main diagonal of the sample covariance matrix.

The EWMA model (J. P. Morgan and Reuters Ltd. 1996) was introduced by JP Morgan's research team to provide an easy but consistent way to assess portfolio covariance. RiskMetrics EWMA considers the variances and covariance driven by an Integrated GARCH process:

$$T_{\text{EWMA},t} \equiv X'X + \lambda T_{\text{EWMA},t-1}, \tag{11}$$

with $T_{\text{EWMA},0} = I_p$ $T_{\text{EWMA},t-1}$ is the target matrix at time $t-1$ and λ is the smoothing parameter: the higher λ, the higher the persistence in the variance.

3.3. The Impact of Misspecification in the Target Matrix

We are now going to show to which extent risk-based portfolios can be affected by misspecification in the target matrix. To do so, we provide a numerical illustration, merely inspired by the one in Ardia et al. (2017). Assume an investment universe made by three securities: a sovereign bond (Asset-1), a corporate bond (Asset-2), and equity (Asset-3), we are able to impose an arbitrary structure to the related 3×3 *true* covariance matrix[5]. We preliminary recall that Σ can be written according to the following decomposition:

$$\Sigma \equiv (diag(\Sigma))^{1/2} P_{\Sigma} (\text{diag}(\Sigma))^{1/2}$$

where $(diag(\Sigma))^{1/2}$ is a diagonal matrix with volatilities on the diagonal and zeros elsewhere and P_{Σ} is the related correlation matrix, with ones on the diagonal and correlations symmetrically displaced elsewhere. We impose

$$(\Sigma_{1,1}^{1/2},\, \Sigma_{2,2}^{1/2},\, \Sigma_{3,3}^{1/2}) = (0.1,\, 0.1,\, 0.2)$$

and

$$(P_{\Sigma;1,2},\, P_{\Sigma;1,3},\, P_{\Sigma;2,3}) = (0.1,\, 0.2,\, 0.7)$$

hence, the *true* covariance matrix is:

$$\Sigma \equiv \begin{bmatrix} 0.010 & 0.001 & 0.004 \\ 0.001 & 0.010 & 0.014 \\ 0.004 & 0.014 & 0.040 \end{bmatrix}$$

---

5 Ardia et al. (2017) imposes Asset-1 and Asset-2 to have 10% annual volatility; Asset-3 to have 20% annual volatility; correlations between Asset-1/Asset-2 and Asset-1/Asset-3 are set as negative and correlation between corporate bonds and equities (Asset-2/Asset-3) is set as positive. However, to better resemble real data, specifically the S&P500, the US corporate index and the US Treasury Index total returns, we assume all three correlation parameters to be positive.

Now assume that the *true* covariance matrix Σ is equal to its shrunk counterpart when $\delta = \frac{1}{2}$:

$$\Sigma \equiv \Sigma_s = \frac{1}{2}S + \frac{1}{2}T$$

that is both the sample covariance matrix S and the target matrix T must be equal to $\frac{1}{2}\Sigma$ and the *true* target matrix is:

$$\mathrm{S} \equiv \mathrm{T} \equiv \begin{bmatrix} 0.005 & 0.0005 & 0.002 \\ 0.0005 & 0.005 & 0.007 \\ 0.002 & 0.007 & 0.020 \end{bmatrix}$$

with few algebraic computations, we can obtain the volatilities and correlations simply by applying the covariance decomposition, ending up with

$$\left(T_{1,1}^{1/2},\ T_{2,2}^{1/2},\ T_{3,3}^{1/2}\right) = (0.0707,\ 0.0707,\ 0.1414);$$

$$(P_{T;1,2},\ P_{T;1,3},\ P_{T;2,3}) = (0.1,\ 0.2,\ 0.7).$$

In this case, we can conclude that the target matrix T is undervaluing all the covariance and correlation values.

At this point, some remarks are needed. First, as summarised in Table 2, we work out the *true* risk-based portfolio weights. Weights are differently spread out: the Minimum Variance equally allocates wealth to the first two assets, excluding equities. This because it mainly relies upon the asset variance, limiting the diversification of the resulting portfolio. The remaining portfolios allocate wealth without excluding any asset; however, the Maximum Diversification overvalues Asset-1 assigning to it more than 50% of the total wealth. The Inverse Volatility and Equal-Risk-Contribution seem to maximise diversification under a risk-parity concept, similarly allocating wealth among the investment universe.

Table 2. *True* weights of the four risk-based portfolios.

Asset	Minimum Variance (MV)	Inverse Volatility (IV)	Equal-Risk-Contribution (ERC)	Maximum Diversification (MD)
Asset-1	0.500	0.400	0.448	0.506
Asset-2	0.500	0.400	0.374	0.385
Asset-3	0.000	0.200	0.177	0.108

Second, assuming Σ as the *true* covariance matrix allows us to simulate misspecification both in the volatility and in the correlation components of the target matrix T by simply increasing or decreasing the imposed *true* values. Since we are interested in investigating misspecification impact on the *true* risk-based portfolio weights, we measure its effects after each shift with the Frobenius norm between the *true* weights and the misspecified ones:

$$||\tilde{\omega}||_F^2 = \sum_{i=1}^{p} \tilde{\omega}_i^2$$

where $\tilde{\omega} = \omega - \hat{\omega}$.

Third, turning the discussion onto the working aspects of this toy example, we will separately shift the volatility and the correlation of Asset-3, as done in Ardia et al. (2017). The difference with them is that we modify the values in the *true* target matrix T. Moreover, in order to also gauge how shrinkage intensity affects the portfolio weights, we perform this analysis for 11 values of δ, spanning from 0 to 1 (with step 0.1). This allows us to understand both extreme cases, i.e., when the *true* covariance matrix is only estimated with the sample estimator ($\delta = 0$) and only with the target matrix ($\delta = 1$). Remember that the *true* shrinkage intensity is set at $\delta = \frac{1}{2}$.

Moving to the core of this numerical illustration, we proceed as follows. First, for what is concerning the volatility, we let $T_{3,3}^{1/2}$ vary between 0 and 0.5, ceteris paribus. Results are summarised in Figure 1, row 1. As expected, there is no misspecification in all the risk-based portfolio at the initial state $T_{3,3}^{1/2} = 0.1414$, i.e., the *true* value. All the portfolio weights are misspecified in the range $[0; 0.1414)$, with the Minimum Variance portfolio showing the greatest departure from the *true* portfolio weights when the Asset-3 volatility is undervalued below 0.12. The absence of misspecification effects in its weights is due to the initial high-risk attributed to Asset-3; in fact, it is already excluded from the optimal allocation at the initial non-perturbated state. Regarding the other portfolios, their weights show a similar behaviour to the one just described: the Maximum Diversification weights depart from the non-misspecified state to reach the maximum distance from the *true* weights of 0.4; however, this effect dissipates as soon as the shrinkage intensity grows. The same applies for the Inverse Volatility and the Equal-Risk-Contribution. On the contrary, when volatility is overvalued in the range $(0.1414; 0.5]$, the Minimum Variance is not misspecified, since Asset-3 is always excluded from the allocation. This fact helps to maintain the stability of its weights: this portfolio is not affected by shifts in the shrinkage intensity when there is over-misspecification. All the remaining portfolios show low levels of misspecification due to diversification purposes. In particular, they react in the same way to shrinkage intensity misspecification, showing an increase in the Frobenius norm especially for low values of Asset-3 variance. A common trait shared by all the considered portfolios is that when weights are estimated with the sample covariance, only the distance from *true* portfolios is at the maximum.

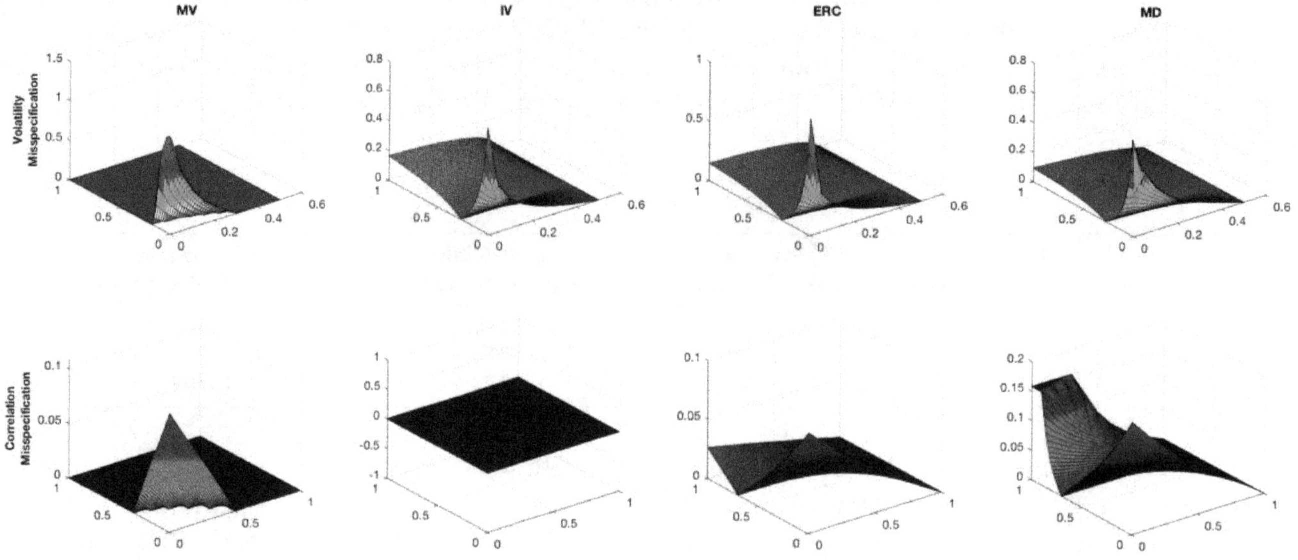

Figure 1. Frobenius norm between *true* and estimated weights; first row reports misspecification in volatility, while second row in correlation. The surfaces' three dimensions are: the shrinkage intensity in y axis (from 0 to 1); the misspecification in the volatility (from 0 to 0.5) or in the correlation (from 0 to 1) in x axis and the Frobenius norm in z axis. Each column refers to a specific risk-based portfolio. From the left to the right: Minimum Variance (MV), Inverse Volatility (IV), Equal-Risk-Contribution (ERC), Maximum Diversification (MD), respectively.

Second, we assess the correlation misspecification impact. We let the correlation between Asset-3 and Asset-2 ($\mathrm{P}_{T;2,3}$) vary from 0 to 1, ceteris paribus. In this case, the greatest signs of perturbation are in the Minimum Variance and in the Maximum Diversification portfolios, while the Equal-Risk-Contribution shows far less distortions, as presented in Figure 1, row 2. The Minimum Variance portfolio is again misspecified in one direction: when the correlation parameter is undervalued and the sample covariance matrix dominates the target matrix in the shrinkage. On the other hand, the Maximum Diversification shows the highest departure from no-misspecification levels in both senses. However, as the Maximum Diversification it seems to benefit from high values of shrinkage intensity. The Equal-Risk-Contribution reacts similarly to the Maximum Diversification, but with a far lower level of misspecification, the Inverse Volatility is not affected at all by misspecification in the correlation structure of the target matrix T. This is due to the specific characteristics of Asset-3 and the way in which the Inverse Volatility selects to allocate weights under a risk-parity scheme.

In conclusion, with this numerical illustration, we assess the effects of target matrix misspecification in risk-based portfolios: the four risk-based portfolios react similarly to what previously found in Ardia et al. (2017), even if in our case, shifts originated in the target matrix. The Minimum Variance and the Maximum Diversification portfolios are the most impacted: the weights of the former are severely affected by volatility and covariance shifts undervaluing the *true* values; the latter shows perturbations in weights when shifts are more extreme. Both portfolios benefit from a higher level of shrinkage intensity. On the other hand, the Inverse Volatility and the Equal-Risk-Contribution weights suffer less from both sources of misspecification. Overall, weights are affected by shifts in the shrinkage intensity: when sample covariance is the estimator ($\delta = 0$), the distance from the *true* weights stands at the maximum level in all the considered portfolios.

4. Case Study—Monte Carlo Analysis

This section offers a comprehensive comparison of the six target matrix estimators by means of an extensive Monte Carlo study. The aim of this analysis is twofold: (1) assessing estimators' statistical properties and similarity with the *true* target matrix; (2) addressing the problem of how selecting a specific target estimator impacts on the portfolio weights. This investigation is aimed at giving a very broad overview about (1) and (2) since we monitor both the p/n ratio and the whole spectrum of shrinkage intensity. We run simulations for 15 combinations of p and n, and for 11 different shrinkage intensities spanning in the interval $[0\,;1]$, for an overall number of 165 scenarios.

The Monte Carlo study is designed as follows. Returns are simulated assuming a factor model is the data generating process, as in MacKinlay and Pastor (2000). In detail, we impose a one-factor structure for the returns generating process:

$$\begin{gathered} r_t = \xi f_t + \varepsilon_t; \\ \text{with } t = 1, \ldots, n, \end{gathered}$$

where f_t is the $k \times 1$ vector of returns on the factor, ξ is the $p \times 1$ vector of factor loadings, and ε_t the vector of residuals of p length. Under this framework, returns are simulated implying multivariate normality and absence of serial correlation. The asset factor loadings are drawn from a uniform distribution and equally spread, while returns on the single factor are generated from a Normal distribution. The bounds for the uniform distribution and the mean and the variance for the Normal one are calibrated on real market data, specifically on the empirical dataset "49-Industry portfolios" with monthly frequency, available on the Kennet French website[6]. Residuals are drawn from a uniform distribution in the range $[0.10; 0.30]$ so that the related covariance matrix is diagonal with an average annual volatility of 20%.

For each of the 165 scenarios, we apply the same strategy. First, we simulate the $n \times p$ matrix of asset log-returns, then we estimate the six target matrices and their corresponding shrunk matrices $\hat{\Sigma}_s$. Finally, we estimate the weights of the four risk-based portfolios. Some remarks are needed. First, we consider the number of assets as $p = \{10, 50, 100\}$ and number of observations as $n = \{60, 120, 180, 3000, 6000\}$ months, which correspond to 5, 10, 15, 250 and 500 years.

[6] http://mba.tuck.dartmouth.edu/pages/faculty/ken.french/data_library.html.

Moreover, the shrinkage intensity is allowed to vary between their lower and upper bounds as $\delta = \{0, 0.1, 0.2, 0.3, 0.4, 0.5, 0.6, 0.7, 0.8, 0.9, 1\}$. For each of the 165 scenarios we run 100 Monte Carlo trials[7], giving robustness to the results.

We stress again the importance of Monte Carlo simulations, which allow us to impose the *true* covariance Σ and hence the *true* portfolio weights ω. This is crucial because we can compare the *true* quantities with their estimated counterparts.

With respect to the point (1), we use two criteria to assess and compare the statistical properties of target matrices: the reciprocal 1-norm condition number and the Frobenius Norm. Being the 1-norm condition number defined as:

$$CN(A) = \kappa(A) = \|A^{-1}\|$$

for a given A. It measures the matrix sensitivity to changes in the data: when it is large, it indicates that a small shift causes important changes, offering a measure of the ill-conditioning of A. Since $CN(A)$ takes value in the interval $[0\,; +\infty)$, it is more convenient to use its scaled version, the $RCN(A)$:

$$RCN(A) = 1/\,\kappa(A) \tag{12}$$

It is defined in the range $[0\,;1]$: the matrix is well-conditioned if the reciprocal condition number is close to 1 and ill-conditioned vice-versa. Under the Monte Carlo framework, we will study its Monte Carlo estimator:

$$E[CN(A_m)] = \frac{1}{M}\sum_{m=1}^{M} CN(A_m) \tag{13}$$

where M is the number of Monte Carlo simulations. On the other hand, the Frobenius norm is employed to gauge the similarity between the estimated target matrix and the *true* one. We define it for the $p \times p$ symmetric matrix Z as:

$$FN(Z) = \|Z\|_F^2 = \sum_{i=1}^{p}\sum_{j=1}^{p} z_{ij}^2$$

In our case, $Z = \hat{\Sigma}_s - \Sigma$. Its Monte Carlo estimator is given by the following:

$$E[FN(A_m)] = \frac{1}{M}\sum_{m=1}^{M} FN(A_m) \tag{14}$$

Regarding (2), we assess the discrepancy between *true* and estimated weights again with the Frobenius norm. In addition, we report the values at which the Frobenius norm attains its best results, i.e., when the shrinkage intensity is optimal.

4.1. Main Results

Figure 2 summarises the statistical properties of the various target matrices.

---

7 Simulations were done in MATLAB setting the random seed generator at its default value, thus ensuring the full reproducibility of the analysis. Related code available at the GitHub page of the author: https://github.com/marconeffelli/Risk-Based-Portfolios.

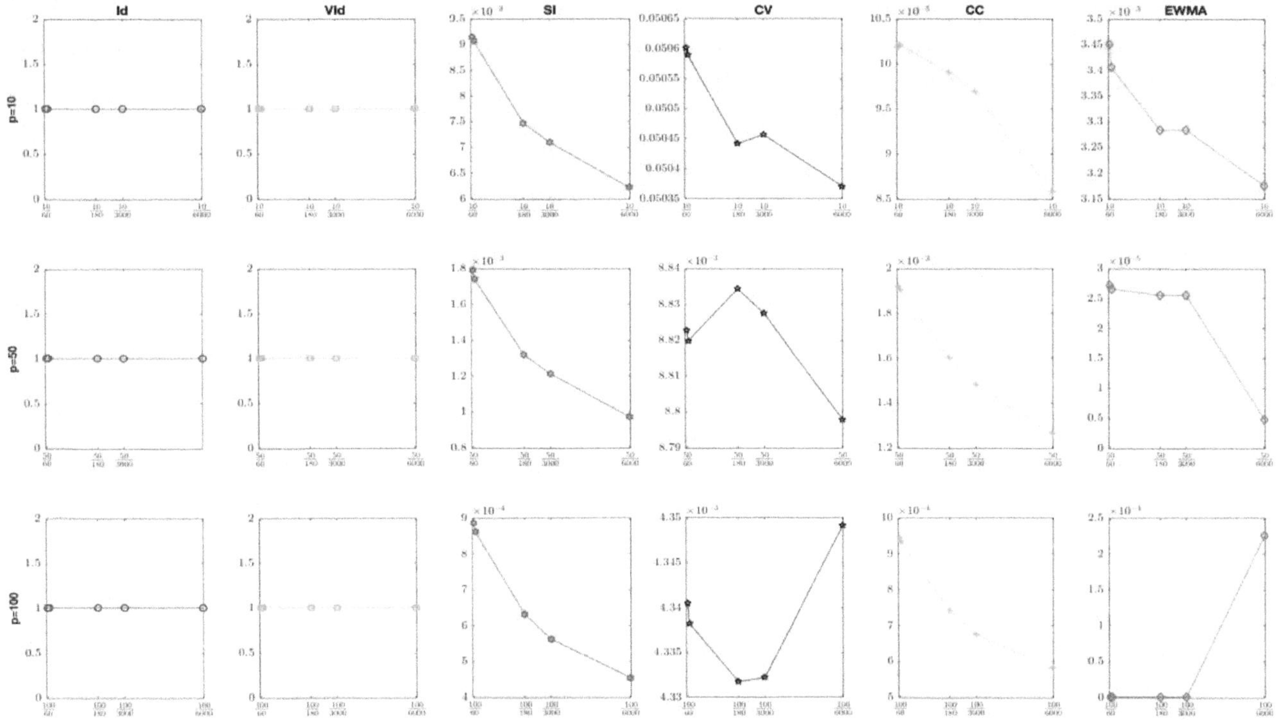

Figure 2. The reciprocal 1-norm condition number (y-axis) as the p/n ratio moves from $\frac{p}{60}$ to $\frac{p}{6000}$ (x-axis). Each column corresponds to a specific target matrix: from left to right, the Identity (Id): blue circle-shaped; the Variance Identity (VId): green square-shaped; the Single-Index (SI): red hexagram-shaped; the Common Covariance (CV): black star-shaped; the Constant Correlation (CC): cyan plus-shaped; and the Exponential Weighted Moving Average (EWMA): magenta diamond-shaped, respectively. Each row corresponds to a different p: in ascendant order from 10 (first row) to 100 (third row).

Figure 2 illustrates the reciprocal 1-norm condition number: the matrix is well-conditioned when the value is closer to 1, vice-versa is ill-conditioned the more it tends to zero. Overall, the Identity and the Variance Identity stem for being always well-conditioned: across all the combinations of p and n their reciprocal condition number is always one. Therefore, we focus our analysis on the remaining target matrices. In the case where $p = 10$, the Common Covariance dominates the other three alternatives, who perform poorly. As the number of assets increases, the reciprocal condition number deteriorates, especially for the EWMA, which now performs worse than the others, and for the Common Covariance, which is now aligned to the Single-Index and the Constant Correlation model. In conclusion, excluding the Identity and the Variance Identity, the considered targets show poor statistical properties.

Then, we turn to the study of similarity among *true* and estimated target matrices. Figure 3 represents the Monte Carlo Frobenius norm between the *true* and the estimated target matrices. The surfaces give a clear overview about the relation among the Frobenius norm itself, the p/n ratio and the shrinkage intensity. Overall, the Frobenius norm is minimised by the Single-Index and the Common Covariance: in these cases, the target matrices are not particularly affected by the shrinkage intensity, while their reactions to increases in the p/n ratio are controversial. In fact, quite surprisingly the distance between *true* and estimated weights diminishes as both p and n increases. For $p = 50$ and $p = 100$, there is a hump for small p/n values; however, the Frobenius norm increases when $\frac{p}{n} \geq 1$. Despite the low condition number, the EWMA shows a similar behaviour to the Single-Index and the Constant Correlation target matrices, especially with respect to p/n values. On the other hand, it is more affected by shifts in the shrinkage parameters; the distance from the *true* weights increases moving towards the target matrix. Lastly, the Identity and the Variance Identity show a similar behaviour: their distances from the *true* target matrix increase for higher values of δ and p/n. Lastly, the Common Covariance is the most far away from the *true* target matrix, being very sensitive both to high shrinkage intensity and p/n values.

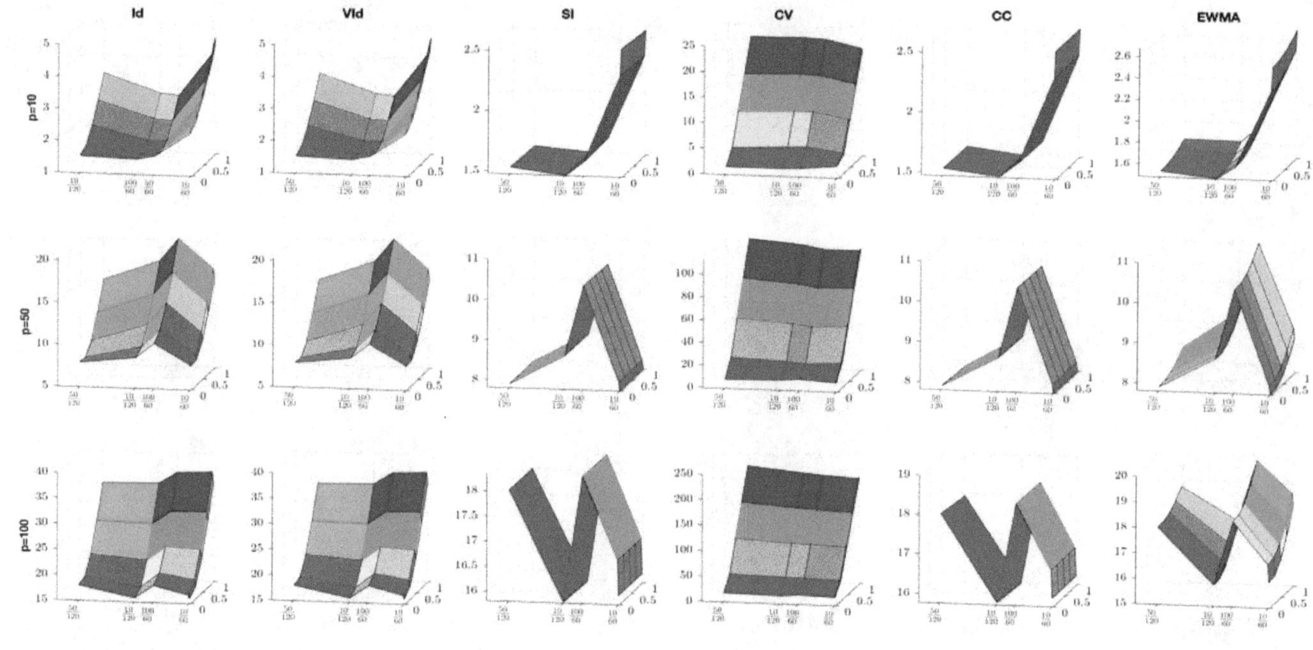

Figure 3. Surfaces representing the Frobenius norm (z-axis) between the *true* and the estimated target matrices, considering the shrinkage intensity (y-axis) and the p/n ratio (x-axis). Each column corresponds to a specific target matrix: from left to right, the Identity (Id), the Variance Identity (VId), the Single-Index (SI), the Common Covariance (CV), the Constant Correlation (CC), and the EWMA, respectively. Each row corresponds to a different p: in ascendant order from $p = 10$ (first row) to $p = 100$ (third row).

To conclude, the Identity and the Variance Identity are the most well-conditioned matrices, being stable across all the examined p/n combinations. Nevertheless, the Single-Index and the Common Covariance target matrices show the greatest similarity with the *true* target matrix minimizing Frobenius norm, while both the Identity and the Variance Identity seem less similar to the *true* target.

4.1.1. Results on Portfolio Weights

Tables 3 and 4 present the main results of the Monte Carlo study: for each combination of p and n, we report the Monte Carlo estimator of the Frobenius norm between the *true* and estimated weights. In particular, Table 3 reports averaged Frobenius norm along with the shrinkage intensity (excluding the case $\delta = 0$, which corresponds to the sample covariance matrix), while Table 4 lists the minimum values for the optimal shrinkage intensity.

In both tables, we compare the six target matrices by examining one risk-based portfolio at a time and the effect of increasing p for fixed n. Special attention is devoted to the cases when $p > n$: the high-dimensional sample. We have this scenario only when $p = 100$ and $n = 60$. Here, the sample covariance matrix becomes ill-conditioned (Marčenko and Pastur 1967), thus it is interesting to evaluate gains obtained with shrinkage. The averaged Frobenius norm values in Table 3 give us a general overview about how target matrices perform across the whole shrinkage intensity spectrum in one goal. We aim to understand if, in average terms, shrinking the covariance matrix benefits risk-portfolio weights. On the other hand, the minimum Frobenius norm values help us understanding to what extent the various target matrices can help reproducing the *true* portfolio weights: the more intensity we need, the better the target is. In both tables, sample values are listed in the first row of each Panel.

Table 3. Frobenius norm for the portfolio weights. Values are averaged along with the shrinkage intensity (excluding the case $\delta = 0$). For each n, the first line reports the Frobenius norm for the sample covariance matrix. Abbreviations in use are: S for sample covariance; Id for identity matrix; VId for Variance Identity; SI for Single-Index; CV for Common Covariance; CC for Constant Correlation and EWMA for Exponentially Weighted Moving Average.

	P = 10				P = 50				P = 100			
	MV	**IV**	**ERC**	**MD**	**MV**	**IV**	**ERC**	**MD**	**MV**	**IV**	**ERC**	**MD**
					Panel A: n = 60							
S	0.834	0.1585	0.1736	0.5842	0.7721	0.0573	0.0637	0.4933	0.7555	0.0409	0.0447	0.4565
Id	0.6863	0.1425	0.1528	0.5045	0.6215	0.0559	0.0631	0.3873	0.4967	0.0404	0.0451	0.3652
VId	0.6935	0.1583	0.1732	0.5176	0.5999	0.0567	0.0634	0.4092	0.5901	0.0404	0.0445	0.3686
SI	0.838	0.1585	0.1736	0.5678	0.7685	0.0573	0.0637	0.4709	0.75	0.0409	0.0447	0.4288
CV	1.2438	0.1583	0.1731	1.011	1.1484	0.0567	0.0628	0.9381	1.1386	0.0404	0.0438	0.9185
CC	0.8353	0.1585	0.1733	0.5361	0.7808	0.0573	0.0635	0.4328	0.7663	0.0409	0.0445	0.3922
EWMA	0.8473	0.1593	0.1745	0.595	0.7811	0.0575	0.064	0.5142	0.7325	0.0411	0.045	0.4431
					Panel B: n = 120							
S	0.9064	0.0877	0.0989	0.4649	0.7814	0.059	0.0656	0.5065	0.6519	0.0424	0.0472	0.4332
Id	0.8157	0.087	0.0983	0.4256	0.6259	0.0613	0.0688	0.4354	0.6307	0.0389	0.0431	0.328
VId	0.8235	0.0871	0.0985	0.4284	0.6259	0.0613	0.0688	0.4354	0.489	0.0421	0.0471	0.3712
SI	0.9097	0.0877	0.0989	0.4563	0.7777	0.059	0.0656	0.4925	0.6458	0.0424	0.0472	0.419
CV	1.3269	0.0871	0.0982	0.9667	1.1806	0.0587	0.0651	1.0138	1.0974	0.0421	0.0467	0.8951
CC	0.905	0.0877	0.0988	0.4357	0.7822	0.059	0.0655	0.4636	0.6566	0.0424	0.0471	0.3856
EWMA	0.9281	0.0883	0.0996	0.4859	0.7994	0.0592	0.0658	0.5246	0.6788	0.0427	0.0475	0.4601
					Panel C: n = 180							
S	0.7989	0.1311	0.1423	0.5007	0.7932	0.0564	0.0627	0.4631	0.6905	0.0404	0.044	0.4065
Id	0.7206	0.1308	0.142	0.4736	0.6705	0.0562	0.0625	0.405	0.5477	0.0375	0.0399	0.3748
VId	0.7273	0.1308	0.1421	0.4757	0.6838	0.0562	0.0626	0.4127	0.5754	0.0402	0.044	0.3556
SI	0.8001	0.1311	0.1423	0.4954	0.7904	0.0564	0.0627	0.4545	0.6873	0.0404	0.044	0.3982
CV	1.2715	0.1308	0.1419	0.9961	1.2073	0.0562	0.0624	0.9988	1.1422	0.0402	0.0437	0.8705
CC	0.7957	0.1311	0.1423	0.4803	0.792	0.0564	0.0626	0.4259	0.692	0.0404	0.044	0.3672
EWMA	0.8415	0.1322	0.1435	0.526	0.8284	0.0567	0.0631	0.5005	0.7206	0.0408	0.0445	0.4429
					Panel D: n = 3000							
S	0.7504	0.1476	0.1596	0.3957	0.734	0.049	0.0539	0.3988	0.513	0.0384	0.0428	0.3259
Id	0.7441	0.1477	0.1597	0.3946	0.7009	0.049	0.0539	0.3872	0.4615	0.0384	0.0428	0.3096
VId	0.7437	0.1477	0.1596	0.3945	0.7043	0.049	0.0539	0.3886	0.4673	0.0384	0.0428	0.312
SI	0.7516	0.1476	0.1596	0.3955	0.7339	0.049	0.0539	0.3984	0.5123	0.0384	0.0428	0.3252
CV	1.2864	0.1477	0.1597	0.963	1.2281	0.049	0.0538	0.9954	1.1041	0.0384	0.0428	0.6822
CC	0.7488	0.1476	0.1596	0.3949	0.7316	0.049	0.0539	0.3904	0.5096	0.0384	0.0428	0.3143
EWMA	0.8563	0.1489	0.1611	0.4452	0.8161	0.0497	0.0547	0.4652	0.6244	0.0389	0.0435	0.4076
					Panel E: n = 6000							
S	0.9672	0.1302	0.1409	0.4821	0.5737	0.0539	0.0589	0.3481	0.5772	0.0402	0.0437	0.3436
Id	0.9496	0.1301	0.1408	0.4813	0.6095	0.0575	0.0639	0.4076	0.5449	0.0402	0.0437	0.3342
VId	0.951	0.1301	0.1409	0.4815	0.5419	0.054	0.0589	0.3401	0.5483	0.0402	0.0437	0.3354
SI	0.9688	0.1302	0.1409	0.482	0.574	0.0539	0.0589	0.3479	0.5772	0.0402	0.0437	0.3434
CV	1.4142	0.1301	0.1408	1.0034	1.1436	0.054	0.0589	0.9706	1.1422	0.0402	0.0437	0.7031
CC	0.9656	0.1302	0.1409	0.4814	0.5709	0.0539	0.0589	0.3415	0.575	0.0402	0.0437	0.3368
EWMA	1.0432	0.1312	0.1422	0.5232	0.6946	0.0547	0.0599	0.4319	0.681	0.0407	0.0444	0.4229

Starting from Table 3, Panel A, the Minimum Variance allocation seems better described by the Identity and the Variance Identity regardless of the number of assets p. In particular, we look at the difference between the weights calculated entirely on the sample covariance matrix and those of the targets: the Identity and the Variance Identity are the only estimator to perform better. In fact, shrinking towards the sample is not as bad as shrinking towards the Common Covariance. By increasing n and moving to Panel B, similar results are obtained. This trend is confirmed in Panel C, while in the cases of $n = 3000$ and $n = 6000$, all the estimators perform similarly. Hence, for the Minimum Variance portfolio the Identity matrix works best at reproducing portfolio weights very similar to the *true* ones. The same conclusions apply for the Maximum Diversification portfolio: when p and n are small, the Identity and the Variance Identity outperform other alternatives. On the other hand, we get very different results for the Inverse Volatility and Equal-Risk-Contribution. Both portfolios seem not gaining benefits from the shrinkage procedure, as the Frobenius norm is very similar to that of the sample covariance matrix for all the target matrices under consideration. This is *true* for all pairs of p and n. In the high-dimensional case ($p = 100$; $n = 60$), the Identity matrix works best in reducing the distance between *true* and estimated portfolio weights, both for the Minimum Variance and Maximum Diversification portfolios. On average, shrinkage does not help too much when alternative target matrices are used; only in the case of Common Covariance is shrinking worse than using the sample covariance matrix. All these effects vanish when we look at the Inverse Volatility and Equal-Risk-Contribution portfolios: here, shrinkage does not help too much, whatever the target is.

Table 4. Frobenius norm for the portfolio weights. Values corresponds to the optimal shrinkage intensity, listed after the Frobenius norm for each portfolio. We report values for the sample covariance matrix ($\delta = 0$) separately in the first row of each panel. For each n, the first line reports the Frobenius norm for the sample covariance matrix. Abbreviations used are: S for sample covariance; Id for identity matrix; VId for Variance Identity; SI for Single-Index; CV for Common Covariance; CC for Constant Correlation and EWMA for Exponentially Weighted Moving Average.

	P = 10				P = 50				P = 100			
	MV	**IV**	**ERC**	**MD**	**MV**	**IV**	**ERC**	**MD**	**MV**	**IV**	**ERC**	**MD**
					Panel A: $n = 60$							
S	0.8340	0.1585	0.1736	0.5842	0.7721	0.0573	0.0637	0.4933	0.7555	0.0409	0.0447	0.4565
Id	0.6778	0.1424	0.1525	0.501	0.5997	0.0558	0.0624	0.3704	0.471	0.0403	0.0446	0.3462
VId	0.6689	0.1581	0.173	0.5084	0.5539	0.0565	0.0627	0.3795	0.5428	0.0402	0.0437	0.3331
SI	0.8345	0.1585	0.1735	0.558	0.7666	0.0573	0.0637	0.4633	0.7479	0.0409	0.0447	0.4195
CV	1.2392	0.1581	0.1729	0.509	1.117	0.0565	0.0627	0.3795	1.1068	0.0402	0.0437	0.3331
CC	0.8335	0.1585	0.1731	0.5081	0.7733	0.0573	0.0634	0.3795	0.757	0.0409	0.0444	0.3332
EWMA	0.8331	0.1586	0.1737	0.5852	0.7706	0.0573	0.0637	0.4953	0.7213	0.0409	0.0447	0.4395
					Panel B: $n = 120$							
S	0.9064	0.0877	0.0989	0.4649	0.7814	0.059	0.0656	0.5065	0.6519	0.0424	0.0472	0.4332
Id	0.8121	0.087	0.0981	0.4241	0.6119	0.0613	0.0685	0.4255	0.613	0.0388	0.0428	0.3111
VId	0.8121	0.087	0.0982	0.4242	0.6119	0.0613	0.0685	0.4255	0.4425	0.042	0.0467	0.3445
SI	0.907	0.0877	0.0989	0.4526	0.776	0.059	0.0656	0.4872	0.6431	0.0424	0.0472	0.414
CV	1.3269	0.087	0.0981	0.4245	1.1756	0.0586	0.0651	0.4302	1.0916	0.042	0.0467	0.3445
CC	0.9043	0.0877	0.0987	0.4241	0.781	0.059	0.0654	0.4302	0.6527	0.0424	0.0471	0.3446
EWMA	0.9052	0.0876	0.0988	0.4651	0.7797	0.0589	0.0655	0.5056	0.6554	0.0424	0.0472	0.4331
					Panel C: $n = 180$							
S	0.7989	0.1311	0.1423	0.5007	0.7932	0.0564	0.0627	0.4631	0.6905	0.0404	0.044	0.4065
Id	0.7177	0.1307	0.1419	0.4724	0.6613	0.0562	0.0624	0.3977	0.534	0.0375	0.0398	0.3645
VId	0.718	0.1307	0.1419	0.4724	0.6614	0.0562	0.0624	0.3979	0.5428	0.0402	0.0437	0.3331
SI	0.799	0.1311	0.1423	0.4929	0.7897	0.0564	0.0627	0.4515	0.6863	0.0404	0.044	0.3955
CV	1.2715	0.1307	0.1418	0.4724	1.2073	0.0562	0.0624	0.3979	1.1422	0.0402	0.0437	0.3331
CC	0.7942	0.1311	0.1422	0.4725	0.7912	0.0564	0.0626	0.3977	0.6904	0.0404	0.0439	0.3331
EWMA	0.8035	0.1312	0.1424	0.5008	0.7951	0.0564	0.0626	0.4653	0.6938	0.0404	0.044	0.4074
					Panel D: $n = 3000$							
S	0.7504	0.1476	0.1596	0.3957	0.734	0.049	0.0539	0.3988	0.513	0.0384	0.0428	0.3259
Id	0.7425	0.1477	0.1596	0.3941	0.6988	0.049	0.0538	0.3859	0.4573	0.0384	0.0428	0.3072
VId	0.7426	0.1476	0.1596	0.3941	0.6988	0.049	0.0538	0.3859	0.4573	0.0384	0.0428	0.3072
SI	0.7506	0.1476	0.1596	0.3953	0.7339	0.049	0.0539	0.3983	0.512	0.0384	0.0428	0.325
CV	1.2864	0.1476	0.1596	0.3951	1.2281	0.049	0.0538	0.3859	1.1041	0.0384	0.0428	0.3072
CC	0.7477	0.1476	0.1596	0.3946	0.7299	0.049	0.0539	0.386	0.5073	0.0384	0.0428	0.3072
EWMA	0.7615	0.1477	0.1597	0.3981	0.7439	0.0491	0.0539	0.4043	0.5263	0.0384	0.0429	0.3346
					Panel E: $n = 6000$							
S	0.9672	0.1302	0.1409	0.4821	0.5737	0.0539	0.0589	0.3481	0.5772	0.0402	0.0437	0.3436
Id	0.9486	0.13	0.1408	0.4811	0.6085	0.0575	0.0639	0.4072	0.5428	0.0402	0.0437	0.3331
VId	0.9486	0.13	0.1408	0.4811	0.5365	0.054	0.0589	0.3381	0.5428	0.0402	0.0437	0.3331
SI	0.9675	0.1302	0.1409	0.482	0.5738	0.0539	0.0589	0.3478	0.5772	0.0402	0.0437	0.3433
CV	1.4142	0.13	0.1408	0.4811	1.1436	0.054	0.0589	0.3381	1.1422	0.0402	0.0437	0.3331
CC	0.9644	0.1302	0.1409	0.4812	0.5687	0.0539	0.0589	0.3381	0.5733	0.0402	0.0437	0.3331
EWMA	0.9765	0.1302	0.1409	0.4832	0.5901	0.054	0.059	0.3561	0.59	0.0402	0.0438	0.3524

Overall, results are in line with the conclusions of the numerical illustrations in Section 3. Indeed, the Minimum Variance portfolio shows the highest distance between *true* and estimated weights, similar to the Maximum Diversification. Both portfolios are affected by the dimensionality of the sample: shrinkage always help in reducing weights misspecification; it improves in high-dimensional cases. On contrary, estimated weights for the remaining portfolios are close to the *true* ones by construction, hence, shrinkage does not help too much.

Switching to Table 4, the results illustrate again that the Identity and the Variance Identity attain the best reduction of the Frobenius norm for the Minimum Variance and Maximum Diversification portfolios. If results are similar to those of Table 3 for the former, results for the latter show an improvement in using the shrinkage estimators. The Identity, Variance Identity, Common Covariance, and Constant Correlation target matrices outperform all the alternatives, including the sample estimator, minimising the Frobenius norm in a similar fashion. This is true also for the high-dimensional case. On the contrary, the other two portfolios do not benefit from shrinking the sample covariance matrix, even in high-dimensional samples, confirming the insights from Table 3. Lastly, we look at the shrinkage intensity at which target matrices attain the highest Frobenius norm reduction. Those values are displayed in Figure 4. The intensity is composed of the interval $[0;1]$: the more it is close to 1, the more the target matrix helps in reducing the estimation error of the sample covariance matrix. Interestingly, the Identity and the Variance Identity show shrinkage intensities always close to 1, meaning that shrinking towards them is highly beneficial, as they are fairly better than the sample covariance matrix. This is verified either for the high-dimensional case and for those risk portfolios (Inverse Volatility and Equal-Risk-Contribution), who do not show great improvements when shrinkage is adopted.

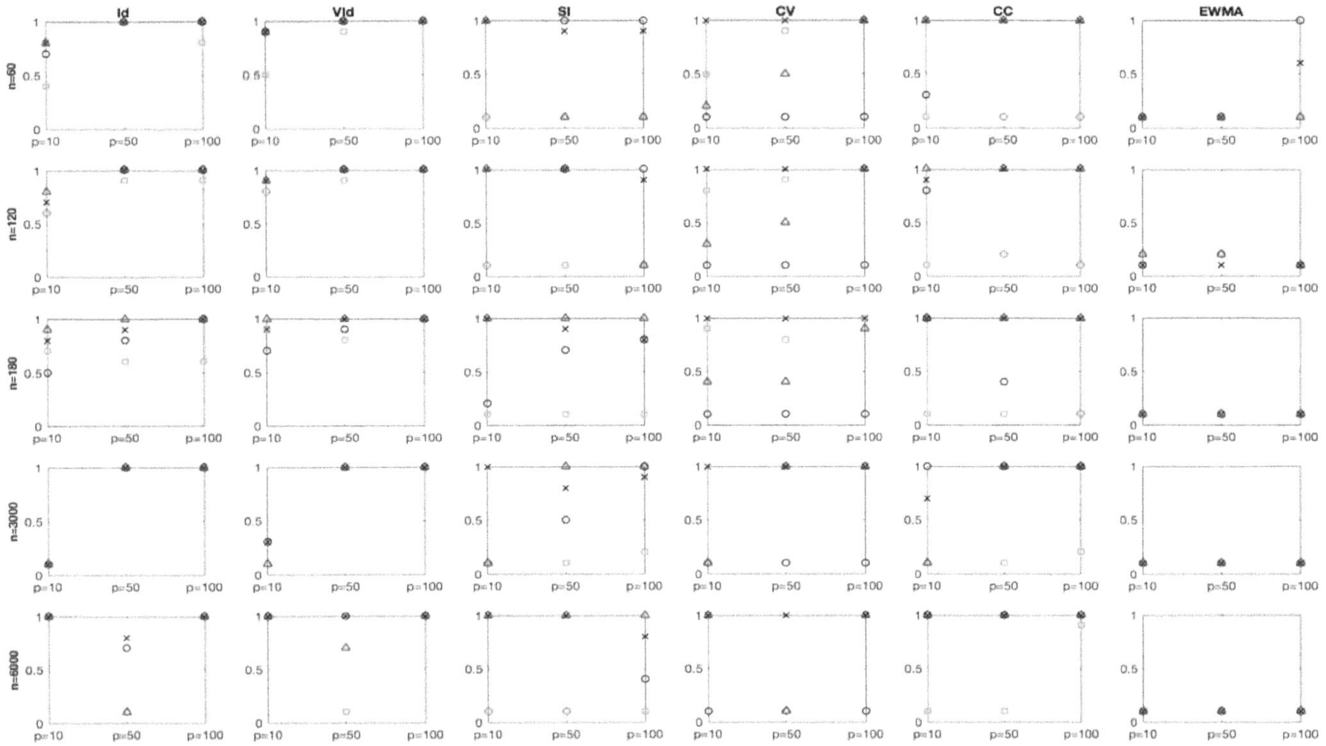

Figure 4. Optimal shrinkage intensity parameters for which the Frobenius norm is minimized. Each column corresponds to a specific target matrix: from left to right, the Identity, the Variance Identity, the Single-Index, the Common Covariance, the Constant Correlation, and the EWMA, respectively. Each row corresponds to a different n: in ascendant order from $n = 60$ (first row) to $p = 6000$ (fifth row). In each subplot, the MV portfolio is blue circle-shaped; the IV is green-square shaped; the ERC is red-triangle shaped; and the MD is black-cross shaped.

4.1.2. Sensitivity to Shrinkage Intensity

To have a view on the whole shrinkage intensity spectrum (i.e., the interval $(0;1)$) we refer to Figure 5, where we report the Frobenius Norms for the weights (y-axis) with regard to the shrinkage intensity (x-axis). Each column corresponds to a specific risk-based portfolio: from left to right, the Minimum Variance, the Inverse Volatility, the Equal-Risk-Contribution, and the Maximum Diversification, respectively. Each row corresponds to the p/n ratio in n ascending order. For each subfigure, the Identity is blue circle-shaped, the Variance Identity is green square-shaped, the Single-Index is red hexagram-shaped, the Common Covariance is black star-shaped, the Constant Correlation is cyan plus-shaped, and the EWMA is magenta diamond-shaped.

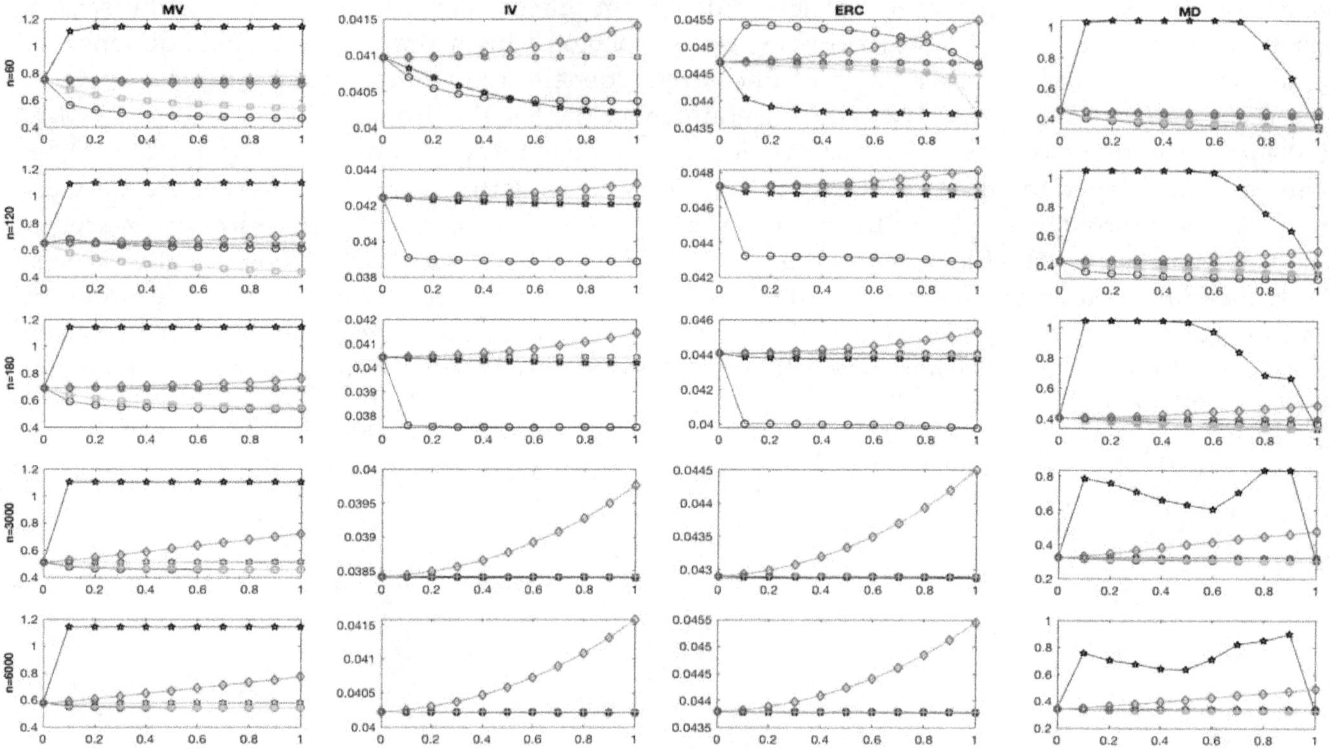

Figure 5. Frobenius norm for portfolio weights with regard to the shrinkage intensity parameter, when $p = 100$.

Figure 5 illustrates the case $p = 100$, as to include the high-dimensional scenario. Starting from the latter (first row, $n = 60$), the Variance Identity is the only target matrix to always reduce weight misspecification for all the considered portfolios, for all shrinkage levels. The Identity do the same, excluding the ERC case where it performs worse than the sample covariance matrix. The remaining targets behave very differently across the four risk-based portfolios: the Common Covariance is the worst in both the Minimum Variance and Maximum Diversification and the EWMA is the worst in both remaining portfolios. The Market Model and the Constant Correlation do not improve much from the sample estimator across all portfolios.

Looking at the second row ($n = 120$), the Identity is the most efficient target, reducing the distance between estimated and *true* portfolio weights in all the considered portfolios. The Variance Identity is also very efficient in Minimum Variance and Maximum Diversification portfolios, while the remaining targets show similar results as in the previous case. The same conclusions apply for the case $n = 180$.

When the number of observations is equal to or higher than $n = 3000$, results do not change much. The Identity, the Variance Identity, the Market model, and the Constant Correlation are the most efficient target matrices towards which to shrink, while the EWMA is the worst for both Inverse

Volatility and Equal-Risk-Contribution portfolios and the Common Covariance is the worst for the Minimum Variance and Maximum Diversification ones.

In conclusion, for the Minimum Variance portfolio, the Common Covariance should not be used, since it always produces weights very unstable and distant from the *true* ones. At the same time, the EWMA should not be used to shrink the covariance matrix in the Inverse Volatility and Equal-Risk-Contribution portfolios. The most convenient matrices towards which to shrink are the Identity and the Variance Identity. Overall, the Minimum Variance and the Maximum Diversification portfolio weights gain more from shrinkage than those of the Inverse Volatility and Equal-Risk-Contribution allocations.

5. Conclusions

In this article, we provide a comprehensive overview of shrinkage in risk-based portfolios. Portfolios solely based on the asset returns covariance matrix are usually perceived as "robust" since they avoid estimating the asset returns mean. However, they still suffer from estimation error when the sample estimator is used, causing misspecification in the portfolio weights. Shrinkage estimators have been proved to reduce the estimation error by pulling the sample covariance towards a more structured target.

By means of an extensive Monte Carlo study, we compare six different target matrices: the Identity, the Variance Identity, the Single-index model, the Common Covariance, the Constant Correlation, and the Exponential Weighted Moving Average, respectively. We do so considering their effects on weights for the Minimum Variance, Inverse Volatility, Equal-risk-contribution, and Maximum diversification portfolios. Moreover, we control for the whole shrinkage intensity spectrum and for dataset size, changing observation length and number of assets. Therefore, we are able to (1) assess estimators' statistical properties and similarity with the *true* target matrix; (2) address the problem of how selecting a specific target estimator affects the portfolio weights.

Regarding point (1), the findings suggest the Identity and the Variance Identity matrices hold the best statistical properties, being well conditioned across all the combinations of observations/assets, especially for high-dimensional datasets. Nevertheless, these targets are both not very similar to the *true* target matrix. The Single-Index and the Constant Correlation target matrices show the greater similarity with the *true* target matrix, minimizing the Frobenius norm, albeit being poorly conditioned when observations and assets share similar sizes. Turning to point (2), the Identity attains the best results in terms of distance reduction between the *true* and estimated portfolio weights for both the Minimum Variance and Maximum Diversification portfolio construction techniques. The Variance Identity shows a similar performance. Both estimators are also stable against shifts in the shrinkage intensity.

Overall, selecting the target matrix is very important, since we verified that there are large shifts in the distance between *true* and estimated portfolio weights when shrinking towards different targets. In risk-based portfolio allocations the Identity and the Variance Identity matrices represent the best target among the six considered in this study, especially in the case of Minimum Variance and Maximum Diversification portfolios. In fact, they are always well conditioned and outperform their competitor in deriving the most similar weights to the *true* ones.

Lastly, the findings confirm that the Minimum Variance and Maximum Diversification portfolios are more sensitive to misspecification in the covariance matrix, therefore, they benefit the most when the sample covariance matrix is shrunk. These findings are in line with what was previously found in Ardia et al. (2017): the Inverse Volatility and the Equal-Risk-Contribution are more robust to covariance misspecification; hence, allocations do not improve significantly when shrinkage is used.

Acknowledgments: I would thank my Ph.D. supervisor Marina Resta for having spent time in reading the manuscript and giving precious suggestions. I also thank three anonymous referees for helpful comments and effort into improving this paper.

References

Ardia, David, Guido Bolliger, Kris Boudt, and Jean Philippe Gagnon-Fleury. 2017. The Impact of Covariance Misspecification in Risk-Based Portfolios. *Annals of Operations Research* 254: 1–16. [CrossRef]

Black, Fischer, and Robert Litterman. 1992. Global Portfolio Optimization. *Financial Analysts Journal* 48: 28–43. [CrossRef]

Briner, Beat G., and Gregory Connor. 2008. How Much Structure Is Best? A Comparison of Market Model, Factor Model and Unstructured Equity Covariance Matrices. *Journal of Risk* 10: 3–30. [CrossRef]

Candelon, Bertrand, Christophe Hurlin, and Sessi Tokpavi. 2012. Sampling Error and Double Shrinkage Estimation of Minimum Variance Portfolios. *Journal of Empirical Finance* 19: 511–27. [CrossRef]

Chopra, Vijay Kumar, and William T. Ziemba. 1993. The Effect of Errors in Means, Variances, and Covariances on Optimal Portfolio Choice. *The Journal of Portfolio Management* 19: 6–11. [CrossRef]

Choueifaty, Yves, and Yves Coignard. 2008. Toward Maximum Diversification. *The Journal of Portfolio Management* 35: 40–51. [CrossRef]

De Miguel, Victor, Lorenzo Garlappi, and Raman Uppal. 2009. Optimal versus Naive Diversification: How Inefficient Is the 1/N Portfolio Strategy? *Review of Financial Studies* 22: 1915–53. [CrossRef]

De Miguel, Victor, Alberto Martin-Utrera, and Francisco J. Nogales. 2013. Size Matters: Optimal Calibration of Shrinkage Estimators for Portfolio Selection. *Journal of Banking and Finance* 37: 3018–34. [CrossRef]

J. P. Morgan, and Reuters Ltd. 1996. *Risk Metrics—Technical Document*, 4th ed. New York: Morgan Guaranty Trust.

Jagannathan, Ravi, and Tongshu Ma. 2003. Risk Reduction in Large Portfolios: Why Imposing the Wrong Constraints Helps. *Journal of Finance* 58: 1651–84. [CrossRef]

James, W., and Charles Stein. 1961. Estimation with Quadratic Loss. In *Proceedings of the 4th Berkeley Symposium on Probability and Statistics, Volume 1*. Paper presented at Fourth Berkeley Symposium on Mathematical Statistics and Probability, Berkeley, CA, USA, June 20–July 30.

Jorion, Philippe. 1986. Bayes-Stein Estimation for Portfolio Analysis. *The Journal of Financial and Quantitative Analysis* 21: 279–92. [CrossRef]

Ledoit, Olivier, and Michael Wolf. 2003. Improved Estimation of the Covariance Matrix of Stock Returns with an Application to Portfolio Selection. *Journal of Empirical Finance* 10: 603–21. [CrossRef]

Ledoit, Olivier, and Michael Wolf. 2004a. A Well-Conditioned Estimator for Large-Dimensional Covariance Matrices. *Journal of Multivariate Analysis* 88: 365–411. [CrossRef]

Ledoit, Olivier, and Michael Wolf. 2004b. Honey, I Shrunk the Sample Covariance Matrix—Problems in Mean-Variance Optimization. *Journal of Portfolio Management* 30: 110–19. [CrossRef]

Leote de Carvalho, Raul, Xiao Lu, and Pierre Moulin. 2012. Demystifying Equity Risk–Based Strategies: A Simple Alpha plus Beta Description. *The Journal of Portfolio Management* 38: 56–70. [CrossRef]

MacKinlay, A. Craig, and Lubos Pastor. 2000. Asset Pricing Models: Implications for Expected Returns and Portfolio Selection. *Review of Financial Studies* 13: 883–916. [CrossRef]

Maillard, Sébastien, Thierry Roncalli, and Jérôme Teïletche. 2010. The Properties of Equally Weighted Risk Contribution Portfolios. *The Journal of Portfolio Management* 36: 60–70. [CrossRef]

Marčenko, Vladimir Alexandrovich, and Leonid Andreevich Pastur. 1967. Distribution of Eigenvalues for Some Sets of Random Matrices. *Mathematics of the USSR-Sbornik* 1: 507–36. [CrossRef]

Markowitz, Harry. 1952. Portfolio Selection. *The Journal of Finance* 7: 77–91. [CrossRef]

Markowitz, Harry. 1956. The Optimization of a Quadratic Function Subject to Linear Constraints. *Naval Research Logistics Quarterly* 3: 111–33. [CrossRef]

Merton, Robert C. 1980. On Estimating the Expected Return on the Market: An Exploratory Investigation. *Topics in Catalysis* 8: 323–61.

Michaud, Richard O. 1989. The Markowitz Optimization Enigma: Is Optimized Optimal? *Financial Analysts Journal* 45: 31–42. [CrossRef]

Pantaleo, Ester, Michele Tumminello, Fabrizio Lillo, and Rosario N. Mantegna. 2011. When Do Improved Covariance Matrix Estimators Enhance Portfolio Optimization? An Empirical Comparative Study of Nine Estimators. *Quantitative Finance* 11: 1067–80. [CrossRef]

Qian, Edward. 2006. On the Financial Interpretation of Risk Contribution: Risk Budgets Do Add Up. *Journal of Investment Management* 4: 41–51. [CrossRef]

Schäfer, Juliane, and Korbinian Strimmer. 2005. A Shrinkage approach to large-scale covariance matrix estimation and implications for functional genomics. *Applications in Genetics and Molecular Biology* 4: 1175–89. [CrossRef] [PubMed]

Sharpe, William F. 1963. A simplified model for portfolio analysis. *Management Science* 9: 277–93. [CrossRef]

Developing an Impairment Loss Given Default Model using Weighted Logistic Regression Illustrated on a Secured Retail Bank Portfolio

Douw Gerbrand Breed [1], Tanja Verster [1], Willem D. Schutte [1,*] and Naeem Siddiqi [2]

[1] Centre for Business Mathematics and Informatics, North-West University, Potchefstroom 2531, South Africa; gerbrand.breed@gmail.com (D.G.B.); tanja.verster@nwu.ac.za (T.V.)

[2] SAS Institute Canada, Toronto, ON M5A 1K7, Canada; naeem.siddiqi@sas.com

* Correspondence: wd.schutte@nwu.ac.za

Abstract: This paper proposes a new method to model loss given default (LGD) for IFRS 9 purposes. We develop two models for the purposes of this paper—LGD1 and LGD2. The LGD1 model is applied to the non-default (performing) accounts and its empirical value based on a specified reference period using a lookup table. We also segment this across the most important variables to obtain a more granular estimate. The LGD2 model is applied to defaulted accounts and we estimate the model by means of an exposure weighted logistic regression. This newly developed LGD model is tested on a secured retail portfolio from a bank. We compare this weighted logistic regression (WLR) (under the assumption of independence) with generalised estimating equations (GEEs) to test the effects of disregarding the dependence among the repeated observations per account. When disregarding this dependence in the application of WLR, the standard errors of the parameter estimates are underestimated. However, the practical effect of this implementation in terms of model accuracy is found to be negligible. The main advantage of the newly developed methodology is the simplicity of this well-known approach, namely logistic regression of binned variables, resulting in a scorecard format.

Keywords: loss given default; weighted logistic regression; International Financial Reporting Standard 9; independence assumption

1. Introduction

The International Accounting Standard Board published the IFRS 9 standard in 2014, (IFRS 2014), which replaced most of International Accounting Standard (IAS) 39. Amongst others, it contains impairment requirements that allow for earlier recognition of credit losses. The financial statements of banks are expected to reflect the IFRS 9 accounting standards as of 1 January 2018 (European Banking Authority (EBA)). Banks found that IFRS 9 had a significant impact on systems and processes (Beerbaum 2015). While the IAS 39 standard made use of provisions on incurred losses, the financial crisis showed that expected losses, instead of incurred losses, are better used to calculate provisioning for banks (Global Public Policy Committee (GPPC)). In addition, under IFRS 9, the expected credit losses (ECL) should be equivalent to the lifetime ECL, if the credit risk has increased significantly. When the converse is true, a financial entity may allow for credit losses equal to a 12-month ECL. The ECL model is a forward-looking model and should result in the early detection of credit losses, which is anticipated to contribute to overall financial stability (IFRS 2014). The ECL is a function of the probability of default (PD), the loss given default (LGD) and the exposure at default (EAD).

In this paper, we focus on the LGD component within the impairment calculation under IFRS 9. There are many methodologies to model LGD, see e.g., Joubert et al. (2018a, 2018b) and the references therein. These methodologies include the run-off triangle method, beta regression, survival analysis, fractional response regression, inverse beta transformation, and Box–Cox transformation. Most of these techniques are quite complex and very difficult to understand, including the monitoring and validation thereof. This is confirmed by Bijak and Thomas (2018), who indicate that more than 15 different performance measures can be found in the literature concerning LGD models, possibly due to the difficulty of modelling the distribution shape of LGD. The LGD can be modelled through either the direct or the indirect approach. When using the direct approach, the LGD is equal to one minus the recovery rate (De Jongh et al. 2017). The indirect approach uses two components that are modelled separately, namely the probability component and the loss severity component. Independent of the methodology, the LGD is always assessed over the life of the lending exposure (Basel Committee on Banking Supervision 2015a).

Different modelling approaches are usually followed for accounts in different stages. An account can reside in one of three stages. Stage 1 accounts are performing accounts, Stage 2 have significant deterioration in credit risk, but are not in default, while defaulted accounts are in Stage 3 (Aptivaa 2016).

This paper describes the proposed new methodology to model the LGD for IFRS 9 purposes. We estimated both the LGD1 and LGD2 values, where the LGD1 was applied to non-defaulted accounts and the LGD2 to defaulted accounts. For the non-defaulted accounts (accounts in Stages 1 and 2, according to the IFRS 9 definition) we used the historically observed the LGD value (LGD1) and segmented this value according to variables with business importance using a lookup table. The weighted logistic regression was applied on the defaulted accounts (accounts in Stage 3, according to the IFRS 9 definition) to obtain the LGD2. This therefore resulted in two models: one for the LGD1 and one for the LGD2. The LGD1 was applied for Stage 1 (12 months) and Stage 2 (lifetime) because, while the PD component differentiates between 12 months and lifetime, the LGD is the loss expected for the remaining life of the account. Since logistic regression is well known and regularly used in banks, established monitoring metrics and governance practices have been embedded in the industry. These metrics, as well as the methodology, are thoroughly understood by stakeholders, which leads to a high degree of confidence in the results. Logistic regression using the scorecard format provides an even more transparent and user-friendly technique that is easy to understand and communicate to stakeholders. For this reason, we propose this new methodology to model the LGD for IFRS 9 purposes.

The paper consists of five sections. The modelling approach is described in Section 2. Section 3 follows with a case study where the proposed methodology is applied to a secured retail portfolio. The effect of the dependency of the observations used in the logistic regression is tested by comparing the results from the logistic regression with that of a generalised estimating equation (that takes dependency into account). We also investigate whether a decision tree could outperform the weighted logistic regression. Section 4 discusses the strengths and weaknesses of our new methodology and Section 5 concludes.

2. LGD Methodology

This section describes the newly proposed LGD methodology. First, the methodology used to estimate the LGD of the non-defaulted accounts is provided (LGD1) under Section 2.1, followed by Section 2.2 that discusses the methodology employed to model the LGD of the defaulted accounts (LGD2).

2.1. LGD1 Methodology

The LGD1 was obtained by calculating the loss as the exposure at default minus the net present value (NPV) of recoveries, divided by the EAD. The LGD1 is typically modelled on a smaller data sample than for the LGD2, since the loss is only calculated on accounts in Stages 1 and 2 that eventually transition into default. The probability of transitioning from Stages 1 and 2 directly into default is typically very low. The data sample for LGD2 is typically much larger as it considers all accounts in default and not only those that transition into it in a specific cohort. In this specific case study, the discounted write-off amount served as a proxy for the NPV of recovery cash flows. A more granular estimate was obtained by using the most important LGD drivers to segment the LGD1 values. The historical LGD values were calculated (and averaged) per segment and the estimated LGD1 values were derived using a lookup table (see e.g., Basel Committee on Banking Supervision (2015b)). The results of the case study are shown in Section 3.1. Note that the number of variables available to use for the LGD2 modelling is much larger than that for the LGD1. The reason is that some of the default related variables are not available at the LGD1 model stage, e.g., months since default.

2.2. *LGD2 Methodology*

We use a weighted logistic regression to model the LGD for the defaulted account including all available data. The actual loss experienced is transformed to a binary format related to the "fuzzy augmentation" technique commonly used to introduce "rejects" in scorecard development (Siddiqi 2006). This means that each observation has both a target of 1 (Y = 1) as well as a target of 0 (Y = 0). Furthermore, a weight variable is created, where the sum of the weights of these two events adds up to the full exposure of the account at observation. This is related to Van Berkel and Siddiqi (2012) who used a scorecard format for modelling LGD. This newly proposed methodology for LGD2 only considers worked-out accounts. A worked-out account can either cure or be written off. Note that the point of write-off is taken as that specific point where the institution (e.g., bank) no longer expects any recovery. This is specifically prescribed by the reporting standard: "IFRS 7 (35F) (e): The Group writes off financial assets, in whole or in part, when it has exhausted all practical recovery efforts and has concluded there is no reasonable expectation of recovery. Indicators that there is no reasonable expectation of recovery include (i) ceasing enforcement activity and (ii) where the Group's effort to dispose of repossessed collateral is such that there is no reasonable expectation of recovering in full" (PWC 2017). In effect, with our methodology, all write-offs and cures are included regardless of the time spent in default and no filter is applied on default cohort.

We calculated the LGD for accounts that cured and for accounts that were written off. The modelling approach can be subdivided into five steps: (1) sample creation; (2) target and weight variables created; (3) input variables; (4) weighted logistic regression; and (5) test for independence.

Note that if any accounts in the considered dataset originated as credit impaired accounts (i.e., accounts starting in default), their loss behaviour will most likely be different from other Stage 3 accounts and should therefore be modelled separately (i.e., segment the portfolio based on this characteristic). In this specific case study here presented, no such accounts existed.

2.2.1. Step 1: Sample Created

This approach would first need to identify all worked-out accounts (i.e., write-off, cure) over an appropriate reference period. Note that one account can appear multiple times, but an account will only appear once per month. This violates the logistic regression assumption of independent observations. The effect of this dependence (Sheu 2000) is tested at the end of the paper, by comparing a generalised estimating equation (GEE) model with the logistic regression model. In statistics, a GEE is used to estimate the parameters of a generalised linear model with a possible unknown correlation between outcomes (Kuchibhatla and Fillenbaum 2003).

The sample of observations was split into two datasets for out of sample testing. Evaluating the performance of a classifier on the same data used to train the classifier usually leads to an optimistically biased assessment (SAS Institute 2010). The simplest strategy for correcting the optimism bias is to hold out a portion of the development data for assessment (Baesens et al. 2016), i.e., data splitting. We therefore split the data into a training and a validation dataset. The validation data is used only for assessment and not for model development.

2.2.2. Step 2: Target and Weight Variables Created

Two rows ($Y = 1$ and $Y = 0$) are created for each observation (i.e., per account per month). Each row is weighted. Cured and written-off accounts are weighted differently. Mathematically, the weight for observation i is defined as

$$w_i = \begin{cases} Exposure_i \times LGD_i & if\ Y_i = 1 \\ Exposure_i \times (1 - LGD_i) & if\ Y_i = 0, \end{cases} \tag{1}$$

where the loss given default of observation i (LGD_i) is defined as

$$LGD_i = \begin{cases} P(Cure) \times P(redefault) \times LGD_{1.Unadj} & \text{if observation } i \text{ is a cured} \\ WO_i / Exposure_i & \text{if observation } i \text{ is written off} \end{cases}, \tag{2}$$

where

- i is the number of observations from 1 to N;
- $Exposure_i$ is the exposure of observation i; and therefore,

$$EAD_i = \sum_{\forall Y_i} Exposure_i = Exposure_i \text{IND}(Y_i = 1) + Exposure_i \text{IND}(Y_i = 0), \tag{3}$$

where $IND(Y_i = 1) := \begin{cases} 1\ if\ Y_i = 1 \\ 0\ if\ Y_i = 0 \end{cases}$ and $IND(Y_i = 0) := \begin{cases} 1\ if\ Y_i = 0 \\ 0\ if\ Y_i = 1 \end{cases}$.

- $P(Cure)$ is the proportion of cured observations over the total number of worked-out accounts (over the reference period);
- $P(redefault)$ is the proportion of observations that re-default over the reference period;
- $LGD_{1.Unadj}$ is the exposure at default (EAD) minus the net present value (NPV) of recoveries from first point of default for all observations in the reference period divided by the EAD—see e.g., PWC (2017) and Volarević and Varović (2018);
- WO_i is the discounted write-off amount for observation i; and
- $P(Cure)$, $P(redefault)$ and $LGD_{1.Unadj}$ are therefore empirical calculated values. This should be regularly updated to ensure the final LGD estimate remains a point in time estimate as required by IFRS (IFRS 2014).

Note that the write-off amount is used in Equation (2) to calculate the actual LGD. An alternative method employs the recovery cash flows over the work out period. A bank is required to use its "best estimate" (a regulatory term, e.g., Basel Committee on Banking Supervision (2019b) and European Central Bank (2018)) to determine actual the LGD. In this case, this decision was based on the data available. Only the write-off amount was available for our case study, not the recovered cash flows. In Equation (2), the write-off amount needs to be discounted using the effective interest rate (PWC 2017), to incorporate time value of money. When recoveries are used, each recovery cash flow needs to be similarly discounted. In the case study, the length of the recovery time period exists in the data and differs for each account. The length of this recovery time period will have an influence on the calculation of LGD: the longer the recovery process, the higher the effective discount rate. In the case study, we used the client interest rate as the effective interest rate when discounting.

Note that, in special circumstances, accounts may be partially written off, leading to an overestimation of provision. This should be taken into account during the modelling process. However, in our case study no such accounts existed.

Illustrative Example

Consider one observation with an exposure of \$50,000. Assume it is a written-off account, for a specific month, with an $LGD_i = 27\%$ (based on the written-off amount divided by the exposure, i.e.,

$WO_i/Exposure_i$). The weight variable for $Y = 1$ will be $27\% \times \$50,000 = \$13,500$ and $Y = 0$ will be $(1 - 27\%) \times \$50,000 = \$36,500$ (see Table 1).

Table 1. Illustrative example of weight variable.

Binary Outcome (Y)	Exposure	Weight Variable
0	$50,000	$13,500
1	$50,000	$36,500

2.2.3. Step 3: Input Variables (i.e., Variable Selection)

All input variables were first screened according to the following three requirements: percentage of missing values, the Gini statistic and business input. If too many values of a specific variable were missing that variable was excluded. Similarly, if a variable had a too low value for the Gini statistic, then that variable was also excluded. Note that business analysts should investigate whether there are any data issues with variables that have low Gini statistics. For example, traditionally strong variables may appear weak if the data has significant sample bias. This forms part of data preparation that is always essential before predictive modelling should take place.

The Gini statistic (Siddiqi 2006) quantifies a model's ability to discriminate between two possible values of a binary target variable (Tevet 2013). Cases are ranked according to the predictions and the Gini then provides a measure of correctness. It is one of the most popular measures used in retail credit scoring (Baesens et al. 2016; Siddiqi 2006; Anderson 2007) and has the added advantage that it is a single value (Tevet 2013).

The Gini is calculated as follows (SAS Institute 2017):

1. Sort the data by descending order of the proportion of events in each attribute. Suppose a characteristic has m attributes. Then, the sorted attributes are placed in groups $1, 2, \ldots, m$. Each group corresponds to an attribute.
2. For each of these sorted groups, compute the number of events $\left((\#(Y = 1)_j\right)$ and the number of nonevents (#(Y=0)_j)in group j. Then compute the Gini statistic:

$$\left(1 - \frac{2\sum_{j=2}^{m}\left((\#(Y=1)_j \times \sum_{j=1}^{j-1} \#(Y=0)_j\right) + \sum_{j=1}^{m}\left((\#(Y=1)_j \times \#(Y=0)_j\right)}{\#(Y=1) \times \#(Y=0)} \times 100\right), \quad (4)$$

where $\#(Y = 1)$ and $\#(Y = 0)$ are the total number of events and nonevents in the data, respectively.

Only variables of sufficient Gini and which were considered important from a business perspective were included in the modelling process. All the remaining variables after the initial screening were then binned. The concept of binning is known by different names such as discretisation, classing, categorisation, grouping and quantification (Verster 2018). For simplicity we use the term binning throughout this paper. Binning is the mapping of continuous or categorical data into discrete bins (Nguyen et al. 2014). It is a frequently used pre-processing step in predictive modelling and considered a basic data preparation step in building a credit scorecard (Thomas 2009). Credit scorecards are convenient points-based models that predict binary events and are broadly used due to their simplicity and ease of use; see e.g., Thomas (2009) and Siddiqi (2006). Among the practical advantages of binning are the removal of the effects of outliers and a convenient way to handle missing values (Anderson 2007). The binning was iteratively done by first generating equal-width bins, followed by business input-based adjustments to obtain the final set. Note that if binned variables are used in logistic regression, the final model can easily be transformed into a scorecard.

All bins were quantified by means of the average LGD value per bin. The motivation behind this was to propose an alternative to using dummy variables. Logistic regression cannot use categorical variables coded in its original format (Neter et al. 1996). As such, some other measure is needed for each bin to make it usable—the default technique of logistic regression is a dummy variable for each class less one. However, expanding categorical inputs into dummy variables can greatly increase the dimension of the input space (SAS Institute 2010). One alternative to this is to quantify (e.g., using weights of evidence (WOE)—see Siddiqi (2006)) each bin using the target value (in our case the LGD value), which will reduce the number of estimates. An example of this is using the natural logarithm (ln) of the good/bad odds (i.e., the WOE)—see for example Lund and Raimi (2012). We used the standardised average LGD value in each bin.

Some of the advantages of binning and quantifying the bins are as follows:

- The average LGD value can be calculated for missing values, which will allow "Missing" to be used in model fit (otherwise these rows would not have been used in modelling). Note that not all missing values are equal and there are cases where they need to be treated separately based on reason for missing, e.g., "No hit" at the bureau vs. no trades present. It is therefore essential that business analysts investigate the reason for missing values and treat them appropriately. This again forms part of data preparation that is always a key prerequisite to predictive modelling.
- Sparse outliers will not have an effect on the fit of the model. These outliers will become incorporated into the nearest bin and their contributions diminished through the usage of bin WOE or average LGD.
- Binning can capture some of the generalisation (required in predictive modelling). Generalisation refers to the ability to predict the target of new cases and binning improves the balance between being too vague or too specific.
- The binning can capture possible non-linear trends (as long as they can be assigned logical causality).
- Using the standardised average LGD value for each bin ensures that all variables are of the same scale (i.e., average LGD value).
- Using the average LGD value ensures that all types of variables (categorical, numerical, nominal, ordinal) will be transformed into the same measurement type.
- Quantifying the bins (rather than using dummy variables) results in each variable being seen as one group (and not each level as a different variable). This aids in reducing the number of parameter estimates.

Next, each of these average LGD values was standardised using the weight variable by calculating the average LGD per bin. An alternative approach could have been to calculate the WOE for each bin. The WOE is regularly used in credit scorecard development (Siddiqi 2006) and is calculated using only the number of 1's and the number of 0's for each bin. Note that our underlying variable of interest (LGD) is continuous. However, since our modelled target variable was dichotomous, we wanted the quantification of the bin to reflect our underlying true target, e.g., the LGD value, which ranges from 0 to 1. This average LGD value per bin was then standardised by means of the weight variable. The weighted mean LGD, $\overline{LGD}_w$ is defined as

$$\overline{LGD}_w = \frac{\sum_i w_i LGD_i}{\sum_i w_i}, \tag{5}$$

where LGD_i is the LGD value of observation i and w_i is the weight of observation i. The weighted standard deviation LGD is defined as

$$s_w = \sqrt{\frac{\sum_i w_i \left(LGD_i - \overline{LGD}_w\right)^2}{N-1}}, \tag{6}$$

where N is the number of observations. The weighted standardised value for LGD, $LGD^*{}_i$, for observation i will then be

$$LGD^*{}_i = \frac{LGD_i - \overline{LGD}_w}{s_w}. \quad (7)$$

The standardisation of all input variables implies that the estimates from the logistic regression will be standardised estimates. The benefit is that the absolute value of the standardised estimates can serve to provide an approximate ranking of the relative importance of the input variables on the fitted logistic model (SAS Institute 2010). If this was not done, the scale of each variable could also have had an influence on the estimate. Note that the logistic regression fitted was a weighted logistic regression with the exposure as weight (split for $Y = 1$ and $Y = 0$) and therefore to ensure consistency, we also weighted the LGD with the same weight variable as used in the logistic regression.

Furthermore, pertaining to the month since default as input variable: The model that is developed does not require the length of default for incomplete accounts in order to estimate LGD. It assumes that the length of default for these accounts will be comparable to similar accounts that have been resolved. This is an assumption that can be easily monitored after implementation.

2.2.4. Step 4: Weighted Logistic Regression

A weighted logistic regression was then fitted using the available data. The log of the odds in a weighted logistic regression is given as:

$$logit(p_i) = \ln\left(\frac{p_i}{1 - p_i}\right) = \beta_0 + \boldsymbol{\beta} w_i \mathbf{X}_i^T, \quad (8)$$

where:

- $p_i = E(Y_i = 1 | \mathbf{X}_i, \beta)$ is the probability of loss for observation i;
- β_0, $\boldsymbol{\beta}$ are regression coefficients with $\boldsymbol{\beta} = \{\beta_1, \ldots, \beta_K\}$;
- $\mathbf{X}_i$ is the vector of the predictor variables $X_{i1,}, \ldots, X_{iK}$ for observation i; and
- w_i is the weight of each observation i, calculated by the actual loss amount ($s) and given in Equation (1).

Note that in this weighted logistic regression, we estimated the regression coefficients where the repeated observation within the same individual was assumed to be independent (i.e., disregarding the dependence among repeated observation of the same account).

2.2.5. Step 5: Test the Effect of the Dependence Assumption

A single account would appear multiple times in our dataset (depending on the number of months the account is present), which violates the assumption of independent observations in logistic regression. We therefore tested the effect of this violation using a GEE that can handle the statistical dependence of repeated data by assuming some correlation structure (Kuchibhatla and Fillenbaum 2003) among observations. This approach estimates regression coefficients without completely specifying the joint distribution of the multivariate responses, but the parameters of the within-subjects correlation are explicitly accounted for in the estimation process (Sheu 2000). It is also shown in Sheu (2000) that the GEE approach is not sensitive to the choice of correlated structure. Kuchibhatla and Fillenbaum (2003) also found that when comparing the model fit using the GEE with that using the logistic regression, the logistic regression overestimated the standard errors of the dependent variables.

3. Case Study: Secured Retail Portfolio from a South African Bank

This section illustrates the newly proposed LGD methodology on a secured retail portfolio from one of the major banks in South Africa. Section 3.1 shows the results for the non-defaulted accounts (i.e., LGD1). Then, Section 3.2 shows results for the defaulted accounts (LGD2). Note that the data was split into LGD1 and LGD2, resulting in 95% of the data in the LGD2 dataset and 5% of the data in the LGD1 dataset. The reason for the much smaller LGD1 dataset is that very few of the "non-defaulted" sub-set of total accounts actually defaulted. In reality, the LGD1 model is applied to the non-defaulted portfolio (which is typically the bigger dataset), whereas the LGD2 model is applied to the defaulted portfolio (which is typically a much smaller dataset). The datasets used for modelling therefore appear counterintuitive to real world conditions.

3.1. LGD1 Results

The empirical observed LGD described in Section 2.1 was applied to the pre-default book, i.e., accounts not in default. This number was further enhanced by using segmentation variables. As it is important that the variables used for segmentation do not change over time, the final set of variables was selected on the basis of stability and business sense. These variables were then binned. The final variables selected for segmentation were loan to value (LTV) at origination, channel/manufacturer and new/old/used indicator (NOU). The channel/manufacturer variable was derived the channel and manufacturer code. The empirical LGDs at the point of default were subsequently calculated by these variables in a matrix type approach (lookup table). The final lookup table for accounts not in default (Stage 1 and 2) is in Table 2. Note that the standardised LGD values are shown to protect the confidential information surrounding this portfolio's observed values. The final segmentation is consistent with business sense (note the LGD separation from very negative to very positive). This lookup table approach—separating risks into different bins (slots)—is closely related to the concept of slotting (Basel Committee on Banking Supervision 2019a).

Table 2. Lookup table for Loss Given Default 1.

LTV	Channel & Manufacturer	New/Old	Standardised LGD
<=1	Group 1	New	−1.0553
<=1	Group 1	Old	−1.00075
<=1	Group 2	New	−0.87389
<=1	Group 2	Old	−0.18252
<=1	Group 1	New	−0.2155
<=1	Group 1	Old	−0.10513
<=1	Group 3	New	−0.67346
<=1	Group 3	Old	0.050902
>1	Group 1	New	−0.22311
>1	Group 1	Old	0.519007
>1	Group 2	New	−0.24721
>1	Group 2	Old	0.532962
>1	Group 1	New	0.365509
>1	Group 1	Old	0.957936
>1	Group 3	New	0.647134
>1	Group 3	Old	1.503425

3.2. LGD2 Results

The results are described according to the five steps discussed in Section 2.2.

3.2.1. Step 1: Sample Created

A 24-month reference period, based on business input, was used. Only worked-out accounts were selected in this reference period. The LGD2 dataset was then split into a 70% training (946,285 observations, 38,352 unique accounts) and 30% validation dataset (405,630 observations, 37,720 unique accounts).

3.2.2. Step 2: Target and Weight Variables Created

Two rows ($Y = 1$ and $Y = 0$) were created for each observation (i.e., per account per month). Each row was weighted, as described in Section 2.2.

3.2.3. Step 3: Input Variables

All input variables were screened using the following three requirements: percentage of missing values (more than 50% missing was used as a cut-off), the Gini statistic (variables with low Gini statistic values were excluded) and business input. All bins were quantified using the average LGD value per bin, which was then standardised with the weight variable. Table 3 lists the binned and quantified variables used in the weighted logistic regression. The final decision on binning was a combination of bucket stability (CSI), logical trends as well as consistency of logical trends over time. Some of the observations on these variables, with respect to LGD values, include (variable names indicated in brackets):

- Higher LTV values are associated with higher LGD values (*LTV*).
- The higher the month on book (MOB) value for a customer, the lower the expected LGD value (*MOB*).
- The more months a customer has been in default, the higher the LGD value (*Default*).
- Customers buying old vehicles are associated with higher LGD values (*New/Old*).
- Certain channels and certain manufacturers are associated with higher LGD values (*Channel Manufacturer*).

Table 3. Binned input variables.

LTV	**LTV Range**	**#**	**Standardised LGD**
Bin 1	LTV <=1	18188	−0.00566
Bin 2	LTV <=1.2	10461	−0.00268
Bin 3	LTV > 1.2	9703	0.004802
MOB	**MOB Range**	**#**	**Standardised LGD**
Bin 1	MOB <=24	17593	0.005193244
Bin 2	MOB <=42	10431	−0.000342394
Bin 3	MOB > 42	10328	−0.006198457
Default	**Default Range**	**#**	**Standardised LGD**
Bin 1	0	1043	−0.005747327
Bin 2	1	7706	−0.004411893
Bin 3	2+	16150	−0.000289465
Bin 4	Other/Missing	13453	0.006032881
New/Old	**New/Old Range**	**#**	**Standardised LGD**
Bin 1	New	15249	−0.004677389
Bin 2	Old	23103	0.004428005
Channel Manufacturer	**Channel Manufacturer Range**	**#**	**Standardised LGD**
Bin 1	Group 1	3870	−0.008325
Bin 2	Group 2	5984	−0.004694
Bin 3	Group 3	26422	0.001172
Bin 4	Group 4	2076	0.011212

This binning approach (separating risks in different bins or slots) is related to the underlying principle used in slotting (Basel Committee on Banking Supervision 2019a).

3.2.4. Step 4: Weighted Logistic Regression

A stepwise weighted logistic regression was fitted on the dataset, with a 5% significance level. The analyses were performed using SAS. The SAS code is provided as Supplementary Material for reference. While the authors of this paper used SAS, users can implement these techniques using any available analytic tool including Python and R. The final variables for accounts in default (Stage 3) are given in Table 4. The Gini statistic on the training dataset was 45.49% and on the validation dataset 36.04%. The difference between the training and validation Gini is quite large and could be an indication of the model not generalising well. However, it should be acknowledged that the Gini describes how well the model distinguishes between the two groups $Y_i = 1$ and $Y_i = 0$ (Breed and Verster 2017), while our underlying target is the LGD value which is a continuous value between 0 and 1. Therefore, a better measure for both model performance and comparing training and validation samples is the mean squared error (MSE), although several other measures could have been used (see Bijak and Thomas (2018) for an extensive list of performance measures applicable to LGD).

Table 4. Weighted logistic regression results.

Analysis of Maximum Likelihood Estimates					
Parameter (X)	**DF**	**Estimate (β)**	**Standard Error**	**Wald Chi-Square**	**Pr > ChiSq**
Intercept	1	−1.0977	0.000012	8528907254	<0.0001
LTV (X_1)	1	32.6329	0.00256	161977546	<0.0001
Months on books (X_2)	1	10.3046	0.00261	15622966.5	<0.0001
Default event (X_3)	1	173.9	0.00253	4709270394	<0.0001
New/Old (X_4)	1	18.5934	0.00252	54593987.2	<0.0001
Channel/Manufacturer (X_5)	1	17.3602	0.00248	48935118.5	<0.0001

The mean squared error was therefore calculated as follows:

$$MSE_i = \frac{\left(\widehat{LGD}_i - LGD_i\right)^2}{N}, \quad (9)$$

where $\widehat{LGD}_i$ is the predicted LGD value of observation i from the model, LGD_i the best estimate of the actual LGD (as defined in Equation (1)) and where i is the number of observations from 1 to N.

The MSE for the training and validation datasets were 0.0473 and 0.0427 respectively, thus showing a small mean squared error.

The R-square value (Bijak and Thomas 2018) was calculated as follows:

$$R\ squared = 1 - \frac{\sum_i\left(\widehat{LGD}_i - LGD_i\right)^2}{\sum_i\left(\widehat{LGD}_i - \overline{LGD}\right)^2}, \quad (10)$$

where $\overline{LGD}$ is the expected value of the actual LGD values. The R-squared value for the training and validation datasets were 0.3202 and 0.2727, respectively.

Furthermore, it showed that the model generalises well, as it also predicted well on the validation dataset (small difference between train and validation datasets). Here, the MSE on the training and validation dataset are very close. Note that the MSE and the R-squared value were calculated on the LGD values and not the standardised LGD values.

3.2.5. Step 5: Test the Effect of the Dependence Assumption

Next, we estimated the regression coefficients using the GEE, first assuming an independent correlation structure and then with an autoregressive correlation structure of the order one. In Table 5, the results of the GEE using an independent correlation structure are shown. The code is provided in the Supplementary Material for reference, although any other analytics tool could be used to fit a GEE model.

Table 5. Generalised Estimating Equations regression results (independent correlation).

Analysis of GEE Parameter Estimates							
Empirical Standard Error Estimates							
Parameter (X)	**Estimate (β)**	**Standard Error**	**95% Confidence Limits**		**Z**	**Pr > |Z|**
Intercept	−1.0978	0.0116	−1.1205	−1.0750	−94.44	<0.0001
LTV (X_1)	32.6348	2.4257	27.8805	37.3891	13.45	<0.0001
Months on books (X_2)	10.3055	2.3708	5.6587	14.9522	4.35	<0.0001
Default event (X_3)	173.8758	1.8297	170.2897	177.4619	95.03	<0.0001
New/Old (X_4)	18.5943	2.4984	13.6976	23.4910	7.44	<0.0001
Channel Manufacturer (X_5)	17.3607	2.5861	12.2921	22.4293	6.71	<0.0001

The Gini on the training and validation datasets came to 45.49% and 36.04%, respectively, while the MSE on the training and validation datasets were 0.0473 and 0.0427. We used a significance level of 5% throughout, and all six variables were statistically significant. We note that the results (parameter estimates, Gini and MSE) are almost identical to that of the weighted logistic regression.

Next, an autoregressive correlation structure to the order of one was assumed. The results are shown in Table 6.

Table 6. Generalised Estimating Equations regression results (autoregressive correlation).

Analysis of GEE Parameter Estimates						
Empirical Standard Error Estimates						
Parameter (X)	**Estimate (β)**	**Standard Error**	**95% Confidence Limits**		**Z**	**Pr > |Z|**
Intercept	−0.7973	0.0080	−0.8131	−0.7816	−99.15	<0.0001
LTV (X_1)	24.8404	1.8335	21.2468	28.4339	13.55	<0.0001
Months on books (X_2)	6.8528	1.7314	3.4592	10.2463	3.96	<0.0001
Default event (X_3)	129.6377	1.3393	127.0126	132.2627	96.79	<0.0001
New/Old (X_4)	12.5228	1.8139	8.9677	16.0779	6.90	<0.0001
Channel Manufacturer (X_5)	11.7312	1.8959	8.0154	15.4470	6.19	<0.0001

The Gini on the training data was 45.48% and on the validation dataset 36.04%, with the MSE values being 0.0522 and 0.0406, respectively, for training and validation. Note that all six variables were again statistically significant.

Next, the three models were compared in terms of parameter estimates, standard errors of the estimates and on model performance. Table 7 provides the parameter estimates comparisons, which indicate similar numbers for the weighted logistic regression (LR) and the GEE (independent correlation). This is similar to the results found by Sheu (2000). The parameter estimates were quite different, however, when using an autoregressive correlation matrix.

Table 7. Comparison of the parameter estimates of the three modelling techniques.

	Weighted LR	**GEE (Ind Corr)**	**GEE (Ar1 Corr)**
β_0	−1.0977	−1.0978	−0.7973
β_1	32.6329	32.6348	24.8404
β_2	10.3046	10.3055	6.8528
β_3	173.9	173.8758	129.6377
β_4	18.5934	18.5943	12.5228
β_5	17.3602	17.3607	11.7312

In Table 8 the most significant difference between using a weighted logistic regression (disregarding the dependence among repeated observations of the same account) and using a GEE (addressing the dependence) can be seen. The weighted logistic regression underestimates the standard error of the parameter estimates. This is also confirmed by Sheu (2000) and Kuchibhatla and Fillenbaum (2003). Disregarding the dependence leads to the incorrect estimation of the standard errors. Although this is a problem from a statistical standpoint, resulting in incorrect inferences of the parameters, the practical effect is negligible, as evident from the goodness-of-fit statistics (MSE) of the different models.

Table 8. Comparison of the standard errors of the three modelling techniques

	Weighted LR	GEE (Ind Corr)	GEE (Ar1 Corr)
β_0	0.000012	0.0116	0.0080
β_1	0.00256	2.4257	1.8335
β_2	0.00261	2.3708	1.7314
β_3	0.00253	1.8297	1.3393
β_4	0.00252	2.4984	1.8139
β_5	0.00248	2.5861	1.8959

Table 9 summarises the model performance of all three models. It is interesting to note that all three models have almost identical performance. From a practical point of view, there was no difference in using any of these three techniques. When the model is productionalised, the bank will use the model to predict a specific LGD value and the accuracy of this predicted LGD was almost identical with either technique. If we suppose that the standard errors are not used by the bank, then there is no reason to refrain from using logistic regression.

Table 9. Comparison of the model performance of the three modelling techniques.

Technique	Train MSE	Valid MSE	Train Gini	Valid Gini
Weighted logistic regression	0.04727719	0.04274367	0.45492145910	0.36039085030
GEE (independent correlation)	0.04727703	0.04274417	0.45492145910	0.36039085030
GEE (AR 1 correlation)	0.05222953	0.04062386	0.45482289180	0.36037450660

One additional issue that bears mentioning is the low number of variables in the model itself. The banking industry prefers to see models that are consistent with how they would make decisions—meaning models must have variables that not only make business sense, but also cover as many of the different information types that should be considered. Typically, between eight to fifteen variables are considered normal in the industry (Siddiqi 2017). In a business setting, it is also common to add weaker variables, albeit those that display satisfactory correlations with the target, into the model itself.

3.3. *Additional Investigation: Decision Tree*

An additional modelling technique, namely the decision tree (Breiman et al. 1984), was considered to determine whether it could improve on the results above. First, the distribution of the actual LGD was analysed, as shown in Figure 1 (training dataset). Note that the LGD values were standardised, by subtracting the average and then dividing by the standard deviation. It can be seen that the LGD has a huge spike to the left and a much smaller spike closer to the right. This bimodal type of distribution is typical of an LGD distribution (Joubert et al. 2018a).

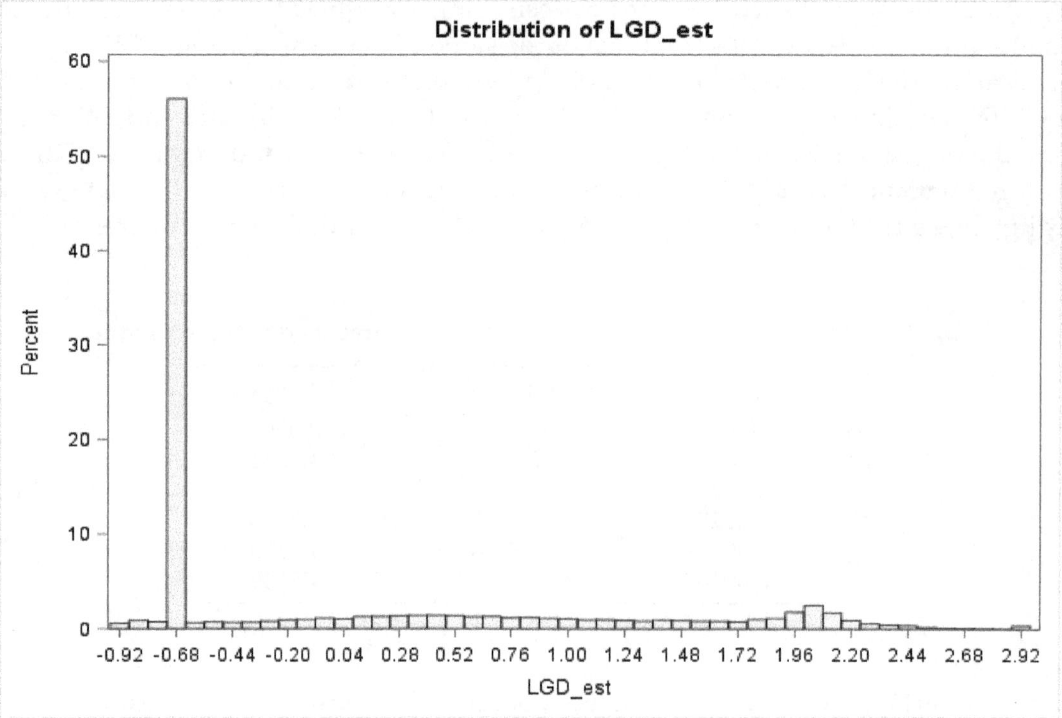

Figure 1. The distribution of the standardised observed LGD (training dataset).

The decision tree (i.e., classification tree), was developed with three different settings (see the Supplementary Material for the specific code used). First, the default settings were used. Second, the decision tree was pruned by means of the average squared error (ASE), and lastly, a setting of "no pruning" was used. For each of the decision trees, we used the same target variable (binary variable), the same weight variable and the same six explanatory variables as with the other models developed in this section. The MSE (Table 10) for the decision tree was worse than the weighted logistic regression and the GEE models that were developed (Table 9). Note that we only show the MSE values here and not the Gini values, because, as noted before, the MSE is a better measure to indicate model performance of the "true" target value, i.e., the LGD values.

Table 10. Model performance of decision trees.

Technique	Valid MSE
Decision tree (default settings)	0.1012884759
Decision tree (prune on ASE)	0.1002412789
Decision tree (no pruning)	0.1041756997

4. Strengths and Weaknesses of the Methodology

The method discussed in this paper presents several advantages. The first is that it is a relatively simplistic approach. Logistic regression is a well-known technique that has a long history in the financial services industry. In contrast, for secured products, indirect more complex methodologies are often used. One example is using a haircut model for the loss severity component and survival analysis for the probability component (Joubert et al. 2018b). Because logistic regression is well known and regularly used in banks, established monitoring metrics and governance practices have been embedded in the industry. These metrics, as well as the methodology, are thoroughly understood by stakeholders, which leads to a high degree of confidence in the results. Logistic regression using the scorecard format provides an even more transparent and user-friendly technique that is easy to understand and communicate to stakeholders.

A second advantage is that all variables are first binned and then quantified using the standardised LGD rate in each bin. Some of the specific advantages of this type of data transformation, as noted earlier in the paper, are:

- Better handling of missing values, and their usage in the model.
- Better way to deal with outliers by minimising their influence.
- Improved generalisation of data.
- Easier way to capture non-linear trends.
- Easier comparison across variables through the usage of standardised average LGD value for each bin and standardised estimates.
- A reduction in the degrees of freedom introduces stability into the model.

A weakness of the weighted regression is that it disregards the assumption of independence and this results in the statistical inference of the parameter estimates being incorrect. In particular, the standard errors of the parameter estimates are underestimated. Yet, there is no apparent difference in model accuracy.

5. Conclusions and Recommendation

This paper presented a new methodology to model LGD for IFRS 9 purposes, consisting of two components. First, the LGD1 model was applied to the non-default accounts and is an empirical value obtained through a lookup table, based on a specified reference period. This LGD1 was further segmented across the most important variables to obtain a more granular estimate. Second, the LGD2 was applied to defaulted accounts and is estimated using an exposure weighted logistic regression. This new methodology was tested by applying it on a real dataset, using a secured retail bank portfolio.

A comparison of this weighted logistic regression was done with GEE models to test the effect of the dependence among repeated observation of the same account. We discovered that when disregarding the repeated accounts, the standard errors of the parameter estimates were underestimated. However, the practical effects of such disregard were found to be negligible.

In conclusion, we propose this new methodology to model LGD for IFRS 9 purposes based on the following reasons mentioned in the paper:

- This methodology presents a relatively simple approach using logistic regression, which is a well-known and accepted technique in the banking industry.
- The results are easy to interpret and understand, and when converted to the scorecard format, provide a transparent user-friendly output.
- The method also uses transformations that offer better alternatives for dealing with issues such as missing data and outliers.
- Most banks have well-established processes for monitoring and implementing logistic regression models and they are well understood by stakeholders.
- From a practical perspective, there was no discernible difference in model accuracy when comparing the logistic regression model to the GEE model or the decision tree.

From a purely theoretical point of view, we recommend using the GEE approach. However, as some banks do not use the parameter estimates or the associated standard errors for any decisions (e.g., variable selection), the weighted logistic regression approach may be preferable in such situations.

We suggest future research ideas to include comparing this new methodology to other LGD modelling techniques. We could also explore alternative data transformations from the current binning and quantification using standardised LGD rates. We also did not include any direct costs in the calculation of the LGD, and determining how to split costs into direct and indirect components could be a further research idea. According to IFRS 9, the LGD should include forward-looking macro-economic scenarios (Miu and Ozdemir 2017). This has also not been considered in this paper and could be researched in future.

Author Contributions: Conceptualization, D.G.B., T.V. and W.D.S.; formal analysis, D.G.B., T.V. and W.D.S.; investigation, D.G.B., T.V. and W.D.S.; methodology, D.G.B., T.V., W.D.S. and N.S.; software, D.G.B., T.V. and W.D.S.; validation, D.G.B., T.V., W.D.S. and N.S.; visualization, D.G.B., T.V. and W.D.S.; writing—original draft, D.G.B., T.V. and W.D.S.; writing—review and editing, D.G.B., T.V., W.D.S. and N.S.

Acknowledgments: This work is based on research supported in part by the Department of Science and Technology (DST) of South Africa. The grant holders at the Centre for Business Mathematics and Informatics acknowledges that opinions, findings and conclusions or recommendations expressed in any publication generated by DST-supported research are those of the author(s) and that the DST accepts no liability whatsoever in this regard.

References

Anderson, Raymond. 2007. *The Credit Scoring Toolkit: Theory and Practice for Retail Credit Risk Management and Decision Automation*. Oxford: Oxford University Press.

Aptivaa. 2016. Cash Shortfall & LGD – Two Sides of the Same Coin. Available online: http://www.aptivaa.com/blog/cash-shortfall-lgd-two-sides-of-the-same-coin/ (accessed on 4 March 2019).

Baesens, Bar, Daniel Rosch, and Harald Scheule. 2016. *Credit Risk Analytics*. Cary: SAS Institute, Wiley.

Basel Committee on Banking Supervision. 2015a. Guidance on Accounting for Expected Credit Losses. Bank for International Settlements. Available online: https://www.bis.org/bcbs/publ/d350.htm (accessed on 31 January 2017).

Basel Committee on Banking Supervision. 2015b. Revisions to the Standardised Approach for Credit Risk. Bank for International Settlements. Available online: https://www.bis.org/bcbs/publ/d347.pdf (accessed on 18 February 2019).

Basel Committee on Banking Supervision. 2019a. CRE33 IRB Approach: Supervisory Slotting Approach for Specialised Lending (CRE Calculation of RWA for Credit Risk). Bank for International Settlements. Available online: https://www.bis.org/basel_framework/chapter/CRE/33.htm?tldate=20220101&inforce=20190101&export=pdf&pdfid=15661993943265707 (accessed on 11 March 2019).

Basel Committe on Banking Supervision. 2019b. Calculation of RWA for Credit Risk: CRE36 IRB Approach: Minimum Requirements to Use IRB Approach. Bank for International Settlements. Available online: https://www.bis.org/basel_framework/chapter/CRE/36.htm?inforce=20190101&export=pdf&pdfid=0 (accessed on 11 March 2019).

Beerbaum, Dirk. 2015. Significant increase in credit risk according to IFRS 9: Implications for financial institutions. *International Journal of Economics and Management Sciences* 4: 1–3. [CrossRef]

Bijak, Katarzyna, and Lyn C. Thomas. 2018. Underperforming performance measures? A review of measures for loss given default models. *Journal of Risk Model Validation* 12: 1–28. [CrossRef]

Breed, Douw Gerbrand, and Tanja Verster. 2017. The benefits of segmentation: Evidence from a South African bank and other studies. *South African Journal of Science* 113: 1–7. [CrossRef]

Breiman, Leo, Jerome Friedman, Richard A. Olsen, and Charles J. Stone. 1984. *Classification and Regression Trees*. Wadsworth: Pacific Grove.

De Jongh, Pieter Juriaan, Tanja Verster, Elzabe Reynolds, Morne Joubert, and Helgard Raubenheimer. 2017. A critical review of the Basel margin of conservatism requirement in a retail credit context. *International Business & Economics Research Journal* 16: 257–74.

European Banking Authority (EBA). 2016. Consultation Paper EBA/CP/2016/10: Draft Guidelines on Credit Institutions' Credit Risk Management Practices and Accounting for Expected Credit Losses. Available online: https://www.eba.europa.eu/documents/10180/1532063/EBA-CP-2016-10+%28CP+on+Guidelines+on+Accounting+for+Expected+Credit%29.pdf (accessed on 3 May 2017).

European Central Bank. 2018. Proposal on ELBE and LGD in-Default: Tackling Capital Requirements after the Financial Crisis. Available online: https://www.ecb.europa.eu/pub/pdf/scpwps/ecb.wp2165.en.pdf?176589bb4b7b020c3d3faffee9b982cd:No2165/June2018 (accessed on 11 February 2019).

Global Public Policy Committee (GPPC). 2016. The Implementation of IFRS 9 Impairment Requirements by Banks: Considerations for Those Charged with Governance of Systemically Important Banks. Global Public Policy Committee. Available online: http://www.ey.com/Publication/vwLUAssets/Implementation_of_IFRS_9_impairment_requirements_by_systemically_important_banks/$File/BCM-FIImpair-GPPC-June2016%20int.pdf (accessed on 25 February 2019).

IFRS. 2014. IRFS9 Financial Instruments: Project Summary. Available online: http://www.ifrs.org/Current-Projects/IASB-Projects/Financial-Instruments-A-Replacement-of-IAS-39-Financial-Instruments-Recognitio/Documents/IFRS-9-Project-Summary-July-2014.pdf (accessed on 31 January 2016).

Joubert, Morne, Tanja Verster, and Helgard Raubenheimer. 2018a. Default weighted survival analysis to directly model loss given default. *South African Statistical Journal* 52: 173–202.

Joubert, Morne, Tanja Verster, and Helgard Raubenheimer. 2018b. Making use of survival analysis to indirectly model loss given default. *Orion* 34: 107–32. [CrossRef]

Kuchibhatla, Maragatha, and Gerda G. Fillenbaum. 2003. Comparison of methods for analyzing longitudinal binary outcomes: Cognitive status as an example. *Aging & Mental Health* 7: 462–68.

Lund, Bruce, and Steven Raimi. 2012. Collapsing Levels of Predictor Variables for Logistic Regression and Weight of Evidence Coding. MWSUG 2012: Proceedings, Paper SA-03. Available online: http://www.mwsug.org/proceedings/2012/SA/MWSUG-2012-SA03.pdf (accessed on 9 April 2019).

Miu, Peter, and Bogie Ozdemir. 2017. Adapting the Basel II advanced internal ratings-based models for International Financial Reporting Standard 9. *Journal of Credit Risk* 13: 53–83. [CrossRef]

Neter, John, Michael H. Kutner, Christopher J. Nachtsheim, and William Wasserman. 1996. *Applied Linear Statistical Models*, 4th ed. WCB McGraw-Hill: New York.

Nguyen, Hoang-Vu, Emmanuel Müller, Jilles Vreeken, and Klemens Böhm. 2014. Unsupervised interaction-preserving discretization of multivariate data. *Data Mining Knowledge Discovery* 28: 1366–97. [CrossRef]

PWC. 2017. IFRS 9 for Banks: Illustrative Disclosures. February. Available online: https://www.pwc.com/ee/et/home/majaastaaruanded/Illustrative_discloser_IFRS_9_for_Banks.pdf (accessed on 8 April 2019).

SAS Institute. 2010. *Predictive Modelling Using Logistic Regression.*. Cary: SAS Institute Inc., Available online: http://support.sas.com/documentation/cdl/en/prochp/67530/HTML/default/viewer.htm#prochp_hpbin_overview.htm (accessed on 6 September 2017).

SAS Institute. 2017. *Development of Credit Scoring Applications Using SAS Enterprise Miner (SAS Course Notes: LWCSEM42)*. Cary: SAS Institute, ISBN 978-1-63526-092-2.

Sheu, Ching-fan. 2000. Regression analysis of correlated binary outcomes. *Behavior Research Methods, Instruments & Computers* 32: 269–73.

Siddiqi, Naeem. 2006. *Credit Risk Scorecards: Developing and Implementing Intelligent Credit Scoring*. Hoboken: John Wiley & Sons.

Siddiqi, Naeem. 2017. *Intelligent Credit Scoring: Building and Implementing Better Credit Risk Scorecards*. Hoboken: John Wiley & Sons.

Tevet, Dan. 2013. Exploring model lift: is your model worth implementing? *Actuarial Review* 40: 10–13.

Thomas, Lyn C. 2009. *Consumer Credit Models: Pricing, Profit and Portfolios*. Oxford: Oxford University Press.

Van Berkel, Anthony, and Naeem Siddiqi. 2012. *Building Loss Given Default Scorecard using Weight of Evidence Bins in SAS®Enterprise Miner™*. SAS Institute Inc Paper 141–2012. Cary: SAS Institute.

Verster, Tanja. 2018. Autobin: A predictive approach towards automatic binning using data splitting. *South African Statistical Journal* 52: 139–55.

Volarević, Hrvoje, and Mario Varović. 2018. Internal model for ifrs 9-expected credit losses calculation. *Ekonomski pregled: Mjesečnik Hrvatskog Društva Ekonomista Zagreb* 69: 269. [CrossRef]

Permissions

All chapters in this book were first published in MDPI; hereby published with permission under the Creative Commons Attribution License or equivalent. Every chapter published in this book has been scrutinized by our experts. Their significance has been extensively debated. The topics covered herein carry significant findings which will fuel the growth of the discipline. They may even be implemented as practical applications or may be referred to as a beginning point for another development.

The contributors of this book come from diverse backgrounds, making this book a truly international effort. This book will bring forth new frontiers with its revolutionizing research information and detailed analysis of the nascent developments around the world.

We would like to thank all the contributing authors for lending their expertise to make the book truly unique. They have played a crucial role in the development of this book. Without their invaluable contributions this book wouldn't have been possible. They have made vital efforts to compile up to date information on the varied aspects of this subject to make this book a valuable addition to the collection of many professionals and students.

This book was conceptualized with the vision of imparting up-to-date information and advanced data in this field. To ensure the same, a matchless editorial board was set up. Every individual on the board went through rigorous rounds of assessment to prove their worth. After which they invested a large part of their time researching and compiling the most relevant data for our readers.

The editorial board has been involved in producing this book since its inception. They have spent rigorous hours researching and exploring the diverse topics which have resulted in the successful publishing of this book. They have passed on their knowledge of decades through this book. To expedite this challenging task, the publisher supported the team at every step. A small team of assistant editors was also appointed to further simplify the editing procedure and attain best results for the readers.

Apart from the editorial board, the designing team has also invested a significant amount of their time in understanding the subject and creating the most relevant covers. They scrutinized every image to scout for the most suitable representation of the subject and create an appropriate cover for the book.

The publishing team has been an ardent support to the editorial, designing and production team. Their endless efforts to recruit the best for this project, has resulted in the accomplishment of this book. They are a veteran in the field of academics and their pool of knowledge is as vast as their experience in printing. Their expertise and guidance has proved useful at every step. Their uncompromising quality standards have made this book an exceptional effort. Their encouragement from time to time has been an inspiration for everyone.

The publisher and the editorial board hope that this book will prove to be a valuable piece of knowledge for researchers, students, practitioners and scholars across the globe.

List of Contributors

Svetlana Drobyazko
European Academy of Sciences, London 71-75, UK

Anna Barwinska-Malajowicz and Boguslaw Slusarczyk
Faculty of Economics, University of Rzeszow, 35-310 Rzeszów, Poland

Olga Chubukova
Faculty of Economics and Business, Kyiv National University of Technology and Design, 01011 Kyiv, Ukraine

Taliat Bielialov
Department of Finance and Financial and Economic Security, Kyiv National University of Technology and Design, 01011 Kyiv, Ukraine

Faridah Najuna Misman
Department of Finance, Faculty of Business and Management, Universiti Teknologi MARA, Segamat 85000, Johor, Malaysia

M. Ishaq Bhatti
Department of Economics, Finance & Marketing, La Trobe Business School, La Trobe University, Melbourne, VIC 3086, Australia

Stanislaus Maier-Paape
Institut für Mathematik, RWTH Aachen University, Templergraben 55, 52062 Aachen, Germany

Qiji Jim Zhu
Department of Mathematics, Western Michigan University, 1903 West Michigan Avenue, Kalamazoo, MI 49008, USA

Takaaki Koike and Marius Hofert
Department of Statistics and Actuarial Science, University of Waterloo, 200 University Avenue West, Waterloo, ON N2L 3G1, Canada

Rasika Yatigammana
Central Bank of Sri-Lanka, Colombo 01, Sri Lanka

Shelton Peiris
School of Mathematics and Statistics, The University of Sydney, Sydney 2006, Australia
Department of Statistics, The University of Colombo, Colombo 03, Sri-Lanka

Richard Gerlach
Discipline of Business Analytics, The University of Sydney, Sydney 2006, Australia

David Edmund Allen
School of Mathematics and Statistics, The University of Sydney, Sydney 2006, Australia
Department of Finance, Asia University, Taichung 41354, Taiwan
School of Business and Law, Edith Cowan University, Joondalup 6027, Australia

Andreas Mühlbacher and Thomas Guhr
Fakultät für Physik, Universität Duisburg-Essen, Lotharstraße 1, 47048 Duisburg, Germany

Wided Khiari
Institut Supérieur de Gestion, University of Tunis, Le Bardo 2000, Tunisia
GEF-2A Laboratory, University of Tunis, Le Bardo 2000, Tunisia

Salim Ben Sassi
Institut Supérieur de Gestion, University of Tunis, Le Bardo 2000, Tunisia
LAREQUAD, FSEG of Tunis, University of Tunis El Manar, Tunis 1068, Tunisia

Marco Neffelli
Department of Economics and Business Studies, University of Genova, Via Vivaldi, 5, 16126 Genova, Italy

Douw Gerbrand Breed, Tanja Verster and Willem D. Schutte
Centre for Business Mathematics and Informatics, North-West University, Potchefstroom 2531, South Africa

Naeem Siddiqi
SAS Institute Canada, Toronto, ON M5A 1K7, Canada

Index

Printed in the USA
CPSIA information can be obtained
at www.ICGtesting.com
JSHW051625061123
51533JS00005B/104

9 781647 254551